AF531002

The Spirituality of the Catholic Church

The Spirituality of the Catholic Church

by
William A. Kaschmitter, M.M.

LUMEN CHRISTI PRESS
Houston, Texas 77019

NIHIL OBSTST:
Reverend Edwin C. Garvey, C.S.B., Ph.D.
Censor Deputatus

IMPRIMATUR:
Most Reverend John L. Morkovsky, S.T.D.

Bishop of Galveston-Houston
October 18, 1982

The Imprimatur and Nihil Obstat are official declarations that a book or pamphlet is free of doctrinal or moral error. No indication is contained therein that those who have granted the Nihil Obstat and Imprimatur agree with the contents, opinions, or statements expressed.

First Printing: November 1982

Library of Congress catalog card number: 82-061066

ISBN 0-912414-33-2

Printed in the United States of America

ACKNOWLEDGEMENTS

For permission to quote from their publications, grateful acknowledgement is made to:

Alba House, for excerpts from *Therese Neumann* by Johnannes Steiner, and *Pattern For a Christian* by A.L. Mennessier.

Andrews & McMeel, Inc., for excerpts from *The Complete Works Of St Teresa* translated by E. Allison Peers from the critical edition of P. Silverio de Santa Teresa, C.D., published in three volumes by Sheed & Ward, and *The Collected Letters Of St Therese Of Lisieux* edited by the Abbe Combes, translated by F.J. Sheed. Copyright c.1949, Sheed & Ward.

Benziger Bruce & Glencoe, Inc., for excerpts from *The Only One* by Albert J. Shamon, and *Sex Education & Training In Chastity* by Kirsch.

The Blue Army, for excerpts from *Mystical City of God* by Blessed Mary of Agreda, Four volumes available from AMI Press, Washington, N.J. 07882.

Burns & Oates, London, England, for excerpts from *By Jacob's Well* by Archbishop James Leen, and *How To Pray & Other Conferences* by Fathers Bruno James, Bernard Dyer and Robert Nash.

The Catholic University of America Press, for excerpts from *Fathers Of The Church* series.

The Christopher Publishing House, for excerpts from *The Catholic Layman & Holiness* by Msgr. R. Bandas.

Confraternity of the Precious Blood, for excerpts from *My Way Of Life* by Fathers Farrell & Healy, and *The Imitation Of Christ* by Thomas A. Kempis.

Daughters of St Paul, for excerpts from *St Pius X, Pope* by Most Rev. Jan Olav Smit, and *Spiritual Diary*.

Doubleday & Company, Inc., for excerpts from *The Little Flowers Of St. Francis,* translated and edited by Raphael Brown. Copyright c.1958 by Beverly H. Brown; *Abandonment To Divine Providence* by Jean-Pierre de Caussade. Copyright c.1975 by John Beevers; *Our Lady Of Fatima* by William Thomas Walsh. Copyright c.1954 by Doubleday & Company Inc.

Franciscan Herald Press, Chicago, IL. 60609, for excerpts from *Rooted In Faith* compiled by Marigiven Schumacher, 1974.

Gill & Macmillan, Ltd., Dublin, Ireland, for excerpts from *The Mother Of Jesus* by Father James, O.F.M. Cap. and *More About Fatima* by Rev. V. Monted de Oca, C.S.Sp.

Harper & Row, Publishers, Inc., for excerpts from *Introduction To A Devout Life* by St Francis de Sales.

Loyola University Press, for excerpts from *Practice Of Perfection And Christian Virtues* by Alphonsus Rodriguez.

Macmillan Publishing Co., Inc., for excerpts from *The True Vine And Its Branches* by Rev. Edward Leen, and *Life Of St Catherine Of Siena* by Bl. Raymond of Capua.

Marian Publications, for excerpts from *On Preparation For Death* by St Alphonsus Marie de Liguori.

The Mercier Press, Cork, Ireland, for excerpts from *Retreat Notes For Religious* by Rev. Edward Leen.

Montfort Publications, Bay Shore, N.Y. 11706, for *The Secret Of The Rosary* by St Louis De Montfort.

New York Province Of the Society of Jesus, for excerpts from *Searchlighting Ourselves* by Fr Timothy Brosnahan, S.J., and edited by Fr Francis P. LeBuffe, S.J. Copyright c.1949.

Paulist Press, for excerpts from *The Love Of God* by St Francis de Sales; *The Nun At Her Prie-Dieu* by Robert Nash, S.J.; *The Person Of Jesus* by Father James, O.F.M. Cap.; *This Tremendous Lover* by Dom Eugene Boylan, O.C.S.O.; *Graceful Living* by John Fearon, O.P.

Prentice-Hall, Inc., for excerpts from *Living Your Faith* by Robert Nash, S.J.

Redemptorist Provincial, for excerpts from the writings of St Alphonsus Marie de Liguori.

Regnery Gateway, Inc., for excerpts from *Faith, Hope & Love* by St Augustine; *The Sunday Sermons Of The Fathers* edited by Rev. M.F. Toal; *Meditations On The Gospel* by Bossuet.

Selesians of St John Bosco, for excerpts from *St John Bosco* by F.A. Forbes.

Rev. Stephen A. Snincak, for excerpts from *Guide To Perfect Christian Living.*

Tan Books and Publishers, Inc., for excerpts from *Dialogue Of St Catherine*; *The Priest, The Man Of God* by St Joseph Cafasso; *The Soul Of The Apostolate* by Dom Jean-Baptiste Chautard, O.C.S.O.; *Christ The Life Of The Soul, Growth In Christ,* and *The Structure of God's Plan* by Dom Columba Marmion, O.S.B.; *The Faithful Servant: Spiritual Retreats & Letters* by Al. Claude de la Colombiere, S.J.;*Ascetical Conferences For Religious* by Henry A. Gabriel; *Spiritual Conferences* by John Tauler; *Contemplative Life In The World* by A.M. Goichon, *St. Dominic* by Sister Mary Jean Dorcy; *St Ignatius & St Francis de Sales* by Charmot; *The Theological Virtues* by Garrigou-Lagrange, O.P.; *Purgatory And Heaven* by J.P. Arendzen.

United States Catholic Conference, for excerpts from the Pastoral Letter, *Behold Your Mother.*

FOREWORD

The quotations contained in this concordance are taken directly or indirectly from approximately two hundred authorities including six ecumenical Councils, seven Popes, many Fathers and Doctors of the Church and a considerable number of more recent writers on things spiritual. Since many pastors and retreat masters like to cite authorities for what they say, the source of each quotation is given at the end of each such quotation.

For the convenience of users of the concordance, nearly all of the entries in the index give a brief indication of the content of each quotation referred to. This is to allow the user of the book quickly to see which, if any, of the quotations are pertinent to the sermon or conference he wishes to give.

All marginal numbers in the index refer to the given quotations, not to pages on which the excerpts are published.

Publisher's Note

Father Kaschmitter is a Maryknoll priest who was ordained in 1924. He spent nine years as a teacher and spiritual director in the society's minor and major seminaries. He was a missionary in Manchuria, Peking, China and Japan for 41 years. During eight of those years he served as head of the official Catholic news service of China. He was sent to Japan after World War II to establish an official Catholic news service there. He directed that for another eight years.

During the 16 years in press work he was unable to find good, new spiritual books. Most of the new books he found stressed psychology so much that God was left much in the background.

When he was assigned to the Maryknoll home for the aged, after 50 years in the priesthood, he began working on *The Spirituality of the Catholic Church,* making great use of the energy he still had. He collected excerpts from the great masters of Catholic spirituality—material which would be helpful, not only for priests when preparing their sermons, conferences and retreats, but also for all serious men and women who want to read the very best.

Father has assembled over 2,000 excerpts, taken directly or indirectly from about 200 authorities, including six ecumenical Councils, seven Popes, many Fathers and Doctors of the Church, as well as the great spiritual writers of the 17th., 18th., 19th., and 20th. centuries.

The book is designed as a concordance of Catholic spirituality and is basically arranged in an alphabetic order. However, the first 157 texts deal with God, the Blessed Trinity, God the Son and Holy Spirit, Divine Providence.

Readers will find the index of great help. Every entry gives a telegraphic summary of each text, so that one may tell at a glance which text is most useful for a particular need.

I hope that this gold mine of the riches of the great spiritual writers will have a myriad of uses—spiritual reading, meditation, study, reference. It will be most useful for those who teach and those who preach. It is an excellent bedside book, from which to read a passage each evening, and when the reader has finished the book he will want to start all over again.

Father Kaschmitter has given us a masterpiece which will make us grateful to him for a long time.

W. Doyle Gilligan

CONTENTS

THE TRIUNE GOD

1. *The Divine Reality*

Let us transport ourselves in spirit into the eternity of God and consider the divine life as it was prior to the existence of all created things. God lived a life of infinite thought, in the contemplation of the boundless reality of the divine; he lived a life of infinite satisfaction springing from the love which the divine beauty evoked. Such was the life of the Blessed Trinity. The Son was the living, divine, adequate expression of God's thought; the Holy Spirit was the divine breath of God's love. It was a life which baffles language and thought. A grain of sand would have more proportion with the vastness of the universe than human words would have with the divine reality they attempt to describe.

James Leen, *By Jacob's Well*, p. 73

2. *Inner Life of the Trinity*

God's thought is infinitely active; it surveys and comprehends all that God is. It proceeds to the divine statement of what it sees in its all-embracing vision. Forthwith there is begotten of the divine energy of the divine mind actively contemplating the whole realm of the divinity, a Word that fully, adequately, completely states what is ineffable for all but God himself. This divinely uttered 'Term' fully expressed what God is. It is the perfect image of God, 'the brightness of His glory and the figure of his substance'. To be an adequate expression of God, this Word must possess the divine substance in its fullness; nothing short of that could express God. To the Word, therefore, is communicated, by the Father, the one, unique, divine substance. This is the Son of God, begotten from all eternity. 'In the beginning was the word, and the Word was with God, and the Word was God.' This divine generation is eternal. It does not begin; it does not end; it always is.

The Father, finding in his Son that which makes his glory and satisfies his love, loves him infinitely. The Son loves the Father with the same intensity. Both love with the same divine nature, which is the infinitely fertile source of all the divine operations. And this infinite movement of love in these two Persons, arising in that one divine nature which is possessed by both, issues in the third divine Person, who personified the love of

God. As the divine thought issues in a Word, so the divine energy of loving flowers in a 'love.' The 'Love' as the 'Thought' possesses the whole reality of the divine nature. It is true God, equal to, because consubstantial with, the Father and the Son. Such is the inner life of God. It unfolds itself in the eternal generation of the Word and the eternal procession of the Holy Ghost. The divine life is a life that is one, yet lived by Three. It finds a faint image in the sun, which is at once all sun, all light, all heart.

James Leen, *ibid.*, pp. 46-47.

3. *The Trinity – Its Nature; Inner Life of God; Reason for Creation*

There are, as you know, three divine Persons in God, the Father, the Son, and the Holy Ghost; three distinct Persons, but all three having one and the same Nature or Divine Essence. Being infinite Intelligence, the Father perfectly knows His perfection. He expresses this knowledge in one Word, the living, substantial Word, the adequate expression of what the Father is. In uttering this Word, the Father begets the Son, to whom He communicates all his Essence, His Nature, His Perfections, His Life 'As the Father hath life in himself, so He hath given to the Son also to have Life in himself' (Jn 5:26). The Son also belongs entirely to his Father, is entirely given up to him by a total donation which pertains to his Nature as Son. From this mutual donation of one and the same love, proceeds, as from one principle, the Holy Spirit, who seals the union of the Father and the Son by being their substantial and living Love.

This mutual communication of the three Persons, this infinite loving union between themselves, assuredly constitutes a new revelation of holiness in God: it is the ineffable union of God with himself in union of his nature and the Trinity of Persons.

God finds all his essential beatitude in this inexpressible unique and fruitful life. To exist, God has only need of himself and all his infinite perfections; finding all felicity in the perfections of his Nature and in the ineffable society of his Persons, he has no need of any creature; he refers to himself, in himself, in his Trinity, the glory which springs from his infinite perfections.

God had decreed, as you know, to make us enter into participation of this intimate life proper to himself alone; he wills to communicate to us this infinite, endless beatitude, which has its source in the fullness of the infinite Being.

Therefore – and this is the first point of St Paul's exposition of the Divine Plan – our holiness is to consist in *adhering to God, known and loved*, not only as the Author of creation, *but as he knows and loves himself* in the bliss of his Trinity; this is to be united to God to the point of sharing his intimate life.

Marmion, *The Structure of God's Plan*, pp. 26-27.

4. *Nature of the Trinity*
In the Godhead, the Son proceeds from the Father as the expression of his knowledge, and the Holy Spirit proceeds from Father and Son as the expression of their mutual love – each of these two Persons (Son and Spirit) is distinct from the other and from the Father; yet they are inseparably one in a Godhead that is utterly simple, indivisible, unique.
St Francis de Sales, *The Love of God*, p. 38.

GOD AND CREATION

5. *Why God Created Us*
The life of God is an ecstatic union of knowledge and love – complete and infinite happiness. God has no need of anything more; his joy and happiness are such that nothing could increase them. Yet, in his infinite goodness, He decided to share them with somebody else. And so, out of the nothingness that was not God, he created us.
Boylan, *This Tremendous Lover*, p. 2.

6. *Man Created for Union with God*
We were created to serve God. That is true, but we are created not merely for that. We are created to use our wills to unite ourselves to God by bringing these wills into conformity with his. . . . We serve God and we keep ourselves submissive to him by so doing (for union with God is impossible if our will is at variance with his) only in order that God may, through that union, be able to give himself to us – to give us a participation in the treasure of his own being – to 'impregnate' our spirit with his life, and so bring us to that fulness of existence after which we are ever thirsting.
Edward Leen, *The Holy Ghost*, p. 134.

7. *Why God Created Intelligent Beings and Lifeless Beings*
Our creation could not be a necessary act, one namely to which the infinitely all-perfect God was compelled by the exigencies of His nature or attributes. . . . Neither, on the other hand, could it be an arbitrary and purposeless act, because, as such, it would be incompatible with God's supreme intelligence and absolute holiness of will. It was, therefore, a divine act performed for a reason worthy of infinite wisdom and an infinite holiness. . . .

The only conceivable reason why God created, the only one that would befit his nature, was the motiveless purpose of diffusing his own inexhaustible perfections, of manifesting outside Himself 'the depths of the riches of the wisdom and knowledge of God' (Rom 11:33), and the depth of the riches of his love and goodness. His only purpose was to communicate being in such a way as to reveal himself in creatures, and to creatures, and by creatures. The purpose of his creation, therefore, entailed the existence, not only of beings that would exhibit passively in orderly and graded sequence and in various degrees the excellence and beauty of their Creator, but the existence of beings also capable of reading the book of creation, of interpreting its revelation, of actively proclaining in thought, in word and deed the perfections and goodness which their Creator wished to manifest.

Brosnahan, *Searchlighting Ourselves*, pp. 20-21.

8. *Our Destiny in God's Creative Plan*

We are those creatures whom God has created a little less than angels, on whom He has bestowed faculties that place us at the summit of his visible creation, in order that we may be the prophets, seers and priests of his revelation, in order that we may know him, and loving him, praise him with the service of mind and heart and body, 'The first commandment of all is: Hear, O Israel: the Lord thy God is one God. And thou shalt love the Lord thy God, with thy whole heart, and with they whole soul, and with thy whole mind and with thy strength . . . ' (Mk 12:29, quoted from Dt 6:4,5). If we fulfill that purpose, that is to say, if during this probationary existence, we direct all our actions to the promotion of God's eternal glory, we shall finally, in the beatific vision of our Creator's internal glory, obtain that fullness of existence which we call eternal life – we shall save our souls. . . . It is manifest that we personally were, throughout the past reaches of eternity, present in the foreknowledge of God, the object of his love, complacency, benevolence, the predestined instruments of his divine designs; that we are not mere chance waifs floating down the stream of life, but men elected from all eternity as ministers of God's glory, chosen to do a special work at a special time in the unfolding of human history, in a specific way.

Brosnahan, *ibid.,* pp. 22-23

9. *Our Total Dependence on Our Creator*

The dominion of God over us is *universal*. 'For of Him, and by Him, and in Him are all things' (Rom 11:36). Everything in me is God's: every fibre of my being, my body and soul, my every faculty, all my actions, the most fleeting thought. I am God's at all times; at every age; on all occasions; at every moment; in every situation. This truth theologians expressed by saying that we are contingent beings; that is to say, beings who have two attributes: (1) who out of absolute nothingness have been called to existence in response to the will of the Creator, and (2) who are kept in existence by that same will; beings whose nature is insufficient of itself to exist even after it is created, who would fall into nothingness if not sustained by the Omnipotent Power that created them; beings who are, as it were, shadows of an infinite, necessary, and self-sustaining Being, cast on a background of nothingness, who had not only to be lifted out of the void of nothingness, but must now and forever be supported above the abyss of nothingness lest they should fall again into the primeval night of non-existence; beings whose existence is like the note of an organ, lasting while God's fingers are on the keys. Conservation, as we know, is the creative act unceasingly continued. Creation is not an act which was once performed at the dawn of time and from which the Creator then ceased. The omnipotence of God could not create a being which, once created, would be wholly or even in part self-sustaining. God is creating us today, and at this moment, as truly as He created the heavens and earth in the beginning.

Brosnahan, *ibid.,* p. 18.

10. *Man as Link Between Creator and the Whole of Creation*

The second Council of the Vatican tells us that 'though made up of body and soul, man is one. Through his bodily composition he gathers to himself the elements of the material world. Thus they reach their crown through him, and through him raise their voice in free praise of the Creator.

'For this reason, man is not allowed to despise his bodily life. Rather, he is obliged to regard his body as good and honourable, since God created it and will raise it up on the last day . . . ' (*Gaudium et Spes,* no. 14).

Seeking a deeper understanding of God's innermost thoughts concerning man, mystics have long since pointed out that man, made up as he is of body and soul, can be looked upon as a representation of the whole of creation. His body contains inorganic elements in common with the material universe. It also has vegetative life in common with the entire plant world, as well as sensible cognition and bodily emotions in common with animals. United to an immortal soul, the body is to share in the joys of the beatific vision in heaven for all eternity. In the Body of Christ, the whole universe is thus to be united vicariously with the creative Word of God eternally by virtue of the hypostatic union. All things came forth from God through the Word. Through that same Word, all things must go back to God.

Kaschmitter, *Spirituality of Vatican II,* p. 23.

11. *Ways God Shares His Causality*

Philosophers say . . . [that] God shared not only his nature but his causality.

This causality is shared by plants which produce seeds . . . by the carpenter, the planter, the sculptor and the teacher. But there are only two instances in which the sharing of divine causality deserves to have the name of Fatherhood as it does in God; in the family and in the priesthood. . . .

It is in terms of this divine plan for creation that the sacraments of Holy Orders and Matrimony make sense. It is from this point of view that they fit into the divine plan in the same way and have something important in common. And it is for this reason that both the head of the family and the priest have the same name as God himself – *Father.*

Fearon, *Graceful Living,* pp. 132-133.

GOD'S PROVIDENCE

12. *Nothing Happens by Chance*

Do not say: 'This happened by chance' and 'That occurred accidentally'. Nothing is casual, nothing indeterminate, nothing happens at random, nothing among things that exist is caused by chance. And do not say: 'It is a bad mishap' or 'It is an evil hour.' These are the words of the untaught. 'Are not two sparrows sold for a farthing? And yet not one of them will fall' without divine will. How many are the hairs of your head? Not one of them will be forgotten. Do you see the divine eye, how none of the least trifles escapes its glance?

St Basil, in *The Fathers of the Church*, vol. 46, p. 232.

13. *Providence – Submission Demanded to What It Disposes*

. . . Someone may say: Who is so mad as to be displeased by God? If I examine you, perhaps I will find that you are the very one to whom God is displeasing. Tell me, I beseech you, have you never murmured against an abundance of rain? Have you never been angry at the violence of the winds? Have you never complained about the dryness of droughts? Have you never murmured against the good fortune of wicked men? And, to speak even further, have you never blasphemed when rather abundant fruit was not gathered from the vines? Now if in all these matters you see and realize that you have never murmured against God, know that you possess true peace with God. In everything which happens to you, exclaim what that most blessed man, Job, cried out with a safe conscience: 'The Lord gave, and the Lord has taken away; blessed be the name of the Lord' (Jb 1:21).

St Caesarius of Arles in *The Fathers of the Church,* vol. 47, p. 399.

14. *God's Providence Draws Good out of Evil*
God's providence has left on mankind vivid traces of his severity – for example, the necessity of dying, disease, troublesome toil, the revolt of sensuality. Yet, for all that, his heavenly graciousness holds sway over all; he delights in transforming all these hardships into blessings for those who love him – drudgery can give birth to patience, the necessity of dying can lessen our attachment to this world, concupiscence can know a thousand defeats.

St Francis de Sales, *The Love of God*, bk. 2, chap. 5, pp. 62-63.

15. *Providence of God – His Patience and His Scourge*
God's patience is an invitation to the wicked to do penance, just as God's scourge is a school of patience for the good. In like manner, God's mercy embraces the good with love, just as his severity corrects the wicked with punishment.

St Augustine, *City of God*, bk. 1, chap. 8.

MERCY AND JUSTICE

16. *God's Mercy Should Encourage Us*
'God is rich in mercy' (Eph 2:4); His mercy surpasses our sins. As wax melts before a fire, so do our faults and sins vanish before the infinite mercy of God. This should greatly encourage us to live always in much content and cheerfulness, to understand that God loves us and wishes us well, and that for all these ordinary faults that we commit, we lose not one point of the sanctifying grace and love of God.

Rodriguez, *Practice of Perfection and Christian Virtues,* vol. 2, p. 470.

17. *God's Mercy Toward Sinners*
. . . This very fact is an evidence of his abundant mercy: that he not only gave his Son, but even postpones the time of the judgment in order that sinners and unbelievers may have an opportunity to wash away their sins.

St John Chrysostom, in *The Fathers of the Church*, vol. 33, pp. 270-71.

18. *God's Mercy as Served by His Wisdom, Power, and Justice*
. . . To quote a splendid metaphor, God's optimism is invincible. Moved with pity when we should expect indignation, he calls on his wisdom, his power and his justice to put themselves at the service of his mercy. Man must be saved and that without robbing God's justice of its rights. God alone, acting and suffering in a human nature that would be personally

his, could satisfy the rigorous demands of that justice. . . .
James Leen, *By Jacob's Well,* p. 77.

19. *God's Mercy Abused by Devil and Sinners*
There are two ways by which the devil endeavours to deceive men to their eternal ruin: after they have committed sin he tempts them to despair on account of the severity of God's justice; but before they have sinned he encouraged them to do so by the hope of obtaining divine mercy. And he effects the ruin of numberless souls as well by the second as by the first artifice. 'God is merciful,' says the obstinate sinner to him who would convert him from the iniquity of his ways. God is merciful. But, as the Mother of God expresses it in her canticle, 'His mercy is to them that fear Him' (Lk 1:50). Yes, the Lord deals mercifully with him that fears to offend him, but not so with the man who presumes upon his mercy to offend him still more.
St Alphonsus Liguori, *The Way of Salvation and of Perfection*, p. 26.

20. *Confidence in God's Mercy Needed to Defeat the Devil*
. . . In order to escape from [the devil's] deceit, and to be pleasing to me, you must enlarge your heart and affections in My boundless mercy with true humility. Thou knowest that the pride of the devil cannot resist the humble mind, nor can any confusion of spirit be greater than the broadness of my good mercy, if the soul only truly hopes therein.
Dialogue of St Catherine of Siena, pp. 162-163.

21. *Justice of God, VS His Mercy*
You cannot take away from the Lord God his justice. Implore his mercy, but heed his justice. He is mercy insofar as he forgives the sinner; He is justice when he punishes sin.
St Caesarius of Arles, in *The Fathers of the Church*, vol. 47, p. 256.

22. *Exterior Observance*
. . . Keeping the commandments exteriorly is meaningless unless they are also kept interiorly through love.
Bossuet, in *Selections from Meditations on the Gospel*, vol. 2, p. 117.

23. *Natural Law is Essential in the Order of Religion*
Do not forget that the natural law is something essential in the order of religion. God need not have created me; but since I have been created, I am and remain a creature, and the relations resulting from that fact are unchangeable. One cannot, for example, conceive that a man could be created for whom it would be lawful to blaspheme his Creator.
Marmion, *Christ, the Life of the Soul,* p. 215.

24. *Natural Law Violated Even by Seemingly Pious People*
[One meets people] even among religious and priests, who are exact, even to scrupulosity, as to their self-chosen practices of piety, and yet hold certain precepts of the natural law very cheaply. These people have it at heart not to miss their exercises of devotion, and this is excellent, but, for example, they do not abstain from attacking a neighbor's reputation, from telling falsehoods, and from failing to keep their word; [from giving] a wrong meaning to what an author has written; from not respecting the laws of literary or artistic property; from deferring, sometimes to the detriment of justice, the payment of their debts, and not . . . observing the clauses of a contract [exactly.]

Such as these 'whose religion spoils their morality,' to use the expression of the great English statesman Gladstone, have not understood St Paul's precept: '*Veritatem facientes*.' There is a want of logic in their spiritual life, there is 'untruth.' Many of these souls may be unconscious of this untruth, but it is not less hurtful, because God does not find in them that order which he wills should reign in all his works.

Marmion, *ibid.*, pp. 215-216.

25. *Commandments Can be Kept with God's Help*
[St Thomas Aquinas is quoted as saying that] 'what we can do with the divine assistance is not altogether impossible to us' (Ia IIae, q. 109, art.4). Nor let it be said that it appears an injustice to order a cripple to walk straight. No, says St Augustine, it is not an injustice, provided always means are given him to find the remedy for his lameness; for after this, if he continues to go crooked, the fault is his own. 'It is most wisely commanded that man should walk uprightly so that when he sees that he cannot do so of himself, he may seek a remedy to heal the lameness of sin' (*De Perf. Just. Hom*., C, 3). Finally, the same holy Doctor says that he will never know how to live well who does not know how to pray well. 'He knows how to live aright who knows how to pray aright' (Serm. 55, E.B., app.). There is no doubt that we are too weak to resist the attacks of our enemies. But, on the other hand, it is certain that God is faithful, as the Apostle says, and will not permit us to be tempted beyond our strength: 'God is faithful, who will not suffer you to be tempted above that which you are able, but will make also with the temptation issue, that you may be able to bear it' (1 Cor 10:13). . . . He, therefore, who falls has no excuse (says St Chrysostom), because he has neglected to pray; for if he had prayed, he would not have been overcome by his enemies. 'Nor can any one be excused who, by ceasing to pray, has shown that he did not wish to overcome his enemy.'

St Alphonsus Liguori, *Great Means of Salvation and of Perfection*, pp. 33-34.

26. *With God's Grace Man Can Keep the Commandments*
. . . The Council of Trent has most clearly defined [that]: 'God does not command impossibilities; but by commanding he admonishes you both to do what you can, and to ask for that which is beyond your power, and by his help enables you to do it' (Sess. 6, cap. 11).

St Alphonsus *ibid.*, p. 134.

KNOWING GOD

27. *How Get to Know God?*
St Bernard says that he learned to know God among the beech trees and oaks better than in all the learned books he had read.

St Alphonsus, *ibid.*, p. 290.

28. *Knowledge of Self and Knowledge of God*
. . . The soul must sometimes emerge from self-knowledge and soar aloft in meditation upon the greatness and majesty of its God. . . . Believe me, we shall reach much greater heights of virtue by thinking upon the virtue of God than if we stay in our own little plot of ground and tie ourselves down to it completely. . . .

As I see it, we shall never succeed in knowing ourselves unless we seek to know God: let us think of his greatness and then come back to our own baseness; by looking at his purity we shall see our foulness; by meditating upon his humility, we shall see how far we are from being humble.

St Teresa, *Interior Castle*, in Peers, vol. 2, pp. 208-209.

29. *Knowledge of God Makes Doing His Work Easier*
. . . The more one gets to know of God, the easier his work becomes. . . .

St Teresa, *Book of Foundations,* in Peers, vol. 3, p. 10.

GOD'S GLORY

30. *Glory Given by the Child Jesus to the Father*
[The Child Jesus] has given more glory and honor to God in the first moment of his creation than all the angels and saints together have given him, or shall give him for all eternity. And therefore did the angels at the birth of Jesus sing, Glory to God in the highest. The Child Jesus has rendered more glory to God than all the sins of men have deprived him of.

St Alphonsus Liguori, *The Incarnation, Birth and Infancy of Jesus Christ,* p. 186.

31. *Doing God's Will is the Greatest Glory We Can Render Him*
The greatest glory we can give God is the fulfillment in everything of his holy will. That is what our Redeemer, whose object in coming upon earth was the establishment of the glory of God, principally came to teach us by His example. See how St Paul makes him address his eternal Father: 'Sacrifice and oblation thou wouldst not; but a body thou hast fitted to Me. . . . '

'Then', said I, 'Behold, I come, that I should do Thy will, O God. Thou hast refused to accept the victims which mankind has offered Thee. It is Thy will that I should sacrifice to Thee the body which Thou hast given Me; lo, I am ready to perform that will of Thine.'

And hence it is that he so often declares that he had come upon earth, not to fulfil his own, but the Father's will only: 'I came down from heaven, not to do my own will, but the will of him that sent me.

St Alphonsus Liguori, *The Way of Salvation and of Perfection,* p. 354.

GOD'S LOVE FOR MAN

32. *God's First Love Is for the God-Man – Then for his Members*
Every well-regulated will, when it makes choice of several objects equally present, loves the most lovable of them first and foremost. This being so, it follows that supreme providence, in forming his eternal plan and scheme of creation, first of all intended and loved with special preference the most lovable part of that creation – the humanity of our Savior. Then he intended and loved each of the other creatures in turn, in proportion to the closeness or remoteness of their relationship to the Savior, their role in his service, their contribution to his honor and glory.

Thus it was for the God-Man that all things were made. For that reason he is described as 'the first birth which precedes every act of creation' (Col 1:15).

St Francis de Sales, *The Love of God,* p. 61.

33. *God's Love for Christ Living in Us Overflows into us*
Our Savior, being in us the love with which the Father loves him, extends also over us by an effusion of his kindness: for it is toward this union that the entire prayer of Jesus Christ bursts forth.

Bossuet, in *Selections from Meditations on the Gospel,* vol. 2, p. 195.

34. *Depth of God's Love for Us*
The Eternal Word has no other end in becoming man than to inflame us with his divine love. . . . How can the Lord call man his delight? Yes, in-

deed, writes St Thomas, God loves man just as if man were his god, and as if without man he could not be happy.

St Alphonsus Liguori, *The Incarnation, Birth and Infancy of Jesus Christ,* pp. 14-15.

35. *Love of God for Men Shown in Redemption*
'He spared not even His own Son, but delivered Him up for us all', (Rom 8:32). But, O God eternal! Consider that this divine Son, whom thou dost doom to die, is innocent, and has ever been obedient to thee in all things. Thou lovest him even as thyself, how then canst thou condemn him to death for the expiation of our sins? The Father eternal replies: 'It was precisely because he was my Son, because he was innocent, because he was obedient to me in all things, that it was my will he should lay down his life, in order that you might know the greatness of that love which we both bear toward you.'

St Alphonsus Liguori, *The Way of Salvation and of Perfection,* p. 117.

36. *God's Love for Men Overcame His Omnipotence*
Our God is omnipotent: who then will ever overcome and conquer him? But no, says St Bernard, love towards man has conquered and triumphed over him (*in Cant.* s. 64): for this his love has caused him to die in torments upon a disgraceful cross to secure man's salvation. O infinite love! Unhappy the soul that loves thee not. . . . [St Gregory says that] 'It appeared folly that the author of life should die for men (St Greg., Hom. 6, in *Evang.*). . . . St Mary Magdalen de Pazzi was led to say: 'My Jesus, thou lovest us unto infatuation.'

St Alphonsus, *ibid.,* pp. 157-158.

37. *Suffering of Christ Needed to Show God's Love for Us*
[St John Chrysostom says:] 'A single prayer of Jesus would have been enough to redeem us, but not enough to show the love our God has for us.' St Thomas confirms this saying: 'By suffering out of love, Christ recompensed God more fully than man's offense required.'

St Alphonsus Liguori, *The Passion of Jesus Christ*, p. 15.

38. *Proofs of God's Love for Us*
In God you possess the Lord most exalted and supreme; but you have also him who loves you with the greatest possible love. He disdains not, but delights that you should use towards him the confidence, that freedom and tenderness which children use towards their mothers. . . . Consider, you have no friend nor brother, nor father, nor mother, nor spouse nor lover who loves you more than your God. . . . He went so far as to become an infant, to become poor, even so far as to die the death of a malefactor

upon the cross. He went yet farther, even to hide himself under the appearance of bread, in order to become our constant companion and unite himself intimately to us. 'He that eateth My Flesh and drinketh My Blood abideth in Me, and I in him (Jn 6:57).

St Alphonsus Liguori, *The Way of Salvation and of Perfection,* pp. 391-392.

39. *God Loved Us from All Eternity*

. . . The world was not yet created, and God loves us; and how long before the creation of the world did he love us? Perhaps a thousand years, or a thousand ages? It is useless to multiply years and ages, for God loved us as long as he has loved himself. . . . Our God, then, loved us as he has been God; and through pure love has drawn us out of nothing; and among so many possible beings that he could but never will create, he has chosen us and has placed us in this world.

St Alphonsus Liguori, *The True Spouse of Jesus Christ*, p. 644.

40. *God's Goodness to Man – How Many Men React to It*

God, who is all-good, never forsakes unless forsaken, never takes away his gifts from us until we take away our hearts from him. We rob God of his due if we pride ourselves on our salvation; but we insult his mercy if we claim that he has failed us. We wrong his generosity if we do not acknowledge his blessings; but we blaspheme his goodness, if we deny that he has been at hand to help us.

St Francis de Sales, *The Love of God*, p. 76.

41. *Adam's Sin Inflamed God's Goodness*

So far was Adam's sin from getting the better of God's goodnaturedness, it stimulated, it inflamed it. The kindness of God, reacting gently and lovingly to human opposition, intervened to overcome it: as our fault was amplified, grace has been more amply bestowed than ever (Rom 5:20). So that holy Church, in an ecstasy of wonderment, cries out at the Easter Vigil: 'O truly necessary sin of Adam, which Christ's death blotted out; and happy fault that merited such a Redeemer! (*Exulted*). . . . Human nature, to be sure, received more grace through being redeemed by its Savior, than ever it would have received from Adam's unsullied innocence.

St Francis de Sales, *ibid.,* p. 62.

42. *God's Love Allowed Barabbas to Be Freed – Jesus to Be Crucified*

As the people had the choice of saving either Jesus or Barabbas, so the eternal Father had the choice of either saving his Son or sinful man. He made the choice, saying: Let my Son die to let sinful man be saved. In the words of the Apostle: 'He has spared not even His own Son, but delivered Him for us all' (Rom 8:32).

St Alphonsus Liguori, *The Passion of Jesus Christ*, p. 103.

GOD'S LOVE FOR EACH OF US

43. *Christ's Love for Each One*
We must remember that [God's] love for men is not merely for humanity in general. God is in love with each human individual, personally and particularly. It is essential to remember that fact. Each of us can rightly regard our Lord's Heart and interest as centered on our own self, for our Lord would have undergone all his passion for any one of us, and each of us was present to his mind just as clearly and as significantly as if there were no one else to redeem.

Boylan, *This Tremendous Lover*, p. 20.

44. *If Necessary, the Redeemer Could Have Come for You Alone*
St John Chrysostom says that God has the same love for each one of us as he has for all men together (in Gal 2). So that, my dear brother, if there had been no others in the world beside yourself, the Redeemer would have come for the sake of you alone, and would have given his blood and his life for you.

St Alphonsus Liguori, *The Incarnation, Birth and Infancy of Jesus Christ,* p. 92.

45. *God Cares for You as Much as If He Had No Other to Think About*
He loves you as much, and has as much care for you, as if he had no others to think about but yourself. He is entirely devoted to your interests as though the only end of his providence were to succor you, of his almighty power to aid you, of his mercy and goodness to take pity on you, to do you good, and gain by the delicate touches of his kindness your confidence and love. Manifest, then, to him freely all your state of mind, and pray to him to guide you to accomplish perfectly his holy will.

St Alphonsus Liguori, *The Way of Salvation and of Perfection*, pp. 398-399.

46. *God's Love for Our Souls Is Eternal*
The love which God bears our souls is eternal and infinite. 'I have loved thee with an everlasting love' (Jer 30:3). So that God has from all eternity

loved every human soul. For the salvation of souls he placed all other creatures in the world: 'All things for the sake of the elect' (2 Tm 2:10). And lastly he sent his only Son into the world, made man for our sake, to die upon the cross for the salvation of souls.

St Alphonsus Liguori, *ibid.*, p. 137.

47. *God Identifies Self with Each to Protect Each*

If a king were to love a courtier of his so much as always to put himself in front of him when any sought to hurt the courtier or murder him, so that they could not touch nor hurt the courtier, nor attack him with musket or sword without wounding and hurting the king first, would not that be an extraordinary love? Now this is what God does for men; he puts himself ever in front of them so that you cannot offend your neighbor without offending him, to the end that you may beware of offending your brother for fear of offending God. 'He who toucheth you,' says the Lord, 'toucheth the apple of mine eye' (Zac 2:8).

Rodriguez, *Practice of Perfection and Christian Virtues*, vol. 1, p. 201.

48. *God's Ambition for Each of His Children*

No parent has an ambition as high for her child as God has for each one of his children. And the sad thing is that God's ambitions are so rarely fulfilled.

Edward Leen, *Retreat Notes for Religious*, p. 15.

49. *God Eager to Impart Himself to Us*

Never does friend desire to enter the house of his friend as God desires to enter into your heart. He is more eager to impart himself to us and do us favours than we can be to receive them.

Rodriguez, *Practice of Perfection and Christian Virtues*, vol. 1, p. 18.

50. *God Cannot Love Sinner with Love of Friendship – Can Show Mercy*

God, being infinitely perfect and holy, cannot love with the love of friendship any but those who participate in his holiness and perfection. Sinners are necessarily debarred from his friendship, though, of course, they are not excluded from his kindness and mercy. There can be nothing in common, morally speaking, between God and the sinner as such. But there is much in common between the God-man and the sinner; there is the humanity common to them both. Hence, though God in his own nature can love but the holy and just, God-made-man can love even sinners.

Edward Leen, *The Holy Ghost*, p. 65.

CHRIST

51. *Son of God Not Younger than Father*
. . . Someone may say: 'How is it possible for him to be the Son of the Father and not be younger?' . . . Now, tell me, does the sunlight burst forth from the very substance of the sun, or from some other source? It must be acknowledged, unless one has been entirely bereft of his senses, that it comes from its substance. Nevertheless, although the light has its origin in the sun, we should not say that it would ever be subsequent to the substance of the sun, since the sun has never appeared without its light.

St John Chrysostom, homily 4, in *The Fathers of the Church,* vol. 33.

52. *Christ's Hidden Life was of Infinite Value*
Certainly God has achieved nothing more wonderful than this, that he should live a life so perfectly simple and natural and human that men should never detect in it, during thirty years, anything divine.

And yet this life in which the Galileans saw nothing wonderful was one of absolute perfection. . . . Each act of Jesus was an object of infinite complacency for him (God) – on account of the great charity in which it had its origin. Though all interior, the life of Jesus was one of wondrous force and power, and each year of his hidden life played as great a part in the redemption of mankind as any of the last three, up to and exclusive of the Passion. His human greatness, as ours consists in the depth of union of the soul with God, and is proportioned to the measure in which God's life is participated in by the soul.

Edward Leen, *In the Likeness of Christ*, pp. 118-119.

53. *Christ Set an Example That Can Be Followed by All*
. . . It is through the example of and by virtue of the life of Christ that we are enabled to walk worthy of our divine vocation. . . . Heaven is not thrown open exclusively to men of heroic calibre. Jesus, in his goodness, has traced for us a human existence which is easy for all to imitate and at the same time one which is eminently pleasing to God. . . . Our Lord . . . had to set up before men an example of the human life they should lead if they were to please God and arrive at their final supernatural end. To the

latter object he consecrated thirty years of his life – whilst to the task of vindicating His divine mission and instructing men in the divine secrets, he devoted but three.

Edward Leen, *ibid.*, pp. 112-113.

54. *Jesus Hid from Those Who Tried to Stone Him*

They took up stones therefore to cast at him. . . . 'But Jesus hid himself and went out of the temple.' He did not hide himself in a corner of the temple as though he were afraid, or take refuge in some dwelling-house, or turn aside behind some column or well; but, by heavenly power, making himself invisible to those who lay in wait for him, he passed through their midst. . . . As a man, he fled from the stones, but woe to them from whose stony hearts God has taken flight.

St Augustine, quoted by St Thomas in *Catena Aurea*, in Toal, vol. 2, p. 137.

55. *How Share the Name of Christ, the Way, Truth and Life?*

. . . How shall we share in the name of Christ, save by being inseparably united with him, who is, as he himself asserted, 'the Way, the Truth and the Life.? The Way . . . of holy living, the Truth of divine doctrine, and the life of eternal happiness.

St Leo the Great, in *The Nicene and Post-Nicene Fathers*, vol. 2, p. 184.

56. *Christ as the Way for Us to the Divinity*

God did not become man in order that we might pass from human imperfection to merely human perfection. The Second Person of the Most Blessed Trinity became man to make us like to God and not simply like to a perfect man. . . . The Sacred Humanity of Jesus, all-perfect as it is, is not for us the *Term* – it is the *Way* that leads to this realm where man comes in contact with God Himself. Hence it was that our Lord, speaking of himself as man, said: 'I am the way.'

In our prayerful relations with the Savior, we should never lose sight of the fact that the Humanity upon which we are fixing the gaze of our souls is a means to lead us on the Divinity, which dwells in him corporally.

Edward Leen, *The Holy Ghost*, pp. 85-86.

57. *Jesus is the Way to God for Ordinary People*

Jesus is the Way that leads to God. . . . Man's interests were consulted in the decisions of divine mercy and goodness. The career of obscurity, simplicity, poverty and suffering chosen by Christ was one of the most appropriate to human needs. It is by the way he lives on earth that man gains heaven. Christ chose the most ordinary, the most common life. He fulfilled God's good pleasure and exhibited moral and spiritual perfection in conditions accessible to the lowliest of men.

Edward Leen, *The True Vine and Its Branches*, p. 19.

58. *Christ Is the Truth*

[Christ] is the 'Truth' because He is the eternal, living, adequate expression of the Godhead. He was the Word that intellectually expressed God fully, He is the 'Truth' because he is the complete, adequate expression of what man must be.

Edward Leen, *ibid.*, p. 18.

59. *By Not Compromising, Christ Became the Most hated, the Most Beloved Man in History*

[Christ's] uncompromising attitude toward his enemies is yet another proof that the man who attacks vice, especially in high places, is not going to escape the vengence of those whom he attacks. Though there never was a man loved as Jesus was loved, it is true at the same time that neither was there ever a man who was hated by men to the same degree.

Nash, *Living Your Faith,* pp. 216-217.

60. *Jesus Dwells in Us Through His Spirit*

Though absent in the Flesh, having placed himself before the Father for our sake, and sitting at the right hand of his Begetter, he (Christ) dwells in the just through his spirit, and remains forever one with his saints: for he has promised that he will not leave them orphans.

St Cyril of Alexandria, in Toal, vol. 2, p. 330.

CHRIST THE INCARNATION

61. *Grandeur of the Incarnation*

If God had created a thousand other worlds, a thousand times greater and more beautiful than the present, it is certain that this work would be infinitely less grand than the incarnation of the Word.

St Alphonsus Liguori, *The Incarnation, Birth and Infancy of Jesus Christ,* p. 175.

62. *Purpose of the Incarnation*

If Jesus was ready to share humanity with men, it was that men might share Divinity with him within the infinite world of life, the Holy Trinity.

O'Mahoney, *The Person of Jesus*, p. 25.

63. *Incarnation – Two Reasons for it*

For two ends, the saints tell us, the Son of God descended from heaven and clothed himself with our flesh, making himself a true man. The one end was to redeem us by his precious blood, the other to teach us by his doctrine the way to heaven and instruct us by his example. For, as it would profit us nothing to know the way if we remained shut up in prison, so, says St Bernard, it would not profit us to deliver us from prison if we did not know the way. . . . St Leo says: 'If He were not true God, he would bring us no remedy; if he were not true man, he would give us no example.'

Rodriguez, *Practice of Perfection and Christian Virtues*, vol. 1, p. 467.

64. *Why the Son of God Came to Redeem Man*

St Bernard, in his contemplations on the Incarnation, imagines a struggle to ensue between the justice and the mercy of God. Justice says 'I no longer exist if Adam is not punished; I perish if Adam die not.' Mercy, on the other hand says: 'I am lost if man be not pardoned; I perish if he does not obtain forgiveness.' In this contest the Lord decides that in order to deliver man, who was guilty of death, some innocent one must die: 'Let one die who is no debtor to death.'

On earth there was not one innocent. 'Since, therefore,' says the Eternal Father, 'amongst men there is no one who can satisfy my justice, let him come forward who will go to redeem men.' The angels, the cherubim and seraphim, all are silent, not one replies; one voice alone is heard, that of the Eternal Word, who says: 'Lo, here am I; send Me.'

'Father,' says the only-begotten Son, 'Thy majesty being infinite, and having been injured by man, cannot be fittingly satisfied by an angel, who is purely a creature; and though thou mightest accept of the satisfaction of an angel, reflect that, in spite of so great benefits bestowed on men, in spite of so many promises and threats, we have not yet been able to gain his love, because he is not yet aware of the love we bear him. If we would oblige him without fail to love us, what better occasion can we find than that, in order to redeem him, I, thy Son, should go upon earth, should there assume human flesh, and pay by my death the penalty due to him. In this manner thy justice is fully satisfied, and at the same time man is thoroughly convinced of our love!'

'But think,' answered the Heavenly Father, 'think, O my Son, that in taking upon thyself the burden of man's satisfaction, thou wilt have to lead a life full of sufferings.' 'No matter,' replied the Son, 'Lo, here am I, send Me.'

Think that thou wilt have to be born in a cave, the shelter of beasts of the field; thence thou must flee into Egypt whilst still an infant to escape the hands of those very men who, even from thy tenderest infancy, will seek to take away thy life.' 'It matters not: Lo, here am I, send Me.'

Think that on thy return to Palestine, thou shalt there lead a life most arduous, most despicable, passing thy days as a simple boy in a carpenter's shop.' 'It matters not: Lo, here am I, send Me.'

Think that when thou goest forth to preach and to manifest thyself, thou wilt indeed have a few, but very few, to follow thes; the greater part will despise thee and call thee an imposter, magician, fool, Samaritan; and finally they will persecute thee to such a pass that they will make thee die shamefully on a gibbet by dint of torments.' 'No matter: Lo, here am I, send Me.'

St Alphonsus Liguori, *The Incarnation, Birth and Infancy of Jesus Christ,* pp. 15-17.

65. *Incarnation and Passion of Christ Morally Necessary*

St Thomas writes: 'It was necessary (with a moral necessity) for man's salvation that God should become man – inasmuch as the pride of man, the chief obstacle to his union with God, might be put to shame and cured by such humility on the part of God.'

Edward Leen: *In the Likeness of Christ*, p. 13.

66. *Incarnation – Basis of Many Virtues – Shows Man's Dignity*

The Incarnation is the firm foundation of the virtues of faith, hope and charity. It is the foundation of faith because in Christ we hear the voice of God himself. It is the foundation of hope because it is a manifestation of the strength of God's love for us. It is the foundation of charity because God's great love for us cannot but enkindle our love for him. Moreover, in the Incarnation men find the example they must follow to reach the vision of God, for in the life and actions of Christ we see the work of the Christian virtues in their full perfection. Lastly, through the Incarnation the divine life of grace is restored to man, and it becomes possible for him to live divinely here on earth so that he may inherit the vision of God in heaven.

The Incarnation withdraws man from evil. First of all, it shows him that he must prefer God and himself to the devil, who brought about the ruin of human nature. Secondly, it shows man his own great dignity. God has united himself to no other nature but the nature of man. Surely, then, man is something wonderful in God's eyes and in the universe. But the Incarnation also preserves man from presumption, for grace is restored to him through Jesus Christ and not because of his own merits. Then, too, in the Incarnation the love of God dissolves the hard ice of human pride. If God is humble enough to become man, can man be too proud to become godlike through divine grace? Most importantly, Jesus Christ, the God-Man satisfied God for man's sins and so merited for him the forgiveness of sins.

Farrell and Healy, *My Way of Life*, p. 445.

67. *Incarnation – Cause of Joy to Sinners, Gentiles*
Let the sinner rejoice, since he is invited to grace. Let the Gentiles exult, for they are called to life. For the Son of God, in the fulness of time, has taken upon himself the nature of our humanity, as the unsearchable depths of the divine counsel hath decreed, in order that the inventor of death, the devil, by that very nature which he had defeated, would be himself overcome.... For the Omnipotent God engaged in combat with his most bitter enemy, not in the strength of his own Majesty, but in our human infirmity; confronting him with our very form and nature, and sharing alike in our mortality, but free from all stain.... Unless he (Christ) were true God, he could bring us no aid; and were he not true man, he could offer us no example.

St Leo the Great, in Toal, vol. 1, pp. 118-119.

68. *Why the Incarnation Is Called the Work of the Holy Ghost*
St Thomas asks why the Incarnation of the Word is called the work of the Holy Ghost: 'And was incarnate by the Holy Ghost.' It is certain that all God's works styled by the theologians *opera ad extra*, or external works, are the works of the three divine Persons. And why, therefore, should the Incarnation be attributed solely to the Person of the Holy Ghost? The chief reason which the Angelic Doctor assigns for it is because all the works of divine love are attributed to the Holy Ghost, who is the substantial love of the Father and the Son; and the work of the Incarnation was purely the effect of the surpassing love which God bears to man: 'But this proceeded from the very great love of God, that the Son of God should assume flesh to himself in the womb of the Virgin' (III, q. 32, art. 1).

St Alphonsus Liguori, *The Incarnation, Birth and Infancy of Jesus Christ,* p. 21.

69. *Incarnation Planned Before Creation*
From all eternity God knew that he could make ... creatures, past all counting, endowed with different perfections, different characteristics, to which he could give himself. Realizing that he could give himself in no better fashion than by uniting himself with a created nature – in such a way as to engraft the creature into the godhead, so as to form one person –his infinite goodness, naturally self-sharing, decided on that method. In God, the divine nature is eternally shared – the Father sharing the whole of his infinite indivisible godhead with the Son in begetting him; Father

and Son together sharing their unique godhead with the Holy Spirit, who proceeds from them. Similarly, that supreme loving kindness could be shared so perfectly with a creature outside itself that the created nature and the godhead, each retaining its characteristic qualities, would be so intimately united as to form a single person.

Now of all possible creatures which God, in his almighty power could produce, his choice fell upon the humanity which he intended later on to be united with the person of God the Son. He destined it for the peerless honor of personal union with his divine Majesty, so that it might enjoy preeminently, for all eternity, the treasures of his infinite glory. After choosing the sacred humanity of our Savior for this felicity, Supreme Providence arranged that the sharing of his goodness should not be limited to the person of his beloved Son: He planned to pour it out, in his benevolence, on many other creatures. From the mass of innumerable possible things, he decided to create men and angels as companions for his Son, to share his graces, his glory, to adore and praise him forever.

St Francis de Sales, *The Love of God*, pp. 58-59.

70. *Incarnation Glorifies Human Nature*
[It was to Christ] no lowering to put on what he himself had made. Let that handiwork be forever glorified which became the cloak of his own Creator.

St John Chrysostom, in Toal, vol. 1, p. 112.

CHRIST – MEDIATOR

71. *Christ Interceding for Us in Heaven*
[Jesus Christ did not end his intercession for us with the Father with his death]. . . . Even at the present moment he is acting as our advocate, and it seems as if he does not know what else to do in heaven, as St Paul writes, but [move] the Father to exercise mercy toward us: 'He lives always to make intercession for them' (Heb 7:25). And the Apostle adds that this is the reason our Saviour ascended into heaven: 'To appear before the face of God on our behalf' (Heb 9:24).

St Alphonsus Liguori, *The Passion of Jesus Christ*, p. 71.

72. *Christ Still Our Mediator in Heaven*
[St Paul goes on to say that Jesus] performs the office of our advocate and intercedes for us with his Father. St Thomas explains this, saying that

Jesus intercedes for us in heaven by showing to his Father the wounds he endured for love of us. And St Gregory [the Great] does not hesitate to assert (in opposition to what some say) that our Redeemer, as truly man even after his death, prays for the Church militant so that we will be faithful to him: 'Christ prays daily for the Church.' and St Gregory Nazianzen before had said: 'He intercedes, that is, he prays for us, as our mediator.'

St Alphonsus, *ibid.*, p. 219.

73. *Christ our Advocate in Heaven*

The Apostle Paul says that Christ has ascended to heaven to do the office of advocate and agent on our behalf in the court of the Father (Heb 9:24). St Bernard says that he is there in heaven, showing and presenting to the eternal Father his wounds, saying that it was for us that he had received them and at his command, and begging him not to let that be lost which has cost him so dear.

Rodriguez, *Practice of Perfection and Christian Virtues*, vol. 2, p. 495.

CHRIST – OUR REDEEMER

74. *Why a Redeemer Was sent – His Qualifications*

. . . When Adam was created, he, being a righteous man, had no need of a mediator. But when sin had placed a wide gulf between God and the human race, it was expedient that a Mediator, who alone of the human race was born, lived, and died without sin, should reconcile us to God, and procure even for our bodies a resurrection to eternal life, in order that the pride of man might be exposed and cured through the humility of God; that man might be shown how far he had departed from God, when God became incarnate to bring him back; that an example might be set to disobedient man in the life of obedience of the God-Man; that the fountain of grace might be opened by the Only-begotten taking upon himself the form of a servant, a form which had no antecedent merit; that an earnest of that resurrection of the body which is promised to the redeemed might be given in the resurrection of the Redeemer; that the devil might be subdued by the same nature which it was his boast to have deceived, and yet man not glorified, lest pride should again spring up; and, in fine, with a view to all the advantages which the thoughtful can perceive and describe, or perceive without being able to describe, as flowering from the transcendent mystery of the person of the Mediator.

St Augustine, *The Enchiridion on Faith, Hope and Love*, pp. 126-127.

75. *Redemption by Christ – Greater Atonement than if Whole Human Race Had Been Sentenced to Hell*

St John Damascene says that, if for sin God had cast into hell forever and ever the whole multitude of men that the world has held and shall hold till it comes to an end, divine justice would not have been satisfied and paid as it has been by God's becoming man and dying.

Rodriguez, *Practice of Perfection and Christian Virtues*, vol. 2, p. 508.

76. *Redemption – Why It Was the Son of God Who Came to Redeem Us*

St Thomas says that just as the idea in a craftsman's mind is the model of the thing he makes, so 'The Word of God, which is His eternal concept, is the exemplar and model of every creature' (*Summa,* III, q. 3., art. 8). Now the Redemption is a new creation or, one might say, a re-creation, and it is, therefore, fitting that the Person in whom is found the original design of creation should be the Person by whom the restoration of all creation should be effected.'

Boylan, *This Tremendous Lover*, p. 14.

77. *Redemption – Why Christ Chose to Suffer*

[Since Christ was both man and God] a single prayer from him would have been sufficient to make satisfaction for the sins of the whole world; but our Saviour would rigorously satisfy divine justice, and hence he chose for himself a life of contempt and suffering, being content for the love of man to be treated as the last and vilest of men. . . .

St Alphonsus Ligouri, *The Way of Salvation and of Perfection*, pp. 83-84.

Note: Commenting on the Passion of Christ, an anonymous writer says that, by accepting the death sentence, Christ wished to atone for the sins of all men, but that his reason for accepting all the extra agonies of Holy Week was that both he and his Father wished to show mankind the malice of sin and to win back men to the love for God.

78. *Redemption – A Greater Work than Creation*

. . . Says St Augustine: 'The creation of the world was a great work; the creation of so many perfect creatures was a sign of God's power. . . . But compared with the redemption of the world, that work was zero. . . . '

Pope St Leo says: 'God raised man to a high degree of being when he created him to his image and likeness; but he raised and ennobled him far more by making himself, God as he was, not merely in the image and likeness of man, but true man. . . . ' The Church on Holy Saturday sings: 'O happy evil by which so great good has come to man! O happy infirmity that has been cured by such a medicine.' . . . More has been given to us by Christ than has been taken away from us by Adam. Greater is the gain of the Redemption than the loss of the fall.

Rodriguez, *Practice of Perfection and Christian Virtues,* vol. 2, pp. 491-492.

79. *Redemption – By It We Gained More than We Lost by Sin*
[Greater, says St Leo,] has been the acquisition which we have made by the grace of our Redeemer, than was the loss which we had suffered by the devil. . . . St Anselm says that the sacrifice of the life of Jesus Christ surpassed all debts of sinners: 'The life of that Man surpasses every debt which sinners owe'. For this reason the Church styles the fault of Adam a happy one: 'O happy fault, which deserved to have so great a Redeemer.'

St Alphonsus Liguori, *Incarnation, Birth and Infancy of Jesus Christ,* pp. 53-54.

80. *Redemption – A Greater Benefit than Creation*
. . . St Ambrose says: 'I owe thee, more, O Lord, for what thou hast done in redeeming me than for what thou hast done in creating me.'

Rodriguez, *Practice of Perfection and Christian Virtues,* vol. 2, p. 513.

81. *Redemption – Greater Blessing than Sinlessness*
The disabilities under which redeemed mankind labours are not due to any vindictiveness on the part of God nor to any desire to make the human race smart for its great betrayal. The truth is that, in spite of these disabilities, the status of those redeemed in Christ is incomparably superior to that status that would have been theirs were they children of an unfallen Adam. To be 'graced' in a sinless Christ confers a far greater dignity than to be graced in a sinless Adam. To be united supernaturally with Christ's humanity, is a much more royal privilege than to be united supernaturally with Adam's humanity. Adam, even when raised by grace to be the adopted child of God, was not united personally with God.

Edward Leen, *The True Vine and Its Branches*, p. 44.

82. *Redemption of Man Done for the Angels Too*
. . . It was not for the angels that Christ died. Yet what was done for the redemption of man through his death was in a sense done for the angels because the enmity which sin had put between man and the holy angels is removed, and friendship is restored between them, and by the redemption of man, the gap which the great apostasy left in the angelic host was filled up.

St Augustine, *The Enchiridion on Faith, Hope and Love*, pp. 72-73.

83. *Redemption – Source of Joy to Angels*
Among the angels in heaven, our Lord tells us, 'there will be more rejoicing

over one sinner who repents than over ninety-nine souls that are purified and have no need of repentance.' So our present condition of being redeemed is a hundred times better, more valuable than that of innocence. . . .

St Francis de Sales, *The Love of God,* p. 63.

CHRIST LOVES US

84. *Christ Would Die Many Times*

Our Lord revealed to St Gertrude that he was willing to die as many times as there were souls in hell if it were possible to redeem them.

St Alphonsus Liguori, *The Passion of Jesus Christ*, p. 12.

85. *Christ Was Always Mindful of Each of Us*

. . . Says St Chrysostom, Christ's love was so great that he would not have refused to do for one individual what he did for the whole world. Moreover, it is true that God bore us in mind individually and had me present before his eyes when he made himself man and when he died on the Cross. 'I have loved thee with a perpetual love' (Jer 31:3). He counted the cost of his death well spent to give me life.

Rodriguez, *Practice of Perfection and Christian Virtues,* vol. 2, p. 517.

86. *Pope Pius XII on Christ's Love for Each Member of Christ*

[Pope Pius XII, in his encyclical *Mystici Corporis Christi,* writes:] 'By means of the beatific vision, which he enjoyed from the time He was received into the womb of the Mother of God, he has forever and continuously had present to him all the members of his Mystical Body, and embraced them all in his saving love. . . . In the manger, on the Cross, in the eternal glory of the Father, Christ sees and embraces all the members of his Church, and he sees them far more clearly and embraces them far more lovingly than does a mother the child of her [womb] – far better than a man knows and loves himself. . . . '

Our Lord's love is infinite, and, therefore, it is not lessened by being shared, so that each of us can say with St Paul: 'He loved me, and delivered himself up for me' (Rom 8:28).

If, then, you say that you were in our Lord's thoughts, in his mind, in his Heart, throughout all his life – that your salvation was the motive of all his actions – you say truth. Because our Lord would have done it all for a single soul. In fact, you can say that if it were necessary for your salvation, He would have suffered it all over and over again.

Boylan, *This Tremendous Lover,* pp. 41-42.

87. *Christ Died for Us – We Should Live unto Him*
Jesus has died for us, that by his love for us he might gain the entire dominion of our hearts. . . . 'Christ died for all that they also who live may not now live to themselves, but unto him who died for them' (2 Cor 5:15).

St Alphonsus Liguori, *The True Spouse of Jesus Christ*, p. 650.

88. *Friendship with Christ*
By becoming man, the only-begotten Son of God can have for his fellow-men that friendship which the upright can feel for their friends even when they have erred grievously. On earth, friendship between two men is not necessarily severed when one of them suffers moral shipwreck. A friendship which could not survive such a catastrophe is neither deep nor true. The true friend is one who knows us through and through, who is not blind to our shortcomings and yet loves us.

Edward Leen, *The Holy Ghost and His Work in Souls*, p. 64.

89. *Mercy of Jesus – Examples Referred to by Archbishop Leen*
In referring to the examples of Christ's mercy, Archbishop Leen mentions the man who would leave the ninety-nine sheep in the desert in order to look for the one that was lost; recalls the father of the Prodigal Son; tells how Jesus wept over Jerusalem; mentions Christ's treatment of Mary Magdalen, and Christ's treatment of Judas in the garden; cites Christ's merciful glance at Peter after the latter's betrayal and Christ's promise to the Good Thief: 'This day shalt thou be with me in paradise.']

See James Leen, in *By Jacob's Well, passim.*

90. *Why Charity of Christ Failed to Win Over Some Men*
The charity of Christ failed to win the Pharisees and scribes because they were swelling with pride and self-sufficiency. The charity of Christ did not penetrate into the heart of Pilate because it was crusted over with love of the world. The charity of Christ only provoked Herod to a display of ill-timed mirth and buffoonery because the heart of Herod was glutted with the unclean sin. And, saddest failure of all, the charity of Christ knocked long and loud at the door of the heart of Judas Iscariot, but the door remained bolted and barred in Christ's face because Judas loved money too well and Jesus too little.

Nash, *Living Your Faith*, pp. 222-223.

CHRIST – HIS PASSION

91. *The Passion – Christ's Greatest Achievement*

He [Christ] was overwhelmed with infamy and reputed among the wicked; and he was being tortured in every nerve and fiber of his innocent body far beyond the limits of human endurance. Yet Jesus, our heavenly King, never achieved anything so wonderful as when he was dying there on Calvary like an imposter, a seducer, an outcast, for the glory of his Father and for the salvation of his brethren. The time for action was past; it only remained for him to suffer. Precisely then it was that he accomplished that most divine of all works, the redemption of fallen man. In this condition of helplessness, of apparent annihilation, he wrought the most sublime deed of mercy and of justice, the most stupendous miracle of power and love. It was by the measureless abjection and torment of the cross that the proud and sensual empire of Satan was completely destroyed.

Gabriel, *Ascetical Conferences for Religious*, pp. 100-101.

92. *Why Christ Suffered So Much When a Tiny Act Could Have Redeemed Men*

The Christ-Child might have glanced around his stable nursery, given one baby smile, of infinite worth because he was God, and then returned to eternal glory. This would have been more than sufficient to redeem men, to attain the principle end of the Incarnation. But would that divine smile have produced all the other things which pertain to the salvation of men over and above the forgiveness of sin?

Would it, for example, have given them that unanswerable protestation of limitless divine love that would stop their human hearts and start them off again in a rapid, eager beat as they attempted to respond to that love? Would men have had that terrifying estimate of the price of their souls with its consequent conviction of the grave necessity of avoiding sin? Would it have flashed before men's eyes the living examples of humility, obedience, constancy, and justice that were struck out from the flint of the cross? Would it have sent men down the ages with their shoulders a little straighter, their heads a little higher, their step a little firmer in the knowledge that man, who had been conquered by the devil, had turned about and given his enemy a beating; that man, who had merited death, had conquered death by dying on the cross?

Farrell, *A Companion to the Summa*, vol. 4, pp. 208-209.

93. *Passion of Christ – Greatest Proof of God's Love for Us*
St Thomas tells us that the Passion is the greatest of the mysteries because it reveals as nothing else could the love of God the Father for us. That is the principle of the Passion. Christ's principle is his love for God. St Thomas says that the Passion was acceptable and agreeable to God the Father because of the immense love that marked it. Christ so loved the Father that when he saw God's desire for our salvation, he willingly accepted all so that that desire would not be frustrated.

Edward Leen, *Retreat Notes for Religious*, p. 122.

94. *Passion of Christ Shows Love of Three Divine Persons for Man*
The surrender to death of the Son of God was the supreme proof of the devoted love of the Three Divine Persons for man, the apparently insignificant work of their hands. . . . God the Son gave himself to death in his human nature on behalf of men that were sinners. God the Father surrendered to the Passion on their behalf the Beloved Son, who was the object of all his complacency. God the Holy Ghost in his turn took upon himself the communication to men of that life that had been purchased for them at such a great price – at the price of the Blood of God.

Edward Leen, *In the Likeness of Christ*, pp. 243-244.

95. *Passion of Christ Shows God's Wisdom*
St John Chrysostom says that the Passion of Jesus Christ was not an ordinary suffering, nor his death a simple death like that of other men.

It has made us know the divine *wisdom*. Had our Redeemer been merely God, he could not have made satisfaction for man; for God could not make satisfaction to himself in place of man, nor could God make satisfaction by means of suffering, being impassible. On the other hand, had he been merely man, man could not have made satisfaction for the grevious injury done by him to the divine majesty. What, then did God do? He sent his own very Son, true God with the Father, to take human flesh so that as man he might by his death pay the debt due to the divine justice, and as God might make it full satisfaction.

St Alphonsus Liguori, *The Way of Salvation and of Perfection*, p. 332.

96. *Passion of Christ Shows God's Justice*
St John Chrysostom says that God reveals to us the greatness of his justice, not so much by hell, in which he punishes sinners, as by the sight of Jesus on the cross; since in hell creatures are punished for the sins of their own, but on the cross we behold a God cruelly treated in order to make satisfaction for the sins of men. What obligation had Jesus Christ to die for us? 'He was offered because it was his own will'. He might have justly abandoned man to his perdition; but his love for us would not let him see us

lost; wherefore he chose to give himself to so painful a death in order to obtain for us salvation: 'He hath loved us, and delivered himself up for us' (Eph 5:2).

St Alphonsus Liguori, *ibid.*, pp. 332-333.

97. *Passion of Christ Shows the Depth of God's Love for Us*

It ought to have been a motive more than sufficient to secure our love had he given us to know that his love for us is from all eternity: 'I have loved you with an everlasting love' (Jer 31:3). But, seeing that this was not enough for our lukewarmness, the Lord, in order to move us to love him according to his desires, has willed thus to give us indeed a practical demonstration of the love which he bore towards us, by making us behold him, covered with wounds, die of anguish, through his love for us, that by means of his sufferings we might understand the immensity and tenderness of the love which he cherished toward us.

St Alphonsus Liguori, *ibid.*, p. 323.

98. *Passion of Christ – School of Virtues*

The whole life of Jesus was one continuous example and school of perfection. Yet never did he inculcate his excellent virtues more effectively than from the pulpit of the Cross. What admirable instruction he gives us there on patience, especially in the time of weakness! See the patience and constancy with which he endures on the cross the pains of his most bitter death! There, by his divine example, he teaches us an exact obedience to God's precepts, a perfect resignation to God's will; and above all, a dedication to God's love. Fr Paul Segneri, the younger, wrote to one of his penitents that she ought to keep these words written at the foot of the crucifix: 'See what it is to love.'

St Alphonsus Liguori, *The Passion of Jesus Christ*, p. 62.

99. *Passion of Christ – School of Humility, Obedience, Patience, Love*

Comforted by the sight of Jesus despised on the cross, the saints have loved contempt more than worldings have loved all the honors of earth. . . . At the sight of the obedience and the conformity to his Father's will that Jesus practiced, they have striven to conquer all longings not in conformity with God's pleasure. Many, though occupied in works of piety, have realized that to be deprived of their own will was the sacrifice most welcome to the heart of God, and they entered some religious Order, to lead a life of obedience and to subject their own will to the will of others. At the sight of the patience of Jesus, who willingly suffered so many pains and insults for love of us, they have borne with patience and joy injuries, infirmities, persecutions and all the torments of tyrants. At the sight of the love our Saviour showed in sacrificing his life on the cross, they have sacrificed to Jesus all they possessed, honors, even their life.

St Alphonsus, *ibid.*, pp. 152-153.

100. *Passion of Christ – Cure for Our Pride*

St Augustine [speaking of the sufferings of Christ in the night before his death] says: 'If this medicine cannot cure our pride, I do not know what can.' My Jesus, how can you be so meek and I so proud? O Lord, give me light. Make me know who you are and who I am.

St Alphonsus, *ibid.*, p. 38.

101. *Passion of the Cross – Drama of Justice, Mercy, Love*

Jesus on the cross was a spectacle that astonished heaven and earth. Here was an Almighty God, the Lord of the World, dying in shame, a condemned criminal between two other criminals. It was a drama of justice, in the sense that it showed the Eternal Father punishing the sins of men in the person of his only Son, whom he loved as himself. It is a spectacle of mercy, showing God's innocent Son dying a shameful and bitter death to save his creatures from the punishment due them. It was, above all, a drama of love, displaying a God offering and giving his life to redeem his slaves and enemies from death.

St Alphonsus, *ibid.*, p. 152.

102. *Christ Accepted Death Freely for Sinners*

[He said to his disciples:] 'I have desired to eat this Pasch with you before I suffer' (Lk 22:15). As other men pursue pleasures and satisfactions, our Lord sought for sacrifice, not, indeed, for its own sake, but as the price of the salvation of men.

Edward Leen, *In the Likeness of Christ*, p. 248.

103. *Christ Delayed His Own Death to Die on the Cross*

[In Gethsemani, Christ said:] 'My soul is sad, even unto death' (Mt 27:38).

And since this anguish was enough to cause death, why did he not die? St Thomas answers that he did not die because he himself prevented his own death. He wished to preserve his life so that he could sacrifice it later on the altar of the cross.

St Alphonsus Liguori, *The Passion of Jesus Christ*, p. 140.

104. *Jesus Died at the Time He Himself Chose*

Liberty is an essential element of merit, for the act is only worthy of praise if the one who accomplishes it is responsible. Where there is no freedom, there can be no merit, says St Bernard. This liberty covers the whole redeeming mission of Jesus. . . .

One day the inhabitants of Nazareth want to cast him down headlong from the brow of the hill; Jesus passes through the midst of them with wonderful calmness (Lk 4:30). Another time, at Jerusalem, the Jews attempt to stone him because he affirms his divinity; he hides himself and goes out of the temple; his hour is not yet come. . . . [In Gethsemani:] 'Whom seek ye?' he asks them. At their reply: 'Jesus of Nazareth,' he says to them simply: 'I am he.' This one word uttered by him is enough to overthrow his enemies and make them fall to the ground. He could have kept them there. Now the hour has struck when, for the salvation of the world, he is about to deliver himself up to his executioners, who only act as the instrument of the powers of Hell. . . . 'This is your hour and the power of darkness. . . . He was offered because it was his own Will.'

Marmion, *The Structure of God's Plan*, pp. 77-79.

105. *Christ's Chalice Was Given by the Father, Not by Judas*

When, on the night of his Passion, he bade St Peter sheathe his sword, he added: 'The chalice that my Father hath given me, shall I not drink it?' (Jn 18:11). He did not say 'the chalice that Judas and the scribes and Pharisees have contrived for me.'

Rodriguez, *Practice of Perfection and Christian Virtues*, vol. 1, p. 501.

106. *Simon of Cyrene Helps Jesus Carry the Cross*

Contemplate Christ Jesus on his way to Calvary, laden with his cross; he falls under the weight of this burden. If he willed, his divinity would sustain his humanity; but he does not will it. Why? Because, in order to expiate sin, he wills to feel in his innocent flesh the burden of sin. But the Jews fear he will not live to reach the place of crucifixion; they therefore constrain Simon the Cyrenean to help to carry his cross, and Jesus accepts his help.

Simon in this, represents us all; as members of Christ's Mystical Body, we must help Jesus to bear his cross. It is a sure sign we belong to him if, following him, we deny ourselves and take up our cross: '*Qui vult venire post me, abneget semetipsum, et tollat crucem suam, et sequatur me*' (Lk 9:23).

Marmion, *Christ, the Life of the Soul*, p. 204.

107. *Christ Carrying His Cross to Calvary*

He goes, therefore, to the place where he was to be crucified. Jesus! Bearing his own cross. Sublime spectacle! For the blasphemous, a great mockery; to the eyes of the just, a great mystery. To the impious looking on, the supreme token of his ignominy; to those who love him, the supreme comfort of the faith. The impious look and laugh at a king bearing upon his shoulder, not the scepter of his kingdom, but the wood of his own torment; piety looks and sees a king bearing the Cross on which he is to be fastened; a cross hereafter to be fastened on the diadems of kings – that was to be mocked by the eyes of the godless, but in which the hearts of saints would glory.

St. Augustine, in Toal, vol. 4, p. 450.

108. *Why Christ Did Not Come Down from the Cross*
[Insulting our Savior, the Jews said to Jesus:] 'He saved others, himself he cannot save' (Mt 27:42). . . . St Leo replies to them that this was not the proper hour for Jesus to display his divine power, and that he would not hinder the redemption of man in order to confound their blasphemies.

St Alphonsus Liguori, *The Passion of Jesus Christ*, p. 156.

109. *Why Jesus Did Not Come Down from The Cross*
St Gregory suggests another motive why Jesus would not come down from the cross: 'If he had come down, he would not have exemplified the virtue of patience.' Christ could indeed have delivered himself from the cross and from these insults, yet this was not the time for making a display of his power. He wanted to teach us patience in our trials so that we will obey God's will. That is why Jesus would not deliver himself from death before he had fulfilled his Father's will. 'Because he wanted to teach patience, he laid aside his power,' says St Augustine. The patience Jesus exercised in enduring the shame of all the insults that were offered him by the Jews obtained for us grace to endure with patience of mind all the humiliations and persecutions of the world.

St Alphonsus, *ibid.,* p. 156.

110. *Passion of Christ – In It He Was Constantly Thinking of Others*
[Throughout his Passion] Jesus is always thinking of somebody else. . . . When his enemies advance to arrest him in the garden . . . he tells them fearlessly who he is. 'I am Jesus of Nazareth. If then you seek Me, *let these go their way*. . . . Daughters of Jerusalem, weep not over me, but weep for yourselves and your children. . . . If this is done in the green wood, what shall be done in the dry?' [During the crucifixion he prays:] 'Father, forgive them; they know not what they do.' [To the Good Thief, he says:] 'Amen, I say to thee, this day thou shalt be with me in paradise.' [Seeing his Mother and St John beneath the cross, he says to the disciple:] 'Behold thy mother.' After that he says to his mother: 'Behold thy son.'

Nash, *Living Your Faith,* pp. 256-259.

111. *'My God, My God, Why Hast Thou Forsaken Me'*
St Leo writes: 'This cry of the Lord [Mt 27:46] was not a lament but a lesson. A lesson, because he wanted to teach us the wickedness of sin, which, as it were, compelled God to abandon his Son to inconsolable torment, since he had undertaken to make satisfaction for our sins. At the same time, Jesus was really not abandoned by God, nor was he deprived of the glory that had been communicated to his blessed soul from the first moment of its creation. He was deprived of that sensible relief by which God is wont to comfort his faithful servants in their sufferings. And he was left in darkness, fear and bitterness – torment that we merited.'

Quoted by St Alphonsus Liguori in *The Passion of Christ*, p. 166.

112. *Death of Christ*
St Ambrose remarks that the evangelist used the expression 'gave up his spirit' to show that Jesus did not die by force of necessity or as a result of violence of the executioners, but voluntarily. He went to his death voluntarily to save men from eternal death. . . .

St Alphonsus, *ibid.*, p. 173.

113. "*Father, into Thy Hands I Commend My Spirit*"
. . . St John Chrysostom writes that he (Christ) cried out with a loud voice to teach us that he submitted to death, not by force of necessity, but by his own free will. He showed this by using such a strong voice at the moment when he was about to breathe his last. This bears out what Jesus had said on a previous occasion, namely, that he was sacrificing his life for his sheep voluntarily, and not through the will and malice of his enemies: 'And I lay down my life for my sheep. . . . No one takes it from me, but I lay it down of myself' (Jn 10:15,18).

St Alphonsus, *ibid.*, p. 171.

114. *Christ's Body Pierced with a Lance*
Then one of the soldiers struck his side with a lance, and from his side blood flowed out, and water (Jn 19:33). Why water? Why blood? Water that it might cleanse; blood that it might redeem.

St Ambrose, in Toal, vol. 3, p. 131.

115. *Burial of Christ a Consolation to Us*
For us . . . there is comfort in watching Christ placed in the tomb; from that time on, men could watch those they loved placed in a tomb and remember that the doors of every tomb are not eternally locked, that every tomb has an exit as well as an entrance, that it is a gate rather than the end of a road.

Farrell, *A Companion to the Summa*, vol. 4, pp. 218-219.

116. *Passion of Christ – Benefits for Mankind*
St Augustine says that there is nothing more useful to the attainment of eternal salvation than to think every day on the pains Jesus Christ has suffered for love of us. And before him, Origen had said that sin cannot reign in the soul that frequently meditates on the death of our Lord: 'It is certain that, when the death of Christ is carried about in the soul, sin cannot reign in it.'
St Alphonsus Liguori, *The Passion of Jesus Christ*, p. 87.

117. *Single Tear of Sympathy with Christ's Passion Better than Pilgrimage*
St Augustine said that a single tear shed in memory of the Passion of Jesus is worth more than a pilgrimage to Jerusalem and a year of fasting on bread and water. Yes, for this very reason did our Savior suffer so much, so that we would recall his sufferings.
St Alphonsus, *ibid.*, p. 7.

118. *Fruits of Christ's Passion Communicated to All Baptized Persons*
[In the *Summa Theologica*, St Thomas Aquinas writes:] 'The Passion of Christ is communicated to every baptized person as if he himself had suffered and died. . . . The result of the pain of the Passion of Christ is communicated to the baptized person as if he himself had undergone the suffering. . . .'
Quoted in Boylan, *This Tremendous Lover*, p. 179.

119. *Passion of Christ Blotted Out the Ancient Trespass*
The blood of the spotless lamb blotted out the consequences of the ancient trespass: there the whole tyranny of the devil's hatred was crushed, and humiliation triumphed gloriously over the lifting up of pride; for so swift was the effect of faith that of the robbers crucified with Christ, the one who believed in Christ as the Son of God entered paradise justified.
St Leo the Great, in *The Nicene and Post-Nicene Fathers*, vol. 12, p. 168.

120. *Devil Conquered Human Nature in Adam – Was Defeated by Christ's Human Nature*
There would be no justice in his (the devil's) losing the immemorial slavery of the human race were he not conquered [that is, through the humanity of Christ] by that which he had subjugated.
St Leo the Great, in *The Nicene and Post-Nicene Fathers*, vol. 12, p. 131.

FEASTS OF CHRIST

121. *Christmas – The Cave, the Most Beautiful Hostelry Ever Seen*
The cave of Bethlehem that God's Providence provided for the shelter of the Holy Family was, after all, the most suitable place to be the scene of God's birth. . . .

The hostelry in which the newborn God found shelter was not, after all, such a mean one. It was the greatest and the most beautiful that earth has seen or ever will see. It was not all lowliness and sordidness that surrounded the nativity of the Savior. Man could not take from him his greatness, nor could the humble circumstances to which their blindness condemned him obscure it. He was great in spite of all that man could say or do or judge, and his greatness burst in splendor through the lowly conditions of the Nativity.

Edward Leen, *In the Likeness of Christ*, pp. 41-42, 46.

122. *Christmas – The Nativity of Christ Includes the Nativity of His Members*
In adoring the birth of our Savior, we find that we are celebrating the commencement of our own life. For the birth of Christ is the source of life for Christian folk, and the birthday of the Head is the birthday of the body.

St Leo the Great, in *The Nicene and Post-Nicene Fathers*, vol. 12, p. 137.

123. *Christmas Peace*
What is it, dearly beloved, to have peace towards God, except to wish what he bids, and not to wish what he forbids?

St Leo the Great, *ibid.*, p. 138.

124. *The Holy Name of Jesus is Light, Food, Medicine*
[St Bernard says that] the name of Jesus is light to the mind, food for the heart and medicine for the soul. It is light to the mind. By this name the world has converted from the darkness of idolatry to the light of faith. . . .

The name of Jesus is also food that nourishes our hearts; yes, because this name reminds us of what Jesus has done to save us. . . .

Lastly, this name is medicine to the soul because it renders it strong against the temptations of our enemies. The devils tremble and fly at the invocation of this holy name, according to the words of the Apostle: 'At the name of Jesus every knee should bow, of those that are in heaven, on earth, and under the earth.'

St Alphonsus Liguori, *The Incarnation, Birth and Infancy of Christ*, p. 256.

125. *Epiphany – The Magi Adore and Bring Gifts*
'Falling down, they (the Magi) adore him', call him king, and profess that he shall rise from the dead; and this they do by offering him from their treasures, gold, frankincense and myrrh.

What are these gifts, offered in true faith? Gold, as to a king; incense, as to God; myrrh, for the dead. For one is the token of the dignity of a king; the other the symbol of the divine majesty; the third is a service of honor to a Body that is to be buried, which does not destroy the body of the dead but preserves it.

St Ambrose, in Toal, vol. 1, p. 213.

126. *Epiphany – Gifts the Faithful Offer*
He that acknowledges Christ the King of the universe brings gold from the treasure of his heart: he that believes the Only-Begotten of God to have united man's true nature to himself, offers myrrh; and he that confesses him in no wise inferior to the Father's majesty, worships him in a manner with incense.

St Leo the Great, in *The Nicene and Post-Nicene Fathers*, vol. 12, p. 150.

127. *Epiphany – Daily Occurence in Our Time*
There are daily epiphanies in our lives. . . . Every cross in our life is, as it were, a reliquary containing God. If we embrace it with faith, it will open and reveal His presence in us.

Edward Leen, *In the Likeness of Christ*, pp. 70-71.

128. *Baptism of Christ – Why Holy Spirit Appeared in Form of a Dove*
For men, the Son of God became man, revealing himself to man as gentle. He willed not to crush sinners but to gather them to himself. He desired to correct with mildness at first, that there might then be those whom afterwards he could save when he came to judge. And so it was fitting that the Spirit should appear as a dove above him who came, not now to punish sinners in his zeal, but that he might bear with them yet a while in mildness.

St Gregory the Great, in Toal, vol. 3, p. 53.

129. *Transfiguration – Shows Power and Glory of Christ's Humanity*
. . . Jesus took Peter and James and his brother John, and ascending a very high mountain with them apart, showed them the brightness of his glory; because, although they recognized the majesty of God in him, yet the power of his Body, wherein his Deity was contained, they did not know. And, therefore, rightly and significantly had he promised that certain of his disciples standing by, should not taste death till they saw 'The Son of Man coming in his Kingdom, that is, in the kingly brilliance which, as specially belonging to the nature of his assumed Manhood, he wished to be conspicuous to these three men.

St Leo the Great, in *The Nicene and Post-Nicene Fathers*, vol. 12, p. 163.

130. *Transfiguration – Expresses Hope for Our Future Glory*
In this transfiguration, the foremost object was to remove the offence of the cross from the disciples' hearts, and to prevent their faith being disturbed by the humiliation of his voluntary Passion by revealing to them the excellence of his hidden dignity. But with no less foresight, the foundation was laid of the Holy Church's hope, that the whole body of Christ might realize the character of the change which it would have to receive and that members might promise themselves a share in that honor which had already shone forth in their Head.

St Leo the Great, *ibid.*, vol. 12, p. 163.

131. *Transfiguration – Peter's Mistaken Ideas*
And so Simon says: 'Lord, it is good for us to be here'. What is it you say, O Simon? If we should remain here, who would fulfill the words of the Prophets? . . . 'They have pierced my hands and my feet' (Ps 22:17). 'They have parted my garments among them, and upon my vesture they have cast lots' (Ps 22:19).

If we should remain here, who would tear up the writ against Adam, and who would pay his debt?. . . How would the Church be built upon you, Peter? And the keys of the kingdom of heaven, how would you receive them from me? Whom would you bind? Whom would you loose? If we should remain here, all these things would remain unfulfilled which were spoken by the Prophets.

St Ephraem, in Toal, vol. 2, p. 47.

132. *Transfiguration – Why Moses and Elias Were Called to Be There*
[Among the reasons given by St John Chrysotom are the following:] that [the Apostles Peter, James and John] might learn that he has power over life and death; and that he has power equally over those in heaven and those on earth. . . ; that he might show them the glory of the cross

and bring comfort to Peter and the others who went in fear of his Passion, and to raise their courage. For when these men appeared, they . . . spoke with him of the glory he was to accomplish in Jerusalem, that is, of his Passion and Cross. . . .

St John Chrysostom, in Toal, vol. 2, pp. 53-54.

133. *Transfiguration – Indicates Our Position as Adopted Sons of God*
The transfiguration of Christ was really a revelation of the full signification of our position as adopted sons of God. By that adoption, we are made conformable to the natural Son of God, imperfectly now by grace with its glory for the soul, perfectly in heaven with its glory for the body and soul.

Farrell, *A Companion to the Summa*, vol. 4, p. 197.

134. *Easter – The Word Means "Crossing Over"*
Pasch means *the crossing over*; and so the festival is called by this name. For it was on this day that the children of Israel crossed over out of Egypt and the Son of God crossed from this world to his Father. What gain is it to celebrate the Pasch unless you imitate him whom you worship; that is unless you cross over from Egypt . . . from the darkness of evildoing to the light of virtue, and from the love of this world to the love of your heavenly home?

St Ambrose, in Toal, vol. 2, pp. 218-219.

135. *Easter – Why Christ Retained the Five Wounds*
[Christ] invites them to handle him with careful scrutiny because the traces of the nails and spear had been retained to heal the wounds of unbelieving hearts, so that, not with wavering faith but with most steadfast knowledge, they might comprehend that the Nature which had lain in the sepulchre was to sit on God the Father's throne.

St Leo the Great, in *The Nicene and Post-Nicene Fathers,* vol. 12, p. 187.

136. *Easter – Why Jesus Said to Mary Magdalen: "Touch Me Not"*
. . . The Lord said after his Resurrection, when Mary Magdalen, representing the Church, hastened to approach and touch him: 'Touch Me not, for I have not yet ascended to my Father'; that is, I would not have you come to me as to a human body, nor recognize me by fleshly perceptions: I put thee off for higher things, I prepare greater things for thee: When I have ascended to my Father, thou shalt handle me more perfectly and truly, for thou shalt grasp what thou canst not touch and believe what thou canst not see.

St Leo the Great, *ibid.,* vol. 12, p. 189.

137. *Reason for the Ascension of Christ*
[The apostles] had grown accustomed to seeing him (Christ) with them as their Master, their Comforter, Consoler, Protector; a man like themselves. . . .

They had thought only for the Man and were unable to give their minds to God. If the Man should be withdrawn from their eyes and from among them, then they would think of God; and so, cutting off the familiar contact which existed between them and the Man, they, in the absence of his Body, would learn to think of his Divinity.

Accordingly, he says to them: *If you loved me, you would indeed be glad, because I go to the Father.* Why? So that when I go to the Father you will be able to think of me as equal with the Father.

St Augustine, in Toal, vol. 2, pp. 417-419.

138. *Ascension of Christ Expedient for the Apostles*
[Christ says to his Apostles:] 'It is expedient to you that I go. For if I go not, the Paraclete will not come to you. . . .'

It appears to me that the disciples were taken up with the human figure of Christ, and, as men, were held by their human love for him as a man. He began now to wish them to have rather a divine love, and so change them from unspiritual men to spiritual: which a man does not become without the gift of the Holy Ghost. Therefore, this is what he says: I shall send you a gift whereby you will become spiritual men; namely, the gift of the Holy Ghost. But you cannot become spiritual men unless you cease to be unspiritual. You will cease to be unspiritual if this human form is taken from before your eyes, so that the form of God may be grafted instead upon your hearts.

It was by this human form, the form that is of a servant, that the Lord 'emptied himself, taking the form of a servant' (Phil 2:7). By this form of a servant the human affection of Peter was held, since he loved him so greatly that he was in great fear lest he should die. For he loved the Lord Jesus Christ as man loves man, as one in the flesh loves a man in the flesh, not as the spiritual man loves the divine Majesty.

St Augustine, in Toal, vol. 3, p. 32.

139. *Even Our Sins May be Stepping-stones for Ascension to Heaven*
'Dearest children,' writes St Augustine in his sermon on Our Lord's Ascension, 'let this be our task, that as our Lord on this day of ours ascended with his body into heaven, so we, insofar as we can, may rise up with him through hope, and follow after him with our hearts. . . . Let this ascent be made even through our very vices and passions themselves. For if each of us strives to subdue his vicious habits and trains himself to trample upon

them, what will then happen is that he will make for himself a stepping-stone by means of which he will succeed in climbing higher still. Our very sins will lift us up to greater heights if they are under our feet.'

Quoted by Nash, in *Living Your Faith*, p. 197.

140. *Sacred Heart – Feast and Devotion*

This admirable devotion is directed to our divine Savior under the aspect of His love symbolized by his Heart of flesh and blood. Its general object is, therefore, the God-man, Jesus Christ, the Word incarnate, the Second Person of the Blessed Trinity. The special object is the very heart of Christ our Lord, eloquent symbol of his infinite love, at once human and divine. This special object comprises two distinct but closely related elements: the one sensible, the organic heart of our Savior; the other spiritual, the ineffable charity of Jesus Christ. According to this definition, the symbolizing heart and the love symbolized are only the partial object of the devotion to the Sacred Heart. The total object of this devotion comprises both the heart and the Person, the heart as special object, the Person as general object.

Gabriel, *Ascetical Conferences for Religious*, pp. 243-244.

141. *Feast of Christ the King*

[Jesus is] called Christ from the chrism, that is, from his anointing. But only kings are anointed, and priests (Ex 30:30). He therefore was anointed as both King and Priest. As our King he did battle for us; as our Priest he offered Himself for our sake. When he fought for us, He was as one defeated; yet he truly conquered. He was crucified, yet from the Cross to which he was fastened, he defeated the devil; and from this he became our King.

St Augustine, in Toal, vol. 4, p. 455.

THE HOLY SPIRIT

142. *Holy Spirit – Bond of Union Between Father and Son, God and Man*

As the Holy Ghost is the link, the bond of union between Father and Son, so too it is in the Holy Ghost and through the Holy Ghost that the creature is united to the Creator. If by love we designate that in the will on which follows the impetuous movement by which the lover is carried with force towards the object of his affection, then truly may the Holy Ghost be said to be the love whereby God loves not only himself but us creatures as well.

Edward Leen, *The Holy Ghost*, pp. 56-57.

143. *Sending of the Holy Spirit – The Crowning Circumstance of Christ's Mission*

The Lord's discourse at the Last Supper shows that for Christ the sending of the Holy Spirit was the crowning circumstance on which converged all those acts culminating in the Passion which he wrought for the salvation of mankind. This mission, the dispatching from heaven to the souls of men of an ambassador wholly divine in Nature and in Person, was evidently looked forward to by the Savior as the full fruit of his whole earthly mission and his life work.

Edward Leen, *ibid.,* pp. 147-148.

144. *Since the Holy Ghost is Omnipresent, How Can He Be "Sent"?*

[In a passage of St Thomas's *Summa Theologica* are to be read these words: 'A Divine Person is *capable of being sent in so far as He exists in someone in a new way*: and of being given, in so far as He is had (that is, held or possessed) by someone; and it is sanctifying grace that accounts for both these results. . . . *Hence it is by reason of sanctifying grace that a Divine Person is sent*, or temporarily proceeds. . . . Hence the Holy Ghost is given and sent.' (I, Q. 43, art. 3, c).

Quoted in Edward Leen, *ibid.,* p. 162.

145. *Why Was It Expedient that Christ Depart and the Holy Ghost Be Sent?*

All that the Lord had to do on earth was now done; but it was necessary that we should become sharers and 'partakers of the divine nature' (2 Pt 1:4) of the Word, or rather, that giving up our old life we should be changed to another, and be reformed in newness of life in a manner pleasing to God. But it was not possible to do this except through the possession and communion of the Holy Spirit. The most fitting and the most appropriate time for the mission of the Holy Spirit, and for his descent upon us was that which now opportunely arose, namely, after the going from our midst of Christ our Savior.

For as long as Christ remained bodily with those who believed in him, He appeared to them, I think, as the Giver of every gift. But when it was time, and imperative that he should ascend to his heavenly Father, then he was to be present to his worshippers by means of the Spirit, and dwell in their hearts by faith, so that possessing him we might with courage cry: 'Abba, Father' and go forward in every virtue, and as having within us the all powerful Spirit, be strong and invincible against the assaults of men and the snares of the devil.

St Cyril of Alexandria, in Toal, vol. 2, pp. 368-369.

146. *Pentecost – The Day of Final Agreement Between God and Man*
[The] final agreement between God and man was consummated on the great morning of Pentecost. It was the Day of Days – the day of the Great and final Pact. God's long and merciful pursuit of his wandering creatures reached its term on that tenth day after the Ascension. . . . With Pentecost is ushered in a new era. . . . A study of the characteristics of this era enables one to differentiate clearly between the role of Jesus Christ and the role of the Holy Spirit in bringing mankind back to God. The difference between the two roles can be summarized in one sentence: To Jesus fell the task of *pacification*; to the Holy Ghost, that of *sanctification*. For when we were enemies, we were reconciled to God by the death of his son . . . . We are therefore reconciled to God by the submission unto death of our elder Brother, Jesus, but we were saved by his life. We have that life in us *when we have in us the spirit of Jesus*. In that lies sanctification and salvation, these two being one. . . . Then the 'Spirit of Christ' becomes the chief actor in the events that open on Pentecost and will unfold themselves until the end of time.

Edward Leen, *The Holy Ghost*, pp. 168-170.

147. *Holy Ghost – His Work Makes It Possible for God to Love us as Friends*
The great aim of a foreign representative in a state is to create in the people among whom he resides a deep sympathy with a strong friendship for his own people. This is precisely the function of the Holy Ghost in the soul. He aims to make that soul love God. . . . To fallen and unredeemed man He could but extend mercy and kindness. He could love many only with the love which he may bestow on creatures that have but a natural participation of his own Perfections. Where man was concerned, God could not rest satisfied with this diminished form of affection. He would love his rational creatures with the love friend has for friend, spouse for spouse, and father for child. Jesus made this possible. God could now set free the torrents of his affection and pour them out on men. *He could at last love them with the love he bears toward himself* because, by the grace of justification, they bear a supernatural likeness to himself. The Holy Ghost is sent in justification and he, the Spirit of Love, labors to impress more and more deeply his own image on the soul – the image of Divine Love. St Paul discloses to us the Divine Envoy at this work saying: 'And because you are sons, God hath sent the Spirit of His Son into your hearts, crying: "Abba, Father."'

Edward Leen, *ibid.,* pp. 174-176.

148. *Why the Holy Spirit Appeared in the Form of Fiery Tongues*
. . . The Lord sends fire on earth when, by the breath of his Holy Spirit,

He sets fire to the hearts of unspiritual men. And the earth catches fire when the heart of flesh, indifferent to its own evil pleasures, puts away the lusts of the present life and becomes inflamed with the love of God. Fittingly then did the Spirit appear in fire; because in every heart that He enters into he drives out the torpor of coldness and kindles there the desire of his own Eternity.

He is shown in form of *tongues* of fire, because the Spirit is coeternal with the Son, and the tongue has the closest connection with the Word. The Son is the Word of the Father and, since one is the substance of the Son and the Spirit, the Spirit should be shown in the form of a tongue. And because a word proceeds from the tongue, the Spirit appears in the form of tongues; because whosoever is touched by the Holy Spirit confesses the Word of God, that is, since he now has in him the tongue of the Holy Spirit.

St Gregory the Great, in Toal, vol. 3, pp. 51-52.

149. *Holy Ghost – God's Ambassador to the Soul*

When a treaty of peace has been struck between two powers, a representative from each is sent to reside close to the seat of government of the other. Christ our Chief has ascended to the court of the heavenly Father, where he lives, 'always living to make intercession for us.' . . . The Creator, on his side, at the request of Jesus, sends his ambassador to represent his interests in the world of souls. That divine envoy is none other than the Holy Ghost. . . . It is to be noted that Christ as man does not send the Holy Ghost. He does so only as God. As man he can but plead with the two Persons of the Blessed Trinity, from whom, as from one principle, the Holy Ghost proceeds, that in view of his merits they should send the Holy Spirit to men.

Edward Leen, *The Holy Ghost*, pp. 172-173.

150. *Indwelling of the Holy Ghost in the Soul as Certain as the Presence of Christ in the Tabernacle*

The Holy Ghost personally and in a special manner dwells in the soul that is in the state of grace. So that through this indwelling we become 'partners of the Divine Nature' as St Peter says (2 Pt 1:4). . . . The fact, therefore, of the substantial indwelling of the Holy Ghost in our souls as in temples is as certain as the indwelling of the sacred Humanity of Christ in the tabernacle. The manner of that indwelling, the mode of his union with us, may be open to discussion; but the fact of his presence cannot be denied. . . . As by the union of the Second Person with the sacred Humanity, the Son of Man became the natural Son of God and true God, so by the union of the Holy Ghost with us, we become adopted sons of God, partakers or sharers of the divine Nature.

Brosnahan, *Searchlighting Ourselves*, pp. 64-65.

151. *See How the Holy Spirit Transforms Believers in Christ*

See then how the Spirit transforms those in whom he dwells! For he readily turns them away from their taste for earthly things to dwell on those that are in heaven; and from unmanly cowardice to a courageous state of soul. And we cannot doubt that we shall find the disciples so changed and so strengthened by the Spirit that they were in no way dismayed by the assaults of their persecutors, and holding fast to the love that is in Christ. What the Savior said then is true: 'It is expedient to you that I go.'

St Cyril of Alexandria, in Toal, vol. 2, pp. 368-369.

152. *The Holy Spirit as Soul of the Church*

We may say that if Christ is the Chief, the Head of the Church, the Holy Spirit is the soul of it. It is the Holy Spirit who guides and inspires the Church, keeping her, as Jesus said, in the truth of Christ and in the light he has brought to us: 'He will teach you all things and bring all things to your mind, whatever I shall have said unto you.'

Marmion, *The Structure of God's Plan*, p. 143.

153. *How the Holy Spirit Serves as Soul of the Church*

The Church has a soul, that is, an inner principle of life. It is self-moving. And as the soul ennobles the human body by its presence and communicates life to the body, so in an analogous manner the Holy Spirit animates the Mystical Body. He is the primal source of the supernatural life for the whole Body and for each of the members. He is totally in the Whole Body, and he is totally in each part, with a totality of substance, though not with a totality of action. He moves each separate member according to the function it has to perform.

James Leen, *By Jacob's Well*, p. 234.

154. *The Holy Spirit Does in the Church What the Soul Does in the Body*

Consider what the soul does within the body. It gives life to all the members. It sees through the eyes, hears through the ears, smells through the nostrils, speaks by the tongue, works by means of the hands, walks by means of the feet. It is present at the same time in all the members, that they may live. It gives life to all; to each it allows duties. . . .

Such is the Church of God. In some of its saints it works miracles, in others of the saints it utters truth; in some saints it cherishes virginity, in others of the sanctified it upholds conjugal modesty, in others this, in others that. Each one does what belongs to him, but they live in the same manner. What the soul is to the body of man, the Holy Spirit is to the Body of Christ, which the Church is. What the soul does in all the members of one body, this the Holy Spirit does throughout the Church.

St Augustine, in Toal, vol. 3, p. 27.

155. *Holy Spirit – Source of Life, Truth Holiness in the Church*

As a natural body is alive, so the Mystical Body of Christ is alive in the supernatural order. As the soul is the source of the life of the human body, so the Holy Spirit, the Third Person of the Most Blessed Trinity, is the life of the Mystical Body of Christ. From heaven, Christ, as the Son of God sends the Spirit into the world to give supernatural life to His Church. The Holy Spirit communicates life to the Church in the order of truth, holiness and discipline. He is the source of truth in the Church, because it is the Holy Spirit who imparts infallibility to the Pope and the bishops in the teaching of Christian doctrine. He is the source of truth for all the members of the Church, for it is he who bestows on all the gift of divine faith whereby they lay hold of God's revealed truth. He is the source of holiness, since he is the principle agent infusing grace – a share in the divine life – into the souls of men. He is the source of discipline, as it is he who chooses – in a mysterious, invisible way – those who will be the visible rulers of the Church in the world. He is the primary source of all vocations to the priesthood or the religious life, to the episcopacy or the papacy. It is for these reasons that the Holy Spirit is called the Soul of the Church, the Soul of the Mystical Body of Christ. He is the source of all supernatural life. He is the source of the charity which binds together all the members of the Church.

Farrell and Healy, *My Way of Life*, pp. 460-461.

156. *The Holy Spirit is Creator*

. . . I am moved to consider how great, as Creator, is the Holy Spirit. . . . He enters into a young boy, disciplined in spirit, and makes him a judge (Dn 13:46). He enters a fisherman, and makes of him a preacher of the Gospel (Mt 4:19). He fills a persecutor of the Church and makes him the Doctor of the Gentiles. He fills a publican and makes him an Evangelist (Lk 5:27-28). What power of creation has this Spirit!

St Gregory the Great, in Toal, vol. 3, p. 54.

157. *The Holy Ghost – Christ's "Pet" Devotion*

One devotion . . . Jesus taught us so directly that we might affectionately call it his pet devotion. That is the devotion to the Holy Ghost. . . . Jesus says: 'If you love me, keep my commandments, and I will ask the Father, and he shall give you another Paraclete, that he may abide with you forever, the Spirit of truth, whom the world cannot receive because it seeth him not nor knoweth him: but you shall know him, because he shall abide with you and shall be in you. I will not leave you orphans' (Jn 14:15). Again the Master comes back to the same subject: 'The Paraclete, the Holy Ghost, whom the Father will send in my name, he will teach you all things and bring all things to your mind, whatever I shall have said to you.' . . . He goes so far as to tell us that we need the Holy Ghost more than we need his own physical presence in our midst. He says: 'It is expedient to you that I go, for if I go not, the Paraclete will not come to you, but if I go, I will send him to you' (Jn. 16:7).

Hoeger, *The Convent Mirror*, p. 18.

ABANDONMENT

158. *Abandonment Not Merely Passive*

We must take God's will as a whole. By 'abandonment' we mean not only a cheerful submission to all that God permits to happen to us, but also a prompt, decisive and generous performance of all he requires us to do.

Boylan, *This Tremendous Lover,* p. 193.

159. *Abandonment to God Expresses Love for God*

. . . St Thérèse of Lisieux realized that she expressed more love for God by abandonment to his will than by desiring to suffer.

Goichon, *Contemplative Life in the World*, p. 93.

160. *Abandoning Self to God's Will as Christ Did on the Cross*

And Jesus cried out with a loud voice and said: Father, into thy hands I commend my Spirit (Lk. 23, 46).

. . . Oh, that we could also say the same when we meet any cross, that we could let ourselves be guided by the Lord in all things according to His good pleasure! This, says St Francis de Sales, is that holy abandonment to God which constitutes all our perfection, particularly at the hour of death; but in order to be able to do so, we must practice it frequently during life.

St Alphonsus Liguori, *The Passion of Jesus Christ*, p. 119.

161. *Abandonment to God's Will, the Road That Makes Saints*

Seeking to console one of her nuns, St Madeleine Sophie Barat Wrote:

'What you lack does not depend on you. Be faithful; count on grace; accept what it costs; and your prayer will be good. If you become more humble, perfectly surrendered to God's will, you will find yourself on the road that makes saints. Think of the many who have endured desolation, temptation, abandonment for years on end. Afterwards when they had passed through these trials, their hearts were purer; they were without self-seeking. Seek Jesus and his glory, not your own satisfaction. All for God; for us nothing but hard work and the cross.'

Brou, *Saint Madeleine Sophie Barat: Her Life of Prayer and Her Teaching,* p. 175.

162. *Even When We Feel Abandoned, We Are not Fighting Single-handed*
To encourage a nun who was discouraged over her aridity in prayer, St Madeleine Sophie Barat wrote that 'if you continue to be faithful . . . the Lord will soon show himself to you as he did to Mary Magdalen, who perseveringly sought him. So, take courage. You are not fighting single-handed, though you feel yourself deserted, alone, and weary of the struggle.'

Brou, *ibid.*, p. 175.

163. *Hope, Not Joy, Promised to One Who Felt Abandoned*
Writing to a much-tried nun, St Madeleine Sophie Barat sought to fill her with hope while not promising her joy: 'The few words you wrote about the state of your soul went straight to my heart. Our good Master continues to treat you as his well-beloved, his generous and faithful spouse, while never taking away one drop of your bitter chalice. He deals with you as his Father dealt with him. What surer proof of his love could he give you? I envy you; your lot is that of strong and truly-loving souls. In your state there are no illusions; you are sure of acting for God alone.

'Do you remember the first retreats we made together? In those days your motto, which you wrote down everywhere possible, was: "God alone." Even then God had given you that attraction proper to souls strongly attached to solid virtue, who walk along the crucifying way of suffering. You have already passed through thirty such years, and in another thirty we shall both have gone to God. Have courage; Jesus is keeping his hundredfold for you. The less joy you have had on earth, the lovelier the crown you will have in heaven. I am convinced that your sorrowful journey is nearly at an end. The last years will be filled with peace and trust.'

Brou, *ibid.,* pp. 176-177.

164. *Abandonment Felt by Christ on the Cross*
My God, my God, why has thou forsaken me! . . . St Leo writes: 'This cry

of the Lord was not a lament but a lesson. A lesson because he wanted to teach us the wickedness of sin, which, as it were, compelled God to abandon his Son to inconsolable torment, since he had undertaken to make satisfaction for our sins. At the same time, Jesus was not really abandoned by God, nor was he deprived of the glory that had been communicated to his blessed soul from the first moment of its creation. He was deprived of the sensible relief by which God is wont to comfort his faithful servants in their sufferings. And he was left in darkness, fear, and bitterness – torments that we merited. Jesus had also endured this deprivation of the sensible presence of God in the Garden of Gethsemani, but that which he suffered on the cross was even greater and more bitter.'

Quoted by St Alphonsus Liguori, in *The Passion of Jesus Christ*, p. 166.

ABORTION

165. *Abortion Condemned by Bishop Over 1400 Years Ago*
No woman should take drugs for purposes of abortion, nor should she kill her children that have been conceived or already born. If anyone does this, she should know that before Christ's tribunal she will have to plead her case in the presence of those she has killed.

St Caesarius of Arles, in *The Fathers of the Church*, vol. 31, p. 221.
Note: St Caesarius died August 27, 543 A.D.

166. *Abortion Condemned by U.S. Bishops in 1972*
Reverence for human life as sacred from the beginning is bound up with the correct understanding and use of sexual love. Abortion arouses in the Christian the same horror as the slaughter of the innocents of St Matthew's gospel. Defenders of unborn life do well to appeal to the first part of the Hail Mary. Elizabeth's words, 'Blessed is the fruit of your womb.' are true in a real sense of every unborn child.

Because she is seen as the Mother of all the living, Mary is viewed properly as guardian of the child in the womb, as well as of the child that enters this earth alive.

. . . We, the Catholic Bishops of the United States, denounce abortion as an affront to the human race, as an unspeakable crime and a serious sin. We call upon all people of good will who reverence life to join in a crusade to protect life on all levels. No court, no matter how prestigious, can make acceptable what is obviously totally opposed to the Law of God and the best interests of our society.

Behold Your Mother, Pastoral Letter on the Blessed Virgin Mary, by the National Conference of Catholic Bishops, November 21, 1973, United States Catholic Conference. 132, 135, 136.

ADOPTION AS CHILDREN OF GOD

167. *Adoption as Children of God – God's Greatest Gift to Us*

To the mind of St Leo, the dignity of divine adoption eclipses all other kinds of greatness with which men could possibly be invested. That God, in calling man his child, and man, in calling God his Father, should be expressing a literal truth – that is the gift which surpasses all other gifts.

James Leen, *By Jacob's Well,* p. 51.

168. *Adoption as Children of God Richer in Meaning than Human Adoption*

In the divine adoption we find all that is involved in human adoption, and something still more excellent. In human relations, the adopted child is admitted to the family hearth; he is given the name of the family and the prerogatives of those who are born members of the household; finally, he shares the property. When God decided to admit us into the circle of the divine life, he planned bestowing all these favors on us. But his goodness did not pause there. His power, placed at the service of his love, gave us a true participation in the nature of our Father in heaven, who adopts us as his children. He begets us in a mysterious and spiritual manner. The divine adoption passing into effect creates a bond of nature between the adopting and the adopted. In adopting us, God 'deifies' us. 'Deification' is a word most frequently employed by the great ecclesiastical writers and exponents of the Christian faith. In that lies the great distinction between human and divine adoption. That we might really be able to enjoy the delights of the divine life, God bestows on our souls a divine and therefore superhuman quality. It is not only superhuman, it is superangelic; it is, in a word, supernatural – that is, beyond all that is created. Man, in adopting a child, cannot bestow on the child anything of himself. . . .

Happily for us, God's power is not limited in this way. His power is commensurate with His love. A man adopting a child of predilection would gladly, if he could, make the child be of his own flesh and blood. It is an impossible desire. God can, in a certain measure, compass this marvel. To love us, God must create in us the attraction which draws him to us. If he is to love us as His children, He must beforehand make us to be his children, sharing in a finite way in his nature. What God loves in us is not what he finds in us but what he creates in us. When He elects to love us with a love like in quality with which he loves His only-begotten Son, he elects, by that fact, to form us to the image and likeness of that Son. He proceeds to transform us and enrich us with interior perfections that correspond to the love he bears us and the dignity He confers on us.

James Leen, *ibid.*, pp. 51-52.

169. *We Must Live as Children of God*

Our preoccupation should not be to die in the state of grace, but to live and grow in the state of grace. Death is not a beginning but a continuation of life. . . . If we congratulate ourselves on having God for our Father, we ought so to bear ourselves that he may be able to congratulate himself on having us as his children. We are in truth the temples of God. Our conduct should show that he dwells in us. We ought to be heavenly in our outlook, and savor only the things of God.

James Leen, *ibid.*, p. 54.

AFFECTIONS

170. *Inordinate Affections Hinder Union with God*

God has declared that he loves all those who love him: 'I love them that love me' (Prv 8:17). But it is not to be supposed that God will give himself entirely to one who loves anything in the world equally with God. At one time, St Teresa was in this state, keeping up an affection, not indeed an impure affection, but an inordinate one, for a certain relative. When, however, she divested herself of this attachment, God was pleased to say to her in a vision, 'Now that thou art wholly mine, I am wholly thine.'

St Alphonsus Liguori, *The Way of Salvation and of Perfection*, p. 151.

ALMSGIVING

171. *Almsgiving Procures Great Benefits for Us*

You give the poor a coin and receive a kingdom from Christ; you bestow a mouthful and are given eternal life; you offer clothes and Christ grants you the forgiveness of your sins.

St Caesarius of Arles, in *The Fathers of the Church*, vol. 31, p. 129.

172. *He Who Gives Is a Minister of God's Mercy*
. . . Let him that gives some portion of his substance (to the poor) understand that he is a minister of divine mercy; for God has placed the cause of the poor in the hand of the liberal man.

St Leo the Great, in *The Nicene and Post-Nicene Fathers*, vol. 12, p. 162.

173. *Alms Are of Two Kinds – Food and Forgiveness*
No one will be able to excuse himself from giving alms, dearly beloved, because Christ has promised a reward for a cup of cold water.

As I have frequently mentioned, there are two kinds of alms, the one good, but the other better; the one that you extend a mouthful to the poor; the other that you immediately forgive a brother who has offended you. . . . [Christ himself] told us: 'If you forgive, your heavenly Father will also forgive you your offenses; but if you do not forgive, neither will your Father forgive you your offenses' (Mt 6:14-15).

St Caesarius of Arles, in *The Fathers of the Church*, vol. 31, p. 130.

174. *Almsgiving – Why and to What Extent in Secret*
[The fact that Christ said that] alms should be given in secret and advised that they be given publicly demands prudent understanding in order that His precepts may not seem to contradict each other. One who gives alms out of the desire to be praised by men gives them publicly even if he bestows them in secret, since he seeks praise from men. However, one who gives alms solely out of love for God, in order that other men may imitate him in this good work and that God, not himself, may be praised, gives them in secret even if he does so in public. In return for those alms, this man desires, not that which is seen, but what is not seen; he does not long to receive praise from men but a reward from God.

St Caesarius of Arles, in *The Fathers of the Church*, vol. 47, p. 309.

175. *Almsgiving May Be a Theological Virtue*
Almsgiving may be an act either of moral or of theological virtue, according to the motives from which it proceeds. If he who relieves the miseries of others be moved merely by the natural goodness that is felt when alleviating the sufferings of a fellowman, he practices a moral virtue. But if his motive in lending them a helping hand be the delight which God takes in such merciful deeds, and he is urged to give alms for the love he bears to God, then he practices a theological virtue.

Scaramelli, *Directorium Asceticum*, vol. 4, p. 228.

ANGELS

176. *Angels – Our Older Brothers in Heaven*
The Angelic Host, though different from us in nature, is not beyond the sphere of the love of the children of men. They are our elder brethren, but brethren none the less. . . . The angels must be closely akin to us, for otherwise God would not have used them as our guardians.

Arendzen, *Purgatory and Heaven*, p. 75.

177. *Angels Guardian – Why They Take Care of Us*
We are guarded by angels. 'Behold, I will send my angel, who will go before thee' is literally true for the least of men in the universe. The guardianship of men is not a lowly work undertaken in a spirit of humility or humiliation by the pure spirits who are so close to God; neither is it a compassionate or patronizing gesture called forth by the pitiable condition of men. This is a part of the general order of the universe, a dictate of the invariable law that leads inferiors to their perfection by superiors. It is an angelic responsibility, consequent on complete, accurate knowledge and irrevocable love, that they should take over the guidance of our stumbling minds and fickle hearts. This is not a small boy's wishful thinking, nor a poet's fragile dream, but an integral part of the divine government of the universe. It is a predictable thing; to be expected; a protection that is in no sense an effect of our will, our morals, or our merits.

This tremendous truth must not be left in the field of generalities. St Jerome probed its significance when he said: 'Great is the dignity of souls, for each one to have an angel deputed to guard it from its birth.' St Thomas explains the truth with words of simple beauty. 'Man, while in this state of life is, as it were, on a road by which he should journey to heaven. On this road man is threatened by many dangers both from within and without. . . . And, therefore, as guardians are appointed for men who have to pass by an unsafe road, so an angel guardian is assigned to each man as long as he is a wayfarer. When, however, he arrives at the end of life, he no longer has a guardian angel; but in the kingdom he will have an angel to reign with him, in hell a demon to punish him.'

From the first moment of human life, a particular angel is assigned to lifelong guardianship of this man. To that work, the angel bends all his mastery over the physical world, all his command of human senses, memory and imagination, all the angelic deposit of truth, all the raging fire of angelic love. That guardianship never relaxes for a moment, night or day, year in and year out, until the last spark of life is extinguished. It is a benefit given to every man, not by reason of his belief or his sanctity, but by reason of his humanity.

Farrell and Healy, *My Way of Life*, pp. 130-131.

178. *Angels Guardian – Their Power*

Nothing in the universe can withstand the angel's powers except our own choice. The angel who guards us is of the lowest of the heavenly choirs; yet his power is more than enough for all the physical universe, more than enough for the greatest devil, bowed as the devils are in punishment to the least of the good angels. The only effective obstacle to the angel's guarding love is our own intellect and our own will. We ourselves can defeat such guardianship, and we do so in every sin.

Farrell and Healy, *ibid.*, pp. 132-133.

179. *Angels Guardian – Why Honor and Invoke Them*

We should devoutly honor and invoke our guardian angel because: (a) he is a great prince of heaven, (b) he is given by God to us as our constant companion, protector and leader.

Be always mindful of his presence and never do anything you would not do in the presence of your mother. Invoke him in all dangers to body and soul and follow his inspirations. Remember that all men have guardian angels; greet them too, frequently, and adjust your behaviour toward your fellowmen accordingly.

Wallenstein, *Guide to Perfect Christian Living*, p. 83.

180. *Angels Guardian – Why So Helpful to Men*

Admirable, my daughter, is the love, the fidelity and the solicitude with which the angelic spirits assist mortals in their necessities; and most horrible is the forgetfulness, ingratitude and grossness on the part of men in failing to acknowledge this debt. In the bosom of the Most High, whose face they see in beatific clearness (Mt 8:15), these heavenly spirits perceive the infinite paternal love of the Father in heaven for earthly men, and therefore they appreciate and estimate worthily the Blood of the Lamb, by which men were bought and rescued, and they know the value of the souls thus purchased with the treasures of the Divinity. Thence arise their watchfulness and attention in securing the interests of souls, which, on account of the value set upon them by the Most High, have been given into their charge.

Mary of Agreda, *City of God: Words of Wisdom,* p. 82.

181. *Angels Guardian – Attitude We Owe God for Their Help*
. . . I wish to instruct thee . . . that thou, by incessant praise and acknowledgment, show thyself thankful for the favour which God vouchsafed in appointing angels to assist thee, teach thee, and guide thee through tribulations and sorrows. Mortals in their abominable ingratitude and grossness ordinarily forget this blessing. They do not consider what great mercy and condescension of the Most High it is to have these holy princes as helpers, guardians, and defenders of men, their earthly fellow-creatures so full of miseries and sins. In forgetting how exalted in glory, dignity and beauty these spirits are, many men deprive themselves of numerous blessings, which they would otherwise obtain at the hands of these angels. Greatly do they rouse the indignation of the Lord on this account.
Advice of the Blessed Mother to Mary of Agreda, *ibid.*, p. 25.

ANXIETY

182. *Anxiety – Next to Sin, The Greatest Evil That Befalls a Soul*
With the single exception of sin, anxiety is the greatest evil that can happen to a soul. Just as sedition and internal disorder bring total ruin to a state and leave it helpless to resist a foreign invader, so also if our heart is inwardly troubled and disturbed, it loses both the strength necessary to maintain the virtues it had acquired and the means to resist temptations of the enemy. He then uses his utmost efforts to fish in troubled waters. . . .

Anxiety proceeds from an inordinate desire to be freed from a present evil or to acquire a hoped for good. Yet there is nothing that tends more to increase evil and prevent enjoyment of good than to be disturbed and anxious.
St Francis de Sales, *Introduction to the Devout Life*, p. 207.

183. *Anxiety – How to Overcome It*
If you can reveal the cause of your anxiety to your spiritual director, or at least to some faithful and devout friend, you may be sure that you will speedily find relief. . . . St Louis, the King, gave this counsel to his son: 'If your heart is disturbed in any way, tell it immediately to your confessor or to some reliable person. In this way you will be enabled to endure the evil very easily because of the relief he will bring you.'
St Francis de Sales, *ibid.*, p. 208.

APOSTOLATE

184. *Apostolate – Men to Be Saved Through Men*
How admirable the plan, the universal law laid down by Providence, that it is through men that men are to find out the way to salvation. . . . [Quoting a letter of Pope Leo XIII to Cardinal Gibbons:] 'Jesus Christ alone has shed the Blood that redeems the world. Alone, too, he might have put its power to work and acted directly, as he does in the Holy Eucharist. But he wanted to have others cooperate in the distribution of his graces. Why? No doubt his Divine Majesty demanded that it be so, but his loving affection for men urged him no less. And if it is seemly for the most excellent king to govern, more often than not, through ministers, what condescension it is for God to deign to give poor creatures a share in his work and his glory!'

Chautard, *The Soul of the Apostolate*, pp. 4-5.

185. *Reservoirs Needed – Not Channels*
Is there anyone who does not know St Bernard's saying to apostles: 'If you are wise, you will be reservoirs and not channels'? The Channels let the water flow away, and do not retain a drop. But the reservoir is first filled, and then, without emptying itself, pours out its overflow, which is ever renewed over the fields which it waters.

Chautard, *ibid.*, pp. 52-53.

186. *Holiness and Success of Apostles Come from God*
. . . Christ chose disciples, whom he called apostles, men of humble birth, undistinguished in letters, so that however great they might become in character and accomplishment, he would be their holiness and their success. Among them he had one bad man, of whom he made good use to carry out the purposes of his Passion and to set an example for his Church, how she should bear with bad men, too.

St Augustine, *City of God*, bk. 18, chap. 49.

187. *Apostolate Requires Kindness*
'You catch more flies,' said St Francis de Sales, 'with a little honey than with a barrel of vinegar.'

Chautard, *The Soul of the Apostolate*, p. 137.

188. *Apostolate – Prayer and Self-sacrifice Needed for Success*
In the heart of the apostle there must . . . be found the spirit of *self-sacrifice.* 'Unless the grain of wheat, falling into the earth, die, itself remaineth alone. But if it die, it will bring forth much fruit.' Prayer attaches the soul to God and imparts the power of drawing others to him. Sacrifice detaches the soul from the world, from self, and, united with the great sacrifice of Jesus on Calvary, it atones to the Father's offended majesty.

It is most true that the Church needs men and women who will organize, and write, and preach, and lecture, and argue. But even more sorely does she need men and women crucified to the world, and to whom the world itself is crucified. Prayer and sacrifice form the solid foundation of the apostolic life.

Nash, *The Nun at Her Prie-Dieu*, p. 43.

189. *Consolation Eternally to Be Derived from Souls Saved*
A day will come, as we may well hope, when we shall see ourselves all united together in that eternal home, never more to be separated from one another, and where we shall find united with us many hundreds of thousands of souls who at one time did not love God, but who, brought back to His grace by means of us, will love him, and will be for all eternity a cause of glory and gladness for ourselves. Should not this thought spur us on to give ourselves wholly to the love of Jesus Christ and to making others love him?

St Alphonsus Liguori, letter to the Fathers and Brothers of the Congregation of the Most Holy Redeemer, July 19, 1774.

190. *Apostolate of St Pius X as a Young Priest*
[In an audience with St Pius X, an influential priest spoke violently against a known enemy of the Church. Pius answered:] 'My dear friend, I do not approve of your vehement language. Listen to a little story of my own experience.

'A young priest who had just received his appointment as pastor thought it his duty to visit every family in the parish without discrimination; he visited not only Catholics but also the Jews and the Masons. His conduct displeased the neighboring pastors, who lodged a complaint with the bishop. The bishop summoned the young priest and gave him a rather sharp warning. The accused humbly bowed his head, but said to the bishop with all due respect and modesty: "Monsignor, Jesus ordered the shepherd in the Gospel to tend all sheep and to lead them to the true sheepfold. But how is that possible if the shepherd does not first go in search of the sheep? Moreover, please understand that I make no concessions in questions of principle. All I do is to show charity to all souls which God has entrusted to me. But if in your opinion, Monsignor, should refrain from it, would you be kind enough to give me such a prohibition in writing so that everybody may know that I do nothing but obey my bishop."

'Moved by the straightforward words of the young pastor, the bishop did not insist. And the future put the priest in the right. For it was a comfort to him that he was able to bring many erring sheep back to the right path and to increase the respect for the Catholic Church in many people of other persuasions.' Then, after a little pause, Pius X added to his story: 'That priest is still living and is talking to you at this moment.'

Smit, *St Pius X, Pope,* pp. 144-145.

ARIDITY

191. *Works Done with Repugnance Can Be Most Meritorious*
[If certain persons] do something with repugnance and weariness, they feel that they have not gained any merit. On the contrary, they have gained greater merit, for a single ounce of good performed with weariness and without satisfaction while the soul is undergoing a period of spiritual darkness is worth more than one hundred pounds of good done with pleasure and satisfaction, because the first was performed with a stronger and purer love than the latter.

St Francis de Sales, in *Spiritual Diary*, pp. 11-23.

192. *Aridity Can Be an Occasion of Merit*
. . . When a man embraces what is good, though he have no feeling nor sensible relish in the matter, he will please God and merit heaven, especially as God is more ready to reward than to punish. Nay, oftentimes these acts are more meritorious and pleasing to God when they are done in dryness without taste of sensible consolation, because they are purer and stronger and more lasting, and a man puts more of his own into them than when he is carried off his feet by devotion.

Rodriguez, *Practice of Perfection and Christian Virtues*, vol. 1, p. 347.

193. *Benefits for Those Who Persevere in Prayer*
Taulerus says that on him who perseveres in prayer in a state of aridity, God will bestow greater graces than had he prayed much with great sensible devotion.

St Alphonsus Liguori, *The Way of Salvation and of Perfection*, p. 381.

194. *Aridity – Its Function*
The purification sent by God to divorce the soul from its feelings, from the desires that yearn more for the consolations of God than for the God of consolations, is generally sensible dryness.
Shamon, *The Only Life*, p. 15.

195. *Aridity – A Time to Practice Humility and Resignation*
As all masters of the spiritual life recommend, in time of desolation we ought especially to exercise ourselves in acts of humility and resignation. There is no better time for learning our own helplessness and our misery than when we are barren in prayer, wearied, distracted, and desolate, without any perceptible fervor, and even without perceptible desires for making progress in divine love. At such times let the soul say, 'Lord, have mercy upon me; behold how powerless I am to do a single good deed.'
St Alphonsus Liguori, *The Way of Salvation and of Perfection*, pp. 286-287.

ASTROLOGY

196. *Astrology Refuted by St Gregory the Great*
. . . You must know that the Priscillian heretics believe that every man is born subject to the rule of the stars . . . they hold [that the star of Bethlehem was the destiny of Christ]. But even if we reflect upon the words of the Gospel which speak of this very star: 'Until it came and stood over the house where the child was,' we see that it is not the Child that hastens to the star, but the star that hastens to the Child, and so, if I may say it thus, it is not the star that is the Child's fate, but rather it is the Child who is the destiny of the star.
St Gregory the Great, in Toal, vol. 1, pp. 231-232.

BEATITUDES

197. *Beatitudes – Exemplified by Christ Himself*
[Consider the beatitudes] and you will find on examining each that he anticipated the teaching contained in the words by his deeds. 'Blessed are the meek.' How, then, shall we learn meekness? 'Learn of me, for I am meek and humble of heart.' 'Blessed are the peacemakers.' Who will teach us the beauty of peace? The Peacemaker himself, who makes peace and

reconciles two men into one new man; who made peaceful by the Blood of His cross both things of heaven and those of earth. 'Blessed are the poor.' He himself is the one who was poor and emptied himself in the form of a slave in order that 'of His fullness we might receive, grace for grace.'

St Basil, in *The Fathers of the Church*, vol. 46, pp. 256-257.

198. *St Augustine on the Poor in Spirit*

What does poor in spirit mean? Those who are poor in their desires, not in their means. For he who is poor in spirit is humble; and God listens to the sighs of the humble. . . .

St Augustine, in Toal, vol. 4, p. 473.

199. *St Leo on the Poor in Spirit*

. . . Saying, *Blessed are the poor in spirit* [Jesus Christ] shows that the kingdom of heaven shall be given to those whom humility of soul commends rather than absence of riches.

But it cannot be doubted that this blessing of humility is more easily attained by the poor than the rich; for while meekness is the companion of those who live in poverty, pride is the familiar of the rich. Yet in many of the rich that spirit is found which uses its abundance, not to increase its own inflated pride, but in works of goodness, and which holds as its greatest gain that which it has bestowed in relieving the misery of another's want. It is given to every kind and rank of men to share in this virtue; because they can be equal in good will, who are unequal in means.

St Leo the Great, in Toal, vol. 4, pp. 480-481.

200. *Blessed Are the Meek*

Those who do not resist the will of God: they are the meek. Who are meek? They, who when things go well with them, give praise to God; and when things go ill, do not speak ill of God. For their good works, they give glory to God; for their sins, they blame themselves.

St Augustine in Toal, vol. 4, p. 476.

201. *Blessed Are They That Mourn over Their Sins*

'Blessed are they who mourn, for they shall be comforted' (Mt 5:5). . . . Does anyone mourn except for one who is dead? But, every sinner ought to mourn for himself, since there is nothing else so dead as a man in sin. Yet, how marvelous! If he mourns for himself, he comes to life again. Let him mourn through repentance, and he shall be comforted through forgiveness.

St Augustine, in *The Fathers of the Church*, vol. 11, p. 365.

202. *Blessed Are They That Mourn*
Blessed are they that mourn, for they shall be comforted. . . . They are torn with grief until a love for eternal things is begotten in them. They shall be comforted therefore by the Holy Spirit – Who is, on this account especially, called the Paraclete, that is Comforter – so that when they have lost temporal happiness, they may fully enjoy the eternal.
St Augustine, in *The Fathers of the Church,* vol. 11, pp. 22-23.

203. *Blessed Are They That Mourn*
Godfearing sorrow mourns either its own sins or those others. It does not grieve over what divine justice has ordered but mourns the evils man's iniquity has committed; when he is more to be sorrowed for who commits iniquity than he who suffers it; for iniquity shall bring the unjust to torment, while to suffer it in patience leads the just to glory.
St Leo the Great, in Toal, vol. 4, p. 481.

204. *Blessed Are the Merciful*
A man is called *misericors* as possessing an unhappy heart; because he regards others' afflictions as his own and grieves for another's misfortune as if it were his own.
St Thomas Aquinas, quoting Remigius, in Toal, vol. 4, p. 466.

205. *Purity of Heart*
'Blessed are the pure of heart, for they shall see God' (Mt 5:8). . . . If you are earnestly striving to make your heart pure, call upon him who will not disdain to make it a clean abode for himself, and who will deign to abide in you.
St Augustine, in *The Fathers of the Church*, vol. 11, p. 366.

206. *The Peacemakers*
'Blessed are the peacemakers, for they shall be called the children of God' (Mt 5:9). . . . Do you see two persons at odds with each other? Try to restore peace between them. To one of them, speak well of the other; to the latter, speak well of the former. After the manner of an angry man, one of them may have told you something bad about the other. Do not reveal it. Bury within your bosom any disparaging remarks you have heard from the man in anger. Let harmony be the constant aim of your advice.
St Augustine, *ibid.,* p. 367.

207. *Peacemakers Are Blessed – But Must War Against Evil*
'Blessed are the peacemakers, for they shall be called children of God' (Mt 5:9). And if a man begins to be a child of God who has begun to be a

peacemaker, he refuses to be a child of God who is unwilling to embrace peace. He who scorns to be a peacemaker denies that God is his Father. The children of God must therefore be peacemakers, kind in heart, simple of speech, united in the peace of love, joined firmly one to another in the bonds of fellowship. . . .

We must ever be at peace with the just, and ever at war with evil; for we must forever hate the evildoing of the wicked. For men themselves, even though they are wicked, must still be loved; for they are creatures of God.

St Augustine, in Toal, vol. 3, p. 40.

BIRTH CONTROL

208. *Birth Control Condemned in Sixth Century A.D.*
Is anyone unable to warn that no woman should accept a potion to prevent conception or to condemn within herself the nature which God wanted to be fruitful? Indeed, she will be held guilty of as many murders as the number of those she might have conceived or borne, and unless suitable penance saves her, she will be condemned to eternal death in hell. If a woman does not want to bear children, she should enter upon a pious agreement with her husband, for only the abstinence of a Christian woman is chastity.

St Caesarius of Arles, in *The Fathers of the Church*, vol. 31, p. 13.

Note: St Caesarius died in 543 A.D.

BODY

209. *Body as Enemy of Salvation*
The world and the devil are very powerful enemies of our eternal salvation; but our own body, because it is a domestic enemy, is a still more dangerous antagonist. 'A domestic enemy,' says St Bernard, 'is the worst of enemies.'

St Alphonsus Liguori, *The True Spouse of Jesus Christ*, p. 207.

210. *Body as Traitor to the Soul – Must Be Mortified*
If they told any one: 'Know that one of your household, and of those who eat and drink at your table, is plotting treason to kill you,' what fear would that inspire? . . . And if he should discover who the traitor was,

what hatred would he conceive and what vengeance he would take on him! Now this is our body, which eats and sleeps with us and knows very well that in doing harm to our soul it is doing harm to itself, and in casting the soul into hell it must go there with it. . . .

Rodriguez, *Practice of Perfection and Christian Virtues*, vol. 2, pp. 18-19.

211. *Body Not Our Master – Seneca*
Even Seneca . . . said a thing divinely true: 'I am too great and born to too great things to become the slave of my body' – *Major sum, et ad majora natus, quam ut mancipium fiam mei corporis.*

Rodriguez, *ibid.*, p. 43.

CATHOLIC ACTION

212. *Catholic Action of the Kind Desired by St Pius X*
An interesting conversation of the Holy Pontiff (Pius X) with a group of cardinals was reported in the French clerical publication *L'Ami du Clergé.* The Pope asked them: 'What is the thing we most need today to save society?' 'Build Catholic schools,' said one. 'No.' 'More Churches, ' said another. 'Still no.' 'Speed up the recruiting of priests,' said a third. 'No, no,' said the Pope. ' *the MOST necessary thing of all, at this time, is for every parish to possess a group of laymen who will be at the same time virtuous, enlightened, resolute, and truly apostolic.* [In a footnote the author adds:] After comparing certain passages from St Pius X's first Encyclical with various later statements made by him, it becomes evident that in the interview we quote here, he is depending on the *fervor of priests* to produce the shock troops he mentions. But that it is on the latter, the *select laymen*, that he counts, more than on any other means, for the increase in numbers of the true faithful.

Chautard, *The Soul of the Apostolate*, p. 165.

CENTURION

213. *Centurion of Capharnaum – First Convert among Gentiles*
[The Centurion] is himself said to have been the first of the Gentiles to believe (St Hilary). . . .

[St Augustine is quoted as follows:] In saying he was not worthy, he showed himself worthy that Christ the Word of the Lord should enter, not into his house, but into his heart.

St Thomas Aquinas, in *Catena Aurea*, in Toal, vol. 1, pp. 294-295.

CHURCH

214. *Church – Her Mission*
Before ascending into Heaven, Christ Jesus bequeathed to his Church its greatest treasure – the mission of continuing his work here below. This work, as you know, is double: it is a work of praise in regard to the Eternal Father, a work of salvation in regard to men.
Marmion, *Christ, the Life of the Soul*, p. 306.

215. *Church, Extension of Incarnation, Shares Christ's Infallibility*
. . . Since his Ascension, Christ has left his Church on earth, and this Church is like the extension of the Incarnation among us. The Church – that is to say the Sovereign Pontiff and the Bishops, with the pastors, who are subject to them – speaks to us with all the infallible authority of Jesus Christ himself. . . .

While he was upon earth, Christ contained infallibility in himself. . . . 'I am the truth; I am the life; he that followeth Me walketh not in darkness, but shall have the light of life.' Before leaving us, he confided these powers to his Church: 'As the Father hath sent me, I also send you; he that heareth you, heareth me, and he that despiseth you, despiseth him that sent me.'
Marmion, *ibid.*, p. 88.

216. *Church as Mystical Body of Christ*
According to the beautiful words of St Augustine, we cannot have a full conception of Christ considered apart from the Church. *Totus Christus caput et corpus est: caput Unigenitus Dei Filius, et corpus ejus Ecclesia (De Unitate Ecclesiae).* Jesus has the glory of his Father in view as the foundation of all his life, of all his acts, but the masterpiece by which he is to procure this glory is the Church.
Marmion, *ibid.*, p. 86.

217. *What Membership in the Mystical Body Demands*
To be a true member of the human body, the organ or constituent in question must be animated by the life of the organism; it must be subject to its vivifying principle; and it must exercise its activity, not merely for

its own benefit, but for the benefit of the whole organism and its other members. . . . So it is in the Mystical Body of Christ. To be a living member, the Christian must be in the state of grace – he must be vivified by the Holy Spirit, who is the Soul of that Body; he must be subject to that vivifying Spirit, which means that he must love God and do his will; and he must act for the good of his fellow members, which means he must love his neighbor.

Boylan, *This Tremendous Lover*, p. 51.

218. *Membership in the Visible Church Necessary*

It is true that the invisible Church, or the soul of the Church, is more important than the visible Church, but, in the normal economy of Christianity, it is only by union with the visible society that souls have participation in the possession and privileges of the invisible kingdom of Christ.

Marmion, *Christ, the Life of the Soul*, p. 86.

219. *Why the Church Is in Crisis*

I do not know why we are astonished that the Church is in so much trouble, when we see those who ought to be an example of every virtue to others so disfigure the work which the spirit of the Saints departed wrought in their Orders.

The Life of St Teresa of Jesus, Written by Herself, p. 40.

CONSCIENCE

220. *How Conscience Becomes Blinded*

There is a terrifying law by which sin succeeds in blinding conscience. The man who keeps on sinning against the light must end by not seeing at all. The Pharisees seem to have reached this pitch of blindness. When Jesus did good, they could think of no other explanation than the spirit of evil, so evil had their souls become. When people showed signs of believing in him, they were concerned only with the effect of this upon themselves.

O'Mahoney, *The Person of Jesus*, p. 79.

221. *Conscience versus "Broadmindedness"*

Religious in their praiseworthy efforts after academic recognition and standing . . . must keep in such close union with God and the supernatural principles of life that they will never be infected by that contagious disease called broadmindedness. Of this our Lord warned us when he said:

'Broad is the way that leads to destruction and many there are who enter that way' (Mt 7:13). A Jewish rabbi, on the occasion of his golden jubilee in one of our large cities, answered those who accused him of not being sufficiently broadminded: "I cannot discard my conscience to gain the reputation of being broadminded. Broadmindedness and friendliness are not the same thing."

Hoeger, *The Convent Mirror*, pp. 46-47.

CONSOLATION

222. *Consolation from God – How to Accept It*
St Bernard excellently observes: 'If God gives you the grace of consolation, receive it not as if you thought that it was to be your lasting possession, belonging to you by an hereditary right, nor esteem that you can keep and retain it, as though it could never be taken away from you: lest, when the time comes that God withdraws his hand and gift, you lose heart and fall into undue gloom and sadness. Rather will you take heed . . . if you savor the counsel of the Wise Man to be mindful in evil days of happier ones, and in happy days to forecast the days of evil."

Scaramelli, *Directorium Asceticum*, vol. 1, p. 202.

CONVERSATION

223. *Conversation – Its Power for Good*
Often a word about God, spoken familiarly in conversation, will produce more fruit than many sermons. We should therefore be careful in all our conversations, however indifferent they may be, to allow some edifying word to glide into it on the eternal truths or on the love of God.

St Alphonsus Liguori, *Dignity and Duties of the Priest* pp. 440-441.

CONVERSIONS

224. *Prayer Needed More than Eloquence*
A great servant of God, Father Vincent Caraffa, writing to some young ecclesiastics who were engaged in studying to qualify themselves for the work of saving souls, said to them: 'To bring about great conversions among souls, it is better to be a man of much prayer than a man of great eloquence; for the eternal truths that convert souls are preached differ-

ently by the heart than by the lips.'
St Alphonsus, *ibid.*, pp. 450-451.

225. *Deep Love for God More Effective than Learning*
Experience permits us to see that a priest with moderate science, but burning with love for Jesus Christ, draws more souls to God than many learned and excellent orators who charm people with their eloquence.
St Alphonsus, *ibid.*, p. 452.

226. *Criminal Condemned to Death Converted by Words of a Nun*
A man had been condemned to death, and a nun visited the cell. All efforts to win him from his sins had failed. Just as she was leaving, the nun said: 'What would not a soul in hell give for your chances?' He thought it over, and grace won.
Nash, *The Nun at Her Prie-Dieu*, p. 140.

227. *Conversion from Crime to Sainthood Can Be Instantaneous*
It is possible, not in five days only, but in one moment of time, to change one's whole life. What, indeed, is worse than a robber and murderer? Is this not the worst form of wickedness? Nevertheless, [the good thief] won his way to the summit of virtue and went to paradise itself without needing days or a half day, but only one brief moment.
St John Chrysostom, in *The Fathers of the Church*, vol. 33, p. 9.

DEATH

228. *Death Will Come, But Its Date Is Uncertain*
Nothing is more certain than death, but nothing more uncertain than the hour of death. It is certain that the year and day of each one's death are already determined by our Lord, though we know them not; and wisely does God conceal them from us, in order that we may always prepare for our departure.
St Alphonsus Liguori, *The Way of Salvation and of Perfection*, p. 91.

229. *Death – Certainty Thereof*
St Cyprian says that we are born with a rope around our necks, and as long as we live on earth we hourly approach the gallows, that is, the sickness that puts an end to our life. It would be madness for anyone to delude himself with the idea that he shall not die.
St Alphonsus, *ibid.*, p. 20.

230. *Uncertainty of Death's Date Is a Blessing*
'God, who has promised pardon to the sinner who repents,' says St Gregory, 'has never promised him that he shall have a tomorrow.'

. . . It is a very great mercy of God that the hour of death should be uncertain, to the end that we may always be prepared for it; for if we knew the time, this assurance would give us occasion to become lax and sin with greater confidence.

Rodriguez, *Practice of Perfection and Christian Virtues*, vol. 1, pp. 111-112.

231. *Life Is a Race Toward Death*
From the first moment that life begins in a mortal body, every movement made hastens the approach of death. . . . For every moment that is lived subtracts from the length of life, and day after day less and less remain. Thus, the course of life is nothing but a race towards death, a race in which no one may stand still or slow down for a moment, but all must run with equal speed and never-changing stride. For, to the short-lived as to the long-lived, each day passes with unchanging pace. Both run with equal speed, one to a nearer, the other to a farther post, but for both the same-lengthed minutes are left equally behind.

St Augustine, *City of God*, bk. 13, chap. 10.

232. *Death – Its Right Use Is Beneficial*
. . . The right use of death, which originally was intended as the punishment of sin, may bring forth abundant fruits of holiness. . . .

. . . In a word, while men are in the throes of death and death is bringing disintegration, death is good for no one, but it may become meritorious if suffered to retain or to gain some good. However, when it is a question, not of dying, but of being dead, then death may well be said to be bad for sinners and good for saints. For, the separated souls of the saints are now in peace, while those of the wicked are in pain.

St Augustine, *ibid.*, bk. 13, chaps. 7-8.

233. *Death, the Time of Truth*
The time of death is the time of truth: then do all worldly things appear as they really are – vanity, smoke, and dust.

St Alphonsus Liguori, *Great Means of Salvation and of Perfection*, p. 313.

234. *Death, a Punishment and a Way to Sainthood*
In the case of the first parents, death was incurred by sinning; now, sainthood is attained by dying. This is true of the holy martyrs. . . .

This does not mean that death, which before was an evil, has now become something good. But it means that God has rewarded faith with so much grace that death, which seems to be the enemy of life, becomes an ally that helps man enter life.

St Augustine, *City of God*, bk. 13, Chap. 4.

235. *Day of Death Is a Day of Loss – and of True Comfort*
The day of death is called the day of loss: *The day of loss is at hand* (Dt 32:35). It is a day of loss because all the goods we have gained on earth must be left on the day of death. Wherefore St Ambrose wisely says that we falsely call these good things *our* good things, because we cannot carry them with us into the other world, where we must dwell forever. It is our holy deeds alone that accompany us, and they alone will comfort us in eternity.

St Alphonsus Liguori, *The Way of Salvation and of Perfection*, p. 261.

236. *Death – Feared on Earth, Desired in Hell*
In this life, death is of all things the most dreaded, but in hell it is of all things the most desired. There they desire and long for death but cannot die. 'They shall desire to die, and death shall fly from them' (Apoc 9:6).

St Alphonsus, *ibid.,* p. 94.

237. *Death Not to Be Feared – Resurrection to Be Hoped For*
Our Redeemer took death upon him that we might not be afraid to die; he showed us his own Resurrection that we might hope that we too shall rise again.

St Gregory the Great, in Toal, vol. 4, p. 123.

238. *Death, the Beginning of Eternal Happiness*
Death merely bursts the bonds so that souls may be free to unite themselves perfectly to God, from whom they are far removed in this land of exile.

Let us then be careful while we are in this exile not to look upon death as a misfortune, but as the end of this pilgrimage of ours, which is full of difficulties and dangers. Let us look upon death as the beginning of the eternal happiness we hope one day to attain through the merits of Jesus Christ.

St Alphonsus Ligouri, *The Passion of Jesus Christ*, p. 176.

239. *Death – the Gateway to Eternal Life*
St Paul writes that Jesus Christ chose to die so that through death He might destroy him who had the power of death; that is, the devil; and

might deliver them who, throughout their life, were kept in servitude by the fear death (Heb 2:14, 15). . . . St Thomas remarks on St Paul's words, 'Christ, by His death, took away the fear of death:' When a man reflects that the Son of God chose to die, he himself loses the fear of death. The gentiles were terrorized by the thought of death because they thought that death was the end of everything. But the death of Jesus Christ gives us the guarantee that, if we die in the grace of God, we shall pass from death to eternal life.'

St Alphonsus, *ibid.*, p. 218.

240. *Death as a Road to Eternal Life and Glory*

From death you shall pass to eternal life, from ignominy in men's sight to glory with God, and from the adversities of this world to eternal peace with the angels. Earth did not accept you as citizens, but heaven will welcome you. The world persecuted you, but the angels bear you aloft to the presence of Christ. You will even be called friend by him and will hear the longed-for word of commendation: 'Well done, good and faithful servant, brave soldier and imitator of the Lord, follower of the King. I will reward you with my own gifts, and I shall pay heed to your words even as you did to mine.'

St Basil, in *The Fathers of the Church,* vol. 9, pp. 11-12.

241. *Death Not Terrible for the Truly Wise*

Death is an awesome thing, and one that inspires great fear – not, however, to those who have knowledge of the true wisdom from above. The man who has no clear understanding of the life to come, but considers death as a kind of annihilation and end of life, with good reason shudders and is afraid under the illusion that it means passing on to a state of non-existence. We, on the contrary, who by the grace of God have learned the mysteries and secrets of his wisdom, and who consider death merely as a transition, have no reason to tremble at it. We ought to rejoice and be of good heart because, leaving behind this ephemeral life, we are going to another, much better and brighter, and one that is without end.

St John Chrysostom, in *The Fathers of the Church*, vol. 41, p. 399.

242. *Happy Death of a Good Religious*

St Bernard says that 'it is very easy to pass from the cell to heaven; because a person who dies in the cell scarcely ever descends into hell, since it seldom happens that a religious perseveres in her cell till death unless she is predestined to happiness.'

. . . Hence, Father Suarez, remembering at the hour of death that all his actions in religion were performed through obedience, was filled with spiritual joy and exclaimed that he could not imagine death could be so full of consolation.

St Alphonsus Liguori, *The True Spouse of Jesus Christ*, pp. 55-56.

243. *Happy Death of a Good Religious*

A certain religious of the Society of Jesus, being observed to smile on his deathbed, some of his brethren who were present began to apprehend that he was not aware of his danger and asked him why he smiled; he answered: 'Why should I not smile, since I am sure of paradise? Has not the Lord himself promised to give eternal life to those who leave the world for his sake? I have long since abandoned all things for the love of him; he cannot violate his own promises. I smile, then, because I confidently expect eternal glory.'

St Alphonsus, *ibid.*, p. 55.

244. *Lawful Desire for Death*

We ought not to fear death but sin, which alone makes death so terrible. A great servant of God, Fr Colombiere, said, 'It is morally impossible for one who in life has been faithful to God to die unhappily.'

He who loves God is desirous of death, which will unite him eternally to God. It is a sign of but little love for God not to desire soon to behold him.

St Alphonsus Liguori, *Great Means of Salvation and of Perfection*, p. 339.

245. *Death as a Reward for the Just*

To the just man, death is not a punishment but a reward; it is not dreaded by him, but desired. How can it be dreadful to him if it is to terminate all his pains, afflictions, and conflicts, all danger of losing God? Those words, 'Depart, Christian soul, out of this world,' which strike such terror into the soul of the sinner, fill the soul that loves God with joy.

St Alphonsus Liguori, *The Way of Salvation and of Perfection*, p. 143.

246. *Death Desirable for All Who Are in the State of Grace*

How can he ever abhor death who is in the grace of God? 'He that abideth in love dwelleth in God, and God in him' (1 Jn 4:16). He, therefore, that loves God is secure in his grace, and, thus dying, he is sure of going to rejoice forever in the kingdom of the blessed. . . . Therefore, everyone who has a hope that he is in the grace of God ought to desire death, repeating the prayer which Christ taught us: 'Thy kingdom come.'

St Alphonsus, *ibid.*, pp. 201-204.

247. *Why Saints Desire Death*
I say . . . that he who has but little desire for Paradise shows that he has but little love for God. One that loves desires the presence of the object loved; but we cannot see God without leaving this world; and therefore it is that all the saints have sighed for death in order to see the Lord, whom they have loved. Thus did Augustine sigh, 'Oh, may I die, that I may see thee!'
St Alphonsus, *ibid.*, p. 384.

248. *Death of the Just to Be Envied*
Dearest Aunt, when we look upon the death of the just man, we cannot but envy his lot. For him the time of exile is no more, there is now only God, nothing but God.
Collected Letters of St Thérèse of Lisieux, p. 60.

249. *Death to Be Desired*
What has God given us through his Only-begotten if we still fear the coming of death? Why glory in being born again in water and the Holy Ghost when we are saddened at the thought of going forth from this world? The Lord himself cries out to us: 'If any man minister to me, let him follow me; and where I am, there also shall my minister be' (Jn 12:26). Do you suppose that if an earthly king were to call someone to his palace, or to a feast, that he would not hasten there gratefully? How much more should we not hasten to the heavenly King, who will not only receive us as guests but shall give us to reign with him, as it is written: 'For if we be dead with Him, we shall also live with Him; if we suffer, we shall also reign with Him' (2 Tm 2:11-12).

For this is the sum total of Christian belief: to look for our true life after death: at the end of life, to look for its return.
St John Chrysostom, in Toal, vol. 4, p. 318.

250. *Preparation for Death Necessary*
Would not that general be thought mad who deferred laying in stores of provisions and arms till he were beseiged? That pilot who neglected to provide himself with anchors and cables till overtaken by the storm? Such precisely is the Christian who waits to settle the affairs of his conscience till death is actually at his door.
St Alphonsus Liguori, *Preparation for Death*, p. 10.

251. *How Obtain a Happy Death*
He who expects death every hour will die well even though he die suddenly.
St Alphonsus, *ibid.*, p. 16.

252. *Lessons from the Death of a King*
Philip III, king of Spain, died a young man at the age of forty-two years; and before he died he said to those who stood by: 'When I am dead, proclaim that . . . to have been a king serves only to make me feel the pain of having reigned.' And then he ended with a sigh, saying: 'Oh, that during this time I had been in a desert, becoming a saint, that now I might appear with more confidence before the tribunal of Jesus Christ!'
St Alphonsus Liguori, *The Way of Salvation and of Perfection*, p. 263.

253. *A Kingdom Useless at the Hour of Death*
It was said by Sister Margaret of St Anne, a nun of the Barefooted Carmelites and daughter of the Emperor Rudolph II: 'What profit is a kingdom in the hour of death?'
St Alphonsus, *ibid.*, pp. 196-197.

254. *A King's Regret on His Deathbed*
Philip II, while dying, said: 'Oh, that I had been a lay-Brother in some monastery and not a king!' Philip III said: 'Oh, that I had lived in a desert! For now I shall appear but with little confidence before the tribunal of God.' Thus at the hour of death do those express themselves who have been esteemed the most fortunate in this world.
St Alphonsus, *ibid.*, p. 312.

255. *Road to a Happy Death*
Happy are the dead who die in the Lord (Apoc 14:13). And who are those blessed dead who die in the Lord but the religious who at the end of their lives are already found dead to the world and all its goods?. . .

Pope Honorious, when dying, wished that he had remained in his monastery, occupied in washing the plates, and had not been Pope.
St Alphonsus Liguori, *Great Means of Salvation and of Perfection*, pp. 420-421.

256. *St John Chrysostom on Preparation for Death*
St Chrysostom says, 'Go to a sepulchre, contemplate dust and worms, and sigh. Look on the graves of the dead; see those skeletons gnawed by worms and crumbling into dust, and say . . . 'Such must I become, and why do I not think of this? Why do I not give myself to God? Alas! Who knows but that the sentiments which I am now reading may be the last call for me?'
St Alphonsus, *ibid.*, p. 315.

257. *A Priest Should Desire Death*
The priest should often desire paradise and, consequently, death itself in order promptly to go to heaven, where he may love Jesus Christ with all his strength during all eternity without fear of ever losing him.
St Alphonsus Liguori, *Dignity and Duties of the Priest*, p. 442.

258. *Death of Pope John XXIII*
Shortly after the death of Pope John XXIII, press reports quoted him as having said: 'My bags are packed and I am ready to go.'

259. *Condemned Prisoner Consoles His Weeping Mother*
About the year 1915, a widow living just across the road from Maryknoll Seminary at Ossining, New York, was forced by the death of her husband to look for work in New York City. She was therefore unable to pay adequate attention to the conduct of her children, one of whom, a young man, became involved with a gang of criminals. He had a pistol with which he hoped merely to threaten a druggist the gang planned to rob, but the druggist caught hold of him and the boy killed the druggist.

He was sentenced to die in the electric chair of Sing Sing Prison. There he tried to console his heartbroken mother by telling her how fortunate it was for him that he had not been shot down in the street without a chance to save his soul. 'Here,' he added, 'I know just when I will die, and I have a good opportunity to save my soul.'

Story told to the seminarians by Bishop James Anthony Walsh, co-founder of Maryknoll.

260. *Let This Thought Influence Your Life*
Strive now so to live that in that hour of death thou mayest rather rejoice than fear.
Thomas a Kempis, *Imitation of Christ*, bk. 1, chap. 23.

261. *Death – Thought Thereof Is Remedy for Sin*
No more useful remedy for the wounds of all sins can be found than for each one to think of the hour when he will leave this world.
St Caesarius of Arles, in *The Fathers of the Church*, vol. 31, p. 279.

262. *Death – Remembrance Thereof Helped Make a Saint*
St Camillus de Lellis, looking at the graves of the dead, was accustomed to say: 'If those who are here interred could now return to life again, what would they not do to become saints! And I who have time at my disposal, what do I do for God?' Thus did the saint animate himself to become

more and more closely united with the Lord.

St Alphonsus Liguori, *The Way of Salvation and of Perfection*, p. 134.

263. *Death – Remembrance Thereof a Great Aid to Salvation*
If . . . you desire to live well, endeavor to spend the remainder of your life in the continual remembrance of death. Oh, how correctly does he judge things and how rightly does he direct all his actions who performs them with a view to his departure hence! The remembrance of death destroys in him all affection for the good things of this world by reminding him that he must soon leave them all behind him.

St Alphonsus, *ibid.,* p. 132.

264. *Death of Unbaptized Children – Their Kind of Happiness*
[St Thomas says that] such children will not only not grieve for the loss of eternal happiness, but will, moreover have pleasure in their natural gifts; and will even in some way enjoy God, so far as is implied in natural knowledge and natural love: 'Rather, will they rejoice in this, that they will participate much in the divine goodness and in natural perfections.' And he immediately adds that, although they will be separated from God as regards the union of glory, nevertheless, they will be united with Him by participation of natural knowledge and love.

St Alphonsus Liguori, *Great Means of Salvation and of Perfection*, p. 132.

DEIFICATION

265. *Soul Becomes Like God*
The word *deification* is used to express the process by which the soul is made like to God.

Edward Leen, *Progress Through Mental Prayer*, p. 162.

Deification consists in the knowledge and love of God, in that knowledge and that love which constitutes God's own life and happiness.

Edward Leen, *The True Vine and Its Branches*, p. 39.

266. *Deification Through Grace*
Grace is in the creature a real, physical, not simply moral imitation of a perfection which is found in God in an infinite degree. By it man does not become the divine nature; he does not become God, he becomes 'deified' or 'deiform.' What the Almighty enjoys in virtue of the divine nature with which he is identified, that the creature enjoys in a certain, finite, limited

manner by reason of the participation of the divine likeness given by habitual grace.

Edward Leen, *The Holy Ghost*, p. 254.

267. *Deification of Rational Creatures Willed by God*
God lovingly and firmly wills to 'deify' each rational creature if the creature on its side consents to accept this 'deification.' Man can frustrate this design of God. He frustrates it completely by mortal sin, by which he stifles utterly the divine life in his soul; he frustrates it partially by each degree of imperfection. But the moment the soul submits itself to God's will and accepts his purposes, it enters on the way of 'deification' and comes under the divine influence in a measure proportioned to the greater or less perfection of its submission.

James Leen, *By Jacob's Well*, p. 123.

268. *Deification Through the Eucharist*
The Eucharist alone among the sacraments has for its direct, immediate, and specific effect the spiritual changing of man into the likeness of Christ. . . . Where the dispositions of the soul do not present any obstacle to the operation of grace, the Blessed Sacrament, under the agency of God, infallibility does its divinizing work. As the block of marble, under the action of the chisel in the hands of the artist, loses its shapelessness and takes form and contour, so the soul, under the action of the Sacrament in the hands of God, begins to assume ever more definitely the spiritual traits of Jesus Christ.

Edward Leen, *The Vine and Its Branches*, pp. 84-85.

269. *Deification Through the Eucharist*
As the Body and Blood of the Redeemer is the matter of the sacrifice by which man propitiates his outraged God, so the Body and Blood of Christ is the matter of the sacrament through which God effects his intent of divinizing man.

Edward Leen, *ibid.*, p. 81.

270. *Deification of the Soul – How Accomplished*
The Christian life in the complete sense is a life that is given. It consists in the gradual divinization of the soul. The Christian incorporated in the Sacred Humanity and making his daily life more in ryhthm with what was the daily life of Christ, is brought into intimate contact with the Word, dwelling in the Savior corporally. . . . The Christian must not content himself with aiming to live according to the law of Christ: he must strive to allow Christ, as it were, to express His life through what the Christian himself does and suffers.

Edward Leen, *ibid.*, pp. 171-172.

DESIRES

271. *Desire to Be A Saint Essential*
An ardent desire of perfection is the first means that a religious should adopt in order to acquire sanctity and to consecrate her whole being to God. . . . But how do fervent desires make a soul fly to God? 'They,' says St Laurence Justinian, 'supply strength and render pains light and tolerable.' . . . Whosoever, through diffidence of attaining sanctity, does not ardently desire to become a saint, will never arrive at perfection.

St Alphonsus Liguori, *The True Spouse Of Jesus Christ*, pp. 80-81.

272. *Desire for the Love of God Needed*
All holiness consists in loving God. The love of God is that infinite treasure in which we gain the friendship of God. God is ready to give this treasure of his love, but He wills that we earnestly desire it. . . . St Teresa said: 'God never gives many favors, except to those who earnestly desire His love.' And again, 'God leaves no good desire without its reward.'

It is a deceit of the devil, according to the opinion of the same saint, which makes us think it is a mark of pride to desire to become saints. It would be pride and presumption if we trusted our own works or intentions; but if we hope for all from God, He will give us that strength which we have not.

St Alphonsus Liguori, *The Way of Salvation and of Perfection*, p. 184.

273. *The Desire to Love God Makes Saints*
Holy desires are wings with which souls fly to God. St Aloysius Gonzaga made himself a saint in a short time through the great desire he had of loving God; and as he knew he should never be able to love him as much as he was worthy of being loved, he consumed himself in ardent desires. On this account, St Mary Magdalene of Pazzi called St Aloysius a martyr of love.

St Alphonsus Liguori, *Great Means of Salvation and of Perfection*, p. 360.

274. *Desire of Holiness – First Step Toward It*
The desire of holiness is the first step toward it. To desire holiness is to tend toward it. To tend toward perfection is to begin to attain it. To

desire to love God is already to love him, for God considers the intention and the heart. The desire of the supernatural expands . . . the soul. It empties the soul of attachment to other goods. It opens the soul wide to the communications of God. The more ardent the desire, the more abundant the graces which we receive: 'Open thy mouth wide, and I will fill it.'

Bandas, *The Catholic Layman and Holiness*, p. 47.

275. *Desires for Earthly Things VS Desires for Heavenly Things*

I desire to exhort you to leave all things, but I do not dare to. If you cannot, then, abandon all that is of the world, so hold what you have of this world that you are not to hold fast to the world because of it; that you so possess things that they do not possess you; that what you possess is subject to the rule of your mind, lest your soul, overcome by love of earthly things, be rather possessed by them. Therefore, let earthly things be for use; eternal things the object of our desires. Let temporal things be for the journey; eternal things for our arrival there.

St Gregory the Great, in Toal, vol. 3, p. 187.

276. *Desires for Impossible Things Are Useless*

If I am sick in bed and yet want to preach, say Holy Mass, visit other sick people, and do the work of a well man, are not these empty desires since it is now beyond my ability to put them into effect? In the meantime, these useless desires usurp the place of virtues I ought to have – patience, resignation, mortification, obedience, and meekness under suffering. . . . I can see no way to approve the idea that a person obligated to a certain duty or vocation should distract himself by longing for any other kind of life but one in keeping with his duties or by engaging in exercises incompatible with his present state. To do so dissipates his heart and renders it unfit for its needed work.

St Francis de Sales, *Introduction to the Devout Life*, p. 178.

277. *We Must Learn to Overcome Desires*

[The Elders] lay it down that a man who has not first learnt to overcome desires, cannot possibly stamp out anger or sulkiness . . . nor can he preserve true humility of heart, or lasting unity with the brethren, or a stable and continuous concord; nor remain for any length of time in the monastery.

Cassian, *Institutes,* in *The Nicene and Post-Nicene Fathers*, vol. 11, bk. 4, chap. 8.

278. *Desire for Crosses Can Be an Abuse*

Do not desire crosses except in proportion to the way in which you have patiently carried those already sent to you. It is an abuse to desire martyrdom and lack the courage to put up with injury. The enemy often supplies us with great desires for absent things that we will never encounter in order to divert our minds from present things, from which, small as they may be, we might obtain great profit.

St Francis de Sales, *Introduction to the Devout Life*, p. 179.

DESPAIR

279. *Why Those Tempted to Despair Should Have Confidence*
Let no one say: I have sinned in many ways and so there is no hope of pardon for me. He who says this does not know that God is the God of the repentant; who came into the world because of those who were sick; who has said: There shall be joy in heaven over one sinner doing penance; who has said: *I am not come to call the just, but sinners to repentance* (Mt 9:13).

St Ephraim, in Toal, vol. 3, p. 308.

280. *Despair — — Most Damning of All Sins*
In speaking of despair, St Thomas hesitates not to say that it is the most damning sin of all sins, unbelief not excepted, nor even open hate of God (IIa IIae, q. 22, art. 3); for, as the soul no longer expects any good from God, it casts aside every virtuous practice and runs headlong down the steep path of vice and perdition. In confirmation of this view he [adduces] the saying of St Isidore of Seville, that 'to commit a crime is to give death to the soul, but to despair is to rush headlong into hell'.

Scaramelli, *Directorium Asceticum*, vol. 4, p. 84.

281. *Despair Does God Greater Injury than Any Other Sin*
God one day told St Catherine of Siena that the sinners who despair of his mercy, by losing hope at the end of their lives, do him more injury by this one sin than by all the others they have committed in the course of their lives; thus showing by this new crime that they esteem their sins to be greater than his infinite mercy.

Scaramelli, *ibid.*, p. 78.

DETACHMENT VS ATTACHMENT

282. *Detachment as Means to Attachment to Jesus*
Detachment is but a means to an end, or rather, it is the reverse side of the real end and process, namely attachment. If we have to detach ourselves from various creatures and from our own selves, from our free will, from our own ways, from our own judgment, from our own strength, from our own pleasures, from our own achievement, from our own life — — spiritual as well as temporal — — it is only in order to become completely attached to Jesus. Attachment to Jesus is the royal road to detachment from self. . . . The purpose of this detachment is to achieve complete union of love with God.

Boylan, *This Tremendous Lover*, pp. 257-258.

283. *Not Necessary to Renounce All Creatures*
The perfection of detachment is the work of a lifetime and is only achieved gradually. We are not obliged to renounce all creatures absolutely, but we are asked to make God our ultimate end in our use and our love of them. Our Lord never ceased to love his Mother; St John was his chosen friend until the end; and yet, for all their excellence, they were only creatures.

Boylan, *ibid.*, p. 265.

284. *Detachment from Earthly Things Needed for Growth in Charity*
In the degree to which we withdraw from the love of earthly things, the more will our soul be strengthened in the love of God. The desire to obtain and retain earthly things is the poison of charity, as St Augustine says. Charity is nourished by the weakness of this cupidity. When perfection is reached, there is no cupidity, since the root of all evils is cupidity. Whoever then wishes to nourish charity must not cease to weaken these earthly desires, for cupidity is the love of obtaining and holding on to temporalities.

Mennessier, *Pattern for a Christian, According to St Thomas Aquinas,* p. 194.

DEVIL

285. *The Devil's Mission Makes Us Trust in God*
How many men are fit to evade all [the devil's] deadly wiles unless God

restrains and watches them? The very difficulty of the matter, however, is useful in this respect, that it prevents men from trusting in themselves or in one another, and leads all to place their confidence in God alone. And certainly no pious man can doubt that this is most expedient for us.

St Augustine, *The Enchiridion on Faith, Hope And Love*, p. 72.

286. *Why God Permits Us to Be Tempted*

The omnipotence of the Son of God, in which through one and the same essence he is the equal of the Father, could have, by a simple act of his Will, saved us from the power of the devil, were it not more perfectly in accord with the divine plan that the hostility of our wicked enemy should be undone through that which he had undone; and that we should be restored by means of the same nature through which slavery was imposed on man.

St Leo the Great, in Toal, vol. 2, p. 149.

287. *The Devil's Place in God's Government of Creation*

For all his malicious energy in the cause of disorder and ruin, the devil in spite of himself falls neatly into place as a factor in the divine government of the universe. Despite his most vicious gestures of hatred of God and man, when the results are totalled, the devil is shown to be, not the prince of the world, but the servant not only of God but also of man. . . . Yet his campaign of disorder is turned to the purposes of God. Let him entice man to sin and in reality he offers man an opportunity for the practice of virtue; irritations are builders, not destroyers, of patience; honesty is stronger, not weaker, for its battles against the lazy ease of injustice. . . . The devil's attacks on men are, in the divine government of the world, for the perfection of the very ones the devil works hardest to destroy. . . . This truth is plain when we understand that temptation really means a trial or test. Thus, tests are imposed on man by God for the refining and strengthening of virtue.

Farrell and Healy, *My Way Of Life*, pp. 133-134.

288. *Why God Permits the Devil to Tempt Us*

If the devil, seeing even one enter paradise, cannot bear it, tell me how he can endure to see so many in heaven. You have aroused this fierce beast; but do not fear! You have received greater power, a sharper sword. Pierce the serpent with it. God suffers the demon to rage against you that you may learn by trial the force of your strength. . . . [Christ] could have removed the enemy from our midst, but that you may learn the superiority of his grace, the greatness of the spiritual strength you have received in your baptism, he allows him to attack you, giving you at the same time

the opportunity to gain for yourself many victories.
St John Chrysostom, in Toal, vol. 2, p. 224.

289. *The Devil's Mission Is to Give Saints a Chance for Victory*
God says: 'The Devil, dearest daughter, is the instrument of my Justice to torment the souls who have miserably offended me. And I have set him in this life to tempt and molest my creatures, not for my creatures to be conquered, but that they may conquer, proving their virtue, and receive from me the glory of victory. And no one should fear any battle or temptation of the devil that may come to him, because I have made my creatures strong and have given them strength of will, fortified by the Blood of my Son, which will neither devil nor creature can move, because it is yours, given by me.'
Dialogue of St Catherine of Siena, pp. 118-119.

290. *How the Devil Tempts Spiritual Persons*
St Francis of Assisi said that the devil tempts spiritual persons who have given themselves to God very differently from the way in which he tempts the wicked: at first he does not try to bind them with a cord; he is content with a hair; then he binds them with a thread, then a string, and at last with a cord, and so at length he draws them into sin. He, therefore, who would be free from danger must from the very first despise those hairs, those occasions, those salutations, presents, notes and the like. And for those especially who have contracted a habit of impurity, it will not be sufficient to avoid the proximate occasions; if they do not avoid even the remote, they will fall back into sin.
St Alphonsus Liguori, *Preparation for Death*, p. 87.

291. *The Devil Attacks According to Each One's Character*
When the devil seeks to overcome any man, he first considers what vice is it to which nature is most inclined, so that, delighting in his bonds, he will not even wish to free himself. For our cunning and deceitful enemy well knows with what sort of bonds he can hold us; that should he force us unwilling into his snares, our soul, quickly breaking them, would soon regain its liberty. And so he embraces each one with bonds that to him are pleasant and agreeable, and to which he cheerfully consents. . . . For one who is held by the bonds of envy, since he is a stranger to lust, will believe himself wholly free. And one given to the vice of calumny believes, because he hates robbery and theft, that he is free of every bond.
St Ephraim, in Toal, vol. 4, p. 10.

292. *The Devil's Techniques*
The old enemy does not cease to 'transform himself into an angel of light,'

and spreads everywhere the snares of his deceptions, and makes every effort to corrupt the faith of believers. He knows whom to ply with the zest of greed, whom to assail with the allurements of the belly, before whom to set the attractions of self-indulgence, in whom to instill the poison of jealousy; he knows whom to overwhelm with grief, whom to cheat with joy, whom to surprise with fear, whom to bewilder with wonderment: there is no one whose habits he does not sift, whose cares he does not winnow, whose affections he does not pry into; and whenever he sees a man most absorbed in occupation, there he seeks opportunity to injure him.

St Leo the Great, in *The Nicene and Post-Nicene Fathers*, vol. 12, p.140.

293. *The Devil Works Harder to Capture One Servant of God than Worldlings*

The devil makes more account of getting one servant of God to fall, one religious who is aiming at perfection, than of many others, men of the world.

Rodriguez, *Practice of Perfection and Christian Virtues*, vol. 3, p. 264.

294. *The Devil Attacks Religious Especially*

The demon, ancient and astute serpent as he is, uses more diligence in his attempts to overcome religious men and women than to conquer all the rest of worldly men; and if one of these religious fall, all hell exerts the greatest solicitude and care to prevent his using the many means which religion affords for rising from a fall, such as obedience and holy exercises and the frequent use of the sacraments.

Words of the Blessed Mother to Mary of Agreda in *City of God: Words of Wisdom*, p. 37.

295. *The Devil Strives for Small Conquests at First*

'The devil,' says the holy Doctor (Jerome), 'does not contend at once against anyone by temptations to great vices, but only to small faults, that he may by some means enter and govern the heart of man, and that he may afterwards impel him to more heinous crimes.'

Quoted by St Alphonsus Liguori in *The True Spouse of Jesus Christ*, p. 116.

296. *The Devil Bores Little Holes*

[Let those who strive for perfection] keep watch over the most trifling things and realize that the devil is always boring little holes through which in time great faults may enter. Let them never say: 'This does not matter. We are too particular about this.' Oh, my daughters, everything matters if it is not helping us to make progress.

St Teresa, *Foundations* in Peers, *Complete Works of St Teresa*, pp. 177-178.

297. *The Devil Does Not Attack His People, but God's People*

[The devil] 'is at no pains to assault those of whom he feels already that he is in undisturbed possession,' says St Gregory. And therefore we should not only not be dismayed by temptations, but rather take them for a good sign, as St John Climacus observes. 'There is no surer sign,' he says, 'that the devils are being beaten by us, than their assaulting us most vigorously.' They do it because you have revolted from them and gone out of their jurisdiction; therefore does the devil persecute you because he envies you; otherwise, he would not persecute you so much.

Rodriguez, *Practice of Perfection and Christian Virtues*, vol. 2, p. 358.

298. *Devil Violently Attacks Holy People – Only Prayer Can Save Them*

Denis the Carthusian says that the more anyone gives himself up to God, the more does hell strive to overcome him: 'The more bravely a man strives to serve God, so much the more fiercely does the enemy rage against him.' . . . There is no defence but prayer against being overcome by the devil. . . . Let us not trust, then, to our resolutions; if we put confidence in them, we shall be lost. When we are tempted by the devil, let us place all our confidence in the help of God; recommending ourselves at such times to Jesus Christ and the most Holy Mary.

St Alphonsus Liguori, *Preparation For Death*, p. 80.

299. *The Devil Seeks to Prevent Prayer*

[The devil] knows full well that prayer is the main remedy for all our spiritual disorders. He knows that herein lies our only security for the attainment of eternal blessings. He knows that as they who are constant in prayer are morally certain of their salvation, so there is a moral certainty of the final ruin of such as live in the constant neglect of it, and therefore he spares no effort to destroy the habit, and uses every evil stratagem to render it burdensome, disagreeable, and all but insupportable to the faithful.

Scaramelli, *Directorium Asceticum*, vol. 1, p. 213.

300. *The Devil's Power Is Limited*

While the devil may tempt, taunt, suggest, call names like a spiteful boy, play the part of a sneak and a coward, unless a man surrenders, the devil can never crash the gates of the human soul.

Farrell, *Companion to the Summa*, vol. 4, p. 63.

301. *The Devil's Temptations Are Limited by God*
The devil can tempt a soul, violently and persistently. He can keep nagging that poor harassed soul, sometimes for years, in his effort to win consent to sin. But this he can do only by God's permission and only to the extent for which that permission is given. When he is allowed to tempt a soul, God, who loves the soul, defines the exact terms according to which the evil one may tempt, and then He apportions for the soul grace sufficient to guarantee complete victory over all serious sin. All the soul has to do is to cooperate, and even in the very act of cooperating, it needs grace, which will be offered by a generous God.

Nash, *Living Your Faith*, p. 136.

302. *The Devil Is Chained but Can Bite Those Who Come Near*
. . . Christ came and bound the devil. Someone may say: if he is bound, why is the devil still so powerful? It is true, beloved brethren, that he has much power, but those he dominates are lukewarm, careless, not fearing God in truth. He is bound like a dog in chains, and can bite no one except the soul which is willingly joined to him with fatal self-assurance. So now you see, brethren, how foolish a man is if he is bitten by someone in the position of a dog in chains. Do not be joined to him by the pleasures and passions of the world, and he will not dare to bite you. He can bark and annoy you but is unable to bite you at all unless you will it. He does not harm you by force, but by persuasion; he does not wrest consent from us, but asks it.

St Caesarius of Arles, in *The Fathers of the Church*, vol. 47, p. 201.

303. *Our Weapons Are Stronger than the Devil's*
For a man to let the devil get the better of him is just like a well-armed soldier giving in to an insect and letting it sting him to death. We have far stronger weapons than the devil has: our holy faith, the Blessed Sacrament, the word of God, the example of saintly people, the prayers of Holy Church, and many other powerful helps. In comparison with us, the devil is weaker than an insect compared with a bear, if only we will stand firm and act like men and anchor ourselves in God, who has conferred all these benefits upon us.

Tauler, *Spiritual Conferences*, pp. 44-45.

304. *The Devil is Weak in Face of Those Who Will Not Give Consent*
St Bernard [referring to the devil's attempt to get Christ to hurl Himself down from the pinnacle] says very well: 'Look and observe, my brethren, how weak our enemy is, since he can only overcome him who wishes to be overcome. St Jerome says: 'This is the voice of the devil, who desires that

all should throw themselves down and fall into the abyss. The devil can urge you to throw yourself down, but he cannot throw you down if you do not wish it.'

Rodriguez, *Practice of Perfection and Christian Virtues*, vol. 2, pp. 388-389.

305. *By Submitting Ourselves to God's Will, we Are Stronger than the Devil*

Without God's permission, the evil spirit has no power against mankind, for he could not even have entered into the swine if God has not permitted it. We must therefore subject ourselves of our own free will to him to whom all opposing forces must subject themselves, even against their own will. By doing so we become stronger than our enemies, for through humility we become one with the Creator of the universe.

St Gregory the Great, in *The Fathers of the Church*, vol. 39, p. 153.

306. *How to Fight the Devil*

The surest way of fighting the demon is to despise him, looking upon him as the enemy of the Most High who has lost all fear of God and all hope of good; who in his stubborness has deprived himself of all means of recovery and is without sorrow for his wickedness. . . .

The devil is proud and is deeply hurt by contempt; in the presumption of his arrogance and vanity, he desires above all the attention of men. . . .

As long as this slave of wickedness is not despised, he never believes himself discovered and he continues, like an importunate fly, to buzz about the spot most tainted by the greatest corruption. . . .

Arm thyself with living faith, unwavering hope, and love of humility, for these are the virtues by which the dragon is crushed and vanquished and against which he dares not take a stand. He flies from them because they are powerful weapons against his pride and arrogance. (Words of the Blessed Mother to Mother Mary of Agreda).

Mary of Agreda, *City of God: Words of Wisdom*, pp. 172, 174-175, 338-339.

307. *The Devil – How To Defeat Him*

[The devil] suggests to thee many evil thoughts that he may weary thee, and frighten thee that he may withdraw thee from prayer and the reading of devout books.

He is displeased with humble confession, and if he could he would cause thee to omit Communion.

Give no credit to him, value him not, although he often lays his deceitful snares in thy way.

Charge him with it when he suggests wicked and unclean things, and say to him: Begone, unclean spirit; be ashamed, miserable wretch, thou art very filthy indeed to suggest such things to me. Depart from me, thou wicked imposter, thou shalt have no share in me, but my Jesus will be with me as a valiant warrior, and thou shalt be confounded.

Thomas à Kempis, *Imitation of Christ*, bk. III, chap. 6.

308. *The Devil – a Way to Combat Him*

[St Francis de Sales] insists especially on perseverance in action with as much good humor as at the time of consolation. 'If the enemy, who seeks by sadness to make us weary of good works, sees that we do not cease on that account to perform them, and that, being performed despite his opposition, they become more meritorious, he will cease to trouble us any longer.' This is an art that we can call 'the deceiver deceived.' The demon, losing at each throw of the dice, no longer seeks to play.

Charmot, *St Ignatius Loyola and St Francis de Sales*, p. 89.

309. *The Devil Foiled by His Own Malice*

If the cruel and proud foe could have known the counsel of God's mercy, he would have aimed at soothing the Jews' minds into gentleness rather than firing them with unrighteous hatred, lest he should lose the thralldom of all his captives in assailing the One who owed him nought. Thus he was foiled by his own malice: he inflicted a punishment on the Son of God, which was turned to the healing of all the sons of men. He shed righteous Blood, which became ransom and the drink for the world's atonement. The Lord undertook that which he chose according to the purpose of his own will. He permitted madmen to lay their wicked hands upon him: hands which, in ministering to their own doom, were of service to the Redeemer's work.

St Leo the Great, in *The Nicene and Post-Nicene Fathers,* vol. 12, p. 174.

DEVOTION

310. *The Essence of Devotion*

The Angelic Doctor says that true devotion consists not in feeling but in the desire and resolution to embrace promptly all that God wills. Such was the prayer that Jesus Christ made in the garden; it was all full of aridity and tediousness, but it was the most devout and meritorious prayer that has ever been offered in this world; it consisted of these words: 'Not what I will, but what thou wilt' (Mk 14:36).

St Alphonsus Liguori, *The True Spouse of Jesus Christ*, pp. 464-465.

311. *Devotion Is Readiness for All That Is Good*
Devotion is nothing else than a promptitude and readiness of will for all that is good; and thus the truly devout man is he who is prompt and disposed for all good: such is the common doctrine of the saints. Now St Thomas says there are two causes of this devotion, one extrinsic and principal, which is God; the other intrinsic on our part, which is meditation. . . . Thus true devotion and fervor of spirit does not consist in the sensible sweetness and relish which some experience in prayer, but in keeping a will prompt and disposed for all points of the service of God. This is devotion that lasts and endures; that other soon comes to an end, consisting as it does of affections and sensible devotion. . . .
Rodriguez, *Practice of Perfection and Christian Virtues*, vol. 1, p. 311.

312. *Devotion Defined*
. . . Devotion is simply that spiritual agility and vivacity by which charity works in us or by aid of which we work quickly and lovingly. Just as it is the function of charity to enable us to observe all God's commandments in general and without exception, so it is the part of devotion to enable us to observe them more quickly and diligently. Hence, a man who does not observe all God's commandments cannot be held to be either good or devout.
St Francis de Sales, *Introduction to the Devout Life,* p. 34.

313. *Not Sweetness but Prompt Service*
. . . [Strong devotion] is based upon a deep realization of God's absolute sovereignty over us, and his right to unqualified subjection on our part; and it means a promptitude of disposition to obey Him in all things and to exhibit a great generosity in His service. [A footnote here quotes St Thomas as follows: 'Devotion is the will to give oneself with promptitude to the things that belong to the service of God'.] The soul possessed of true devotion is not content merely with carrying out God's orders, it aims at anticipating his wishes. Devotedness is something far higher than mere duty. It is inventive to discover ways of giving pleasure to the Person who is its object. . . . Often, devotion is exercised without any feeling of relish and in the darkness of faith; this absence of feeling is called spiritual dryness. For faithful souls, such dryness is a test of their sincerity and a trial sent by God to purify and deepen their faith.
Edward Leen, *Progress Through Mental Prayer*, pp. 206-207.

314. *In What Devotion Consists*
Devotion, St Thomas says consists in a readiness of the will to carry out all that belongs to obeying, serving, and pleasing God. In this readiness of

the will to perform acts of service and love, however devoid they may be of sensible fervor, the whole substance of real devotion really consists.

Scaramelli, *Directorium Asceticum*, vol. 1, p. 158.

315. *Our Heart Becomes God's Altar*

When raised to God, our heart becomes his altar; his only Son is the Priest who wins for us his favor. It is only by the shedding of our blood in fighting for his truth that we offer him bloody victims. We burn the sweetest incense in his sight when we are aflame with holy piety and love. As the best gifts, we consecrate and surrender to him our very selves, which He has given us.

St Augustine, *City of God,* bk. 10, chap. 3.

DIGNITY OF CHRISTIANS

316. *Members of Christ, Temples of the Holy Spirit*

Acknowledge, O Christian, the dignity that is yours! Being made a partaker of the divine nature, do not by an unworthy manner of living fall into your former abjectness of life. Be mindful of whose Head, of whose Body, you are a member. . . . By the sacrament of baptism, you have become the temple of the Holy Spirit. Do not by evil deeds drive from you such a One dwelling with thee and submit yourself again to the bondage of the devil. Because your price was the Blood of Christ; because in strictness He shall judge you who in mercy redeemed you.

St Leo the Great, in Toal, vol. 1, p. 120.

317. *Discouragement to Be Avoided*

The saints set so much value on our keeping up our courage and cheerfulness that they say we should not be discouraged even over our falls, nor lose heart, nor go about sad and melancholy. Sin being one of the things for which we may reasonably be sad, as we shall say presently, nevertheless, says St Paul this sadness should be tempered and allayed by the hope of forgiveness and the mercy of God, so as not to cause discouragement and disheartenment, 'lest perhaps it happen that such a one be overwhelmed with excess of sadness' (2 Cor 2:7).

Rodriguez, *Practice of Perfection and Christian Virtues*, vol. 2, p. 468.

318. *Discouragement – How to Be Cured*
. . . Discouragement is a tight bond which binds fast the spirit, keeps it captive, holding it back, cramping and stopping its onward movement. A Director in this case should help the disciple to draw from the sense of his feelings and miseries, not depression of spirit and loss of energy, but honest humility full of trust in God.
Scaramelli, *Directorium Asceticum*, vol. 1, pp. 92-93.

319. *Discouragement – A Disaster*
Discouragement and loss of heart are the great disasters of the spiritual warfare. Discouragement is never justifiable. For though there may be many a failure in the fight, nevertheless, if the fight is not abandoned, these failures can be turned to good account. They help the soul to grow in the realization of its own weakness. They teach it humility and a sane distrust of self. They reveal to it the wisdom of relying on God alone. Much is allowed to happen to the soul in order that it might become practically convinced of its own powerlessness for good. Occasional failures, proceeding from weakness, should produce, not discouragement, but detachment from self. It is for this purpose, very often, that they are permitted by the Lord. Disappointment and irritation with oneself always comes from wounded self-love and from having too much confidence in one's own power to achieve good.
Edward Leen, *The True Vine and Its Branches*, p. 197.

DISSENTION

320. *The Evil of Causing Strife*
. . . Since nothing is more precious with God than the virtue of loving kindness, nothing is more acceptable to the devil than the extinction of charity. Whosoever, then, by sowing strife destroys the loving kindness of neighbors serves God's enemy as his familiar friend.
St Gregory The Great, in *The Nicene and Post-Nicene Fathers,* vol. 12, p. 50.

DOCTRINE

321. *Doctrinal Errors Are Like Spots of Leprosy*
True doctrine mixed without order with what is false, in a man's discussion or conversation, and showing like the colors in a body, resembles the leprosy that spots and blemishes the human body with patches of true and false color. Such persons are to be excluded from the Church so that, if it is possible, placed afar off, they may with a loud voice cry out to Jesus.
St Bede, in Toal, vol. 4, p. 83.

322. *Knowledge of Doctrine should balance with secular knowledge*
Quite a number of educated Catholics try to be satisfied with what they have learned of doctrine at school; this would seem to be a mistake. A man's mind develops after he leaves school, his knowledge and experience increases, his view broadens, his judgment matures, and he meets many problems that require a doctrinal solution. To expect the grown and mature mind . . . to be satisfied with the hazy memory of what [the] immàture mind had acquired from . . . limited instruction . . . is, at the least, imprudent; one runs the risk of having religion rejected as inadequate.
Boylan, *This Tremendous Lover*, p. 103.

323. *Professionals Need Special Knowledge of Doctrine*
In one field of knowledge at least, [the professional classes] are familiar with a complete and scientific treatment of a subject. Their trained minds, consciously or unconsciously, tend to estimate things by the reasons lying behind them, and if their knowledge of [the Faith] is not sufficiently wide or deep to show them something of its solid foundations and extraordinary logic, and to enable them to see that it can hold its own as a science with their own subject, they may be led to contempt for what little they know of religion, and may be tempted to abandon it altogether. Certainly, they are not likely to make it the driving force of their whole life, as God wants them to do.
Boylan, *ibid.*, pp. 103-104.

324. *How Doctrine Developed*
[Explaining the development of doctrine, Mr Frank J. Sheed says:] A

rough comparison may make the position clear: a man brought into a dark room begins by distinguishing little: then he sees certain patches of shadow blacker than the rest: bit by bit he sees these as a table and chairs: then, as his eyes grow accustomed to the obscurity, he sees things smaller still – pictures, books, ash trays—and so on to the smallest detail. Nothing has been added to the contents of the room: but there has been an immense growth in his knowledge of the contents of the room. So with the Church. She has, generation by generation, seen deeper and deeper. This development of the Church's understanding of what has been committed to her is not like anything else in the world. Science, for instance, progresses, but its progress consists in discovering and discarding its own errors. The teaching of the Church develops by seeing further truths. At every stage the Church adds something: but not at the cost of discarding anything. At every stage all she teaches is true: at no stage does she teach all that is contained in the Truth.

Sheed, *A Map of Life*, pp. 71-72.

DYING

325. *The Priest's Duty*
The priest should be occupied in assisting the dying, which is a work of charity most dear to God, and most conducive to the salvation of souls; for the dying are more strongly tempted by the devils and are less able to assist themselves. St Philip Neri frequently saw angels suggesting words to priests who were attending dying persons. For parish priests this work is an obligation of justice, but for every priest it is a duty of charity.

St Alphonsus Liguori, *Dignity and Duties of the Priest*, p. 181.

EATING

326. *Eating Without Preference*
We should listen with great reverence to the words said to his disciples by our Savior and Redeemer: 'Eat what is put before you.' It is, I believe, a greater virtue to eat without preference what is put before you and in the same order as it is put before you, whether you like or dislike it, than always to choose the worst. Although the latter way of life seems more austere, the former demands more resignation, for by it we renounce not

only our taste but our choice as well. Moreover, it is no little mortification to adapt our taste to all kinds of food and keep it under control at all times. Again, mortification of this kind doesn't show in public, bothers no one, and is well adapted to social life.

St Francis de Sales, *Introduction to the Devout Life*, p. 152.

EDUCATION

327. *Education Demands a Supernatural Foundation*
For more than thirty years we have been able to observe, from afar, the progress of two orphanages for little girls, maintained by two separate congregations. Each one had to go through a period of evident decline. To be frank: out of sixteen orphans, all of whom had entered under the same conditions and had left upon coming of age, three from the first house and two from the second had passed, in from eight to fifteen months, from the practice of frequent Communion to the most degraded level of the social scale. Of the eleven others, one alone remained deeply Christian. And yet every one of them had been placed, on leaving, in a good situation.

In one of these orphanages, eleven years ago, there was a single change: a new Mother Superior was installed. Six months afterwards a radical transformation was apparent in the spirit of the house.

The same transformation was observed three years later in the other orphanage because, while the same superior and the same sisters remained, the chaplain had been changed.

Now, since that time, not a single one of the poor girls who left, at the age of twenty-one, has been dragged down by Satan into the gutter. Every one, every single one of them without exception, has remained a good Christian.

The reason for these results is very simple. At the head of the house, or in the confessional, the spiritual direction previously given had not been really supernatural.

Chautard, *The Soul of the Apostolate*, pp. 107-108.

EFFORT

328. *Effort Is What Counts in God's Sight*
The Apostle St Paul says: 'I have laboured more than all' (1 Cor 15:10). He does not say: "I have produced more fruit than all," because he knew well, as he had been taught by God, that 'Everyone shall receive reward and recompense according to his labor' (1 Cor 3:8), not according to the success and fruit that has been gained. . . . The increase and fruit does not stand to your account. The Lord will give it when he pleases. . . .
Rodriguez, *Practice of Perfection and Christian Virtues*, vol. 3, p. 109.

ETERNITY

329. *Thinking about Eternity Sanctifies*
One thought upon eternity, well weighed, is enough to make a saint.
St Alphonsus Liguori, *The Way of Salvation and of Perfection*, p. 253.

330. *The Thought of Eternity Saves*
He who frequently meditates upon eternity does not become attached to the goods of this world and thus secures his salvation.
St Alphonsus, *ibid.*, p. 83.

331. *The Thought of Eternity Steadies Us*
St Gregory wrote that they who meditate on eternity are neither puffed up by prosperity nor cast down by adversity; for they desire nothing and they fear nothing in this world. When it happens to us to suffer infirmities and persecutions, let us think of the hell which we have deserved through our sins.
St Alphonsus, *ibid.*, pp. 173-174.

332. *The Thought of Eternity Changes One's Whole Life*
St Philip Neri, speaking one day to a young man named Francis Zazzera, who expected to make his fortune in the world by his talents, said: 'Be of

good heart, my son, you may make a great fortune, you may become an eminent lawyer, you may then be made a prelate, then perhaps a cardinal, and then, who knows, perhaps even pope'. And then? And then?' 'Go,' continued the saint, 'and reflect on these two words'. The young man went on his way, and after having meditated on the two words *and then? and then?* abandoned all his worldly prospects and gave himself entirely to God. Leaving the world, he entered into the same congregation that St Philip had founded, *and then* he died in the odor of sanctity.

St. Alphonsus, *ibid.*, p. 86.

333. *Eternity – the Great Thought*

Thus did St Augustine designate the thought of eternity: 'The great thought – *magna cogitatio*.' It was this thought that induced so many solitaries to retire into deserts; so many religious, even kings and queens, to shut themselves up in cloisters; and so many martyrs to sacrifice their lives in the midst of torments in order to acquire a happy eternity in heaven and to avoid a miserable eternity in hell. The Venerable John of Avila converted a certain lady with these two words: 'Reflect,' said he to her, 'on these two words: *Ever* and *Never*.' . . . The same John of Avila says that he who believes in eternity and becomes not a saint should be confined as one deranged.

St Alphonsus, *ibid.*, p. 23.

334. *We Should Live for Eternity*

Whatever the world may promise you, the kingdom of heaven is greater; whatever the world threatens you, the punishment of hell is worse. And so if you wish to rise above all human fears, fear the eternal punishments that God threatens. And do you wish to crush the impulses of concupiscence? Desire the eternal life God promises us. By this you close the door to the devil; by this you open it to Christ.

St Augustine in Toal, vol. 4, p. 405.

335. *Let Eternal Things be Our Goal*

Let temporal things serve thy use, but the eternal be the object of thy desire.

Thomas a Kempis, *Imitation of Christ*, bk. 3, chap. 16.

336. *The Thought of Eternity is Effective*

Nothing is so effective as the *mindfulness of eternity* in keeping the soul directed to God in all its acts.

Chautard, *The Soul of the Apostolate*, p. 248.

337. *The Lodestar of St Aloysius Gonzaga*
[The thought of eternity had been the lodestar of St Aloysius.] When faced with a decision to be made, he would ask himself: 'What shall I wish to have decided in eternity?' When he had to make a choice, his choice was governed not by caprice but by the same momentous question. Eternity realized, not merely believed in, dwarfed all else, and Aloysius scaled the heights.

Nash, *Living Your Faith*, p. 7.

EVIL

338. *God Draws Good out of Evil*
God would never have created a single angel – not even a single man – whose future wickedness he foresaw, unless, at the same time, he knew of the good which could come of the evil.

St Augustine, *City of God*, bk. 11, chap. 18.

339. *Why Evil Is Permitted by the Creator*
[The Creator] judged it better to bring good out of evil than not to permit any evil to exist.

St Augustine, *The Enchiridion on Faith, Hope and Love*, p. 33.

340. *God's Concurrence in Evil Actions*
'Good things and evil, life and death . . . are from God' (Ecclus 11:14): Prosperity and adversity, life and death, come from the Lord. It is necessary to know that in every action there is a physical entity which belongs to the material part of the action, and a moral entity that appertains to reason: the moral entity of the action, or the sin of the person who persecutes you, belongs to his malice, but the physical entity appertains to the divine concurrence; so that God wills not the sin, but he wills that you suffer the persecution, and it is he who sends it. . . . Hence, Job said: 'The Lord gave, and the Lord hath taken away, as it hath pleased the Lord, so it is done; blessed be the name of the Lord' (Jb 1:21).

St. Alphonsus Liguori, *The True Spouse of Jesus Christ*, pp. 428-429.

341. *Evil Permitted by God*
Comparatively little of what befell Christ at the hands of men was the will of God. Much, in fact, emanated from the will of men in positive opposi-

tion to the will of God. But this perversity of men had no power to oust the beneficent influence of the Almighty from those events. God can achieve his purpose even through the perversity of his creatures. What occurred may not have been God's will, but it was God's will that the victims of these circumstances should, relying on the help of his Heavenly Father, embrace the sufferings involved, and in this way make them serve for the purification of mankind from sin. It is thus that God enables his faithful servants to meet the Divine Will, even in what runs counter to that will. God does not will the wrong and injustice from which his servants suffer; but he wills that his servants should bear themselves virtuously in their sufferings and in this way make them redound to the glory of God and the spiritual advantage of their own souls.

James Leen, *By Jacob's Well*, pp. 114-115.

EXAMPLE

342. *Good Example Is Best Means of Doing Good*

[St Ignatius writes:] 'The first thing that will help will be a good example of all propriety and Christian virtue, that by good works even more than by good words they may edify those with whom they deal.' A good and holy life, being oneself under control and discipline to begin with, is the principal and most efficacious means of doing much good to our neighbor.

Rodriguez, *Practice of Perfection and Christian Virtues*, vol. 3, p. 51.

343. *Importance of Good Example*

St Augustine says that so great is the infirmity and weakness of man, that it is difficult for him to do good unless he first sees the example of it in others; and on that account he says that it is very important for a teacher and preacher of the Gospel to be a good man, to give a pattern for those who hear him to imitate.

Rodriguez, vol. 3, p. 52.

344. *Good Example Gives Glory to God*

How can the Lord say: 'Let your light shine before men in order that they may see your good works and give glory to your Father in heaven' (Mt 5: 16)? This means that he orders the person who is following the precepts of God to do everything with an eye toward God and to be pleasing to

God alone without searching for any reputation among men. In ordering us to flee from the praise and approbation of men on the one hand, and, on the other, to be known to all because of our life and deeds, he does not say that the beholders of these deeds should admire the person who does them, but that they should give glory to the Father in heaven. He orders us to refer all glory and to direct all action to the will of that One with whom lies the reward of virtuous deeds.

St Gregory of Nyssa, in *The Fathers of the Church*, vol. 58, p. 135.

345. *Giving Good Example Is Not for Our Glory*

'So let your light shine before men,' [Christ] told them, 'that they may see your good works and glorify your Father in heaven' (Mt 5:16). Not, notice, 'that you may be seen by them,' not, that is, with the intention that they be converted to you – since you by yourselves are nothing – but 'that they may glorify your Father, who is in heaven,' so that, by being converted to him, they may become as you are.

St. Augustine, *City of God*, bk. 5, chap. 14.

346. *Example of St. John the Baptist and St John Vianney*

Without working a single miracle, John the Baptist attracted great crowds. St John Vianney had a voice so weak that it could not reach most of those in the crowds that surged about him. But if people could hardly hear him, they saw him; they saw a living monstrance of God, and the mere sight of him overwhelmed those who were there and converted them.

A lawyer had just returned from Ars. Someone asked what it was that had impressed him. He said: 'I have seen God in a man.'

Chautard, *The Soul of the Apostolate*, pp. 121-122.

347. *Example of a Lay Brother*

[A captain of the dragoons in the Franco-Prussian War, in 1870, Brother Gabriel made a vow at the battle of Gravelotte to join the Trappists as a lay brother. Chautard says of him:] 'Brother Gabriel, the Trappist brother, did much more to revive the faith of numerous visitors to his monastery, merely by carrying out his duties as assistant to the guest master, than could have been done by a learned priest whose words might appeal more to the mind than to the heart. General Miribel frequently came to converse with the humble brother and used to say: "I came here to revive my faith."'

[In a footnote, Chautard says that] the duties of the assistant to the guest Master are the simple ones of washing dishes, waiting on table, making beds, and so on; but those in this position are allowed to speak with the guests.

Chautard, *ibid.*, pp. 123-124.

348. *Giving Good Example Is Not Pride*
To appear devout, mortified, observant of rule, devoted to mental prayer and to frequent Communion, in order to give good example to the other Sisters, is not an act of vanity, but an act of charity, very pleasing to God.
St Alphonsus Liguori, *The True Spouse of Jesus Christ*, p. 370.

349. *Bad Example Is Ruinous for Religious Life*
. . . You cannot do more harm in religion than by giving bad example in it; and the older and more gifted you are, the more harm you will do, because example is the most effectual of forces to move and carry others away, as the saints and experience show us; and example is far more potent for evil than for good.
Rodriguez, *Practice of Perfection and Christian Virtues*, vol. 3, pp. 406-407.

FASTING

350. *The Usefulness of Fasting*
Let not anyone listen to the tempter inwardly suggesting such things as these: 'What do you do that prompts you to fast? You are cheating your soul; you are not giving it what pleases it; you are imposing punishment upon yourself; you are your own torturer and executioner. Does it please God to have you torment yourself? Then he is cruel, since he is pleased by your suffering.' Answer a tempter of this sort with these words: 'Certainly I punish myself so that he may spare me; I take vengeance on myself so that he may come to my aid, so that I may be pleasing in his eyes, so that I may delight in his graciousness. For the victim is tortured so that it may be placed on the altar. My flesh will thus weigh less heavily upon my mind. . . .'
St Augustine, in *The Fathers of the Church*, vol. 16, p. 407.

351. *The Usefulness of Fasting*
He [Adam] from whom we were born received the punishment of death, and we drag along that which we are to conquer. On that account, we strive against the flesh so that we may render it, when subdued, subservient to us, and so that we may draw it to obedience. Do we then hate that which we wish to give obedience to us? . . . You subdue your son so that he may obey you. Do you hate him? Do you consider him your enemy? . . . 'I chastise my body and bring it into subjection; lest perhaps while preaching to others, I myself should be found lacking' (1 Cor 9:26-28).

Your flesh is below you; above you is your God. When you wish your flesh to serve you, you are reminded of how it is fitting for you to serve your God. You notice what is under you; notice, also, what is above you.
St Augustine, *ibid.*, p. 410.

FATE

352. *Fate Vs. Free Will – Wrong Notion of Fate*
We do not deny, of course, an order of causes in which the will of God is all-powerful. On the other hand, we do not give this order the name of fate, except in a sense in which the Word 'fate' is derived from *fari*, to speak. For, of course, we cannot reject what is written in Holy Scripture: 'God hath spoken once, these two things I have heard, that power belongeth to God and mercy to thee, O Lord, for thou wilt render to everyone according to his works' (Ps 61:12). The 'once' here means 'once and for all'. God spoke once and for all because he knows unalterably all that is to be, all that he is to do. In this way, we might use the word 'fate' to mean what God has 'spoken' (*fatum*), except that the meaning of the word has already taken a direction in which we do not want men's minds to move.

However, our main point is that, from the fact that to God the order of all causes is certain, there is no logical deduction that there is no power in the choice of our will. The fact is that our choices fall within the order of the causes, which is known for certain to God and is contained in his foreknowledge . . . for human choices are the causes of human acts. It follows that he who foreknew the causes of all things could not be unaware that our choices were among those causes which were foreknown as the causes of our acts.
St Augustine, *City of God*, bk. 5, chap. 9.

FAULTS

353. *Faults Are to Be Uprooted While They Are Still Weak*
St Dorotheus tells of an aged monk who was directing a novice on how to uproot faults. The monk told the novice to pull up a plant that had just appeared above the ground. This, the young man did easily. Then the monk told him to pull up a plant that had already struck root. The novice did so with one hand, but with a certain amount of effort. Then the monk

ordered him to pull up a sapling. The novice had to use both hands and succeeded only with difficulty. Then the monk told him to pull up a tree. This he could not do even with extreme effort. The monk then drew the conclusion that it is easy to control passions when they have just begun, but that it is more and more difficult as the passions grow stronger, and said that in the end only the all-powerful hand of God can give success.

Scaramelli, *Directorium Asceticum*, vol. 2, pp. 183-184.

FEAR OF GOD

354. *A means of Gaining and Keeping Grace*

. . . Says St Bernard: . . . I have found by experience that there is no means so effectual for gaining the grace of God and keeping it, and recovering it if lost, as to walk always in fear before God, not presuming on myself. . . .

Rodriguez, *Practice of Perfection and Christian Virtues*, vol. 3, p. 259.

355. *Fear That Disciplines Our Life Is Good*

'Fear the Lord, all ye His saints; for there is no want to them that fear him' (Ps 33:10). Unless fear disciplines our life, it is impossible successfully to attain holiness in body.

St Basil, in *The Fathers of the Church*, vol. 46, p. 259.

356. *Fear of the Lord That Is Based on Love*

Whoever . . . has been established in this perfect love is sure to mount to a higher stage to that still more sublime fear belonging to love, which is the outcome of no dread of punishment or greed of reward, but of the greatest love; whereby a son fears with earnest affection a most indulgent father . . . while there is no dread of his blows or reproaches but only a slight injury to his love. . . . To this fear, then, not sinners but saints are invited by the prophetic word where the Psalmist says: 'O fear the Lord, all ye saints; for they that fear him lack nothing.'

Abbot Chaeremon, quoted by Cassian in *The Nicene and Post-Nicene Fathers*, vol. 11, p. 421.

357. *Fear of the Lord Cuts Off Wicked Desires*

The fear of the Lord is like a two-edged sword, cutting off every wicked desire. Keep, therefore, ever in mind the fear of the Lord, being mind-

ful at all times of that last dreadful day . . . when the Son of Man shall appear.
St Ephrem, in Toal, vol. 1, p. 11.

358. *Fear of Christ the Judge*
Keep before your mind this so fearful Judge. Fear his coming, so that when he comes you may be able to look upon him, not in fear, but in confidence. He is now to be feared, so that then we shall not fear him. Let the fear of him make you eager in doing good. Let fear of him keep your soul from evil. Believe me, brethren, the more we are now in earnest to keep ourselves free from sin, the more confident shall we be in his presence.
St Gregory the Great, in Toal, vol. 2, p. 287.

359. *Fear of God, Vs. Love for God*
It is filial fear which is the gift of the Holy Spirit. It is filial fear which really perfects hope by leading man to make certain of his salvation by avoiding sin. . . .

Men often say that love casts out fear. When we apply this saying to the love and fear of God, it is partly true and partly false. It is true that the love of God takes away the servility or cravenness of servile fear. For the more a man loves God, the less he fears punishment. For the more he loves God, the less he thinks of himself, even from the point of view of punishment. And the more he loves God, the more confident he is that he will escape punishment and attain happiness. . . .

Filial fear, the gift of the Holy Spirit, increases as a man's love for God increases. For the more a man loves someone, the more he fears to offend him or be separated from him. So too, the more a man loves God, the more he will fear to offend Him or be separated from Him.
Farrell and Healy, *My Way of Life*, pp. 335-336.

360. *Filial Fear Vs. Servile Fear*
'Thou shalt love', he says, not: 'Thou shalt fear'. For it is a greater thing to love than to fear. To fear is the character of slaves; to love, of children. Fear springs from coercion; love from liberty. He who serves God in fear will indeed escape punishment but does not receive the reward of justice; because he did good, not freely, but because of fear. God, therefore, does not wish men to fear him in a servile manner, as an owner, but love him as a Father; since he gave men the spirit of adoption.
St Thomas Aquinas, in Toal, vol. 4, p. 155.

361. *Servile Fear Vs. Filial Fear*
A soul that always walks in the single way of the fear of punishment, and

from this single motive avoids sin, is always in great danger of making a relapse before long into sin; but he that attaches himself to God by love is sure not to lose him as long as he loves him, and for this reason we must continually beg God to grant us the gift of His holy love, always praying and saying: O Lord, keep me united with thee, never suffer me to be separated from thee and from thy love. The fear which we ought rather to desire and beg of God is filial fear, the fear of displeasing this our good Lord and Father.

St Alphonsus Liguori, *The Incarnation, Birth and Infancy of Jesus Christ*, p. 59.

362. *Hostile Fear*
Every fear is not a good and saving feeling, but there is also a hostile fear, which the Prophet prays may not spring up in his soul, when he says: 'Deliver my soul from the fear of the enemy' (ps 63:2). . . . He . . . who is easily scared by the demons has the fear of the enemy in him. On the whole, such a fear seems to be a passion born of unbelief. For no one who believes that he has at hand a strong helper is frightened by any of those who attempt to throw him into confusion.

St Basil, in *The Fathers of the Church*, vol. 46, p. 262.

FORGIVENESS

363. *Forgiveness of Sin Shows Christ's Divinity*
'Son', he says, 'thy sins are forgiven thee'. Saying this, he intimates that it is his will that men should know he is God: though now as man still hidden to human eyes. Through his signs and wonders he was already compared with the prophets who, through him, had also wrought signs and wonders. Now he began to implant in human breasts that he is God; for to forgive sin, since it is beyond the power of man, is the particular sign of divinity. The envy of the Pharisees proves this; for when he said 'Thy sins are forgiven thee, the Pharisees answered: He blasphemeth. Who can forgive sin but God alone?'

St Peter Chrysologus, in Toal, vol. 4, pp. 190-191.

364. *Forgiveness of Sins – an Act of Justice Toward Christ*
'Father, forgive them for they know not what they are doing' (Lk 23:34). By those words Jesus also prayed on the cross for us sinners. Let us, there-

fore, turn to the Eternal Father and say to him with confidence: O Father, hear the voice of your beloved Son, who implores you to forgive us. To forgive is an act of mercy because we do not deserve pardon. But it is also an act of justice to Jesus Christ, who superabundantly atoned for our sins. You have obliged Yourself to forgive us through his merits and to receive into favor all who are sorry for the offenses they have offered you: My Father, I am sorry with my whole heart for having offended You.

St Alphonsus Liguori, *The Passion of Jesus Christ*, p. 116.

365. *Christ prays for His persecutors*

'Father, forgive them, for they know not what they are doing' (Lk 23:34). . . . Why did Jesus pray to his Father to pardon them when He himself could have forgiven them? St Bernard replies that He prayed to the Father, 'not because he could not himself forgive them, but to teach us to pray for those who persecute us.' . . . 'Look,' says St Augustine, 'at your God upon his cross; see how he prays for those who crucify him; and then deny pardon to your brother who has offended you!'

St Alphonsus, *ibid.*, p. 159.

366. *God Is Obliged to Forgive Us – Under Due Conditions*

'Justice,' comments St Bernard, 'Is the washing away of sins.' Yes, for God, accepting on our behalf the torments and death of Jesus Christ, is obliged to pardon us by virtue of the compact made: 'Him that knew no sin, for us He hath made sin, that we might be made the justice of God in Him' (2 Cor 5:21).

St Alphonsus Liguori, *The Incarnation, Birth and Infancy of Jesus Christ*, p. 66.

367. *God Is Anxious to Forgive Sinners*

Art thou a sinner, and wilt thou have pardon? 'Doubt not,' says St John Chrysostom, 'that God has more desire to pardon thee than thou hast to be pardoned'.

St John Chrysostom, in *The Fathers of the Church*, vol. 33, homily 36.

368. *Forgiveness as We Forgive*

'Forgive us as we forgive'. How admirable it is that God makes the forgiveness which we expect from him depend on the forgiveness which he commands us to grant to those who have offended us. Not content with having everywhere inculcated the obligation, he places it in our own mouths, in our daily prayer, in order that, were we to fail to forgive, he might say to us: 'I judge you through your own mouth, you wicked servant' (Lk 19:22). You have asked me to forgive on condition of your own forgiveness. Therefore you have pronounced your sentence when you refused to forgive your brother. Go to the unhappy place where there is neither forgiveness nor mercy.

Bossuet, in *Selections from Meditations on the Gospel*, vol. 1, p. 56.

369. *Forgiveness Demanded by the Our Father*
When we say: 'forgive us our debts, as we also forgive our debtors' (Mt 6: 12), we bind ourselves in the most enduring bonds unless we fulfill what we profess. And if the most sacred contract of this prayer has not in every respect been fulfilled, let every man now at least examine his conscience and gain the pardon of his sins by forgiving those of others.

St Leo the Great, in Toal, vol. 2, p. 127.

370. *Ways Not to Say the Our Father*
. . . [Those] utter the Lord's Prayer with their lips to their own judgment, rather than as a remedy, if they have not forgiven debts to their neighbors and are shown to have failed to fulfill it in deed. Moreover, to no purpose do they say 'Deliver us from evil' when they themselves do not cease to return evil for evil.

St Caesarius of Arles, in *The Fathers of the Church*, vol. 31, p. 343.

371. *The Our Father Demands We Forgive, Not Insult, our brother*
You called God *Father*, and straightway insult your brother. Think of why you call God your Father! By nature? No, you cannot for that reason. Because of your virtue? No, not for that reason either. Why then is it? Solely because of his love toward man, because of his kindness, because of his mercy. So when you call God *Father*, remember this, that not alone do you do what is unworthy of your dignity when you insult another, but remember also that it is only from his kindness and mercy that you possess this dignity. Do not dishonor it . . . by using cruelty and unkindness against your brethren. . . . The work of the Son of God is to forgive his enemies, to pray for those who crucified him, to shed his Blood for those who hated Him.

St John Chrysostom, in Toal, vol. 3, p. 240.

372. *Forgiveness of Enemies*
Let us remember that we are justified in asking forgiveness of our sins only if we have previously forgiven those who wronged us. The offering will not be accepted unless discord is first removed from the heart, as Christ says: 'If thou art bringing thy gift, then, before the altar and rememberest there that thy brother has some ground of complaint against thee, leave thy gift lying there before the altar and go home; be recon-

ciled with thy brother first, and then come back to offer thy gift'. Since all sins are forgiven by the offering of a gift, the gravity of the sin of discord becomes apparent when we see that no gift will be accepted for it. We are therefore obliged to go to our neighbor in spirit, no matter how far removed or separated from us he may be, and in spirit bow down before him, and through our humility and good will be reconciled with him.

St Gregory the Great, in *the Fathers of the Church*, vol. 39, p. 274.

373. *Forgiveness of Injuries Regarded as Alms*

This alms whereby we forgive those who injure us is not offered from the cellar or granary or shrine, but from the treasury of the heart. Of this, the Lord himself says: 'The good man from the good treasury of his heart brings forth good things' (Mt 12:35). Many poor people can excuse themselves from giving things which we mentioned before – gold, silver, grain, wine and oil – but with what boldness or what kind of conscience will any man say he cannot possess the alms which is bestowed from the heart.

St Caesarius of Arles, in *The Fathers of the Church*, vol. 31, p. 150.

374. *An Unforgiving Priest Loses Crown of Martyrdom – His Enemy Receives It*

At Antioch in the days of the emperors Valerianus and Gallus there lived a priest named Sapricius and a layman named Nicephorus. They had been intimate friends, but for some reason this friendship was changed to bitter enmity. Nicephorus finally admitted it was his fault and made three attempts to heal the breach. Meanwhile, a violent persecution broke out. Sapricius was arrested and showed remarkable endurance under torture. Sentenced to death by the Governor of Antioch, he was led out to the place of execution. When Nicephorus heard this, he ran out to meet Sapricius and knelt down to ask again for forgiveness but was again refused. When the executioner ordered him to kneel down to have his head struck off the unhappy Sapricius cried out: 'For mercy sake, do not behead me! I'll obey the emperor's command; I'll sacrifice to the idols.'

Nicephorus then called to the executioners: 'Friends, I am a Christian and I believe in Jesus Christ, whom this man has denied. Take me then and strike off my head.' The officers informed the governor, who ordered Sapricius to be set free and Nicephorus to be put to death.

According to Metaphrastes and Surius, this incident took place on February 9, about the year 260 A.D.

Summarized from *The Love of God*, by St Francis de Sales, pp. 420-422.

FREE WILL

375. *Why God Left Men Free to Sin*
. . . No one would dare believe or declare that it was beyond God's power to prevent the fall of either angel or man. But, in fact, God preferred not to use this power, but to leave success or failure to the creature's choice. In this way God could show the immense evil that flows from a creature's pride and also the even greater good that comes from His grace.

St Augustine, *City of God*, bk. 14, chap. 27.

FRIENDSHIP

376. *Particular Friendships in Community and in the World*
Many people say, 'We should not have any particular friendship or affection, since it fills our hearts, distracts our minds, and causes envy.' They are mistaken in their advice. They have read in the writings of many holy and devout authors that particular friendships and unusual affections cause the very greatest harm to persons in the religious life, and they therefore imagine that it is the same for the rest of the world. There is a difference. In a well-ordered monastery the common purpose of all the members tends to true devotion. Hence it is not necessary to form particular associations, lest by seeking among individuals what is common to the whole community they should fall from particularities to partialities.

For those who live in the world and desire to embrace true virtue, it is necessary to unite together in holy, sacred friendship. By this means they encourage, assist, and lead one another to perform good deeds. Men walking on level ground do not have to lend one another a hand, while those who are on a rugged, slippery road hold on to one another to walk more safely. . . .

St Thomas says that friendship is a virtue. He speaks of particular friendships, since, as he says, perfect friendship cannot be extended to many persons.' Hence perfection consists, not in having no friendships, but in having only those which are good, holy, and sacred.

St Francis de Sales, *Introduction to the Devout Life*, pp. 143-144.

377. *The Value of a True Friend*
The Saints and Doctors of the Church, Ambrose, Augustine, Jerome, and Bernard, say that one of the greatest comforts that a man can have in this life is to have a faithful friend whom he can lean upon, discovering to him all his heart and all his secrets, according to that saying of the Wise Man: 'A faithful friend is a medicine for life' (Ecclus 6:16). There is no medicine so effectual for the cure of wounds, says St Augustine, as a friend who can comfort you in your afflictions, counsel you in your doubts, rejoice with you in your adversities.
Rodriguez, *Practice of Perfection and Christian Virtues*, vol. 3, p. 422.

378. *Particular Friendships Rooted in Self-love*
Particular friendship is the fly in the ointment of community charity. Charity unites, particular friendship divides. An affinity complex is that unaccountable something which lures characters to pair off, not because they love each other, but because they love themselves so much that they scheme to steal the affection of a particular individual from the whole community.
Hoeger, *The Convent Mirror*, p. 84.

379. *Particular Friendships – a Seed Plot of Envy, Suspicion*
St Basil says that particular friendships in religion are a great seed plot of envy and suspicion and hatreds and enmities: and further, cause divisions, private meetings and cliques, which are the pest of religious life, for there one discovers his temptations, another his judgments, another his complaints and other secret things that ought to be hushed up. There go on detractions and criticisms of one another and sometimes of the superior. There people infect one another with their mutual faults in such sort that each catches the fault of the other in a few days.
Rodriguez, *Practice of Perfection and Christian Virtues*, vol. 1, pp. 259-260.

FRUITS OF THE HOLY SPIRIT

380. *Fruits of the Holy Spirit*
When we let ourselves be guided by the promptings of the Holy Spirit of love . . . our souls produce those fruits which are at once the term of the Holy Spirit's action in us, and by their sweetness, are the anticipated reward of our fidelity in this action. These fruits, as enumerated by St Paul, are charity, joy, peace, patience, benignity, goodness, longanimity, mildness, faith, modesty, continence and chastity.
Marmion, *Christ, the Life of the Soul*, pp. 121-122.

GIFTS OF THE HOLY SPIRIT

381. *The Function of the Gifts*
The specific function of the Gifts is to adapt the soul to receive effectively the illuminations and the impulses of the Holy Ghost dwelling in it.
Edward Leen, *The Holy Ghost*, p. 331.

382. *Gifts of the Holy Ghost Compared with Virtues*
The gifts are not of themselves inspirations of the Holy Ghost, but dispositions which cause us to obey these inspirations promptly and easily. . . .

By those gifts, the soul is made capable of being moved and directed in the path of supernatural perfection and of divine filiation; it possesses, as it were, a supernatural tact, a divine instinct of spiritual things. The soul that, in virtue of these dispositions, lets itself be guided by the Spirit, acts in all security and becomes a child of God. . . .

By the virtues, the soul in a state of grace acts supernaturally, it is true, but it acts in a manner conformable to its rational and human conditions as likewise by its own movement and initiative. By the gifts it is disposed to act directly and solely under the divine impulsion (while keeping, of course, its liberty, which is manifested by acquiescence to the inspiration from on high), and this in a manner which does not always fit in with its rational, natural way of seeing and considering things.
Marmion, *Christ, the Life of the Soul*, pp. 115-116.

383. *Gifts of the Holy Ghost are Necessary*
St Thomas expressly teaches that the Gifts of the Holy Ghost are necessary for the securing of salvation.
Edward Leen, *The Holy Ghost,* p. 313.

384. *Gifts of the Holy Ghost are Like Wind on a Sailboat*
It can happen . . . that the Holy Spirit himself may act on man's soul and move it to supernatural action. Man, as aided only by his reason and will informed by the divine virtues, may be compared to a vessel which moves forward slowly and painfully under the impetus given by the oars. As coming under the immediate influence of the Holy Spirit in his course

heavenwards, man may be likened to a ship borne forward by the favourable wind and under full canvas.

James Leen, *By Jacob's Well*, p. 80.

385. *The Gift of Wisdom – Its Nature and Effects*
. . . The gift of wisdom is concerned above all with the divine mysteries in themselves. It judges everything in the light of these mysteries, including those vast and vibrant intentions of prayer that see the evil and misery of this world from God's viewpoint, and flow, so to speak, from the Heart of Christ into our own.

Goichon, *Contemplative Life in the World*, p. 126.

386. *The Gift of Wisdom – Its Nature*
The gift of wisdom is an intimate, a deep knowledge that relishes the things of God. . . . It is not – far from it – what is called sensible devotion, but a spiritual *experience* of what is divine, that the Holy Spirit wills to produce in us.

Marmion, *Christ, the Life of the Soul*, pp. 117-118.

387. *The Gift of Understanding*
For man to penetrate the supernatural truth of faith, he has need of the supernatural light called the gift of understanding. . . . The gift of understanding offsets dullness of mind, just as knowledge counters ignorance and wisdom counters folly. . . . Outside the state of sanctifying grace, nobody possesses the infused gift of understanding.

Garrigou-Lagrange, *The Theological Virtues*, vol. 1, pp. 369, 371, and 381.

388. *The Gift of Understanding – Its Effects*
The gift of understanding makes us search deeply into the truth of faith. . . . It is this gift which seems to have been granted in a special measure to those in the Church who have shone by the depth of their doctrine, those whom we call 'Doctors of the Church,' but every baptized soul possesses within itself this precious gift.

Marmion, *Christ, the Life of the Soul*, p. 118.

389. *The Gift of Understanding – What the Holy Ghost Achieves by It*
. . . The gift of understanding brings a sort of spontaneous discernment of error. This is of inestimable value in the Christian's continual contacts with various sophisms and religions. . . .

All bitterness is banished from the atmosphere created under the influence of the Holy Ghost. Conversation is carried on in a spirit of serenity and with mutual efforts at comprehension, without becoming heated even when there is no agreement. . . .

Through understanding, we are attuned to God when we judge everything about us; we are united to spiritual realities, not in the order of being, but in the order of love.

Goichon, *Contemplative Life in the World*, pp. 120-121.

390. *The Gift of Knowledge*
According to Aquinas, 'Knowledge is a gift of the Holy Ghost which takes the form of right judgment in things that are to be believed, never confusing them with what ought not to be believed, once the Church has committed itself in deciding which is which. . . . The gift of knowledge is concerned only with things created and human.'

Noted by Garrigou-Lagrange, in *The Theological Virtues*, vol. 1, pp. 393, 395.

391. *The Gift of Knowledge – Its Effects*
The gift of knowledge makes us see created things in a supernatural way as only a child of God can see them. . . . The child of God sees creation in the light of the Holy Spirit, as the work of God wherein His eternal perfections are reflected. This gift makes us know created things, including ourselves, from God's viewpoint; it makes us know our supernatural end and the means of arriving at it.

Marmion, *Christ, the Life of the Soul*, p. 120.

392. *The Gift of Knowledge – What the Holy Ghost Does by It*
The gift of knowledge clarifies an experience of the heart that distinguishes created things from God and sees them in their proper relationship to Him. Things are weighed in terms of their true properties and effects, and not those that are merely apparent and superficial. That is why judgments made with the gift of knowledge are at once clearer and more far-reaching. They are made without passion because nothing is dreaded except what displeases Him.

Goichon, *Contemplative Life in the World*, p. 118.

393. *The Gift of Counsel*
By the gift of counsel, the Holy Spirit responds to this prayer of the soul: '*Lord, what wilt Thou have me to do?*'

Marmion, *Christ, the Life of the Soul*, p. 118.

394. *The Gift of Counsel – What It does*
The gift of counsel completes the other three (knowledge, wisdom and understanding) which are in the speculative domain. . . . Counsel relates to the particular. It is the gift that guides action by providing its immediate

rule, as distinct from the lofty rule provided by the gift of wisdom. . . .

Above all, counsel appeals to fortitude and to hope; to fortitude because it takes courage and integrity to conform to God's commands and views, whatever the cost. Man then seeks guidance from what he knows of God's wishes, and God does not refuse to lead him according to his own counsel.

Goichon, *Contemplative Life in the World*, p. 128.

395. *The Gift of Fortitude*
Owing to our fallen nature, we often need strength to carry into effect what God requires of us; it is the Holy Spirit who, by the gift of fortitude, sustains us in particularly difficult moments.

Marmion, *Christ, the Life of the Soul*, p. 119.

396. *The Gift of Piety*
The gifts of piety and of fear are the complements, the one of the other. The gift of piety is one of the most precious because it concurs directly in regulating the attitude we ought to keep in our relations with God: the blending of adoration, respect and profound reverence toward the Divine Majesty, of love, confidence, tenderness, perfect abandonment and holy liberty in the presence of Him who is our Heavenly Father. . . . The gift of piety bears another fruit: it reassures timid souls who in dealing with God are afraid of not employing the right formulae in their prayers. This scruple is dispelled by the Holy Spirit when one listens to his inspirations. He is 'the Spirit of Truth.'

Marmion, *ibid.*, p. 120.

397. *The Gift of Fear*
. . . There are two kinds of fear of God: first there is the fear which only thinks of the chastisements due to sin; that is servile fear, wanting in nobility but not always without use. Then there is filial fear, but it remains imperfect as long as the fear of punishment is mingled with it.

Marmion, *ibid.*, p. 121.

GRACE IN GENERAL

398. *Only God Can Bestow Grace There by Deifying the Soul*
There is [according to St Thomas Aquinas] no being in nature that contains in its potentiality the least element of grace. There is no created energy that can call it forth. It does not exist in the tiniest degree in the whole vast possibilities of created reality. Were all the natural forces of the

worlds of angels and men marshalled together and combined in effort, they would prove utterly and absolutely powerless to call forth a spark of divine grace in a spiritual substance. God alone can be its cause. The divine nature itself is the exemplary cause, whilst the life and death of Jesus are the meritorious cause of this mysterious entity. But to be the efficient cause of it – that is reserved to God himself inalienably. With no creature, not even the Sacred Humanity of his Divine Son, can he share this principality in the causation of grace. It is only as instrument that creatures can be employed in the process of 'deifying' the soul. The Humanity of Jesus, and the Sacraments instituted by him, are instruments in the hands of the Holy Ghost in this work.

St Thomas likens the action of God in infusing grace into the soul to the act of 'creation', while pointing out that the word is not quite applicable in this connection. Grace in its genesis is like creation in this, that it does not come to be out of preexisting conditions. But the production of grace in the soul is unlike the act of calling beings from nothing in this, that the act of creation terminates in a subsistent thing. Whatever is created is something having an independent existence of its own. Grace has not this independence in existence. It is an accident, not a substance.... God, directly using his supreme power, causes the soul to be modified by a form which gives it a divine quality.

Edward Leen, *The Holy Ghost*, pp. 281-283.

399. *Calvary a Reservoir of Grace Flowing to All*

Outside every city you have a great reservoir, the purpose of which is to keep the place supplied with water. The reservoir is connected with the city by means of many conduit pipes through which the water is borne along till it reaches the spot required. Now the hill of Calvary is something like that reservoir. In it are contained all the merits of Christ's sacred Passion and death. Because he came and atoned for our sin, the heavenly Father's just anger has been turned away from us and sanctifying grace has once more been given back to us. But how is the grace of Christ to be borne from him into our souls? Our Lord has laid down seven 'conduit pipes' for this purpose. These are his seven Sacraments. . . .

Nash, *Living Your Faith*, p. 279.

400. *Grace as Principle of Our Spiritual Life*

Grace becomes the principle of the divine life in us. What is it to *live*? For us, to live is to move in virtue of an interior principle, the source of actions which tend to the perfection of our being. Another life is engrafted, so to speak, upon our natural life, a life of which grace is the principle; grace becomes in us the source of actions and operations which are supernatural and tend toward a divine end, namely, one day to possess God, to rejoice in him, as he knows himself and rejoices in his perfection.

Marmion, *Christ, the Life of the Soul*, p. 16.

401. *Grace and Charity – Their Mutual Relationship*

It is true that supernatural charity is not grace; but charity and grace always go together. . . . Grace elevates our *being*; but charity transforms our *activities*: the degree of the one marks the degree of the other. . . .

Sanctifying grace should be the source from which our activity is nourished; without it, we cannot produce any supernatural act having any meritorious proportion with the beatitudes of eternal life. . . . A being only accomplishes actions by reason of its nature: we only accomplish human actions if we first possess human nature; in the same way, we can only perform the acts of the supernatural life if we first possess, by grace, what is, as it were, a new nature: *Nova creatura*. . . .

Sanctifying grace is the inward principle whence all supernatural activity emanates. If the soul possesses this grace, it can produce acts of life, supernaturally meritorious; if not, the soul is dead in the sight of God. '. . . Without me, you can do nothing. . . . As the branch cannot bear fruit of itself unless it abide in the vine, so neither can you, unless you abide in me.'

Marmion, *ibid.*, pp. 219-220.

402. *God Gives Power to Those Who Are Faithful*

. . . Where there is faith, reverence, and a blameless life, there is present the power of Christ, there is flight from evil and from death which robs us of life. For shameless things do not have in themselves sufficient power to vie with the power of the Master. . . . Those who approach the Spirit with guileless intent, in perfect faith, with no defilement in their conscience, the power of the Spirit cleanses according to the one who says: 'For our gospel was not delivered to you in word only, but in power also; and in the Holy Spirit and in much fullness, as you know.

St Gregory of Nyssa in *The Fathers of the Church*, vol. 58, p. 129.

403. *Grace Never Wanting to Those Who Do What They Can*

The Council of Trent . . . was inspired by God to teach all children of the Holy Church that grace is never wanting to those who do what they can, who ask for God's help; that God never deserts souls once they have won his acceptance, his approval, unless they first desert him; so that, as long as they are not unfaithful to grace, they will come to the possession of glory.

St Francis de Sales, *The Love of God*, pp. 160-161.

404. *Grace Given to All Who Do What in Them Lies*
[There is an axiom] universally received in the schools [which says:] 'To him who does what in him lies, God does not refuse his grace.' That is, to the man who prays, and thus makes good use of the sufficient grace which enables him to do such an easy thing as prayer, God does not refuse the efficacious grace to enable him to execute difficult things.
St Alphonsus Ligouri, *Great Means of Salvation and of Perfection*, p. 203.

405. *The Fruits of Grace Surpass the Value of the Universe*
. . . St Thomas says that the perfection that results for a single soul from the gift of grace surpasses all the natural riches of the entire universe. 'What doth it profit a man,' says Jesus, 'if he gain the whole world,' if he win its esteem, yet, not possessing grace, be shut out forever from the Kingdom of Heaven? (Mt. 16:26).
Marmion, *Christ, the Life of the Soul*, p. 225.

406. *Perseverance in Grace Impossible Without God's Special Help – Trent*
The Council of Trent condemns those who say that we can persevere in grace without a special help from God. 'If any man shall say that the justified can persevere in the justification he has received without special help from God, let him be accursed.' Thus we cannot persevere in grace without a special, extraordinary help from God: but this special help God will justly deny to one who makes no account of committing many venial sins with his eyes open.
St Alphonsus Liguori, *The Way of Salvation and of Perfection*, p. 299.

407. *Grace Absolutely Necessary for a Supernatural Act*
This much may be said: that the living plant is no more different from the dead earth, nor the rational man more different from the brute beast, than is the supernatural from the natural. A dog has a better chance of proving Euclid's Fifth Proposition, or of writing a symphony, than a man without grace has of performing a supernatural act. The supernatural is utterly beyond his powers, and yet, for the Christian, his whole happiness depends upon his achieving a supernatural end.
Boylan, *This Tremendous Lover*, p. 169.

408. *Without Grace We Can Do Nothing*
[St Augustine] says that without the grace of God we are no more than what a body is without a soul. As a dead body cannot move or handle anything, so we without the grace of God cannot do works of life or value before God. . . . Elsewhere he says that, as the bodily eyes can see no-

thing, even though they are quite healthy, without the aid of light, so man, however justified he be, cannot lead a good life without the light and grace of God.

Rodriguez, *Practice of Perfection and Christian Virtues*, vol. 2, pp. 310-311.

409. *Without Grace We Can Do Nothing Supernatural*

. . . St Paul . . . When he speaks of our weakness . . . goes so far as to say that we cannot even have a good thought, a thought worth anything for heaven, of ourselves . . . . All that is good in us, all that is meritorious for eternal life comes from God through Christ: our sufficiency is from God. It is God who enables us to act, and not only to act but even to will, in a supernatural manner; it is God who worketh in us, both to will and to accomplish according to his good will, for such is his pleasure. So we see that of ourselves we can neither will, nor act, nor pray supernaturally. . . . Are we to be pitied for this? In no wise. St Paul, after having detailed our weakness, adds: 'I can do all things,' not of myself, but 'in him who strengtheneth me."

Marmion, *The Structure of God's Plan*, p. 86.

410. *The Help of God's Grace Is Essential*

'To make a lame man walk without a limp is less absurd than to try and succeed without Thee, my Savior' (St Augustine). Why do my resolutions bear no fruit? It can only be because my belief that '*I can do all things*' is not followed by: '*in Him Who strengtheneth me*' (Phil 4:13).

Chautard, *The Soul of the Apostolate*, p. 208.

411. *Grace of Christ Essential for Progress*

As a fish cannot swim without water, and a bird cannot fly without air, so a Christian cannot advance a single step without Christ.

St Gregory Nazianzen, in *The Nicene and Post-Nicene Fathers*, vol. 7, p. 199.

412. *Grace Needed to Strive for Grace*

. . . As St Prosper asserts, without grace, no one strives for grace.

St Francis de Sales, *The Love of God*, p. 106.

413. *Grace Brings Victory*

He is victorious who hopes for the grace of God, not he who presumes upon his own strength.

St Ambrose, in *The Fathers of the Church*, vol. 22, p. 318.

414. *Grace Asked in Order to Fulfill the Commandments*
Grant what thou dost command, and command what thou wilt.
St Augustine, *Confessions*, bk. 10, chap. 29.

415. *God Is Anxious to Give Us Grace*
So great is the desire which God has to give us his graces that, as St Augustine says, he has more desire to give them to us than we have to receive them from him.
St Alphonsus Liguori, *The Way of Salvation and of Perfection*, p. 221.

416. *If God Gives Commandments, He Is Bound to Give Needed Graces*
On the one hand, it is true that God is not bound to give us his grace, because what is gratis is not of obligation; but, on the other hand, supposing that he gives us commandments, he is obliged to give us the assistance necessary for observing them.
St Alphonsus, *ibid.*, p. 204.

417. *Grace a Greater Thing than What We Lost by the Devil's Envy*
. . . St Leo says: 'We have gained greater things by the grace of Christ than we had lost through the envy of the devil.
St Alphonsus , *ibid.*, p. 122.

418. *By Grace, the Trinity Makes Its Home in Our Souls*
The Trinity, Father, Son and Holy Ghost, living the infinitely intense divine life, abide within us as we share that divine life by the gift of sanctifying grace. . . . We begin to be at home in the family of God when the Trinity makes its home within the house of our soul.
Farrell and Healy, *My Way of Life*, p. 52.

419. *Grace Gives Us a Share in the Divine Nature*
God gives a mysterious share in his nature, which we call grace. *Efficiamini divinae consortes naturae.*

[In a footnote we read:] 'St Peter does not say that we become participants in the Divine *Essence*, but in the Divine *Nature*, that is to say, of that activity which constitutes the life of God and consists in the knowledge and the beatifying love of the Divine Persons.'
Marmion, *Christ, the Life of the Soul*, p. 15.

420. *How Sanctifying Grace Enables Us to Share in God's Nature*
Through the operation of the Holy Ghost in the justified soul there is produced there a physical reality endowed with the properties of the intimate nature of God. The nature of God – itself undergoing no change or

diminution – is reproduced in the created spiritual substance. One shrinks from the attempt at illustrating this mystery by an example from experience, for all such comparisons will, necessarily, under one aspect or another, be misleading. The most serviceable illustration is perhaps taken from light. It was the one habitually employed by the great Doctors of the Church. A mirror exposed to the sun's rays becomes itself a source of radiance and illumination without thereby taking from or adding to the illuminating power of the sun. It participates in the sun's power to dazzle and illuminate. So the soul exposed to the action of the Source of all grace and clarity, namely the Holy Spirit, becomes charged with the radiance and the power of the Divine Being. The physical reality produced in the soul by the Spirit of Sanctification endows it with the aptitude to be associated hereafter in the blissful life of God, and with the capacity of being able here, in time, to perform supernatural acts that are, at once, a preparation for and a meriting of that divine life.

Edward Leen, *The Holy Ghost*, p. 274.

421. *How Sanctifying Grace Unites Us to God*

For us, participation in this divine life is brought about by grace, in virtue of which our soul becomes capable of knowing God as God knows himself, of loving God as he loves himself, of enjoying God as he is filled with his own beatitude, and thus living the life of God himself.

Such is the ineffable mystery of our divine adoption. . . . This act of adoption has so much efficacy that we really become, through grace, partakers of the divine nature. And as participation in the divine life constitutes our holiness this grace is called *sanctifying*. Grace becomes the principle of the divine life in us. What is it *to live*? For us, to live is to move in virtue of an interior principle, the source of actions which tend to the perfection of our being. Another life is engrafted, so to speak, upon our natural life, a life of which grace is the principle; grace becomes in us the source of actions and operations which are supernatural and tend toward a divine end, namely, one day to possess God, to rejoice in him, as he knows himself and rejoices in his perfection.

Marmion: *The Structure of God's Plan*, pp. 30-31.

422. *By Sanctifying Grace We Abide in Christ and God Works in Us*

When we possess divine grace within us, we fulfill the wish of our Lord: we 'abide in him' . . . and he 'abides in us.' He abides with the Father and the Holy Spirit. . . . The Holy Trinity, dwelling truly within us as in a temple, does not remain inactive, but unceasingly sustains us so that our soul may exercise its supernatural activity. . . .

We can never act supernaturally unless God gives us the grace so to act.

This grace, on account of its transitory effect, is called *actual* in opposition to sanctifying grace, which, being in its nature permanent, is called *habitual* grace.

Marmion, *Christ, the Life of the Soul*, p. 222.

423. *Sanctifying Grace Divinizes the Soul*

The soul itself, as transformed by divine grace, possesses the 'super-nature.' The faculties of this super-nature are the infused virtues. The dispositions which enable the faculties to function with ease are the gifts of the Holy Ghost. Sanctifying grace divinizes the soul. The infused virtues aid it to act in a human-divine manner. The gifts render the actions that spring from the infused virtues more agreeable, more prompt, more joyous and more energetic.

The function of sanctifying grace, then, is to divinize the soul. In consequence, the soul enjoys a supernatural mode of being. God himself comes to the spirit he has created. He possesses it, penetrates it, transforms it. The spirit of man, becoming thus full of the fullness of God, reflects the Godhead as a mirror. It becomes able to express God and to reproduce an image of His life. Henceforth, it has the power to see God as he sees Himself and to love God as he loves himself.

James Leen, *By Jacob's Well*, p. 59.

424. *Sanctifying Grace Renders the Soul Fruitful*

In the realm of nature, the effect of water is to purify, refresh, irrigate—and render fruitful. . . . Water gives fertility to the soil. Where it is plentiful, earth clothes itself with a rich mantle of green, flowers dapple its surface, and fruits come forth in abundance to yield a rich and varied harvest. Where it fails, the land becomes a desert and a scene of aridity, desolation and death. Such a parched, barren and lifeless scene is an apt image of the soul through which the streams of grace have ceased to flow. Nothing blooms there for eternal life. Whereas, on the other hand, when the soul of man's heart is plentifully watered by the channels of divine grace, it produces an abundant harvest of virtues and merits, enriching it with the wealth of God.

James Leen, *ibid.*, p. 61.

425. *Sanctifying Grace Enables God to Love the Soul as a Friend*

The sanctifying grace which we receive through union with our Redeemer makes us sons of God, as St John states (Jn 1:12). One has a totally inadequate conception of the effect of sanctifying or habitual grace, as it is called, if it be regarded as producing a condition of soul characterized by merely negative properties – such as freedom from sin and from punishment due to sin. The infusion of habitual grace into our souls is the genesis of a life, the vital activities of which far transcend the energies of the highest form of moral life. Grace does not merely purify the heart; it does not merely aid it to withdraw its affections from what is unworthy of a man; nor does it merely create in the human heart a love for moral good. It does far more than this. The grace that comes to us from Jesus Christ bestows on the soul a life which surpasses and leaves behind all that can find its origin in the limited resources of the whole realm of nature. By grace we are empowered to love not only the Man in the Man-God, but even the God in Him, and that, too, with the love of friendship.

. . . Jesus can love us humanly, but God Himself as God cannot love except divinely, and cannot love with the love of friendship anything that is not divine. If we are to reciprocate this affection on the part of God, we must be able to love with a love greater than any created heart is capable of. We must be able to love with an affection which is divine in its principle.

Who can free the soul from its created limitations, lift itself above itself and establish terms of intimacy between the created and the uncreated Spirit? It is the Third Person of the Blessed Trinity that by means of sanctifying grace accomplishes this marvel – because the charity of God is poured forth in our hearts by the Holy Ghost, who is given to us (Rom. 5:5). We have seen that the Holy Spirit, in the work of the Incarnation, brought God down to man. He crowns this wonder by one more dazzling still. He raises man up to God . . . The Holy Ghost, by communicating himself to the soul in the inpouring of divine charity, makes the soul *deiform* or like unto God. By the imparting of grace, of which he, Subsistent Grace, is the Source, he *divinizes* the soul. He bestows on it the condition of God, in a finite measure, and thus permits the creature and the Creator to embrace in an affection which is in its mode divine and truly bears the name of friendship. God, becoming man, became a friend of man. Man, being made *deiform* by the Holy Ghost, becomes a friend of God. The Holy Ghost *humanized* God to effect a community of nature between Creator and creature on the human plane, now *divinises* man to effect that community of nature on the divine plane. He has made it possible that God should love us with the love of friendship, not only humanly but divinely. . . .

Edward Leen, *The Holy Ghost*, pp. 96-99.

426. *Sanctifying Grace Confers Greatness on the Soul*

It is possible to form an idea, true as far as it goes but necessarily very inadequate, of the grandeur and beauty of this new life [of sanctifying grace] by a consideration of the immense distances which separate the different realms of creation. What a wide chasm yawns between inert matter and the kingdom of plant life! between the most perfect plant and the least of the animal world! between the irrational animal and man! The distance which lies between the highest in each realm and the lowest in the one that follows next mounting upwards is immense and impassable. Yet such distances dwindle when compared with that which divides the natural from the supernatural being in man. Quasi-infinite in extent is the gulf that lies between the soul left to its own natural resources and the same soul transformed by grace.

James Leen, *By Jacob's Well*, p. 59.

427. *Sanctifying Grace Is Increased by Sacraments, Prayer, Good Works*
Since grace can increase in the soul, since it ought to increase, the question remains as to how this increase can be effected. Grace grows in the soul in three ways: by the sacraments, by prayer, and by good works. The sacraments are the normal and most efficacious ways provided by God for this growth. Of their very nature they cause an increase – and infallibly, provided no obstacle is put in their way. As sunlight on a sunny day will surely stream into a room unless the blinds are drawn, so the sacraments confer grace on all whose dispositions offer no impediment. Of course *how much* grace is given will depend on the fervor of the recipient. . . .

Another most powerful means of increasing grace is prayer. 'Ask and it shall be given you; seek, and you shall find; knock, and it will be opened to you' (Mt 7:9). Prayer differs from the sacraments in that prayer does not work independently of the merits of a person (that is *ex opere operato*): and it differs from a meritorious act in that prayer at times is not meritorious – for example, when a person is in mortal sin. . . . The important thing to remember about prayer, however, is the fact that it *is* impetratory, addressed to the mercy of God. . . . Because it is, it surpasses every other meritorious act; prayer can obtain what can be increased by good works in the sense that our good works merit a right to an increase in grace; but they do not produce this increase – only God does. 'I have planted, Apollos watered, but God has given the growth' (1 Cor. 3:6)

Shamon, *The Only Life*, pp. 35-36.

428. *It's Good Business to Increase Our Supply of Grace*
A businessman who wants to succeed will be very keen to keep his shop well stocked. In times of emergency he will redouble his efforts . . . so as to get a better price. . . .

In the spiritual order, what are the 'supplies' except the man's store of sanctifying grace? He knows that if he possesses this treasure he is on the straight road that leads to God, here and hereafter. . . . He is always on the watch to increase what he has. So you will see him regular and fervent in his reception of the sacraments, frequent and persevering in his prayer. Why? Because through prayer and the sacraments, he is adding to his supplies. . . .

In heaven, all will be perfectly happy, but not all will be by any means equally happy. One man dies after a life of sin, but on his deathbed he makes a really good confession; another dies after having watched his opportunities all through his life to increase his supplies. . . .

Nash, *Living Your Faith*, p. 52.

429. *How Is Sanctifying Grace Increased in the Soul?*

If a man contending with another in a race of speed and being successful were rewarded by an increase of the physical powers which give him his victory, one could have an image of what takes place in the world of grace. Successful action in that world is *grace-full* action. It is rewarded by a further infusion of grace, the effect of which is to make possible, normally speaking, action still more vigorous with the vitality of grace. The reward of *grace-full* action is more grace. It always remains a reward freely given by God, the arbiter in the spiritual combat, for grace is not generated from within by meritorious action; it is always infused from without.

Edward Leen, *The Holy Ghost*, pp. 188-189.

430. *Cooperation with Actual Grace Increases Sanctifying Grace*

When the soul corresponds to the actual graces received, sanctifying grace, following the inborn tendency of all vital things, waxes strong. Sanctity is directly measured by the amplitude that divine grace has reached and the degree in which it influences the faculties in their operations. As grace expands, there is a proportionate weakening of evil habits and evil inclinations; there is, as well, a steady elimination of faults and imperfections. . . . It happens, too, that as habitual grace develops, actual graces find less obstacles to their efficacy and, hence, operating more freely, produce effects of more intense charity.

Edward Leen, *The True Vine and Its Branches*, p. 104.

431. *Action of Will and Intellect Needed*

Grace unites us to God by assimilating us to him; but it is imperative that we be united to him by the operation of will and intellect.

Edward Leen, *In the Likeness of Christ*, p. 134.

432. *Why God Does Not Let Us Know Whether We Are in the State of Grace*

Whether your name is or is not inscribed in the book of life is a secret which it is not the will of God that any should know; that so, through the fear of damnation, everyone should be diligent by means of good works to secure his salvation. Thus St Peter writes: wherefore, brethren, labor the more that by good works you make sure of your calling and election (2. Pt 1:10).

St Alphonsus Liguori, *The Way of Salvation and of Perfection*, p. 469.

433. *Special Graces a Reason for Humility*

Many men neither wish nor dare to . . . reflect on the particular graces God has shown them because they are afraid this might arouse vain-glory and self-complacence. They deceive themselves in this. Since the true means to attain to love of God is consideration of His benefits, as the great Angelic Doctor states, the more we know about them, the more we shall love him. As the particular benefits He has conferred on us affect us more powerfully than those we share with others, they must be considered more attentively.

Certainly nothing can so effectively humble us before God's mercy as the multitude of his benefits and nothing can so deeply humble us before his justice as our countless offenses against him. Let us consider that what he has done for us and what we have done against him, and so reflect on our sins one by one; let us also consider his graces one by one. There is no need to fear that knowledge of his gifts will make us proud if only we remember this truth, that none of the good in us comes from ourselves. Do mules stop being dull, disgusting beasts simply because they are laden with a prince's precious, perfumed goods? What good do we possess that we have not received?

St Francis de Sales, *Introduction to the Devout Life*, p. 110.

HEAVEN

434. *God Wishes to Share His Eternal Happiness with Us*

This is the will of God, your sanctification (1 Thes 4:3). It is in our good that God has placed his own glory, being, as St Leo says, in his own nature goodness infinite – 'God whose nature is goodness' – and it being the nature of goodness to desire to spread itself abroad, God has a supreme desire to make the souls of men partakers of his own bliss and glory. And if, in this life, he sends us tribulations, they are all for our own good.

St Alphonsus Liguori, *The Way of Salvation and of Perfection*, p. 367.

435. *The Basis of the Saint's Happiness Is Seeing God's Happiness*
The blessed are not so much blessed through the delight which they experience in themselves, as the joy with which God rejoices; for the blessed love God so infinitely much more than themselves that the blessedness of God delights them infinitely more than their own blessedness, through the love which they bear to him; which love makes them forget themselves, and all their delight is to please their Beloved.
St Alphonsus, *ibid.*, p. 256.

436. *St Teresa's Desire for Greater Glory in Heaven*
If I were asked which I preferred, to endure all the trials of the world until the end of it, and then receive one slight degree of glory additional, or without any suffering of any kind, to enter into glory of slightly lower degree, I would accept – Oh, how willingly – all those trials for one slight degree of fruition in the contemplation of the greatness of God; for I know that he who understands best, loves him and praises him best.
The Life of St Teresa of Jesus, Written by Herself, p. 365.

437. *The Saints Know Our Problems and Can Help Us*
It is a mistake to picture souls as existing in heaven completely isolated from the events of the world. . . . In the vision of God, they see all that pertains to them of the events of this earth; indeed, they see much more than ever they could in this life, for they are seeing with the eyes of God, which do not stop at the face of man. It is with very good reason that we ask our Lady and the saints to intercede for us, even though their time of strict merit is over at death; they are tried and true friends of God, living in an eternal intimacy with him, and fully conversant with our condition. They can and they do help us immensely.
Farrell, *Companion to the Summa*, vol. 4, p. 425.

438. *Saints in Heaven Know the Condition of Loved Ones on Earth*
The blessed in heaven see God face to face and in his eyes as in a mirror can see what passes on this earth. They are in a perfect state of bliss, and the knowledge of their near and dear ones in this world, therefore, is not withheld from them.
Arendzen, *Purgatory and Heaven*, p. 43.

439. *The Saints in Heaven Know and Love Their Own*
In heaven the affection of husband and wife, of parents and children, of brothers and sisters will retain all its force and intimacy. These affections will retain their characteristic qualities, enhanced, not diminished, by divine love. No jealousy can find a place in these holy friendships.

As for those whom we have left behind on earth, we shall continue to know them, and to intercede for them. According as it may seem good to God, we may be permitted to come to their assistance. The blessed in heaven retain an immense desire for the salvation of souls, especially of the souls of those dearest to them.

James Leen, *By Jacob's Well*, pp. 255-256.

440. *We Will Know Our Friends in Heaven*

Yes, we shall know our friends in heaven, and we shall know them better than we ever understood them on this earth. . . .

No doubt the natural love of parents and kindred will be spiritualized, but it will certainly not be destroyed. In heaven we shall be supernatural, not unnatural. He that has decreed the resurrection of the body certainly wished us eternally to lead natural human lives, glorified and exalted, indeed, but not changed into something inhuman and alien to the instincts he himself has instilled into our breasts.

Arendzen, *Purgatory and Heaven*, pp. 72-74.

441. *Intimacy with the Saints in Heaven*

If we think their number [all the saints and angels] too great ever to become intimate with us, let us not forget that we shall have an eternity in which to form our friendships, and that the heavenly city will be an easy meeting place even for those who during their earthly days were far apart in many ways.

Arendzen, *ibid.*, p. 75.

442. *Heaven Is Our Goal*

That traveller is very foolish who, looking at the pleasant scenery around him, forgets to advance towards his journey's end. Therefore, let us long with all our hearts to reach our enduring home.

St Gregory the Great, *Parables of the Gospel*, p. 169.

HELL

443. *The Need for Meditation on Hell*

How comes it, writes Salvian, that men believe in death, judgment, hell and eternity, and yet live without fearing them? Hell is believed, and yet how many go thither! But, O God! while these truths are believed, they are not dwelt upon, and hence are so many souls lost.

St Alphonsus Liguori, *The Way of Salvation and of Perfection*, p. 85.

444. *The Threefold Remorse of the Souls in Hell*

The condemned soul is tormented with three kinds of remorse. The first arises from reflecting for what a mere trifle it has incurred everlasting misery. For how long does the pleasure of sin last? Only for a moment. To a man at the point of death, how long does his past life appear? A mere moment. But to one in hell, what do the fifty or sixty years of his sojourning upon the earth appear, when, in the gulf of eternity, he foresees that after a hundred or a thousand millions of years, he will be only beginning eternity? . . .

The second kind of remorse arises from the reflection of the condemned soul of the little which it need have done to be saved, but did not do it; and now there is no remedy. . . .

The third and most bitter kind of remorse arises from the consciousness of the wretched soul of the great happiness which it has forfeited through its own fault. It recollects that God offered it abundant means of gaining heaven . . . and that all have been rendered useless through its own fault.

St Alphonsus, *ibid.*, pp. 138-139.

445. *Hell's Greatest Torment*

This will be their greatest torment in hell, the thought that they have lost a God who, to draw them to love him, gave his life on the cross, the thought that of their own choice they have perished, and that there will be no remedy for their misery through all eternity.

St Alphonsus Liguori, *The Passion of Jesus Christ*, p. 151.

446. *What Must Be Done to Avoid Hell*

[Christ said, concerning the judgment:] 'These will go into everlasting punishment, but the just into everlasting life.' . . .

Anyone who does not awaken at such thunder is evidently not asleep but dead. Indeed, we have heard the irrevocable sentence: the one which the just will hear, never to depart from heaven; and the other which sinners will hear, never to leave hell. However, the kind and merciful Lord will not utter these sentences to lead us to despair, but to make us watchful and careful. . . .

[The fact that great evils] happen in the world and he still does not avenge them indicates patience, not carelessness. God has not lost his power, but is preserving us for repentance . . . God does not want to kill the sinner but his sin. Like a good doctor, he wants to strike the disease, not the person who is ill.

St Caesarius of Arles, in *The Fathers of the Church*, vol. 31, pp. 91-92.

447. *St Teresa's Vision of Hell*
I was one day in prayer when I found myself in a moment, without knowing how, plunged apparently into hell. I understood that it was our Lord's will I should see the place which the devils kept in readiness for me. . . . This vision was one of the grandest mercies of our Lord. It has been to me of the greatest service because it has destroyed my fear of trouble and of the contradictions of the world, and because it made me strong enough to bear up against them, and to give thanks to our Lord, who has been my Deliverer, as it now seems to me, from such fearful and everlasting pains.
The Life of St Teresa of Jesus, Written by Herself, pp. 298 and 301.

448. *Those Who Delayed Repenting*
Hell is filled with souls who said, 'By and by, by and by.' Death came in the meantime and they were lost.
St Alphonsus Liguori, *Great Means of Salvation and Perfection*, p. 309.

449. *Thought of the Hell He Deserved Helps Sinner*
Let him who has committed a mortal sin cast a glance upon the hell he has deserved, and thus he will suffer with patience every contempt and every pain.
St Alphonsus Liguori, *The Way of Salvation and of Perfection*, p. 238.

450. *The Thought of Hell Will Save Us from It*
When the devil tempts you to sin again, think of hell; have recourse to God, to the Blessed Virgin; the thought of hell will deliver you from hell: *Remember thy last end and thou shalt never sin*, because the thought of hell will make you have recourse to God.
St Alphonsus Liguori, *Preparation for Death* p. 77.

451. *A Soul in Hell Would Rejoice If There Were Hope It Would End*
If an angel were to say to one of the damned: 'Thou shalt leave hell, but when as many ages have passed as there are drops of water, leaves on the trees, and grains of sand on the seashore' – he would rejoice more than a beggar on hearing he was made a king. . . . The trumpet of divine justice will sound forth in hell nothing but 'Forever! Forever! Never! Never!'
St Alphonsus Liguori, *Preparation for Death*, p. 71.

HOLINESS

452. *Holiness consists essentially in the soul being intimately united to God by supernatural love.* This love, which is usually called charity, is the immediate effect of sanctifying grace. Sanctifying grace constitutes the supernatural life of the soul; it is that wonderful gift of God by which we become his adopted children, members of the divine family, brothers of our Savior, Jesus Christ, and accordingly the objects of an altogether special love on the part of the Blessed Trinity.

Gabriel, *Ascetical Conferences for Religious*, p. 182.

453. *Perfection – According to St Alphonsus*
Perfection consists in conforming ourselves to the will of God in those things which are disagreeable to us. The Venerable Father Avila says: 'It is of more use to say once, 'Blessed be God,' in any contradiction than to thank him six thousand times when we are pleased.'

St Alphonsus Liguori, *Great Means of Salvation and of Perfection*, p. 367.

454. *Perfection – According to St Teresa*
The highest perfection consists not in interior favors or in great raptures or in visions or in the spirit of prophecy, but in bringing our wills so closely into conformity with the will of God that, as soon as we realize he wills anything, we desire it ourselves with all our might . . . bitter with the sweet, knowing that to be his Majesty's will.

St Teresa, *Foundations*, in Peers, vol. 3, p. 23.

455. *Holiness – According to St Thérèse of Lisieux*
Holiness does not consist in this or that practice; it consists in a disposition of the heart which makes us always humble and little in the arms of God, well aware of our feebleness, but boldly confident in the Father's goodness.

St Thérèse of Lisieux, *Novissima Verba*, p. 78.

456. *Holiness as Union with God*
[Holiness] is a permanent union with God, a constant abiding in Christ by

lovingly doing his will, always and in all things.
Boylan, *This Tremendous Lover*, p. 181.

457. *Holiness an Obligation – Desiring It Is Not a Sin*
[Pope Pius XI] in his Encyclical, written in 1923 for the third centenary of St Francis de Sales, declared: 'Christ has made his holy Church the source of holiness, and he wills that all those who take her as guide and teacher should strive for personal holiness. "This is the will of God," says St Paul, "your sanctification" (1 Thes 4:3). But what kind of holiness? Our Lord himself tells us: "Be you perfect, as also your heavenly Father is perfect" (Mt 5:48). Let no one think, [continues the Pope] that this invitation is addressed to a small and exclusive number, and that it is permissible for the rest to remain in a lower degree of virtue. It is clear that this law obliges everybody without exception. . . . ' Hence there is no pride in desiring genuine sanctity, since God enjoins us to do so; and there is no presumption in striving for this lofty ideal, since we count not on ourselves but on God.
Gabriel, *Ascetical Conferences for Religious*, p. 110.

458. *All Are Called to Holiness*
It is a mistake to believe that the spiritual life is only for a chosen few; that sanctity is in much the same category as genius and only within the scope of a tiny minority. . . .

The Catechism tells us that we are made to know, love and serve God in this life; and sanctity consists in nothing more than the fulfillment of this end. It is the object for which we were made and, if we live accordingly, we shall achieve the full spiritual development in which sanctity consists. This does not entail, of necessity, any extraordinary mortifications, any visions or ecstasies such as we sometimes read about in the lives of some saints; these may be the effects of sanctity, but they are accidental to it and do not belong to its essential character. The essence of sanctity is the perfect love of God, and to be saints it is necessary only that we should love much. We cannot all of us undertake great physical mortifications, we are not all called to the priesthood or the cloister, but we can all of us love.

Fr Bruno S. James, 'The One Thing Necessary,' in Nash, *How to Pray and Other Conferences*, pp. 14-15.

459. *Holiness Is Achieved Gradually Through the Holy Spirit*
Justification takes place in an instant. Sanctification is a process that is extended over the entire period of the soul's union with the body. It consists in this, that God, who is the chief agent in the process, imparts him-

self to the soul in ever-increasing measure, according as the soul's power of receptivity develops. To the Holy Ghost is appropriately attributed the beginning, the continuance, and the crowning of this mysterious process. All the activities that are concerned with the sanctifying of the rational creature are rightly considered to be peculiarly his by reason of his personal characteristics. He is the Subsistent Sanctity of God because he is the Subsistent Love of God – sanctity being nothing else than love of the Divine Essence.

Edward Leen, *The Holy Ghost*, p. 232.

460. *Holiness Through Faith*

All holiness for us consists of participation in the holiness of Christ Jesus, the Son of God. But how are we to participate in it? – By receiving Jesus Christ, who is the one source of holiness. . . . How do we receive Christ? . . . First and before all, by faith: '*His qui credunt in nomine ejus. . . .*' St Augustine says the same: 'It is primarily faith that subjects the soul to God.'

Marmion, *Christ, the Life of the Soul*, pp. 131-132.

461. *Holiness – Love Of Conformity with, Preference for God*

God, the infinite Good, as revealed by faith, is made the supreme object of desire to the rejection of the claims of all other good things that can be selected in his stead and substituted for him as an object to which the will should adhere. This adherence of the will to God is nothing else but the conformity of the human will with the divine; man wills the same things that God wills; he rejoices in what pleases God and is saddened by what displeases him; he does God's holy will with all care and accepts from his hands the daily cross. This total surrender to and conformity with the divine will implies that the soul has willingly yielded to the attractiveness of God, and this willing yielding is love. That man is a saint for whom the attraction of God is supreme above all other attractions.

Edward Leen: *Progress Through Mental Prayer*, pp. 6-7.

462. *Holiness Is Loving That Which Is Worthy of the Most Supreme Love*

For men and angels also, sanctity lies in the love of that which is worthy of most supreme love. It is synonymous with the love of God, and is measured by that love. It is scarcely necessary to remark that this love of God is not a sentiment, a feeling, or an emotion. It is of the will, not of sensibility. It consists in a deliberate election, choice, and preference of the Supreme and Infinite Good above all else.

Edward Leen, *ibid.*, p. 6.

463. *What Is Needed to Become a Saint*
... He who wishes to be a saint must wish only what God wishes. All our good consists in uniting ourselves to the will of God. . . . The most acceptable offering, then, that we can present to God is the oblation of our will, saying with the Apostle: 'Lord, what wilt Thou have me do?' (Acts 9:6).

But we must remember that our merit consists in embracing the divine will, not so much in things that are pleasing to us as in those that are opposed to self-love. In these we show the strength of the love we bear to God.

St Alphonsus Liguori, *Dignity and Duties of the Priest*, pp. 403-404.

464. *Holiness Even Without Miracles*
I believe there still are many such [holy] men in the world, Peter. One cannot conclude that there are no great saints just because no great miracles are now worked. The true estimate of life, after all, lies in acts of virtue, not in the display of miracles. There are many, Peter, who without performing miracles, are not at all inferior to those who perform them.

St Gregory the Great in *The Fathers of the Church*, vol. 39, p. 51.

465. *Holiness Is Easy – It is Merely Loyalty to God*
If the business of becoming holy seems to present insufferable difficulties, it is merely because we have a wrong idea about it. In reality, holiness consists of one thing only: complete loyalty to God's will. Now everyone can practice this loyalty, whether actively or passively. To be actively loyal means obeying the laws of God and the Church and fulfilling all the duties imposed on us by our way of life. Passive loyalty means that we lovingly accept all that God sends us at each moment of the day. Now is there anything here too difficult for us? Certainly nothing in active loyalty, for if the duties are beyond our powers, we are not expected to attempt to fulfill them. If we are too ill to go to Mass, we need not. And it is the same for all other precepts which lay down duties. But, of course, there can be no exemption from precepts which forbid wrongdoing, for we are never allowed to sin. Can anything be more sensible? Or easier? We are left with no excuse. Yet God asks nothing more than this. But he does require it from everyone without exception. Class, time and place mean nothing. Everyone must obey.

Caussade, *Abandonment to Divine Providence*, p. 24.

466. *Easy Road to Holiness for All*
I believe that people trying to be holy would be saved a lot of trouble if they were taught to follow the right path, and I am writing of people who live ordinary lives in the world and of those specially marked by God. Let

the former realize what lies hidden in every moment of the day and the duties each one brings, and let the latter appreciate the fact that things they regard as trivial and of no importance are essential to sanctity. And let them both be aware that holiness means the eager acceptance of every trial sent them by God. This is vastly superior to the enjoyment of all extraordinary experiences. It is the philosopher's stone which changes into gold all their worries, all their troubles, all their sufferings. . . . I am asking nothing extraordinary from you. All I want is for you to carry on as you are doing and endure what you have to do – but change your attitude to all those things. And this change is simply to say 'I will' to all that God asks. What is easier? For who could refuse obedience to a will so kind and so good? By this obedience we shall become one with God.

Caussade, *ibid.*, pp. 34-35.

467. *Holiness Through Ordinary Actions*
If we remember that the most fruitful life of any human being was that lived by our Lady, and that her life was essentially ordinary, obscure and laborious, we shall, perhaps, find a new value in the ordinary things in the day's round when done for God.

Boylan, *This Tremendous Lover*, p. 187.

468. *A Simple Road to Sanctity*
One single holy maxim, well ruminated, is sufficient to make a saint. St Francis Xavier left the world in consequence of the impression made on him by that sentence of the Gospel: 'What doth it profit a man if he gain the world and suffer the loss of his soul'?

St Alphonsus Liguori, *Great Means of Salvation and of Perfection*, p. 295.

469. *What Is Needed for a Priest to Become a Saint*
. . . The priest who wishes to be a saint must do all his actions for the sole purpose of pleasing God. . . . Works performed without the proper intention, are victims without marrow, which God rejects. In the oblations made to him, he regards not the value of the offering, but the affection with which it is presented. 'God,' says Salvian, 'looks not so much at the value of the offering as at the disposition with which it is offered.'

St Alphonsus Liguori, *Dignity and Duties of the Priest*, pp. 395-396.

470. *What Is Needed for a Priest to Become Holy*
. . . The priest who wishes to be holy must be ready to suffer in peace for God all things – poverty, dishonor, infirmity and death. . . . Sometimes we shall be reproved for a fault which we have not committed; but, 'What

matter?' says St Augustine, 'We ought to accept the reproof in atonement for other sins to which we have consented.' . . . If, then, on account of past sins, we find ourselves debtors to divine justice, we should not only accept with patience the tribulations that befall us, but should pray with St Augustine: 'Here burn, here cut, here do not spare, that thou mayest spare me in eternity.'

St Alphonsus, *ibid.*, pp. 339 and 401-402.

471. *Holiness Achieved Through Work in the Kitchen*
[The following is a quotation from *The Practice of the Presence of God,* written by Brother Lawrence, a lay brother of the Barefoot Carmelites, at Paris during the latter part of the seventeenth century.]

'The time of business' said the Brother, 'does not with me differ from the time of prayer; and amid all the racket and excitement of the kitchen, while several persons are at the same time clamoring for various things, I possess God in as great a peace as if I were upon my knees before the Blessed Sacrament.' In fact, so had he learned how to combine action with contemplation that, in spite of very active occupations, for the space of more than forty years he hardly ever turned from the presence of God.

Gabriel, *Ascetical Conferences for Religious*, pp. 206, 213-214.

472. *Holiness is Acquired Through Work as Well as Through Prayer*
It is a great mistake to think that the time devoted to exercises of piety ought to differ from other times; we are as strictly obliged to adhere to God, by action as by prayer, whenever the hour for either has arrived. Our sanctification does not depend on changing our occupations, but on doing for the sake of God what men commonly do for their own. Hence the most excellent method of going to God consists in performing our ordinary occupations without any view to pleasing men, but, as far as we may, purely for the love of God.

Gabriel, *ibid.*, p. 211.

IDLENESS

473. *The Dangers of Idleness*
[St Joseph Calasanctius says:] 'The devil goes in pursuit of idle religious.' And according to St Bonaventure, a religious assiduously employed is molested with one temptation, but an idle religious shall be assailed by a thousand.

St Alphonsus Liguori, *The True Spouse of Jesus Christ*, p. 491.

IMITATION OF CHRIST

474. *A Lesson From a Portrait Painter*
Gregory of Nyssa makes a delightful comparison when he says that we are all artists and that our souls are blank canvasses which we have to fill in. The colors we must use are the Christian virtues, and our Model is Jesus Christ, the perfect living Image of God the Father. Just as a portrait painter who wants to do a good job places himself before his model and glances at him before making each stroke, so the Christian must always have the life and virtues of Jesus Christ before his eyes so that he may never say, think or do the least thing which is not in harmony with his model.
St Louis de Montfort, *The Secret of the Rosary*

475. *Imitation Of Christ*
Let us become like Christ, since Christ became like us.
St Gregory Nazianzen in Toal, vol. 2, p. 220.

476. *Comparison Taken from an Artist's Work*
Suppose an amateur artist is in front of an easel with the purpose of painting the face and form and character of Michelangelo, who sits as model. The artist may be good, and may produce a fair likeness, but how far more successful would he be if the model had the power to infuse his own genius and skill into the artist at work. How much greater the result would be. It would be a masterpiece, produced entirely by the amateur, yet stamped by the genius of the master. Christ sits as model for us, but he does not leave us laboriously working to reproduce his features with our own abilities. He sits there and causes his own divine power to pass into our hands. That is what is called the 'Spirit of Jesus' in our souls, and if we allow the Holy Spirit to work, he will produce the likeness of Christ in our souls. That is what the Holy Spirit does.
Edward Leen, *Retreat Notes for Religious*, p. 86.

IMPERFECTIONS

477. *Our Imperfections Are to Be Detested*
As long as we detest our imperfections, there is hope that we may still become saints; but when we commit faults and make little of them, then, says St Bernard, the hope of becoming saints is lost.
St Alphonsus Liguori, *Great Means of Salvation and of Perfection*, p. 436.

478. *Imperfections Vs. Perfection*
The work of purging the soul neither can nor should end except with our life itself. We must not be disturbed at our imperfections, since for us perfection consists in fighting against them. How can we fight against them unless we see them, or overcome them unless we face them? Our victory does not consist in being unconscious of them but in not consenting to them, and not to consent to them is to be displeased with them.
St Francis de Sales, *Introduction to the Devout Life*, p. 41.

INJURIES

479. *Injury to Others Must Be Repaired*
If, therefore, thou offer thy gift at the altar, and there thou remember that thy brother hath anything against thee; leave there thy offering before the altar. God is not angered because you put your gift aside for a while: God waits for you rather than for your gift. For if with evil in your heart against your brother you draw near to God with a gift, he will say to you: 'You are lost; why bring a gift to me? You offer a gift, and you are not yourself a gift worthy of God.' Christ looks more for you, whom he redeemed with his Blood, than for that which you found in your garden.
St Augustine, in Toal, vol. 3, p. 96.

INTENTION

480. *The Nature and Importance of a Good Intention*
A good intention consists in doing, omitting or enduring something for a supernatural motive. . . . Supernatural motives are:

(a) Fear of God's punishment,
(b) Hope of being rewarded by God,
(c) Desire to please God.

A good intention is of very great importance:

(1) It is necessary if an act is to be at all pleasing to God and meritorious for heaven.
(2) It gives great value to the most insignificant acts.
(3) It changes indifferent works into good works.

Wallenstein, *Guide to Perfect Christian Living*, p. 31.

481. *The Value of Things Done with a Pure Intention*
The Venerable Beatrice of the Incarnation, the first daughter of St Teresa, said, 'No price can be put on anything, however small, that is done entirely for God.' And with great reason she said this, for all works done for God are acts of divine love. Purity of intention makes the lowest actions become precious, such as eating, working, recreation, when they are done from obedience and from a desire to please God.

St Alphonsus Liguori, *The Way of Salvation and of Perfection*, p. 302.

482. *Our Intention Is More Important than What We Do*
It is not so much *what* we do that matters as *why* we do it. It is not so much what we *do* as what we *become* that is of value of God's eyes. His design for the soul is that it become transformed interiorly. The walls of selfishness and sin must be levelled. The poison of pride must be drawn off. Then there will ensue that 'more abundant life' which flows into the soul from its close contact with Christ.

Nash, *How to Pray and Other Conferences*, p. 124.

483. *Intention to Please God Alone Cures Vanity*
St Teresa says: 'When we seek to please God only, the Lord will give us strength to conquer all vainglory.'

Quoted by St Alphonsus Liguori in *The True Spouse of Jesus Christ*, p. 602.

484. *Purity of Intention*
'Do nothing,' said the Cure of Ars, 'that you cannot offer to Jesus.' It is pithy advice for one who would make a particular examen on purity of intention. It will ensure that nothing be offered except gold, frankincense and myrrh.
Nash, *The Nun at Her Prie-Dieu*, p. 78.

485. *Intention Can Elevate the Most Ordinary Actions*
[If we do] all in the name of the Lord Jesus Christ . . . the most ordinary incidents of our daily life, such as taking food, attending to our business or work, fulfilling our social duties, taking rest or recreation; all these actions that occur every day and literally weave, in their monotonous and successive routine, the thread of our entire life, can be transformed, by grace and love, into acts very pleasing to God and rich in merit. To use another simile, each is like a grain of incense which seems nothing in itself but, when thrown into the fire, becomes a fragrant perfume. When grace and love take hold of everything in our life, then all our existence is like a perpetual hymn to the glory of the heavenly Father; it becomes for him, through our union with Christ, like a censor from which arise perfumes that rejoice him.
Marmion, *Growth in Christ*, p. 151.

486. *Three Kinds of Good Intentions*
Our intentions may be good in three ways: first, when we perform an act in order to obtain from God temporal goods. . . . Secondly, when we do an act in order to make satisfaction to the divine justice for the pains due to our sins, or to obtain from God spiritual goods such as virtue, or an increase of merits and of glory in heaven; this intention is far more perfect than the former. But the most perfect of all is when, in our works, we seek only to please God and do his holy will. This intention is also the most meritorious; for the more we forget ourselves in our good actions, the more God will remember us, and the more abundantly he will pour his grace upon us. . . .
St Alphonsus Liguori, *The True Spouse of Jesus Christ*, p. 602.

487. *The Effect of a Good Intention*
The right intention is called by the masters of the spiritual life a heavenly alchemy which converts into gold all our actions, even corporal alleviations, such as sleep, eating and recreation.
St Alphonsus Liguori, *Dignity and Duty of the Priest*, p. 439.

488. *Purity of Intention Needed*
Purity of intention consists in performing all our actions through the sole motive of pleasing God. It is necessary to know that the good or bad intention with which an act is performed makes the act good or bad in the sight of God. . . . Before God, the value of an act increases in proportion to the purity of intention with which it is performed.
St Alphonsus Liguori, *The True Spouse of Jesus Christ*, p. 597.

489. *Intention to Do God's Will Is Better than Any Other*
When you taken in hand any work to the end that some good, general or particular, may thence accrue to your neighbor, have not chiefly in view the fruit and good success of the work, but the doing therein of the will of God. Thus when we hear confessions, preach, or lecture, we must not have chiefly in view the conversion or amendment and profit of those with whom we speak, or whose confessions we hear, or to whom we preach, but the doing of the will of God in that work, and doing therein the best we can to please God. The success of such work, the amendment of our neighbor and his actually drawing from the sermon . . . that is not our affair, but God's. 'I planted, Apollo watered, but God gave the increase' (1 Cor 3:6).
Rodriguez, *Practice of Perfection and Christian Virtues,* vol. 1, p. 162.

490. *Purity of Intention*
Purity of intention consists in doing everything from a simple desire to please God. . . .
The prophet Aggaeus says that works, however holy in themselves, if not done for God, are nothing better than bags full of holes; which means, that they are all lost directly, and that no good comes of them. On the contrary, every action done with an intention of pleasing God, of however little value in itself, is worth more than many works done without such pure intention.
St Alphonsus Liguori, *The Way of Salvation and of Perfection*, p. 300-301.

JOY

491. *Joy in Tribulations*
Jesus wishes that under injuries and persecutions we not only be not disquieted, but that we even rejoice and exult in expectation of the great

glory that he has prepared for us in heaven as a reward of our sufferings. 'Blessed are ye when they shall revile and persecute you. . . . Be glad and rejoice, for your reward is very great in heaven.'

St Alphonsus Liguori, *The True Spouse of Jesus Christ*, p. 344.

492. *Rejoice as If Rejoicing Not* – 1 Cor 7:30

[St] Paul says: 'And they that rejoice [should live] as if they rejoiced not'; so that, should you rejoice in this present world, let you so take your joy of it that the remembrance of the judgment to come is at the same time never far from your mind. For in the measure that the anxious soul is penetrated with the fear of final punishment, the more its present delight is taken with moderation, the more shall the wrath to come be tempered.

St Gregory the Great, in Toal, vol. 3, p. 350.

JUDGING OTHERS

493. *Judging Others Is Wrong – Judge Yourself*

. . . You have perverted the right order of things when you exact no account of yourself for your own sins, great and small, but instead search carefully into the sins of others. Make an end of this; and putting from us this perversion of right order, let us set up a tribunal within ourselves, and become in it the accuser, the judge, and the punisher of our own crimes.

St Gregory the Great, *ibid.*, vol. 1, p. 379.

494. *A Rash Judgment Forbidden – Not Obligatory Judgment*

'Judge not that you may not be judged' . . . . Why then has Christ set up so many to reprove, and not alone to reprove, but to punish? For he has commanded that he who will not hear any of these is to be looked upon as the heathen and sinner.

Why then did he give them the power of the keys? For if they are not to judge, they are without authority, and in vain have they received the power of binding and loosing. And besides, if this were to be the case, everything would come to an end, in the churches, in the cities, in homes; for if the master did not correct the servant, and the mistress the maid, the father the son, the friend his friend, everything would go to the bad. . . . Unless we correct our enemies also, we shall never put an end to enmity, and everything would be turned upside down. Let us then carefully study the meaning of what is said here, so that no one may think that the remedies of our salvation and the laws of peace, are really laws of disorder and confusion. For he has, in what follows, made as clear as possible to those who have understanding, the perfection of this law, saying to us: 'And why seest thou the mote in thy brother's eye, and seest not the beam in thy own?. . . '

'What then, you will say, if the neighbor has committed fornication; am I not to say that fornication is a wicked thing, am I not to correct his evil conduct? Correct him, yes; but not like a foe, an enemy, one out for vengeance, but like a physician administering healing remedies. For the Lord did not say: Do not restrain the sinner from his sins, but *Do not judge*, that is, do not be a harsh judge.

St John Chrysostom, in Toal, vol. 3, pp. 91-93.

495. *Judging Others Is Like Murdering God's Will*
It is inherent in man's nature to be so full of prejudice that he is willing to judge others and yet incapable of passing sound judgment on himself. . . .

What do you know of your neighbor's inmost heart? What do you know of God's will for him or by what God has called or attracted him? And yet you would direct and rule his doings according to your own mind. You would murder God's will and order it according to your own false notions.

This murderer does an inconceivable amount of harm among religious persons. . . . One should never pass judgment on any action unless it is an external mortal sin. If a man is in a position in which it is his duty to pass judgment and he has to do it, then it should be the Holy Spirit who judges through him. It should be done at the right time and place, with kindliness and humility, so as not to inflict ten wounds while healing one; not roughly and violently, but kindly and patiently. People who behave otherwise are acting in darkness and not in the light.

Johannes Tauler, *Spiritual Conferences*, pp. 72-73.

THE JUDGMENT

496. *The Particular Judgment – When and Where It Will Occur*
It is the common opinion amongst theologians that the particular judgment takes place at the very moment in which a man expires; and that in the very place where the soul is separated from the body, she is judged by Jesus Christ, who will . . . come himself to judge her cause: 'At what hour

you think not, the Son of man will come' (lk 12:40). 'For the just He will come in love,' says St Augustine, 'for the wicked in terror.'

St Alphonsus Liguori, *Preparation for Death*, pp. 40-41.

497. *Why Priests Must Remind People of God's Judgment*
I beseech you, dearly beloved, and I exhort you with great humility that no one get angry with me or think that I am unreasonable or foolish when I frequently and purposely strive to impress upon you the fearful and dreadful day of judgment. If anyone is displeased by this, he should consider my danger and hear the Lord threaten priests in the terrible words of the prophet: 'If thou declare not to the wicked his iniquity, I will require his blood at thy hand' (Ez 3:18). In another place he says: 'Cry, cease not, lift up thy voice like a trumpet, and show my people their wicked doings' (Is 58:1).

St Caesarius of Arles, in *The Fathers of the Church*, vol. 31, pp. 281-282.

498. *A Man's Works Will Be His Accusers at the Judgment*
It is certain that when his days of trial are ended, man will have to stand up for himself and behold his soul in the mirror of his heart, while witnesses will be brought against him, not from the outside, but within his very soul. Not the evidence of strangers will be produced, but that which is only too familiar, namely, his own works. His faults and sins will be lined up before his unhappy soul to overcome him with their evidence and to confound him with their knowledge.

St Caesarius, sermon 58, *ibid.*, p. 286.

499. *The Terrors of the Wicked on Judgment Day*
... What shall we do, I ask you, when God will come down in anger and dreadful wrath, and sit on the Throne of his Glory, and summon to him all the earth from the rising of the sun to the going down thereof, and all the ends of the earth, so that he may judge his people and render to each according to his works? Oh, Woe! Woe! ... Where now is the pride of the flesh? ... Where the delight of sin, sordid and unclean? ... Where the monstrous pride that disposes all things, and thinks to itself that it alone exists? ... Where now is the tyrant? Where the king? Where the prince? Where the leader? Where the magistrate? Where are they who reveled in luxury, who gloried in the multitude of their riches and despised God?

St Ephraem, in Toal, vol. 1, p. 12.

500. *Fear of Judgment as Motive for Amendment*
... That we may not rise again unto judgment, let us, putting away sorrowing over death, take to ourselves this other sorrowing, which is true

repentance, and give ourselves to good works and to a better life. And in the presence of the dead, or of a burial, let this be our thought: the reflection that we too are mortal. And while we have time, while yet we may, let us through reflection be zealous for our salvation: namely, either by yielding better fruits in our lives, or by amending our present life.

St John Chrysostom, in Toal, vol. 4, p. 364.

501. *Vain Excuses Sinners Might Make at the Judgment*

At the last day, when we shall appear before God, we shall not be able to say to him: 'My God, I have had to surmount too great difficulties; to triumph over them was impossible; my many sins have discouraged me.' For God would reply: 'That would have been true if you had been alone; but I gave you my Son, Jesus; he has expiated and paid for all. . . . In my divine designs, he is not only your salvation, but the source of your strength: for all his satisfactions, all his merits, all his riches – and they are infinite – were yours from Baptism, and since he is seated at my right hand, he has offered for you unceasingly all the fruits of his sacrifice; you should have leaned on him, for in him I would have given you a superabundance of strength to overcome all evil.'

Marmion, *The Structure of God's Plan*, p. 87.

502. *Where the General Judgment Will Take Place*

People often do wish to know where on earth the judgment is to take place. Some have mentioned the Valley of Jehoshaphat, spoken of in the prophet Joel. This valley, however, is but a symbolic designation of the place of judgment, wherever it shall be. Jehoshaphat is but the Hebrew for 'Jehovah judges.' . . . According to St Paul, we shall at the resurrection be carried up toward Christ into the clouds. If in such a matter a guess is allowed, we may imagine that the Judgment will indeed be somewhere on earth, but risen bodies are not subject to laws of earthly gravity and they may therefore rise as in a vast amphitheatre, encircling the throne of the Judge placed in the height of the heavens.

Arendzen: *Purgatory And Heaven*, pp. 83-84.

503. *The Joys of the Just on Judgment Day*

With what joy will we be filled if we are directed to the right hand of the King? What must we be like when the just embrace us there . . . Of what kind shall be that unspeakable delight which we are to receive when the King shall with joyfulness say to those who will be on his right hand: 'Come ye blessed of my Father, possess the kingdom prepared for you from the foundation of the world'.

St Ephraem, in Toal, vol. 1, p. 13.

KNOWLEDGE

504. *Knowledge of God – Not Merely Knowledge About Him*
Those . . . who are consecrated to God's service . . . must try not only to know *about God*, but they must try to *know him* as he is manifested in all the varieties of things he has made, know him in the miracles of Christ, know him in the Passion of Christ, know him in their own souls.
Hoeger, *The Convent Mirror*, p. 72.

505. *Knowledge of Christ Is the Science of the Christian*
The knowledge of Jesus Christ is the science of Christians and the science of salvation; St Paul says that it surpasses all science in value and perfection. This is true:

(1) because of the dignity of the object, which is the God-man, compared to whom the whole universe is but a drop of dew or a grain of sand;
(2) because of its helpfulness to us; human sciences, on the other hand, but fill us with the smoke and emptiness of pride;
(3) and finally, because of its utter necessity: for no one can possibly be saved without the knowledge of Jesus Christ – and yet a man who knows absolutely nothing of any of the other sciences will be saved as long as he is illuminated by the science of Jesus Christ.

St Louis de Montfort, *The Secret of the Rosary*, p. 65.

506. *Knowledge of Self Is the Highest Science – St Augustine*
Men greatly esteem, says St Augustine, the knowledge of the things of heaven and earth, astronomy, cosmography, the study of the movements of the heavens, the courses of the planets, their properties and influences; but the knowledge of oneself is the highest science and most profitable of all. Other sciences *puff up* and make people vain, as St Paul says (1 Cor 8:1), but this *edifies* and humbles.
Rodriguez, *Practice of Perfection and Christian Virtues*, vol. 2, p. 211.

507. *Knowledge of God and of Self*
[Prayer of St Augustine:] 'Lord, that I may know thee and know myself in order that I may love thee and hate myself.'
Quoted by Nash in *How to Pray and Other Conferences*, p. 107.

THE LAW OF GOD

508. *Law of God – Not a Mere Whim*

[The sinner says] 'Here am I, a being full of possibilities of development. Yet my development is checked at every turn by some absurd law' This view arises from a failure to understand the nature of God's laws. His laws are no mere whims, like the laws of some stupid despot. They are, on the contrary, the expression by God, of his knowledge of man's nature and destiny. He knows the kind of being man is, for he made him. And for the same reason, he knows what man is made for. God's laws, then, are a precise statement of how this particular kind of being may avoid destruction and reach his particular goal. The man who makes an engine is not limiting your freedom when he tells you not to run it beyond a certain speed. He knows that if you do you will smash the engine. And if you should plead that your nature demands more speed, that you feel stifled by such slow running – he may very well grow impatient. He knows what speed is right for the engine because he made it.

God's laws then are best thought of as 'makers' instructions,' directions for the right use of ourselves. His prohibitions warn us of wrong ways of using ourselves or our neighbors. Earlier I used the simile of a razor to illustrate the point that to misuse a thing was to destroy it. Emancipate the razor from its old humdrum task of removing hair from the face – defy the maker's statement that razors are only meant for shaving – use your razor for chopping wood and you will have a twisted metal, fit only for the scrap heap. . . .

The act of running counter to God's law is sometimes justified on the ground of 'self-expression.' It certainly is not an expression of self, for God, who made the self, has declared that such action is contrary to its nature. And a man who commits sin – any sin – is to that extent less a man, just as a motor car whose engine has been used in violation of its maker's instructions is less of a motor car.

Sheed, *A Map of Life*, pp. 96-97.

LAY APOSTLES

509. *Lay Apostles Can be "Angels"*
. . . Each one among you, in as far as he is able, in as far as he responds to the grace of the heavenly invitation, should recall his neighbor from evil-doing; should he seek to encourage him in doing what is good; when he reminds him of the eternal kingdom, or of the punishment of wrongdoers; whenever he employs words of holy import, he is indeed an angel. . . .

It is a greater thing to strengthen with the nourishment of a word that will feed the mind forever, than to fill with earthly bread a stomach of perishable flesh. . . . Direct your idle conversation toward a fondness for what will edify . . . and so you also may with John (the Baptist) merit to be called angels.

St Gregory the Great, in Toal, vol. 1, pp. 48-49.

510. *Learning Without Virtue Is Tragedy*
The more learned and capable a member of the Society be, if he has no great fund of virtue and mortification, the more is disunion to be feared and his giving trouble in religion. They say very well that letters and high talents in an unmortified man are like a good sword in the hands of a madman, to the hurt and harm of himself and others. But if learned men are mortified and humble, 'not seeking themselves but the things of Jesus Christ', as St Paul says (Phil 2:21), then much peace and union will ensue, since their example will be of great benefit to the rest and will draw them to follow their path.

Rodriguez, *Practice of Perfection and Christian Virtues,* vol. 1, p. 198.

LENDING

511. *Lending with No Hope of a Return Lauded*
'Lend to those from whom you do not hope to receive in return' (Lk 6: 35). . . . Consider the force of the statement, and you will admire the kindness of the Lawmaker. Whenever you have the intention of providing for a poor man for the Lord's sake, the same thing is both a gift and a

loan, a gift because of the expectation of no return but a loan because of the great gift of the Master who pays in his place, and who, receiving trifling things through a poor man, will give great things in return for them. 'He that hath mercy on the poor, lendeth to God' (Prv 19:17).

St Basil, in *The Fathers of the Church*, vol. 46, p. 190.

LENIN

512. *Lenin on St Francis of Assisi and the Saving of Russia*
Perhaps no man ever worked so hard at what he thought was the salvation of a nation as Lenin did. Yet in his last illness, Lenin confessed: 'I have been mistaken. It was, I suppose, necessary to liberate a multitude of oppressed people; but our method has provoked other oppressions, frightful massacres. You know that my most awful nightmare is to feel myself drowning in an ocean of the blood of countless victoms. *To save Russia, what we needed (but it is too late now) was ten men like Francis of Assisi. Ten like him, and we should have saved Russia.'* . . . A Hungarian priest, a former classmate and confidant of Lenin, heard him speak these words during a lucid interval in his last illness and repeated them verbatim to Father Michael D'Herbigny, S.J.

Shamon, *The Only Life*, pp. 9-10.

LENT

513. *Lent Not only for Fasting but for Practising Virtues*
. . . Our fast does not consist chiefly of mere abstinence from food, nor are dainties withdrawn from our bodily appetites with profit unless the mind is recalled from wrongdoing and the tongue restrained from slandering. This is a time of gentleness and long-suffering, of peace and tranquility; when all the pollutions of vice are to be eradicated and continuance of virtue is to be attained by us. Now let godly minds boldly accustom themselves to forgive faults, to pass over insults, and to forget wrongs.

St Leo the Great, in *The Nicene and Post-Nicene Fathers,* vol. 12, p. 156.

514. *Lent – Time for Spiritual Housecleaning*
[St Paul says:] 'You are the temple of the living God' (2 Cor 6:16); we

must then strive with all vigilance that the dwelling of our heart be not unworthy of so great a Guest. . . . [As damaged or old houses are repaired,] so must we with unceasing concern take care that nothing disordered be found in our souls, that nothing unclean be found there.

St Leo the Great, in Toal, vol. 2, p. 125.

LEPER

515. *In Touching the Leper, Christ Showed He Is above the Law*
'And Jesus, stretching forth His Hand, touched him'. Because it was laid down in the Law that he who touched a leper would be unclean until sundown, he touched the leper, not as a servant of the Law, but as its Lord. For the Law is under the Lawgiver; it is not the Lawgiver that is subject to the Law.

St John Chrysostom, in Toal, vol. 1, p. 306.

516. *In Curing the Leper Christ Showed Himself Superior to Moses*
. . . From the healing of the leper it was clearly evident that Christ, in an incomparable manner, far transcended the law of Moses. For Mary, the sister of Moses, because she had murmured against him, was stricken with leprosy. And Moses at this affliction of his sister was profoundly grieved; but since he was unable to banish the disease from the woman, falling down before God, he besought him saying: 'O God, I beseech thee, heal her' (Nm 12:13).

Now, observe carefully. In the one case there is entreaty: with prayer he sought to obtain the divine clemency; but the Savior of mankind, with the authority that was truly divine, says: 'I will. Be thou made clean.' This healing of the leper served, therefore, as a warning to the priests that from it they should learn that those who gave precedence to Moses were wandering far from the truth. Without doubt they should reverence Moses as the minister of the Law, a helper of grace made known by angels (Gal 3:19), but much more is Emmanuel to be praised and glorified as the true Son of God and the Father.

St Cyril, in Toal, vol. 1, p. 310.

LIFE

517. *Spiritual Life as Intimacy with God*
The spiritual life may be . . . simply and correctly described as the 'culti-

vation of intimacy with God. . . .' God has smoothed the path for the human soul by becoming man. To become intimate with God, the soul has only to become intimate with Jesus, who is like to the soul in his humanity, like to it in all things except sin.

Edward Leen, *Progress Through Mental Prayer*, p. 9.

518. *Sanctifying Grace Is Not Enough*

To have sanctifying grace is the prime requisite for having the interior life. But for adults, the interior life, as understood by spiritual writers, implies more than the mere possession of sanctifying grace. *Having* the divine life of grace is but half the story; *doing* the works of grace is the other half. The interior life is more than merely *being* a child of God; it means, in addition, *acting* as his child.

This brings us to the heart of the question. The proper activities of human life are to know and to love; the interior life, being a higher life, must be capable of knowing and loving in a higher way. Furthermore, knowledge and love must have objects. No one merely knows or loves; he knows and he loves someone or something. . . .

What, then, must be the object of man's thoughts and desires if his life is to be truly interior? . . .

There is only one answer: God! The truly interior life must have for the object of its thoughts and desires, not one's self – but God himself, dwelling within the soul. Only now are we ready to answer the question: What is the interior life? Life, as we have said, is the principle of immanent activity. Viewed from its principle, the interior life is sanctifying grace, or the divine life a man has when he is in the state of grace (the habitual interior life). But viewed from the angle of its activity, *the interior life is the activity of the soul in grace striving to know, love, and serve God within it* (*the actual interior life*).

Shamon, *The Only Life*, pp. 4-6.

519. *Spiritual Life, the Source of Greatness*

[Christ's] thirty years of silence . . . were the natural preparation for [his] three years of activity; in the career of the servants of God, it is from the hours of silence and communing with God that is derived the efficiency that marks the hours of active service.

The lesson to be drawn from this is important. It is not *what we do* that matters in God's eyes, so much as *how we do it*; it is not *what we effect* that he regards, but *what we are*. An action of the most trivial kind, as far as human estimation goes, may be wonderfully pleasing in God's eyes if it proceeds from a soul in which charity is great and grace abundant. . . . To accomplish great things, we must be great.

Edward Leen, *In the Likeness of Christ*, pp. 120-121.

520. *Three Modes of Life*
. . . Take the three modes of life: the contemplative, the active, the contemplative-active. A man can live the life of faith in any of these three and get to heaven. What is not indifferent is that he love truth and do what charity demands. No man must be so committed to contemplation as, in his contemplation, to give no thought to his neighbor's needs, nor so absorbed in action as to dispense with the contemplation of God.

St Augustine, *City of God*, bk. 19, chap. 19.

521. *Spiritual Life Vs. Intellectual Life*
Cardinal du Perron, at the hour of his death, expressed his sorrow at having been more devoted during his life to perfecting his intellect by science than his will by the exercises of the interior life.

Chautard, *The Soul of the Apostolate*, pp. 88-89.

522. *Life in Christ – How and Why*
He made us his by baptism; he has cared for us, soul and body, with a love that passes knowledge; to win life for us, he suffered death; his own Body and Blood have been our food. After that, we have no choice but to come to the only conclusion possible: that being alive should no longer mean living with our own life, but with his life who died for us. In other words, we are to dedicate every moment of life to the divine love that inspired our Savior's death; we are to deliver to his glory . . . all our victories, our virtues, our activities, our thoughts, everything on which our hearts are set.

St Francis de Sales, *The Love of God*, p. 294.

523. *Life Eternal, Our Final Goal*
We are not created for this earth: the end for which God has placed us in the world is this, that with our good deeds we may inherit eternal life. . . .

St Augustine . . . said that a man who believes in eternity, and yet is not converted to God, has either lost his senses or his faith. 'O Eternity!' (these are his words), 'he who meditates upon thee and repents not, either has no faith, or has no heart.' In reference to this, St John Chrysostom relates that the Gentiles, when they saw Christians sinning, thought them either liars or fools. If you believe not (they said) what you say you believe, you are liars; if you believe in eternity and sin, you are fools.'

St Alphonsus, *Way of Salvation and of Perfection*, pp. 171-173.

524. *Thinking about Eternal Life Helps Us Despise Present Things*
A man will despise all things present as transitory, when he has securely fixed his mental gaze on those things which are immovable and eternal,

and already contemplates in heart – though still in the flesh – the blessedness of the future life.
Cassian, in *The Nicene and Post-Nicene Fathers*, vol. 11, p. 239.

525. *Eternal Life to Be Desired with Longing*
Let us, I beseech you, long for this [eternal] life. For if we long for this life, we shall place no value on the things of the present time.
St John Chrysostom, in Toal, vol. 4, p. 110.

LITTLE THINGS

526. *Little Things Done with Love Are Great*
Without love the most brilliant deeds are nothing; but with love, the most trivial deeds are diamonds for the eternal crown.
Nash, *The Nun at Her Prie-Dieu*, p. 282.

527. *The Value of Little Things*
'It is true, little things are little, but to be faithful in little things is something great' (St Jerome). Fidelity in little things is the secret of sanctity.
Wallenstein, *Guide to Perfect Christian Living*, p. 28.

528. *Little Things Can Be Great*
Nothing is little that God commands. Christ did little things. Great and little are relative. The will makes things great. It requires great fervor and loyalty to do the little things, so that doing little things is doing a great thing. Little things guard great things and beget great things.
Bronsnahan, *Searchlighting Ourselves*, p. 110.

529. *Fidelity in Little Things Brings God's Special Help*
. . . He who is very careful and diligent to please God, not only in matters of obligation, but also in those of supererogation and perfection, and not only in greater but also in lesser things, he is liberal to God. Now to them that are thus liberal, God also is very liberal. These are God's favorites to whom he shows his bounties; to these he gives not only those general aids which are sufficient to resist and overcome temptations, but also those special and superabundant and efficacious aids wherewith they will nowise fall when they are tempted. But if you are not liberal to God, how can you expect God to be liberal to you? If you are niggardly with God, you deserve that God should be niggardly with you. If you are so mean and close as to go sounding and measuring as with rule and compass – 'Am I

bound or not bound? Am I bound under sin or not bound under sin? Does it amount to a mortal sin or to no more than a venial?' – all this is being niggardly with God, since you want to give him no more than you are obliged, and even in that possibly you fail: God then will be niggardly with you and give you no more than he is obliged by his word. . . .

Rodriguez, *Practice of Perfection and Christian Virtues*, vol. 1, pp. 51-52.

530. *The Value of Little Things in God's Sight*

[St Francis de Sales does not] hesitate to write to Madame Brulart: 'In the house of a prince it is not so great to be the scullery maid in the kitchen as it is to be valet of the chamber; but in the house of God, the menials are most often the greatest because when they become soiled, it is for the love of God, for his will. God's will gives value to our actions, not only to their exterior appearances.'

Charmot, *Ignatius Loyola and Francis de Sales*, p. 233.

LOYALTY

531. *Loyalty to God Vs. Loyalty to Man*

[Speaking of her youth, St Teresa of Spain says:] I was then so imprudent as to think it a virtue to be grateful and loyal to one who liked me. Cursed be that loyalty which reaches so far as to go against the law of God. It is a madness common in the world, and it makes me mad to see it.

The Life of St Teresa of Jesus, Written by Herself, p. 28.

MAN

532. *Man Is Three Men*

Man is really, as it were, three men: an animal man who lives according to his senses, a rational man, and finally a higher man, formed and re-formed in the likeness of God. We must all withdraw into this highest and innermost part of ourselves. It is with this higher man that we must come face to face with the divine abyss, become detached from ourselves and give ourselves as captives to God.

Tauler, *Spiritual Conferences*, p. 124.

533. *Distinction Between 'Person' and 'Nature'*

The distinction between person and nature is not some deep and hidden thing to which philosophy only comes after centuries of study. It is, on the contrary, a distinction so obvious that the smallest child who can talk at all makes it automatically. If in the half-light he sees a vague outline that might be anything, he asks: 'What is that?' If, on the other hand, he can see that it is a human being but cannot distinguish or does not recognize the features, he asks: 'Who is that?' The distinction between *what* and *who* is the distinction between *nature* and *person*. Of every man the two questions – What is he? and Who is he? – can be answered. Every man, in other words, is both a nature and a person. Into my every action nature and person enter. For instance, *I* speak. I, the person, speak. But I am able to speak only because I am a man, because it is my nature to speak. I discover that there are all sorts of things I can do; and all sorts of things I cannot do. My nature decides. I can think, speak, walk: these actions go with the nature of man, which I have. I cannot fly, for this goes with the nature of a bird, which I have not.

Sheed, *A Map of Life*, pp. 46-47. (This is in connection with the one Person and the two Natures in Christ.)

534. *Man's Dignity as an Image of God*
Let us make recognition of our own dignity. Let us give honor to him in whose likeness we were made. Let us dwell upon this mystery that we may understand for what Christ died.

St John Chrysostom, in Toal, vol. II, p. 220.

535. *Man's True Dignity and Value*
Being in such great honor because he was created in the image of the Creator, man is honored above the heavens, above the sun, above the choirs of stars. For which of the heavenly bodies was said to be an image of the most high God? . . .

If you are not mindful of your first origin, because of the price paid for you, accept at least some idea of your dignity; look at that which was given in exchange for you and realize your worth. You were bought with the Precious Blood of Christ; do not become a slave of sin. Understand your own honor in order that you may not be like the senseless beasts.

St Basil, in *The Fathers of the Church*, vol. 9, pp. 325-326.

536. *Man's Worth Seen from the Care God Takes of Him*
To remember that there is not a single thought, word, or act done by me or to me, which affects my life remotely or proximately, but it is permitted by [God] with a view to helping my soul; that the Lord is indeed solicitous for me, and that his solicitude is constant; to recognize this, to be convinced of this, gives me at least a faint idea of my true importance

as being loved thus by the heavenly Father. . . . 'Can a mother forget her infant so as not to have compassion of the child of her womb? And, even if she should forget, yet will I not forget thee.' So it is he who arranges my life, he who plans all the details and circumstances of each day and hour, always with a view to cultivating in my soul the seed of sanctifying grace sown therein on the day of my baptism.

Nash, *Living Your Faith*, p. 63.

537. *Man's Purpose Is to Obey God*

. . . [Christ's infallible explanation of man's purpose, briefly,] is that man belongs to God and that therefore he has only one business to do in life – to obey God. Man is not here just in order to enjoy himself or amass wealth; still less, to wallow like an animal in the gutter of sin. Even the doing of kindly deeds, or the heroic life among lepers, or the service of cancerous patients, or the prayer and penance and solitude of the monk's cell do not constitute the ultimate purpose of life. These are of value in God's eyes in so far as they are the expression of what he wills to be done, and he wills them because they are objectively right in themselves.

Nash, *ibid.*, p. 26.

538. *Man Can Find Rest Only in God*

'Thou hast made us, O Lord, for thyself, and our heart is restless till it rests in thee' (St Augustine, *Confessions*, bk. 1, chap. 1).

A very good comparison, and one which illustrates this matter very well, is that common comparison which is drawn from the needle of a mariner's compass. The nature of that needle, after it has been touched by the magnet, is to point to the north, God having given it that natural inclination; and you will see how restless that needle is and how many times it turns and turns back again until it takes the direction to the north. . . . Now, in this way God has created men, with this natural inclination in respect of Himself.

Rodriguez, *Practice of Perfection and Christian Virtues*, vol. 1, pp. 487-488.

MARTYRS

539. *How We Can All Become Martyrs*

The following is the way in which we acquire the glory of martyrdom: It is by accepting death to please God and to conform to his will; for, as we have remarked . . . with St Augustine, not the pain but the cause of death, or the end for which one submits to it, is that which makes martyrs. It follows that he who dies, in courageously accepting death and all the pains that accompany it to accomplish the divine will, though he does not receive death by the hands of the executioner, dies, however, with the merit of martyrdom, at least with a very similar merit. . . . Hence we shall see in heaven a great number of saints doubly crowned with the merit of martyrdom, without having been martyred.

St Alphonsus Liguori, *Victories of the Martyrs*, pp. 39-40.

540. *"I am Hastening Not to Death but to Life"*

St Pionius, the martyr, standing by the instruments of death, showed himself so full of joy that the people who stood by wondered at his delight and asked how he could be so happy when he was just going to die. 'You are mistaken,' said he, as Eusebius relates – 'you are mistaken; I am not hastening to death but to life.'

St Alphonsus Liguori, *The Way of Salvation and of Perfection*, pp. 296-297.

541. *Martyrs Seek Eternal Life*

The martyrdom of St Vitus. . . . shows us the wonderful assistance of grace which never fails the servants of the Lord. . . . When only fourteen years of age, St Vitus was scourged, racked, and torn with irons. His father, who was a gentile, wept with anguish to see his son expire in such torments. 'No, Father!,' explained the boy, 'I do not die; I go to live with Christ forever.'

St Alphonsus Liguori, *Victories of the Martyrs*, p. 36.

542. *Fifty-two Die On Burning Crosses in Japan*

While the warlords reigned supreme in Japan in the early seventeenth century, many Christians were imprisoned in the capital city of the country, then called Miyako, but now known as Kyoto. When the warlord visited the city in 1619, he ordered fifty-two men, women and children to be attached to crosses and burned to death. Only about twenty-seven crosses had been erected, so two or more were attached to many of the crosses. Since most of them were tied loosely, they could have escaped death, but not one of them made the attempt. One woman, named Thecla, died with five of her children, three of whom expired in her arms.

St Alphonsus, *ibid.*, pp. 369-370.

543. *A Martyr Thanks the Governor*

[St] Phileas had dischared some of the first offices of state in the city of Thmuis, in Egypt. . . . He was somewhat advanced in age when he became a Christian but was soon named bishop of Thmuis. From his prison he wrote a letter, still extant, in which he urged the Christians to be true despite all the tortures that might be inflicted on them. The governor of Egypt, Culcian, said to him: 'Thy conscience should make thee sacrifice for the sake of thy wife and children.' But the Saint replied: 'Conscience obliges me to prefer God to all things, since the Scriptures say that thou shalt love thy God, who created thee, above all things.' On the way to the place of execution, the bishop's brother cried out that Phileas had demanded an appeal, but the Saint answered: 'I have not demanded any appeal. Give not ear to this wretched man. I am much beholden to the judges who have made me a co-heir with Jesus Christ.'

St Alphonsus, *ibid.*, pp. 112-115.

544. *Father and Four-year-old Son Die Together*

In the daimyate of Bungo, Japan, a Christian named Balthasar, who had served as superintendent of the treasury, on account of his faith was arrested, deprived of his property and sent into exile. There, the governor of the region sentenced him to death. Balthasar thanked the governor for delivering him from the miseries of this life. Balthasar's four-year old son insisted on going along and kissed the garment of his dead father, after which he, too, was beheaded as his father had been.

St Alphonsus, *ibid.*, pp. 367-368.

545. *Persecutor Cured by Victim Becomes a Martyr*

In the days of Diocletian, St Sabinus, Bishop of Spoleto, travelled through his whole diocese to encourage Christians to persevere. Arrested by order of Venustianus, then governor of Tuscany, he was ordered to worship an image of Jove. Sabinus dashed the image to the earth, breaking it into pieces. Venustianus had the Saint's hands cut off and sent him to prison hoping he would die of his wounds or of starvation. A pious widow, Serena, found ways to support the Saint. Meanwhile, Venustianus was tortured by excessive pain in his eyes. Friends urged him to ask help from St Sabinus, who visited him and told him he would be cured if he believed and were baptized. After baptism, Venustianus was cured instantly and was himself beheaded along with his wife and children by order of the emperor, Maximian.

St Alphonsus, *ibid.*, pp. 87-89.

546. *Heroism of a Martyr's Mother*

When Symphorian's mother saw her son led away to martyrdom, she cried after him: 'My son, my son, remember eternal life! Look up to heaven and think of him who reigns there! Your approaching end will quickly close the brief course of this life.'

St Francis de Sales, *Introduction to the Devout Life*, p. 239.

547. *Martyrs Hope for Eternal Life*
Hope for eternal life and happiness in heaven is the theme stressed most frequently by the hundreds of martyrs whose victories are narrated by St Alphonsus in his book *Victories of the Martyrs*.

MERCY

548. *Mercy Toward the Poor – Means for Obtaining Mercy*
Let those who wish Christ to spare them, have mercy on the poor; let them give freely to feed the wretched, who desire to attain to the society of the blessed. Let no man consider his fellow vile, nor despise in any one that nature which the Creator of the world made his own. For who that labors can deny that Christ claims that labor as done unto himself? Your fellow slave is helped thereby, but it is the Lord who will repay.
St Leo the Great, in *The Nicene and Post-Nicene Fathers*, vol. 12, p. 119.

549. *To Obtain Mercy, We Must Practice It*
'Would you, ' says St Augustine, 'gain God's mercy for the sins you have been guilty of? Be merciful to your neighbors, for God measures to you the same measure that you measure to your brethren.'
Quoted by Scaramelli, in *Directorium Asceticum*, vol. 4, pp. 238-239.

550. *St Augustine's Prayer for Mercy*
Let us, then pray to the Lord, according to the prayer of St. Augustine: 'Here burn, here cut, here do not spare, that Thou mayest spare in eternity.'
St Alphonsus Liguori, *Preparation for Death*, p. 68.

551. *Mercy Is of Two Kinds*
There is . . . both an earthly and a heavenly mercy, the one human and the other divine. What is human mercy? It is to care for the miseries of the poor. And what is divine mercy? Doubtless it is that which grants forgiveness of sins. Whatever human mercy gives on the way, divine mercy pays in the heavenly country. In this world God is cold and hungry in the person of all his poor, for he said: 'As long as you did it for one of these, the least of my brethren, you did it for me' (Mt 25:40, 42). Therefore, God, who deigns to give from heaven wants to receive on earth. What kind of creatures are we if we want to take when God gives, but are unwilling to give when he asks it? If a poor man hungers, Christ is in need, as he himself said: 'I was hungry and you did not give me to eat.' . . . Therefore, grant earthly mercy and you will receive the heavenly.
St Caesarius of Arles, in *The Fathers of the Church*, vol. 31, pp. 127-128.

MERIT

552. *Desire for Merit and Reward Not Mercenary*
[Do not say that the desire for merit and a reward] is a mercenary thought. Certainly it is to our interest to make the divine life increase in us, for the more we advance in grace and charity, the more our merits increase and the greater will be our future glory and eternal beatitude. But God himself in the magnificence of his generosity has willed it to be so; if it concerns our joy throughout eternity, it also concerns the will of God and the glory that the accomplishment of this will procures for our heavenly Father.

Marmion, *Growth in Christ*, pp. 156-157.

553. *Merit Gained by the Simplest Actions*
Every one of our actions, however insignificant it may seem, if performed in a state of sanctifying grace and for God's glory, is meritorious unto life eternal. The least act of mortification and self-denial, the performance of our humblest daily duties – if done in union with Christ our Head and with the right intention – will be rewarded in heaven. In the Catholic life there is nothing trifling and unimportant . . . Says Fr Tanquerey: 'From the moment we awake until we retire at night, the meritorious acts which we can perform, if we are recollected and generous, may be numbered by the hundreds. Indeed, there is growth of the godlike life of grace in our souls, not only through every act of the day, but through every effort to make each action more perfect; through every effort to dispel distractions in prayer, to apply our minds to our tasks, to keep back an unkind word, to render service to others. Likewise every word inspired by charity, every good thought turned to good account in short, all the movements of the soul directed by our free will toward good are so many means of increasing merit.'

Bandes, *The Catholic Layman and Holiness*, p. 214-215.

554. *In What Merit Consists*
Our Lord said this to me one day: 'thinkest thou, my daughter, that meriting lies in fruition? No; merit lies only in doing, in suffering and in loving.'

The Life of St Teresa of Jesus, Written by Herself, p. 452.

555. *Life on Earth a Wonderful Opportunity*
[One day in a vision St Mechtildis] heard the saints exclaiming: 'Oh, how fortunate and blessed are you who still live on earth for the amount of merit that you may gain!' If a man knew how much we might merit every day from the moment of his rising, his heart would be filled at once with joy and satisfaction to think that that day had dawned on which he might live to God, our Lord, and with his grace, to the honor and glory of God, might increase his merit; and this would give him courage and strength to do and suffer all things with the utmost cheerfulness.

Rodriguez, *Practice of Perfection and Christian Virtues,* vol. 2, p.90.

556. *Merit Due To Christ, Holy Spirit*
Our deeds, then, like a grain of mustard seed, bear no comparison with the tree of glory they become. Their strength, their power of growth, is due to the fact that they proceed from the Holy Spirit. By a wonderful infusion of grace into our souls, he makes our deeds his own, yet at the same time leaves them ours. We are members of a body whose Head is Christ, but whose soul is the Holy Spirit; we are branches grafted upon a tree of which he is the divine life-force. Because, in this way, he is responsible for our actions, and we cooperate with him, he leaves us all the merit, all the profit of our service, our good deeds; we, in turn, leave him all the glory, all the praise – acknowledging that every work of ours begins, continues and ends through him, through his mercy. In his mercy he comes to us, prompting us; he dwells in us, helping us; he lives in us, guiding us – until he brings to perfection what he first began.

God in his goodness shows us great mercy in thus going shares with us, heaven knows! We give him the glory of our praise, indeed, but he gives us the glory of possessing him. In a word, for these light and momentary labors of ours we receive the reward of blessings that will last forever. Amen.

St Francis de Sales, *The Love of God*, p. 473.

MIRACLES

557. *Cure of the Centurion's Son – Why Christ Volunteered to Go*
Why is it that when the ruler [royal official] asks Jesus to come to his son, he refuses to go there bodily, while, though not asked to come to the servant of the centurion, he offers to go there at once? He does not think it fitting that he should go to the ruler's son, while he did think it fitting that He should hasten to the centurion's servant.

What is this but rebuking our pride, which leads us to honor in men, not their nature, in which they are made to the image of God, but their dignity and riches?

St Gregory the Great, in Toal, vol. 4, pp. 260-261.

558. *Son Cured; Father's Lack of Faith Criticized*

. . . Without doubt, this man who came praying for the health of his son believed. He would not have asked healing from one he did not believe was a healer. Why then were the words 'Unless you see signs and wonders, you believe not' said to one who believed even before seeing a sign? But remember what he asked and you will see clearly that his faith was doubtful.

For he asked that Jesus should come down and heal his son. He asked, therefore, for the bodily presence of the Lord, who in spirit is present in all places; and so he had little faith in him who, he believed, could not heal unless he were present in body with the sick. Had his faith been perfect, he would have known without doubt that there is no place where God is not. And so in great part he was unbelieving; for he was not honoring Christ's divine majesty, but his corporal presence.

St Gregory the Great, *ibid.*,

MORTIFICATION

559. *Mortification – Its Meaning*

Mortification consists in making the sacrifices necessary to resist our corrupt inclinations and to do God's holy will.

The main thing, therefore, is not hurting our bodies but fulfilling God's will. Mortification is something that has a deep influence on our life. This is indicated by the terms:

(a) To 'mortify' means to control the inferior appetite so that it seems to be dead and can do no more harm.

(b) To 'deny' ourself means not to recognize our lower self, not pay any attention to it, but to be heedless of it.

(c) To 'overcome' ourself means to fight against our lower self until it is conquered.

Wallenstein, *Guide to Perfect Christian Living*, p. 113.

560. *Mortification – Its Function*

Mortification aims at replacing disorder with order, revolt against God and reason by subjection to Christ and his faith, disordered nature by vivifying grace, and self-indulgence by purity and justice. The ultimate effect is to reduce our senses to the control of our reason, our imagination to our will, and our will to God. It may be defined then as a deliberate renouncement of disorderly satisfaction of our concupiscence, and a curbing of every inordinate exercise of our external and internal faculties.

Edward Leen, *Progress Through Mental Prayer*, p. 237.

561. *Mortification – What It means and Why We should Practice It*

Some are terrified by the word 'mortification.' They think it means killing or destroying nature and its faculties. Now our nature and its powers are the handiwork of the Creator and, hence, are good in themselves. They were not corrupted by the Fall. But there is disorder – a lack of harmony and coordination – in fallen nature. The body, senses, imagination and passions are continually striving to emancipate themselves from the control of reason and will. The flesh is continually at odds with the spirit. Mortification is simply the application of will power, strengthened and elevated by God's grace, to this disorder in nature. The negative aim of this toil and effort is to guard our senses and powers from going astray and from indulging in activities harmful to our salvation; to withdraw them from dangerous occasions and from all that flatters sensuality; to prevent any passion from dominating and enslaving us. The positive aim of this self-mastery and self-discipline is to guide, educate and improve human nature, to make it prompt and pliable in the service of God, to restore, as far as possible, its original harmony, to make us live in conformity with the dictates of Christ's teaching, of conscience and right reason. If there is any suffering, constraint or violence in mortification, these are not an end in themselves but a means of attaining self-mastery, inward peace and complete liberty. . . .

Just as weeds must be continually hoed in the garden, so we must constantly strive to uproot the inordinate tendencies which crop up in the garden of the soul.

Bandas, *The Catholic Layman and Holiness*, p. 119-120.

562. *Mortification of the Body and Its Resurrection*

Revelation bids us consider, not only the Fall, which caused the disorder in man's nature, but also divine grace, with the aid of which man controls and disciplines the body and prepares it for the resurrection when body and soul will unite once more and live forever in perfect accord and harmony. The germ of this glorious bodily immortality is divine grace in our soul. That life of the soul must be protected and developed by a constant warfare against the flesh and by close union with God.

Bandas, *ibid.*, p. 123.

563. *In What Mortification Consists*
[Mortification] consists in regulating what was irregular, in ordering and moderating our passions and evil inclinations and our disorderly self-love. In the words of Christ, our Redeemer: 'If anyone would come after Me, let him deny himself, and take up his cross and follow me' (Mt. 16: 24). St Jerome says: 'He denies himself and takes up his cross who before was unchaste and becomes now chaste and pure, who before was intemperate and becomes now very abstemious, who before was timid and weak and becomes now strong and constant.'

Rodriguez, *Practice of Perfection and Christian Virtues*, vol. 2, pp. 14-15.

564. *Mortification Likened to a Cataract Operation*
All the mortification undertaken in the development of the spiritual life should be a kind of cataract operation, made worthwhile because it gradually removes the obstacles to the vision of God through faith, hope and charity.

Hoeger, *The Convent Mirror*, p. 12.

565. *Exterior and Interior Mortification*
We have a soul and a body. External mortification is necessary in order to mortify the disorderly appetites of the body; and interior mortification is necessary to mortify the irregular affections of the soul. All this is comprised in the following words of the Savior: 'If any man will come after me, let him deny himself, and take up his cross, and follow me' (Mt 16: 24). External mortification is included in the words, 'let him take up his cross. . . . ' Interior mortification is still more important and necessary – 'let him deny himself. . . . ' The interior mortification restrains the affections of the heart in order to subject them to reason and God; hence it has been called by the Apostle: 'The circumcision is that of the heart, in the spirit.' (Rom 2:29).

St Alphonsus Liguori, *Dignity and Duties of the Priest*, p. 341.

566. *Fruits of Exterior Mortification*
Let us now attend to the fruits of external mortification.

First, it satisfies for the pains due to the pleasures in which we indulged: these pains are far milder in this than in the next life. . . . 'If you do not wish to be punished,' says St John Chrysostom, 'be your own judge – chastise and amend yourself.'

Second, mortification detaches the soul from earthly pleasures and gives her facility of flying to God and of uniting herself with him. St Francis de Sales used to say that 'If the flesh is not mortified and depressed, the soul will never be able to raise herself up to God.'

Third, penance merits for us eternal goods, as St Peter of Alcantara revealed from heaven to St Teresa, saying: 'O happy penance that has merited for me so much glory.'

St Alphonsis, *ibid.*, pp. 365-366.

567. *Bodily Mortification Helps Conquer the Devil*

'Mortify your body and you will conquer the devil,' says St Augustine.

St Alphonsus, *ibid.*, p. 378.

568. *Mortification of the Body Defended by St Bernard*

. . . St Bernard said to some seculars who were horrified at his monks treating their bodies so badly, saying that they bore a deadly hatred to them: to whom the saint answered that it was they in the world who really detested their bodies, since to give them a little enjoyment of sensual delights, they bound them over to everlasting torments; while the monks truly loved their bodies, since they affiicted them for a little time to merit a lasting repose.

Rodriguez, *Practice of Perfection and Christian Virtues*, vol. 2, p. 40.

569. *Mortification of the Body is Needed*

St Ambrose has written that he who does not cease to indulge the body shall cease to please God. . . .

We are born for a more noble end than to be the slaves of the body, said the pagan Seneca.

St Alphonsus Liguori, *Dignity and Duties of the Priest*, p. 364.

570. *Mortification Needed to Combat Evil Desires*

. . . We must always carry in our hand the mattock of mortification to cut down evil desires that constantly spring up and bud forth within us from the infected roots of concupiscence; otherwise the soul will become a forest of vices.

All our sanctity and salvation consist in following the example of Jesus Christ: 'For whom he foreknew, he also predestined to be made conformable to the image of his Son' (Rom 8:29). But we shall not be able to imitate Jesus Christ unless we deny ourselves and embrace by mortification the cross that he gives us to carry: 'If any man will come after me, let him deny himself and take up his cross and follow me' (Mt 16:24).

St Alphonsus, *ibid.*, pp. 338-339.

571. *Mortification Is Not Merely Negative*

Mortification . . . is not performed in any morbid sense of self-hatred or contempt of the body; it is not a mere negative thing, a foolish frustration or self-suppression. It is something quite positive; an 'assertion' of Jesus rather than a denial of self; for we only deny ourselves to find him, that he may live in us and that we may be united to him.

Boylan, *This Tremendous Lover*, pp. 236-237.

572. *The Nature and Function of Interior Mortification*

'To regulate the motions of the soul is,' as St Augustine says, 'the office of interior mortification.'

The human soul is a garden in which useless and noxious herbs constantly spring up: we must, therefore, by the practice of holy mortification continually hold the mattock in our hands to root them up and banish them from our hearts; otherwise, our souls will become a wild, uncultivated waste, covered with briers and thorns.

St Alphonsus Liguori, *The True Spouse of Jesus Christ*, pp. 130-131.

573. *Mortification of a Dying Son*

A mother was watching at the bedside of her dying Son. 'Mother,' he gasped. 'Water! I am tortured with this thirst.' And the mother held the glass to his lips. Just at that moment, the clock in the town struck three. 'My son,' she whispered, 'it is three o'clock, and today is Friday. It is the day and the hour of Christ's death. He thirsted too.' The boy put the glass of water, untasted, back into the hands of his mother. Which of them displayed the greater courage?

Nash, *Living Your Faith*, pp. 91-92.

574. *Mortification of the Eyes*

'Through the eyes,' says St Bernard, 'the dart of impure love enters the heart.' 'What is not seen,' says St Francis de Sales, 'is not desired.'

Seneca justly said that blindness is a great help to preserve innocence.

St Alphonsus Liguori, *Dignity and Duties of the Priest*, pp. 367-368.

MYSTERY

575. *What Mystery Means*

As used by theologians, the word [*mystery*] does not mean a truth of which we cannot know anything; it means a truth of which we cannot know everything. Mystery there must be once we touch on the nature of God. He is the Infinite, the Immeasurable, the Limitless. We are finite, measured, limited on all sides. It is impossible that we should totally contain God in our minds so as totally to comprehend him.

Sheed, *A Map of Life*, pp. 77-78.

NATURE VS GRACE

576. *Temporal Nature and Eternal Grace*
Nature is crafty and draws away many; she ensnares and deceives them, and always has herself for her end. . . . Nature is not willing to be mortified, or to be restrained, or to be overcome; or to be subject; neither will she of her own accord be brought under. . . . Nature has regard to temporal things, rejoices at earthly gain, is troubled at losses, and is provoked at every slightly injurious word. But grace attends to things eternal, and cleaves not to those which pass with time; neither is she disturbed at the loss of things, nor exasperated with hard words, for she places her treasure and her joy in heaven, where nothing is lost.

Thomas à Kempis, *Imitation of Christ*, bk. III, chap. 54.

PARABLES

577. *Parable of the Cockle*
This speaks of those who receive the corrupters of the Word. For it is the guile of the spirit of evil to commingle his own errors with the sowing of the truth, so that they have the shape and color of truth, and so deceive the trusting. He then here speaks not of any seed, but only of tares, which resemble wheat.

Then he speaks of the manner of this guile, while men are asleep. Here lies no small danger of headlong disaster for the rulers of the Church, to whom has been confided the care of the field; and not only to the rulers but to the subjects as well. . . . Something of this evil, happened in the beginning of the Church. For many among the bishops, not being vigilant, received into the Church men who were evil and unworthy, secretly heretics, and gave them authority and opportunity to lay snares of this kind.

St John Chrysostom, in Toal, vol. 1, p. 335.

578. *Why Not Pull Up the Cockle?*
Wilt thou that we go and gather it up?. . . They are forbidden [to do so], lest they uproot the good wheat together with the tares, that is, so that

the sinner may not be cut off while in his mind there is yet a possibility of repentance. . . . Nor did he slay Matthew who had given himself to the exacting of tribute, so that he might not thus impede the preaching of the Gospel. Neither did he destroy the harlots who served lust and immodesty, lest models of repentance might be wanting. He avenged not Peter's denial, because already he beheld his burning tears of repentance. Nor did he strike down with death the persecuting Saul, lest the ends of the earth be deprived of salvation.

St Isidore, in Toal, vol. 1, pp. 339-340.

579. *Parable of the Wedding Garment at the King's Dinner*
Rightly is charity called a wedding garment; for our Creator wore this upon him when he came to the marriage of himself with the Church. It was solely through the charity of God that his Only-begotten joined to himself the souls of the chosen among men. It was because of this that John says: 'For God so loved the world as to give his only-begotten son for us' (John 3:16).

St Gregory the Great, in Toal, vol. 4, p. 231.

580. *The Man Without a Wedding Garment Is Forced Out*
. . . God gives us the love with which we are to love him; more than that, he gives us the gift of wisdom by which we acquire a taste and a relish for God and for his friendship and his ways. Both the love and the wisdom come from God; this will help us to understand the otherwise seemingly harsh treatment of the guest who, in the Gospel parable, came to the wedding feast without the ceremonial garment. Unless one realizes that such garments were provided by the host, one will not understand the host's resentment at the guest's refusal to avail of his kindness, and one will completely miss the parallel with the man who comes to the service of God without love in his heart. For if there is one gift that is to be had for the asking – and there are many – it is the gift of love for God.

Boylan, *This Tremendous Lover*, p. 60.

581. *Many Called, Few Chosen*
When this one has been cast forth, in whom manifestly the whole body of the wicked is set before us, straightway he adds a general sentence which says: 'For many are called but few are chosen'. . . . That we are called, we know; that we are chosen, we do not know. And so, the more each one of us knows not whether he is chosen, so much the more do we need to humble ourselves in humility.

St Gregory the Great, in Toal, vol. 4, p. 234.

582. *Parable of the King Calling Servants to Account*
. . . By this word *servants* he means kings and rulers and princes, rich, poor, slaves, and free; every kind of men; all are referred to here: 'for we must all be manifested before the judgment seat of Christ' (2 Cor 5:10). . . . And we shall render an account, not only of our deeds, but also of our words. . . . Money foolishly expended does not do so much harm as rash and foolish words spoken without need. For money foolishly spent may sometimes do harm, but speech imprudently used may bring sadness to whole families and undo and ruin souls. The loss of money can be made good; but the word once gone forth can never be recalled.
St John Chrysostom, in Toal, vol. 4, p. 281-282.

583. *Parable of the Laborers Who Received Each a Denarius*
Because eternal life will be equally the possession of all the blessed, the denarius, which is the wage of all, is given to each alike.
St Augustine, quoted by St Thomas Aquinas in Toal, vol. 1, p. 364.

584. *Parable of the Laborers Who Received Each a Denarius*
It may be said that the whole life of men is but one day, according to the parable, and that they who are called by the Master of the vineyard in the morning early are they who from their childhood were called to do the things of the kingdom of God. They who, after they had come to adolescence, begin to serve God are they who are called about the third hour. They who began as men fully grown are they who were called at the sixth hour. They who in mature age are converted to the work of God are those of the ninth hour, who, after the heat of youth and before the burden of old age, take on themselves the word of the Lord. And the old, who are near to death, are signified by those who were called at the eleventh hour to labor in the vineyard.
Origen, in Toal, vol. 1, p. 373.

585. *The Good Thief at the Eleventh Hour*
Did not the Good Thief come at the eleventh hour? . . . The Householder began indeed from the last to pay the denarius that was due, for even before Peter, he leads the Thief into the repose of paradise.
St Gregory the Great, in Toal, vol. 1, p. 381.

586. *Laborers Rewarded According to the Measure of Love*
. . . Every man will receive a price, according to the measure of his love . . . as my Truth [Christ] told you in the Gospel by the example of those who were standing idle and were sent by the Lord of the vineyard to labor; for he gave as much to those who went out at dawn, as to those

who went at prime or at tierce, and those who went at sext, or none, or even at vespers receiving as much as the first; my Truth showing you in this way that you are rewarded, not according to time or work, but according to the measure of your love. Many are placed in their childhood to work in the vineyard; some enter later in life, and others in old age; Sometimes these latter labor with such fire of love, seeing the shortness of time, that they rejoin those who entered in their childhood, because they have advanced but slowly.

Dialogue of St Catherine of Siena, p. 320-321.

587. *Parable of the Leaven*

. . . If twelve men could leaven the whole world, how unprofitable are we though so great in number, yet we cannot convert those that remain: we who should be enough to leaven a thousand worlds. . . . You will say, [the spostles] worked miracles. It was not because of their miracles that they were remarkable. How long must we speak of miracles to cover up our own laziness? Look upon the number of the saints. They shone forth, but not because of their miracles. . . .

What then, you may ask, was it that made them great? Their rejection of wealth and their contempt of vainglory, their turning away from the things of this world. Because had they been wanting in this regard or had they indulged their passions, then even though they had raised thousands from death to life, they would have been not merely worthless, but would have been held as deceivers and frauds. . . . It is their life which shines forth on every side and draws down on them the graces of the Spirit.

St John Chrysostom, in Toal, vol. 1, p. 353.

588. *Parable of the Pharisee and the Publican in the Temple*

What did [the Pharisee] ask of God? Search his words and you will find nothing. He went up to pray. He had no desire to ask God for anything. He wished to praise himself. And it was not enough not to ask God for anything, but only to praise himself; he wished also to insult the other man praying there.

'The publican [was] standing afar off'. And yet he began to draw near to God. The conscience of his heart held him 'afar off'; his piety brought him close to God. . . . 'He struck his breast, saying: O God, be merciful to me a sinner.' Hear how he prays. What wonder that God forgives him when he accuses himself in this manner. . . . 'This publican went down into his house justified rather than the Pharisee. . . . ' Why? . . . 'Because everyone that exalteth himself shall be humbled: and he that humbleth himself shall be exalted'.

St Augustine, in Toal, vol. 3, p. 368.

589. *Parable of the Prodigal Son*
[Christ] craves our love, but he is too delicate to force it. It has no value for him unless it is freely given.

No matter how sinful we have been, at the first word of repentance, at the first indication that our heart has turned away from created things and turned again to him, he forgets all that has passed and like the father in the parable, he clasps the soul to his embrace, clothes it with the robe of sanctifying grace, bestows on it those actual helps that it needs to walk once more in the ways of holiness, and gives it the ring which is the pledge of affection and union.

Edward Leen, *In the Likeness of Christ*, p. 214.

590. *Joy over the Lost Sheep That was Found*
Let us note that he does not say, 'Rejoice with the sheep that was found,' but 'Rejoice with me'; for our life is his joy, and when we are brought back to heaven we shall complete the feast of his rejoicing.

St Gregory the Great, in Toal, vol. 3, p. 202.

591. *Parable of the Good Shepherd*
. . . Who is the thief that steals there? It is a treacherous twist in man's nature, a detestable parasite; it is the possessiveness and false attachment which makes a man desire to draw everything to himself, to snatch whatever he can from God or from creatures. He will lay hands on everything, seeking to satisfy his own sensibility and his own self-will. If he thinks he has achieved some good, he attributes it to his own doing. He wants to have pleasure, consolation, experience and feeling; to be great, holy and blessed, with experience and knowledge of all things. He wants to be somebody and is never willing to lose himself. This is the thief, who, in such a devilish way, slinks in to rob God of the honor and men of all truth and perfection.

Tauler, *Spiritual Conferences*, pp. 71-72.

592. *The Parable of the Sower*
'Why . . . is the greater part of the seed lost? Because . . . of the soul that heeded not.' . . .

[Christ] desired in this parable to form and to educate his disciples so that should many of those who would receive the preaching of the apostles be lost, they should not lose heart. For this happened also to their Teacher; who, though knowing what was yet to be, ceased not from sowing.

St John Chrysostom, in Toal, vol. 1, p. 393.

593. *The Parable of the Sower*
. . . For what reason have some brought forth fruit a hundredfold, and some sixty and some thirty? Here, obviously, the difference depends upon the nature of the earth; and even where the ground is good, there is a great variety here likewise. You see then that the Sower is not the cause of this, nor the seed, but the earth which received it. The difference therefore arises not from our nature but from our will. . . . All this he said so that those who were listening to him might not think that merely to listen is sufficient for salvation.

St John Chrysostom, *ibid.*, pp. 394-395.

594. *The Parable of the Unjust Steward*
Why then did he command [the steward] to be sold, when in his own mind he had no intention of doing so? In order to increase his fears by means of a threat; to compel him to humble himself in supplication so that he might have reason to forgive him. He could, even before he besought him, have freed this man from this debt, but this he did not do for fear he might become worse. . . . Let us learn from this how careless we are in our own prayer, and also how great is the power of fervent prayer. Even fasting has not shown this, nor poverty, nor anything of this nature; but here was a man, helpless, void of all virtues, yet when he cried out in fervent supplication to his Maker, by this act alone he was able to obtain mercy.

St John Chrysostom, *ibid.*, vol. 4, pp. 284-285.

595. *The Parable of the Unjust Steward*
Let us not lose heart, nor be slothful or timid in prayer. Even if we have been brought down to the depths of evil, prayer can speedily draw us back. For no one has sinned as this man had: he had fallen into every kind of wickedness; for this is what the ten thousand talents mean. No one is so wanting in virtue as he was; and this we understand from the fact that he had not wherewith to pay. Yet, however abandoned and destitute he was, the power of prayer was able to deliver him.

Has prayer then, someone will ask, the power to deliver a man from correction and retribution who has offended the Lord by countless evil deeds? Yes, it has this power, O man. For it is not alone in accomplishing this, but has as its most powerful help and ally the great loving kindness of God himself, who receives our prayers, by whose power all things are accomplished, and which makes our prayer efficacious. And Jesus implies this when He goes on to say: 'And the lord of that servant, being moved to pity, let him go and forgive him the debt' that you might learn that before prayer and after prayer . . . the compassion of the Master does all.

St John Chrysostom, *ibid.,* p. 286.

596. *The Parable of the Unjust Steward*

'When that servant was gone out, he found one of his fellow servants that owed him an hundred pence; and laying hold of him he throttled him, saying: Pay what thou owest'. What could there be more abominable than this? With the voice of forgiveness still sounding in his ears, he has forgotten the loving kindness of his Master.

See what a good thing it is to be mindful of your own sins. Had this man kept them clearly in remembrance he would not have been so cruel, so inhuman. . . . It is truly most profitable and most necessary to keep clearly before us the remembrance of our own offenses. For there is nothing makes the soul so truly wise, so truly gentle and compassionate as the continuous remembrance of our own sins. . . . For, remembering them, we not only wipe them away, but through the practice of humility, we grow milder toward all men and begin to serve God with more fervor and good will: coming through this humble remembrance of our own sins, to understand his ineffable compassion for us.

But this the wicked servant in the parable did not do, but forgetful of the magnitude of his own debt, he also forgets the compassion his lord had shown him. And through this forgetfulness of his compassion, he becomes cruel towards his own fellow servant. And in his wickedness he loses all he had gained through the goodness of God.

St John Chrysostom, *ibid.,* pp. 286-287.

597. *The Parable of the Unjust Steward*

The Lord . . . is more tolerant toward those who offend against himself than toward those who sin against their neighbor. . . . Nothing, nothing whatsoever does God so hate and turn away from as cherishing remembrance of past offenses, and fostering anger against another. This he reveals especially in this place, and also in the prayer in which he commands us to say: 'Forgive us our trespasses as we forgive those who trespass against us' (Mt 6:12). Instructed, therefore, in all these things, and with this parable inscribed in our hearts, let us, when the thought comes of what our fellow servants have done to us, think also of what we have done against our Lord; and then through remembrance of our own sins we shall be able at once to banish the anger we feel at others' sins against us. . . . He says at the end of this parable: 'So also shall my heavenly Father do to you, if you forgive not everyone from your hearts.'

St John Chrysostom, *ibid.,* pp. 288-289.

598. *Parable of the Vine and the Branches*
Says the Council of Trent: 'Jesus Christ continually exercises his influence on the justified, as the head upon the members and as the vine upon the branches. And this influence always precedes and accompanies and follows their good works, which without it could not in any wise be pleasing and meritorious before God.'
Gabriel, *Ascetical Conferences for Religious*, p. 22.

599. *Parable of the Vine and the Branches*
. . . Holiness is for us an essentially supernatural order, and God is its source; the more our souls, by means of mortification, free themselves from sin and are detached from self and creatures, the more the divine action is powerful within us. Christ tells us so; he even tells us that his Father makes use of suffering to render the life of the soul more fruitful: 'I am the vine, and my Father is the husband-man; you are the branches. Every branch that beareth fruit, my Father will purge that it may bring forth more fruit.'. . . When the Eternal Father sees that a soul, already united to his Son by grace, resolutely desires to give herself fully to Christ . . . he himself enters into this work of renunciation and detachment, because that is the preliminary condition of our fruitfulness. He prunes away all that could prevent the life of Christ from producing its full effects. . . . Our corrupt nature contains roots that tend to produce evil fruits; by the repeated and deep sufferings he permits or sends, by humiliations and contradictions, God purifies us, digs and ploughs up the ground of our souls, as it were, detaches us from creatures, and empties us of self that we may produce numerous fruits of life and holiness. . . .
Marmion, *Christ, the Life of the Soul*, pp. 209-210.

600. *The Parable of the Vine and the Branches*
According to the beautiful remark of St Augustine, it is as man that Christ is the vine; as God, one with his Father, he is the vine-dresser who works, not like the vine-dresser of this world, outside, but interiorly, thereby to give increase of grace and life; for, adds the great Doctor, quoting St Paul, he who plants is nothing, neither is he who waters, but God gives the increase.
Marmion, *ibid.*, p. 82.

601. *The Parable of the Vine and the Branches*
He is the vine and we the branches. Just as the sap flows from the parent stem out into the branch and in this way communicates its life to the branch, so does sanctifying grace flow from him into us. The more freely it flows and the more fully we share in it, the greater will be our holiness.

Holiness consists precisely in the possession of the grace poured into the soul by Christ, and the measure of the soul's holiness is in exact proportion to the amount of grace it possesses.
Nash, *Living Your Faith*, p. 279.

PARENTS

602. *Parenthood a Reason for Humility – and Holy Pride*
For the humility of parents, the fact is plain that their child is more God's than theirs. They cannot create anything, let alone a spirit that will never die; yet, in every human conception, an immortal soul comes into being. Procreation is a work done under God and directly with him; the parents in each case prepare the material for union with a soul that comes directly, in each case, from God himself. Parents have a right to be proud, but their pride must focus on the beneficence of God in giving them so humble a share in so great a work. They people the earth with citizens of heaven; and in deepest humility, they dedicate themselves to the children that have come to them from God.
Farrell and Healy, *My Way of Life*, p. 144.

PASSIONS

603. *Dangers Involved in the Passions*
St Francis says that it is the devil's art to bind souls first with a hair, that he may afterwards bind them with a chain and secure them. Let us therefore be on our guard not to be entangled by any of the passions. A soul that is entangled by passion is either lost or in great danger of being lost.
St Alphonsus Liguori, *Great Means of Salvation and of Perfection*, p. 330.

604. *Tyranny of the Passions to Be Opposed*
[Meyer, in *Science of the Saints*, illustrates the tyranny of the passions] with the following story: 'Where are you going?' shouted one man to another who was galloping at headlong speed upon a public highway. 'Don't know, ask my horse!' said the latter. He had lost all control of the animal and was completely at its mercy. Ask the slave of passion: 'Where are you going?' and if he is sincere, he will answer: 'Don't know, ask my passion.' He is at its mercy, and nothing but a special Providence can save him from destruction.
Bandas, *The Catholic Layman and Holiness*, p. 130.

605. *How Best to Control the Passions*

. . . In order that we may have confidence in being able to rid ourselves of them . . . we should change the matter and the objects of our passions. . . . The desire, nay the hankering that we feel for the transient things of earth may be directed to the things of heaven; and thus our fear of temporal losses may be changed into a wholesome dread of such as are eternal: thus can our hopes at once become heavenly, and our harmful terrors be changed into a saving fear. . . . This, beyond question, is the easiest, the most agreeable, and the most effectual way of subduing the unruly passions of our souls; giving them, that is to say, a new sphere of action, a different food, and occupying them with good, profitable and holy objects. In a word, to pretend to conquer our concupiscences by mere resistance, without supplying them with other objects, is too violent a strain to be lasting; for, as St Augustine says, the heart of man cannot live long without some affection and some pleasure which it must seek either in the creature or the Creator, in things of time or in things of eternity.

Scaramelli, *Directorium Asceticum*, vol. 2, p. 189-190.

606. *Passions to Be Uprooted While They Are Still Weak*

St Dorotheus narrates that one day, while an old monk was travelling through the woods with one of his disciples he commanded the latter to uproot several cypress trees. First he pointed to one that was but a little shoot; then to one that was beginning to take root; next to one that was already a tree, and finally to one that was a full-grown tree. The disciple then began to uproot them. The first one he picked up with one hand and with no difficulty whatsoever; the second he uprooted with the same hand, but with some difficulty. In order to uproot the third he had to use both hands and pull several times with all his might; but when he tried to uproot the full-grown tree, try as he might with all his strength and in every conceivable way, he could not move the tree a single bit. Thereupon the saintly old monk said: 'This, my son, is precisely what happens with our passions. When they make their first appearance, a little vigilance and some mortifications on the part of the one tempted and he will succeed in overcoming them and eradicating them, but if we let them take root in our soul, no human strength will be able to overcome them – only the omnipotent hand of God. So, my son, if you wish to acquire virtue, watch the first movements of your soul, and study to repress them instantly.'

In *Spiritual Diary*, p. 65.

PEACE

607. *Peace Impossible Without Justice*
. . . In his first Encyclical, 4 October 1903, Pope St Pius X wrote: 'Where God is driven out, justice is expelled, too. And when justice disappears, it is idle to hope for peace.'
Smit, *St Pius X, Pope*, p. 110.

608. *Three Things That Disturb Our Peace*
Be assured that all disturbing, upsetting thoughts do not come from God, who is the Prince of Peace. They come either from the devil, or from our self-love, or from the high opinion we entertain of ourselves. These are the three fonts of all our troubles. When such thoughts come to our mind, we should banish them immediately and pay no attention to them.
St Francis de Sales, in *Spiritual Diary*, p. 120.

PENTECOSTALISM

609. *Guidance by the Holy Spirit*
. . . There are times when the Spirit directs a soul entirely from within. In such cases the guidance of this divine Teacher supplies for the absence of any human instruction. Weaker souls, however, must not try to imitate this freedom in their own lives. For if, on the vain presumption that they, too, are filled with the Holy Spirit, they refuse to be guided by another human being, they will only become teachers of error.
St Gregory the Great, in *The Fathers of the Church*, vol. 39, p. 8.

PERFECTION

610. *Perfection Defined by St Thomas*
[St Thomas] unhesitatingly decides that the whole essence of Christian perfection consists in the love of God and our neighbor; with this distinc-

tion, however, that the love of God must hold the first place, the love of neighbor the second.

Scaramelli, *Directorium Asceticum*, vol. 1, p. 10.

611. *Perfection a Duty for All Christians*

Every Christian is bound to tend to perfection. When I speak of a Christian, says St Ambrose, 'I mean a perfect man.' The precept by which all are commanded to love God with all their strength imposes upon all the obligation of perfection.

St Alphonsus Liguori, *The True Spouse of Jesus Christ*, p. 77.

612. *Perfection as Understood by St Francis de Sales*

I, for my part, know of no other perfection than that of loving God with one's whole heart and one's neighbor as oneself. He who conceives any other type of perfection deceives himself, because the accumulation of all the other virtues without this love is nothing but the amassing of stones. And if we do not immediately and perfectly enjoy this treasure of holy love, it is our own fault, because we are too parsimonious and hesitant with God, and we do not give ourselves entirely to him as did the Saints.

St Francis de Sales, in *Spiritual Diary*, p. 11.

613. *How Perfection Is to Be Achieved*

When Bishop [Jean Pierre] Camus asked St Francis de Sales for the secret of perfection, de Sales answered him thus: 'There are many besides you who want me to tell them of methods, and systems and secret ways of becoming perfect, and I can only tell them the sole secret is a hearty love of God, and the only way of attaining that love is by loving. You learn to speak by speaking, to study by studying, to run by running, to work by working; and just so you learn to love God and man by loving. All those who think to learn in any other way deceive themselves.' . . . Together with habitual charity, operative charity, or love in action, is required for perfection.

Shamon, *The Only Life*, p. 116.

614. *Surest Way to Perfection*

The surest road to perfection is to accomplish purely in Christ, without excessive eagerness, and according as they present themselves, the daily duties of life. The true Christian will acquire the habit of pausing occasionally in the midst of his activity and asking himself in what way would the Lord act were he placed in the present situation.

Edward Leen, *The True Vine and Its Branches*, p. 146.

615. *The Perfection of an Action*

The perfection of an action consists, first, in that it is done through the sole motive of pleasing God; for it is not the external act, but the purity of intention that constitutes perfection. . . . The perfection of an action consists, secondly, in doing it well; that is, with promptness, attention and exactness. The following are the means of performing our actions well:

1. The first means is to preserve during the discharge of your duties a lively sense of the presence of God, that thus every act may be worthy of His divine eyes.
2. The second is, to perform every act as if it were the only duty you have to fulfill. . . .
3. The third means is to perform every action as if it were the last of your life. St Anthony frequently recommanded this means to his disciples: 'In every work,' says St Bernard, 'let each one say to himself: If I were about to die, would I do this?'

St Alphonsus *The True Spouse of Jesus Christ*, pp. 186-187.

616. *Perfection Attainable Through Little Things*

If we demanded of you daily disciplines to blood, or fasting on bread and water, or going barefoot with a perpetual hairshirt, you might say that you did not feel strong enough for that; but that is not what we demand of you, not in that does your perfection lie, but in doing the very thing that you are doing, taking care that it is well done. With the same works that you are doing, if you like, you can become perfect.

Rodriguez, *Practice of Perfection and Christian Virtues*, vol. 1, p. 99.

617. *Three Degrees of Christian Perfection*

[According to St Thomas Aquinas] the lowest degree of charity consists in loving nothing more than God, or in opposition to God, or equally with God. . . . This degree is to be found even in abandoned women . . . from the moment that by a true conversion they regain the grace of God. . . . The highest degree of charity . . . we cannot have . . . in our present life of misery (but only in heaven). . . . The intermediate degree consists in this, that when all obstacles have been removed and the necessary dispositions are acquired, the soul is able with ease and fervor to perform those acts of divine charity which are the perfection of our life on earth, and to which we should aspire.

Scaramelli, *Directorium Asceticum*, vol. 1, p. 26.

618. *The Desire for Perfection Pleases God*

. . . St Ambrose says that when a man has a great desire of his improvement and growth in virtue and perfection, God is so pleased therewith that he enriches and fills him with bounties and rewards; and he applies to this effect that which the most holy Virgin said in her canticle: 'He hath filled the hungry with good things' (Lk 1:53).

Rodriguez, *Practice of Perfection and Christian Virtues*, vol. 1, pp. 16-17.

619. *When Is a Christian Perfect?*

A Christian is perfect when he loves God with his whole heart, above all things, and his neighbor as himself. All teachers of the spiritual life agree that Christian perfection consists in the love of God, and that love of neighbor is inseparably united with it. Our divine Lord himself calls the love of God the greatest commandment, and places love of neighbor on the same level (Mt 22:37-38).

Wallenstein, *Guide to Perfect Christian Living*, p. 2.

620. *Ten Superiors Not Enough for One Monk*

[Christ] said to that young man in the Gospel: 'If thou wilt be perfect' (Mt 19:21). But if you do not will it, all the contrivances and methods that superiors can apply will never suffice to make you perfect. This is the solution to the question which St Bonaventure raises: How is it that in former times one superior sufficed for a thousand monks, and for three thousand, and five thousand (for so St Jerome and St Augustine say there used to be under one superior); and now one superior is not enough for ten monks and even less? The reason is that those monks of old had in their hearts a living and ardent desire of perfection, and the fire that burned within made them greatly take to heart their own advancement and press on their way with great fervor. . . . But in the absence of this desire, not only will one superior not suffice for ten monks, but ten superiors will not suffice for one monk nor be able to make him perfect if he does not want it.

Rodriguez, *Practice of Perfection and Christian Virtues*, vol. 1, pp. 13-14.

621. *Religious Are Bound to Tend Toward Perfection*

Religious are strictly obliged to aspire after perfection. 'He that enters the religious state,' says St Thomas, 'is not commanded to have perfect charity; but he is bound to tend to it. It is not,' continues the saint, 'obligatory on him to adopt all the means by which perfection may be attained; but it is his duty to perform the exercises prescribed by the Rule, which at his profession he promised to observe.'

St Alphonsus Liguori, *The True Spouse of Jesus Christ*, p. 84.

622. *God's Special Love for Those Who Aim at Perfection*

St Teresa after her death revealed to one of her Sisters that God has a greater love for one soul that aspires to perfection than for a thousand others that are in a state of grace, but are tepid and imperfect.

St Alphonsus Liguori, *The Way of Salvation and of Perfection,* pp. 151-152.

PHARISEES

623. *Religious Who Are Really Pharisees*
. . . There are . . . people who are devoted to religious life . . . and yet in their hearts they are Pharisees, full of self-love and self-will, and in fact interested in nothing but themselves. . . . Even outwardly there is one way of distinguishing them from those who truly love God; you will always find them sitting in judgment upon other people, even upon God's lovers, but never upon themselves; whereas those who truly love God judge only themselves.

Tauler, *Spiritual Conferences*, p. 59.

PLEASURES

624. *Pleasures of the Body Vs. Pleasures of the Soul*
There is this difference, dearly beloved brethren, between the delights of the body and those of the soul, that the delights of the body when we do not possess them, awaken in us a great desire for them; but when we possess them and enjoy them to the full, they straightway awaken in us a feeling of aversion. But spiritual delights work in the opposite way. While we do not possess them, we regard them with dislike and aversion; but once we partake of them, we begin to desire them, and the more we partake of them, the more do we hunger for them. In one case the appetite pleases, the reality brings displeasure; in the other it is the appetite displeases, the reality delights us more and more. In the one case appetite leads to fullness, and fullness to disgust; in the other, appetite begets fullness, and fullness in turn begets appetite. For spiritual delights, when they fill the soul, increase in us the desire for them: and the more we savor them, the more do we come to know what we should eagerly love.

St Gregory the Great, in Toal, vol. 3, p. 180.

POPULARITY

625. *The Right Kind of Popularity*

The apostle . . . says, 'If I were still trying to please men, I should not be the servant of Christ' (Gal 1:10). But elsewhere he says: 'Please all men in all things, even as in all things I also try to please all men' (see 1 Cor 10: 32ff; Rom 15:2). Those who do not understand this saying of his consider it contrary to the other. But he said he was not trying to please men because he was doing good in order to please God, and not in order to please men; for, by the very act of trying to please men, he was trying to turn their hearts toward the love of God. Therefore, he could rightly say that he was not trying to please men, for even in his efforts to please men, he was aiming to please God. Although the pleasing of men ought not to be sought as a reward for good works, he could consistently prescribe that we ought to please men, for – since no one can try to imitate a man who is not pleasing to him – a man could not please God unless he were present himself as a model for imitation by those whose salvation he was seeking.

St Augustine, in *The Fathers of the Church*, vol. 11, pp. 111-112.

POVERTY

626. *Poor in Spirit – What It Means*

By 'the poor in spirit' is meant those poor in earthly desires, but not without affection, because they live contented even in this life; and, therefore, the Lord does not say, 'Theirs *will be* the kingdom of heaven,' but 'theirs *is*,' because even in this life they are rich in spiritual blessings which they receive from God; and thus, however poor they are in temporal goods, they live content with their condition.

St Alphonsus Liguori, *The Way of Salvation and of Perfection*, p. 283.

627. *Poverty of Spirit – What It Is*

Poverty of spirit means detachment of heart from all things here below, that freely and without impediment we may follow Christ and give ourselves wholly over to seeking perfection, which is the end at which we aim and for which we came to religion.

Rodriguez, *Practice of Perfection and Christian Virtues,* vol. 3, p. 167.

628. *Why Christ Loved Poverty*

Christ's love of poverty was simply the expression of his splendid independence of wealth and its advantages. One of the aspects of his task was to lead men back to the knowledge, the love and the pursuit of that true greatness to which they were called. *He had to teach them that they were great, not by what they had or what they did, but by what they were.*

Edward Leen: *In the Likeness of Christ*, p. 26.

629. *Poverty Demands That We Master Riches*

If you cannot abandon everything, at least possess what you have in such a way that you are free of it; so that temporal wealth is possessed, and does not possess you. Preserve your mastery over it, rather than allow your heart to be swayed and dominated by things of lesser value than itself. Let these earthly things be of use to us, while our desires speed toward what is eternal. The former are of value while we are on our way, but we desire the latter at our journey's end.

St Gregory the Great, *Parables of the Gospel*, p. 118.

630. *Poverty of Spirit as a Beatitude*

. . . The poor in spirit are rightly understood . . . as the humble and God-fearing – that is to say, those who do not have a bloated spirit.

St Augustine in *The Fathers of the Church,* vol. 11, p. 21.

631. *Poverty – Vow Vs. Spirit*

. . . The vow of poverty does not suffice to make one a true follower of Jesus Christ if one does not afterwards embrace with joy of spirit all the inconveniences of poverty. 'Not poverty, but the love of poverty is a virtue,' says St Bernard, and he means to say that for one to become a saint it is not enough to be poor only, if one does not love also the inconveniences of poverty.

St Alphonsus Liguori, *Great Means of Salvation and of Perfection*, p. 402.

632. *Deliberate Poverty In Spirit Is Blessed*

. . . Not he who is poor is by all means blessed, but he who has considered the command of Christ better than the treasures of the world. These the Lord also pronounces blessed when he says: 'Blessed are the poor in spirit,' not those poor in resources, but those who from their soul have chosen poverty. For nothing that is not deliberate is to be pronounced blessed.

St Basil, in *The Fathers of the Church*, vol. 46; p. 256.

633. *Ways in Which We Fail to Be Poor in Spirit*
. . . If we who give up the world with its property and riches do not also give up affection for such things, we are not poor in spirit, since the poverty consists not merely in bodily and external separation from the things of the world but, further, in a detachment of will and affection for them; and this is the main point of poverty in spirit. . . .

Secondly, it follows that a religious who has given up and despised the wealth and riches of the world, and here in religion gets a passion for little things, for a room, an article of clothing, a book, a picture and other like things, is not truly and perfectly poor in spirit.

Rodriguez, *Practice of Perfection and Christian Virtues*, vol. 3, p. 174.

PRAYER

634. *Conversation Between God and Ourselves*
Prayer has been defined as a familiar intercourse or conversation with God. . . . A conversation is not a speech delivered before a person, it involves an interchange of thought; and as our thought is directed toward God, so God's thought is directed toward us.

God is intensely operative, and if the soul has willed to draw near to God, he on his side tends to draw near to it. The effect of the contact of two spirits is one of assimilation; i.e., one is made like the other. The soul by its activity cannot assimilate God to itself, for God cannot change; the activity of God therefore is directed toward assimilating the soul to himself. God therefore takes up the soul and assimilates it to himself, and this in proportion as the soul by its own acts, helped by grace, abdicates itself and lives the life of God by acting habitually and intensely under a motive of faith and of charity.

Edward Leen, *Progress Through Mental Prayer*, pp. 52-53.

635. *How God Speaks To Us In Prayer*
[God] speaks to us through the deepening of our faith, through the illumination he supplies to our intelligence, through the penetration into the mysteries of our religion that he grants, and through the impulse to good that he gives to our wills. Note: [St Francis de Sales says:] 'Prayer is a colloquy, a discourse or a conversation of the soul with God; by it we

speak to God and he again speaks to us; we aspire to him and breathe in him; and he reciprocally inspires us and breathes in us.'

Edward Leen, *ibid.*, p. 55.

636. *Prayer Is a Loving Contact With a Beloved*
Prayer is not a number of reflections and resolutions; it is personal, intimate, loving contact and converse with a friend who is loved and by whom the soul understands that it itself is loved.

Nash, *Living Your Faith*, p. 162.

637. *The Excellence of Prayer*
St John Chrysostom, speaking of the excellence of prayer and wishing to say great things of it, says that one of the greatest of great things that it is possible to say of it is that whoever is at prayer is dealing and conversing with God. 'Consider the height, dignity, and glory to which the Lord has raised you, in that you can speak and converse with God, hold conversations and colloquies with Jesus Christ, desire what you would, and ask for what you desire.'

Rodriguez, *Practice of Perfection and Christian Virtues* vol. 1, p. 282.

638. *The Final End of Prayer*
The final end of prayer, considered as a potent means for the development of God's life in the soul, is to emancipate us from natural habits of thought and affection and elevate us to a supernatural manner of thinking and willing, to change our natural outlook on life and things to make it supernatural.

Edward Leen, *Progress Through Mental Prayer*, p. 20.

639. *The Disposition Required for Real Prayer*
The dispositions for prayer are the dispositions for healthy membership of Christ: faith, hope, charity, humility and submission to God's will.... Obviously, a man must believe in God's existence and in his willingness to take notice of us; this is implied in the very act of turning to God. Our request springs from the hope we have of being heard. Charity must be added to our prayer, at least in desire; for if we are in the state of mortal sin, and have not some desire to be reconciled to God, we are really in rebellion against him. Fraternal charity is also necessary for prayer, for we remember how our Lord insisted that even the man offering his gift at the altar should first go and be reconciled with his neighbor who had something against him, and come to offer his gift.... The need of humility is illustrated in the parable of the proud Pharisee and the humble publican;

and God himself warns us that he resists the proud and giveth his grace to the humble.

Boylan, *This Tremendous Lover*, pp. 87-88.

640. *Prayer Should Be Fervent, but Not a Burden*

It is better to say one Our Father sincerely than to rush through a whole Rosary without thinking of God. The prayers we decide to say every day should not be long enough to become a burden to us; otherwise it is very likely that we shall often say them badly, and that sooner or later we shall dispense ourselves from saying them at all. Further, prayer is so essential to our spiritual life that we should never let it be associated with the idea of a burden. In any case, it is not for 'much speaking' that we shall be heard, but rather for the dispositions of our heart.

Boylan, *ibid.*, p. 86-87.

641. *Prayer – Quantity to Be Lessened, Quality Improved*

Should the Director . . . meet with persons who have burdened themselves with a huge weight of prayer – which they recite hurriedly, without attention or feeling, caring much more for the completion of their self-imposed task than for the interior devotion of the heart – he must correct this extravagance and reduce the prayers to a third, a fourth, or even a fifth part, as he shall judge expedient. But he must remind them, meanwhile, to make up for number by the strictness of their attention, to recite the prayers appointed for them at full leisure, with application of mind and with frequent pauses, in order to relish the affections which the prayers express, not as something learned by rote, but as the expression of a feeling proceeding from the heart and made vocal by the tongue.

Scaramelli, *Directorium Asceticum*, vol. 1, p. 253.

642. *Prayer Is Possible under All Circumstances*

It is possible while sitting in your workshop stitching leather to consecrate your heart to God. It is possible . . . for the person standing over a pot cooking to make fervent and frequent prayer though it is not possible to enter a church. For God takes no thought of place. This alone he requires of us: a mind and soul that loves the things of God.

St John Chrysostom, in Toal, vol. 2, p. 394.

643. *Prayer, the Key to Heaven*

The glorious St Augustine says that prayer is the key of heaven that fits all the gates of heaven and all the coffers and treasures of God, and nothing hidden from it. And elsewhere he says that what bread is to the body.

prayer is to the soul.

Rodriguez, *The Practice of Perfection and Christian Virtues*, vol. 1, p. 285.

644. *Jesus Prays IN and FOR Us*

Let St Augustine have the last word: 'Jesus prays *for us*, as our Priest; Jesus prays *in us*, as our head; Jesus is prayed to *by us*, as our God.'

James O'Mahoney, OFM Cap., *The Person Of Jesus*, p. 71.

645. *Angels Love It; Devils Hate It*

The angels have a great esteem for fervent prayer and, consequently, do much to promote it. The devils, on the contrary, have an intense dislike for it and, as a result, strongly combat and disturb it.

St John Chrysostom, in *Spiritual Diary*, p. 184.

646. *Prayer of a Lay Brother More Pleasing to Mary than Choir Song*

A Cistercian lay-brother of Clairvaux was watching the sheep during the night of the Assumption. He did his best, chiefly by reciting the Angelic Salutation, to unite himself to the Matins which the monks were singing in choir, the distant bells of which reached him out in the hills. God revealed to St Bernard that the simple and humble devotion of this Brother had been so pleasing to our Lady that she preferred it to that of the monks, fervent as they were.

Chautard, *The Soul of the Apostolate*, p. 220.

647. *Why Pray for Our Enemies?*

We ought to pray for our enemies so that we may then with more confidence pray for ourselves.

St John Chrysostom, in Toal, vol. 2, p. 398.

648. *Aridity in Prayer Suffered by St Teresa*

Are you, peradventure, troubled with dryness in prayer? Are you callous and insensible to every supernatural truth? St Teresa suffered more than you; for during eighteen years she lived plunged in a distressing desolation; yet she bore it with calm, and never gave up her accustomed devotions.

Scaramelli, *Directorium Asceticum*, vol. 3, p. 278.

649. *Prayer in the Midst of Aridity – St Thérèse of Lisieux*

For me, prayer is an uplifting of the heart, a glance toward heaven, a cry of gratitude and love in times of sorrow as well as of joy. It is something noble, something supernatural, which expands the soul and unites it to

God. When my state of aridity is such that not a single good thought will come, I repeat very slowly the Our Father and the Hail Mary which suffices to console me and provides divine food for my soul.

St Thérèse of Lisieux, *Autobiography and Letters,* p. 180.

650. *Prayer Valuable in Periods of Aridity*

St Francis de Sales used to say an ounce of prayer made amid desolations, is of greater value than a hundred pounds of it in the midst of consolations.

St Alphonsus Liguori, *Dignity and Duties of the Priest*, p. 294.

651. *Prayer of Christ in Gethsemani*

The prayer of Jesus Christ in the Garden of Gethsemani was dry and arid to the last degree; nay, full even of weariness, melancholy and deadly languor; yet it was the holiest and most meritorious prayer ever made on earth; because our Savior, praying in his Father's presence, though no sensible devotion came to cheer him, nevertheless submitted himself promptly to the will of his Eternal Father, offering himself a voluntary victim to suffer and to die for the redemption of mankind.

Scaramelli, *Directorium Asceticum*, vol. 1, p. 184.

652. *Requirements for Vocal Prayer*

To acquit ourselves perfectly of vocal prayer, it is necessary to raise to God our mind by attention, our heart by devotion and our will by submission.

Edward Leen: *Progress Through Mental Prayer*, p. 44.

653. *Affections Are the Real Part of Prayer*

These 'acts' or 'affections,' as they are called, are the important, and in fact, the real part of prayer. The whole purpose of considerations is to lead up to these acts. The word 'affections,' which is generally applied to these acts, has a meaning in this context quite different from its ordinary connotation in English. It does *not* imply feeling, emotion, or tenderness. Affections in prayer are essentially acts of the will, by which it moves toward God and elicits other acts of the different virtues, such as faith, hope, love, sorrow, humility, submission, gratitude, or praise.

Boylan, *This Tremendous Lover*, p. 118.

654. *Prayer of Adoration – Its Necessity*

Adoration is the obligation of elementary justice that the creature owes its God. It is the first, the elemental right of God, a right so inalienable that to God alone it belongs, and could be shared by nothing short of God.

James O'Mahoney, OFM, Cap., *The Person of Jesus*, p. 65.

655. *Prayer of Thanks in Adversity*
Father Master Avila well says that to give thanks to God in time ot consolation is the part of all; but to give thanks in time of tribulations and adversities is proper to the good and the perfect; and so it is a music that sounds very sweet and pleasant in the ears of God. Better is one 'Thanks be to God!' he says, in adversities, than 'Blessed be God!' a thousand times in time of prosperity.
Rodriguez, *Practice of Perfection and Christian Virtues*, vol. 1, p. 522.

656. *Prayer Taught by the Angel at Fatima*
While the Fatima children were praying one day in September or October, 1916, an angel appeared holding a chalice, and over it a Host which he left suspended in the air while he prostrated himself on the ground and said: 'Most Holy Trinity, Father, Son, Holy Spirit, I adore you profoundly and offer you the most precious Body, Blood, Soul and Divinity of Jesus Christ, present in all the tabernacles of the earth, in reparation for the outrages, sacrileges and indifference with which he himself is offended. And through the infinite merits of his most Sacred Heart and of the Immaculate Heart of Mary, I beg of you the conversion of poor sinners.'
Walsh, *Our Lady of Fatima*, pp. 41-42.

PRAYER FOR THE POPE'S INTENTION

657. *St Thérèse of Lisieux*
Like our Holy Mother, St Teresa, I wish to be a true daughter of the Church, and make prayer for all the intentions of Christ's Vicar, the one great aim of my life.
St Thérèse of Lisieux, *Autobiography and Letters*, p. 190.

658. *Contemplative Prayer Surpasses Petitions*
Contemplative prayer far surpasses the prayer of petition, which too often is the only prayer about which many Christians think, to the scandal of Moslems, for example. On the contrary, it is a prayer of praise, admiration, of delight in God and silent love.
Goichon, *Contemplative Life in the World*, p. 145.

659. *Seeds of Contemplative Life Given in Baptism*
Every Christian receives the seed of the contemplative life through the primordial effect of baptism, which is incorporation in Christ. Having become members of Christ, Christians are called to live by the same sentiments as

he. From him they receive a certain spiritual sense, an intimate knowledge of the truth, and an impulsion to good acts.

Goichon, *ibid.*, p. 72.

660. *Contemplation Needed in Active Apostolate*

The Angelic Doctor says that those who are called to the works of the active life would be mistaken if they thought that this duty dispensed them from the contemplative life. This duty is *merely added to that of contemplation without diminishing its necessity.* And so these two lives, far from excluding one another, mingle together and complete one another. And if there is question of giving greater importance to one than to the other, it is the contemplative life that merits our preference, as being the more perfect and the more necessary.

[A footnote here explains] . . . Dom Chautard uses the terms active and contemplative *life*, not in the sense of the active or contemplative *states*, such as are explicitly intended as the aim of the various active and contemplative religious orders, but merely in the sense of exterior works of virtues and of mercy on the one hand, and interior union with God by prayer on the other. Every Christian is bound to practice both of these, and without them there is no Christian life.

Chautard, *The Soul of the Apostolate*, pp. 58-59.

KINDS OF PRAYER – ROSARY

661. *Why the Rosary Begins with the Apostles' Creed*

The Apostles' Creed is a prayer that has great merit because faith is the root, foundation and beginning of all Christian virtues, of all eternal virtues and also of all prayers that are pleasing to Almighty God. 'He that cometh to God must believe . . . ' (Heb 11:6). Whosoever wishes to come to God must first of all believe and the greater his faith the more merit his prayer will have, the more powerful it will be and the more it will glorify God.

'I believe in God.' . . . [These were] the last words of St Peter Martyr; a heretic had cleft his head in two by a cruel blow of his sword and St Peter was almost at his last gasp, but he somehow managed to trace words in the sand with his finger before he died. (*Note*: St Peter of Verona, O.P., 1206-1253, was a Dominican who fought heresy courageously. He had the honor of receiving the habit from the hands of St Dominic himself.)

St Louis de Montfort, *The Secret of the Rosary*, pp. 32-33.

662. *Devotion to Rosary Restored at Christ's Command*
[After the practice of saying the Rosary had fallen into disuse for many years, Blessed Alan de la Roche was commanded by Christ himself to revive it.] One day when he was saying Mass, our Lord, who wished to spur him on to preach the Holy Rosary, spoke to him in the Sacred Host: 'How can you crucify me again so soon?' 'What did you say, Lord?' asked Blessed Alan, horrified. 'You crucified me once before by your sins.' answered Jesus, 'and I would willingly be crucified again rather than have my Father offended by the sins you used to commit. You are crucifying me again now because you have all the learning and understanding that you need to preach my Mother's Rosary, and you are not doing so. If you only did this, you could teach many souls the right path and lead them away from sin – but you are not doing it and so you yourself are guilty of the sins they commit.'

St Louis de Montfort: *ibid.,* p. 23.

663. *Why Meditate on the Mysteries of the Rosary?*
The Blessed Virgin said to Blessed Alan de la Roche: 'When people say one hundred and fifty Angelic salutations, this prayer is very helpful to them and is a very pleasing tribute to me. But they will do better still and please me even more if they say these salutations while meditating on the life, death and passion of Jesus Christ – for this meditation is the soul of this prayer.'

For, in reality, the Rosary said without meditating on the sacred mysteries of our salvation would be almost like a body without a soul: excellent *matter* but without the *form*, which is meditation – this latter being that which sets it apart from all other devotions.

St Louis de Montfort, *ibid.,* p. 54-55.

664. *The Mysteries of the Rosary*
These mysteries are the most signal results of our Lord's love for us and the greatest presents that he could possibly give us, because it is by virtue of such presents that the Blessed Virgin herself and all the saints are in their glory in heaven.

St Louis de Montfort, *ibid.,* p. 57.

665. *The Rosary – St Dominic's Appraisal of Its Value*
St Dominic, who had received the revelation of the Rosary, said in a sermon: 'After the Divine Office and the Holy Mass, no homage is as agreeable to Jesus and his Blessed Mother as the fervent recitation of the Rosary!' And to confirm this he worked a miracle!

De Oca, *More About Fatima and the Immaculate Heart of Mary*, p.73.

666. *Rosary Effective in Converting Sinners*
One day our Lady said to Blessed Alan: 'Just as Almighty God chose the Angelic Salutation to bring about the Incarnation of his Word and the Redemption of mankind, in the same way those who want to bring about moral reforms and who want people reborn in Jesus Christ must honor me and greet me with the same salutation. I am the channel by which God came to men, and so, next to my Son, Jesus Christ, it is through me that men must obtain grace and virtue.'

I, who write this, have learned from my own experience that the Rosary has the power to convert even the most hardened hearts. I have known people who have gone to missions and who have heard sermons on the most terrifying subjects without being in the least moved; and yet, after they had, on my advice, started to say the Rosary every day, they eventually became converted and gave themselves completely to God.

St Louis de Montfort, *The Secret of the Rosary*, pp. 84-85.

667. *Rewards from Mary for Saying the Rosary*
[Our Lady said to Blessed Alan:] 'Whosoever shall persevere in the devotion of the Holy Rosary, saying these prayers and meditations, shall be rewarded for it; I shall obtain for him full remission of the penalty and of the guilt of all his sins at the end of his life. Do not be unbelieving, as though this is impossible. It is easy for me to do so because I am the Mother of the King of Heaven, and he calls me full of grace. And, being full of grace, I am able to dispense grace freely to my dear children.'

St Louis de Montfort, *ibid.*, p. 68-69.

668. *How the Blessed Mother Wants the Rosary Recited*
When someone asked little Jacinta about the message of our Lady at Fatima she answered: 'What Our Lady of the Rosary especially recommended to us is to recite the Rosary every day, adding after each decade the short prayer: O my Jesus, forgive us our sins, save us from the fire of hell, lead all souls to heaven, and help especially those who most need your mercy.' . . . [Montes de Oca adds:] The devout and constant recitation of the Rosary always works miracles. It tires neither the lips that recite it nor the heart that loves; but it finally tires God, who, importuned by our Lady, grants at last the graces requested.

De Oca, *More About Fatima and the Immaculate Heart of Mary*, p. 71.

669. *Why Say the Our Father*
The Our Father contains all the duties we owe to God, the acts of all the virtues and the petitions for all our spiritual and corporal needs. Tertullian says that the Our Father is a summary of the New Testament. Thomas

à Kempis says that it surpasses all the desires of all the saints; that it is a condensation of all the beautiful sayings of all the Psalms and Canticles; that in it we ask God for everything we need; that by it we praise him in the very best way; that by it we lift up our souls from earth to heaven and unite them with God. . . . God the Father listens more willingly to the prayer that we have learned from his Son rather than those of our own making, which have all our human limitations.

St. Louis de Montfort, *The Secret of the Rosary*, p. 34.

[When giving a course on the methods of teaching religion at the Catholic University of America, the late Monsignor Edward A. Pace devoted eight lectures to an explanation of the Our Father and concluded by saying that, judged from the purely pedagogical viewpoint, it is the most perfect document that has ever been composed. A child can understand it sufficiently while the greatest theologian cannot fully understand it. It is so perfect, said Monsignor Pace, that only the divine Mind could have composed it.]

670. *The Our Father*

The mystery of this boon is great, dearly beloved, and this gift exceeds all gifts, that God should call man son, and man should call God Father. . . .

St Leo the Great, in *The Nicene and Post-Nicene Fathers,* vol. 12, p.138.

671. *Why Say the Hail Mary*

By each Hail Mary we give our Lady the same honor that God gave her when he sent the Archangel Gabriel to greet her for him. How could anyone possibly think that Jesus and Mary, who often do good to those that curse them, could ever curse those that bless and honor them by the Hail Mary? . . . St Bonaventure says that Mary will greet us with grace if we greet her with the Hail Mary.

St Louis de Montfort, *The Secret of the Rosary*, p. 47.

672. *Why Say the Hail Mary*

One day St Gertrude had a vision of our Lord counting gold coins. She summoned up the courage to ask him what he was doing. He answered: 'I am counting the Hail Mary's that you have said; this is the money with which you can pay your way to heaven.'

The holy and learned Jesuit, Father Suarez, was so deeply aware of the value of the Angelic Salutation that he said that he would gladly give all his learning for the price of one Hail Mary that had been said properly.

St Louis the Montfort: *ibid.,* p. 48.

673. *How Say the Hail Mary*
One single Hail Mary that is said properly is worth more than one hundred and fifty that are badly said.

St Louis de Montfort, *ibid.*, p. 87.

674. *Why Say the Hail Mary*
'Greet [Mary] with the Angelic Salutation,' says Thomas à Kempis, 'for it makes her very happy to hear that prayer.' Our Lady revealed to St Matilda that no one could greet her in a more pleasing way than by reciting the Hail Mary.

St Alphonsus Liguori, *The Glories of Mary*, vol. 2, p. 177.

PRAYER – ITS POWER

675. *The Excellence and Power of Prayer*
Our prayers are so dear to God that he has appointed the angels to present them to Him as soon as they come forth from our mouths. 'The angels,' says St Hilary, 'preside over the prayers of the faithful and offer them daily to God.' . . . This is that smoke of the incense, which are the prayers of saints, which St John saw ascending to God from the hands of angels (Apoc 8:3).

. . . In order to understand better the value of prayer in God's sight, it is sufficient to read both in the Old and the New Testaments the innumerable promises which God makes to the man who prays. 'Cry to me, and I will hear thee' (ps 49:15). 'Call upon me and I will deliver thee.' (Jer 33:3) 'Ask and it shall be given you; seek and you shall find; knock and it shall be opened to you. . . . He shall give good things to them that ask him' (Mt 7:7). 'Everyone that asketh receiveth, and he that seeketh, findeth' (Lk 9: 10). 'Whatsoever they shall ask, it shall be done for them by my Father' (Jn 15:7). 'All things whatsoever you ask when you pray, believe that you shall receive them, and they shall come to you' (Mk 11:24). 'If you ask me anything in my name, that I will do. You shall ask whatever you will, and it shall be done unto you. Amen, Amen, I say if you ask the Father anything in my name, he will give it to you.' (Jn 14:14; 16:23). . . .

'The powers of hell are mighty,' says St Bernard; 'but prayer is stronger than all the devils.

St Alphonsus Liguori, *Great Means of Salvation and of Perfection*, pp. 50-52.

676. *The Efficacy of Prayer*
St John Climacus asserts that prayer is so powerful before God that it, as it were, constrains him to give us all the graces we ask.

St Alphonsus Liguori, *The True Spouse of Jesus Christ*, p. 612.

677. *How Prayer Is Related to Predestination*
Holy men cannot obtain what has not been predestined. Whatever they accomplish through prayer has been predestined for accomplishment through prayer. Even our predestination to heaven has been so ordained that we must exert ourselves to attain it; for it is only through prayer that we obtain the kingdom decreed for us by God from all eternity.
St Gregory the Great, in *The Fathers of the Church,* vol. 39, pp. 32-33.

678. *The Fruits of Prayer*
Prayer: (a) Unites us to God and makes us mindful of heaven. (b) Arms us against evil and gives us strength to do good. (c) Brings comfort in affliction and help in need. (d) Obtains for us the grace of perseverance until death.

The chief fruit of prayer we must strive for is utter devotion to God. Where this fruit is lacking, prayer is powerless or downright suspicious. Anyone who prays, especially anyone given to longer devotional practices (Mass, Breviary, Rosary, Stations, Spiritual Reading) must have the purpose: I want to become better, to fulfill God's will more perfectly. This is a basic teaching of the spiritual life, which many do not understand.
Wallenstein, *Guide to Perfect Christian Living*, pp. 38-39.

679. *Prayer That Moves God Most Forcefully*
. . . The disposition of heart which exercises a constraining force on God is a readiness to quit self and leave the soul open for the invasion of God.
Edward Leen, *The True Vine and its Branches*, p. 124.

680. *Prayer – Our Most Powerful Weapon*
'With all prayer and supplication, pray at all times in the Spirit; and therein be vigilant in all perseverance and supplication for all the saints' (Eph 6: 18). Prayer is the most powerful weapon the Lord gives us to conquer our evil passions and the temptations of hell. But this prayer must be a thing of the spirit. We must pray not with the mouth only but with the heart. Moreover, prayer must be persevering; it must last through life. As long as the struggle endures, so must our prayer.
St Alphonsus Liguori, *The Passion of Jesus Christ*, p. 206.

681. *Prayer Saves Us in Time of Temptation*
. . . All those who are tempted and have recourse to God, and invoke Him through Jesus Christ, invariably come off victorious; and, on the contrary, those who in temptation (especially of impurity) neglect to recommend themselves to God, fall miserably and perish. And they excuse themselves by saying they are but flesh and are very weak. . . . What excuse, I say, would that man have for having been vanquished by his enemy, who,

when the requisite arms for his defense were presented him, had despised and refused them? Were such a man to allege his weakness, who would not instantly condemn him with these words: And you, knowing as you did your own weakness, why did you not avail yourself of the arms that were offered you?

St Alphonsus Liguori, *The Incarnation, Birth and Infancy of Jesus Christ,* pp. 79-80.

682. *The Power of Prayer Against Temptation*

God knows the great good it does to us to be obliged to pray, and therefore permits us . . . to be assaulted by our enemies in order that we may ask him for the help he offers and promises us. But as he is pleased when we run to him in our dangers, so he is displeased when he sees us neglectful of prayer. 'As the king,' says St Bonaventure, 'would think it faithlessness in an officer, when his post is attacked, not to ask him for reinforcements, he would be reputed a traitor if he did not request help from the king'; so God thinks himself betrayed by the man who, when he finds himself surrounded by temptations, does not run to him for assistance. . . .

What is prayer? It is, as St Chrysostom says, 'the anchor of those tossed on the sea, the treasure of the poor, the cure of diseases, the safeguard of health.' . . .

'He who uses this great weapon,' says St Chrysostom, 'knows not death, leaves the earth, enters heaven, lives with God.' . . . He falls not into sin; he loses affection for the earth, he makes his abode in heaven, and begins even in this life, to enjoy conversation with God. . . .

The learned Cardinal Gotti writes that . . . 'God is bound, when we are tempted and fly to his protection, to give us by the grace prepared and offered to all such strength as will not only put us in the way of being able to resist, but will also make us resist; 'for we can do all things in him who strengthens us by his grace if we humbly ask for it.

St Alphonsus Liguori, *Great Means of Salvation and of Perfection*, pp. 52-56.

683. *Son Dies But Is Saved from Hell*

Simon Metaphrastes, in his life of St John the Almoner, Archbishop of Alexandria, relates how a rich man had a son whom he loved very much, and to obtain from God the preservation of his life and health he asked the saint to pray for him, and gave him a great quantity of gold to distribute in alms to the poor for that intention. The saint did so, and at the end of thirty days the son died. The father was smitten with great grief, thinking that the prayer and alms that had been offered for him had gone for nothing. The patriarch, knowing his sadness, offered prayer for him, asking God to console him. God heard his prayer and sent one night a holy angel from heaven, who appeared to the man and told him that he should know that the prayer made for his son had been heard by God; and that his son was alive and well in heaven and that his death at that time was the right thing for him in view of his salvation; for, if he had lived, he would have turned out badly and made himself unworthy of the glory of God.

Rodriguez, *Practice of Perfection and Christian Virtues*, vol. 1, pp. 571-572.

684. *Without Prayer All Other Means Are Ineffective*

. . . What profit is there in sermons, meditations, and all other means pointed out by the masters of the spiritual life, if we forget to pray? Since our Lord has declared he will grant his graces to no one who does not pray. 'Ask and ye shall receive' (Jn 16:24). Without prayer, in the ordinary course of Providence, all the meditations we make, all our resolutions, all our promises will be useless. If we do not pray, we shall always be unfaithful to the inspirations of God and to the promises we make to him. Because, in order actually to do good, to conquer temptations, to practice virtues, and to observe God's law, it is not enough to receive illumination from God and to meditate and make resolutions, but we require, moreover, the actual assistance of God; and, as we shall soon see, He does not give this assistance except to those who pray, and pray with perseverance.

St Alphonsus Liguori, *Great Means of Salvation and of Perfection*, p.20.

685. *Prayer Is Necessary for Salvation*

. . . Lessius wrote that it is heresy to deny that prayer is necessary for salvation in adults; as it evidently appears from Scripture that prayer is the means without which we cannot obtain the help necessary for salvation.

The reason for this is evident. Without the assistance of God's grace we can do no good thing: 'Without me, ye can do nothing.' St Augustine remarks on this passage that our Lord did not say: 'Without me you can complete nothing,' but 'Without me ye can do nothing. . . . ' Nay, more, St Paul writes, that of ourselves we cannot even have the wish to do good. 'Not that we are sufficient to think anything of ourselves, but our sufficiency is from God.' If we cannot even think a good thing, much less can we wish it. The same thing is taught in many other passages of Scripture: *'God worketh all in all. I will cause you to walk in my commandments, and to keep my judgments, and to do them.'* So that, as St Leo says, 'Man does no good thing, except that which God by his grace enables him to do,' and hence the Council of Trent says: 'If any one shall assert that without the previous inspiration of the Holy Ghost, and his assistance, man can believe, hope, love or repent, as he ought in order to obtain the grace of justification, let him be anathema.'

St Alphonsus, *ibid.*, pp. 24-25.

686. *Prayer Is Necessary as Precept and as Means of Salvation*
Prayer is necessary, not only as a matter of strict precept, but according to St Basil, St Augustine, St John Chrysostom, Clement of Alexandria, and others, it is also necessary as a means of salvation, without which it is absolutely impossible for us to preserve ourselves in the grace of God and to be saved. 'It is simply impossible,' says St John Chrysostom, 'to lead, without the aid of prayer, a virtuous life.'

St Alphonsus, *The True Spouse of Jesus Christ*, p. 610.

687. *Grace Is Generally Not Given to Those Who Do Not Pray*
Man is completely unable to provide for his own safety, since God has willed that whatever he has, or can have, should come entirely from the assistance of grace.

But this grace is not given in God's ordinary Providence except to those who pray for it; according to the celebrated saying of Gennadius, 'We believe that no one approaches to be saved except at the invitation of God; that no one who is invited works out his salvation except by the help of God; that no one merits this help unless he prays.' From these two premises, on the one hand that we can do nothing without the assistance of grace; and on the other, that this assistance is only given ordinarily by God to the man that prays, who does not see the consequence that follows, that prayer is absolutely necessary for us for salvation? And although the first graces that come to us without any cooperation on our part, such as the call to faith or to penance, are as St Augustine says, granted by God even to those who do not pray; yet the Saint considers it certain that the other graces, and especially the grace of perseverance, are not given except in answer to prayer: 'God gives us some things, as the beginning of faith, even when we do not pray. Other things, such as perseverance, he has only provided for those who pray.'

St Alphonsus, *Great Means of Salvation and of Perfection,* pp. 25-26.

688. *Prayer Is Necessary for Salvation*
As moisture is necessary for the life of plants, to prevent them from drying up, so, says Chrysostom, is prayer necessary for our salvation. Or, as he says in another place, prayer vivifies the soul, as the soul vivifies the body: 'As the body without the soul cannot live, so the soul without prayer is dead and emits an offensive odor.' He uses these words because the man who omits to recommend himself to God at once begins to be defiled with sins. Prayer is also called the food of the soul because the body

cannot be supported without food; nor can the soul, says St Augustine, be kept alive without prayer: 'As the flesh is nourished by food, so is man supported by prayers.' . . .

St Charles Borromeo, in a pastoral letter, concludes that prayer is 'the beginning and progress, and the completion of all virtue.'

St Alphonsus, *ibid.*, pp. 27-29.

689. *Prayer Is Necessary, According to an Eternal Decree of God*
. . . That prayer is the only ordinary means of receiving divine gifts is more distinctly proved by St Thomas in another place, where he says, that whatever graces God has from all eternity determined to give us, he will only give them if we pray for them. St Gregory says the same thing: 'Man by prayer merits to receive that which God had from all eternity determined to give him.' . . . Not, says St Thomas, that prayer is necessary in order that God may know our necessities, but in order that we may know the necessity of having recourse to God to obtain the help necessary for our salvation, and may thus acknowledge him to be the author of all our good.

St Alphonsus, *ibid.*, p. 27.

690. *Prayer Is Needed to Observe the Commandments*
It is true, says St Augustine, that man, in consequence of his weakness, is unable to fulfill some of God's commandments with his present strength and the ordinary grace given to all men; but he can easily, by prayer, obtain such further aid as he requires for his salvation: 'God commands not impossibilities, but by commanding he suggests to you to do what you can, to ask for what is beyond your strength; and he helps you, that you may be able.' This is a celebrated text, which was afterward adopted and made a doctrine of faith by the Council of Trent. . . .

The Holy Doctor adds that by prayer we may obtain a remedy for our weakness; for when we pray, God gives us strength to do that which we cannot do for ourselves.

[St Augustine is quoted here also as saying that] 'By the very fact that it is absurd to suppose that God could have commanded us to do impossible things, we are admonished what to do in easy matters and what to ask for in difficulties.' . . . But why, it will be asked, has God commanded us to do things impossible to our natural strength? Precisely for this, says St Augustine, that we may be incited to pray for help to do that which of ourselves we cannot do. 'He commands some things which we cannot do, that we may know what we ought to ask of him.'

St Alphonsus, *ibid.*, pp. 30-31.

691. *The Need for Urging the Absolute Necessity of Prayer*

. . . Many poor souls lose God's grace and continue to live in sin and are finally damned for this very reason, that they do not pray nor have recourse to God for assistance. The worst of the matter is (I cannot help saying so), that so few preachers and so few confessors have any definite purpose of indoctrinating their hearers and penitents with the use of prayer, without which it is impossible to observe the law of God and to obtain perseverance in his grace.

Having observed that so many passages, both of the Old and the New Testament, assert the absolute necessity of prayer, I have made it a rule to introduce into all the missions, as given by our Congregation for several years, a sermon on prayer; and I say, and repeat, and will keep repeating as long as I live, that our whole salvation depends on prayer; and, therefore, that all writers in their books, all preachers in their sermons, all confessors in their instructions to their penitents, should not inculcate anything more strongly than continual prayer. They should always admonish, exclaim, and continually repeat: Pray, pray, never cease to pray; for if you pray, your salvation will be secure; but if you leave off praying, your damnation will be certain.

St Alphonsus, *ibid.*, p. 240.

692. *Prayer Is Better than Meditation or Spiritual Reading*

There is no doubt that spiritual reading and meditation on the eternal truths are very useful things; 'but,' says St Augustine, 'It is of more use to pray.' By reading and meditation we learn our duty; but by prayer we obtain the grace to do it. 'It is better to pray than to read; by reading we know what we ought to do; by prayer we receive what we ask.' . . .

. . . As St Isidore observes, the devil is never more busy to distract us with the thoughts of worldly cares than when he perceives us praying and asking God for grace: 'Then mostly does the devil insinuate thoughts, when he sees a man praying.' . . . And why? Because the enemy sees that at no other time do we gain so many treasures of heavenly goods as when we pray. . . .

St Chrysostom wrote that 'there is nothing more powerful than a man who prays.' . . .

[St Bernard is quoted as saying:] 'Let no one undervalue his prayer, for God does not undervalue it. . . . He will either give what we ask, or what He knows to be better.'

St Alphonsus, *ibid.*, pp. 60-63.

693. *The Importance and Effects of Prayer*

[Prayer] is the only means of purifying us, of uniting us to God and of

having God unite himself with us to do something for his glory.
Blessed Claude de la Colombiere, *Faithful Servant*, p. 40.

694. *Prayer Is Needed by Those Who Say They Don't Need It*
. . . You say: what need have I of prayers? You need them for this reason: because you think that you have no need of them.
St John Chrysostom, in Toal, vol. 2, p. 397.

695. *The Meaning and Necessity of Prayer*
What air and light are to the living body, that prayer is to the soul living with a supernatural life. . . . All prayer that is true prayer is a practical recognition that God is the only source of our real good. [A footnote adds:] St Thomas writes: 'By prayer man displays reverence towards God, inasmuch as in praying he subjects himself to the Lord and professes that he needs God as the source of all that which constitutes a good for him.'
Edward Leen, *The True Vine and Its Branches*, p. 108.

696. *Prayer Is Necessary for Salvation*
. . . Theologians, such as Suarez, Habert, Layman, F. Segneri, and others, with Clement of Alexandria, St Basil, St Augustine and St Chrysostom, conclude that prayer is necessary to adults, if not as an end, yet as a means; that is to say, in the ordinary course of Providence, no Christian can be saved without recommending himself to God, and asking him for the graces necessary for salvation. St Chrysostom says that as the soul is necessary for the life of the body, so is prayer necessary for the soul to preserve it in the grace of God.
St Alphonsus Liguori, *The Way of Salvation and of Perfection*, p. 430.

697. *Prayer Needed for Salvation*
St Augustine teaches that with the exception of the first motions of grace – such as the first call to faith or to penance, which come to us without our concurrence – all other graces, especialy that of perseverance, are only given to those persons who pray for them . . . : 'We believe that no one comes to be saved except by the call of God. That no one works out his own salvation except by the assistance of God; and that no one merits this assistance except by prayer.'
St Alphonsus, *ibid.*, p. 429.

698. *Prayer Is Necessary for Salvation*
Prayer is not only useful, but necessary for salvation; and therefore God, who desires that we should be saved, has enjoined it as a precept, 'Seek, and it shall be given you' (Mt 7:7). It is an error of Wyckliff, condemned by the Council of Constance, to say that prayer was a subject of divine

counsel to us and not of command. 'It is necessary' – not, it is advisable or fitting – 'always to pray' (Lk 18:1). Wherefore, Doctors of the Church always say that he cannot be held innocent of grevious sin who neglects to recommend himself to God at least once in a month and at all times when he finds himself assaulted by severe temptation.

The reason of this necessity of recommending ourselves often to God arises from our inability to do any good work, or to entertain any good thought of ourselves: 'Without me ye can do nothing' (Jn 15:5). We are not sufficient of ourselves to think anything of ourselves. Therefore, St Philip Neri said that he despaired of himself. On the other hand, St Augustine wrote that God desires to bestow graces, but only on those who beg them. . . . And especially, said the saint, 'God only gives the grace of perseverance to those who seek it.

St Alphonsus, *ibid.*, p. 191-192.

699. *Prayer Was in God's Plan from All Eternity*
St Thomas, treating of prayer, gives one very good and substantial reason for its necessity, and it is the teaching of Saints Damascene, Augustine, Basil, Chrysostom, and Gregory that what God by his divine Providence and disposition has determined from eternity to give to souls, that he gives them in time by means of prayer, and on this means depend the deliverance, salvation, conversion and cure of many souls and the progress and perfection of others.

Rodriguez, *Practice of Perfection and Christian Virtues*, vol. 1, p. 284.

700. *Prayer Necessary – Trent, Augustine, Etc.*
. . . We have so many enemies that continually combat against us, and we are so weak that if God does not assist us with special helps, or if he gives us only the common graces given to all, we shall not have strength to resist. This is even a dogma of the faith defined by the Council of Trent in the following words: 'If anyone shall say that a person who has been justified can, without special aid from God, persevere in the justice which he has received, or cannot persevere with such aid, let him be anathema.' It is necessary to know, secondly, that this special aid to persevere in grace (at least ordinarily speaking) is given only to those who ask it. 'It is evident,' says St Augustine, 'That God gives, even to those that do not pray, some gifts, such as the beginning of faith; and that he prepares other graces, such as perseverance to the end, only for those who ask them.' . . . In a word, the holy Doctor says, that except for the first graces, such as vocation to the faith or to repentance, all other graces, and particularly perseverance, God gives only to him who prays for them.

St Alphonsus Liguori, *The True Spouse of Jesus Christ*, p. 611.

701. *Why Prayer Is Necessary and under What Circumstances*
'Every man,' says the Angelic Doctor, 'Is bound to pray, because he is bound to procure spiritual goods which cannot be obtained unless they are asked.' . . . A person is obliged to pray particularly in three cases: first, when he finds himself in the state of sin; second, when he is in danger of death; third, when he is assailed by violent temptation. Theologians teach that ordinarily he who neglects prayer for a month, or at most for two months, is guilty of a mortal sin.

St Alphonsus, *ibid.*, 609-610.

702. *The Necessity of Prayer*
With regard to the necessity of prayer, it is necessary to be persuaded that we cannot perform any good action without the actual grace of God. But the Lord declares that these graces he gives only to those who ask them of Him. 'Ask and it shall be given to you' (Jn 16:24). He, then, says St Teresa, who does not ask will not receive.

St Alphonsus, *ibid.*, p. 609.

703. *Prayer Necessary for a Man to Enter Heaven*
The Angelic Doctor teaches . . . : 'After baptism, continual prayer is necessary for a man, in order to enter heaven.' . . . Because, adds the saint, though sins are cancelled by baptism, we still have temptations to conquer which we shall not have strength to overcome without prayer. Hence, he says in another place: 'After a man is justified by grace, he requires to ask of God the gift of perseverance that he may be preserved from evil to the end of life.'

St Alphonsus, *ibid.*, p. 610.

704. *Prayer, the Key to Right Living*
'He knows how to live well, who knows how to pray well,' says St Augustine.

Rodriguez, *Practice of Perfection and Christian Virtues*, vol. 1, p. 285.

705. *St Alphonsus Complains that Priests, and Others Do Not Stress Prayer*
. . . I cannot help saying how grieved I feel when I see that though the Holy Scriptures and the Fathers so often recommend the practice of prayer, so few religious writers or confessors or preachers ever speak of it; or, if they do speak of it, just touch upon it in a cursory way and leave it. But I, seeing the necessity of prayer, say that the great lesson which all spiritual books should inculcate on their readers, all preachers on their hearers, and all confessors on their penitents, is this: to pray always; they should thus admonish them to pray, and never give up praying. If you

pray, you will certainly be saved; if you do not pray, you will certainly be damned.

St Alphonsus Liguori, *The Way of Salvation and of Perfection*, p. 446.

706. *Prayer of Petition Is Necessary*

The Angelic Doctor . . . affirms as certain in several of his works, that 'everyone is obliged to use the prayer of petition, for the very reason that everyone is bound to gain for himself those spiritual gifts which can be given by no one but God alone, nor obtained from Him except by way of earnest petition.' . . . St John Chrysostom illustrates by a striking and most apt comparison the grave obligation we all lie under, of unceasingly begging God to help us. 'Take a fish out of the water,' says the saint, 'and shortly you will see it expire under your very eyes. In the same manner, cease, yourself, from prayer, you too will soon die to grace and to God; for what water is to the bodily life of the fish, that prayer is to man's spiritual life.'

Scaramelli, *Directorium Asceticum,* vol. 1, pp. 210-211.

707. *Prayer as Pleasing Violence to God*

St Gregory says that God wishes us to do him violence by our prayers; for such violence does not annoy, but pleases him: 'God wills to be called upon, he wills to be forced; he wills to be conquered by importunity. . . . Happy violence by which God is not offended but appeased!

St Alphonsus Liguori, *Great Means of Salvation and of Perfection*, p. 97.

708. *Prayer of Petition in Trials and Troubles*

. . . Say to him, 'My God, in thee are all my hopes; I offer to thee this affliction and resign myself to thy will; but do thou take pity on me – either deliver me out of it, or give me strength to bear it.' And he will truly keep with you that promise he made in the Gospel to all those who are in trouble, to console and comfort them as often as they have recourse to him: 'Come to Me, all you that labor and are burdened, and I will refresh you' (Mt 11:28).

He will not be displeased that in your desolation you should go to your friends to find some relief; but he wills you chiefly to have recourse to himself. At all events, therefore, after you have applied to creatures, and they have been unable to comfort your heart, have recourse to your Creator. . . .

St Alphonsus, *Way of Salvation and of Perfection,* p. 400.

709. *Merit Not Needed for Effective Petition*

'Everyone that asketh receiveth' (Lk 11:10). 'It is not necessary,' says St Thomas, 'that the man who prays should merit the grace for which he asks. By prayer, we obtain even those things which we do not deserve.' In order to receive, it is enough to pray. The reason is (in the words of the same holy Doctor), 'Merit is grounded in justice, but the power of prayer (*impetratio*) is grounded in grace.' The power of prayer to obtain what we ask does not depend on the merit of the person who prays, but on the mercy and faithfulness of God, who has gratuitously, and of his own goodness, promised to hear the man who prays to him. When we pray, it is not necessary that we should be friends of God in order to obtain grace; indeed, the act of prayer, as St Thomas says, makes us his friends: 'Prayer itself makes us of the family of God.'

St Alphonsus, *ibid.*, pp. 440-441.

710. *The Reason for Prayers of Petition*
Say not. 'But where is the need of disclosing to God all my wants if he already sees and knows them better than I?' True, he knows them; but God makes as if he knew not the necessities about which you do not apeak to him, and for which you seek not his aid.

St Alphonsus, *ibid.*, p. 399.

711. *Prayer of Petition Is Easy*
There is nothing easier than prayer. What does it cost us to say: 'Lord, stand by me! Lord, help me! Give me thy love!' and the like? What can be easier than this? But if we do not do so, we cannot be saved.

St Alphonsus, *Ibid.*, p. 445.

712. *Why God's Answer to Prayer Is Often Delayed*
The answer to our prayer is [often] put off to some future date; just as when . . . we daily pray the Father: 'Thy kingdom come'. . . . We know that this is ordered by the kind Providence of the Creator, so that, for example, our desires may intensify by the prolongation of our devotion, and by daily increase grow more and more, until at last they come perfectly to possess the joys they seek.

St Bede, in Toal, vol. 2, pp. 404-405.

713. *Prayer for Deliverance from Temptation*
Often we ask God to deliver us from some troublesome temptation which would persuade us to forfeit his grace; but God does not deliver us, in order that our soul may be more closely united in love with him. It is not temptation or bad thoughts that hurt us and separate us from God, but consent to evil. When the soul, through the assistance of God's grace, resists a temptation, it makes a great advance in the way of perfection.

St Alphonsus Liguori, *The Way of Salvation and of Perfection*, pp. 442-443.

714. *If God Does Not Give What We Ask, He Gives Something Better*
'If,' says St Bernard, 'at times God does not give us the grace which we ask, we ought to feel quite convinced that he is giving us in its stead some grace that is more needful to us.'

Quoted by St Alphonsus, in *ibid.,* p. 432.

715. *God Wishes to Grant Genuine Petitions*
God can be trusted to bestow on us all that we need for the attainment of life's purpose. Having created us for a supernatural destiny, that is, for the happiness proper to himself, he, by the very fact, undertakes to give us all that is required for gaining that happiness. . . . But it is not to be expected that he will give ear to our requests when these do not bear on what makes for a good life, as God understands a good life. His help is extended to us to have a good life, but not, certainly, to have a good time. . . . God alone knows what will work in favor of our sanctification and what will prove adverse to it. We are poor judges in this matter.

Edward Leen, *The True Vine and Its Branches*, pp. 110-111.

716. *God Is Always Ready to Hear Our Prayers*
St Chrysostom writes that . . . 'God is always prepared for the voice of his servants, nor did he ever, when called upon as he ought to be, neglect to hear.' . . .

St Mary Magdalene of Pazzi said that 'God feels Himself so honored and is so delighted when we ask for his grace that he is, in a certain sense, grateful to us; because when we do this we seem to open to him a way to do us a kindness, and to satisfy his nature, which is to do good to all.'

St Alphonsus Liguori, *Great Means of Salvation and of Perfection*, pp. 57, 59.

717. *Prayer of Petition – in the Name of Jesus*
Since the name of the Son is Jesus, and since Jesus signifies Savior; or also, salvation, he therefore asks in the name of the Savior who asks for what relates to the true health of his soul. Should he ask for what is not expedient for salvation, he does not ask the Father in the name of Jesus. . . . Paul's prayer also was not heard: because it was not to the profit of his soul's salvation that he should be delivered from temptation (2 Cor 12:9). . . .

Think whether you are asking in the name of Jesus; that is, if you are asking for the joys of eternal salvation? For in the House of Jesus, you do not seek Jesus if, in the temple of eternity, you are asking for the things of time.

St Gregory the Great, in Toal, vol. 4, p. 174.

718. *Conditions Required for Prayer's Efficacy*
St Thomas lays down four conditions necessary in order that our prayers may be efficacious. First, that we pray for our own wants. Second, that we ask for things necessary for salvation. Third, that we ask in faith. Fourth, that we pray with perseverance. The holy Doctor had already mentioned another condition as necessary for obtaining the favors we desire; this is humility in prayer.
Scaramelli, *Directorium Asceticum*, vol. 1, p. 232.

719. *Prayer of Petition – Conditions for Its Efficacy*
[After listing the four conditions laid down by St Thomas for efficacious prayer of petition, Fr Leen says:] Three of these conditions we fulfill readily enough. . . . We desire more ardently what makes for gratification than what makes for our salvation. . . . It is undeniable that temporal needs may form the theme of our communication with the Lord; but if they do, they must have a connection with the obtaining of grace and glory. It is quite legitimate to ask the Lord for all that is required to be able to lead a truly human life. It is only when the necessaries of existence are easily secured that man can have proper scope to attend to the development of the higher life and serve his God in peace.
Edward Leen, *The True Vine and Its Branches*, pp. 120-121.

720. *Prayer of Petition – Confidence Needed for Its Efficacy*
. . . It is necessary to determine what is this faith – or, to speak more accurately, this confidence – failing which God declares that he will withhold his gifts from us. I will state briefly that it is a virtue which resides partly in the understanding and partly in the will. In the understanding, in as much as the suppliant believes most firmly that God, impelled thereto by his sovereign goodness and bound by his oft-repeated promises, will assuredly grant the graces for which we ask. In the will, because, adhering to a belief so solidly grounded, this power undoubtedly and unhesitatingly trusts, as St James requires, that these favors will be obtained. . . . As St Augustine says: 'If confidence fail, prayer disappears; it is without a soul, vigor, force, efficacy: it languishes and dies.'
Scaramelli, *Directorium Asceticum*, vol. 1, pp. 233-234.

721. *Prayer of Petition – Confidence Needed for Its Efficacy*
Prayer must be confident: 'No one hath hoped in the Lord and been confounded' (Ecclus 2:2). The Holy Ghost assures us that it never has happened that anyone who placed his trust in God has been deceived. He once said to St Gertrude that a person who prays to him with confidence does him, in a certain way, such violence that he cannot but listen to him and

grant all his requests. 'Prayer,' said St John Climacus, 'is a pious way of forcing God,' Prayer does violence to him; but a violence which he loves and delights in. 'This violence,' he says, 'is pleasing to God.' In the Our Father . . . which Jesus Christ himself taught us as a means whereby to obtain all the graces necessary for salvation, how are we made to address God? Not as Lord, not as Judge, but as Father, 'our Father,' because he wishes us to ask God for grace with the same confidence as a son, when he is hungry or ill, asks his own father for food or medicine. . . . Our Savior has told us: 'All things whatsoever you ask when you pray, believe that you shall receive, and they will come unto you' (Mk 11:24). . . . 'He would not have exhorted us,' (says St Augustine,) 'to ask, unless he had been willing to grant.'

St Alphonsus Liguori, *The Way of Salvation and of Perfection,* pp. 435-436.

722. *Prayer of Petition – on What our Confidence Is Based*
Confidence is necessary to obtain what we ask of God. But on what, it may be said, are we to found this confidence? On the goodness of God and on the promise which he made when he said, 'Ask and you shall receive.'

St Alphonsus Liguori, *ibid.,* p. 437.

723. *Prayer of Petition – Conditions for Its Efficacy*
It is necessary, in the first place, to pray with humility. 'God,' says St James, 'resisteth the proud and giveth grace to the humble' (Jas 4:6). . . .

It is necessary to pray with confidence. . . . We should as St James says, pray without wavering and with a secure confidence of being heard: 'Let them ask in faith, nothing wavering' (Jas 1:6). The apostle adds: 'For he that wavereth is like a wave of the sea, which is moved and carried about by the wind. Therefore, let not that man think that he shall receive anything from the Lord' (Jas 6:7). He says that the man that prays with a doubt of being heard, being tossed like a wave of the sea, encouraged by one thought and disheartened by another, shall receive nothing from the Lord. . . .

It is, finally, necessary to pray with perseverance. St Hilary says that to obtain the divine graces depends on our continuance in prayer.

St Alphonsus Liguori, *The True Spouse of Jesus Christ*, pp. 613-614, 616.

724. *The Kind of Prayer God Cannot Resist*
When the soul says, 'Lord, I ask thee not for riches, honors, the goods of this world, but I only beg for thy grace; deliver me from sin, give me a good death, give me paradise, and meanwhile give me thy love: (which is

the grace that, as St Francis de Sales says, we ought to pray for above all others). . . . When the soul prays thus, how is it possible that God should refuse to hear it?

St Alphonsus Liguori, *The Way of Salvation and of Perfection*, p. 444.

725. *Humility Needed for Effective Petitions*

Prayer must be humble: 'God resists the proud, but gives grace to the humble' (Jas 4:6). Here St James tells us that God does not listen to the prayers of the proud, but resists them; while, on the other hand, he is always ready to hear the prayers of the humble. . . . However sinful such a soul may be, God can never despise a heart that repents of its sins and humbles itself: 'A contrite and humble heart, O God, thou wilt not despise' (Ps 1:19).

St Alphonsus, *ibid.*, p. 435.

726. *Prayer of Petition – Humility Needed*

He that prays must have one eye fixed on himself and on his miseries, that the sight may humble him and fill him with confusion, by bringing home to him his unworthiness to receive any favor; the other eye must rest upon God's mercy, his liberality and his promises, so as to make the heart expand with lively hope of receiving every good and perfect gift. Humility and confidence are the two wings on which prayer soars aloft to God; the two arms which force his hands to shed every blessing.

Scaramelli, *Directorium Asceticum*, vol. 1, p. 236.

727. *The Devil Uses False Humility to Frustrate Prayer*

[Some people] will have it that their sins and their wickedness render them unworthy to be heard. And the worst of it is that they believe such vile faintheartedness to be true humility. The director must open the eyes of these blind people and show them that such depression of spirit is not humility but its poisonous counterfeit, which the devil puts into their minds in order to disgust them with prayer or, at all events, to render their prayers ineffectual with God. True humility, which comes from above, has this property, that the more it lowers us in our own estimation by the knowledge it gives of our own misery, the more does it raise us to confidence in God by the knowledge it brings of His goodness and promises.

Scaramelli, *ibid.*, p. 251.

728. *Prayer of Petition – Perseverance Needed*

[One] condition which our prayers must have, in order to move effectively the heart of God, is perseverance in asking. . . . For although God has promised to grant the favors we seek at his hands, provided they help us to attain our last end, eternal life, he has not promised to grant them immediately, nor even soon.

Scaramelli, *ibid.*, p. 237.

729. *Prayer of Petition – Perseverance Needed*
Prayer should be persevering, otherwise it will not obtain eternal life. The grace of salvation is not a single grace, but is a chain of graces, all united with the grace of final perseverance. Now to this chain of graces there must be a corresponding chain of prayers on our part. . . .

Men cannot endure importunity; but God not only endures it, but wishes us to be importunate in begging for his grace, and especially for the grace of final perseverance.

St Alphonsus Liguori, *The Way of Salvation and of Perfection*, pp. 437-438.

730. *Prayer of Petition – Perseverance Needed*
St Gregory teaches that God wishes to give us perseverance, but in order to give it, he wishes to be importuned, and, as it were, forced by our prayers. 'God,' says the holy Doctor, 'wishes to be asked, he wishes to be forced, he wishes, in a certain manner, to be overcome by importunity.'

St Alphonsus Liguori, *The True Spouse of Jesus Christ*, p. 617.

731. *Prayer Is Answered in God's Way*
What did [St Monica] ask of thee, O my God, with so many tears, but that thou wouldst not permit me to sail away [to Italy]? But thou, taking counsel on high and giving ear to the main point of her request, didst not provide what she then asked in order that thou mightest do with me what she always sought.

St Augustine, *Confessions*, bk. 5, chap. 8.

732. *What to Pray For*
'The principal objects of our prayer, 'says St Thomas, 'are spiritual benefits, which are the only real goods of the soul, making us absolutely good and leading us to the highest good, that is, to everlasting happiness.' . . . .

Temporal blessings may also form the object of prayer, but, as St Thomas again teaches, ' . . . in a secondary and subordinate manner'; for Christ says expressly, 'seek first the kingdom of God and his justice, and all these things shall be added to you' (Mt 6:33). . . . St Augustine explains the text as follows: 'In saying that the kingdom of God is to be sought for in the first place, he means that temporal goods are to be asked in the order of dignity, not of time. The kingdom of heaven is our chiefest good; temporal blessings are necessary – necessary, that is, to secure our chiefest good.'

Scaramelli, *Directorium Asceticum*, vol. 1, pp. 217-218.

733. *Temporal Favors Not Necessarily Granted*

The Lord, then, hears the prayers of all because he has promised to hear them: but it is necessary to know that this promise does not extend to temporal favors – such as bodily health, the acquisition of wealth, or the attainment of a post of honor, and the like. For God frequently and justly refuses these gifts because he knows that they would be injurious to the soul. 'The physician,' says St Augustine, 'knows better than the patient what is useful for him.' It is not the sick man but the physician that cures his malady, that knows what is most conducive to his recovery. If these temporal favors be the object of prayer, they should be asked with resignation, and on condition that they will be conducive to our eternal salvation; if we ask them without this resignation, the Lord will not listen to our prayers. But in praying for spiritual blessings, we must pray, not conditionally, but absolutely and with a firm confidence of obtaining them.

St Alphonsus Liguori, *The True Spouse of Jesus Christ*, pp. 618-619.

734. *Prayer of Petition – Concerning Temporal Goods*

. . . I repeat, all temporal gifts which are not necessary for salvation ought to be asked conditionally; and if we see that God does not give them, we must feel sure that he refuses them for our greater good. But with regard to spiritual graces, we must be certain that God gives them to us when we ask him.

St Alphonsus Liguori, *The Way of Salvation and of Perfection*, p. 443.

735. *Evil Never to Be asked For*

. . . Whatsoever is incompatible with the soul's health or the honor due to God, cannot, on any account, be the lawful object of our prayers. . . . As we cannot tell whether the temporal favors we ask for will be advantageous or prejudicial to our souls, whether they redound to the glory of God or turn to his dishonor, it behooves us to pray for them under condition of their being expedient both to our own welfare and to the honor of our Maker.

Scaramelli, *Directorium Asceticum*, vol. 1, p. 219.

736. *If Prayer Is Not Answered, It is Because We Pray Amiss*

. . . How does it come to pass that some persons pray but yet do not receive? They pray, indeed, but they do not pray as they ought, and this is why they obtain nothing: 'You ask and receive not, because you ask amiss' (Jas 4:3). Many persons ask for grace but do not observe the proper conditions.

St Alphonsus Liguori, *The Way of Salvation and of Perfection*, p. 434.

737. *God Hears Prayers of Sinners – With One Exception*
. . . A person might say, 'I am a sinner, and God does not hear sinners.' . . . [This] proposition, if taken absolutely, is false; there is only one case in which it is true, as St Thomas says, and that is when sinners pray as sinners; that is, ask something they require to assist them in their sin; as, for instance, if a man asked God to help him take vengeance of his enemy; in such cases God certainly will not hear. But when a man prays and asks for those things that are requisite for his salvation, what matters it whether he is a sinner or not? Suppose he were the greatest criminal in the world, let him only pray, he will surely obtain all that he asks.

St Alphonsus Liguori, *ibid.*, p. 440.

738. *Prayer of Sinners – Its Effectiveness*
If God did not hear sinners, says St Augustine, in vain would the Publican have asked forgiveness: 'If God does not hear sinners, in vain would that Publican have said, 'God, be merciful to me, a sinner.' But the Gospel assures us that the Publican did by his prayer obtain forgiveness: "This man went down to his house justified." (Lk 18:14).

But further still, St Thomas examines this point more minutely, and does not hesitate to affirm that even the sinner is heard if he prays; for though his prayer is not meritorious, yet it has the power of impetration – that is, of obtaining what we ask; because impetration is not founded on God's justice, but on his goodness. 'Merit,' he says, 'depends on justice; impetration, on grace.' . . . Therefore, when we pray, says St Thomas, it is not necessary to be friends with God in order to obtain the grace we ask; for prayer itself renders us his friends; 'Prayer itself makes us of the family of God.' Moreover, St Bernard uses a beautiful explanation of this, saying that the prayer of a sinner to escape from sin arises from the desire to return to the grace of God. Now this desire is a gift which is certainly given by no other than God himself; to what end, therefore, says St Bernard, would God give a sinner this holy desire, unless he meant to hear him?

St Alphonsus Liguori, *Great Means of Salvation and of Perfection*, pp. 90-91.

739. *Prayer for Others, Sinners, Non-Christians*
Let us pray for ourselves, and, if we have zeal for the glory of God, let us pray also for others. It is a thing most pleasing to God to be entreated for unbelievers and heretics, and all sinners. 'Let all the people confess to

thee, O God! Let all the people confess to Thee' (Ps 66:6). Let us say, 'O Lord! make them know thee, make them love Thee.'

St Alphonsus Liguori, *The Way of Salvation and of Perfection*, p. 219.

740. *Prayer – Urged for Sinners*

. . . If you love Jesus Christ, do not fail to recommend to Him every day unfortunate sinners. St Teresa and St Mary Magdalen de Pazzi always prayed for sinners. If we know how much God is offended by infidels, heretics, and so many others, and we neglect prayer to the Lord for their conversion, this would be a sign that our love for God is very feeble.

St Alphonsus, *ibid.,* p. 484.

741. *Prayer for Others Pleases God More than Prayer for Ourselves*

Pray for one another, that ye may be saved (Jas 5:16). St John Chrysostom . . . adds . . . that the prayers we offer for others are more pleasing to God and therefore gain more merit for ourselves than those which we make on our own behalf, as they receive a special luster and price, gilded as they are by fraternal charity. 'We are compelled, ' he says, 'by necessity to pray for ourselves; but the love of our brethren engages us to pray for others also. Now, far more acceptable to God is the prayer that proceeds, not from the pressure of our wants, but from the love of our neighbor.'

Scaramelli, *Directorium Asceticum*, vol. 1, p. 220.

742. *Prayer For Sinners*

It is quite certain that the prayers of others are of great use to sinners, and are very pleasing to God. . . . He once complained to St Mary Magdalen of Pazzi, to whom he said one day: 'See, my daughter, how the Christians are in the devil's hands; if my elect did not deliver them by their prayers, they would be devoured.' But God especially requires this of priests and religious.

[God one day said to the same Saint:] 'I have given you, my chosen spouses, the City of Refuge [the Passion of Jesus Christ] that you may have a place where you may obtain help for my creatures. Therefore, have recourse to it, and thence stretch forth a helping hand to my creatures who are perishing, and lay down your lives for them.'

. . . How is it possible for a person who loves God, and knows what love he has for our souls and what Jesus Christ has done and suffered for their salvation, and how our Savior desires us to pray for sinners – how is it possible, I say, that he should be able to look with indifference on the numbers of poor souls who are living without God and are slaves of hell, without being moved to importune God with frequent prayers to give light and strength to those wretched beings, so that they may come out from the miserable state of living death in which they are slumbering.

St Alphonsus Liguori, *Great Means of Salvation and of Perfection*, pp. 67-68.

743. *Prayer for Those in Mortal Sin*

Let us take special pains, Sisters, to pray to him for them and not be negligent. To pray for those who are in mortal sin is the best kind of almsgiving – a much better thing than it would be to loose a Christian whom we saw with his hands bound behind him, bound with a stout chain, made fast to a post and dying of hunger, not for lack of food, since he has beside him the most delicious things to eat, but because he cannot take them and put them in his mouth, although he is weary to death and actually knows that he is on the point of dying, and not merely a death of a body, but one which is eternal. Would it not be extremely cruel to stand looking at such a man and not give him food to eat? And supposing you could loose his chains by means of your prayers? You see now what I mean? For the love of God, I beg you always to remember such souls in your prayers.

St Teresa, *Interior Castle*, in Peers, vol. 2, pp. 330-331.

744. *Prayer for Sinners Always Profitable*

Should we pray for sinners and cannot obtain their conversion, we are not, however, deprived of the fruit of our prayer. For though they are not worthy of being saved, we shall be given the reward of the love devoted to them. And so, in prayer of this kind, that promise of Christ is fulfilled in which He says: 'If you ask the Father anything in my name, He will give it to you.' For we should note that He does not simply say, 'He will give it; He says: He will give it to you.' For though He will not give it to those for whom you pray, He will give us the reward of our charity who intercede with Him for those who were going astray.

St Bede, in Toal, vol. 2, p. 405.

745. *Prayer for Sinners Taught at Fatima*

Some months after Portugal entered the first World War, which occurred in March 1916, the children of Fatima saw a 'transparent young man' of about fourteen years of age – more brilliant than a crystal penetrated by the rays of the sun – who said: 'Don't be afraid; I am the Angel of Peace. Pray with me.' And kneeling on the ground, he prostrated himself until his forehead touched it, saying: 'My God, I believe, I adore, I hope, and I love you! I beg pardon of you for those who do not believe, do not adore, do not hope, and do not love you!'

Walsh, *Our Lady of Fatima*, pp. 34-36.

746. *Meditation – Its Nature and Effects*
[Meditation means that we] make one or more considerations in order to raise our affections to God and the things of God. Hence meditation differs from study and other thoughts and considerations done not to acquire virtue or love of God but for other ends and intentions, such as to become learned, to write, or to reason. . . .

Meditation produces devout movements in the will, the affective part of the soul, such as love of God and neighbor, desire for heaven and glory, zeal for the salvation of souls, imitation of the life of our Lord, compassion, awe, joy, fear of God's displeasure, judgment, hell; hatred of sin, confidence in God's goodness and mercy, and deep sorrow for the sins of our past life.

St Francis de Sales, *Introduction to the Devout Life*, pp. 72-73.

747. *Meditation – a Private Audience with God*
Vocal prayer usually follows someone else's formulas. Mental prayer . . . is the soul's personal contact with God. It is our private audience with God.

Hoeger, *The Convent Mirror*, p. 185.

748. *Meditation – a Root of Virtue and Salvation*
Meditation [says the Venerable Bartholomew a Martyribus] is like fire with regard to iron, which, when cold, is hard and can be wrought only with difficulty. But placed in the fire, it becomes soft and the workman gives it any form he wishes.

Man becomes docile and tender to the influence of grace, which is communicated in mental prayer. By the contemplation of the divine goodness, the great love which God has borne him, and the immense benefits which God has bestowed on him, man is inflamed with love, his heart is softened and made obedient to divine inspirations. But without mental prayer, his heart will remain hard and restive and disobedient, and thus he will be lost. . . .

St Teresa used to say that he who neglects mental prayer needs not a devil to carry him to hell, but that he brings himself there with his own hands.

St Alphonsus Liguori, *Great Means of Salvation and of Perfection*, pp. 254-256.

749. *Meditation – Its Main Aim*
We must meditate in order to unite ourselves more completely to God. It is not so much good thoughts in the intellect as good acts of the will, or holy desires, that unite us to God; and such are the acts we perform in meditation – acts of humility, confidence, self-sacrifice, resignation and,

especially, love, and of repentance for our sins. Acts of love, says St Teresa, are those that keep the soul inflamed with holy love.

But the perfection of this love consists in making our will one with that of God. . . . St Teresa always says, 'All that he who exercises himself in prayer should aim at is to conform himself to the divine will, and he may be assured that in this consists the highest perfection; he who best practices this will receive the greatest gifts from God and will make the greatest progress in the interior life.'

We must meditate in order to obtain from God the graces that are necessary to advance in the way of salvation, and especially to avoid sin, and to use the means which will lead us to perfection.

The best fruit which comes from meditation is the exercise of prayer. Almighty God, ordinarily speaking, does not give grace to any but those who pray. St Gregory writes: 'God desires to be entreated; he desires to be constrained; he desires to be, as it were, conquered by importunity.'

St Alphonsus, *ibid.,* pp. 263-264.

750. *Meditation – and Union with God*

The less a man has God in his thoughts, the less is his soul subject to God.

St Augustine, *City of God*, bk. 19, chap. 4.

751. *Meditation – Morally Necessary Because Petition is Absolutely Necessary*

Without petitions on our part, God does not grant the divine helps; and without aid from God, we cannot observe the commandments. From the absolute necessity of the prayer of petition arises the moral necessity of mental prayer; for he who neglects meditation and is distracted with worldly affairs will not know his spiritual wants, the dangers to which his salvation is exposed, the means which he must adopt in order to conquer temptations, or even the necessity of the prayer of petition for all men; thus he will give up the practice of prayer, and by neglecting to ask God's graces, he will certainly be lost.

Someone may say: 'I do not make mental prayer, but I say many vocal prayers.' But it is necessary to know, as St Augustine remarks, that to obtain divine grace it is not enough to pray with the tongue, it is necessary also to pray with the heart. . . .

In general, vocal prayers are said distractedly with the voice of the body, but not of the heart, especially when they are long, and still more especially when said by a person who does not make mental prayer; and, therefore, God seldom hears them and seldom grants the graces asked. Many say the Rosary, the Office of the Blessed Virgin, and perform other works of devotion; but they still continue to sin. But it is impossible for him who perseveres in mental prayer to continue to sin; he will either give up meditation or renounce sin.

St Alphonsus Liguori, *Great Means of Salvation and of Perfection*, pp. 256-258.

752. *Meditation Is Necessary*

Mental prayer is . . . necessary in order that we may have light to go on the journey to eternity. Eternal truths are spiritual things that are not seen by the eyes of the body but only by the reflection of the mind. He that does not meditate does not see them; and thus he advances with difficulty along the way of salvation. And, further, he who does not meditate does not know his own failings, and thus, said St Bernard, he does not detest them. So, also, he does not see the perils of his state, and therefore does not think of avoiding them. But when we meditate, our failings and perils quickly present themselves; and when we see them, we seek to remedy them. St Bernard said that meditation regulates our affections, directs our actions, and corrects defects.

At Alphonsus Liguori, *The Way of Salvation and of Perfection*, pp. 214-215.

753. *Meditation – Its Necessity*

. . . St Teresa of Jesus used to say that he who neglects mental prayer does not stand in need of devils to carry him off to hell, but brings himself to that land of woe. . . .

He who attends to mental prayer scarcely ever falls into sin, and should he have the misfortune of falling into it, he will hardly continue to live in so miserable a state; he will either give up mental prayer, or renounce sin. Meditation and sin cannot stand together.

St Alphonsus Liguori, *Dignity and Duties of the Priest*, p. 292.

754. *Meditation Indispensable for Attaining to Perfection*

All the saints have become saints by mental prayer. Mental prayer is the blessed furnace in which souls are inflamed with the divine love. . . . St Catherine of Bologna used to say, 'He who does not practice mental prayer deprives himself of the bond that unites the soul with God; hence, finding her alone, the devil will easily make her his own.' 'How,' she would say, 'Can I conceive that the love of God is found in the soul that cares but little to treat with God in prayer?'

'A man of prayer,' says David, 'is like a tree planted near the current of waters, which brings forth fruit in due time; all his actions prosper before God. 'Blessed is the man who shall meditate on his law day and night! And he shall be like a tree which is planted near the running waters, which shall bring forth its fruit in due season, and his leaf shall not fall off: and all whatsoever he shall do shall prosper' (Ps 1:2-3). Mark the words 'in due season'; that is, at the time when he ought to bear such a pain, such an affront, etc.

St Alphonsus Liguori, *Great Means of Salvation and of Perfection*, pp. 258-259.

755. *Meditation Needed to Know the Will of God*

. . . We must apply ourselves to meditation, not for the sake of consolations, but chiefly in order to learn what is the will of God concerning us. 'Speak, Lord', said Samuel to God, 'for thy servant heareth (1 Kgs 3:9)'. Lord, make me know what thou wilt, that I may do it.

St Alphonsus Liguori, *The Way of Salvation and of Perfection*, p. 219.

756. *Meditation Essential for Religious*

St Philip Neri used to say: A religious without mental prayer is a religious without reason. I add: she is not a religious, but the corpse of a religious.

St Alphonsus Liguori, *The True Spouse of Jesus Christ*, p. 441.

757. *A Priest Without Meditation Is Only the 'Corpse of a Priest'*

A priest without mental prayer is a garden without water. . . . He is not even a priest; he is the corpse of a priest, according to the saying of St John Chrysostom: 'As the body cannot live without the soul, so the soul without prayer is dead and malodorous.'

St Alphonsus Liguori, *Dignity and duties of the Priest*, p. 461.

758. *Meditation – Its Necessity*

. . . According to St John Chrysostom, meditation is just as necessary to perserve the spiritual life of the soul as the soul is necessary to the body, to preserve its physical life.

Wallenstein, *Guide to a Perfect Christian Life*, p. 48

759. *Meditation Needed for an Active Apostolate*

. . . For a man in the active life to give up his meditation is tantamount to throwing down his arms at the feet of his enemy. 'Short of a miracle,' says St Alphonsus, 'a man who does not practice mental prayer will end up in mortal sin.' And St Vincent de Paul tells us: 'A man without mental prayer is not good for anything; he cannot even renounce the slightest thing.'

Chautard, *The Soul of the Apostolate*, p. 82.

760. *Meditation – Its Value*
Father Suarez used to say he would rather lose all his knowledge than one hour's meditation.

St Alphonsus Liguori, *Dignity and Duties of the Priest*, p. 298.

761. *Meditation Is Easy*
Meditation is easy because we have nothing else to do with regard to a religious subject than what we often do without trouble in our daily life with regard to worldly matters, namely: (a) We recall something of the past, by means of our memory; (b) We make corresponding considerations by means of our intellect; (c) We take measures and make resolutions by means of our will.

Wallenstein, *Guide to a Perfect Christian Life*, p. 49.

762. *Subjects to Be Dealt with in Meditation*
The Holy Spirit says, 'In all thy works remember thy last end and thou shalt never sin'. He who often meditates on the four last things, – namely death, judgment and the eternity of hell and paradise, will not fall into sin....

If we, moreover, do not meditate especially on our obligation to love God on account of his infinite perfections and the great blessings that he has conferred upon us, and the love that he has borne us, we shall hardly detach ourselves from the love of creatures in order to fix our whole love on God....

Louis Blosius relates that our Lord revealed to several holy women – to St Gertrude, St Bridget, St Mechtilde and St Catherine of Siena – that they who meditate on his Passion are very dear to him. According to St Francis de Sales, the Passion of our Redeemer should be the ordinary subject of the meditation of every Christian.

St Alphonsus Liguori, *Great Means of Salvation and of Perfection*, pp. 267-268.

763. *Greatest Fruits of Mental Prayer*
It should be remembered that the advantage of mental prayer consists not so much in meditating as in making affections, petitions, and resolutions: these are the three principal fruits of meditation. 'The progress of a soul,' says St Teresa, 'does not consist in thinking much of God, but in loving him ardently; and this love is acquired by resolving to do a great deal for Him.' ...

The act of love, as also the act of contrition, is the golden chain that binds the soul to God. An act of perfect charity is sufficient for the remission of all our sins: 'Charity covereth a multitude of sins' (1 Pt 4:8). The Lord has declared that he cannot hate the soul that loves him: 'I love them that love Me' (Prv 8:17).

. . . The Angelic Doctor teaches that by every act of love we acquire a new degree of glory. 'Every act of charity merits eternal life.' . . .

In meditation, among the acts of love towards God, there is none more perfect than taking delight in the infinite joy of God. This is certainly the continual exercise of the blessed in heaven; so that he who often rejoices in the joy of God begins to do in this life that which he hopes to do in heaven through all eternity.

St Alphonsus Liguori, *ibid.*, pp. 276-277.

764. *Prayer and Mediitation – Two Feet for Walking to Perfection*

St Bernard, arguing that we are not to mount to perfection by flying but by walking, says that walking and mounting to perfection must be done with two feet, meditation and prayer; since meditation shows the way, and prayer carries us along it; by meditation we know the dangers that encompass us, and by prayer we escape and are delivered from them.

Rodriguez, *Practice of Perfection and Christian Virtues*, vol. 1, p. 305.

765. *Distractions and Aridities*

Let us remember that the devil labors hard to disturb us in the time of meditation in order to make us abandon it. Let him, then who omits mental prayer on account of distractions be persuaded that he gives delight to the devil. . . .

St Teresa says that 'the devil knows that he has lost the soul that perseveringly practices mental prayer.' . . . She says also: 'By aridities and temptations the Lord proves his lovers.' Though aridity should last for life, let not the soul give up prayer: the time will come when all shall be rewarded.

St Alphonsus Liguori, *Great Means of Salvation and of Perfection*, pp. 281-283.

766. *Dryness in Prayer Can Please God*

. . . Though one never feels any sap or moisture of devotion at meditation, but very much dryness, and is assailed by thoughts and temptations, and passes all the time in this way, not for that does the meditation cease to be very pleasing to God our Lord and of great merit in his august, divine presence; nay, often it is more pleasing and meritorious than if the time had passed in much devotion and consolation, because the person has suffered and borne more labor and difficulty in it for the love of God.

Rodriguez, *Practice of Perfection and Christian Virtues*, vol. 1, p. 371.

767. *Distractions During Meditation*

St Francis de Sales said that if in meditation we did nothing but drive away or seek to drive away distractions, our meditation would be of great profit.

St Alphonsus Liguori, *The Way of Salvation and of Perfection*, p. 276.

768. *Distractions in Prayer Displease God Only if Voluntary*

For the comfort of those who are troubled with these temptations [to distraction while at prayer]. St Basil observes that God is offended by these thoughts and distractions only when they are voluntary, when a man is distracted with advertence. . . .

Rodriguez, *Practice of Perfection and Christian Virtues*, vol. 1. p. 370.

769. *The Evil of Distraction*

[St Augustine says that] if I went before a judge to complain of someone who had done me wrong, and then left him in the midst of the proceedings and stayed chatting with some one of the onlookers in court, think you not that the judge would take me for an ill-mannered man and bid such an ill-bred suitor be off from his tribunal where he is sitting in judgment? But this is what they do who go to prayer to speak with God and then give way to distractions, thinking of other things quite out of place there.

Rodriguez, *ibid.*, p. 365.

770. *Presence of God – What the Practice Consists In*

Let us now come to the practice of this excellent exercise of the divine presence. This exercise consists partly in the operation of the understanding, in beholding God present; of the will, in uniting the soul to God by acts of humiliation, of adoration, of love, and the like.

St Alphonsus Liguori, *The True Spouse of Jesus Christ*, p. 500.

771. *God Cannot Help Seeing Us*

As a bird in flight is wholly surrounded by air, as an atom dancing in a sunbeam is penetrated by the light; as a fish gliding about in the depths of the ocean has the sea around it on every side: so too are we, whithersoever we may go, wheresoever we may stay, surrounded by the omnipresence of the Lord. . . . St Augustine observes, God cannot help seeing our every movement, every step we take, every action, however unimportant, that we perform – just as though, having banished the rest of the world from His mind, He were wholly absorbed in the contemplation of each one of us alone.

Scaramelli, *Directorium Asceticum*, vol. 1, p. 274.

772. *Presence of God – Benefits from This Practice*

The practice of the presence of God is justly called by spiritual writers the foundation of the spiritual life, which consists in three things: the avoidance of sin, the practice of virtue, and union with God. These three effects the presence of God produces: it preserves the soul from sin, leads it to the practice of virtue, and moves it to unite itself to God by means of holy love.

St Alphonsus Liguori, *The True Spouse of Jesus Christ*, p. 495.

773. *Imagining Christ Present Is Not Always Good*

With regard to the intellect, the presence of God may be practiced in four ways: . . . .

By imagining that our Redeemer, Jesus Christ, is present, that he is in our company, and that he sees us in whatsoever place we may be. . . . But it is necessary to remark that though this method is good, it is not the best, nor is it always profitable; first, because it is not conformable to truth, [for Christ], as God and man together, is present with us only after communion, or when we are before the Blessed Sacrament. Besides, this mode is liable to illusion. . . .

St Alphonsus, *ibid.,* pp. 500-501.

774. *On the Basis of the Omnipresence of God*

The second method, which is more secure and more excellent, is founded on the truth of faith, and consists in beholding with the eyes of faith, God present with us in every place, in considering that he encompasses us, that he sees and observes whatever we do. . . . Our God, says St Augustine, observes every action, every word, every thought of each of us, as if he forgot all his other creatures and had only to attend to us. . . . Hence, observing all we do, all we say and think, he marks and registers all, in order to demand an account on the day of accounts, and to give us then the reward or the chastisement we have deserved.

St Alphonsus, *ibid.,* pp. 501-502.

775. *By seeing Him in Creatures*

The third means of preserving the remembrance of the presence pf God is to recognize him in his creatures, which have from him their being and their power of serving us. God is in the water to wash us, in the fire to warm us, in the sun to enlighten us, in food to nourish us, in clothes to cover us, and in like manner in all other things that are created for our use. . . . St Augustine says . . . 'Learn to love your creator in creatures; and fix not your affections on what God has made, lest you should become attached to creatures and lose Him by whom you, too, have been created.'

St Alphonsus, *ibid.,* pp. 502-503.

776. *The Best Method – God's Presence in Us*
The Fourth and most perfect means of remembering the divine presence is to consider God within us. We need not ascend to heaven to find our God; let us be recollected within ourselves, and in ourselves we shall find him. To treat in prayer with God as at a distance causes great distraction. St Teresa used to say: 'I never knew how to make mental prayer as it ought to be made till God taught me this manner of praying: in this recollection within myself I have always found great profit.'

To come to what is practical: it is necessary to know that God is present in us in a manner different from that in which he is present in other creatures; in us He is present as in his own temple and His own house. 'Know you not,' says the Apostle, 'that you are the temple of God and that the spirit of God dwelleth in you? . . . If anyone love me . . . my Father will love him and we will come and we will make our abode with him' (Jn 14:23).

St Alphonsus, *ibid.*, pp. 503-504.

777. *Three Ways of Applying Our Will to the Practice*
The first method consists in frequently raising the heart to God by means of short but fervent ejaculations, or loving affections toward God present in us.

The second method of preserving the presence of God by acts of the will is to renew always in distracting employments the intention of pleasing God. . . .

The third method is, when you find yourself very much distracted during the day and the mind oppressed with business, to procure leave from the Superior to retire, at least for a little, to the choir or to the cell, in order to recollect yourself with God.

St Alphonsus, *ibid.*, pp. 508 and 510.

778. *How to Practice the Presence of God*
The very intention of pleasing God in our actions, kept up constantly or at least renewed frequently, is of itself a loving remembrance of God, and, therefore, a true and very useful act of his presence. St Basil makes this plain by the comparison of a smith or other artisan who has been charged to produce a work. . . . The workman ever bears in mind the person who has given him the order, and executes it according to the plans and directions which he has received. Thus, continues the saint, provided that in the performance of our outward actions we try to carry out the will of God, who requires us to do them, and that we have in view not our own private ends but his good pleasure alone, not only will our works be perfect, but we shall thus be able to keep God before us. . . .

Scaramelli, *Directorium Asceticum*, vol. 1, p. 282.

779. *The Presence of God – Practice Thereof*
Do everything as though you really saw His Majesty before you; by acting thus a soul gains greatly.
Maxim 21 of St Teresa of Jesus, in Peers, vol. 3, p. 257.

780. *The Presence of God – Benefits Derived from This Practice*
. . . St John Chrysostom concludes: 'If we keep ourselves always in the presence of God, the thought that he sees all our thoughts, that he hears our words and observes all our actions will preserve us from thinking any evil, from speaking any evil, and from doing any evil.'
St Alphonsus Liguori, *The True Spouse of Jesus Christ*, p. 498.

781. *The Presence of God – This Practice Enables Us to Avoid Sin*
. . . There is no more efficacious means of subduing our passions, of resisting temptations, and consequently avoiding sin, than the remembrance of God's presence. The Angelic Doctor says: 'If we always thought that God was looking at us, we would never, or scarcely ever, do what is displeasing in His eyes.' . . . And St Jerome has written that the remembrance of God's presence closes the door against all sins. 'The remembrance of God,' says the holy Doctor, 'shuts out all sins.'
St Alphonsus, *ibid.,* pp. 495-496.

782. *The Presence of God – God Working in Us*
The artist is more present to the work which engages all his powers than to that which can be executed with less effort and absorption of mind. Now, in conferring grace on a creature, God calls upon the resources not only of his omnipotence but also of his goodness. The magnitude of the effect aimed at in the sanctification of a soul demands (speaking figuratively) an 'intentness' on the part of God not required in the creation of the universe. St Augustine assures us that it is a more stupendous work to justify a sinner than to call a world into being.
Edward Leen, *The Holy Ghost*, p. 161.

783. *Presence of God Vs Presence of Christ in Communion*
In human language it is true to say that the presence of God by sanctifying grace is more permanent than the sacramental presence of Jesus through Holy Communion. This latter ceases with the disappearance of the sacramental species, but the presence of God by grace remains. This helps us realize how real is the presence of God in the sanctified soul.
Hoeger, *The Convent Mirror*, p. 13.

784. *The Presence of God – Importance of the Practice*
What thief would dare to steal, seeing the judge looking on hard by? But God is looking at us: He is our Judge.... And so St Augustine [says:] 'When I consider, O Lord, that thou beholdest me always and watchest over me night and day with as much care as if in heaven and earth thou hadst no other creatures to govern but myself alone; when I consider well that all my actions, thoughts and desires lie open clearly before Thee, I am full of fear and covered with shame.'
Rodriguez, *Practice of Perfection and Christian Virtues*, vol. 1, pp. 402-403.

785. *The Presence of God – Different Modalities*
God is present in all things by Essence, Presence and Power. He can be in a still more intimate way even in sinners, enlightening their intelligence and moving their wills by actual graces. But He 'inhabits' exclusively the souls of the just.
Edward Leen, *The Holy Ghost*, p. 185.

786. *The Presence of God – in Heaven and in Our Heart*
By reason of his immensity, our God is in every place; but there are two places above all where he has his own particular dwelling. One is in the highest heaven, where he is present by that glory which he communicates to the blessed; the other is on earth – it is within the humble soul that loves Him: 'who dwelleth with a contrite and humble spirit.'
St Alphonsus Liguori, *The Way of Salvation and of Perfection*, pp. 396-397.

PREACHING

787. *Love for Christ Needed for Good Preaching*
Justly did Father John d'Avila say to a person who asked what rule he should follow in order to preach well, that the best means of preaching well was to love Jesus Christ ardently. 'He,' says St Gregory, 'who is not on fire does not inflame.' . . . The divine love must first burn in the preacher, that he may afterwards kindle it in others. St Francis de Sales used to say that the heart speaks to the heart. . . .
St Alphonsus Liguori, *Dignity and Duties of the Priest*, p. 267.

788. *Love of God Makes Preaching Fruitful*
A single word from a priest who truly loves God will produce more fruit in others than a thousand sermons of the learned who love God but little.
St Alphonsus, *ibid.*, p. 296.

789. *How Jesus Preached*

Jesus not only proclaimed the necessity of a return to God in religion: He was himself the embodiment of religion, the very union of man and God in one Person. The simple manifestation of himself to the people was the greatest sermon ever preached. Jesus preached by what he was; he preached by the way he loved; he preached more by his Person than by his words.

O'Mahoney, *The Person of Jesus*, p. 9.

790. *Preaching – a duty of the Priest*

A zealous priest ought to be employed in preaching. . . . 'Faith cometh by hearing; and hearing by the word of Christ.' . . . Priests who feel themselves unable to preach should at least endeavor as often as possible, in their conversations with friends and relatives, to edify by words of edification, by relating examples of virtues practiced by the saints, by inculcating some maxims of eternity, by impressing on them the vanity of the world, the importance of salvation, the certainty of death, the peace enjoyed by those who are in the grace of God, and similar truths.

St Alphonsus Liguori, *Dignity and Duties of the Priest*, p. 181.

791. *The Penalty for Not Preaching*

We ought to fear that the souls of as many as have perished through a famine of the word of God due to our negligence will be required of our souls on the day of Judgment. As the Prophet says: 'I will require his blood at thy hand' (Ez. 3:18).

St Caesarius of Arles, in *The Fathers of the Church*, vol. 31, p. 17.

792. *Preaching on the End of the World and the Last Judgment*

. . . Priests of the Lord should not stop . . . preaching about the last things, namely, the end of the world and the future Judgment. By ceaselessly proclaiming the rewards of the just and the punishments of sinners, they may arouse the good to better things and recall the wicked from their sinful actions through fear of the future Judgment.

St Caesarius, *ibid.*, p. 7.

793. *Preaching Should Be Simple*

. . . All my priests of the Lord should preach to the people in simple, ordinary language which all the people can grasp, fulfilling what the Apostle says: 'I became all things to all men, that I might gain all' (1 Cor 9:22). Moreover, according to the holy and salutary advice of St Jerome: 'When a priest preaches, he ought to arouse groans of compunction rather than applause.'

St Caesarius, *ibid.*, p. 23.

794. *Saving Souls More Important than Filling Stomachs*
It is more important to refresh a mind that will live forever with the food of the word, than to satisfy with food the stomach of the body that is going to die.
St Caesarius, *ibid.*, p. 53.

PRIESTHOOD

795. *A continuation of Christ's priesthood*
The priesthood of the New Law is a continuation of the priesthood of Christ, not merely a memory of it. It is as dependent upon Christ the Priest as an echo on the voice that gave it birth; in fact, it is dependent on the priesthood of Christ as the existence of man is on the existence of God, or the miracle of a saint on the efficacy of divine power.
Farrell, *A Companion to the Summa*, vol. 4, p. 123.

796. *Christ's Death Was Necessary to Establish the Priesthood*
. . . To institute the priesthood, the death of Jesus Christ was necessary. Had he not died, where would we find the Victim that the priests of the New Law now offer? A Victim altogether holy and immaculate, capable of giving to God an honor worthy of God.
St Alphonsus Liguori, *Dignity and Duties of the Priest*, p. 26.

797. *Priesthood – Its Powers*
[The priest] is a priest by reason of the real power he has of changing bread and wine into the real Body and Blood of Christ, and of changing sinners into the members of the Mystical Body of Christ. In these actions he is not just an exhorter or a pleader. In these actions he is a living instrument in the hands of God. . . . In the Priesthood is vested the responsibility of being Father to members of the Mystical Body who now live in the society which we call the Church. To the priesthood belongs the responsibility of bringing to man this higher life of grace and nurturing it to maturity.
Fearon, *Graceful Living*, pp. 134-135.

798. *The Priest – "Creator of His Creator"*
The priest may, in a certain manner, be called the creator of his Creator, since by saying the words of consecration, he creates, as it were, Jesus in

the sacrament, by giving him a sacramental existence, and produces him as a victim to be offered to the eternal Father. As in creating the world it was sufficient for God to have said 'Let it be made,' and it was created – he spoke and they were made (Ps 32:9) – so it is sufficient for the priest to say '*Hoc est corpus meum*' and, behold, the bread is no longer bread but the body of Jesus Christ. 'The power of the priest,' says St Bernardine of Siena, 'is the power of the divine Person; for the transubstantiation of the bread requires as much power as the creation of the world.'

St Alphonsus Liguori, *Dignity and Duties of the Priest*, pp. 32-33.

799. *The Dignity of the Priest*

The dignity of the priest is so great that he even blesses Jesus Christ on the altar as a victim to be offered to the eternal Father. In the sacrifice of the Mass, writes Father Mansi, Jesus Christ is the principal offerer and victim; as minister he blesses the priest, but as victim, the priest blesses him.

St Alphonsus, *ibid.*, p. 33.

800. *The Power of Absolving Involves God's Omnipotence*

The priest holds the place of the Saviour himself, when, by saying '*Ego te absolvo*,' he absolves from sin. This great power, which Jesus Christ has received from his eternal Father, he has communicated to his priests. . . . To pardon a single sin requires all the omnipotence of God. 'O God, who chiefly manifesteth thy almighty power by pardoning and showing mercy . . . ' says holy Church in one of her prayers.

St Alphonsus, *ibid.*, pp. 34-35.

801. *Priesthood's Aim*

For this end Jesus Christ gave [the Apostles] the Holy Ghost, that they might save souls by remitting their sins. 'He breathed on them and said to them, Receive ye the Holy Ghost; whose sins you shall forgive, they are forgiven them.' Hence the theologian Habert has written that the essence of the priesthood consists in seeking ardently to procure first the glory of God, and then the salvation of souls.

St Ambrose calls the sacerdotal office 'an office that should acquire not money but souls.'

St Alphonsus, *ibid.*, pp. 45-46.

802. *In Absolving a Sinner, the Priest Performs the Office of the Holy Spirit*

According to St Ambrose, a priest, in absolving a sinner, performs the very office of the Holy Ghost in the sanctification of souls. Hence, in giving priests the power of absolving from sin, the Redeemer 'breathed on them, and said to them, Receive ye the Holy Ghost: whose sins you shall forgive, they are forgiven; and whose sins you shall retain, they are retained' (Jn 20:22).

St Alphonsus, *ibid.,* p. 36.

803. *Power over Christ's Mystical Body*

With regard to the mystical body of Christ, that is, all the faithful, the priest has the power of the keys, or the power of delivering souls from hell, of making them worthy of paradise, and of changing them from the slaves of Satan into the children of God.

St Alphonsus, *ibid.,* p. 27.

804. *Priesthood as Mediatorship Between God and Man*

God and man are like two extreme points; between them a certain intercourse and communication must be maintained, and God has selected among men a certain class of persons and has appointed them mediators between himself and men. He has made them priests and charged them with the duty of looking after his interests with men, and the interests of men with him; and in this consists the essence of our state.

St Joseph Cafasso, *The Priest, the Man of God,* p. 157.

805. *Power of Absolving Given to Priests Alone*

The power of the priest surpasses that of the Blessed Virgin Mary; for, although this divine Mother can pray for us and by her prayers obtain whatever she wishes, yet she cannot absolve a Christian from even the smallest sin. 'The Blessed Virgin was eminently more perfect than the Apostles,' says Innocent III; 'it was, however, not to her but only to the apostles, that the Lord entrusted the keys of the kingdom of heaven.'

St Alphonsus Liguori, *Dignity and Duties of the Priest*, pp. 31-32.

806. *The Dignity of the Priest Surpasses All Others*

. . . The sacerdotal dignity is the most noble of all the dignities in this world. 'Nothing,' says St Ambrose, 'is more excellent in this world.' . . . It transcends, says St Bernard, 'all the dignities of kings, of emperors and of angels.' . . . According to St Ambrose, the dignity of the priest exceeds that of kings as the value of gold surpasses that of lead. . . . The reason is, because the power of kings extends only to temporal goods and to the bodies of men, but the power of the priest extends to spiritual goods and to the human soul. Hence, says St Clement, 'as much as the soul is more noble than the body, so much is the priesthood more excellent than royalty.' . . .

St Alphonsus, *ibid.,* p. 29.

807. *Priesthood – Saints Feared to Accept Its Responsibilities*
St Cyprian said that all those that had the spirit of God were, when compelled to take the order of the priesthood, seized with fear and trembling as if they saw an enormous weight placed on their shoulders by which they were in danger of being crushed to death. . . .

St Gregory Nazianzen says: 'No one rejoices when he is ordained a priest.' In his life of St Cyprian, Paul the Deacon states that when the saint heard that his bishop intended to ordain him priest, he through humility, concealed himself. . . . It is related in the life of St Fulgentius that he too fled away and hid himself. . . . St Athanasius also, as Sozomen relates, took flight in order to escape the priesthood. St Ambrose, as he himself attests, resisted for a long time before he consented to be ordained. . . .

St Alphonsus, *ibid.,* pp. 39-40.

808. *The Difficulties and Blessings of the Priesthood*
St Augustine has said: 'There is nothing more difficult or more laborious than the office of the priesthood, but with God, there is nothing more blessed.'

Quoted by St Joseph Cafasso, in *The Priest, the Man of God*, p. 259.

809. *Priesthood – Its Dignity*
In his epistle to the Christians of Smyrna, St Ignatius, Martyr, says that the priesthood is the most sublime of all created dignities: 'The apex of dignities is the priesthood.' St Ephrem calls it an infinite dignity: 'The priesthood is an astounding miracle, great, immense and infinite.' St John Chrysostom says that though its functions are performed on earth, the priesthood should be numbered among the things of heaven. According to Cassian, the priest of God is exalted above all earthly sovereignties and above all celestial heights – he is inferior only to God. Innocent III says that the priest is placed between God and man: 'inferior to God, but superior to man.'

St Alphonsus Liguori, *Dignity and Duties of the Priest*, pp. 23-24.

810. *The Priesthood of the Laity*
All who are born again in Christ, the sign of the Cross makes kings, and the anointing of the Holy Spirit consecrates priests; so that, apart from the special service of our ministry, let all spiritual and reasoning Christians know that they are of royal birth and sharers in the priestly office. For what is so kingly as the soul that is subject to God and the ruler of its own body? And what is so priestly as to dedicate to the Lord a pure conscience and to offer him on the altar of our hearts the unstained gift of

our love? . . . By God's grace this has been given to us all.
St Leo the Great, in Toal, vol. 4, p. 457.

811. *The Basis of the Laity's Priesthood*
It is true that priests alone who participate through the Sacrament of Holy Orders . . . have the right of officially offering the Body and Blood of Jesus Christ. However, all the faithful can, in a real manner, although by a lesser title, offer the Sacred Host. By our baptism we share in some manner in Christ's priesthood, because we share in the divine being of Christ, in his qualities and his states. He is King; we are kings with him. He is Priest, we are also priests. Hear what St Peter says to the baptized: 'You are a chosen generation, a kingly Priesthood, a holy nation, a purchased people.' . . . The faithful can therefore offer the Sacred Host in union with the priest.
Marmion, *Christ, the Life of the Soul*, p. 274.

812. *The Priest – the Most August Person in the World*
The word *priest*, says Denis the Areopagite, 'connotes the most august person in the world, a person truly divine.' The great pontiff Innocent III, speaking of the priest and of the dignity to which he is raised because of his office, says that he is placed between God and man, beneath God, but above man. He cannot be called God, but neither can he be called a mere man. He is like a middle person between God and man, but nearer and more closely belonging to God than to man.
St Joseph Cafasso, *The Priest, the Man of God*, p. 22.

813. *The Priest as Ambassador for Christ*
[St Paul called Timothy] 'a man of God', and with reason, for the ambassador belongs rather to him who sends him than to those to whom he is sent. The priest is indeed ordained for men, but that does not make him one of them or cause him to belong to them. He belongs to him who sent him and is 'a man of God.'
St Joseph Cafasso, *ibid.*, p. 22.

814. *The Priest's Aim Is to Inspire All with Love for God*
Jesus Christ came into the world for no other purpose than to light up the fire of divine love. 'I am come to cast fire on the earth, and what will I but that it be kindled' (Lk 12:49). And the priest must labor during his whole life, and with his whole strength, not to acquire riches, honors and worldly goods, but to inspire all with the love of God.
St Alphonsus Liguori, *Dignity and Duties of the Priest*, p. 43.

815. *The Priest's Functions*
. . . Priests are placed in the world to make known to men God and his perfections, his justice and mercy, his commands, and to procure the respect, obedience and love that he deserves. They are appointed to seek the lost sheep and, when necessary, to give their lives for them. This is the end for which Jesus Christ came on earth, for which he has constituted priests: 'As the Father hath sent Me, I also send you'.
St Alphonsus, *ibid.,* pp. 42-43.

816. *The Grandeur and Glory of the Priest's Work*
. . . Let us . . . turn over in our mind this truly great and consoling thought: I live, I work, I labor for God, and under this aspect, I am greater, more fortunate, more blessed than any man in the world, even the inhabitants of heaven, since the blessed in heaven gain in God because they delight in him, while on earth God gains in the priest who expands and extends his honor and glory. . . .

I think that ever so many priests who are now in heaven would be ready to descend to the earth and to accept as many days as God would allow them in this vale of tears and misery in exchange for an equal number of days in heaven, just to be able to have the satisfaction of increasing even a little the glory of their Lord.
St Joseph Cafasso, *The Priest, the Man of God*, p. 261.

817. *The Power of the Priest over Christ's Real Body*
With regard to the power of priests over the real Body of Christ, it is of faith that when they pronounce the words of consecration the Incarnate Word has obliged himself to obey and come into their hands under the sacramental species. . . .

'Never', [says St Laurence Justinian,] 'did divine goodness give such power to the angels. The angels abide by the order of God, but the priests take him in their hands, distribute him to the faithful, and partake of him as food for themselves.'
St Alphonsus Liguori, *Dignity and Duties of the Priest*, pp. 26-27.

818. *The Priest Is Elected to Glory or Condemned to Hell*
St Bernard says that the priest 'holds a celestial office, that he is made an angel of the Lord and as an angel he is elected to glory or condemned to hell.'
St Alphonsus, *ibid.,* p. 68.

819. *Priests Should Be 'Angels'*
Christ said of John: 'This is he of whom it is written: behold, I send my

angel before thy face, who shall prepare the way for thee' (Mal 3:1). That which is called *angelus* in Greek, is in Latin *messenger* (*nuntius*). Fittingly, therefore is he called *angel* who is sent to announce the Heavenly Judge; so that he may be in name that which he fulfills in his office. . . .'

Would, my dear brethren, that we say not this to our own condemnation, namely: that all who are called . . . priests are also . . . angels, as the prophet testifies, saying: 'For the lips of the priest shall keep knowledge, and they shall seek the law at his mouth, because he is the angel of the Lord of hosts' (Mal 2:7).

St Gregory the Great, in Toal, vol. 1, p. 48.

820. *The Priest as Representative of God*

God, who is invisible to the human eye on earth, has willed to give the consolation of his presence in a certain manner to men in order that they may contemplate him, approach him and speak to him; and in order to accomplish this, what has he done? He has selected a man, separated him from other men, invested him with his powers and elevated him so high as to constitute him his minister and representative on earth, so that the believer who sees him could say within himself: 'Behold my God,' that is to say, 'behold a person who reminds me of God, who represents God for me, who resembles God, and in a certain manner makes me see God with my eyes.'

St Joseph Cafasso, *The Priest, the Man of God*, p. 50.

821. *The Priest in the Presence of and Representing God*

. . . This God who sees me, who is looking at me is the same God who has charged me with the office of representing him. If I speak, it is as if God speaks, if I look, it is as if God looks; if I sit or walk or amuse myself, it is as if God did these things: I am his representative, his instrument, all my acts are his rather than mine, because I do them through him on his account, and this is so in every case, even in the least of my actions. He gains from them or he loses by them.

St Joseph Cafasso, *ibid.*, p. 62.

822. *Things That Can Comfort a Priest*

There are three principal thoughts which should animate and sustain a priest in the exercise of his ministry and be a source of great comfort to him. The first is that our apostolate is not a human institution, a work of man, but a work of God, and that accordingly it will remain firm and unshakeable in the midst of all the shocks and assaults of the world. The second is that God, having called us to the apostolate, has at the same time strengthened us and furnished us with all the gifts and qualities that are necessary for us to fulfill and exercise this apostolate. The third is that God, not content with furnishing us with these lights and graces, has pledged his word and promised us very special assistance reserved for us alone.

St Joseph Cafasso, *ibid.*, pp. 251-252.

823. *Saints Feared to Accept the Priesthood*

In entering the sanctuary, even after God himself called them to it, the saints trembled. When his bishop ordered St Augustine to receive ordination, the saint through humility regarded the command as a chastisement for his sins. . . . To escape the priesthood, St Ephrem of Syria feigned madness; and St Ambrose pretended to be a man of cruel disposition.

St Alphonsus Liguori, *Dignity and Duties of the Priest*, p. 186.

824. *Priest's Life-style Should Reflect His Vocation*

. . . The Fathers of the Council of Trent . . . laid down rules for the whole body of the clergy: . . . It is most fitting that clerics called to the service of the Lord should all so arrange their life and conduct that they show nothing in their dress, their carriage, their walk and in all other things, but what is grave and moderate, and befitting their calling.' St Augustine had already recommended in almost the same terms to the clergy of his time: 'In walk, in posture, in dress and in all your movements, let there be nothing that will give offense to anyone who sees you.'

St Joseph Cafasso, *The Priest, the Man of God*, p. 60.

825. *The Duty of Pastors to Protect Their Flocks from Devils*

. . . If it does not please us that our vinedressers, in the vineyard itself or out of it, eat, drink, or sleep as much as they want, and do not guard the vineyard entrusted to them by keeping awake and do not defend it by condemning or frightening intruders, how, then, do we think we can please God if we do not strive with all solicitude, warning and rebuking, to defend the Lord's flock, the spiritual vineyard of souls, as we already said, from most wicked beasts and birds, that is, from the Devil and his angels.

St Caesarius of Arles, in *The Fathers of the Church*, vol. 31, p. 6.

826. *The Greatness of a Good Priest*

The whole world combined would not be able to estimate or recompense the work that a priest does when he prevents a sin or when he saves a soul. It is a work so great that all the Saints together could do nothing nobler or greater; this work the priest accomplishes and often obtains with a groan, with a word or a prayer.

St Joseph Cafasso, *The Priest, the Man of God*, p. 266.

827. *What It Means to Be Christ's Representative*
We know that we are truly and really the representatives, the viceregents of Jesus Christ, so that in a certain sense it can be said of every priest: 'Behold another redeemer of the world, behold another Jesus Christ'

. . . If there is a difference between us and Jesus Christ, a difference in name and person which is infinite, we should endeavor that there be no difference in the works and in the manner of performing them.

St Joseph Cafasso, *ibid.*, pp. 124-125.

828. *Holiness Demanded in the Priest*
The priest should be holy, because he holds the office of dispenser of the sacraments and also because he is a mediator between God and sinners. 'Between God and man the priest stands,' says St John Chrysostom. 'By communicating to us God's benefits, and by offering him our petitions: he reconciles the angry Lord, and wards from us the blows of justice.'

St Alphonsus Liguori, *Dignity and Duties of the Priest*, pp. 59-60.

829. *Holiness Required in a Priest*
St Thomas says that greater sanctity is required in a priest than in religious, on account of the most sublime functions of his ministry, particularly in the oblation of the sacrifice of the Mass.

St Alphonsus, *ibid.*, p. 55.

830. *Good Example Is the Priest's Most Effective Weapon Against Sin*
The destiny of the priest is to struggle against sin. . . . Among the many means which the priest has to fight this battle with success, the first and indispensible means, without which all the others avail little or even nothing, is his own blameless conduct and exemplary life. . . . Good example is everything in a priest, and a priest is everything if he has it. With it he shines, he preserves, he teaches. . . . With it he is everything because it suffices for everything.

St Joseph Cafasso, *The Priest, the Man of God*, p. 164.

831. *The Good Example of Priests Is a Form of Unending Preaching*
. . . The Fathers of the Council of Trent have said . . . : 'There is nothing which more efficaciously draws others to piety and to the assiduous worship of God than the life and example of those who have dedicated themselves to the divine ministry.' . . . This example, according to the same Council . . . '*is an unending form of preaching*.' . . . It is a continuous sermon, a manner of preaching that makes the priest all tongue from head to foot. He preaches with his eyes, with his hands, with his feet, and even with his hair, and this manner of preaching is so strong and efficacious

that it never goes without fruit, because it either gains the person who sees it or condemns him. It either spurs him on to do good or it confounds him and puts him to shame for his evil conduct.

St Joseph Cafasso, *ibid.*, pp. 56-57.

832. *Priests Must Give Good Example*

The Council of Trent ordains that they only are to be admitted to the priesthood who are 'conspicuous for piety and chasteness of morals, as that a shining example of good works and a lesson how to live may be expected from them.' . . . But observe that good example should be first expected, and afterwards salutary instructions; the Council calls good example a perpetual kind of preaching. Priests, then, should preach, first by example, and afterwards by words. 'Their life,' says St Augustine, 'must be a sermon of salvation to others.' . . . And St John Chrysostom writes: 'Good example gives forth a louder sound than trumpets . . . for people pay more attention to our deeds than to our words.' . . .

St Alphonsus Liguori, *Dignity and Duties of the Priest*, p. 238.

833. *Priests Must Be Clothed with Love for God and Man*

The priest must be clothed . . . with charity toward God and man: toward God, living in an entire union of his soul with God, and making his heart, by means of mental prayer, an altar on which the fire of divine love always burns; and toward man, fulfilling the instruction of the Apostle: 'Put ye on, therefore, as the elect of God, holy and beloved, the bowels of mercy' (Col 3:12); and endeavouring to the best of his ability to relieve all in their spiritual and temporal necessities.

St Alphonsus, *ibid.*, pp. 66-67.

834. *Priests Must Be Pure*

'Since,' says St Chrysostom, 'the priest represents Jesus Christ, he ought to have as much purity as would entitle him to stand in the midst of the angels.'

St Alphonsus, *ibid.*, p. 52.

835. *What Should a Priest's Qualification Be?*

According to St Gregory, the sermons of a priest whose life is not edifying excite contempt and produce no fruit. . . . St Thomas adds, 'For the same reason are disregarded all the spiritual functions of such a one.' . . . Speaking of the priest of God, St Gregory Nazianzen writes: 'The priest must first be cleansed before he can cleanse others; he must first himself approach God before he can lead others to him; he must first sanctify himself before he can sanctify others; he must first be himself a light before he can illumine others. . . .

St Alphonsus, *ibid.*, p. 63.

836. *Injury Suffered by God Through Bad Example of Priests*

'God', writes St Gregory, 'suffers from no one more than from priests whom he has appointed for the salvation of others, and whom he sees giving bad example.'

St Alphonsus, *ibid.*, p. 231.

837. *Malice of a Sacrilegious Mass*

'The sacrilegious priest', says St Vincent Ferrer, 'is guilty of greater impiety than if he cast the most holy Sacrament into a sink'.

[St Peter Damian says that] no one sins more greviously than the priest that offers sacrifice unworthily. . . . St Augustine teaches: 'Those that unworthily offer Jesus Christ in heaven sin more greviously than the Jews who crucified him when he was on earth. . . . St Augustine teaches that a priest that approaches the altar with a soul stained with mortal sin is far worse than a devil. . . .

St Alphonsus, *ibid.*, pp. 128-129.

838. *The Prayer of a Bad Priest*

Speaking of bad ecclesiastics, St Augustine says: 'To the Lord is more pleasing the barking of dogs than the prayer of such priests.'

St Alphonsus, *ibid.*, p. 62.

839. *Priests Who Give Scandal*

I do not think it is possible to imagine any sin or disorder more fatal than scandal in a priest, whether it be considered in relation to God or with respect to our neighbor or to the unfortunate priest who commits it. It would have been better if he had never been born, if he had never heard of the ecclesiastical state.

St Joseph Cafasso, *The Priest, the Man of God*, p. 166.

840. *Bad Priests Are Enemies of the Church and of Souls*

St Jerome said that among those that had infected the Church and perverted people, he found in history the names only of priests. And Peter de Blois says: 'On account of the negligence of priests, heresies came into existence.'

St Alphonsus Liguori, *Dignity and Duties of the Priest*, p. 150.

841. *The Tragedy of Fallen Priests*

'Great is the dignity of priests', [says St Jerome]; 'but also, when they sin, great is their ruin. Let us rejoice at having been raised so high, but let us be afraid of falling. . . . Lamenting, St Gregory cries out: 'Purified by the hands of the priest, the elect enter the heavenly country, and, alas! priests precipitate themselves into the fire of hell.'

St Alphonsus, *ibid.*, pp. 37-38.

842. *A Shame for Priests to Be Equalled in Virtue by Laymen*
'What a great shame,' repeats St Jerome, 'for a priest to allow himself to be equalled in virtue by a layman.' . . . 'And what could be more unseemly,' exclaims St Peter Damian, 'than that an ecclesiastic should not distinguish himself from a layman in his conduct? He would be like a great lord whose manners differ in no way from an unlettered peasant.'

Cafasso, *The Priest, the Man of God*, p. 30.

843. *Ruin for the Church if People Can Say: 'The Priest Is Juse Like I Am'*
Woe to the place where the people can say: the priest is just the same as I am; our chaplain, our parish priest, our confessor, our pastor is the same as the rest of us. St Jerome says that this is sufficient to ruin the Church. . . .

St Joseph Cafasso, *ibid.*, p. 31.

844. *Priests Are to Be Holy and Not Cruel*
[God says:] Even as these ministers require cleanness in the chalice in which this Sacrifice is made, even so do I require purity and cleanness of their heart and soul and mind. And I wish their body to be preserved, as the instrument of the soul, in perfect charity; and I do not wish them to feed upon and wallow in the mire of filth or to be inflated by pride, seeking great prelacies, or to be cruel to themselves or to their fellow creatures, because they cannot use cruelty to themselves without being cruel to their fellow creatures; for, if by sin they are cruel to themselves, they are cruel to the souls of their neighbors in that they do not give them an example of life, nor care to draw them out of the hands of the Devil.

Dialogue of St Catherine of Siena pp. 240-241.

845. *A Priest's Duty Is to Wage War Against Sin*
Woe to the priest who does not aim at this end [fighting sin], who does not strive toward it and labor for it! He is guilty and must answer for every sin that he could have prevented and did not try to do so: 'I will require his blood at thy hand' (Ez 3:18). . . . If instead of being dilligent and patient, he is careless and rough with the penitents, they will come more rarely, and will show no improvement. Who will answer for this consequence? Naturally, the priest. . . .

By the very fact that we have the state and character of priests, we are bound not only in charity, but by the office we hold and duty that accompanies it, to look after the interests of our God zealously, and among these duties, the greatest is to see that no one outrages or offends Him.

St Joseph Cafasso: *The Priest, the Man of God*, pp. 155-156.

846. *Priests Are Accountable for Souls Lost Through Their Negligence*

St Thomas, speaking of a simple priest, says that the priest that fails either through negligence or ignorance to assist souls, renders himself accountable for all the souls that are lost through his fault. . . . St. John Chrysostom says the same: 'If priests take care only of their own souls and neglect the souls of others, they will be condemned to hell with the damned.'

St Alphonsus Liguori, *Dignity and Duties of the Priest*, p. 164-165.

847. *Priests Are Accountable for the Souls They Have Sent to Hell*

. . . 'If,' says St Augustine, 'We shall scarcely be able to give an account of ourselves, what shall become of the priest that shall have to render an account of the souls he has sent to hell?' . . .

And St John Chrysostom says: 'If priests sin, all the people are led to sin. Hence every one must render an account of his own sins, but priests are also responsible for the sins of others.'

St Alphonsus, *ibid.,* p. 152.

848. *Priests Do Not Go to Heaven or Hell Alone*

A priest who is damned does not go to hell alone, and the priest that is saved is certainly not saved alone.

St Alphonsus, *ibid.,* p. 175.

849. *Priest Who Does not Rebuke Is Responsible for Loss of Sinner's Soul*

Your charity has frequently heard in Sacred Scripture, beloved brethren, in what danger priests are situated if they are unwilling to fulfill what the Apostle enjoins: 'Preach the word, be urgent in season, out of season; reprove, rebuke, entreat with all patience and teaching' (II Tm 4:2). So heavy a weight hangs over our necks, to whom it is said: 'If you do not dissuade the wicked from his wicked conduct, I will hold you responsible for his death' (see Ez 3, 18). For this reason it is necessary for us to rebuke, either in secret or in public, those who are careless.

St Caesarius of Arles, in *The Fathers of the Church*, vol. 47, p. 304.

PURGATORY

850. *A Soul with Venial Sin Would Want to Go to Purgatory*
[We might say] with St Catherine of Genoa, that if, to suppose the impossible, a soul could enter heaven in the state of venial sin, it would of its own accord rush thence to the cleansing flames of purgatory. To endure the holiness of God without being free of every stain would be a more horrible torture for the soul than to suffer the agony of Purgatory.

Nash, *Living Your Faith*, p. 111.

851. *Souls Go to Purgatory Willingly after Particular Judgment*
[For the soul to] appear before God in its present state [of venial sin] would mean an insult to God, who is supremely loved. . . . The exile, in consequence is accepted [by a poor soul] willingly, eagerly, in the certainty of ultimate purification and final holiness, and as the only means to purge away the stain.

They lament, but do not complain. Purgatory is the one great *mea maxima culpa*, and a loving glorification of God, who is infinitely just.

Arendzen, *Purgatory and Heaven*, p. 24.

852. *Purgatory, Though Terrible, Has Consoling Features*
I know that the torments of Purgatory are fearful. But I also know that they honor God and can do no more harm to souls, that there, one is certain of never opposing God's will; that one will never be able to find fault with his severity: that one will even love his severity; that one will patiently wait until all is fully satisfied. I have most willingly given all my satisfactions to the souls in Purgatory, and surrendered to others even all the suffrages that will be offered for me after my death, so that God will be glorified in heaven by souls which shall have merited to be raised there to a higher glory than mine.

[This act by which one resigns all one's expiatory merit is called in the Church the 'heroic act.']

Blessed Claude de la Colombière, *Faithful Servant*, p. 14.

853. *The Pains of Purgatory Far Exceed Those of Earth*
St Antonine relates that an angel proposed to a sick man the choice of remaining three days in Purgatory or of being confined for two years to his

bed by the infirmity under which he labored. The sick man chose the three days in Purgatory; but he was scarcely an hour there when he began to complain to the angel that his Purgatory, instead of continuing for three days, had lasted for several years. 'What!' replied the angel, 'your body is still warm on the bed of death and you speak of years!'

St Alphonsus Liguori, *Dignity and Duties of the Priest*, p. 365.

854. *Can the Poor Souls Help Us?*

[Unlike the Saints in heaven, the Poor Souls] do not see God face to face; they are in a state of sorrow and punishment, though it be a loving punishment and they be holy souls. [The fact that the Saints in heaven know what concerns their relatives on earth cannot be taken as proof that the Poor Souls also have such knowledge about us.] Two things, however, can be urged in its favor; the fact of occasional apparitions of the dead, betraying a knowledge of earthly affairs, and the fact that the Church allows private prayers asking the intercession of the Holy Souls for the living.

Arendzen, *Purgatory and Heaven*, pp. 43-44.

RECONCILIATION

855. *Refusal to Be Reconciled Leads to Rejection by God*

'If . . . you will not be reconciled to your brother', [God says] 'how can you seek forgiveness and pardon from me? . . . Just as you turn away your face from your brother, so shall I turn my eyes from your prayers and from your offerings.'

St Ephraem, in Toal, vol. 3, p. 233.

RECREATION

856. *Recreation in the Life of St John the Evangelist*

It is sometimes necessary for us to relax both in mind and body by some kind of recreation. As Cassian relates, when a hunter one day found St John the Evangelist holding a partridge in his hand and stroking it by way of amusement, he asked how a man like him could spend time on so common and trivial a thing. St John replied to him: 'Why don't you always carry your bow taut?' 'If it were always bent, I'm afraid it would lose its spring and be useless when I needed it', the hunter answered. To this the apostle replied: 'Don't be surprised then if I sometimes relax my close application and attention of mind a bit and enjoy a little recreation so that I may afterwards apply myself to contemplation.' It is undoubtedly a defect to be so strict, ill-bred, uncouth, and austere as neither to take any recreation ourselves nor to allow it to others.

St Francis de Sales, *Introduction to the Devout Life*, p. 170.

RELIGIOUS

857. *The Aim of Religious Life Is to Become a Saint*
A brother in religion once said to the Venerable Father John Joseph of Alcantara that he had become a religious to save his soul. The Venerable Father replied: 'My child, do not say that you left the world to secure your salvation; say rather that you entered religion to become a saint; for the object of a religious should be to love God in the highest degree'.

St Alphonsus Liguori, *The True Spouse of Jesus Christ*, pp. 65-66.

858. *The Purpose of All Convents*
All convents have this in common, that their raison d'être ultimately is to cooperate with God in the divine work of saving and sanctifying souls. If a convent were to lose sight of this, the only object for which it exists, if an individual religious were to forget this, that convent and that religious would henceforth be a dismal failure. There might still be spectacular results – 'successes' in examinations, unprecedented numbers on the rolls, stately buildings erected, high tributes to the efficiency with which this institute is run, given by those who estimate success by mere visible results. But the nun knows, or she should know, and never should she permit herself to forget, that true success is to be estimated by the depth of the interior spirit of prayer and union with Christ which actuates all these external labors.

Nash, *The Nun at Her Prie-Dieu*, pp. 10-11.

859. *Religious Owe Loyalty to God and the Rules of Their Community*
[In the quiet of meditation, the prayer] 'Thy Will be done on earth as it is in heaven . . . ' suggests many phases of concrete service in our vocation. Venial sin seems inconsistent with such a pledge of loyalty to our heavenly Father. We despise the man who is willing to give up his citizenship for the mess of pottage which communism has to offer. What are we to think

of the loyalty of a religious who is morally so weak that he dares not take a stand against fifth columnists in religious life, who break down respect for rule and customs.

Hoeger, *The Convent Mirror*, p. 76.

860. *Evangelical Counsels – Their Relation to Perfection*

To renounce all worldly possessions, to lead a life of virginity, to subject one's self to the will of another, constitute Christian perfection, and this to an exalted degree; but only as instruments which help to acquire divine charity, as any one may clearly see, if he take the trouble to consider these things one by one.

Scaramelli, *Directorium Asceticum*, vol. 1, pp. 17-18.

861. *The Holy Family – a Model for Religious*

[Speaking of recommendations made by St Francis de Sales, Dom Mackey says:] To propose the most perfect and most divine model which he could find of a life of consummate sanctity, though common in appearance, he offered the Holy Family at Nazareth for the contemplation of his daughters. It is the humility, the silence of the most Blessed Virgin, and the obedience, the equanimity of soul, the abnegation of St Joseph which he recommends to their imitation. According to him, the putative father of the Savior is the 'true religious' par excellence.

Charmot, *Ignatius Loyola and Francis de Sales*, p. 236.

862. *The Religious State as Holocaust*

. . . The religious state may be considered as a holocaust whereby a man offers himself and all his belongings entirely to God. This he does completely by the three vows, because all we hold here on earth is reducible to three heads – exterior goods of property and riches, and these we renounce and offer to God by the vow of poverty; bodily goods and pleasures, and these we renounce and offer to God by the vow of chastity; interior goods of the soul, and these we offer by the vow of obedience, whereby we renounce our will and understanding, handing them over and subjecting them to the superior in the place of God.

Rodriguez, *Practice of Perfection and Christian Virtues*, vol. 3, p. 119.

863. *Religious Life Is a Cross*

. . . The life of a good religious man is a cross, but it is a cross that conducts him to paradise.

Thomas à Kempis, *Imitation of Christ*, bk. III, chap. 57.

864. *Community Life – a Great Mortification*
'The common life is my greatest mortification.'
St John Berchmans, quoted in de la Colombière, *Faithful Servant*, p.24.

865. *Religious State Described as Martyrdom*
. . . So great and heroic is this act of dedicating and surrendering oneself entirely to God by the three vows, that the saints compare the religious state to martyrdom, and say that such is the life of a religious, and that not a short struggle like that of the martyrs, but continual and prolonged. St Bernard says: 'It does not look so horrible as the martyrdom of rack and knife, of gridiron and fire, but in point of duration it is much more irksome and painful.'
Rodriguez, *Practice of Perfection and Christian Virtues*, vol. 3, p. 127.

866. *Faithful Religious Can Equal Martyrs in Merit*
. . . I assure thee, my dearest, that those who are perfect and punctual in their religious obligations can equal and even surpass the martyrs in merit.
Blessed Virgin Mary, quoted by Mary of Agreda in *City of God: Words of Wisdom*, p. 41.

867. *Religious Superiors Not to Follow Own Will*
. . . Superiors must realize that they have been given their position, not that they may choose a road for their daughters which is to their own liking, but in order that they may guide them along the road of the Rule and Constitutions of the Order even if they have to force themselves to do so and would prefer to act otherwise.
St Teresa of Jesus, *Foundations*, in Peers, vol. 3, p. 89.

868. *Rules of Community to Be Observed for Love of Christ*
You should observe the rules, not to escape the rebukes of the Superior, nor to win the admiration of the Sisters, but through the spirit of love and to please Jesus Christ. Hence the same saint [Ignatius] has declared, that in not annexing the penalty of sin to the violation of the Rule of the Society of Jesus, his object was 'to make love take the place of fear of offending God.'
St Alphonsus Liguori, *The True Spouse of Jesus Christ*, p. 185.

869. *Disobedience of the Rules Shows Lack of Love for Christ*
He who makes no account of the Rules makes no account of the love of Jesus Christ; and experience proves that he who commits a fault against the Rule with his eyes open, and especially if this fault is repeated, soon becomes dry and cold in the love of God. . . .

To love Jesus Christ is the greatest work that we can perform on this earth; but it is a work and a gift that we cannot have of ourselves: it must come from him, and he is ready to give it to those who ask for it; so that if we are wanting in it, it is through our own fault and our own negligence that we have it not.

St Alphonsus Liguori, *Letters of St Alphonsus,* vol. 3, p. 32.

870. *Though Rules Do Not Bind under Sin, Infractions Can Be Sinful*
Supposing that the infraction takes place through some small yielding to passion, or to self-love, ever jealous of its liberty and averse to restraint and mortification (though in this case the religious is not guiltless of venial sin on account of the motives, more or less unreasonable, which impel him to violate the rule), yet if such transgressions proceed from contempt of the rule, they are greviously sinful. . . . And this, as Cajetan observes, because contempt of the Rule implies contempt of God, who has specially inspired saintly founders of religious orders to draw up such rules, and to impose them upon their communities.

Scaramelli, *Directorium Asceticum*, vol. 1, p. 48.

871. *Relaxation of Discipline in Communities to Be Opposed*
When manifest abuses and relaxations of discipline steal into a convent, it is not pride or temerity, but an act of virtue and zeal, to exclaim against them, and even to oppose the Superiors themselves should such opposition be necessary to correct the abuses.

St Alphonsus Liguori, *The True Spouse of Jesus Christ*, p. 180.

872. *Example More Effective than Sermons*
A good religious in a house does more by his good example than any number of conferences and sermons can do, for men are more apt to believe what they see with their eyes than what they hear with their ears.

Rodriguez, *Practice of Perfection and Christian Virtues*, vol. 1, p. 63.

873. *Importance of Training Given to Novices*
[The first rule for the Master of Novices in the Society of Jesus says:] 'Let the Master of Novices understand well that he has given over to his charge a thing that is of the highest importance.' And the rule gives two very solid reasons to make the Master of Novices open his eyes and understand the weightiness and importance of his charge. The first is that on this first training and formation of the novices there usually depends all their future progress. The second is that all the hope of the Society pivots on this, and on this depends the wellbeing of the order.

Rodriguez, *ibid.,* p. 122.

874. *Dress and Ornamentation of Religious*
. . . St John Chrysostom says that a religious who attends to the ornamentation of her person manifests the deformity of her soul. 'Attention to the ornaments of the body indicates internal deformity.' . . . St Jerome observes that 'The soul is defiled in proportion as the body is adorned.'. . . St Mary Magdalen de Pazzi saw many nuns in hell for violating poverty, and especially by vanity in dress.

St Alphonsus Liguori, *The True Spouse of Jesus Christ*, p. 266.

875. *The Dress of Religious – Example of Daughter of Maximilian II*
When the venerable Sister Margaret of the Cross, a daughter of Maximilian II and a barefooted Clare, appeared before her brother, the Archduke Albert, in a patched habit, he was struck with astonishment and expressed his surprise at seeing her dressed in such a manner. 'Brother', replied the good religious, 'I am more happy in these rags than all the monarchs of the earth in their purple'.

St Alphonsus, *ibid.*, p. 267.

876. *Religious Should Be Fit for Social Life – and Keep away from It*
. . . A religious should work to acquire those natural decent graces of speech, manners and carriage that will make him accessible to well-bred gentlemen. He ought to be fit to go into the best society – and then stay away from it.

Brosnahan, *Searchlighting Ourselves*, p. 117.

REPENTANCE

877. *The Effects of Repentance*
Our good God adds that if the sinner repent of the evil he has done, He is willing to forget all his sins: 'If the wicked do penance . . . living he shall live and shall not die. I will not remember all the iniquities that he hath done' (Ez 18:21).

St Alphonsus Liguori, *The Way of Salvation and of Perfection*, p. 112.

878. *Joy in Heaven over repenting Sinner*
God himself says that there is more joy in heaven over one sinner that repenteth than over ninety and nine just persons. St Gregory explains the reason of this by saying that very often sinners, when pardoned, are more

fervent in loving God, while those who have not thus fallen grow lukewarm in their security.

St Alphonsus, *ibid.*, p. 224.

879. *Repentance Involves Sorrow for and Avoidance of Sin*
St Gregory . . . says that 'to repent is neither more nor less than to grieve over the evil we have done, and not to do again the evil that we grieve over. . . . He that mourns over his sins yet continues to commit them, either knows not what repentance really is, or else acts as if he did not know'.

Scaramelli, *Directorium Asceticum*, vol. 1, p. 300.

REPUTATION

880. *Guarding Our Good Reputation Is Not Pride*
Humility agrees with the counsel of the Wise Man who warns us to 'take care of our good name', because to esteem our good name is not to esteem an excellence but only ordinary honesty and integrity of life. Humility does not forbid us to acknowledge this within ourselves or to desire a reputation for it. It is true that humility would despise a good name if charity had no need for it, but because a good name is one of the bases of human society and without it we are not only useless but harmful to the public by reason of the scandal it would provoke, charity requires and humility agrees that we should desire to have a good name and carefully preserve it.

St Francis de Sales, *Introduction to the Devout Life*, pp. 116-117.

881. *Reputation of Others to Be Protected*
When you hear anyone spoken ill of, make the accusation doubtful if you can do so justly. If you cannot, excuse the intention of the accused party. If that cannot be done, express sympathy for him, change the subject of conversation, remembering yourself and causing the rest to recall that those who do not fall into sin owe it all to God's grace. Recall the slanderer to himself in a mild way and tell of some good deed of the offended party if you know of any.

St Francis de Sales, *ibid.*, p. 168.

RESOLUTION

882. *The Need of Strong Resolution*
'Resolution, resolution', said St Teresa: 'The devil has no dread of irresolute souls'. On the contrary, he who resolves to give himself truly to God will overcome even what seemed impossible.
St Alphonsus Liguori, *The Way of Salvation and of Perfection*, p. 186.

RESURRECTION

883. *Christ's Resurrection Lays a Foundation for Ours*
'I have power,' Christ says, 'to lay down my life; and I have power to take it up again. No man taketh it away from me'. Great was this power by which he could also not die; but greater his mercy because of which he willed to die. He went toward this through mercy, which he could, because of which he willed to die. He went toward this through mercy, which he could, because of his power, not suffer; that he might lay the foundation of our resurrection; so that that mortal body which he bore for us might die, because we shall die; and rise again to immortality, that we might hope for immortality.
St Augustine in Toal, vol. 4, pp. 386-387.

884. *It Is Easy for God to raise Our Bodies from Death*
How can ashes be brought again to life; To which we briefly answer: that for God to restore what was, is far less than to create what was not. And what great wonder should it be that He renews man from the dust who created all things from nothing? It is more wondrous by far, that he should make heaven and earth from nothing that previously existed, than that he should restore man from the earth.
St Gregory the Great, in Toal, vol. II, p. 287.

885. *The Doubts of the Apostles Strengthen Our Faith*
That the Apostles were slow to believe in the Lord's Resurrection happen-

ed, not so much because of their weakness of faith, but rather, if I may say so, for the future firmness of ours. For it was because of their doubting that the fact of the Resurrection was made clear to us by many proofs; and as we read them, we must confess that nothing else than their doubt has made us so certain. Of less help to me is Mary Magdalene, who believed so readily, than Thomas, who doubted so long. For he by his doubting came to touch the scars of the wounds, and removed from our breast the wound of uncertainty.

St Gregory the Great, *ibid.*, p. 426.

886. *The Qualities of the Risen Bodies*

The resurrected bodies of men will have quality. This means that men will rise with perfect bodies, at the age of perfection – St Thomas thinks this is at the age of thirty. Quality also implies that, since the bodies of men will be immortal for all eternity, there will be no need for men to eat and drink to sustain their lives.

The bodies of the saints will also have the qualities of impassibility, subtlety, agility and clarity. After the resurrection, the glorified souls will have complete mastery over their bodies. This mastery will manifest itself in impassibility: by the power of the soul, the body will not be subject to any injury or suffering. By the power of the soul, the body will also be subtle: the body will be spiritual, that is, completely subject to the spirit of man. The risen body will also be agile: by the power of the soul, the body will be able to move from place to place almost with the speed of thought. The glorified bodies of the saints will also be gifted with clarity: the splendor of the soul enjoying the vision of God will flow over, as it were, into the body and give it the beauty of divine light.

Farrell and Healy, *My Way of Life*, p. 592.

887. *The Condition of Our Risen Bodies*

Glorified bodies shall be *impassible*. No pain or harm of any kind can approach them. Sickness and frailty, hunger and thirst, weariness or exhaustion, are things that have forever passed away. . . . The second gift is called *subtlety*. . . . We know from the Gospels that [Christ] . . . entered the upper room, the doors being closed. . . . Our body is sown in infirmity, it shall rise in power. This is summed up in the gift of *agility*. . . . At present we are cribbed, cabined and confined in the small area which we can influence by our mortal body. The time will come when the wide expanse of the universe, the remotest recesses of the starry skies, will be accessible to us with the swiftness of thought, and all God's world shall be our home. . . . At the transfiguration, Christ's face shone like the sun and His garments were as white as snow. . . .

Arendzen, *Purgatory and Heaven*, pp. 92-94.

888. *After Resurrection, Our Bodies Will Be Mature*
. . . Each one will receive again his own stature, as he had it in youth, if he died an old man, or as he was to receive it, had he died before that age. And for this reason the Apostle does not say, 'unto the measure of the stature', but 'unto the measure of the age of the fullness of Christ' (Eph 4:12) because the bodies of the dead shall rise in that age of youth and strength which, we know, Christ attained.
St Thomas Aquinas, quoting St Augustine, in Toal, vol. 4, p. 93.

889. *Condition of the Bodies of Saints after the Resurrection*
[After the resurrection] the saints will be robed in bodies so adorned with the certain and utterly inviolable gift of immortality that they will feel no need to eat, although able to do so if they choose.
St Augustine, *City of God*, bk. 13, chap. 22.

890. *After Resurrection We Will Be Able to Eat, But Need Not*
This power to eat and to drink shall remain, but not the need. This then was the reason why the Lord did this; (viz., to eat) because they were still in the flesh with whom he desired to be in harmony, to whom he also willed to show His wounds.
St Augustine, in Toal, vol. 4, p. 386.

891. *Souls in Heaven Will receive Added Bliss after Resurrection*
The just will . . . see an increase in their reward on the day of judgment inasmuch as up till then they enjoyed only the bliss of the soul. After the judgment, however, they will also enjoy bodily bliss, for the body in which they suffered grief and torments will also share in their happiness.
St Gregory the Great, in *The Fathers of the Church*, vol. 39, p. 218.

892. *Joy of the Saints Increased after Resurrection*
The happiness of the saints will be greater after the general judgment than before. It is true that the saints will have achieved the essential element of their happiness – the vision of God – before the judgment. But after the general resurrection and the last judgment, their bodies also will find the essence of human happiness. Or perhaps we should say, that after the resurrection, man – body and soul – will find his complete happiness. For then he will be happy as man, as a composite of both body and soul. His soul will be eternally happy in the vision of God, and his body will be happy in its immortality and in its union with the glorified soul.
Farrell and Healy, *My Way of Life*, p. 601.

893. *After the Resurrection, bodies will be 'spiritual'*
The bodies of the saints, then, shall rise again free from every defect, from every blemish, as from all corruption, weight and impediment. For their ease of movement shall be as complete as their happiness. Whence their bodies have been called *spiritual*, though undoubtedly they shall be bodies and not spirits. For just as now the body is called *animate*, though it is a body, and not a soul [*anima*], so then the body shall be called *spiritual*, though it shall be a body, not a spirit. . . . The Apostle . . . says: 'It is sown a natural body: it is raised as a spiritual body' (1 Cor 15:44).
St Augustine, *Enchiridion on Faith, Hope and Love*, p. 105-106.

894. *One Resurrection for Christ, Two for Us*
Adam . . . died in both body and soul; he died by sin, he died by nature. . . . The first death was of the soul; afterwards came that of the body . . . . From a single death, [Christ] rose in a single Resurrection from the dead. But we who have died a twofold death rise by a twofold resurrection. Until now we have risen by one resurrection: that is from sin. For we were buried with him in baptism, and we have risen with him through baptism. This resurrection is deliverance from our sins; the second is the resurrection of the body. He has given us the greater; we await the lesser. The first is greater than the second. For it is a greater thing to be delivered from sin than for the body to see resurrection.
St John Chrysostom, in Toal, vol. 2, p. 222.

RICHES

895. *Riches Engender Pride*
. . . Riches, more than anything else, engender pride. Of course, if the rich man is not proud, he has already scorned his riches and fixed his hopes in God. On the other hand, if he is proud, he does not possess his riches; he is possessed by them. . . . A man's regard for his riches ought to be so moderated that he will bear in mind that what he has can perish. Let him lay hold, therefore, on that which he cannot lose. . . . Let your true riches be God himself, who provides all things in abundance for our enjoyment.
St Augustine, in *The Fathers of the Church*, vol. 11, pp. 360-361.

RIDICULE

896. *Scoffing Is One of the Worst Offenses Against Charity*
To scoff at others is one of the worst states a mind can be in. God detests this vice and in past times inflicted strange punishments on it. Nothing is so opposed to charity, and much more to devotion, than to despise and condemn one's neighbor. Derision and mockery are always accompanied by scoffing, and it is therefore a very great sin. Theologians consider it one of the worst offenses against one's neighbor that a man can be guilty of. Other offenses may be committed with some esteem for the person offended, but by this he is treated with scorn and contempt.

St Francis de Sales, *Introduction to the Devout Life*, p. 160.

RIGHTEOUSNESS

897. *True and False Righteousness*
[St Gregory says:] 'True righteousness makes us have compassion on our brother, false righteousness breeds disdain and indignation.'

Rodriguez, *Practice of Perfection and of Christian Virtues*, vol. 2, p. 338.

SACRAMENTS

898. *Principal Sources of Divine Life in Us*
The sacraments are the principal sources of divine life in us. They act in our souls *ex opere operato*, as the sun produces light and heat; it is only necessary that there should be no obstacle within us to oppose their operation.

Marmion, *Christ, the Life of the Soul*, p. 230.

899. *Sacraments Are a Two-way Bridge*
. . . The sacraments are a two-way bridge. In the use of the sacraments, our worship goes to God while our sanctification comes from Him.

Farrell, *A Companion to the Summa*, vol. 4, p. 254.

900. *Christ Is the Principal Minister of Sacraments*
. . . In every sacrament the principal minister is Christ, the secondary and human minister only acts in his name. Christ still lives in his Church – he has promised to be with her all days even to the end of the world – and nowhere is his living power more evident than in the administration of the sacraments, nowhere can he be found in such an effective way as by approaching them. There he speaks to us, there he forgives us, there he strengthens us, there he sanctifies us, there he gives us the kiss of reconciliation and of friendship, there he gives us his own merits and his own power, there he gives us himself.
Boylan, *This Tremendous Lover*, pp. 128-129.

901. *Sacramental Effects Produced by Christ as God and as Man*
Christ is both God and man. He produces the interior spiritual effects of the sacraments both as God and as man. As God he has both the power and authority to produce grace in the souls of men. As man, he produces these effects meritoriously and efficiently, but instrumentally. He uses his human nature as an instrument in the production of grace. But his human nature is the chief instrument used by God to produce grace in the sacraments. By his Passion he won the grace which is given to men in the sacraments. Hence he had the power to institute the sacraments. Hence all other human ministers of grace derive their power from Him. They act in his name.
Farrell and Healy, *My Way of Life*, pp. 515-516.

902. *Causality of Sacraments Compared with the Action of a Carpenter*
The carpenter is the principal cause of the nail being driven. His hand is an instrument, but a conjoined instrument, one immediately united to the principal cause, indeed an integral part of the carpenter. The hammer is also an instrument, not conjoined but separated, put to work through the medium of the conjoined instrument, the carpenter's hand. In the sacraments, the principal cause is God. The humanity of Christ, substantially united to the Word of God, is the conjoined instrument, finite, created. The sacraments themselves, matter and words, are separated instruments wielded by the principal cause only through the medium of the conjoined instrument, the humanity of Christ, for it is by the passion of Christ that grace has been given to us and the sacraments are an application, a continuation of the work of the God-man, Christ.
Farrell, *A Companion to the Summa*, vol. 4, p. 260.

903. *Sacraments as Instruments Used by Christ to Dispense Graces*
Look at an artist in his studio; with his chisel he hews and sculptures the

marble in order to realize the ideal that haunts his genius. When the masterpiece is finished, it is exact to say that the artist created it but the chisel was the instrument that transmitted the artist's idea. The work is due to the chisel, but it was guided by the master's hand, itself directed by the genius which conceived the work.

So it is with the sacraments: they are signs that produce grace, not as the principal cause – it is from Christ alone that sanctifying grace glows as from one source – but as instruments, in virtue of the power they receive from the humanity of Christ united to the Word and filled with divine life. In the person of the priest, it is Christ himself who baptizes; who absolves. 'Peter baptizes,' says St Augustine, 'it is Christ who baptizes; Judas baptizes, it is Christ who does so.'

Marmion, *The Structure of God's Plan*, p. 99.

904. *Sacraments Bring Grace and Participation in God's Life*
The sacraments are a means instituted by God to incorporate man into the Mystical Body of Christ and elevate him to the supernatural plane, to allow him to participate in the life of God, knowing and loving God as God knows and loves himself. That participation in the divine life is, radically, habitual and sanctifying grace, which inheres in the essence of the soul and does for a man supernaturally what conception and birth do for him naturally. It gives him life. . . . It is God himself who is the principal cause of grace in a man's soul; it is he who possesses divine life essentially and from him it must be shared. The words and matter of the sacraments are the instruments of the divine Workman, especially selected by him for effects that only he can produce.

Farrell, *A Companion to the Summa*, vol. 4, pp. 258-259.

905. *Why Sensible Signs Are Used*
Just as he does for all other things, so also for man, God provides according to his condition. Now, man's condition is such that he is brought to grasp the spiritual and intelligible through the senses. Therefore, spiritual remedies had to be given man under sensible signs.

Mennessier, *Pattern for a Christian, According to St Thomas Aquinas*, p. 154.

BAPTISM

906. *Roots of the Vine*
[The Sacraments] are the roots of the vine of which we are to be the branches. This is so true of the Sacrament of Baptism that St Thomas can write: 'Baptism incorporates us into the Passion and Death of Christ . . .

whence it follows that the Passion of Christ is communicated to each baptized person as a remedy, *just as if each one had himself suffered and died*. . . . For the Passion of Christ is sufficient satisfaction for all the sins of all men.' And again: 'Inasmuch as he becomes a member of Christ, the baptized person shares in the penal value of Christ's Passion, as though he had himself endured the penalty.'. . . And more generally, he states: 'Since Christ's Passion preceded our sins as a kind of universal cause of the remission of sins, it needs to be applied to each one for the cleansing of his personal sins. Now this is done by Baptism and Penance and the other Sacraments which derive their power from the Passion of Christ.'

Boylan, *This Tremendous Lover*, p. 129.

907. *Baptism of Desire and of Blood*
. . . Neither baptism of blood nor baptism of desire is the sacrament of baptism. Hence, they do not imprint on the soul the baptismal Character which enables a man to participate in the priesthood of Christ.

Farrell and Healy, *My Way of Life*, p. 524.

908. *Baptism Needed for Us to Know Self, God, Neighbor*
Man must be born to live and grow to manhood; he must be born again, enter into another life and reach another manhood if he is to have full understanding of his fellowmen, his own life, and his God.

Farrell, *A Companion to the Summa*, vol. 4, p. 293.

CONFIRMATION

909. *Confirmation – Our Pentecost*
Confirmation is our Pentecost. Just as Pentecost made all the difference in the world in the Apostles' morale, so too this sacrament should make us strong and contageous like them, once they had received the fullness of the Spirit.

Fearon, *Graceful Living*, p. 52.

910. *Character of Confirmation Gives Us Right to Needed Graces*
The confirmational character gives us a right to the graces that a strong and perfect Christian needs, the graces that a soldier of Christ requires in the battle of life. . . .

The grace comes, not right in Church while the bishop is consigning us with the sign of the Cross, but in the marketplace years later, or wherever a man fights the good fight as a soldier of Jesus Christ.

Fearon, *ibid.*, pp. 69 and 71.

911. *Significance of the Chrism*
The grace of confirmation is aptly symbolized in the matter and form of the sacrament. The person to be confirmed is anointed on the forehead with chrism. Chrism is a mixture of olive oil and balsam. Oil is a familiar symbol of strength and fullness. It signifies the spiritual fullness of grace that comes in confirmation. Balsam is a fragrant substance. Its fragrance is intended to show that the interior grace of the man confirmed must make itself known in the world by the odor of good works and constancy in the faith. While the man being confirmed is anointed with chrism, the bishop says: 'I sign thee with the sign of the Cross, I confirm thee with the chrism of salvation, in the name of the Father and of the Son and of the Holy Ghost, Amen.' In this formula the Church expresses the cause of the grace of confirmation, the Trinity; the strength given by the sacrament is expressed in the word 'confirm'.

Farrell and Healy, *My Way of Life*, pp. 527-528.

912. *Why the Forehead Is Anointed*
St Thomas Aquinas noted that speech is meaningless unless it proceeds from the mind, and to indicate that the confession of faith should be both free and intelligent, the forehead is anointed instead of the tongue. . . . That makes the forehead the ideal spot for consigning with the sign of the Cross.

Not only are the face and forehead the most prominent portion of a man, but it is in the face especially that fear and shame become evident. Fear makes the face turn white and shame makes it turn red. It is fear and shame that interfere with the public profession of the faith. Confirmation strengthens us against these things.

Fearon, *Graceful Living*, pp. 62-63.

THE EUCHARIST

913. *The nature and Purpose of the Eucharist*
Perhaps the best plan is to quote the Council of Trent as follows: 'Our Savior, when about to depart out of this world to the Father, instituted this Sacrament, in which he poured forth, as it were, the riches of his divine love toward men, making a remembrance of his wonderful works; and he commanded us in the participation thereof to venerate his memory and to show forth his death until he comes to judge the world. And he willed also that this Sacrament should be received as the spiritual food of souls, whereby may be fed and strengthened those who live with his life, who said: 'He that eateth me, the same shall live by me,' and as an antidote whereby we might be freed from daily faults and be preserved from

mortal sins. He willed, furthermore, that it should be a pledge of our glory to come, and of everlasting happiness, and thus be a symbol of that one body, whereof he is the head, and to which he would fain have us as members be united by the closest bonds of faith, hope and charity,' that we might all speak the same things, and there might be no schisms among us.'

Boylan, *This Tremendous Lover*, pp. 142-143.

914. *Effects in Those Who receive Holy Communion*
The Council of Florence says . . . all the effects which bodily nourishment works in bodies, this divine food works spiritually in souls. . . . As bodily nourishment sustains the life of the body and renews its strength, and at a certain age makes it grow, so too this Most Holy Sacrament sustains the spiritual life, restores the powers of the soul, repairs the feebleness of virtue, fortifies the man against temptations of the enemy and makes him grow to his due perfection.

Rodriguez, *Practice of Perfection and Christian Virtues*, vol. 2, p. 567.

915. *Why Christ Established the Eucharist*
. . . On the last night of his life, realizing that the long-desired hour of his death for the love of man had come, our Redeemer did not have the heart to leave us alone in this valley of tears. He did not want to be separated from us even in death, and so he decided to leave us himself as food in the sacrament of the altar. He wanted us to understand by this that, having given us this infinite gift, there was nothing left he could give us to prove his love.

St Alphonsus Liguori, *The Passion of Jesus Christ*, p. 25.

916. *Christ Is in the Eucharist as Our Sympathetic Friend*
Wherever is the white Host, there is present our Lord in all his reality, with the same understanding, the same affection, the same divine power and the same profound sympathy with everything human as he had during those days on earth. . . . For he is there in our tabernacles, not solely as an object of our worship, but as the intensely human Friend that looks forward to our visits and awaits our communications. He is always ready to receive us, with an infinite sympathy and tenderness; we can pour all our confidence into his Sacred Heart and entrust all our anxieties to Him.

Edward Leen: *In the Likeness of Christ*, p. 258.

917. *The Eucharist Is Christ's Pledge of love for Each Individual*
'No tongue, ' says St Peter of Alcantara in his meditations, 'is able to ex-

press the love which Jesus has for every soul. And so that souls could not forget him after his departure from this world, he left to his spouse this most holy Sacrament, in which he himself remained, wishing that between them there should be no other pledge than Himself to keep alive the remembrance of Him.' We can imagine then how pleasing it is to our Lord that we remember his Passion, since he has instituted this Sacrament of the altar for this very purpose, that we preserve a continual remembrance of the immense love he has shown us in his death.

St Alphonsus Liguori, *The Passion of Jesus Christ*, pp. 94-95.

918. *Eucharist Bestows Sanctifying Grace*

Manifold are the graces received through the Sacrament of the Body and Blood of Christ. It gives a rich communication of the life of God, called habitual and sanctifying grace. This bestows on the soul the power to exercise a vital energy which is a participation of that which distinguishes the inner life of the Blessed Trinity.

Edward Leen, *The True Vine and Its Branches*, p. 103.

919. *Eucharist as Strength for Soul and Body*

. . . Oue may ask, why do we need to possess Jesus Christ in our bodies? Say, rather, why must we possess his Body in truth and in substance? Why do we need the flesh of this sacrifice? . . . If it is true that the flesh combats the spirit, we may well ask: Who can better mollify this struggle than Jesus Christ, through the agency of His own body? If there is a mortal combat between the desires of the flesh and those of the spirit, who can better show us how to weaken the power of the flesh and place our mortal members under the yoke of the spirit than Jesus?

Bossuet, in *Selections from Meditations on the Gospel*, vol. 2, p. 59.

920. *Eucharist Helps All to Lead a Christ-like Life*

From the Eucharist the child derives the grace to play his role with the graciousness of the Child of Nazareth. From it the adult draws the strength to reproduce the fortitude that marked the career of the Divine Master. The Sacrament enables the ruler to govern with the prudence, justice and mercy of the King of men. It enables the worker to toil with the dignity and nobility that distinguished the Carpenter of Nazareth. The Holy Eucharist, if its effects are not impeded, aids each one, in every sphere of life, every condition, every age, every rank and every occupation, to express a life that is truly Christian.

Edward Leen, *The True Vine and Its Branches*, p. 102.

921. *Eucharist Gives Us a Right to Actual Graces*

In addition to sanctifying grace, the Blessed Sacrament gives a soul a right to those actual graces it needs in order to produce acts that Jesus can claim as his own. . . . By it the intelligence is illuminated so as to be able to see clearly what line of action to adopt when a decision is to be taken. . . . Then the will is, by divine impulse, stirred to adopt the particular course which has been shown to be good. . . . The actual graces to which the Blessed Sacrament entitles the soul serve in this manner, to strengthen and to develop in the Christian the participated divine life of the Word. Every action done in and through grace is to this inner life as dry wood heaped on a fire.

Edward Leen, *ibid.*, pp. 103-104.

922. *Eucharist Demands Love for God and Neighbor*

Since the Eucharist is the Sacrament of Charity, we should excite ourselves to a great love of him who gives himself to us. And since this love would be false, did we not include in it those who are his members, those who partake with us of the same spiritual food, those who receive the same supernatural life as ourselves, we must bring to the holy Table a spirit of forbearance and love, free from all feelings of jealousy, envy or dislike of our fellow Christians.

Edward Leen, *In the Likeness of Christ*, p. 256.

923. *Eucharist Welds the Faithful into Union of Charity*

The Eucharist, to the extent that its action is not impeded, welds the faithful into the union of charity. . . . A firm grasp of this doctrine by an intelligence enlightened by a living faith is sufficient to transform man's life. It makes reasonable and recommendable the duty of fraternal charity. It is not easy to love the average man in all the unpleasing asperities of his ways and character, unless he is regarded in the light of faith. The difficult exterior is recognized as the commonplace human veil that contains and hides the Christ. It is not the harsh and unpleasant human exterior that we are asked to love, but that divine thing which it contains actually, or potentially. My fellow creature can have a character and temperament entirely opposed to mine. He may be psychologically antipathetic to me. But he is a creature not only of flesh and blood born to the will of man, but one that is, like myself, born of God, called to share in the same divine life, and destined for the same beatitude. He is, in the supernatural sphere, a member of that body of which I myself also am a member. It is utterly unnatural to hate one's own flesh. Besides, one cannot have a true supernatural love of God and not love one's neighbor. On the other hand, one cannot be reassured as to the reality of one's own love for God if a true charity is not extended to the neighbor in spite of incompatibility of temperament, character, education and the rest.

James Leen, *By Jacob's Well*, pp. 235-236.

924. *Eucharist as Defense Against Temptations and Devils*
St Thomas says that one of the reasons why this most holy Sacrament defends and delivers us from temptations and falls is because it is a memorial of the Passion of Christ. Now it was by the Passion of Christ that the devils were overcome; so when they see in us the Body and Blood of Christ, they take to flight, while the holy Angels accompany and aid us.
Rodriguez, *Practice of Perfection and Christian Virtues*, vol. 2, p. 569.

925. *God's Humility in the Eucharist*
... St Thomas, speaking of [the] most holy Sacrament, says that God has so humbled himself with us that it is as if He were our servant and each of us his God: 'As though he were their servant, and each of them were God's God.'
St Alphonsus Liguori, *The Way of Salvation and of Perfection*, pp. 320-321.

926. *Emperor Maximilian Is Saved on a Mountain*
Maximilian I, Emperor of Austria, having ascended the steep mountain in the neighborhood of Innsbruck to so great a height that he could neither venture to descend again, nor could anyone come to his aid, cried to the people below to bring the Blessed Sacrament as near to him as possible in order (as in his great peril he was unable to receive it) that he might at least honor it as well as he could by adoring it and recommending himself to Jesus Christ from the rock above. Accordingly, the Blessed Sacrament is carried thither; the Emperor adores it with most profound respect and great devotion, and implores Jesus Christ to help him. What happens? No sooner had the Emperor commenced to pray to Jesus in the Blessed Sacrament, than he saw a beautiful youth behind him, probably his Guardian Angel, who led him safely down among the most frightfully steep rocks, by a path hitherto unperceived, and when the Emperor was about to reward him, he suddenly disappeared.
Müller, *Blessed Eucharist, Our Greatest Treasure,* pp. 90-91.

927. *Rudolph of Hapsburg Lends His Horse to a Priest*
Rudolph, Count of Hapsburg, while hunting one day, observed a priest carrying the Viaticum to the sick, whereupon he immediately alighted and insisted on the priest mounting in his place. The offer was accepted. The priest, having gone through his sacred and pastoral duty, returned the animal with many marks of gratitude. But this noble and Christian Count could not be prevailed upon to accept it. 'No,' said he, 'Keep it, for I am not worthy to ride upon a horse which has borne my Lord.'
Müller, *ibid.,* pp. 52-53.

928. *King Philip II Accompanies Eucharist on Sick Call*
[On one occasion,] while the Blessed Sacrament was being carried a great distance to a sick person, Philip II (King of Spain) accompanied it all the way on foot. The priest, observing this, asked him if he were tired. 'Tired?' replied he, 'Behold my servants wait upon me both by day and by night, and never have I heard one of them complain of being tired. Shall I, then, complain of fatigue, when I am waiting upon my Lord and my God, whom I can never sufficiently serve and honor!'

Müller, *ibid.*, p. 52.

MASS

929. *Greatest and Holiest Act*
'It must be confessed,' says the Council of Trent, 'that man can perform no action more holy than the celebration of the Mass.'

. . . God himself could not enable man to perform a more sublime or sacred action than the celebration of Mass.

St Alphonsus Liguori, *Dignity and Duties of the Priest*, pp. 58 and 122.

930. *Christ Performed No Greater Action than the Mass*
The priest who has not a just idea of the Mass shall never offer that holy Sacrifice as he ought. Jesus Christ performed no action on earth greater than the celebration of Mass. In a word, of all actions that can be performed, the Mass is the most holy and dear to God; as well on account of the oblation presented to God, that is, Jesus Christ, a victim of infinite dignity, as on account of the first offerer, Jesus Christ, who offers Himself on the altar by the hand of the priest. 'The same now offering,' says the Council of Trent, 'by the ministry of priests, who then offered himself on the Cross.'

St Alphonsus, *ibid.*, p. 209.

931. *The Nature and Effects of the Mass*
The Council of Trent teaches that . . . forasmuch as in this divine sacrifice which is celebrated in the Mass, the same Christ, who once offered himself in a bloody manner on the altar of the Cross, is contained and immolated in an unbloody manner, the Holy Synod teaches that this Sacrifice (of the Mass) is truly propitiatory, and that by means thereof this is effected that we obtain mercy and find grace in seasonable aid if we draw near

to God contrite and penitent, with a sincere heart and upright faith, with fear and reverence. For the Lord, appeased by the oblation thereof (of the Mass) granting grace and the gift of penitence, forgives even heinous crimes and sins. For the Victim is one and the same, and the one who now offers by the ministry of the priests is the very same one who then offered himself on the Cross, the manner alone of the offering being different. The fruits of that oblation – namely that bloody one – are received most plentifully by this unbloody one.

Boylan, *This Tremendous Lover*, pp. 158-159.

932. *The Significance of the Mass*

In the Mass the minister represents not only Christ, but also the whole Mystical Body and each one of us, its members. Through the priest we offer to God the Victim, in praise and propitiation for the needs of the whole Chruch. As on the Cross, Christ offered himself as the Head of the whole human race, so in the Mass he offers himself not only as Head of the Church but in himself he encloses each of its members, for he encloses us all – even the weakest of us – most lovingly in his heart.

In the Mass, then, each of us can say: Christ is offering himself as a perfect Sacrifice to God; I, too, am offering him; he is offering me in himself; *am I also offering myself with Him?*

Boylan, *ibid.*, p. 162.

933. *What Christ Gives Us in the Mass*

Christ offers us with himself in the Mass in a complete surrender of devotion to God the Father, and then in the Communion of the same Mass, he gives himself in complete surrender to us, so that we may be able to live the Mass, and carry out what we have promised. In the Mass he puts the fruit of his whole life at our disposal; his adoration and thanksgiving, his praise and satisfaction, his atonement and impetration, are all ours without limit, so that we may walk with him before God and be perfect. The more we give ourselves to him in the Mass, the more he gives himself to us in Holy Communion.

Boylan, *ibid.*, p. 312.

934. *Benefits Conferred in the Mass*

St Bonaventure says that in each Mass God bestows on the world a benefit not inferior to that which he conferred in his incarnation. . . . This is conformable to the celebrated words of St Augustine: 'O venerable dignity of the priests, in whose hands, as in the womb of the Virgin, the Son of God became incarnate!'. . . Moreover, St Thomas teaches that since the Sacrifice of the altar is nothing else than the application and renewal of the sacrifice of the cross, a single Mass brings to men the same benefits and salvation that were produced by the sacrifice of the cross. . . . St John Chrysostom says: 'the celebration of a Mass has the same value as the death of Christ on the cross.'

St Alphonsus Liguori, *Dignity and Duties of the Priest*, pp. 210-211.

935. *Mass as Sacrifice and Sacrament*

Sacrifice is the channel of the creature's approach to God. The Sacrament is the Creator's way of approach to man. The one naturally calls for the other. Sacrifice would be inconclusive were it not followed by sacrament. Man's attempt to establish union with the divine would be pathetic and ineffectual as the helpless groping of an infant, did not God stoop and take his creature to himself.

Edward Leen, *The True Vine and Its Branches*, p. 79.

936. *The Value of the Mass as Sacrifice*

The entire Church cannot give to God as much honor, nor obtain so many graces, as a single priest by celebrating a single Mass; for the greatest honor that the whole Church without priest could give to God would consist in offering to Him in sacrifice the lives of all men. But of what value are the lives of all men compared with the sacrifice of Jesus Christ, which is a sacrifice of infinite value?

St Alphonsus Liguori, *Dignity and Duties of the Priest*, p. 25.

937. *Mass to Be Permanent in the Church*

[The Council of Trent says (Sess. 22)] that Christ, the Redeemer of the world, coming to be sacrificed and die on the Cross to redeem us, would not have his sacrifice end there, being as he was 'a priest forever' (Heb 5:5, 10), but would have his Church possess it, and the sacrifice to be permanent.

Rodriguez, *Practice of Perfection and of Christian Virtues*, vol. 2, p. 591.

938. *Mass as Sacrifice*

. . . We can say that the Catholic who assists at Mass is as near to the sacrifice of our Lord on the Cross, in all that concerns its supernatural essentials, as were those who stood at the foot of the Cross, for the Mass [as St Thomas says] is the 'perfect sacrament of the Passion.'

Boylan, *This Tremendous Lover*, pp. 24-25.

939. *The Four Ends of the Mass*

It is . . . necessary to know that the sacrifice of the Mass has been instituded for four ends: (a) to honor God; (b) to satisfy for our sins; (c) to

thank God for his benefits; (d) to obtain divine grace.
St Alphonsus Liguori, *The True Spouse of Jesus Christ*, p. 702.

940. *The Mass Gives God Greater Glory than All the Angels and Saints*
All the honors that the angels by their homages, and men by their virtues, penances, and martyrdoms, and other holy works, have ever given to God could not give Him as much glory as a single Mass. For all the honors of creatures are finite honors, but the honor given to God in the sacrifice of the altar, because it proceeds from a divine Person, is an infinite honor.
St Alphonsus Liguori, *Dignity and Duties of the Priest*, p. 209.

941. *Mass Gives the Greatest Honor to God*
. . . By the celebration of a single Mass, in which he offers Jesus Christ in sacrifice, a priest gives greater honor to the Lord than if all men by dying for God offered him the sacrifice of their lives. By a single Mass, he gives greater honor to God than all the angels and saints, along with the Blessed Virgin Mary, have given or shall give him; for their worship cannot be of infinite value like that which the priest celebrating on the altar offers to God.
St. Alphonsus, *ibid.,* p. 25.

942. *The Mass Gives More Honor to God than Could All Saints and Angels Together*
. . . Father Paul Segneri says well in his *Homo Christianus* . . . : 'If, on the one hand, the Blessed Mother of God and all the saints and angels of heaven were to prostrate themselves before God in the deepest humility and reverence, and on the other hand, the humblest priest on earth were to offer but one Mass, the offering of the priest would give more honor to God than the united adoration of all those angels and saints.'
Müller, *Blessed Sacrament, Our Greatest Treasure,* pp. 288-289.

943. *The Mass Is an Act of Thanksgiving And Petition*
. . . In the holy Mass, the priest offers to God an adequate thanksgiving for all the graces bestowed even on the Blessed in Paradise; but such a thanksgiving all the saints together are incapable of offering to him. Hence it is, that on this account also the priestly dignity is superior even to all celestial dignities. Besides, the priest, says St John Chrysostom, is an ambassador of the whole world, to intercede with God and to obtain graces for all creatures.
St Alphonsus Liguori, *Dignity and Duties of the Priest*, p. 25.

944. *The Mass Enables Us to Obtain Graces*

During the Mass, we can obtain all the graces that we desire for ourselves and for others. We are unworthy of receiving any grace from God, but Jesus Christ has given us the means of obtaining all graces if, while we offer him to God in the Mass, we ask them of the eternal Father in his name, for then Jesus himself unites with us in prayer.

St Alphonsus Liguori, *The True Spouse of Jesus Christ*, p. 703.

945. *Expiatory Value of the Mass*

Whatever be our offenses and ingratitude, one Mass gives more glory to God than all the wrongs, so to speak, take from him.

Marmion, *Christ, the Life of the Soul*, p. 270.

946. *The Mass Gives Complete Satisfaction for All Sin*

By the oblation of Jesus Christ in the Mass, we offer to God a complete satisfaction for all the sins of men, especially for the sins of those that are present at Mass; to whom is applied the same divine Blood by which the human race was redeemed on Calvary. Thus, by each Mass, more satisfaction is made to God than by any other expiatory work. But although the Mass is of infinite value, God accepts it only in a finite manner, according to the dispositions of those that are present at the holy Sacrifice, and therefore it is useful to hear several Masses.

St Alphonsus Liguori, *The True Spouse of Jesus Christ*, pp. 702-703.

947. *God Is the Principal Agent in the Mass*

If thou hadst the purity of an angel and the sanctity of St John the Baptist, thou wouldst not be worthy to receive or handle the Sacrament. For this is not due to any merits of men, that a man should consecrate and handle the Sacrament of Christ, and receive for his food the bread of angels. Great is this mystery, and great the dignity of priests, to whom that is given which is not given to angels. For priests alone, rightly ordained in the Church, have power to celebrate and to consecrate the Body of Christ.

The priest, indeed, is the minister of God, using the word of God, and by the command and institution of God; but God himself is there, the principal author and invisible worker, to whom is subject all that he wills, and to whose command everything is obedient.

Thomas à Kempis, *Imitation of Christ*, bk. IV, chap. 5.

948. *Effects of the Mass*

When a priest celebrates [Mass], he honors God, he rejoices the angels, he edifies the Church, he helps the living, he obtains rest for the dead and

makes himself partaker of all that is good.
Thomas à Kempis, *ibid.*

949. *Results of Not Saying Mass*
Attend to the words of Venerable Bede: 'A priest who without an important reason omits to say Mass robs the Blessed Trinity of glory, the angels of joy, sinners of pardon, the just of divine assistance, the souls in Purgatory of refreshment, the Church of a benefit, and himself of a medicine.'
St Alphonsus Liguori, *Dignity and Duties of the Priest*, p. 228.

950. *The Priest Should Sacrifice Self First*
St Ambrose says that to offer sacrifice worthily, the priest ought first to sacrifice himself by the oblation of his whole being to God.
St Alphonsus, *ibid.*, p. 50.

951. *How We Should Say Mass*
We need to sacrifice ourselves to God in a sincere immolation of the heart whenever we offer Mass, because we who celebrate the mysteries of the Lord's Passion ought to imitate what we are enacting. The Sacrifice will truly be offered to God for us when we present ourselves as the victim.
St Gregory the Great, in *The Fathers of the Church*, vol. 39, p. 273.

952. *How We Should Say Mass*
The Mass is without doubt the most excellent and most holy ceremony, the most acceptable to God, and most beneficial to us. While Mass is being celebrated, the angels assist with attention and reverence, in deep silence and with great wonder and veneration. What purity, attention, devotion and reverence the priest who celebrates it must have! He must approach the holy altar as Jesus Christ, assist at it as an angel, perform his ministry there as a saint, offer the prayers of the people as a pontiff, intercede for peace between God and the world as a mediator, and pray for himself as any other man.
St Laurence Justinian, in *Spiritual Diary*, pp. 169-170.

953. *The Mass and Our Victimhood*
The Mass is the implicit protestation on the part of the Christian of his resolve to tend toward adopting the most characteristic disposition of the soul of Christ. This disposition is one of uncalculating submission to the will of God. Such a protestation implies the resolve to renounce all that is in opposition to the divine will. . . .

St Gregory writes: 'We must, when we offer the sacrifice, immolate ourselves to God by contrition of heart, because in celebrating the Lord's

Passion we ought to imitate what we do, Then truly shall there be a victim.' . . . Victimhood and the abnegation of self in the interests of God are one and the same thing.

Edward Leen, *The True Vine and Its Branches*, pp. 73-74.

954. *How to Offer Ourselves as Victims with Christ*

Christ 'is the High Priest, but likewise the Victim, and the desire of his Sacred Heart is that we too should share in this state of victimhood. It is above all by this that our souls will be transformed and become holy. . . .

At the moment of the Offertory, the priest pours a little water into the chalice already containing the wine. . . . The wine represents Christ, the water represents the people, as was said by St John in the Apocalypse and was confirmed by the Council of Trent: *Aquae populi sunt*. . . .

We must be united to Christ in his immolation and offer ourselves with him; then he takes us with him, he immolates us with him, he bears us before his Father, *in odorem suavitatis*.

Marmion, *Christ, the Life Of the Soul*, pp. 275-276.

955. *How to Offer Ourselves as Victims with Christ*

How are we to unite ourselves to Christ Jesus in this character of victim? By yielding ourselves, like him, to the entire accomplishment of the divine good pleasure.

It is for God to fully dispose of the victim offered to him; we must be in this essential attitude of giving all to God, of making our acts of self-renunciation, of accepting the sufferings and trials of each day for love of him. . . .

Marmion, *ibid.*, p. 227.

956. *We Form One Victim with Christ*

The Mass is our sacrifice united with that of Christ. It is our gesture of submission to God expressed in and through him. It is the outward sign of our readiness to face suffering in fulfillment of the will of God. In the sacrifice of the altar we are at one with Christ in this. We form one victim with him. All this was projected by Jesus when he instituted the Eucharist as at once a sacrifice and a Communion. It is a mistake to regard one of these aspects of the Eucharist as independent of the other. Communion is the normal complement of sacrifice, for it works towards unifying mystically the Head and members of the Mystical Body. The Eucharist in this unifying process calls forth in our souls the sentiments and dispositions of Jesus as victim. The faithful, then at Mass do not assist simply as interested spectators at something being done in their presence. They tend, in a greater or lesser degree, to associate themselves with the Savior in his great saving act.

James Leen, *By Jacob's Well*, pp. 164-165.

957. *The Faithful Unite Selves to Christ as Priest and as Victim*
. . . At Mass the faithful are united to Christ in two ways. In union with the priest they offer up the sacrifice, uniting themselves to Christ as Priest. Besides, they themselves are offered up with the matter of the Sacrifice as they unite themselves to Christ the Victim.

Goichon, *Contemplative Life in the World*, p. 165.

958. *The Mass as Sacrifice*
Sharing in the priesthood of Christ, the faithful necessarily are united with him in his Victimhood. Being co-offerers, they are co-offered. . . . [St Augustine says:] 'The whole society of the redeemed is a universal sacrifice offered to God by the Great High Priest, who offered himself in the Passion on our behalf. He offered this sacrifice to make us one with his humanity. It is his humanity that he offered to God. It is as Man that he makes the offering. For it is as man that he is the Mediator, Priest and Victim. Because of this the Apostle exhorts us to make of our bodies a living sacrifice holy, pleasing to God. . . . That is the sacrifice of the Christian Church. That is the mystery that is perpetually enacted on the altar. The faithful are taught that in making the oblation, it is themselves that they sacrifice to God. For all together form one body in the Church.'

Edward Leen, *The True Vine and Its Branches*, p. 70.

959. *Mass Offered by Priest and Bystanders for Selves and Others*
It is . . . a very consoling fact that the priest, when he says Mass, offers the sacrifice for himself and others, and at the same time all who are there hearing it offer along with him this sacrifice for themselves and others. . . . The priest alone, who is chosen by God for that purpose, can consecrate and do what is done in the Mass, but all the rest who serve or assist at it likewise offer this sacrifice. And so the priest says in the Mass: 'Pray, brethren, to God that my sacrifice and yours may be acceptable to Almighty God.' And in the Canon he says: 'For whom we offer to thee, or who themselves offer.'

Rodriguez, *Practice of Perfection and Christian Virtues*, vol. 2, pp. 594-595.

960. *Hearing Mass is to Offer to Share Christ's Cross*
To offer sacrifice – and that is what hearing Mass means – is to offer to share the Cross of Christ, to consent to endure what must be, in adhering

to God's will, to be victim with the Savior, to make reparation for our sins, even to volunteer to expiate the sins of others.
James Leen, *By Jacob's Well,* p. 164.

961. *Mass Attendance Leads to Oneness with Christ*
On the Cross, the Great High Priest was alone in his grand gesture of submission: at the altar, the faithful are drawn into this sublime act and profess their acquiescence in it. The participation of the faithful in the Holy Sacrifice implies their 'oneness' with Christ in that interior oblation made on the Cross and perpetually reenacted at the altar. This 'oneness' is aptly typified by the bread and wine, the remote materials of the oblation. The host is formed of many grains of wheat ground into one substance. So too Christ, his ministers and the faithful are kneaded together in *one thing*, the Mystical Body.
Edward Leen, *The True Vine and Its Branches*, p. 68.

962. *The Mass Is a Picture of the Christian Life*
The Mass is the perfect picture of the Christian Life. We offer ourselves to God and he gives us Christ. The more sincerely we offer ourselves and the more faithfully we carry out the promise contained in that offering by doing the will of God – the more closely shall we be united to Christ and, losing our old selves, the more wonderfully shall we find new selves in him.
Boylan, *This Tremendous Lover*, p. 194.

963. *Symbolism of Water Poured into Chalice at Offertory*
We should, with all our trials and efforts in the service of God, place ourselves in the chalice, as the drop of water is mingled with the wine at the offertory. This gesture of our soul will intimate our desire that our humble acts of expiation and sacrifice should be associated with the sacrifice of the Savior, and that our oblation and His should form a unity.
James Leen, *By Jacob's Well*, p. 166.

964. *'Lift Up Your Hearts'*
After ['The Lord be with you'], you heard ['Lift up your hearts']. The whole life of true Christians is an uplifting of the heart. Of course, it is not the whole life of those who are Christians in name only, but it is the whole life of those who are Christians in reality and truth. What does an uplifted heart mean? It means trust in God, not in yourself. You are from beneath, but God is from above. If you rely on yourself, your heart is not lifted up, it is directed downwards. Accordingly, when you hear ['Lift up your hearts'] said by the priest, you give the response, ['We lift them up

to the Lord']. Strive to make this response correspond with the truth, because your response is recorded at God's tribunal. Let your heart be as you say it is. Let not your conscience deny what your tongue affirms. But this uplifting of the heart is a gift from God, not a natural endowment of your own. Therefore, when you respond that you have your hearts lifted up to God, the priest immediately says, ['Let us give thanks to the Lord our God']. Why should we give thanks? Because we have our hearts lifted up, for, if God had not lifted them up, we would be groveling on the earth.

St Augustine, in *The Fathers of the Church*, vol. 11, p. 324.

965. *Why We Say 'Forgive Us Our Trespasses'*

Why is this prayer [the Our Father] recited before receiving the Body and Blood of Christ? It is recited because of human frailty. If, perchance, our mind has conceived any thought that is not proper, if our tongue has spoken any words that were indecent, if our eye has gazed on any object that was immodest, if our ear has been rather pleased to listen to something unbecoming – if, through human frailty, we have contracted any such stains from the world's temptation, they are wiped out by the recitation of the Lord's Prayer when we say: 'Forgive us our trespasses.'

St Augustine, *ibid.*, p. 325.

966. *Mass Is Offered to God Alone*

The Council of Trent observes that, though the Church is accustomed to say Mass in reverence and memory of the saints, yet this Sacrifice of the Mass is not offered to the saints.

Rodriguez, *Practice of Perfection and Christian Virtues*, vol. 2, p. 593.

967. *How St Francis de Sales Prepared to Say Mass*

At the time of his ordination to the priesthood, St Francis de Sales took the resolution of making every action of the day a preparation for the Eucharistic Sacrifice of the morrow, so as to be able to reply truly if any one asked him the reason for his conduct: 'I am preparing myself to celebrate Mass.'

Marmion, *Christ, the Life of the Soul*, p. 294.

968. *St Louis, King, Attended Several Masses Daily*

St Louis, King of France, used to hear two Masses every day; sometimes even three or four. Some of his courtiers murmured at this, but the King gave them a sharp reprimand, saying: 'If I were to ask you to play, or to go hunting with me three or four times a day, you would find no time too long, and now you feel weary of staying in the Church during one or two

Masses for the honor of Our Lord and Savior.'

Müller, *Blessed Sacrament, Our Greatest Treasures,* p. 307-308.

969. *Origin of the Gregorian Mass*

[Gregory the Great says that about three years before he wrote the 'Dialogues' a monk named Justus was on his deathbed. Noted for his medical skill, he had treated Gregory himself during his many illnesses. Knowing he was about to die, he told his brother, Copiosus, who was still practicing medicine in Rome, that he had hidden three gold pieces for his own use. . . . Gregory ordered the Prior, Pretiosus, to forbid any monk to visit the sick man and also ordered that Justus be buried 'in a grave dug in a manure pile. And as you throw the gold pieces into the grave after him, have all the monks say together, 'Take your money with you to perdition.' Of these two commands, one was meant to benefit the dying man, the other to instruct the living. . . . Thirty days later, Gregory the Great felt strong compassion and gave orders that Mass should be offered for Justus every day for thirty days. On the day when the thirtieth Mass was said, Justus appeared to his brother, Copiosus, and said: 'Up to this moment I was in misery, but now I am well because this morning I was admitted to communion.' [After comparing the dates of the Masses and the apparition of Justus to Copiosus, the monks] were convinced that Justus was then freed from punishment through the Sacrifice of the Mass.

St Gregory the Great, in *The Fathers of the Church*, vol. 39, pp. 267-270.

970. *Communion – Christ's Desire to Come to Each of Us*

Jesus Christ . . . is not satisfied with the visits and reverence which we pay to him. He wishes especially that we should receive him in Holy Communion; this is his chief object in remaining among us under the sacramental species. Now, if you ask why it is that Jesus Christ wishes us to receive him, I answer, it is because he so ardently desires to be united to us. Yes, strange as it may seem, our Lord's Heart yearns to be united to us.

Müller, *Blessed Sacrament, Our Greatest Treasure,* p. 97.

971. *Why Christ Wants to Come to Each of Us*

What . . . is it that induces him to come to us? It is love, pure undeserved love. He comes to apply to our souls the fruits of his Redemption, which he accomplished on Calvary; for, in this Sacrament, he becomes, to each one of us, a Savior in a special sense. He comes to accomplish the work for which he created us, to prepare us for the place in heaven which he has destined for us. It is he that works in this Sacrament, not we. He created us; he redeemed us; now he comes to pour out upon us all the riches of his love; he comes to give us light to know, and strength to do his will. He comes to repair what is decayed, and to restore what was wasted; to forgive rebellion and unthankfulness; in a word, to receive us as children....

Müller, *ibid.,* p. 122.

972. *Christ Does Not Want to Stay in the Ciborium*
It is not to remain in a golden ciborium that Christ comes down from heaven each day, but to seek another Heaven – the Heaven of our souls wherein he takes such delight.

St Thérèse of Lisieux, *Autobiography and Letters,* p. 92.

973. *Communion Is The Greatest Proof of God's Love for Us*
. . . In order to unite himself more closely to us, Jesus has left himself, after his Death, upon our altars, where he makes himself one with us, that we might understand how burning is the love wherewith he loves us. 'He hath mingled himself with us,' exclaims St John Chrysostom, 'that we may be one and the same thing; for this is the desire of those who ardently love.'. . . And St Francis de Sales, speaking of the Holy Communion, adds: 'There is no action in which we can think of our Savior as more tender or more loving than this, in which he, as it were, annihilates himself and reduces himself to food, in order to unite himself to the hearts of his faithful.'

St Alphonsus Liguori, *The Way of Salvation and of Perfection,* pp. 336-337.

974. *Communion – a Challenge to Us to Love Christ*
'O man', says St John Chrysostom, 'why are you stingy and so reserved in your love of that God who has given himself so selflessly to you?' The Angelic Doctor [St Thomas] is our authority that this is precisely what Jesus has done in the Sacrament of the Altar: 'In the Eucharist, God has given us everything that he is and everything that he has.' And St Bonaventure adds that the immense God whom the world cannot contain becomes our prisoner and our captive when we receive him into our hearts in Holy Communion.

St Alphonsus Liguori, *The Passion of Jesus Christ,* p. 30.

975. *Reception of Holy Communion Is Best Way to Please God*
A soul can do nothing that is more pleasing to God than to communicate in a state of grace. The reason for this is, that love tends to perfect union with the object loved; as, then, Jesus Christ loves a soul that is in grace with an immense love; he ardently desires to unite himself to it. This is what Holy Communion does; by it Jesus Christ is wholly united to the

soul. 'He that eats My flesh dwells in Me and I in him'. (Jn. 6-57).
St Alphonsus Liguori, *Great Means of Salvation and of Perfection*, p.361.

976. *Trinity Present and Active in Us in Holy Communion*
The presence of the triune God in our soul begins the very moment we acquire sanctifying grace. But Communion is the most effectual means of intensifying this supernatural indwelling of the Blessed Trinity. Each time we receive Holy Communion, the presence of the three divine Persons within our hearts is being wonderfully confirmed and augmented. This intimate presence of the Trinity is not limited, like the physical presence of the Sacred Humanity, to the physical presence of the eucharistic species. . . . Thus our soul becomes a haven, a permanent dwelling, a sacred temple of the Blessed Trinity and our earthly existence becomes a prelude to eternal bliss. . . .

The Mystery of the Trinity is realized in the active love which the three Persons exercise in our souls; in other words, we are being loved distinctly by each of them, yet with a single love. This love is single because the three divine Persons, in all their outward acts, act as one.
Gabriel, *Ascetical Conferences*, pp. 23-24.

977. *Inner Life of the Trinity Realized in Us in Holy Communion*
The Father eternally expresses an intellectual Word, absolutely equal to himself, so that he completely manifests himself by this substantial and living Word. On seeing the Word, the perfect image of himself, the Father embraces it with an infinite love, and the Word also returns an infinite love, in all respects equal to that of the Father, a living, subsistent love, which is the Holy Ghost. . . . Now this sublime mystery is brought to us in Holy Communion. Though, as St Thomas teaches, 'by sanctifying grace the entire Trinity is the guest of our souls,' yet this is eminently true at the moment we receive Communion because then Jesus comes to us as the bread of life, expressly to bestow upon us that life which he derives from his eternal Father. . . . The soul of every communicant in the right disposition becomes, as it were, the heaven of the Blessed Trinity. At the moment of Communion, the Father utters his Word, engenders His Son, and in so doing gives him to me. Descending within my soul, the Father and the Son exchange their mutual love and breathe forth the divine Spirit.

In this way, Holy Communion associates us with the inner life of the Blessed Trinity. By the Communication of this life we share in the marvelous interchange of love of the three divine Persons. Jesus permits us to penetrate into his Sacred Heart, aflame with love for God. . . . The Father in turn includes us in his infinite love for his only begotten son. . . . Led to the Father by Jesus and to Jesus by the Father, we are immersed as it were, in the Holy Spirit, the eternal love that unites the Father and the Son.

Gabriel, *ibid.*, pp. 19-20.

978. *By Communion We Become Tabernacles of Father, Son & Holy Ghost*

Since the Incarnate Word is inseparable from the other two Persons (they all have the one and the same divine nature), and since the second Person becomes united to us at Holy Communion in a new, more intimate and physical manner, the other two Persons also come to dwell in us in a special way. In Holy Communion, we become tabernacles of the God-Man, and through him, of the Father and of the Holy Ghost. We become temples where angels adore and where we anticipate the joys of Paradise.

Bandas, *The Catholic Layman and Holiness*, p. 32.

979. *Sacrifice and Communion Lead to Deification*

Sacrifice prepares for Communion. All the elements that compose the whole supernatural system converge towards these two – Sacrifice and Communion. They are the synthesis of the operations on the part of God and of man by which the deification of the soul is accomplished.

James Leen, *By Jacob's Well*, p. 141.

980. *One Communion Can Make a Saint*

Truly, indeed, can one Communion make a Saint. There is nothing in our self or in our past that one Communion cannot more than repair – if we have but enough faith. Listen to St Thomas: 'This Sacrament contains in itself Christ crucified. Whence, whatever is the effect of the Passion of our Lord all that is likewise the effect of this Sacrament. . . . ' That is why we made bold to say above that even a lifetime of sins should not discourage us. Because whatever our sins may have done to *us*, the Holy Communion can repair; and whatever our sins have done to *God*, the Mass – which is part of the Eucharist – can restore.

Boylan, *This Tremendous Lover*, p. 148.

981. *Graces Produced in Us by Holy Communion*

Holy Communion unites us most intimately with Jesus Christ, the Source of all grace; the particular effects are:

(1) It increases the supernatural life of our soul.
(2) It cleanses us from venial sins and preserves us from mortal sin.
(3) It weakens our evil inclinations and gives us both the desire and the power to do good.
(4) It is a pledge of our glorious resurrection and everlasting happiness.

Wallenstein, *Guide to Perfect Christian Living*, p. 22.

982. *Grace of Immense Value Added to Communicant*
The soul . . . receives an immense increase of sanctifying grace at each Communion. . . . St Thomas tells us that the lowest degree of sanctifying grace is worth more than all the riches of the world.
Müller, *Blessed Sacrament, Our Greatest Treasure,* p. 149.

983. *Increase of Charity, Infused Virtues, Gifts of the Holy Ghost*
Through Eucharistic Communion, the increase of charity brings with it a proportionate increase in all infused virtues and the seven gifts of the Holy Spirit, as inseparable accompaniments.
Garrigou-Lagrange, *Theological Virtues*, vol. 1, p. 34.

984. *A Means to Union with the Divinity*
The presence of the Sacred Host in our bodies is only a means to something much greater, namely the union of our soul with the Divinity of Christ – the incorporation of our whole being into the Mystical Body in which we are united to him in a new way, as to our head.
Boylan, *This Tremendous Lover*, p. 145.

985. *Purpose and Function of Eucharist*
. . . St Thomas says . . . that the other sacraments have been instituted by Jesus Christ to prepare men either to receive or to administer the Blessed Eucharist, which, according to the holy Doctor, is the consummation of the spiritual life; because from this sacrament is derived all the perfection of the soul. For all perfection consists in a union with God; and of all the means of uniting the soul to him there is none better than Holy Communion, by which, as Jesus Christ himself has said, the soul becomes as it were one thing with him. 'He that eateth My flesh . . . abideth in me and I in him' (Jn 6:57).
St Alphonsus Liguori, *The True Spouse of Jesus Christ*, p. 564.

986. *A Gift to and for Each One of Us*
The Apostle says that with Jesus Christ we have been enriched with every good gift and every grace if we ask it through his merits. . . .

And this gift which God has made us of his Son is a gift to each one of us; for he hath given him entirely to each of us, as if he had given him to each one alone, so that every one of us may say: Jesus is all mine; his Body is mine; his Blood is mine; his life is mine; his sorrows, his death, his merits are all mine.
St Alphonsus Liguori, *Incarnation, Birth and Infancy of Jesus Christ*, p. 178.

987. *We Should Give Ourselves to Him*
The Son of God . . . gives himself to us as food in this most holy Sacrament, his whole self, his Body, Blood, soul and divinity; it will be only reasonable that we should offer and deliver ourselves over wholly and entirely to him.
Rodriguez, *Practice of Perfection and of Christian Virtues*, vol. 2, p.576.

988. *Gift of Self Pleases Christ Most*
. . . You say: 'What have I to offer (to Christ)?' . . . I will tell you. Imitate Aeschines, a disciple of Socrates, of whom Seneca relates that not being able, on account of his poverty, to make such rich presents to his master as his fellow disciples did, he went out and said to him: 'Master, my extreme poverty leaves me nothing to give you as a token of my gratitude, I offer you, then, myself to be yours forever.' 'Truly,' said Socrates, 'you have given me more than all the rest.' Act thus with Jesus Christ; you have no occasion to die for him; you cannot do for him what He has done for you, but you can give him that which he values more than anything else – your heart.

There is nothing that gives so much pleasure to Jesus Christ as a heart truly resolved to serve him. . . . Offer yourself to him to be disposed of as he pleases.
Müller, *Blessed Sacrament, Our Greatest Treasure*, pp. 133-134.

989. *Communion to be Received in a Spirit of Sacrifice*
Union with [Christ] by means of the Eucharist demands on our part a oneness with him in this spirit of sacrifice. The love which binds us to him must be a love modeled on that which in him found expression at the Last Supper. It must be a love which is prepared to deliver itself, to devote itself, to recoil before no sacrifice.
James Leen, *By Jacob's Well*, p. 161.

990. *Communion Makes Us Participators in the Mass*
The Mass does not exist to give us Communion; on the contrary, Holy Communion exists to make us participators in the Mass.
Boylan, *This Tremendous Lover*, p. 163.

991. *Dispositions Required for Communion*
Just as corporal food only produces its full effects when properly digested, so the Eucharistic food may be frustrated from producing the fullness of its effects by lack of the proper dispositions in the soul of the recipient. Faith, hope, charity, humility and submission to the will of God are the

fundamental dispositions required.
Boylan, *ibid.*, p. 150.

992. *Communion an Antidote to Temptation*
The Eucharist is an antidote to temptaion. (a) It is an antidote to the attacks of the devil. The Eucharist is a renewal of Christ's Passion and death, by which Satan was overcome. It contains the Blood of Christ, by which we are made terrible to the evil one. (b) In Holy Communion we are sanctified by the contact with the most sacred Body and Blood of Christ and strengthened against making our bodies or our powers the instruments of sin. (c) Our tongues are consecrated by the Body and Blood of Christ and fortified against being made the vehicles of sin. (d) In Holy Communion Christ's soul unites to our soul. His imagination and memory unite to our imagination and memory in order to discipline and sanctify them. His intelligence enlightens our mind and turns it from worldly and transitory things to the things of God. His holy will strengthens our inconstant and weak will. His Heart, aglow with love of God and souls, enkindles our heart, so cold towards God and yet so tender towards creatures.
Bandas, *The Catholic Layman and Holiness*, p. 34.

993. *Communion Helps Us Fight Off Impurity*
A special fruit of Holy Communion is the aid it gives in fighting off temptations of impurity. Holy Communion is indeed 'the bread of the elect, and the wine springing forth virgins' (Zec 9:17). Blessed Don Bosco made splendid men of some 200,000 boys, of whom 6,000 became zealous priests. He used to say: 'I know only two educational instruments – Holy Communion and the rod, and I have given up the rod and use only Holy Communion.'
Kirsch, *Sex Education and Training in Chastity*, p. 370.

994. *Communion – a Remedy for Sin*
. . . The Council of Trent calls Holy Communion a remedy which relieves us from venial and preserves us from mortal sins: 'An antidote by which we are freed from daily faults, and are preserved from mortal sins.
St Alphonsus Liguori, *Incarnation, Birth and Infancy of Jesus Christ*, p. 79.

995. *Communion Remits Venial Sin*
The Roman Catechism teaches that venial sins are remitted by Holy Communion; and the generality of divines agrees with St Thomas, that the Holy Eucharist excites in the soul acts of divine love by which venial sins

are pardoned.
St Alphonsus Liguori, *The True Spouse of Jesus Christ*, p. 582-583.

996. *Effects of Frequent Holy Communion – St Thomas Aquinas*
Enumerating the effects of frequent Holy Communion, St Thomas says that this Sacrament is given under the form of food and drink, whence it produces in the soul the same effects as meat and drink produce in our bodies; and as by our food the life of the body is sustained, increased, and made glad, and the wasting effects of all that tends to destroy it are repaired, so, too, does the Holy Eucharist work the same results in the spiritual life of the soul. . . . Hence, according to the Angelic Doctor, this divine Sacrament produces within us these four salutary effects: it supports the life of the soul lest it fail; it fortifies it against whatever might prove hurtful and tend to its destruction; it brings to it growth and increase; it causes pleasure.
Scaramelli, *Directorium Asceticum*, vol. 1, p. 371.

997. *Preparation for Communion*
. . . A good and holy life, doing all things to the best of one's power in order to please God, must be the principal preparation for receiving Holy Communion, and also the principal fruit to be gathered from it.
Rodriguez, *Practice of Perfection and Christian Virtues*, vol. 2, p. 580.

998. *Things We Should Pray for at Communion Time*
Pray to him for humility, for patience, for meekness, for contempt of the world, for a lively faith, a firm hope, ardent charity; for brotherly love, for love of your enemies, for the prosperity of the Church, for the conversion of sinners, heretics and infidels; for the souls in Purgatory; for devotion to his Passion, to the Blessed Sacrament, to his Immaculate Mother for the crowning grace of perseverance. . . .
Müller, *Blessed Sacrament, Our Greatest Treasure,* p. 137.

999. *Negotiation with Christ after Receiving Communion*
St Teresa used to say: 'After Communion let us not lose so good an opportunity of negotiation. God does not repay with ingratitude the abode in which he is well received.'
St Alphonsus Liguori, *The True Spouse of Jesus Christ*, pp. 576-577.

1000. *Thanksgiving after Communion*
. . . Since we have neither the knowledge nor the power to render due thanks for such a high favor [as Communion], to make up our insufficiency we should offer to the Lord all the thanks and praises that have been given

and are being given him by all the seraphim and choirs of angels from the beginning of the world, and by all the blessed saints while they lived in the world, and chiefly now what they offer in the glory of heaven, and what they are to give him for all eternity. . . .

Rodriguez, *Practice of Perfection and of Christian Virtues*, vol. 2, p. 563.

1001. *Communion Brings Spiritual, Not Bodily, Immortality*
. . . Lest they should think that they who were promised eternal life through partaking of this Food and Drink, would not now, through receiving it, die in the body, he deigned to anticipate this thought. For when he had said: 'He that eateth my flesh and drinketh my Blood, hath everlasting life', He went on to say: 'And I will raise him up on the last day. . . . '

St Augustine, in Toal, vol. 3, p. 147.

1002. *Good Effects of Communion hindered by Deliberate Venial Sin*
There are two sorts of venial sins: the one committed by inadvertence, although with some carelessness and negligence; the other committed with advertence and of set purpose. Venial sins, inasmuch as for want of advertence . . . befall God-fearing persons who are diligent in his service, do not this harm; but those that are committed deliberately, on purpose and advisedly, by people slack and remiss in the service of God, do hinder in great measure the divine effects of this Most Holy Sacrament.

Rodriguez, *Practice of Perfection and of Christian Virtues*, vol. 2, p. 584.

1003. *Obstacles to Christ's Action When He Comes in Communion*
To remain attached to venial sin, to deliberate imperfections, to wilful negligences, and premeditated infidelities, all these things cannot but fail to impede our Lord's action when he comes to us. . . .

The least wilful coldness, the least resentment harbored in the soul towards our neighbor form a great obstacle to the perfection of that union which our Lord wishes to have with us in the Eucharist.

Marmion, *Christ, the Life of the Soul*, pp. 291-292.

1004. *Rancor Toward Others Frustrates Effects of Holy Communion*
The Christ that comes to us in the Eucharist is he who is Head of the Mystical Body and indissolubly united to all its members. He cannot come shorn of the members of His Mystical Body, or any of these members. Hence, he who, preserving antagonism in his heart for any one of his fellows, [hoping nevertheless] to receive Jesus with suitable dispositions, would be grievously in error.'

James Leen, *By Jacob's Well*, p. 157.

1005. *The Guilt of Sacriligious Communion*
'Whosoever shall eat this bread, or drink the chalice of the Lord unworthily, shall be guilty of the body and of the blood of the Lord' (1 Cor 11:29); that is, he shall have the same guilt, and the same punishment, as those who crucified Christ. For, as those butchers became guilty of his Blood, so likewise are they who partake unworthily of the Eucharist.
St John Chrysostom, in Toal, vol. 2, p. 143.

1006. *Priest's Duty to Prevent Sacriligious Communion*
. . . Should you [as a priest], while knowing that a man is unworthy, permit him to partake of the Sacred Table, his Blood will be required at your hands. And should he be a general of the imperial army, or a prefect, or even one whose head is encircled by the imperial diadem, and should he approach while unworthy, forbid him. Yours is a higher authority than his.
St John Chrysostom, *ibid.*, p. 144.

1007. *Devil Forced to Admit Himself Defeated by Frequent Communion*
A person whom, by special permission of God, the devil was allowed to harass very much and even drag about on the ground, was exorcised by a priest of our Congregation and the devil was commanded to say whether or not Holy Communion was very useful and profitable to the soul. At the first and second interrogatory he would not answer, but the third time, being commanded in the name of the Blessed Trinity, he replied with a howl: 'Profitable! Know that if this person had not received Communion so many times, we would have had her completely in our power.' Behold, then, our great weapon against the devil! 'Yes,' says St John Chrysostom, 'after receiving the Body and Blood of Jesus Christ in the Holy Eucharist, we become as terrible to the devil as a furious lion is to men.'
Müller, *Blessed Sacrament, Our Greatest Treasure,* p. 157.

1008. *Communion Urged by Pius XII*
Pius XII admonishes bishops in his Encyclical on the Holy Liturgy. . . . 'Arouse, Venerable Brethren, in the hearts of those committed to your care, a great and insatiable hunger for Jesus Christ. Under your guidance, let the children and youth crowd to the altar rails to offer themselves, their innocence and their works of zeal to the divine Redeemer. Let husbands and wives approach the holy table so that, nourished on this food, they may learn to make the children entrusted to them conformed to the mind and heart of Jesus Christ.

'Let workers be invited thither to partake of this sustaining and never failing nourishment that it may renew their strength and obtain for their labors an everlasting recompense in heaven; in a word, invite all men of whatever class and compel them to come in; since this is the bread of life which all require.'

Wallenstein, *Guide to Perfect Christian Living*, p. 23.

1009. *Communion as Substitute for Bodily Food for Several Saints*

St Catherine of Siena, from Ash Wednesday to Ascension Day, took no other food than Holy Communion. . . . Nicholas de la Flue . . . for fifteen successive years lived without other nourishment than the Sacred Body of the Lord.

Müller, *Blessed Sacrament, Our Greatest Treasure,* pp. 168-169.

1010. *Communion Valued by English Noblemen*

In the time of the penal laws in England, under Queen Elizabeth I, a Catholic nobleman was fined four hundred crowns for having received Holy Communion; but, regardless of the iniquitious law, he continued to communicate, cheerfully paying the fine each time he was detected, although he was thereby obliged to sell two of his best estates. He declared that he never spent any money with greater joy than that which he was obliged to pay for the privilege of receiving his Lord.

Müller, *Blessed Sacrament, Our Greatest Treasure,* pp. 109-110.

1011. *Pagan Duke Sees Child in Host*

Tilman Bredenbach tells uf a certain Duke of Saxony, named Wetterkind, that, while he was an unbeliever, was seized with a curiosity to see what went on in the Catholic realm of Charlemagne; and that to do this with more ease, he put on the habit of a pilgrim and went there. It was the time of Holy Week and Easter, when all the world went to Communion. He went about with attention, looking at everything. . . . When the priest was giving Communion to the people, he saw a very beautiful and shining infant in every host; and he said that into the mouths of some who received, the Infant went with such alacrity and pleasure and good will, that it seemed he himself were going and bestirring himself to come in; with others he seemed to come in very unwillingly and as if perforce, turning away his head and hands and kicking with his feet, as though struggling not to enter into their mouths. This miracle led to [his] conversion to Christianity [with] all his people.

Rodriguez, *Practice of Perfection and of Christian Virtues*, vol. 2, p. 586.

1012. *Spiritual Communion Sometimes More Effective than Actual Communion*

Spiritual Communion . . . as St Thomas defines it, consists in a lively desire of partaking of this most Holy Sacrament. . . . 'To eat spiritually of Jesus Christ concealed under the sacramental veils, is to believe in Christ with the earnest desire of receiving him in this Sacrament.'. . . And this is not merely a spiritual partaking of Christ, but a spiritual receiving of the Sacrament itself. When such desires are very earnest and very fervid, a Communion thus made in spirit will sometimes be more acceptable to God, and more profitable, than many sacramental communions made lukewarmly; and this not through any defect of the Sacrament itself, but on account of the want of fervor of the recipient.

Scaramelli, *Directorium Asceticum*, vol. 1, pp. 404-405.

1013. *Nature and Effects of Spiritual Communion*

[Spiritual Communion] is performed by making an act of faith in the presence of Jesus Christ in the Blessed Sacrament, and then an act of love, and an act of contrition for having offended him. The soul then invites him to come and unite himself to her and make her entirely his own; and lastly, she thanks him, as if she had really received him sacramentally.

Müller, *Blessed Sacrament, Our Greatest Treasure*, p. 215.

1014. *Spiritual Communion Recommended by Trent*

The Holy Council of Trent . . . extols the advantages of spiritual Communion and exhorts the faithful to practice it.

St Alphonsus Liguori, *The True Spouse of Jesus Christ*, p. 586.

1015. *Spiritual Communion*

That Holy Communion is the proper daily food of the soul is obvious; and those who can approach the altar daily should do so. But that is not always possible, and it is well to remember that we have the authority of St Thomas for the statement that the effects of this Sacrament can be obtained by a sincere desire; but our desire is not sincere if we do not avail of the opportunity of reception.

Boylan, *This Tremendous Lover*, p. 151.

PENANCE

1016. *It is Christ himself who Absolved*

'Can one forgive the offense committed against another? No; yet the priest says: "I absolve thee". How can he say it? Because it is Christ who says it by his mouth.'

Marmion, *Growth in Christ*, p. 91.

1017. *Jesus reassures the sinner in Sacrament of Penance*
All the gentle kindness that Jesus exercised in reassuring and restoring the bruised and guilty spirit of the woman who was a sinner in the city and the woman taken in adultery, Jesus exercises in the sacrament of penance. . . .

Just as the ear [of the priest] that listened was an agent of the heavenly Father, so too the voice that absolves is armed with the power of God. The sinner can be sure that his wickedness is taken away by the passion and death of Jesus, and not by his own efforts or by the priest's kindliness. . . . The faithful sinner can be just as certain of his forgiveness as the woman who was a sinner in the city or the woman taken in adultery. The voice falls from different lips, but the meaning and power are the same.

Fearon, *Graceful Living*, pp. 84-85.

1018. *How contrition gains by Penance*
The grace of the sacrament of penance is to destroy sin in the soul, to weaken the remnants of sin and to restore life; or if there are only venial faults, to remit them and increase grace. In this sacrament, the hatred of sin felt by Christ in his agony on the Cross . . . passes into our soul there to produce the destruction of sin. This destruction of sin effected by Christ's substitution of himself for us in the passion is reproduced in the penitent. Contrition remains what it is even outside the sacrament, i.e., an instrument of death to sin; but in the sacrament, Christ's merits give to this instrument, as it were infinite and supreme efficacy.

Marmion, *Growth in Christ*, pp. 85-86.

1019. *Kind Way Christ Gave Power to Forgive Sin*
The power to acquit sin was not given to the Apostles after they had proved themselves by heroic service of Christ. It was given them at a time when they were bowed down under a sense of their own infidelity to their Lord and Master. They had believed that Christ had failed them; now they were but too well aware that it was they who had failed Christ. . . . And it was while the sense of their own sin and failure was upon them that they were appointed by Christ to the office of taking away the sins of man. In bestowing that office, the Master never made reference to their own prevarication. There were no words of reproach nor of remonstrance. Still less were there words of anger and upbraiding. Jesus dealt with them as trustfully and lovingly as if they had been all that they should have been. . . . From all this they were to learn how they, in their turn, were to treat souls filled with shame and remorse for their faults. Gentleness, tact, sympathy and understanding were to mark all their dealings with sinners. Harshness to others would be utterly unbecoming men who themselves had been treated without harshness in spite of having greviously erred.

James Leen, *By Jacob's Well*, pp. 28-29.

1020. *Cardinal Newman Calls Confession a 'Heavenly Idea'*
[Concerning confession, Cardinal Newman says:] 'How many are the souls, in distress, anxiety or loneliness, whose one need is to find a being to whom they can pour out their feelings unheard by the world? Tell them out they must; they cannot tell them out to those they see every hour. They want to tell them and not to tell them; they want to tell them out, yet be as if they be not told; they wish to tell them to one who is strong enough to bear them, yet not too strong to despise them; they wish to tell them to one who can at once advise and can sympathize with them; they wish to relieve themselves of a load, to gain a solace, to receive assurance that there is one who thinks of them, and one to whom in thought they can recur, to whom they can betake themselves, if necessary from time to time.... If there is a heavenly idea in the Catholic Church, looking at it simply as an idea, surely, next to the Blessed Sacrament, confession is such.'

Quoted in Kirsch, *Sex Education and Training in Chastity*, pp. 374-375.

1021. *The Meaning of Penance*
... Penance is a sacrament, as baptism and the Eucharist are. To prepare for that sacrament you must know what *penance* means. It means a complete change of mind. It is completely opposed to sin. Sin is a turning of creatures from God. Penance means turning from creatures to God; a conversion from misuse of creatures to God. A change of heart is essential.

Edward Leen, *Retreat Notes for Religious*, p. 44.

1022. *What the Sacrament of Penance Entails*
It must not be thought that penance – or, as it is popularly known, confession – gives man license to commit sin at will. The sacrament of Penance demands acts of the virtue of penance. By the virtue of penance, a man detests his past sins as offenses against God. He is determined to destroy these sins as far as it is possible to do so. This does not mean that he can undo his past sinful acts. What is done cannot be undone. But he can remake his will. He can withdraw it from his sins, by renouncing them, by determining never to forsake God again through sin, and by resolving to make satisfaction to God for his sins. By his sins he sought creatures to the exclusion of God. In penance he renounces creatures for God. In this way he restores the order of justice which was destroyed by his sins. By his sins he refused God the obedience which was due to him. In penance he turns once again to God in obedience. The penitence of the sinner may begin with servile fear. The sinner is in terror of the pains of hell which await him, or he fears the loss of heaven. But then he begins to hope for pardon. This leads him to love God, who is merciful, and so to

fear God as a child fears a loving Father. This true repentance gives the sinner a habitual displeasure at his past sins. It leads him to resolve never to do anything contrary to the love of God.

Farrell and Healy, *My Way of Life*, p. 554.

1023. *Confession Most Helpful for Young and Old*

Confession is a most helpful prophylactic in that it offers to youth during the critical years of adolescence the protection of a paternal friend. It has curative power in that it wipes out past guilt and offers the incentive of starting anew on the upward path. Even naturally speaking, we must recognize that the interior acts called for in the sacrament have a purgative and curative effect upon the soul. The pedagogy of the confessional makes use, in fact, of all the means offered by Christian education. It offers effective motivation, powerful graces, and ideals that may well inspire young and old to make the greatest sacrifices. There is nothing that psychoanalysis promises that cannot be obtained to an infinitely higher degree by a proper use of this sacrament that was instituted for the healing and strengthening of the soul.

Kirsch, *Sex Education and Training in Chastity*, p. 379.

1024. *What the Devils Think about Penance*

'See that thou always approach this sacrament of confession with fervor, esteem and veneration, with a heartfelt sorrow for thy sins; for this sacrament inspires the dragon with great terror, and he exerts himself diligently to hinder souls by his deceits in order to cause them to receive this sacrament lukewarmly, out of habit, without sorrow, and without proper disposition. He is so eager in this matter not only because he wishes to cause the loss of souls, but also to avoid the fierce torments of being oppressed and confounded in his malignity by the true penance and justification of his escaped victims' (Blessed Virgin Mary to Mary of Agreda).

Mary of Agreda, *City of God: Words of Wisdom,* p. 487.

1025. *Examination of Conscience with Fear and Love of God*

St Augustine says: 'Set up a tribunal within thyself and judge the cause of the life thou hast this day led. Let thy thoughts go in search of thy sins, and let them accuse thee before God. Let thy conscience stand as witness against thee. Let the fear and love of God be thy holy executioners to slay thy sins with the sword of repentance.'

Scaramelli, *Directorium Asceticum*, vol. 1, p. 349.

1026. *Examination of Conscience with contrition*

St Augustine says, 'God loves to pardon those who confess their faults to him with lowly repentance, and forbears from judging those severely who, with a contrite heart, do judgment upon themselves.'

Scaramelli, *ibid.,*vol. 1, p. 348.

1027. *Examination of Conscience Is a Kind of Confession*

There are two kinds of confession whereby a devout person may cancel the sins which sully his conscience: the first is sacramental, and is made at the feet of a confessor; the other is wholly secret, and takes place between God and the soul; and this is called the daily examination of conscience.... In both we have to accuse ourselves of our sins: in the first, to the ears of the priest, in the second, in the presence of God. If our repentance in the solitary accusation of ourselves reach to perfect contrition, both the one and the other kind of confession avail to obtain pardon and to restore the soul to its former purity.

Scaramelli, *ibid.,* vol. 1, p. 334.

1028. *Looking for the Roots*

As a physician has effected not a little but a great deal when he has diagnosed the root of the illness, because then he will hit upon the right remedies, and the medicines will take effect; so we have achieved not a little but a great deal, if we hit upon the root of our infirmities and ailments, because that will be to hit upon the cure of them by applying the remedy and medicine of the examen. One of the reasons why many make little profit of their examen is because they do not apply it where they ought to apply it. If you cut the root of the tree and tear up the weed by the roots, all the rest will soon wither and die; but if you go for the branches and leave the root, it will soon sprout and grow again.

Rodriguez, *Practice of Perfection and Christian Virtues*, vol. 1, p.427.

1029. *Examination of Conscience, Contrition, Purpose of Amendment*

In this sentiment of compunction and repentance and in the firm purpose not to fall again, all the force and efficacy of the examen as a means of self-amendment lies; and therefore, on this most of the time should be spent.... Ask our Lord for grace to that end.... You will never amend yourself if you do not do that. These two things, grief for the past and purpose of amendment for the future, are so akin to one another that the one goes at the same rate as the other, for it is certain that where we really abhor a thing, we take care not to plunge into it.

Rodriguez, *ibid.,* pp. 449-450.

1030. *Particular Examination of Conscience*

The particular examination . . . consists in nothing else than discovering what is our predominant passion and what are the faults to which we are the most liable, and then setting to work to uproot them. . . .

Scaramelli, *Directorium Asceticum*, vol. 1, p. 355.

1031. *Particular Examination Good for Uprooting Faults*

The particular examen . . . is preeminently a reasonable and business-like manner of proceeding to uproot faults and implant virtues. It is, if you wish, a species of spiritual bookkeeping, and as such has sometimes been highly spoken of. But if the children of this world, who are wise in their generation, keep their books, why should not the children of light? The businessman who fails to keep his books or fails to balance them at stated intervals is, we are told by men conversant with mercantile affairs, a prospective bankrupt. Such men, if known, would get credit from no bank.

Brosnahan, *Searchlighting Ourselves*, p. 205.

1032. *Teaching of Pythagoras, Cicero, Senaca*

Pythagoras prescribes [the examination of one's heart] to his disciples, many of whom were in the habit of searching themselves regularly every evening. Cicero tells us of himself that always at the close of each day he called himself to account for everything that he had spoken, heard or done during the whole course of the day. . . . Seneca tells us that every night he sat thus in judgment over his own actions. 'Each night,' he writes, 'when the lamp is put out in my chamber, and my wife, aware of my custom, keeps silence, I examine the whole course of the past day. I think over all I have said and done, concealing nothing from myself, passing over nothing. If I discover anything amiss, I say to myself: "I forgive thee this time, but do so no more".'

Scaramelli, *Directorium Asceticum*, vol. 1, pp. 344-345.

1033. *Examination of Conscience by a Pagan Philosopher*

That great philosopher, Pythagoras, as St Jerome and St Thomas relate, among other instructions that he gave his disciples, gave them this main point, that every one should have two times marked out, one in the morning and one at night, at which to examine himself and take account of three things: What have I done? How Have I done it? What have I left undone of what I ought to do?

Rodriguez, *Practice of Perfection and Christian Virtues*, vol. 1, p. 422.

1034. *Plutarch's Example*

Listen to what Plutarch says of himself: 'Being a lover of meekness no less than of wisdom, I determined within myself to spend some days without yielding to anger; just as I might have bound myself to abstain from drunkenness and wine, as is the custom in certain feasts, where the use of this drink is forbidden. I next continued to exert special efforts for one or two months, and made short trials of my strength. Thus, in course of time, I came to bear with greater troubles and annoyances, being able to maintain my mastery over myself so as to remain calm, gentle, and devoid of all anger. By this means I kept myself untainted by evil words, debasing actions and the shameless lusts which, for a passing gratification, leave the soul pierced through and through with deep remorse and poignant regrets.

Scaramelli, *Directorium Asceticum*, vol. 1, pp. 356-357.

1035. *Penance*

It is to be observed that the sorrow necessary for confession, as the Council of Trent and that of Florence says, includes two things: regret and repentance for sin, and purpose not to sin any more.

Rodriguez, *Practice of Perfection and Christian Virtues,* vol. 1, p. 459.

1036. *Essential Quality of Contrition*

Contrition is sorrow for sin. Now there are two kinds of sorrow. There is the passion, or feeling of sorrow, and there is that rational detestation of sin as an offense against God, which is a deliberate choice of the will. It is this second type of sorrow that is necessary in penance. The glutton may be very sad because his overeating has given him indigestion, but this sorrow will not bring forgiveness. He is sorry for his indigestion, not for his offense against God. The contrition which brings forgiveness of sin in penance is a rational sorrow for sin because it is an offense against God. It extends to all the actual personal sins which the sinner has committed. It includes a resolve to avoid all mortal sins in the future. Contrition is based on the love of God. The sinner renounces his sins because they are offenses against God, who is all good and supremely lovable in himself.

Farrell and Healy, *My Way of Life*, pp. 556-557.

1037. *Contrition Needed, Not Emotion*

. . . So all divines and saints, dealing with contrition and sorrow for sin, advise penitents who are disconsolate because, taking into account the gravity of mortal sin, they cannot burst into tears nor feel in themselves that sensible grief that they would have wished, so that their very hearts should have broken with grief. They tell them, true contrition and sorrow for sin is not in the sensitive appetite, but in the will. Be grieved for having sinned because it is an offense against God, worthy of being loved above all things, for that is true contrition. As for that feeling, when the Lord gives it, receive it gratefully; and when he does not, be not distressed, for it is not that that God asks of us. Clearly he cannot ask you what is not in your power. Now this feeling that you would like to have is a taste of sensible devotion, which is not in our power; and thus God does not ask it of us, but only what is in our power, which is grief of the will, a thing quite independent of that feeling. And the same with acts of love for God; love God with your will above all things, for this is a strong and appreciative love, and what God asks of us; that other is a love of tenderness, which is not in our power.

Rodriguez, *Practice of Perfection and Christian Virtues*, vol. 1, p. 346.

1038. *How to Arrive at Deep Contrition*

The highest motive for purging out all affection for sin is a strong, living conviction of the great evils sins bring upon us. In this way we arrive at a deep, intense contrition.

St Francis de Sales, *Introduction to the Devout Life*, p. 43.

1039. *Contrition Needed for Sacrament of Penance*

The sorrow necessary for confession is an act of the will by which through the help of God's grace we turn away from our sins, resolving to avoid them in future, and turn toward God. The motive must be supernatural; the fear of hell, the loss of heaven, or the love of God are such motives. Since the sorrow is an act of the will, *it need not be felt*. . . . Most souls, even very holy souls, would *feel* more sorrow at some painful loss, for example, the death of a parent, than they would *feel* for their sins. That, however, does not lessen the value of their sorrow for sin in the least. Feelings have nothing to do with it; the real measure and test of the depth of sorrow is the *will* and the *decision* to avoid sin in the future. In fact, that is the real meaning of 'doing penance'; for the old word for penance meant 'change of heart.'

Boylan, *This Tremendous Lover*, p. 135.

1040. *When is Contrition Genuine?*

A reliable touchstone of good contrition is a definite and practical resolution to amend. . . . A determined resolve to shun the proximate occasion of sin is the best test of our contrition, and of our purpose of amendment. This determined resolve and purpose should be accompanied by humble distrust of our own strength and firm confidence in God's grace and his help.

Wallenstein, *Guide to Perfect Christian Living*, pp. 14-15.

1041. *Attrition Suffices for Absolution*
The merits of his Precious Blood imparted to the words of absolution have the strange power to take imperfect contrition . . . called attrition . . . and enable it to expel sin from the soul. This, without the sacrament, attrition cannot do, though contrition, which is sorrow springing from perfect charity, has this efficacy. . . . It would be, for men who have the faith, a cruel suffering to have the conscience burdened with the thought of past sin and at the same time to pass their days in uncertainty as to whether their sorrow for it had been perfect. Of course, as things are, one can never know, apart from a special revelation, whether one is worthy of love or hate. But after an earnest confession, it is legitimate to comfort oneself with the assurance that one's sins are forgiven. If the remission of sins were solely conditioned by perfect contrition, death would be attended by dreadful fears and anxiety.

James Leen, *By Jacob's Well*, p. 30.

1042. *The Devil not worried by general resolutions*
St Alphonsus Liguori has written well that the devil cares little about a vague general purpose of amendment in confession. He smiles contentedly when the penitent promises 'to do his best' or to 'change his life' or to 'make a new start.' All these formulae will probably lead nowhere because they do not face the issue in a practical way. But if the sinner promises from his heart: 'I am not going to meet that companion again. It is not in any way necessary for me to meet him or her, and I know if I do there is imminent danger of serious sin. Therefore I am not going to take that risk.'

Or: 'I will not read that kind of book again'. That is a practical resolution to refuse point blank to give the wild animal the first stimulus, and if the penitent perseveres, the rest of his troubles will gradually die a natural death. It is a resolution of this kind that makes the evil one gnash his teeth in impotent rage.

Nash, *Living Your Faith*, p. 126.

1043. *Frequent Reception of Penance Urged*
By cooperating with the grace of the sacrament [of penance], we can acquire a new horror of those sins, a new delicacy of conscience, and a more correct notion of our own weakness. To quote . . . Pius XII in his encyclical on the Mystical Body: 'For a constant and speedy advancement in the path of virtue, we highly recommend the pious practice of frequent confession . . . for by this means we grow in a true knowledge of ourselves and in Christian humility, bad habits are uprooted, spiritual negligence and apathy prevented, the conscience is purified and the will strengthened, salutary spiritual direction is obtained, and grace is increased by the effi-

cacy of the Sacrament itself.'

Boylan, *This Tremendous Lover*, p. 134.

1044. *Effects of Frequent Confession*

. . . Purity of heart . . . cannot, of course, consist in entire freedom from faults of every kind, but in carefully watching over self, in guarding against any defilement, and in frequently purifying the conscience.

Now these are precisely the two effects which frequent confession produces in the soul. . . . No detergent in the world can cleanse our soiled garments so completely as sacramental confession can purify our souls from every stain.

Scaramelli, *Directorium Asceticum*, vol. 1, p. 293.

1045. *Frequent Confession Harms the Devil*

Ceasarius . . . relates that a theologian of blameless life, being about to die, beheld the devil lurking in a corner of his room; and he addressed the fiend in the words of St Martin: 'What are you doing here, thou cruel beast?' . . . The Priest conjured the demon in the name of God, to answer him, and answer with truth what it was that injured him most. The fiend thereupon made this reply: 'There is nothing in the Church which does us so much harm, which so unnerves our power, as frequent confession.'

Scaramelli, *ibid.*, pp. 311-312.

1046. *Confession Not a Mere Narration*

Confession is not a narration; it is an accusation; one must come to it like a criminal before his judge.

Marmion, *Growth in Christ*, p. 90.

1047. *Confession Must Be Accompanied by Faith and Hope*

[Our confessions should be] made in a spirit of faith and hope: they should be accompanied with a sorrow not only humble, but full of faith and trust in God. 'Let thy confessions, ' says St Bernard, 'be faithful, that thou mayest confess in hope without any distrust of forgiveness.'. . . Without such hope we should never obtain pardon, were we to seek it for all eternity, because sorrow for sin unaccompanied by hope of forgiveness, far from appeasing, only irritates divine mercy. Cain repented . . . but said his sin is 'greater than may deserve pardon' (Gn 4:13). Judas Iscariot . . . repented and, further, made restitution. . . .

Scaramelli, *Directorium Asceticum*, vol. 1, pp. 304-305.

1048. *Why We Should Not Be Ashamed to Confess Sins*

Why should the sinner be ashamed to make known his sins, since they are already known and manifest to God, and to his angels, and even to the blessed in heaven? Confession opens the door to heaven. Confession brings hope of salvation. Because of this the Scripture says: 'First, tell thy iniquities, that you may be justified' (Is 43:26). Here we are shown that the man will not be saved who, during his life does not confess his sins. Neither will that confession deliver you which is made without true repentance. For true repentance is grief of heart and sorrow of soul because of the evils a man has committed. True repentance causes us to grieve over them with a firm intention of never committing them again.

St Ambrose in Toal, vol. 2, pp. 13-14.

1049. *Why God Wants Us to Confess and the Devil Does Not*

God wants us to confess our sins, not because he himself cannot know them, but because the devil longs to find something to charge us with before the tribunal of the eternal Judge and wants us to defend rather than acknowledge our sins. Our God, on the contrary, because he is good and merciful, wants us to confess them in this world so we will not be confounded by them later on in the world to come. If we confess our sins, he spares us; if we acknowledge them, he forgives. . . .

Now, just as the Serpent told man not to observe the command not to sin, so he now urges man not to obey the words: Confess your sin. As he made the one who was standing fall, so now he tries to prevent the one who has fallen from rising.

St Caesarius of Arles, in *The Fathers of the Church*, vol. 31, pp. 290-291.

1050. *Voluntary Satisfaction*

You resolved firmly in confession to watch one fault in particular, your harsh conversation, for instance. But you slipped up at the very next opportunity. Very well; the broken resolution is now going to be followed up by a penance. You are not going to that show tonight although you have a ticket, although you have been told it is a fine show, although you have been looking forward to it all week. Why not? Because you broke your promise about that harsh speech of yours. Or you deprive yourself of a little treat you had promised yourself, or you go without reading that interesting book – all for the same reason. Do something like that every time and your habits of venial sin will disappear like mists before the rising sun.

Nash, *Living Your Faith*, p. 115.

CONFESSORS

1051. *Hearing Confessions Is a Priest's Prime Duty*
. . . It is necessary to be persuaded that the work which is most conducive to the salvation of souls is the administration of the sacrament of penance. The Venerable Louis Fiorillo of the Order of St Dominic used to say that by preaching the priest casts out the net, by hearing confessions he draws it ashore and takes the fish.
St Alphonsus Liguori, *Dignity and Duties of the Priest*, p. 182.

1052. *By Absolution a Priest Raises the Dead to Life*
It is in those moments when he is absolving a really first-rate sinner that the priest's life seems most worthwhile to him. And the bigger the sinner, the deeper is the priest's sense of the miraculous. For he knows that at the words of absolution a human heart is raised to life again just as truly as at the command of Christ, Lazarus came back to life again. The same sense of awe that a priest has when, at the words of consecration which fall from his lips, ordinary bread and wine are changed into the Body and Blood of Christ, comes when, at the words of absolution, ordinary human sinners are changed into the Mystical Body of Christ. The miracle is much alike, and so is the sense of awe.
Fearon, *Graceful Living*, pp. 90-91.

1053. *Confessors Can Become Saints Quickly*
. . . In the administration of the holy sacrament of penance, every one of the virtues is brought into play. Thus charity may be practiced in a very high degree; sometimes by instructing, sometimes by giving counsel. . . . We may exercise our zeal for God's honor by hindering people from offending the Divine Majesty. Mortification, too, is shown, by overcoming the repugnance which a ministry of its own nature so irksome must needs inspire. Humility, again, is exercised when we see in the faults of others what we ourselves would have been were it not for the grace of God. The rude and ignorant will call out our loving kindness. In a word, a priest can become a saint by hearing confessions sooner than by any other religious exercise.
Scaramelli, *Directorium Asceticum*, vol. 1, pp. 332-333.

1054. *Qualities Needed for Hearing Confessions*
The great pontiff St Pius V said: 'Give us fit confessors and surely the whole of Christianity will be reformed.'

St Gregory said: 'The directing of souls is the art of arts.'. . . St Gregory Nazianzen writes: 'To direct men seems to me to be the greatest of sciences'. St Francis de Sales used to say that the office of confessor is of all offices the most important and the most difficult. It is the most important because on it depends the eternal salvation of souls, which is the end of all sciences. It is the most difficult, because the science of moral theology requires a knowledge of many other sciences, and embraces an immense variety of matter.

St Alphonsus Liguori, *Dignity and Duties of the Priest*, pp. 271 and 273.

1055. *God Corrects the Severity of St. Bernard*
At the beginning of his career, St Bernard was full of rigor and sharpness toward those put under his direction and would tell them they must leave the body behind and come to him in soul only. When he heard their confessions he reprimanded with extraordinary severity faults of every kind, no matter how slight, and urged on those poor apprentices to perfection in such a way that instead of pushing them on he pulled them back. They lost heart and breath at seeing themselves unrelentingly driven up so steep and high an ascent. Philothea notes that it was most ardent zeal for perfect purity that induced this great saint to adopt this method. His zeal was a great virtue but a virtue open to criticism. Hence, God himself in a holy vision corrected him and infused into his soul a spirit so meek, gentle, amiable and tender that he was completely changed by it. He not only charged himself with being too severe, but became so gracious and considerate to everyone that he became 'all things to all men' in order to save all of them.

St Francis de Sales, *Introduction to the Devout Life*, pp. 102-103.

1056. *Greatness of Victories Gained in the Sacrament of Penance*
What comparison can those gains, those acquisitions, those conquests of this earth, and even the victories of all the armies of the world bear with the successes, the victories which a priest gains on this battlefield!

St Joseph Cafasso, *The Priest, the Man of God*, p. 195.

1057. *St Chrysostom as Confessor*
St John Chrysostom, as Baronius relates, preached and insisted with people that if any of them should fall into sin, they should come and seek him out immediately, even if they had to arouse him from sleep.

St Joseph Cafasso, *ibid.*, p. 196.

MATRIMONY

1058. *Matrimony – Let Peace Be Preserved in the Family*
Let us not be one of those who are angels in public and devils at home.
St Francis de Sales, quoted in *Spiritual Diary*, p. 115.

1059. *Three Needed for a Happy Marriage*
. . . It takes three to make a happy marriage: a man, a woman and God. . . . The man and the woman are both members of Christ; to receive the grace of the sacrament, they must be living members in the state of grace. Otherwise no supernatural love between them is possible.
Boylan, *This Tremendous Lover*, pp. 280-281.

1060. *Love in Partnership with Christ needed in Marriage*
Marriage, then, implies a complete donation of one partner to the other, and a love that symbolizes the love of Christ and his Church. The very obstacles put by human nature to the fulfillment of this ideal can make marriage the foundation of an intense spiritual life. For it will soon become apparent that neither party is an angel: both are human. And the love and sacrifice demanded on both sides are so great and so costly that the questions soon arise: Is any human being worth all that? Can any human being give all that? The answer lies in the fact that it is not a mere human being that gives, nor is it a mere human being who receives. Each one loves, and sacrifices self, in partnership with Christ; each one is loved and is served, in union with Christ. . . . Beyond his wife, and in her heart, the husband loves and serves Christ.
Boylan, *ibid.*, p. 283.

1061. *Duties of a Husband to His Wife*
[If a man] is married, he is married. And he must devote himself in the first place adequately and generously to his wife and family. It is utterly wrong, for example, on the excuse of important social work, to rush out on all or many evenings of the week after the evening meal to some philanthropic work or meeting, or even to some exercise of devotion. Yet one often finds good Catholics doing that. The point is that they are giving away something that is not their own; they are stealing from their wife to

serve – as they imagine – God. God does not want such service. Far, far better for a man, and more meritorious, to spend the evening at home with his wife, or to take her to some entertainment which they can both share, and so develop and manifest his love for his wife and their community life. He will find Christ in his wife on such occasions more certainly, more fruitfully, and more intimately than he will in all his needy neighbors, or even – we would venture to say – in a visit to the Blessed Sacrament. For Christ is present and is received wherever his will is done. And his will is that they whom he has joined together should not be put asunder by any man.

Boylan, *ibid.*, pp. 286-287.

1062. *Subjection of Wife to Husband Must be Rightly Understood*

St Paul's exhortation to wives to be subject to their husbands as the Church is to Christ raises much comment. . . . As Pius XI says, this subjection merely 'forbids that in this body which is the family, the heart be separated from the head to the detriment of the whole body and the proximate danger of ruin. For if the man is the head, the woman is the heart, and as he occupies the chief place in ruling, so she may and ought to claim for herself the chief place in love' (encyclical on Marriage). The wife is not her husband's servant. They are partners. They complement and supplement one another. She has a right to her opinion and her husband ought to take cognizance of it.

Boylan, *ibid.*, pp. 289-290.

1063. *The Standard for Husband and Wife*

No lower standard can be safely set for husband and wife – for father or mother – than to be 'another Christ'. . . . In marriage, as in all else, we may set up the essential of the spiritual life and of generous acceptance of God's will. Thus we put on Christ, and he is 'all in all.'

Boylan, *ibid.*, p. 293.

SACRAMENT OF THE SICK

1064. *The Sacrament of the Sick Should Not Be Delayed*

Only when lies and syringes have failed do many Catholics think it is time to call the priest. They call the priest as a last desperate chance of curing the patient after all the doctors have failed.

Nothing could be more horribly wrong. There could be no greater perversion of charity. Human cruelty can reach no crueler depths. If you have any spark of real charity in your hearts and any love at all for those who are sick unto death, do not delay to call the priest as soon as there is danger of death in the proximate future.

Fearon, *Graceful Living*, pp. 158-159.

SACRIFICE

1065. *Sacrifice – Its Function*

By sacrifice man acknowledges God as the author of his being and as the unique source of his beatitude; that is, as his first principle and his last end.

Edward Leen, *The True Vine and Its Branches*, p. 51.

1066. *Sacrifice of Self to God*

. . . Let us offer him ourselves, which, to God is the most precious and becoming of gifts. Let us offer to his Image what is made in the image and likeness of this Image.

St John Chrysostom, in Toal, vol. 2, p. 220.

1067. *How We Can Become a Living Sacrifice*

A man is both living and a sacrifice when he has died to the desires of his body, though he has not departed from this life. It is the pleasure-loving body that leads us to sin; mortification leads us back to forgiveness.

St Gregory the Great, in Toal, vol. 2, p. 35.

1068. *Sacrifice for Sinners Urged at Fatima*

In the summer of 1916 while the children of Fatima were playing listlessly in the extreme heat, an angel appeared to them behind the Abobora home and said: 'What are you doing? Pray! Pray a great deal. The hearts of Jesus and Mary have merciful designs for you. Offer prayers and sacrifices constantly to the Most High.' 'How must we sacrifice?' asked Lucia. 'With all your power offer a sacrifice as an act of reparation for the sinners by whom He is offended, and of supplication for the conversion of sinners. Thus draw peace upon your country. I am its Guardian Angel, the Angel of Portugal. Above all, accept and endure with submission the suffering which the Lord will send you.'

Walsh, *Our Lady of Fatima*, p. 39.

1069. *Communists Get Leaders Because They Demand Huge Sacrifices*
Douglas Hyde, a noted British convert from Communism, stated that Communists get the leaders they do because 'they make big demands on members, requiring them to sacrifice their time, their money, their energy; if necessary, life itself. They prove that modern twentieth-century man is willing to make huge sacrifices. . . . We want men to sacrifice, but we are too afraid to ask much of them; so we call for mean little sacrifices and get mean little responses as a consequence.'

Shamon, *The Only Life,* p. v.

SADNESS

1070. *Best Remedy for Sadness*
Cassian says that for all sorts of sadness, by whatever way or from whatever source they come, an excellent method is to betake ourselves to prayer and think of God and the hope of everlasting life that is promised us.

Rodriguez, *Practice of Perfection and Christian Virtues*, vol. 2, p. 474.

1071. *Two Kinds of Sadness*
Is there any sadness that is good? To this St Basil answers that there is a sadness that is very good and profitable; for one of the eight beatitudes which Christ our Lord lays down in the Gospel is: 'Blessed are they that mourn, for they shall be comforted' (Mt 5:5). St Basil says, and St Leo Pope, and Cassian also mentions that there are two sorts of sadness. One is worldly, when one is sad for something of this world, the adversities and troubles; and that sadness they say the servants of God ought not to have. . . .

Another sadness there is that is spiritual and according to God, good and profitable, and becoming the servants of God.

Rodriquez, *ibid.,* pp. 481-482.

1072. *Sadness That Is Good*
Another sadness there is that is spiritual and according to God, good and profitable. This, St Basil and Cassian say is engendered in four ways, and of four things. First, of the sins that we have committed against God, according to the saying of the Apostles: 'I rejoice, not that ye have been made sad, but that your sadness hath led you to repentance'. . . .

Secondly, this sorrow is engendered and springs from the sight of the sins of others, seeing how God is offended and made light of and his law broken. . . .

Third, this sadness may spring from desire of a perfection, which means being so anxious to advance in perfection as to be ever sighing and groaning that we are not better. . . .

Fourth, there may spring up in the servants of God a holy sadness at the contemplation of the glory of heaven and desire of heavenly goods, seeing themselves in exile. . . .

Cassian specifies the signs by which we may know what sadness is good and according to God and what is evil and of the devil. He says that the former is obedient, affable, gentle and patient; in short as springing from the love of God. . . . But the evil sadness that is of the devil is rude, impatient, full of rancor and fruitless bitterness, inclining to diffidence and despair. . . .

Rodriguez, *ibid.,* pp. 482-484.

SAINTS

1073. *The Science of the Saints Lauded*
Blessed is he who has received from God the science of the saints. . . . The science of the saints is to know the love of God. . . . Blessed is he, said St Augustine, who knows God, even if he know nothing else. . . . He that knows God and loves him, though he be ignorant of what others know, is more learned than the learned who know not how to love God.

St Alphonsus Liguori, *The Way of Salvation and of Perfection*, p. 189.

1074. *The Saints Are Also Tempted*
A saint does not differ from a sinner in this, that he is not himself tempted in the same way, but because he is not worsted by any great assault, while the other is overcome even by a slight temptation.

Abbot Piamun, as quoted by Cassian, in *The Nicene and Post-Nicene Fathers,* vol. 11, p. 485.

1075. *Young Saints a Striking Example*
. . . The Lord has, within recent times, raised up a number of young saints, who without *apparent* effort, have attained to a high degree of sanctity. Their lives as a rule present nothing remarkable in the way of external achievement. Many of us when comparing our lives with theirs may easily

find, perhaps, that we are called upon to face greater trials, accomplish harder work, and make as painful decisions in the service of God as they. . . . [The young saints] did not live for themselves, they brought God into everything. Love of him was the source from which each act sprang. . . . Desire to please Him was the sole objective toward which it was directed.

Edward Leen, *In the Likeness of Christ*, pp. 332-333, 335.

1076. *Invocation of Saints Is a Duty*

It is . . . most useful to us, in order to obtain the divine grace, that we have recourse to the intercession of the saints, who have great power with God, especially for the benefit of those who have a particular devotion to them. And this is not a mere devotion dependent upon our private fancy, but it is a duty. . . . The divine Law requires, [St Thomas Aquinas says,] that we mortals should receive aid which is necessary for our salvation, through the prayers of the saints. Especially this aid comes through the intercession of Mary, whose prayers are of more value than those of all the saints. . . .

St Alphonsus Liguori, *The Way of Salvation and of Perfection*, p. 193.

SAINTS – THE BLESSED VIRGIN

1077. *Christ Died for Mary*

. . . Never forget this truth: Christ above all died for his Mother, to pay for her privileges. The singular graces Mary received are the first fruits of the Passion of Jesus. The Blessed Virgin would not have enjoyed any prerogative without the merits of her Son; she is the greatest glory of Christ because she received the most from him.

Marmion, *Christ, the Life of the Soul*, p. 375.

1078. *Mary's Immaculate Conception*

[After quoting many of the Fathers and Doctors of the Church as teaching the Immaculate Conception of the Blessed Virgin, St Alphonsus says:] Actually this opinion is defended by the universities of the Sorbonne, Salamanca, Coimbra, Cologne, Mainz, Naples and many others. All who take their degrees there are obliged to swear that they will defend the doctrine of [Mary's] Immaculate Conception.

St Alphonsus Liguori, *The Glories of Mary*, vol. 2, p. 16.

1079. *Mary's Humility as Precondition for Incarnation*

[The first disposition] so conspicuously present in our Blessed lady is a humility that is altogether admirable. Had it not been for that humility, the Spirit of God would not have rested on her, and had not the Holy

Spirit overshadowed her, the Incarnation would not have taken place. 'Upon whom shall my spirit rest,' asks the Lord, 'except upon one who is humble and quiet? . . . It was pride that prompted Eve to be like unto God 'knowing good and evil', it was humility in Mary that captivated the heart of God. Without humility the creature is closed to God and cannot fulfill its vocation. . . . It is humility alone that keeps the soul open to the power and might of God.

O'Mahoney, *The Mother of Jesus*, pp. 40-41.

1080. *Mary's Part in the Miracle at Cana*

[At Cana, Jesus said to Mary,] 'My hour is not yet come.' He meant the hour marked in the eternal decrees. . . . The knowledge of the acute want [lack of wine] does not move Him to action. The hour of need – that is, the moment when the need was felt – was not the hour of divine Providence. Some other circumstance distinct from the need and over and above was required if Jesus was to act. That circumstance was the intervention of Mary. When that intervention had taken place, the hour decided from all eternity had come. . . . As the decree of the Incarnation hung on her fiat, so the decree of the miracle that ushered in the life of power of the Incarnate God was suspended to her words of intercession.

Edward Leen, *In the Likeness of Christ*, pp. 167-168.

1081. *Mary's Grief at the Foot of the Cross*

The Blessed Mother revealed to St Bridget: 'When Jesus saw me [at the foot of the Cross], he grieved more for me than for Himself.' This led St Bernard to say: 'O good Jesus, great as are your bodily sufferings, much more do you suffer in your Heart through pity for your Mother.'

St Alphonsus Liguori, *The Passion of Jesus Christ*, p. 65.

1082. *Mary's Inspiring Example on Calvary*

A prominent Catholic laymen made the statement in public that, under the cross of daily duty, he finds his greatest inspiration in the text: 'There stood by the Cross of Jesus his Mother.'

Hoeger, *The Convent Mirror*, p. 30.

1083. *Mary's Love for Us*

[Mary loves men] for the reason that God loves them and in the manner he desires her to love them. She reveres in them the image of the Blessed Trinity, she recognizes in them the brethren of her own dear Jesus, she longs to bring about their conversion, to obtain their perseverance, to secure their eternal happiness.

Gabriel, *Ascetical Conferences for Religious*, p. 8.

1084. *Mary Is Most Solicitous for Our Salvation*
Of what use, says St Bonaventure, would Mary's power be to us if she had no regard for us? But, adds the saint, let us hold for certain that as the Virgin is the most powerful of all the saints before God, so she is the most solicitous of all for our salvation.
St Alphonsus Liguori, *The True Spouse of Jesus Christ*, p. 627.

1085. *Mary, Mother of Mercy*
[Kings] must not neglect to exercise justice toward the guilty when this is necessary. Mary, however, is different. Though she is queen, she is not a queen of justice. That is to say, she is not concerned with punishing. She is queen of mercy, committed to pity and pardon. Holy Church expressly wants us to call her a queen of mercy.
St Alphonsus Liguori, *The Glories of Mary*, vol. 1, p. 14.

1086. *Mary, Advocate Of Sinners*
[Mary] glories in being called their [sinners'] special advocate, as she herself declared to the Venerable Sister Mary Villani, when she said: 'Next to the title of Mother of God, I am most happy with that of Advocate of Sinners.'
St Alphonsus, *ibid.*, p. 121.

1087. *Mary, Hope of Sinners*
St Bonaventure encourages a sinner by saying to him: 'If you are afraid that God in his anger will take revenge on you because of your sins, what can you do? Go, appeal to Mary, who is the hope of sinners. And if you are afraid she may refuse to listen to your case, be assured that she cannot do this, for God himself has imposed on her the duty of helping the hopeless.
St Alphonsus, *ibid.*, p. 130.

1088. *Mary's Power Over the Devil*
[St Bonaventure says:] 'No enemy on earth fears a powerful hostile army as much as the demons of hell fear the name and protection of Mary.'
Quoted by St Alphonsus, *ibid.*, p. 91.

1089. *Devils Give Witness to Mary's Power*
[In exorcising a man possessed by various devils, St Dominic asked them various questions, which they would not answer until the Saint asked the Blessed Virgin:] 'Force your enemies to proclaim the whole truth and nothing but the truth about this here and now, before the multitude.'...

[The devil's response was:] 'Then listen well, you Christians: the Mother of Jesus Christ is all-powerful and she can save her servants from falling into hell. She is the sun which destroys the darkness of our wiles and subtlety. It is she who uncovers our hidden plots, breaks our snares and makes our temptations useless and ineffectual.

'We have to say, however reluctantly, that not a single soul who has really persevered in her service has ever been damned with us; one single sigh that she offers the Blessed Trinity is worth far more than all the prayers, desires and aspirations of all the saints.

'We fear her more than all the other saints in heaven together, and we have no success with her faithful servants. Many Christians who call upon her when they are at the hour of death and who really ought to be damned according to our ordinary standards are saved by her intervention.

'Oh, if only that Mary [it is thus in their fury that they called her] had not pitted her strength against ours and had not upset our plans, we should have conquered the Church and have destroyed it long before this; and we would have seen to it that all the Orders in the Church fell into error and disorder.

. . . Now that we are forced to speak, we must also tell you this: nobody who perseveres in saying the Rosary will be damned, because she obtains for her servants the grace of true contrition for their sins and by means of this they obtain God's forgiveness and mercy. . . . '

St Louis de Montfort, *The Secret of the Rosary*, pp. 78-79.

1090. *Conversion Through Picture Of The Immaculate Conception*
St Alphonsus tells of a woman who visited a Redemptorist monastery, saying her husband had not been to confession for years and beat her when she urged him to go to confession. The priest told her to give him a small picture of the Immaculate Conception. Almost immediately after he received it he asked her when she wanted him to go to confession. . . . He went the next morning and told the priest he had not gone to confession for twenty-eight years but that after receiving the picture of the Immaculate Conception he suddenly wanted to go. 'Last night every minute seemed like a thousand years.'

St Alphonsus Liguori, *The Glories of Mary*, vol. 2, p. 17.

1091. *Mary's Promise to Those Who Practice the Five First-Saturdays devotion*
. . . On 10 December 1925, the Blessed Virgin, with the Infant Jesus beside her, appeared again to Lucy. . . . The Blessed Virgin said: 'See, my child, this Heart of mine, surrounded with thorns with which men transfix it at every moment by their blasphemy and ingratitude. Do you at least

try to console me, and announce in my name that I promise to assist at the hour of death with the graces necessary for salvation, all those who, on the first Saturday of five successive months, go to confession and receive Holy Communion, recite the Rosary, and keep me company for a quarter of an hour while meditating on the mysteries of the Rosary, with the intention of making reparation.'

Two months later, on 15 February 1926, the Infant Jesus again appeared to Lucy, encouraging her to spread the devotion to the Immaculate Heart of Mary. . . .

De Oca, *More About Fatima and the Immaculate Heart of Mary*, p. 82.

1092. *Mary's Dignity as the Mother of God*

St Albert the Great asserts that 'to be the Mother of God is the highest dignity after that of being God'. And he adds: 'Mary could not have been more closely united to God than she was without becoming God'.

St Alphonsus Liguori, *The Glories of Mary*, vol. 2, p. 51.

1093. *God himself could not make a Greater Mother than Mary*

. . . St Bonaventure said that God could make a world greater than this world but not a greater mother, for no mother can have a son greater than the Son of God. Since the office is unique, so must its graces be.

Shamon, *The Only Life*, p. 88.

1094. *Mary Owes Her Privileges to Sinners*

William of Paris invoked Mary saying: 'O Mary, you are obliged to help sinners because of all the gifts, graces, and high honors which are comprised in the dignity of Mother of God, which you have received. You owe everything, so to say, to sinners; it is because of them that you were made worthy to have God for a Son'. 'Therefore', concluded St Anselm, 'If Mary was made Mother of God because of sinners, how can I, no matter how great my sins may be, ever despair of forgiveness?'

St Alphonsus Liguori, *The Glories of Mary*, vol. 1, pp. 129-130.

1095. *Mary's Right to Have Prayers Heard by Jesus*

'Because the Incarnate God is Son of Mary, and it is the duty of every son to cherish his mother, what is liberality on His part towards others becomes an obligation as regards the Virgin Mary' (Bossuet, third sermon on the Nativity of the B.V.M.). The right that the Mother of Jesus has to be loved by Him involves a right to have her prayers heard and her desires fulfilled.

Edward Leen, *In the Likeness of Christ*, p. 172.

1096. *Mary's Zeal for Christ's Interests in Us*
Wherever the interests of Jesus are to be promoted or are in any way imperilled, there all her mother-love is focused at once. She is *our* Mother, nor *can* she ever be indifferent to our lot, since we mean so much to Jesus. And further, Jesus has given to us his Mother that by her intercession his interests in us may be promoted, and may triumph.

It follows that the more Jesus lives and reigns in us, the more truly are we children of Mary. And the converse is true: any conscious trying to attain heaven by Mary's help, rosaries or scapulars, while making no effort to grow in his likeness, and to love him above all, would be doomed to failure. It would be superstition. . . .

But given that we do love her Son, or want to love him, then Mary's power to help seems boundless; and she becomes the quickest and surest way to reach him.

Dyer, in *How to Pray and Other Conferences*, p. 68.

1097. *Mary, Our Mother*
In his encyclical *Ad Diem Illum*, St Pius X Asks: 'Is not Mary Mother of God? She is, in consequence, our mother, for it is laid down as a principle that Jesus, being the Word made flesh, is, at the same time Savior of the human race. But as God made man He has a body like other men. As Redeemer of our race, He has a spiritual body, or as it is generally named, a Mystical Body, which is nothing else than the whole Christian corporation united to Him by faith. . . . Hence in the chaste womb of the Virgin Mary, when Jesus took human form, he has also taken to himself a spiritual body formed of all those who were to believe in him: so it can be said that Mary, bearing Jesus in her womb, bore also those whose life is contained in the life of the Savior. This is the reason why we are all called in a spiritual and mystical sense the children of Mary, and that she is, on her side, the Mother of us all. . . . Mother according to the spirit, but, nonetheless real Mother of the Members of Jesus Christ, which we are'.

Edward Leen, *The True Vine and Its Branches*, pp. 240-241.

1098. *Mary, Mother of Us All*
St Gertrude relates that hearing one day, in the chanting of the Divine Office, those words of the Gospel naming Christ: *Primogenitus Mariae Virginis* [the Firstborn Son of the Virgin Mary], she said to herself: 'The title of Only Son would seem to be more befitting for Jesus than that of Firstborn. While she was dwelling on this thought, the Virgin Mary appeared to her: 'No', she said to the holy nun, 'it is not only Son but Firstborn Son which is most befitting; for, after Jesus my sweetest Son, or more truly, in him and by him, I have given birth to you all in my heart, and you have

become my children, the brothers and sisters of Jesus'.
Marmion, *Christ, the Life of the Soul*, pp. 378-379.

1099. *Mary, Our Mother*
The Fathers tell us that Mary became our spiritual Mother on two occasions. The first, according to St Albert the Great, was when she merited to conceive in her virginal womb the Son of God. . . .

The second occasion on which Mary became our spiritual Mother was on Mt Calvary, when she so sorrowfully offered the life of her beloved Son to the Eternal Father for our Salvation. 'As she cooperated by her love in the birth of the faithful to the life of grace', says St Augustine, 'so has she become the Mother of all who are members of the one Head, Jesus Christ'.
St Alphonsus Liguori, *The Glories of Mary*, vol. 1, pp. 21-22.

1100. *Mary's Spiritual Motherhood Promulgated on Calvary*
This great mystery of the spiritual maternity of Mary called for a solemn promulgation. The solemn promulgation took place when Jesus said: 'Woman, behold thy son,' for it was then only that the Blessed Virgin became completely the Mother of men. Up to that moment she was such only in an incomplete manner just as her Son, until the consummation of the Passion, was but incompletely Savior of men.
Edward Leen, *The True Vine and Its Branches*, p. 258.

1101. *The Love Mary Has for Us*
If the Little Flower could promise to spend her heaven doing good on earth, can we think that the Queen of all saints will do less? Mary's interest for mankind was maternal even on earth; how much more now in heaven! On earth, she scarcely knew the full power of her intercession, nor did she know all her children. But now in heaven, through the beatific vision, she is fully aware of her power and knows each one of us. And what is more wondrous, she knows us, not in the cold manner in which the scientist grasps his science, but like a mother. Remember, Mary has her body in heaven; hence her love has the deep emotional overtones of a mother's love. Like every holy mother, she has in her heart great ambitions and desires and hopes for all of us; and she constantly petitions her Son for the fulfillment of these desires.
Shamon, *The Only Life*, p. 95.

1102. *Mary Is Eager to Help All Repentant Sinners*
The Virgin herself said one day to St Bridget these consoling and encouraging words to sinners: 'let a sinner be ever so abandoned, if he come to me

I am ready to receive him the moment he returns. Nor do I attend to the sins he has committed, but only to the intention with which he comes to me.... But she herself declared to the same St Bridget that she is a mother only to those that wish to amend their lives.

St Alphonsus Liguori, *The True Spouse of Jesus Christ*, pp. 634-635.

1103. *Mary as Co-Redemptrix*

It is this association with Jesus on Calvary which accounts for a title given [Mary] by a Pope, the title of co-Redemptrix of the human race. 'With Christ suffering and dying,' wrote Pope BenedictXV, 'she, too, suffered almost unto death. For man's salvation, she abdicated her rights as mother over her Son. In order to appease Divine Justice, she immolated him as far as it lay within her power, so that we may justly say that she has, with Christ, redeemed mankind'.

O'Mahoney, *The Mother of Jesus*, p. 126.

1104. *Mary, Co-Redemptrix*

As God 'delivered up his Son' for the salvation of men, so Mary, too had to 'deliver up her Son' to death for the same object.... Because of this subordinate cooperation with Jesus in presenting to God a humanity living with a supernatural life, she is styled Co-Redemptrix of the human race.... The title of Co-Redemptrix is given her because of the intimate and personal way in which she was associated with the immolation of Calvary, first, by providing the Victim through her consent to the Incarnation, and then, by offering that Victim in union with God the Father for the salvation of men.

It was by that 'fiat', murmured at the foot of the Cross, that Mary's spiritual maternity of men reached its consummation.

Edward Leen, *The True Vine and Its Branches*, pp. 255-256.

1105. *Mary as Co-Redemptrix*

Just as Eve stood by the tree in Eden and played a cardinal part in our fall, so the new Eve – Mary – the Mother of Christ, stood by the cross on Calvary and played so important a part in our redemption that theologians do not hesitate to call her the Co-Redemptrix.

Boylan, *This Tremendous Lover,* p. 20.

1106. *Mary Vs. Eve – Gabriel Vs. Satan*

'An angel of darkness has a hand in our fall. An angel of light plays a part in our restoration. The angel of darkness whispers in the ear of Eve, as yet a virgin. The angel of light speaks to Mary, who will remain forever a virgin. Eve hearkens to the tempter and obeys him; Mary listens to the angel of life, and shows herself in turn, docile to his suggestion. The ruin of the race, consummated by Adam, began in Eve. So. too, the salvation consummated by Christ began through Mary. She occupied the same position in our redemption that Eve did in our enslavement. Jesus wrought our salvation as Adam wrought our loss. All that we lost has been restored in a more excellent state. Before our eyes appear a new Adam, a new Eve, and a new angel. There shall also be a new Tree which shall be that of the Cross. There shall be on this Tree a new fruit that will undo all the evil caused by the eating of the forbidden fruit.'

Bossuet, quoted by James Leen, in *By Jacob's Well*, p. 225.

1107. *Mary's Part in the Redemption*

[Mary] was not merely a passive channel through which God made his entry into the world. God had too much regard for her to assign her but this impersonal part in the Incarnation. He allowed the great mystery of his taking flesh to depend on her free choice. He formally demanded her consent to it. . . . God, knowing what was involved in his proposal to her, would not, unless she was perfectly willing, make her a party to the Incarnation. This would not have been so necessary were Mary simply called upon to give of her flesh and blood for the formation of the Sacred Humanity, and then to remain a simple spectator of the drama of Calvary and a happy recipient of its blessed fruits. But she was destined not to be a mere spectator but a real actor in that terrible drama. She was invited to enter with the Son born of her into the dread struggle with the forces of sin, which was to issue in the regeneration of mankind. Being asked to become the Mother of the Savior, she was asked to share in the task of salvation. Jesus was not to be alone in the decisive combat with sin.

Edward Leen, *The True Vine and Its Branches*, pp. 245-246.

1108. *Mary's Part in the Redemption*

Being impelled by the urging of the Holy Spirit to Calvary, it was decreed that she should not assist as a mere brokenhearted and sympathetic onlooker. Neither was it granted to her to indulge, free and unrestrained, her mother's grief. It was demanded of her that she should, herself, take an intimate part in the Sacrifice that was being offered on the altar of the Cross. That act of will which had existed in disposition from the angel's visit at Nazareth, had to be definitely formulated. It now became incumbent on her actually, and no longer habitually, to 'will' the life of mankind and hence to will its cause – namely, the sacrificial death of her Child. . . . As she gazed upon Jesus fixed on the Cross, Mary underwent a veritable passion. A most suitable word has been framed to express what this was: it is called her compassion. . . . Every wound to his Body and to his soul

pierced her through with pain. She suffered all his sufferings in herself.
Edward Leen, *ibid.*, pp. 253-254.

1109. *Reparatrix of the World, Dispensatrix of Gifts*
Pope St Pius X in his encyclical on the jubilee of the Immaculate Conception, February 1904, has said: 'When the supreme hour of the Son came, beside the Cross of Jesus there stood Mary his Mother, not merely occupied in contemplating the cruel spectacle, but rejoicing that her only Son was offered for the salvation of mankind, and so entirely participating in His Passion that if it had been possible, she would have gladly borne all the torments that her Son bore. And from this community of will and suffering between Christ and Mary she merited to become most worthily the Reparatrix of the lost world and Dispensatrix of all the gifts that our Savior purchased by his death and by his Blood.'
Quoted by O'Mahoney, in *The Mother of Jesus*, p. 127.

1110. *Mediatrix of Grace*
It is well known that the Church Fathers and the theologians give Mary this title of Mediatrix because, by her powerful intercession and her merit 'of congruity', she procured the great benefit of redemption for the world. We say 'of congruity' because, as the theologians say, Jesus Christ alone is our Mediator by justice and 'condign' merit, since He offered His merits to the eternal Father, who accepted them for our salvation. Mary, therefore, is a mediatrix of grace by way of simple intercession and merit 'of congruity', since, as theologians maintain with St Bonaventure, she offered her merits to God for the salvation of all men, and God, as a favor, accepted them with the merits of Jesus Christ. Because of this, Arnold of Chartres says: 'Mary brought about our salvation together with Christ'....

St Bernard concludes that the Church teaches that Mary is the universal mediatress of our salvation.... St Basil declares that she received this plenitude that she might be a worthy mediatress between God and men; 'Hail, full of grace, and for this reason, mediatress between God and men by your intercession'.
St Alphonsus Liguori, *The Glories of Mary,* vol. 2, pp. 24-25.

1111. *Mary as Mediatrix and Almoner of Heavenly Grace*
Said Leo XIII: 'The Virgin Mary is the Mediatrix of our peace with God, and the Almoner of heavenly graces' (encyclical *Supremi Apostolatus*, 1 September 1883). 'The cataracts of divine grace', he says, 'pour down upon us from Mary as through an overflowing channel.' In her hands are the treasures of divine mercies.' 'God wishes her to be the source of all that is good' (encyclical *Diuturni Temporis*, 5 September 1898). Pius X

said: 'Assuredly, the dispensing of these treasures belongs to nobody but Christ from the point of view of right, for they were purchased by his death alone, and he, of natural right, is Mediator between God and man. Yet, because of the union and anguish and sorrow between Mother and Son, this august Virgin has become for the whole world the most powerful Mediatrix and Advocate with her Holy Son. The fountain, therefore, is Christ, and of his fullness we have all received. But Mary, as St Bernard truly observes is the Aqueduct' (encyclical *Ad Diem Illum Laetissimum*, 2 February 1904).

O'Mahoney, *The Mother of Jesus*, p. 133.

1112. *Mary Obtains Grace for Us*

Jesus is the Mediator of justice; Mary obtains for us grace; for, as St Bernard, St Bonaventure, St Bernardine of Siena, St Germanus, St Antoninus, and others say, it is the will of God to dispense through the hands of Mary whatever graces he is pleased to bestow upon us. With God, the prayers of the saints are the prayers of friends, but the prayers of Mary are the prayers of his Mother. Happy they who confidently and at all times have recourse to this divine Mother! This, above all others, is the most pleasing devotion to the Blessed Virgin, ever to have recourse to her and to say: O Mary! intercede for us with thy Son, Jesus.

'It is impossible', says St Antoninus, 'that this Mother should ask any favor of her Son for those who are devout to her, and the Son not grant her request'.

St Alphonsus Liguori, *The Way of Salvation and of Perfection*, pp.38-39.

1113. *All Graces Come to Us Through Mary*

'If it is true – and I hold it to be true, according to the common opinion – if it is true that all graces given us by God come through Mary's hands, then it is also true that only through the help of Mary are we able to hope for and obtain the greatest grace of all, the grace of final perseverance. We will certainly obtain it if we constantly and confidently ask it of Mary.

St Alphonsus Liguori, *The Glories of Mary*, vol. 1, p. 50.

1114. *Mary's Power for Saving Those Who Beg Her Help*

St Thomas says that through the abundant grace which God has given them, the saints can save many, but that the Blessed Virgin has merited grace sufficient to save all.

St Alphonsus Liguori, *Dignity and Duties of the Priest*, p. 410.

1115. *Mary – Omnipotent by Grace*

. . . Richard of St Laurence has written: 'From the omnipotent Son the

Mother was made omnipotent.'... The Son is omnipotent by nature, the Mother by grace, inasmuch as she obtains from God whatever she asks.

St Alphonsus, *ibid.*, p. 414.

1116. *The Incarnation Confounded the Devil*

Because the devil had deceived the Virgin Eve; accordingly, to Mary, who was a Virgin, Gabriel bore a message of joy. As Eve, being deceived, uttered a word that was the cause of death, so Mary brought forth in the flesh a Word that gave us eternal life. The word of Eve led to the tree, because of which Adam was driven from Paradise; the Word which the Virgin brought forth led to the Cross, because of which the Thief, standing in the place of Adam, was led into Paradise.

St John Chrysostom, in Toal, vol. 1, p. 116.

1117. *Mary's Intercession Is Not Only Useful but Necessary*

[Father Suarez says] that it is the universal mind of the Church today that Mary's intercession is not only useful for us, but necessary. Not absolutely necessary . . . because only the mediation of Christ is absolutely necessary. But morally necessary, because the Church feels, with St Bernard, that God has determined that no grace be given except through Mary's hands.

St Alphonsus Liguori, *The Glories of Mary*, vol. 1, p. 100.

1118. *Mary Asked Privilege of Sharing Christ's Passion*

'. . . In the vision of the Divinity . . . I was made to comprehend the high value which the Lord sets upon the labors, the passion and death of my Son, and upon all those who were to imitate and follow Jesus in the way of the Cross. Knowing this, I not only offered to deliver my Son over to passion and death, but I asked him to make me his companion and partaker of all his sorrows, sufferings and torments, which request the eternal Father granted. Then, in order to begin following in the footsteps of His bitterness, I besought my Son and Lord to deprive me of interior delights; and this petition was inspired in me by the Lord Himself, because he wished it so, and because my own love taught me and urged me thereto. This desire for suffering and the wishes of my divine Son led me on in the way of suffering. He himself, because he loved me so tenderly, granted my desire; for those whom he loves, he chastises and afflicts. . . . I as his Mother was not to be deprived of this blessed distinction of being entirely like unto him, which alone makes this life estimable. Immediately this will of the Most High, this my earnest petition, began to be fulfilled: I began to feel the want of his delightful caresses and he began to treat me with greater reserve. That was one of the reasons why he did not call me Mother but

Woman, at the marriage feast at Cana and at the foot of the Cross . . . and also on other occasions, when he abstained from words of tenderness. So far was this from being a sign of a diminution of his love, that it was rather an exquisite refinement of his affection to assimilate me to him in the sufferings which he chose for himself as his precious treasure and inheritance.'

The Blessed Virgin Mary to Mary of Agreda, in *City of God: Words of Wisdom*, pp. 320-321.

1119. *Mary Complains: Sinners Refuse Her the Glory of Saving Them*
. . . If I cannot experience grief now, I may justly complain of men, that they load themselves with eternal damnation and refuse me the glory of saving their souls.'

The Blessed Virgin Mary to Mary of Agreda, in *ibid.*, p. 575.

1120. *Devotion to Mary is Necessary*
No piety would be truly Christian if it did not include in its object the Mother of the Incarnate Word. Devotion toward the Blessed Virgin is not only important, but necessary, if we wish to draw abundantly at the source of life. To separate Christ from his Mother in our piety is to divide Christ; it is to lose sight of the essential mission of his holy humanity in the distribution of divine grace. Where the Mother is left out, the Son is no longer understood.

Marmion, *Christ, the Life of the Soul*, pp. 370-371.

1121. *Mary Is Most Praiseworthy*
. . . St Augustine declares: 'If all the tongues of men were put together, and if each of their members were changed into tongues, they would not suffice to praise Mary as much as she deserves.'

St Alphonsus Liguori, *The Glories of Mary*, vol. 1, p. 7.

1122. *To Honor Mary Is to Gain Eternal Salvation*
St Bonaventure maintains that those who make the glories of Mary known to others are certain of salvation. This opinion is confirmed by Richard of St Lawrence, who declares that to honor Mary is to gain eternal life. He says: 'Our Lady will honor in the next world those who honor her in this.'

St Alphonsus, *ibid.*, p. 8.

1123. *Devotion to Mary Is a Sign of Salvation*
St Bernard wrote that 'devotion to the Mother of God is the surest sign of obtaining eternal salvation.'

St Alphonsus, *ibid.*, p. 157.

1124. *The Value of Devotion to Mary*
Father Suarez was so devoted to Mary that he claimed he would be willing to exchange all his knowledge for the merit of a single *Hail Mary*. As a result of his devotion, he died so cheerfully that he was able to say: 'I never thought it was so sweet to die.'
St Alphonsus, *ibid.,* p. 60.

1125. *The Attitude We Should Take Toward Mary*
There is no doubt about the attitude the Church would have us assume in our approach to the holy Mother of God. It is that of the Publican in the temple, it is that of the Magdalen weeping over our Lord's feet, it is the attitude of the Prodigal Son, in short it is the attitude that our Lord never rejects or repulses. So long as we strive to be among those that esteem themselves 'wretched, and miserable, and poor and blind and naked,' we are sure of a welcome and of a helping hand both from our divine Saviour and from his blessed Mother. . . .

She is the 'refuge of sinners'; the more wretched we are, the greater is our claim. Like the beggars at the church doors, our miseries are our stock-in-trade. 'Sinful and sorrowful – about our sinfulness there is no doubt, but if we plead that sinfulness with our sinless Mother, it is her province to help us to become truly and supernaturally *sorrowful*.
Dyer, 'Ave Maria', in *How to Pray and Other Conferences,* pp. 86-87.

1126. *The Reason for Our Trust in Mary*
St Anselm makes the pertinent remark that when we pray to Mary for graces, it is not because we lack confidence in God's mercy, but rather because we distrust our own worthiness. We commend ourselves to Mary that her worthiness may supply for our insufficiency.
St Alphonsus Liguori, *The Glories of Mary*, vol. 1, p. 95.

1127. *The Confidence We Can Have in Mary*
In all our needs, temporal and spiritual, we can have recourse to Mary with confidence; the more confidence we have, the more likely are we to be heard. She will not inevitably take the cross from our shoulders. She will do better. She will give us strength to bear it and show us how to draw patience and fortitude from it. She will teach us how to unite our crosses with her own and that of Jesus, and, in this way, to find consolation and comfort in our trials.
James Leen, *By Jacob's Well*, p. 226.

1128. *Devotion to the Sorrows of Mary*
Our Lord revealed to Blessed Veronica of Binasco that He is more pleased

to see compassion shown to his Mother than to himself. He said to her: 'My daughter, I certainly appreciate the tears shed for my passion. However, because I love my Mother so intensely, meditation on the torments she suffered at my death is even more agreeable to me.'

And so we may say with reason that Jesus promises extraordinary grace to those who are devoted to the sorrows of Mary. Pelbart relates that it was revealed to St Elizabeth that, after the Assumption of the Blessed Virgin into heaven, St John the Evengelist was eager to see her again. God granted this favor and Mary appeared to him, accompanied by her Son. The saint then heard Mary ask Jesus to grant some special grace to all those who are devoted to her sorrows. So Jesus promised her four principal ones. First, those who invoke Mary in the name of her sorrows will obtain before death true repentance for their sins; second, He will protect in all the trials of life and especially at the time of their death all those who practice this devotion; third, he will impress on their minds the remembrance of his passion and will reward them in heaven for their devotion; and fourth, he will place such devout servants in Mary's hands to do with them as she wishes and to obtain for them all the graces she desires.

St Alphonsus Liguori, *The Glories of Mary*, vol. 2, pp. 112-113.

1129. *Mary's Solicitude for Souls*

If the saints in their charity are so inclined to favor men in the dangerous conflicts with the devils, thou must not be surprised, my dearest, that I am merciful with sinners who take refuge in my clemency; for I desire their salvation infinitely more than they do themselves. Innumerable are those whom I have saved from the infernal dragon because of their devotion to me, even though they have recited only one Ave, or said only one word in my honor and invocation. So great is my love for them, that if they would call upon me in time and with sincerity, none of them would perish. But the sinners and the reprobates do no such thing; because the wounds of sin, not being of the body, do not distress them, and the oftener they are committed, the less regret or sorrow do they cause'.

The Blessed Virgin to Mary of Agreda, in *The City of God: Words of Wisdom,* pp. 484.

1130. *The Devotion of St Thérèse to Mary*

The last words penned by the hand of St Thérèse of Lisieux were: 'O Mary, were I queen of Heaven, and wert thou Thérèse, I should wish to be Thérèse that I might see thee Queen of Heaven.'

St Thérèse in *Autobiography and Letters,* p. 330.

1131. *Devotion to Mary Demands Freedom from Mortal Sin*
[The first homage for which Mary] looks at the hands of her devout clients is that they most carefully avoid every mortal sin. Failing this, no one can claim to be considered dutiful to the Queen of Heaven, and hence no one can be called her devout servant.
Scaramelli, *Directorium Asceticum*, vol. 1, p. 431.

1132. *Lack of Devotion to Mary Is Dangerous*
St Francis Borgia used to fear for the perseverance of those in whom he found no devotion to Mary. He warned the novice master to keep an eye on such unfortunate novices. It happened that every one of those eventually lost his vocation and left the Order.
St Alphonsus Liguori, *The Glories of Mary*, vol. 1, p. 52.

1133. *Folly of Those Who Sin Because of Mary's Mercy*
When we say that it is not possible for a servant of Mary to be lost, we are not speaking, of course, of those who take advantage of their devotion to sin all the more freely. Those who disapprove of saying so much about Mary's mercy to sinners, on the grounds that this only causes them to sin all the more, do so without cause, for such presumptious sinners deserve punishment, not mercy, for their rash confidence. We are referring rather to those clients of Mary who, with a sincere desire to mend their ways, are faithful in honoring and recommending themselves to her.
St Alphonsus, *ibid.*, vol. 1, p. 140.

1134. *Mary Could Have Gone to Heaven Without Dying*
Thou hast already recorded that the Lord offered me the choice of entering into beatific vision either with or without passing through the portals of death. If I had preferred not to die, the Most High would have conceded this favor, because sin had no part in me, and hence, also, not its punishment, which is death. Thus it would also have been with my divine Son, and with a greater right, if he had not taken upon himself the satisfaction of the divine justice of men through his passion and death. Hence I chose death freely in order to imitate and follow him as also I did during his grievous Passion. Since I had seen my Son and true God die, I would not have satisfied the love I owe him if I had refused death, and I would have left a great gap in my conformity to, and my imitation of my Lord the God-Man, whereas He wished me to bear a great likeness to him in his most sacred humanity. As I would thereafter never be able to make up for such a defect, my soul would not enjoy the plenitude of the delight of having died as did my Lord and God.

'Hence my choosing to die was so pleasing to him and my prudent love therein obliged him to such an extent that, in return, he immediately conceded to me a singular favor for the benefit of the children of the Church and conformable to my wishes. It was this, that all those devoted to me, who would call upon me at the hour of death, constituting me as their Advocate in memory of my happy transition and of my desiring to imitate him in death, shall be under my special protection in that hour, and shall have me as a defense against demons, as a help and protection, and shall be presented to me before the tribunal of his mercy and there experience my intercession'.

The Blessed Virgin to Mary of Agreda in *City of God: Words of Wisdom,* pp. 565-566.

1135. *Joseph – Next to Mary, Greatest in Grace*

After Mary, no human being was brought into closer or more intimate relations with the Incarnate Word, the Source of all grace than Joseph. It follows . . . that the grace of Joseph must come next in greatness to that of Mary. . . . It was supernatural charity infused into his soul, enabling him to shadow forth on earth with regard to the Incarnate God the relation that exists in heaven between God the Father and his eternally begotten Son.

Edward Leen, *In the Likeness of Christ*, pp. 136-137.

1136. *Joseph's Part in Christ's Life Compared with That of Mary*

When it is a question of preserving Jesus for his lifework, it is Joseph who holds the principal place, but when it is a question of that lifework itself, then it is Mary who steps into prominence.

Edward Leen, *ibid.*, p. 158.

1137. *St Teresa's devotion to St Joseph*

To other saints our Lord seems to have given grace to succour men in some special necessity; but to the glorious St Joseph, I know from experience, to help us in all; and our Lord would have us understand that, as he was himself subject to him on earth – for St Joseph, having the title of Father and being his guardian, could command him – so now in heaven he performs all his petitions.

The Life of St Teresa of Jesus, written by Herself, p. 37.

1138. *Devotion to St Joseph Urged by Blessed Virgin*

'The whole human race has much undervalued the privileges and prerogatives conceded to my beloved spouse and they know not what his intercession with God is able to do. I assure thee, my dearest, that he is one of the greatly favored personages in the divine presence and has immense power to stay the arms of divine vengeance. . . .

From now on, during the rest of thy mortal life, see that thou advance in the devotion and in hearty love toward my spouse, and that thou bless the Lord for thus having favored him with such high privileges and for having rejoiced me so much in the knowledge of all his excellences. In all thy necessities thou must avail thyself of his intercession. Thou shouldst induce many to venerate him and see that thy own religious distinguish themselves in their devotion to him. That which my spouse asks of the Lord in heaven is granted upon the earth, and on his intercession depend many and extraordinary favors for men if they do not make themselves unworthy of receiving them. All these privileges were to be a reward for the amiable perfection of this wonderful saint and for his great virtues; for divine clemency is favorably drawn forth by him and looks upon St Joseph with generous liberality, ready to shower down its marvellous mercies upon all those who avail themselves of his intercession'.

The Blessed Virgin to Mary of Agreda in *City of God: Words of Wisdom,* pp. 302-303.

OTHER SAINTS

1139. *Mary, Elizabeth, and John the Baptist*
'And it came to pass that when Elizabeth heard the salutation of Mary, the infant leaped in her womb'.

Note the distinctness of each of those words, and their particular significance. Elizabeth was the first to hear her voice; but John was the first to be aware of the divine favor. She heard in a natural manner; he leaped for joy because of the mystery. She sees Mary's coming; he the coming of the Lord.

St Thomas, in Toal, vol. 4, p. 412.

1140. *Augustine Influenced by Story of St Anthony of the Desert*
[Ponticianus, a fellow African and an official at court visited Augustine and told him about two officials of the Emperor, then at Treves in Germany, who were converted by the reading of the life of St Anthony of the Desert and had themselves adopted the life of hermits. After recording this story in his Confessions, St Augustine confessed:] Thou, indeed, O Lord, didst twist me back upon myself while his words were being uttered, taking me away from behind my own back, where I had placed myself because I was unwilling to look at myself, and thou didst set me right in front of my

face so that I might see how ugly I was, how deformed and vile, how defiled and covered with sores. I saw and was filled with horror, yet there was no place to flee from myself. If I had attempted to turn my gaze away from myself, he kept on telling his story, and thou didst again place me before myself, thrusting me up before my eyes so that I would discover my iniquity and detest it.

St Augustine, *Confessions,* bk. 8, chaps. 6 and 7.

1141. *St Ambrose Assures St Monica*

St Ambrose, impatient at St Monica's insistence that he should intervene in the matter of St Augustine said to her: 'Leave me now; as I hope for your salvation, it is impossible for the son of these tears to perish'.

St Augustine, *ibid.,* bk. 3, chap. 12.

1142. *Final Stage of Augustine's Conversion*

[In the midst of his final crisis, Augustine heard the voice of a child in a nearby house:] 'Take it, read it! Take it! Read it!' Feeling that this was a divine command, I hastened back to where Alypius was sitting. I had placed there the copy of the Apostle, when I had gone up from the place. Snatching it up, I opened it and read in silence the first passage on which my eyes fell: 'Not in revelry and drunkenness, not in debauchery and wantonness, not in strife and jealousy, but on the Lord Jesus Christ, and as for the flesh, take no thought of its lusts' (Rom.13, 13). No further did I desire to read, nor was there need to read. Indeed, immediately with the termination of this sentence, all the darkness of doubt dispersed, as if by a light of peace flooding into my heart. . . . My mother . . . was exultant, triumphant, and she blessed thee, who art able to accomplish far more than we ask or understand.

St Augustine, *ibid.,* bk. 8, chap. 12.

1143. *Christ's agreement with Catherine of Siena*

[Christ] did many comforting favors for [St Catherine of Siena], and among them, one in particular. He appeared to her one day and said: 'Daughter, forget thyself to remember me; and I will think of thee and take care of thee'.

Rodriguez, *Practice of Perfection and of Christian Virtues*, vol. 1, p.520.

1144. *Conversion of Dismas Greater Work than Splitting Rocks of Calvary*

Not only did Christ not diminish his glory by the crucifixion, but he even augmented it not a little. For, to convert the thief on the cross and conduct him to paradise was an achievement in no way inferior to that of splitting open the rocks.

St John Chrysostom, in *The Fathers of the Church*, vol. 41, p. 429.

1145. *Virtues Practiced by Good Thief Dismas on the Cross*

Arnold of Chartres in his treatise on the seven words enumerates all the virtues the good thief practiced at the time of his death: He believed, he repented, he confessed, he preached, he loved, he trusted, he prayed. He exercised faith when he said: 'When Thou comest into Thy kingdom.' He believed that Christ, after his death, would enter into his glorious kingdom. He believed, says St Gregory, that the one he saw dying was about to enter upon his reign. He repented and made confession of his sins, saying: 'We suffer indeed justly, for we are receiving what our deeds deserved.' St Augustine points out that before his confession he did not have the boldness to hope for pardon: 'He did not dare to say "Remember Me", until, by the confession of his guilt, he had thrown off the burden of his sins'. And St Athanasius exclaims: 'O fortunate thief, you stole a kingdom by the confession.'

St Alphonsus Liguori, *The Passion of Jesus Christ*, pp. 160-161.

1146. *Francis de Sales, Winner Of Converts*

[Bossuet quotes Cardinal du Perron as saying that] 'Anyone could convince the erring, but if he wished to convert them he should conduct them to our prelate' [St Francis de sales].

Charmot, *Ignatius Loyola and Francis de Sales*, p. 51.

1147. *Ignatius: Would Master Greatest Grief in 15 Minutes*

[One day when St Ignatius was ill, a doctor told him not to think gloomy thoughts. Thereupon Ignatius] began to think attentively within himself what occurrence could possibly happen to him so disagreeable and hard as to affect the peace and tranquility of his soul; and having turned the eyes of his reflection over many things, one thing alone presented itself that he would most take to heart, and that was if by any chance our Society were broken up. He went on reflecting how long this affliction and pain would last, in case it happened; and he thought that, if it happened without any fault on his part, within a quarter of an hour of recollection and prayer he would be rid of that great grief and recover his ordinary peace and cheerfulness although the Society were dissolved like salt in water.

Rodriguez, *Practice of Perfection and Christian Virtues,* vol. 1, p. 337.

1148. *John the Baptist Came in Spirit and Power of Elias*

Our Savior, being questioned by His disciples concerning the coming of Elias, replied: 'Elias is already come, and they knew not, but have done unto him whatever they had a mind and if you will receive it, John himself is Elias' (Mt 17:12, 11:14). John, however, being questioned, says: 'I am not Elias. What is this, Brethren, that what truth affirms, the prophet of truth denies? . . . The Angel said to Zachary, concerning John: 'And he shall go before Him in the spirit and power of Elias' (Lk 1:17). He is said to come in the spirit and power of Elias because, as Elias will precede the second coming of the Lord, so John precedes his first coming. As the former is the Precursor of the Judge to come, the latter was made the Precursor of the Redeemer.

St Gregory the Great, in Toal, vol. 1, pp. 66-67.

1149. *Why John the Baptist Sent Disciples to Question Christ*
[John the Baptist, in prison, feared his disciples might remain separated from Christ.] What then does he do? He waits till he hears from them that Christ is working signs and wonders. . . . [Since, then, Christ] knew with what purpose John had sent these men, he forthwith heals the blind, the lame, and many others; not so as to instruct John; for why instruct one who already knew and believed: but that he might confirm the minds of John's doubting disciples. And then when he had cured many, He says: 'Go and relate to John what you have seen and heard. The blind see, the lame walk.' . . . Then he adds: 'And blessed is he that shall not be scandalized in Me'; showing that he knew the secret thoughts of their hearts. . . . [By this last sentence, Christ secretly rebuked John's messengers for he knew] they had been scandalized in him.

St John Chrysostom, in Toal, vol. 1, pp. 39-40.

1150. *Christ's Appearance to Mary Magdalen after the Resurrection*
We know nothing whatsoever of Christ's first visit with his Mother, though merely on human grounds, leaving aside his divine thoughtfulness, we can have no doubt, that his first appearance was to her. We do know, however, that, of all his other appearances, the first was to a woman, Mary Magdalen. That appearance was the climax of a story which has meant more to sinners than anyone but God can tell, showing them what they know deep in their hearts, namely, that their capacity for great love is not less but more than their capacity for sin. Even on Calvary, Magdalen had hardly reached such heights of loyalty, of unselfish devotion and complete, unquestioning love.

Farrell, *Companion to the Summa*, vol. 4, p. 234.

1151. *Mary of Egypt Aided by the Blessed Virgin*
The history of St Mary of Egypt, as told in *The Lives of the Fathers*, is very well known. At the age of twelve she ran away from home at Alex-

andria, where she led an infamous life and became a scandal to the whole city. After living eighteen years in sin, she was seized with the desire of going to Jerusalem. She was roaming around the city on the Feast of the Holy Cross. More through curiosity than devotion, she determined to enter a church. At the very door, she felt herself repulsed by an invisible force. She tried again and again to enter, and the same thing was repeated a third and a fourth time. Then the poor soul retired to a corner of the vestibule where, enlightened by God, she understood that it was on account of her sinful life that she was driven away. In a fortunate moment she raised her eyes and noticed a picture of Mary painted on the vestibule wall. With tears in her eyes she turned to the picture and said 'O Mother of God, have pity on a poor sinner. I know that because of my sins I do not deserve that you look at me. But you are the refuge of sinners. For the love of your Son, Jesus, help me and bring me into the church. I promise to change my life and do penance in whatever place you appoint for me.'

She immediately heard an interior voice which she took to be that of Mary, saying, 'Very well, since you come to me and promise to amend, enter the church. It is no longer closed for you.' The sinner entered, adored the Holy Cross, and wept unceasingly. then, returning to the picture, she said: 'My Lady, I am ready. Where do you want me to go and do penance?' 'Go', said the voice, 'across the Jordan. There you will find your place of rest.'. . .

When she had spent fifty-seven long years in the desert and had reached the age of eighty-seven years, she was found by the Abbot Zozimus. She told him her life's story and begged him to return after a year and bring her Holy Communion. This the Abbot did. Then she requested that he come again to see her. He returned and found her dead. Her body was surrounded by dazzling light, and at her head he found this note: 'Here bury the body of a wretched sinner, and pray to God for me.' A lion came and with its claws dug the grave in which the Abbot laid the body. On his return to the monastery, Zozimus related the marvels of God's mercy toward this happy penitent. [A footnote says St Mary of Egypt was probably converted in 383 and died in 431.]

St Alphonsus Liguori, *The Glories of Mary*, vol. 1, pp. 54-55.

1152. *Monica's Grief and Her Prayers for Augustine*

Thou didst 'put forth thy hand from on high' and draw forth my soul from this deep darkness of mind, while my mother, one of thy faithful, wept for me before thee, far more than do mothers at bodily deaths. She saw my death in the spirit of faith and the spirit which she had received from thee, and thou didst hear her, O Lord. Thou didst hear her and didst not despise her tears as they flowed forth and watered the ground beneath her eyes in every place of her prayers; thou didst hear her.

St Augustine, *Confessions*, bk. 3, chap. 11, p. 68.

1153. *Monica Reassures Sailors Who Feared Shipwreck*

My mother, strong in her piety, had already come to me, following me over land and sea, safe in Thee through all dangers. For, at moments of dangers during the sea passage, she had reassured the sailors themselves, by whom inexperienced travelers across the bottomless depths are usually reassured when frightened; she promised them a safe arrival for thou hadst promised this to her in a vision.

St Augustine, *ibid.*, bk. 6, chap. 1.

1154. *Monica Saw Nothing to Live for after Augustine's Conversion*

Shortly before her death, St Monica said to Augustine: 'Son, for myself, I find no pleasure, now, in anything in this life. What am I doing here, now, and why I am here, I do not know; my hope for this world is already fulfilled. There was but one thing for which I yearned to remain a little longer in this life. That was to see you a Catholic Christian before I died. My God has more abundantly satisfied my desire, inasmuch as I see you now, having spurned earthly felicity, become his servant. What am I doing here?'

She also said: 'Bury this body anywhere. Let its care give you no concern. One thing only I ask of you, that you remember me at the altar of the Lord, wherever you may be.' Later, speaking with others, she talked with my friends about the contempt for this life and the value of death.

St Augustine, *ibid.*, bk. 9, chaps. 10-11.

1155. *Monica, Model of a Patient and Understanding Wife*

[Though Patricius, father of Augustine] was outstanding for his kindness, he was also quick to anger. But Monica had learned not to oppose any angry husband, either by action or even by word. Eventually, she would observe that his mood had changed and become tranquil, whereupon she would seize the opportune moment to explain her action to him, if, by chance, he had been thoughtlessly disturbed. In short, while many matrons whose husbands were of milder dispositions bore the marks of beatings, even in the form of facial disfigurement, and during their friendly conversations they criticized their husbands, she criticized their talkativeness. ... [When such matrons] expressed amazement, knowing as they did what a bad-tempered husband she had to put up with, that there had never been any rumor or indication to suggest that Patricius had beaten his wife, or that they had quarrelsomely disagreed with each other, even for one day, they asked her in a friendly manner for an explanation, and she told them her way of getting along, which I have noted above. Those who adopted it were grateful as a result of their own experience; those who did not observe it continued to be annoyed at their subjugation.

St Augustine, *ibid.*, bk. 9, chap. 9.

1156. *Peter's Conceit Leads to a Fall, Which Taught Him Compassion*

[Since Peter] spoke out of very great conceit when he said: 'Although all shall be scandalized in Thee, I will never be scandalized' (Mt 26:33), he was delivered over to human cowardice, and sank down to denial of him; so that from his own fall he might learn to be compassionate to the weak and acquire discretion.

St Basil, in Toal, vol. 3, p. 363.

1157. *Cardinal Gibbons Persuades Pius X to Accept the Papacy*

[On the night before his election as Pope Pius X, Cardinal Gibbons came to see Cardinal Giuseppe Sarto at a late hour and said:] 'Your Eminence, I heard you walking in your room' (their rooms were next to each other). 'Don't be worried, my dear friend, if God wants you to be Pope, and the choice of the cardinals will decide that, you should not say no. 'Do you really mean that?' stammered Sarto. 'Certainly, you may not refuse,' answered Cardinal Gibbons in a kindhearted tone. 'Yes, but you know, too, that I am not really suited for it. I know nothing of the big world and know less of the world of politics. Don't forget that I was raised out in the country, that my father was a poor mailman and my mother a simple seamstress.'

'So much the better. In that case you know from your own experience how the common people live and what they need. Don't worry. And please, stop walking and making yourself more excited. Go to bed quietly and leave the rest to God's Providence.' The calm words of the fatherly Gibbons had some effect on Sarto. He regained even something of his usual sense of humor and he answered with a smile on his face that he had a return ticket in his wallet to Venice. "All right,' the American said, 'If that is all, I'll reimburse you for it. And now, good night.'

[After the election Sarto remained seated for a long time.] Finally, he said with trembling lips: 'If it is then impossible that this cup pass away, God's will be done. I accept the election as a cross.' When asked what name he would choose he said: 'Because the popes who in this century suffered most for the Church carried the name of Pius, I will take that name.'

Smit, *St Pius X, Pope*, pp. 90, 92-93.

1158. *The Personality of Pius X*
It was said of [Pius X] that he achieved power over people through his humility, and power with God through his piety. . . .

Cardinal Baudrillart, Rector of the Institut Catholique in Paris, said: 'Leo XIII impressed me as a great man, Pius X as a saint. He judged everything from the supernatural viewpoint. One noticed all the time that he stood in continuous relationship with him whose representative he was in the world. . . . '

Pius X was asked on the day of his election where in the Vatican he wished to have his private apartment fixed up. 'On the third floor in the rooms where Cardinal Rampolla used to live. But, please don't make it too pretty. I was born poor and I hope to die poor.'

Smit, *ibid.*, pp. 139-140.

1159. *Pius X on Seminary Training*
[When he was still bishop of Mantua, he found the seminary a big disappointment and made a passionate appeal for money to help him rebuild. Rich and poor responded, with the result he was able to enlarge and reorganize the seminary and put it on a sound financial footing.] He restored discipline and put capable men in charge of the scholastic and spiritual training of the candidates for the priesthood, so that a few years later the seminary of Mantua had the reputation of being one of the most flourishing and scholarly seminaries in Italy.

Smit, *ibid.*, pp. 52-53.

1160. *Pius X Replies to a Woman Who Called Him a Saint*
At one of the audiences, a lady ventured a tactless remark as follows: 'Holy Father, I hear that you work miracles and are a saint (un santo).' The Pope smiled and said: 'I beg your pardon, Signora, you are wrong in one letter; my name is *Sarto*, not *Santo.*'

Smit, *ibid.*, p. 154.

Note: On pp. 154-156, Bishop Smit tells the stories of numerous miracles worked by the saint.

1161. *Pius X Pokes Fun at People Who Say He Works Miracles*
. . . A rumor spread about miraculous answers to prayers which were said to be obtained because of the Pope's blessing. Eventually such rumors came, of course, to the ears of the Pope, who reacted in his inimitable way: 'Can you beat that! Now they are saying that I can perform miracles, as if I had nothing else to do.

Smit, *ibid.*, p. 152.

1162. *Teresa of Avila, Foundress of Reformed Carmelite Convents*
This witness [Sister Teresa de Jesus, a niece of St Teresa] remembers her once saying: 'I do not know why they are calling me a foundress: it is God who founded these houses, not I.' [From testimony given in 1596, fourteen years after her death.]

In *Complete Works of St Teresa,* Peers edition, appendix to vol. 3, p. 366.

1163. *Teresa of Avila – Growth of Her Reform*
'... In the space of no more than the twenty years which must have gone by since the Mother made her first foundation, Spain is now full of her houses, in which God is served by more than a thousand religious. ...'

Testimony of Master Fray Luis de Leon, as published in the first edition of the works of St Teresa, published in 1586 and quoted in vol. 3, p. 371, of the *Complete Works of St Teresa*, Peers edition.

1164. *How Teresa of Avila suffered from misunderstandings*
There were times when hardly any priest would hear her confessions, for they believed her to be deceived and deluded by the devil.

Testimony given by Sister Teresa of Jesus, niece of the saint, in 1596. Quoted in *ibid.,* p. 366.

1165. *Thérèse of Lisieux Uses an 'Elevator' to Sainthood*
You know, Mother, that I have always desired to become a saint, but in comparing myself with the Saints I have ever felt that I am as far removed from them as a grain of sand trampled under foot by passers-by is from the mountain whose summit is lost in the clouds. Instead of feeling discouraged by such reflections, I concluded that God would not inspire a wish which could not be realized, and that in spite of my littleness I might aim at being a great Saint. 'It is impossible', I said, 'for me to become great, so I must bear with myself and my many imperfections, but I will seek a means of reaching heaven by a little way – very short, very straight and entirely new. We live in an age of inventions: there are now lifts [elevators] which save us the trouble of climbing stairs. I will try to find a lift by which I may be raised unto God, for I am too small to climb the steep stairway to perfection. ... O Jesus! Thy arms, then, are the lift which must raise me even unto heaven'.

St Thérèse of Lisieux, in *Autobiography and Letters,* pp. 151-152.

1166. *The mission of Thérèse Was to Make People Love God as She Did*
Speaking to Pauline [Mother Agnes of Jesus], St Thérèse said: 'I feel that my mission is soon to begin – to make others love God as I love him – to teach souls my little way. ... I will spend my heaven in doing good upon

earth. This is not impossible, for the angels keep watch over us while they enjoy the beatific vision. No, there cannot be any rest for me till the end of the world – till the angel shall have said: "Time is no more".'

St Thérèse, *ibid.*, p. 231.

1167. *Thérèse of Lisieux – Her Mission Declared by the Holy Spirit*

. . . Shortly before her holy death . . . St Thérèse gave expression to a peculiar conviction. She said: 'I feel that my mission is soon to begin – my mission to make others love God as I love him, to teach souls my little way, the way of spiritual childhood, the way of boundless trust and absolute self-surrender.' At first blush, it seems strange that a saint should speak of herself in this way. But Pope Benedict XV, in his discourse affirming the heroicity of her virtues, made the following solemn declaration: 'Since Sister Thérèse had been so humble all her life, it could only have been through a special inspiration that in her last illness she spoke in an apparently contrary sense. In this occurrence we may well recognize God's special design to exalt the merits of spiritual childhood.' Hence this remarkable utterance is to be attributed, not so much to St Thérèse as to the Holy Spirit.

Gabriel, *Ascetical Conferences for Religious*, pp. 108-109.

1168. *Thérèse – Her Conformity with the Will of God*

[Speaking of her maturer years, St Thérèse said:] Then also, as in the days of my childhood, I cried out: 'My God, I choose everything – I will not be a saint by halves, I am not afraid of suffering for thee. One thing only I fear, and that is, to follow my own will. Accept then the offering I make of it, for I choose all that thou willest.

St Thérèse of Lisieux, in *Autobiography and Letters*, p. 40.

1169. *St Thérèse Finds Love to Be Her Vocation*

The Apostle . . . explains how all the better gifts are nothing without love, and that charity is the most excellent way of going safely to God. At last, I found rest. . . . Beside myself with joy, I cried out: 'O Jesus, my Love, my vocation is found at last – *my vocation is love*. I have found my place in the bosom of the Church, and this place, O my God, thou hast thyself given me: in the heart of the Church, my Mother, *I will be love!* . . . Thus shall I be all things and my dream will be fulfilled'.

St Thérèse, *ibid.*, p. 203.

1170. *Why the Apostle Thomas was Permitted to Doubt*

. . . The divine clemency acted in this so wondrous a manner that the doubting Disciple, when he touched the wounds of the Body of his Master, healed in us the wounds of our unbelief. For more did the unbelief of Thomas profit us than the faith of the believing disciples; for when he through touching is brought back to faith, our soul, setting all doubt aside, is made steadfast in the faith.

So the Lord of a certainty suffered his disciple to doubt after his own Resurrection, yet he did not abandon him to doubt. . . .

. . . While Thomas looked, while he touched, why did he say to him: 'Because thou has seen Me, thou hast believed'? But he saw one thing, and believed another. The Godhead could not be seen by mortal man. And so, seeing man, he confesses God, saying: 'My Lord and my God'. Seeing, then he believed; he who as he carefully scrutinizes a true man, exclaims that he is the God whom he could not see.

St Gregory the Great, in Toal, vol. 2, pp. 285-286.

SALVATION

1171. *God Wills Our Salvation*
God is more desirous of our salvation than the devil is for our perdition.
St Alphonsus Liguori, *Great Means of Salvation and of Perfection*, p.338.

1172. *Neglect of Soul's Salvation Is Madness*
St Philip Neri . . . had good reason for calling those persons mad who bestow pains in this life for gaining riches and honors, and give little heed to the salvation of the soul. 'All such', said the Venerable John Avila, 'deserve to be shut up in an asylum for lunatics'.
St Alphonsus Liguori, *The Way of Salvation and of Perfection*, p.254.

1173. *Salvation at All Costs*
We should resolve and say: 'I will save my soul, cost what it may', Perish all things else – property, friends, life itself – if I can but save my soul! . . . Eternity is at stake, the being happy or miserable forever. 'No security can be too great', says St Bernard, 'where eternity is at stake'.
St Alphonsus, *ibid.*, p. 131.

1174. *We Save Our Souls or Lose Them Eternally*
'With fear and trembling', says the Apostle, 'work out your salvation' (Phil 2:12). In order to be saved we should tremble lest we be lost, for there is no medium; we must either be saved or lost forever. He who trembles not is in great danger of being lost, because he takes but little care to employ the means of obtaining salvation. . . .

St Philip Neri used to say: 'Heaven is not made for the slothful'.

Would that we were fully impressed with the meaning of the great maxim of St Francis Xavier: 'There is but one evil, and there is but one good in the world!' The only evil is damnation; the only good, salvation.

St Alphonsus, *ibid.*, pp. 97-98.

SCRUPLES

1175. *Scruples Are Used by the Devil*

[The devil] realizes, treacherous creature that he is, that he cannot get a soul to sin if that soul wants to belong wholly to Jesus, so he only tries to make it *think* it is in sin. It is already much for him to have put confusion into that soul, but his rage demands something more; he wants to deprive Jesus of a beloved tabernacle; since he cannot enter that tabernacle himself, he wants at least to have it remain *empty* and without Master!

Collected Letters of St. Thérèse of Lisieux, p. 107.

1176. *Scruples Sometimes Useful, Sometimes Harmful*

A scruple is nothing else than a vain fear of sinning that arises from false and groundless apprehensions.

These scruples are useful in the beginning of conversion. For a soul that has but a short time renounced sin stands in need of repeated purgations. Scruples produce this effect: they cleanse the soul and at the same time make it careful to avoid real sins, and they also render it humble; so that distrusting its own opinion, it places itself in the hands of its spiritual Father to be directed as he pleases. St Francis de Sales used to say that 'the fear that begets scruples in those that have lately gone from the confines of sin, is a certain presage of future purity of conscience.'...

But, on the other hand, scruples are hurtful to those that seek perfection and have for a long time given themselves to God. In such persons, says St Theresa, scruples produce extravagant impressions, which bring the soul to such a state that it will not advance a single step toward perfection. St Francis de Sales has written: 'Be diligent, but guard against inquietudes; for there is no greater obstacle to advancement to perfection.'

St Alphonsus Liguori, *The True Spouse of Jesus Christ*, p. 545.

1177. *Best Cure for Scruples Is Obedience to a Confessor*

All the anxieties of scrupulous persons consist in the fear lest, in what they do, they are not acting with scruple merely, but with real doubt as to the act being simple, and are therefore incurring sin. But the chief thing they ought to consider is this: that he who acts under obedience to a learned and pious confessor, acts not only with no doubt but with the greatest security that can be had on earth – on the divine words of Jesus Christ himself: 'he that heareth you, heareth me' (Lk 10:16). . . .

Let them read the lives of the saints, and they will find that they know no safer road than obedience.

St Alphonsus Liguori, *The Way of Salvation and of Perfection*, p. 451.

[*Note:* St Alphonsus expands this advice to scrupulous persons in many of the following pages of his book.]

SELF-CONQUEST

1178. *Self-Conquest, Great Victory*
. . . It is a greater thing to overcome oneself than to overcome others.

Rodriguez, *Practice of Perfection and Christian Virtues,* vol. 2, p. 67.

1179. *How to Achieve Self-Conquest*
If we would use but a little violence upon ourselves in the beginning, we might afterwards do all things with ease and joy. . . .

But if thou dost not overcome things that are small and light, when wilt thou overcome greater difficulties?

Thomas à Kempis, *Imitation of Christ*, bk. I, chap. 11.

1180. *Self-Control Is Difficult*
'It is more difficult for a person to rule over himself than over others. To exercise control over one's mind, to restrain one's wrath, and to integrate the conflicting ordinances of soul and body are characteristics of a man who is immortal by nature, a man whom the infernal portals shall not enclose.'

St Ambrose, in *The Fathers of the Church*, vol. 42, p. 382.

1181. *Self-Conquest Is Necessary*
Who hath a stronger conflict than he who striveth to overcome himself? And this must be our business, to strive to overcome ourselves, and daily to gain strength over ourselves, and to grow better and better.

Thomas à Kempis, *Imitation of Christ,* bk. I, chap. 3.

1182. *Self-Conquest, Perfect Victory*
The perfect victory is to triumph over one's self. For he that keeps himself in subjection, so that his sensuality is ever subject to reason, and reason in

all things obedient to me, he is indeed a conqueror of himself, and lord of all the world.

Thomas à Kempis, *ibid.,* bk. III, chap. 53.

1183. *Self-Conquest and Conquest of the Devil*

To fight against the evil motions of the mind which arise, and to despise the suggestions of the devil, is a sign of great virtue and of great merit.

Thomas à Kempis, *ibid.,* bk. III, chap. 6.

1184. *Self-Conquest Needed for the Apostolate*

Conquer self and the conquest of other souls will come as a consequence; overcome and master your own heart and you will, no matter what your position, however humble or however important and elevated, lead other hearts in submission to the standard of Christ. Leave self unconquered and, no matter what labors you perform in what position you have in your community, a curious and disappointing sterility will dog your every effort.

Brosnahan, *Searchlighting Ourselves,* p. 186.

1185. *Self-Surrender to God*

We have seen that man is bound to give himself to God. But what of himself must he give? Four things: our heart, our soul, our mind, our strength. Mark (12:30) writes: 'Thou shalt love the Lord thy God with thy whole heart, and with thy whole soul, and with thy whole mind, and thy whole strength'.

Mennessier, *Pattern for a Christian*, p. 197.

1186. *Self-Surrender Is Imperative*

God is relentless in his demands. He will be content with nothing short of ourselves.

James Leen, *By Jacob's Well*, p. 10.

1187. *Self-denial Not Merely a Counsel but a Command*

Self-denial is not, like poverty, chastity and religious obedience, a counsel of perfection. It is a command obligatory on all who wish to be true disciples of Christ. He said to all: 'If any man will come after me . . . let him deny himself'.

Edward Leen, *The True Vine and Its Branches*, p. 200.

SELF PRAISE

1188. *Self-praise Can Be Good*

Self-praise may be good and holy if it is done as it ought to be, as we see that St Paul, writing to the Corinthians (2 Cor 4:2), began to praise and recount grand things of himself, telling the great favors that the Lord had done to him, and saying that he had worked harder than the other apostles, and beginning to relate the revelations that he had had, and raptures even to the third heaven. But this he did because it was then proper and necessary for the honor of God and the profit of his neighbors to whom he was writing, that so they might regard and venerate him as an apostle of Christ, and receive his doctrine and profit thereby. And he said these things with a heart that not only despised honor, but loved disparagement and dishonor for Jesus Christ's sake. For when it was necessary for the good of his neighbor, he knew how to disparage and debase himself, saying that he was not worthy to be an apostle because he had persecuted the Church of God (1 Cor 15:9).

Rodriguez, *Practice of Perfection and Christian Virtues*, vol. 2, p. 294.

SELF-RELIANCE

1189. *Self-reliance as a Tool of the Devil Against Monks*

By no other fault does the devil drag down a monk so precipitately and lead him away to death, as when he persuades him to despise the counsel of the elders and to rely on his own opinion and judgment.

Abbot Serapion, quoted by Cassian, in *The Nicene and Post-Nicene Fathers,* vol. 11, p. 313.

1190. *Self-conquest According to Socrates*

'There is something ridiculous', one of the interlocutors in Plato's *Republic* . . . declares, 'in the expression "master of himself". The master would be the servant, and the servant the master; in all these modes of speaking, the same person is denoted.' To whom Socrates replies: 'The meaning is, I believe, that in the human soul there is a better and a worse principle.

When the better has the worse under control, then a man is said to be master of himself; and this is a term of praise. But when, owing to evil education or association, the better principle, which is also the smaller, is overwhelmed by the greater mass of the worse – in this case he is blamed and is called the slave of self and unprincipled.'

Brosnahan, *Searchlighting Ourselves,* p. 187.

SELF-SACRIFICE

1191. *Self-sacrifice Needed in a Minister of God*

St Gregory says that no man is fit to be a minister of God, and to offer the sacrifice of the altar unless he has first sacrificed himself entirely to God.

St Alphonsus Liguori, *Dignity and Duties of the Priest*, p. 362.

1192. *One's Self Is the Gift Most Acceptable to God*

'There is no offering', says St Augustine, 'that we can make to God more acceptable to himself than to say to him: "Take possession of us". . . No, we cannot offer to God anything more precious than by saying to him, 'Lord, take possession of us; we give our whole will to thee; make us understand what it is that thou dost desire of us, and we will perform it.'

St Alphonsus Liguori, *The Way of Salvation and of Perfection*, p. 357.

1193. *Sacrifice of Our Own Will*

The sacrifice of our own will is the most acceptable sacrifice we can make to God; and God pours forth his graces abundantly upon him who makes it. This sacrifice, however, in order to be perfect, must have two conditions: it must be *without reserve*, and it must be *constant*. . . .

Sister Margaret of the Cross, a daughter of the Emperor Maximilian, and a Bare-footed Nun of St Clare, when she became blind, was wont to say, 'How can I desire to see, when God wills it not?'

St Alphonsus, *ibid.*, pp. 234-235.

1194. *Dying with Christ*

'If we have died with him, we shall also live with him'. To die with Christ means to deny ourselves, that is, our own inclinations. If we do not deny them, we shall deny Christ, who will justly deny us on the day of judgment. And here let me remark that we deny Jesus Christ, not only when we deny the faith, but also when we refuse to obey him in anything he wants of us; for example, when we will not forgive an injury, when we compromise ourselves out of love for empty honors, when we will not break off a friendship that imperils our friendship with Jesus Christ. . . .

St Alphonsus Liguori, *The Passion of Jesus Christ*, p. 193.

1195. *The Value of Self-sacrifice*

St John Vianney is . . . explicit on the necessity of self-renunciation. 'There is only one way of giving oneself to God, and that is the exercise of self-renunciation and sacrifice; by surrendering one's whole self without keeping anything back. The little that we keep serves only to embarrass us and to make us suffer. . . . We have nothing of our own but our will; it is the only thing we can draw from our own being to offer in homage to the good God. Whenever we are able to renounce our own will to do the will of others, we acquire great merit, which is known to God alone. What is it that makes religious life so meritorious? It is the renunciation of our own will, this continual death to what is most alive in us. . . . Yet, even in the world we may at every moment find some occasion of giving up our own way. . . . I have known beautiful souls living in the world who had no will of their own and who were entirely dead to themselves. This is what makes us saints.

Gabriel, *Ascetical Conferences for Religious*, pp. 272-273.

1196. *Priest's Self-sacrifice Obtains Release of Many Prisoners*

[The following story concerning the saintly priest Sanctulus was recorded by St Gregory the Great in his *Dialogues* only forty days after the priest had visited the pope. The Lombards threatened to kill a deacon, but Sanctulus asked that the deacon be committed to his custody. The Lombards agreed on condition that if the deacon escaped, they would kill Sanctulus. At midnight, Sanctulus awakened the deacon and urged him to flee. When the Lombards threatened to kill Sanctulus he told them:] 'Kill me in whatever way God will allow you to kill me.' [The Lombards decided to behead him, but allowed him to say some prayers before carrying out their threat. When the executioner raised his sword, his arm stiffened so that he could not bring down the sword. Then the Lombards asked Sanctulus to heal the executioner's arm but Sanctulus answered:] 'I will not pray for him unless he first take an oath not to kill another Christian with that arm.' [Recognizing the exceptional powers of Sanctulus, the Lombards offered him presents, but he refused, saying:] 'If you wish to give me anything, give me all the prisoners you have in your power. Then I will have good reason to pray for you.' [His request was granted, and all of the prisoners were told to go with him to their freedom.]

St Gregory the Great, in *The Fathers of the Church,* vol. 39, pp. 178, 181-183.

SELF-KNOWLEDGE

1197. *Self-knowledge Through Knowledge of God*
It is only in the light of God that we see ourselves for what we are.
Edward Leen, *Progress Through Mental Prayer*, p. 123.

1198. *Why Self-Knowledge Is Difficult*
The most difficult of all things seems to be to know one's self. For not alone does our eye look outwardly and not use its power to look at itself, but our mind also; so sharp to note the sins of others, it is slow to see its own sins. Neither should you be too severe, or too prompt in rebuking others.
St Basil, in Toal, vol. 4, pp. 140-141.

SELF-LOVE

1199. *Self-Love – good and bad*
There are two sorts of self-love: the one good, the other pernicious. The former is that which makes us seek eternal life – the end of our creation; the latter inclines us to pursue earthly goods and to prefer them to our everlasting welfare and to the holy will of God.
St Alphonsus Liguori, *The True Spouse of Jesus Christ*, p. 129.

1200. *Self-love – Right and Wrong*
. . . Who is he, you will say, who does not love himself? This is who it is: 'He that loveth iniquity hateth his own soul' (Ps 10:6). Does he love himself who loves his body, but hates his soul, to his own loss, to the loss of soul and body? And who loves his soul? He who loves God with his whole heart and with his whole mind. To such a one I would then entrust a neighbor. Love your neighbor as you love yourselves.
St Augustine, in Toal, vol. 4, p. 222.

1201. *Self-love of the Right Kind is Obligatory*
We are bound to love our neighbor insofar as he belongs to God. Therefore, our love for our own self comes under the same principle. God died for

our salvation, and hence our first duty of charity is to save our own soul. In desiring our own good, we should be guided by this principle; and we may, and often should, seek health, pleasure, safety, learning, honor, fame and the goods of this world insofar as they assist us to reach our supernatural end. Insofar as these things come between us and God, or lead us away from him to seek them, their pursuit is not true Christian love of ourselves. Because we are personally responsible for our own salvation, we must put that first.

Boylan, *This Tremendous Lover*, p. 197.

1202. *Self-love of the Right Kind Vs. Love of Neighbor*

God wants us to love our neighbor as ourselves, but *never more than ourselves*, that is, never to such an extent that we harm our own souls.

Chautard, *The Soul of the Apostolate*, p. 41.

1203. *Self-love Vs Love of Neighbor*

Gregory comments that 'two things must be guarded against in the works of the Lord – deceit and negligence. Too much love of self engenders deceit; too little love of others brings on negligence.'

St Bonaventure, *Rooted in Faith*, p. 40.

1204. *Self-love an Obstacle to Divine Love*

. . . The only obstacle that prevents the Holy Spirit from enkindling in our hearts the fire of divine love is our inordinate self-love, which is entirely rooted in our foolish worship of self, our pride. Hence our whole energy must be centered on humbling ourselves, not only before God, the sovereign excellence, but also before every one of his creatures insofar as God deigns to manifest himself through them by his various gifts in the natural and the supernatural order.

Gabriel, *Ascetical Conferences for Religious*, pp. 10-11.

1205. *Self-love to Be Overcome by Love for God*

'To overcome our self-love and to deny ourselves in all things', says St John of the Cross, 'we require another and nobler love, the love of God, so that, placing all our joy in him . . . we may muster such courage and determination as will enable us effectually to abandon everything else.' . . .

Louis of Granada is even more explicit in teaching this same truth. He says: 'Among the various means we have of overcoming ourselves, the principal one is divine charity; because the love of God, being directly opposed to the love of self, wages the strongest war against it and soon expels it from the soul.'

Gabriel, *ibid.*, pp. 68-69.

1206. *Self-love Is Our Most Dangerous Enemy*
Unhappy the soul that suffers itself to be ruled by its own inclinations. 'A domestic enemy,' says St Bernard, 'is the worst of foes.'. . . The devil and the world continually seek our destruction, but self-love is a still more dangerous enemy. 'Self-love', says St Mary Magdalene de Pazzi, 'is a worm that corrodes the roots of a plant, deprives us not only of fruit, but of life.'
St Alphonsus Liguori, *The True Spouse of Jesus Christ*, p. 130.

1207. *Who Is Governed by Self-love?*
He is governed by self-love who improperly seeks his own natural interests and hates and avoids everything opposed to them.

Self-love is self-respect corrupted by original sin, but self-respect was created in us by God. Therefore, self-love cannot be rooted out, but must be purified and ennobled. It is the basic cause of the eleven passions and the seven capital sins; it therefore plays a most important role in our lives. Self-love is most frequently and clearly seen in the different kinds of sensuality, in pride and in unkindness. Self-love knows only too well how to deceive even the best-intentioned, for it tries to represent what it loves as right, and what is repugnant to it as evil. 'What we desire, we easily believe.'
Wallenstein, *Guide to Perfect Christian Living*, p. 125.

1208. *A Kingdom Hostile to the Supernatural*
The kingdom of self is in irreconcilable hostility to the supernatural. Loyalty to it is the most rooted instinct in fallen human nature, and the most difficult to be eradicated. It resists the action of God strongly. Man must will to destroy it and invite God's aid to accomplish this destruction. If this vile self-love is dethroned in the realm of a man's soul, the divine charity can invade it and in its train the other virtues.
Edward Leen, *The True Vine and Its Branches*, p. 176.

1209. *Self-Love Ruinous in Religious Communities*
Men who seek admission to religious institutes of exact observance must be altogether detached from all self-esteem. Many leave their country, their comforts and parents, but carry with them a certain esteem for themselves; but this is the most hurtful attachment of all. The greatest sacrifice that we can make to God is to give him not only goods, pleasures, and home, but ourselves also, by leaving ourselves. This is that denying of self which Jesus Christ recommends. . . .

Better would it be, perhaps, that a religious Order should be destroyed than that there should enter into it that accursed pest of ambition, which, when it enters, disfigures the most exemplary of communities and the most beautiful works of God.

St Alphonsus Liguori, *Great Means of Salvation and of Perfection*, p. 406-407.

SELF-WILL

1210. *Self-will, the Source of All Evil*

Nothing but self-will can separate us from God. Neither all the men on earth nor all the devils in hell can deprive us of his grace. 'Let self-will cease,' says St Bernard, 'and there will be no hell.'... St Anselm says that 'the will of God is the foundation of all good, and the will of man the source of all evil.'... 'Whoever', says St Bernard, 'constitutes himself his own master, becomes the disciple of a fool.'

St Alphonsus Liguori, *The True Spouse of Jesus Christ*, p. 143.

1211. *Self-will Made the Devils; Denying It Makes Saints*

St Augustine asserts that 'the devil has been made a devil by self-will.'... 'You will', says St Jerome, 'advance in proportion as you deny your own self-will.'

St Alphonsus Liguori, *The True Spouse of Jesus Christ*, pp. 143 and 145.

1212. *Self-will Makes Even Good Actions Ugly*

... The most attractive things and apparently the holiest become ugly in God's sight when our self-will is found in them.

Blessed Claude de la Colombière, *Faithful Servant*, p. 352.

1213. *Self-will Ruinous for Religious*

What does it avail to leave comforts, parents and honors, if we still carry into religion our own will? In this principally consists the denial of ourselves, the spiritual death, and the entire surrender to Jesus Christ. The gift of the heart – that is, of the will – is what pleases him most, and what he wishes from the children of religion. Otherwise, if we do not entirely detach ourselves from our own will and renounce it in all, all mortifications, all meditations and prayers, and all other sacrifices will be of little avail.

St Alphonsus Liguori, *Great Means of Salvation and of Perfection*, p. 409.

1214. *The Sacrifice of Self-will*

Since nothing is more dear to us than self-will, the sacrifice of it is the most acceptable offering we can present to the Lord.

St Alphonsus Liguori, *The True Spouse of Jesus Christ*, p. 421.

1215. *Self-will, Self-love to Be Conquered*
Our principal care . . . should be to conquer ourselves. *Conquer thyself.* St Ignatius of Loyola appeared not to consider any lesson more important than that which is contained in the words: *Conquer thyself*: his familiar discourses were ordinarily on conquering self-love and subduing self-will.
St Alphonsus Liguori, *Dignity and Duties of the Priest*, p. 342.

1216. *Self-will Vs The Will of God*
St Philip Neri used to say that sanctity consists in the mortification of self-will. Blosius has asserted that he who mortifies self-will does an act more pleasing to God than if he gave life to the dead. . . .

It is necessary to understand that all our good consists in a union with the divine will.
St Alphonsus, *ibid.*, pp. 357-358.

1217. *Sacrificing Self-will produces saints*
It is not retirement nor long conversations with God that produces saints. It is the sacrifice of our own will in even the holiest things, and an inseparable attachment to God's will.
Blessed Claude de la Colombière, *Faithful Servant*, p. 349.

1218. *Self-denial Not the Same as Mortification*
'If any man will come after me, let him deny himself and take up his cross daily and follow me' (Lk 9:23).

What is self-denial? A definition of it presents some difficulty. It is almost as subtle and elusive as its opposite, self-love. It is not to be taken as synonymous with mortification. It is something that strikes much deeper. The etymology of the word serves as a good guide in the analysis of what the word stands for. To 'deny self' is the contrary of 'to assert self' or 'to put self forward'. Self-seeking in all its forms is an evil tendency surviving in man as an effect of original sin. Under its prompting, man aims at making himself the center of all things. The honor that is due from a dependent being to the being on whom he depends is given by fallen man not to God but to himself. Instead of glorifying God, he has an inveterate inclination to glorify himself. This 'self' which claims man's fealty is but another name for what St Paul calls the 'old man' or the fallen Adam in each human being.
Edward Leen, *The True Vine and Its Branches*, p. 178.

SEMINARY TRAINING

1219. *Asceticism, Spiritual Direction Urged*
We compliment those ever more numerous bishops who follow Pius X in believing that a course of ascetic and even mystical theology is more valuable in their major seminaries than lectures on sociology.

To emphasize the importance of direction, they demand above all that their seminaries be faithful to it for the sake of their own personal progress, and that all the professors hold it in high esteem and *prove that they do so by radiating the interior life.*

Chautard, *The Soul of the Apostolate*, p. 173.

SEX

1220. *When It Ceases Being a Servant, it Becomes a Tyrant*
Chesterton insists rightly that 'sex cannot be admitted to a mere equality among elementary emotions or experiences like eating and sleeping. The moment sex ceases to be a servant, it becomes a tyrant. There is something dangerous and disproportionate in its place in human nature, for whatever reason; and it does really need a special purification and dedication. The modern talk about sex being free like any other sense, about the body being beautiful like any tree or flower, is either a description of the Garden of Eden or a piece of thoroughly bad psychology, of which the world grew weary two thousand years ago' (*St Francis of Assisi*, pp. 40-41).

Quoted by Kirsch, in *Sex Education and Training in Chastity*, p. 383.

SICKNESS

1221. *'Lessons to Be Learned from Sickness*
. . . The sick are to be admonished that they feel themselves to be sons of God in that the scourge of discipline chastises them. For, unless he purposed to give them an inheritance after correction, he would not have a care to educate them by afflictions. For hence the Lord says to John by the angel, 'Whom I love I rebuke and chastise' (Rv 3:19) Prv 3:11). . . .

The sick are to be told that, if they believe the heavenly country to be their own, they must needs endure labors in this as in a strange land.

St Gregory the Great, in *The Nicene and Post-Nicene Fathers,* vol. 12, p. 35.

1222. *Sickness, Afflictions to Be Borne as God's Will*

Father Master Avila says very well, writing to a sick priest: 'Do not reckon up what you would have done if you had been well, but how much you will please God by acquiescing in being ill. . . . ' St Bonaventure says the same: 'There is more perfection in bearing with patience and conformity afflictions and adversities than in being hard at work on excellent good works'.

Rodriguez, *Practice of Perfection and Christian Virtues,* vol. 1, pp. 548-549.

SILENCE

1223. *Silence as a Virtue*

As the virtue of temperance does not consist in not eating but in eating when necessary and what is necessary, and for the rest abstaining, so the virtue of silence does not consist in not speaking but in knowing how to be silent at the proper time. They quote to this effect that saying of Ecclesiastes: 'There is a time to speak and a time to be silent' (3:7).

Rodriguez, *ibid.,* vol. 2, p. 129.

1224. *Silence Advised Except When Speech Is More Useful*

Behold the excellent rule of St John Chrysostom: 'Then only should we speak when it is more useful to speak than to be silent.'. . . Hence the saint gives the following advice: 'Either remain silent or say what is more profitable then silence.'

St Alphonsus Liguori, *The True Spouse of Jesus Christ*, p. 474.

1225. *Silence a Sign of a Spiritual Man*

The really spiritual man is known by the kindness of his speech, and still more by the kindness of his silence.

Boylan, *This Tremendous Lover*, p. 200.

SIN

1226. *The Nature and Effects of Sin*

According to the definition of St Thomas, sin consists of turning away from God in order to turn toward creatures. . . . It is an act committed knowingly and willfully, by which man turns away from God, his Creator,

Redeemer, Father, Friend and Last End, on account of some creature. . . .

Such then is grievous deliberate sin. It is as if one said to God: 'My God, I know thou dost forbid this thing, that in doing it I shall lose thy friendship, but I shall do it just the same'.

Marmion, *Christ, the Life of the Soul,* p. 175.

1227. *The Only Real Evil*

. . . There is one good, which is God, and one evil which is sin. Sin! This is the monster that has emptied heaven, for which hell was created, on account of which there has been wailing and lamentation for so many centuries, that will go on for all eternity and never have an end; this is the evil to be avoided at all costs, as the Holy Spirit says in the Book of Ecclesiasticus: 'Flee from sins as from the face of a serpent. . . . The teeth thereof are the teeth of a lion, killing the souls of men. All iniquity is a two-edged sword: there is no remedy for the wound thereof' (Ecclus 21:2-4).

However, there is another great evil in the world, and in a certain sense still greater, and it is this: that the great evil of sin is not known or recognized. People have lost the sense of sin, and from this arises an immense, incalculable evil. Sin is committed with the greatest facility and, as it were, for fun.

St Joseph Cafasso, *The Priest, the Man of God*, p. 154.

1228. *Sin as Incredible Stupidity*

[Sin] is incredible stupidity: rebellion against God is one of the most ludicrous things in the world. For whether we are obedient or rebellious we are at every moment totally in the hands of God. He made us out of nothing; by his almighty power he keeps us above the surface of our native nothingness.

Sheed, *A Map of Life*, p. 95.

1229. *Sin Is the Fuel That Feeds the Fires Hereafter*

What other things shall the fire feed on but thy sins? The more thou sparest thyself now and followest the flesh, the more grievously shalt thou suffer hereafter and the more fuel dost thou lay up for that fire.

Thomas à Kempis, *Imitation of Christ*, bk. I, chap. 24.

1230. *What God Thinks of Sin*

If we want to know what God thinks of sin, let us look at Jesus in his passion. When we behold God strike his Son, whom he infinitely loves, with the death of the cross, we understand a little what sin is in God's sight.

Marmion, *Christ, the Life of the Soul*, p. 174.

1231. *Christ's Sorrow over Our Sins*
St Thomas says that this sorrow which Jesus Christ felt at the knowledge of the injury done to his Father, and of the evil that sin would occasion to the souls he loved, surpassed the sorrows of all the contrite sinners that ever existed, even those who died of pure sorrow; because no sinner ever loved God and his own soul as much as Jesus loved his Father and our souls.
St Alphonsus Liguori, *The Incarnation, Birth and Infancy of Jesus Christ,* p. 200.

1232. *The Grief Sin Causes Christ*
In proportion as the eternal Word loved his Father, to that extent did he hate sin. He understood very well the malice of sin. And so, in order to deliver the world from it and no longer see his Father offended, He came down to earth and became man and decided to undergo such an agonizing passion and death. But then he saw that in spite of all his sufferings there would still be many sins committed in the world. And the sorrow this caused him (in Gethsemani), according to St Thomas, exceeded the sorrow any penitent ever felt for his own sins. 'It surpassed the sorrow of all contrite souls'. says the Angelic Doctor.
St Alphonsus Liguori, *The Passion of Jesus Christ*, p. 33.

1233. *Christ Hates Sin*
[Christ] cannot but look with hatred on sin, and cannot love us insofar as we are sinners.
Edward Leen, *In The Likeness of Christ*, p. 202.

1234. *Each Sin Afflicted Jesus Grievously*
St Bernardine of Siena writes that Jesus Christ 'had a particular regard to every single sin.'... Each of our sins was present continually to our Savior, even from his infancy, and afflicted him grievously.
St Alphonsus Liguori, *The Incarnation, Birth and Infancy of Jesus Christ,* p. 295.

1235. *How the Sins of Christians Afflict Christ*
Jesus one day appeared to St Teresa crowned with thorns. The saint began to show pity for him; but the Lord said: 'Teresa, do not pity me for the wounds which the thorns of the Jews produced. Pity me on account of the wounds the sins of Christians occasion me.'
St Alphonsus Liguori, *The Passion of Jesus Christ*, p. 49.

1236. *The Sins of Religious Are More Terrible than Persecutions*
I am more frightened by the faults of the subjects than by the persecutions that assail us. I also entreat each one to fear lest the Lord should also expel him, as He lately expelled several.

St Alphonsus Liguori, in *Letters of St Alphonsus*, vol. 3, p. 170, (a letter to the Fathers and Brothers of the Congregation of the Most Holy Redeemer, November 1776).

1237. *Sin Is Hurtful to the Sinner*
Every sin is more hurtful to the sinner than to the sinned against.

St Augustine, *Enchiridion on Faith, Hope and Love*, p. 20.

1238. *Sin Defiles the Image of God in Our Souls*
. . . Since we have all been created interiorly in our souls according to God's image, as often as we say or do something shameful we defile God's image. . . . If you put your image on a tablet of wood or stone, and someone impudently wanted to shatter that image with stones or to stain it with dirt, I wonder whether you would not take up arms against him. I ask you, if you are so jealous of your image that was painted on a lifeless tablet, what kind of injury do you suppose God suffers when his living image in us is defiled by dissipation? Therefore, if we do not restrain ourselves for our own sake, let us do so for the sake of God's image, according to which we have been made.

St Caesarius of Arles, in *The Fathers of the Church*, vol. 31, pp. 224-225.

1239. *Sin Clouded the Mind*
It is true that sin has clouded the mind to the knowledge of eternal truths and has introduced into the soul concupiscence of sensible good, forbidden by the divine command; yes, but what helps and means has not Jesus Christ obtained for us by his merits, in order to procure us light and strength to vanquish all our enemies, and to advance in virtue? The holy sacraments, the sacrifice of the Mass, prayer to God through the merits of Jesus Christ – ah! These are indeed arms and means, sufficient, not only to gain the victory over all temptations and concupiscences, but even to run forward and fly in the way of perfection. It is certain that by these very means given to us, all the saints of the new law have become saints. Ours, then, is the fault, if we do not avail ourselves of them.

St Alphonsus Liguori, *Incarnation, Birth and Infancy of Jesus Christ*, p. 54.

1240. *Sin to Be Feared*
Better fear sin than death.
Rodriguez, *Practice of Perfection and Christian Virtues,* vol. 1, p. 110.

1241. *Our Sins Should Displease Us above All Else*
Fear nothing so much, blame and abhor nothing so much as thy vices and sins, which ought to displease thee more than any losses whatsoever.
Thomas à Kempis, *Imitation of Christ*, bk. III, chap. 4.

1242. *Learning to Hate Sin*
One of the means of attaining this necessary destruction of sin is to hate it; one makes no compact with any enemy one hates. In order to have this hatred of sin, it is necessary to know its deep malice and infernal ugliness. But who can know the malice of sin? To be able to fathom it we should have to know God himself, whom it offends. . . . It puts God beneath the creature. . . . It is the practical contempt of God's rights. . . .
Marmion, *Christ, the Life of the Soul*, pp. 170-171.

1243. *If We Remember Our Sins, God Will Not*
'Turn away thy face from my sins, and blot out mine iniquities' (Ps 1:11). So Jerome, on these words, observes: 'If you keep your sin before you, God will not keep it before Him'. . . . St Clement relates of the glorious Apostle St Peter, that at the recollection of his having denied Christ he wept so much that the tears burned his face and made furrows down his cheeks. At the first cock crow he arose every night to pray and slept no more all that night; and this custom he kept all his life.
Rodriguez, *Practice of Perfection and Christian Virtues*, vol. 2, pp. 510-511.

1244. *God Wishes to Draw Good from Our Defects*
Blosius relates of the holy virgin Gertrude that she afflicted and scolded herself much for a small defect that she had, and desired and begged God to deliver her from it altogether. And the Lord replied very gently and sweetly: 'Why wishest thou me to be deprived of great honor and thyself of great reward? For every time that thou dost recognize this defect or any other like it, and purposest to avoid it in the future, thou gainest a great reward; and every time that anyone endeavors to overcome his defects for my love, he honoreth me as much as a soldier would honor his king by fighting manfully in war against his enemies and trying to overcome them.'
Rodriguez, *ibid.*, pp. 380-381.

1245. *Sin "Works Together unto Good"*
'All things work together unto good' (Rom 8:28). 'Even sins,' subjoins the gloss. Yes, even the remembrance of the sins we have committed contributes to the advantage of the sinner who bewails and detests them, because this very thing will . . . make him more humble and more pleasing to God, when he sees how God has welcomed him into the arms of His loving mercies: 'There shall be joy in heaven upon one sinner that doth penance, more than upon ninety-nine just.'
St Alphonsus Liguori, *Incarnation, Birth and Infancy of Jesus Christ*, p. 70.

1246. *The Guilt of Sin Remitted*
In dealing with the objection that guilt is only remitted by expiation, St Thomas repeats the principle that the baptized, inasmuch as he is a member of Christ, communicates in the expiation of his passion as if he himself had undergone it. . . . The member of Christ, then, can call the infinite merits of Christ his own and offer them to God for all his needs; and that special title of them acquired in Baptism endures as long as he is not in mortal sin. What limit then is there to his hope?
Boylan, *This Tremendous Lover*, p. 56.

1247. *Sin Gives Us a Right to Go to Christ*
When cavilled at because he [Jesus] frequented the society of those who were not remarkable for the rectitude of their lives, his answer was that he 'was not come to call the just but sinners'. Our sins, then, far from creating a barrier between us and him, really constitute a reason and give us a title or right to come to him, as they also constitute a reason for his coming to us. To the Pharisees he said equivalently: 'I frequent sinners because they need me more than others – the physician passes his time with and gives all his attention and care to those that are ill, and not to those that are in health. I am the Physician of souls. That is my work, and they that are in health need not a physician but they that are ill' (Mt 9:12).
Edward Leen, *In the Likeness of Christ*, p. 207.

1248. *Our Sins Are Only a Cobweb*
[With St John Chrysostom, the director may] likewise suggest [that all our sins], though most grievous, are, when set side by side with God's mercy, but a cobweb which is blown away by a single puff of wind. . . . And if the confessor were to go further and say that were the whole piled-up heap of our enormities to be cast into the boundless ocean of God's mercy, it would be but a drop of gall in a sea of milk, he would in no wise exaggerate, but fall short of the truth.
Scaramelli, *Directorium Asceticum*, vol. 4, p. 86.

1249. *Sin Forgiven, Prevented by God's Grace*
To thy grace and thy mercy do I attribute the fact that thou hast melted away my sins like ice. So, also, to thy grace do I attribute whatever evil things I did not do, for what could I not have done, who even loved an evil action for itself?
St Augustine, *Confessions*, bk. 2, chap. 7.

1250. *Cross and Eucharist Help Us Overcome Sin*
. . . Innocent III says . . . 'The mystery of the cross delivers us from the power of sin; the mystery of the Eucharist, from the will to sin.'
St Alphonsus Liguori, *Incarnation, Birth and Infancy of Jesus Christ*, p. 79.

1251. *Motives for Avoiding Sin*
. . . There is a great difference between one who puts out the fire of sin within him by fear of hell or hope of future reward, and one who from the feeling of divine love has a horror of sin itself. . . .
Abbot Shaeremon, quoted in *The Nicene and Post-Nicene Fathers*, vol. 11, p. 418.

1252. *Preventing Sin Is the Greatest Work of All*
There is no greater or more noble work either in heaven or on earth than this: to prevent offenses against God. . . . It is sufficient to say that neither the angels nor the saints nor our Blessed Lady herself could do greater work than that which a priest does when he opposes the commission of sin and prevents it.
St Joseph Cafasso, *The Priest, the Man of God*, pp. 161-162.

1253. *Sin Honors the Devil*
. . . We believe that, as in good works, God is honored, so in wicked works the enemy is honored. . . . Let us fear lest, by bringing glory and occasions of exultation to the devil through our sins, we may be handed over to everlasting shame with him.
St Basil, in *The Fathers of the Church*, vol. 46, p. 197.

1254. *The Sins of Men Give Satisfaction to the Devils*
'Thou already knowest that my Son and Lord in the Gospel says that the angels have joy in heaven whenever any sinner does penance and is converted (Lk 15:10). . . . Now that which happens among the heavenly inhabitants in the conversion of sinners and in the increase of the just has a counterpart in what happens with the demons at the sins of the just and the deeper falls of sinners; for no sin is committed by men, however small,

in which the demons do not take pleasure. . . . '

The Blessed Virgin Mary to Mary of Agreda, in *City of God: Words of Wisdom,* p. 465.

1255. *The Devil Hates Sermons on Avoiding Occasions of Sin*
. . . The devil once confessed, being compelled to do so by exorcisms, that of all sermons, that which is most displeasing to him is the sermon on avoiding occasions of sin; and with reason, for the devil laughs at the resolutions and promises of the repentant sinner if he does not quit dangerous occasions.

St Alphonsus Liguori, *Preparation for Death*, p. 85.

1256. *Occasions of Sin Must Be Avoided*
. . . Not to remove the proximate occasion of mortal sin is in itself a mortal sin. And, as I have already shown in my *Moral Theology* (Lib. 6, n. 454), he that receives absolution without a firm purpose of removing the proximate occasion of mortal sin commits a new mortal sin, and is guilty of sacrilege.

St Alphonsus Liguori, *The True Spouse of Jesus Christ*, p. 531.

1257. *What Mortal Sin Is*
What is mortal sin? According to St Thomas and St Augustine, it is a *turning away from God*; an act of contempt for his grace and love; and a throwing off of all respect for him before his face, by which the sinner declares: I will not serve thee; I will do as I please, and it matters not to me if by so doing I displease thee and forfeit thy friendship.

St Alphonsus Liguori, *Great Means of Salvation and of Perfection*, p. 324.

1258. *The Nature and Effects of Mortal Sin*
St Augustine and St Thomas define mortal sin to be a *turning away from God*: that is, the turning of one's back upon God, leaving the Creator for the sake of the creature. . . .

God complains and says: Ungrateful soul, thou hast forsaken Me! I should never have forsaken thee hadst thou not first turned thy back on me. . . . O God, with what consternation will these words fill the soul of the sinner when he stands to be judged before thy divine tribunal!

St Alphonsus Liguori, *The Way of Salvation and of Perfection*, pp. 68-69.

1259. *Meaning and Effects of Mortal Sin*
The sinner must be sensible that God cannot dwell in a soul together with

sin. When, therefore, sin enters the soul, God must depart from it. So that the sinner, by admitting sin, says to God: As thou canst no longer remain with me, unless I renounce sin, depart from me; it is better to lose thee than the pleasure of committing sin. At the same time that the soul expels God, it gives possession to the devil. Thus does the sinner eject his God, who loves him, and makes himself the slave of a tyrant who hates him.

St Alphonsus, *ibid.*, p. 155.

1260. *Requirements for Mortal Sin*

. . . It is certain that for the commission of a mortal sin, there is required a full perception on the part of the reason, and a complete, deliberate consent on the part of the will, and to will something which greviously offends God.

St Alphonsus Liguori, *The Way of Salvation and of Perfection*, p. 458.

1261. *Four Effects of Mortal Sin*

. . . Keep in mind these four things: that by [mortal] sin you have lost God's grace, given up your place in paradise, chosen the eternal pains of hell and rejected God's eternal love.

St Francis de Sales, *Introduction to the Devout Life*, p. 41.

1262. *The Gravity of Mortal Sin*

It must be that sin is a great evil, since God, who is mercy itself, is obliged to punish it with an eternal hell. But what more? In order to satisfy divine justice for sin, a God was obliged to sacrifice His own Life.

St Alphonsus Liguori, *Great Means of Salvation and of Perfection*, p. 325.

1263. *The Sight of Man's Mortal Sins Saddened Christ*

It was because our loving Redeemer had our sins constantly before his eyes that his life was so painful and full of bitterness. This was the cause of his sweating blood and suffering the agonies of death in the garden of Gethsemane, where he declared that his 'soul was sorrowful even unto death.' What made him sweat blood and caused him so dreadful an agony but the sight of the sins of men?

St Alphonsus Liguori, *The Way of Salvation and of Perfection*, p. 103.

1264. *Merits Lost by Sin Revived by Grace*

When people lose charity, their good deeds are forgotten because they are useless as long as sin renders eternal life – their reward – an impossibility. Thus, as soon as charity reinstates us as God's children, so disposing us for immortal glory, God recalls our past virtues, which prove valuable to us once more. It would not do for sin to have greater influence than charity; after all, sin is the result of our weakness, while charity is due to God's power. If bad will amplifies our sin to be the end of us, grace is more amply bestowed than ever to put things right. God's mercy, by which he blots out sin, ever triumphs over the severity of his justice, through which he forgot the good deeds sin had veiled. Always, therefore, in our Lord's miraculous healings of the sick, he not only gave them back their health, but additional blessings they never knew before. The cure should far outweigh the ill – so good is God to man.

St Francis De Sales, *The Love of God*, p. 494.

1265. *Our Actions Rendered Valueless by Sin*

. . . All the activity of a soul in a state of mortal sin is fruitless for heaven, however brilliant this activity may appear in the eyes of the world in the natural domain; a withered branch, by its own fault no longer receiving the divine sap of grace, the soul that remains in this state is likened by Christ himself to dead wood, good for nothing but to be cast into the fire to be burnt. . . .

Marmion, *Christ, the Life of the Soul*, p. 176.

1266. *Worst Punishment of Sin Is Abandonment by God*

It is a grievous chastisement of God when he cuts the sinner off in his sins; but still worse is that whereby he abandons him and suffers him to add sin upon sin. 'No punishment is so great,' says Bellarmine, 'as when sin is made the punishment of sin.'. . .

When the master cuts down the fence of his vineyard and leaves it open for any one to enter therein, it is a sign that he considers it not worth cultivating, and abandons it. In like manner does God proceed when he forsakes a sinful soul: he takes away from it the hedge of his holy fear, of his light, and of his voice; and hence the soul being blinded and enslaved by its vices, which overpower it, despises everything, the grace of God, heaven, admonitions, and censures; it thinks lightly even of its own damnation, and thus, enveloped in darkness, is certain to be lost forever.

St Alphonsus Liguori, *The Way of Salvation and of Perfection*, pp. 79-80.

1267. *Means of Avoiding Mortal Sin*

To protect ourselves from mortal sin we should:

(1) Vigorously root out even venial sin.
(2) Be ever mindful of the presence of God and our Guardian Angel.
(3) Keep as far as possible from dangers and occasions of sin.

(4) Pray instantly at the beginning of temptation and resist it immediately and firmly.
(5) Above all, flee idleness.
(6) Be dominated always by the firm resolve to die a thousand times rather than commit one mortal sin.

Wallenstein, *Guide to Perfect Christian Living*, p. 6.

1268. *Better to Die than Commit Mortal Sin*
It is related of St Louis, King of France, that sometimes his holy mother, Queen Dona Blanca (Blanche of Castile) would say to him: 'My son, I would rather see you dead before my eyes than in mortal sin.'

Rodriguez, *Practice of Perfection and of Christian Virtues*, vol. 1, p. 566.

1269. *Distinction Between Mortal and Venial Sin*
The distinction between mortal and venial sin is very important. Between two breaches of law there may not only be a difference of degree, but actually a difference of kind. Consider the law of the land. A man may break it by not taking out a dog licence. Or he may break it by fighting against his country in war. It is not simply that one breach of the law is more serious than the other. The two breaches are totally different in their nature. So with the law of God. There are breaches of his law which do not involve rejection and rebellion, others which do.

Sheed, *A Map of Life*, p. 95.

1270. *Venial Sin Is Not a Light Matter*
. . . We must not be misled by popular usage of the word 'venial sin' into looking upon it as trifling. Theologians tell us that nothing can justify the commission of a deliberate venial sin, that it is a greater evil than any possible temporal evil, that no conceivable temporal good can outweigh the evil of its commission; that, once committed, no creature of himself could make reparation for it, that, consequently, it was expiated by the sufferings of Christ, and that we obtain pardon for it only through the merits of Christ.

Brosnahan, *Searchlighting Ourselves*, p. 69.

1271. *Next to Mortal Sin, Venial Sin Is the Greatest Evil*
Sound doctrine teaches us that, mortal sin alone excepted, venial sin is the greatest of all evils. In spite of the erroneous impression caused by its name, it must not be forgotten that it is a slight inflicted on God himself, all holy, all-loving. Because of this, it dwarfs all calamities of the natural order – plagues, wars and convulsions of nature. An offence derives its gravity from the dignity and status of the offended party. Sin, even when

it does not assume the proportions of a mortal sin, is an offence levelled not at a creature, however eminent, but at the great God himself. It is for this reason that no consideration of loss or calamity could possibly justify it. Honors and life itself do not weigh against it. The destruction of the whole creation, rational or irrational, is a less serious calamity than that Almighty God should be offended.

James Leen, *By Jacob's Well*, p. 171.

1272. *The Gravity of One Venial Sin*

. . . It is certain that one single venial sin displeases God more than all the good works that we can do please him.

St Alphonsus Liguori, *The Way of Salvation and of Perfection*, p. 384.

1273. *The Harm One Venial Sin Can Do Us*

'One venial sin can do us more harm than all hell together'.

The Life of St Teresa of Jesus, Written by Herself, p. 226.

1274. *Venial Sin Does Not Separate Us from God But Disposes us to Mortal Sin*

No matter how many venial sins we commit, they can never amount to a mortal sin, nor suffice to kill the soul or sever us from the grace and friendship of God. But they dispose the soul, debilitating, weakening and unnerving it, so that it is easily overcome by any temptation or occasion which presents itself and so comes to fall into mortal sin.

Rodriguez, *Practice of Perfection and Christian Virtues*, vol. 3, p. 390.

1275. *Danger Involved in Venial Sin*

St Isidore writes that he who makes no account of venial sins is permitted by Almighty God to fall into mortal sins in punishment of his want of love. . . .

The Council of Trent . . . teaches that we cannot persevere in grace without the special assistance of God; but he is too undeserving of such special assistance who offends God by voluntary venial sins, without any thought of amendment.

St Alphonsus Liguori, *Great Means of Salvation and of Perfection*, p. 329.

1276. *Tragic Consequences of Venial Sin*

Venial sin is a great evil in itself; it is, as well, a great evil in its consequences. It has a most baleful influence on the spiritual life.

It closes to the soul the channel of many actual graces. It paralyzes to some extent the effects of the sacraments. It sets up a barrier to the floods of grace which might sweep through souls when they receive the Blessed Eucharist. It would be difficult to estimate the loss this means for the spiritual life.... The smallest degree of sanctifying grace is infinitely more precious than all the treasures of earth. It is this great treasure that men forfeit in large measure by their ill-advised attachment to venial sin.

James Leen, *By Jacob's Well*, p. 172.

1277. *The Effects of Venial Sin*

... What are the effects of venial sin? They diminish the lights, the helps, and the protection of God; so that the soul, being darkened, weak and dry, will lose all affection for the things of God, will become attached to things of the world, and thus exposed to great danger of renouncing the grace of God for the sake of earthly goods. Besides, in punishment of venial sins, Almighty God permits the soul to be assailed with more violent temptations.

St Alphonsus Liguori, *The True Spouse of Jesus Christ*, pp. 105-106.

1278. *Habitual Venial Sin More Dangerous than Occasional Mortal Sins*

Let us suppose a soul that sincerely seeks God in all things, that truly loves him and yet happens through weakness to consent voluntarily to grievous sin. That does occur sometimes. In the world of souls there are abysses of frailty. For this soul such a fall is an immense misfortune, for divine union is severed; but this grave sin, being of a passing nature, is much less dangerous and above all less fatal for the soul than venial faults of habit or of full deliberation are for another. Why is this? The first soul is humbled, rises again, and finds in the remembrance of the sin it has committed an excellent motive for remaining in a state of humility, and a powerful incentive to a more generous love and a greater faithfulness than ever. While, on the other hand, the venial faults frequently consented to without remorse, place it in a *state* in which the supernatural action of God is constantly being thwarted. Such a soul can in no way aspire to a high degree of union with God; on the contrary, the divine action becomes ever weaker within it; the Holy Spirit is silent; and this soul will almost infallibly fall before long into more grievous sin. Doubtless, like the former, it will at once seek to enter again into God's grace; but this is not so much from the love of God as from fear of punishment.... Its supernatural life will continue to be mediocre, ever exposed to the least shaft of the enemy and to fresh falls.

Marmion, *Growth in Christ*, p. 74.

1279. *Some Venial Sins Due to Weakness – Others Dangerous*

There are certain venial faults which escape us by surprise, which often result from our temperament, faults that we regret and seek to avoid; these are miseries which in no wise prevent the soul from attaining a high degree of divine union; they are effaced by acts of charity, by a good communion; moreover they keep us humble.

But what must be greatly dreaded are venial faults which have become habits or are fully deliberate; they are the real peril for the soul; they are too often a step toward a complete severance from God. When a soul is in the habit of responding with a *deliberate* 'no' to God's will (in a small matter, since the question is of venial sins), it cannot expect to remain long united to God. Why so? Because these faults, committed with cool deliberation, pass to a state of habit unstriven against, without the soul's feeling any remorse, and this necessarily results in diminution of supernatural docility, of watchfulness and strength to resist temptation. Experience shows that, from a succession of wilful negligences in small things, we glide imperceptibly, but nearly always fatally, into grave faults.

Marmion, *Christ, the Life of the Soul*, pp. 181-182.

1280. *Callousness Towards Venial Sin Endangers Soul's Salvation*

If . . . a person wishes only to avoid mortal sins, without making any account of those which are venial, he will easily fall into mortal sin and lose his soul. . . .

If [God] should grant you only grace barely sufficient, would you be saved? You would be able to obtain salvation, but you would not obtain it because in this life temptations frequently occur so violent that it is morally impossible not to yield to them without a special assistance from God. But God does not afford his special assistance to those who deal sparingly with him: *He who soweth sparingly shall also reap sparingly*.

St. Alphonsus Liguori, *The Way of Salvation and of Perfection*, pp. 118-119.

1281. *Venial Sin Disposes to Mortal Sin*

Venial sin disposes to mortal sin first by the *effect* it produces *on the will*.

Sin being of its nature a violation of order, the will that habituates itself to violate order in smaller matters comes by gradual steps to violate it in matter that is increasingly more serious. Habits of self-restraint are weakened. It becomes more and more difficult to put forth the effort required to overcome torpidity in prayer, to observe rules, to dismiss suggestions of evil, to control desire. Communion with God becomes more and more strange and artificial, and creature comforts more and more attractive. Graces that once would have been efficacious become from day to day less and less so; temptations that once would have been easily and instantly rejected are now with difficulty rejected. Imprudences that once would have been impossible are now almost habitual. The soul finally sinks into a state of contented debility, which is not death, but is a condition in which death could easily be inflicted.

Venial sin disposes the soul to mortal sin also by the *effect* it produces *on the intellect.*

From the nature of the relation between our will and intellect, every disorder in the will induces a corresponding disorder in our judgment and ideas. We instinctively attempt to justify our inclinations before the tribunal of our reason when we are about to act in accordance with them, or at least we attempt to excuse or palliate them. This self-deception, by which we fashion our practical judgment to suit the inclinations of our corrupt nature, begins at first in little things, but gradually enlarges its sphere until vanity, sensuality and attachment to our own comforts dim the light of reason and faith.

Brosnahan, *Searchlighting Ourselves*, pp. 71-72.

1282. *The Evil of Venial Sin Illustrated*

A shrewd man of business sees to it that his shop is kept spotless. No customer worth while is going to deal with him if the counter is covered with dust, if the windows are dirty and filled with cobwebs, if the man himself is habitually unshaved, with hands always soiled, with clothes that are stained and in tatters. No. He understands well that he and all around him must be spick and span.

Here, too, that man who makes God's will the law of his life will find a page to ponder for his guidance. He understands that his life must be free, first from all stain of serious sin, but also he will labor to acquire an ever-deepening sense of the hideous nature of even venial sin. He realizes that his soul is God's dwelling place; the abode of a divine Guest. Just as the efficient man of business is careful to have everything spotless upon which the eyes of the patrons fall, so the man of God has a horror of any stain in his soul, realizing that all is naked and open before the eye of God.

Nash, *Living Your Faith*, p. 51.

1283. *Desire Death Rather than Commit a Venial Sin*

'. . . Not only for the avoiding of mortal sins, but for the avoiding of venial sins, of which we are full in this life, it is good to desire death. The servant of God should be resolved to die rather than tell a lie, which is a venial sin; and any one who should die on that score would be a martyr'.

St Thomas Aquinas, quoted in Rodriguez, *Practice of Perfection and Christian Virtues,* vol. 1, p. 567.

1284. *Remission of Venial Sin – Three Ways*
[St Thomas says:] 'The remission of venial sins is brought about in three ways: (1) By infusion of divine grace; in this way by means of the Holy Eucharist and the other sacraments, such sins are remitted; (2) By acts that include a movement of detestation, and thus by a general confession of sins, by striking the breast, by reciting the Our Father, we obtain the remission of such sins; (3) By every act of religion toward God and the things of God, such as receiving the blessing from a bishop, taking holy water, praying in a consecrated church.'

St Thomas Aquinas, quoted by St Alphonsus Liguori, in *Dignity and Duties of the Priest*, p. 103.

1285. *Nine Specially Harmful Groups of Venial Sins*
One of the most effective means to keep ourselves free from mortal sin is the firm resolve to avoid all, even the smallest willful venial sins. Particularly detrimental to the spiritual life are the following nine groups of venial sins:

(a) To keep in our hearts evil suspicion, wrong judgment and contempt for our fellowmen.
(b) To foster anger and ill-will.
(c) To mention the faults of our fellowmen in our conversations and to destroy love and unity by talebearing.
(d) To omit spiritual exercises out of slothfulness or to perform them with willful distractions.
(e) To retain inordinate love in our hearts; to intentionally entertain impure thoughts or be negligent in suppressing them.
(f) To have a high opinion of ourselves, to despise others and to have an inordinate complacency in ourselves.
(g) To receive the sacraments without earnest preparation, with tepidity, distracting thoughts or other irreverences.
(h) To accept adversities with impatience and without view to the hand of God, thereby destroying the ways of God and the designs of Divine Providence for us.
(i) To hide the state of our soul with forethought and deliberation, to hide our evil inclinations, weaknesses, faults and mortifications from those who ought to know about them; to walk in the way of virtue not according to the guidance of obedience but following our own will.

If you cannot resolve to avoid these venial sins, you will not draw the least fruit from your spiritual exercises; you never will climb even to the lowest step in spiritual perfection; you will never attain either to union with God or to interior peace of heart; nor will you ever be in a condition in which you could expect death without fear.

Wallenstein, *Guide to Perfect Christian Living*, pp. 7-8.

1286. *Frequent Confession of Venial Sin Urged*

'The opinions of those who assert that little importance should be given to the frequent confession of venial sins are false, hinder spiritual progress of the faithful and contribute deplorably to their ruin. . . . It is true indeed that venial sins may be expiated in many ways which are to be highly commended. But to hasten daily progress along the path of virtue, we wish the pious practice of frequent confession to be earnestly advocated. Not without the inspiration of the Holy Spirit was this practice introduced into the Church. By it, genuine self-knowledge is increased, Christian humility grows, bad habits are corrected, spiritual neglect and tepidity are countered, the conscience is purified, the will strengthened, a salutary self-control is attained, and grace is increased in virtue of the sacrament itself. Let those, therefore, among the young clergy who make light of or weaken esteem of frequent confession realize that what they are doing is foreign to the spirit of Christ, and disastrous for the Mystical Body of our Savior.'

Pius XII, *Encyclical on the Mystical Body*, quoted in Wallenstein, *ibid.*, p. 12.

1287. *Hideousness of Venial Sin*

Our Lord once showed St Catherine of Siena the hideousness of one venial sin; and such was the dread and sorrow of the saint that she fell senseless to the ground.

St Alphonsus Liguori, *Incarnation, Birth and Infancy of Jesus Christ*, p. 197.

AMBITION

1288. *Ambition of the Apostles James and John*

'We desire that whatsoever we shall ask, thou wouldst do it for us' (Mk 10:35). And Jesus asked them: 'What would you that I should do for you?' Not because he did not know, but that he might compel them to answer and so lay bare the ulcer, that he might apply a remedy for it. . . .

God is opposed to nothing so much as to pride. . . .

Fot it is the nature of pride that not alone does it add nothing to our life, but it takes from us that which we have. But humility takes from us nothing that we have, but rather adds that which we have not.

St John Chrysostom, in Toal, vol. 1, pp. 413-414.

1289. *Ambition Vs Charity*
Peter of Blois says that the ambition of honors is the ruin of souls. . . . For ambition disturbs regularity of life and injures charity toward God. Ambition, as the same author says, pretends to resemble charity, and is quite opposed to it. Charity suffers all things, but only for the attainment of eternal goods; ambition bears all things . . . but only for things perishable. Charity is all benignity to the poor, but ambition is kind to the rich. Charity bears all things in order to please God; ambition submits to all evils for the sake of vanity. Charity believes and hopes for all that appertains to eternal glory; ambition believes all things, hopes for all things, that tend to the glory of this life.
St Alphonsus Liguori, *Dignity and Duties of the Priest*, p. 351-352.

1290. *Ambition for Worldly Honors Is Ruinous*
'All worldly honor', says St Hilary, 'is the business of the devil.' . . . Worldly honors are the means by which Satan gains many souls for hell. And, if the ambition of honors occasions great ruin in a worldling, it is productive of far greater havoc in a religious. 'The body of the Church,' says St Leo, 'is defiled by the contention of the ambitious.'
St Alphonsus Liguori, *The True Spouse of Jesus Christ*, p. 325.

1291. *Ambition Ruinous for Convents*
'I would rather see this monastery burnt to the ground than ever see ambition enter into it' (St Teresa). . . .

Similar were the sentiments of St Jane Frances de Chantal. 'I would', says the saint, 'sooner see my monastery buried in the sea, than to see ambition or the desire of office enter it.'
St Alphonsus, *ibid.*, p. 325.

EVILS OF ANGER

1292. *Anger Impedes Reason*
As far as concerns reason, says the Angelic Doctor, among all the passions which run riot in our hearts, none impedes reason so much as anger.
Scaramelli, *Directorium Asceticum*, vol. 3, p. 338.

1293. *Anger as a Sign of Weakness*
When . . . anyone is overcome by a wrong, and blazes up in a fire of anger, we should not hold that the bitterness of the insult offered to him is the *cause* of his sin, but rather the *manifestation* of a secret weakness.
Abbot Piamun, in *The Nicene and Post-Nicene Fathers*, vol. 11, p. 485.

1294. *Anger Can Make a Man Bestial*
'A wrathful man is not seemly' (Prv 11:25). . . . Indeed, this vice, when it has once succeeded in banishing reason, itself usurps the domination over the soul. It makes a man wholly bestial and, in fact, it does not even allow him to be a man, since he no longer has the aid of his reason.
St Basil, in *The Fathers of the Church*, vol. 9, pp. 447-448.

1295. *Anger and Justice*
. . . There never was an angry man who thought his anger unjust.
St Francis de Sales, *Introduction to the Devout Life*, p. 121.

1296. *The Fuel of Anger*
Noisy speech is the fuel of anger. . .
Let us clip the wings of anger, and no longer will the evil rise to its peak. . . . It is ridiculous to be able to tame wild beasts yet to allow our own minds to be savagely angry.
St John Chrysostom in *The Fathers of the Church*, vol. 33, pp. 257-258.

1297. *A Cure for Anger*
How can anger be cured 'except by Our Savior's patience?' [asks St Augustine].
St Alphonsus Liguori, *The Passion of Jesus Christ*, p. 208.

1298. *How to Resist Temptations to Anger*
Were you struck in the face? So, too, was the Lord. Were you spat upon? And so was our Lord. . . . Were you falsely accused? So, too, was your Judge. . . . You have not been condemned to death; nor fastened upon a cross. Many things are wanting before you become like him.
Let each one of these considerations enter into your thoughts; and let them be a restraint on angry passion. For it is by such considerations and affections that we calm the throbbing, the violent impulse of the heart, and bring our mind to sanity and peace.
St Basil, in Toal, vol. 4, p. 275.

1299. *How to Correct Anger and Practise Meekness*
The passion of anger may be weakened, says St Gregory, in two ways. The first is that, before acting, we unfold to our mind's eye all the insults that may be showered upon us, to the end that considering what our dear Lord has been pleased to endure for love of us, we may dispose ourselves to put up with them for his sake. . . .
St Gregory proceeds to set forth the second remedy which he prescribes for curbing anger and acquiring meekness. The second means for acquiring

meekness under injury is, on beholding the excesses of others against ourselves, we call to mind the shortcomings whereby we, in our turn, have transgressed at other times. For the consideration of our weakness will help us to excuse that of others.

Scaramelli, *Directorium Asceticum*, vol. 3, pp. 357 and 360.

1300. *How to Control Anger and Make It Profitable*

When a friend vexes you, or some member of your household stirs you to anger, consider your transgressions against God and that, by the . . . clemency you exercise toward those who have offended you, you may render that judgment of His milder for yourself. Scripture, in fact says: 'Forgive, and you shall be forgiven' (Lk 6:37), and so your passion will quickly depart. . . .

Accordingly, when you have been angered, do not say . . . 'I will not allow that rogue to make a fool of me and get away with it'. Indeed, no one will ever make a fool of you, except you yourself when you have been vindictive; and if someone does ridicule you, even when you have exercised self-control, he will be acting like a fool.

St John Chrysostom, in *The Fathers of the Church*, vol. 33, pp. 53-54.

1301. *How to Quench Anger*

How then shall we soften this anger? How extinguish a flame like this? By turning over in our mind the remembrance of our own sins, and of how much we ourselves have to answer for before God. By reflecting that we are wreaking vengeance, but on ourselves, not on our enemy. By thinking of how we are delighting the devil . . . who is truly our enemy, and because of whom we are inflicting injury on our own members. Do you wish to be both an enemy and forgiving at the same time? Then be an enemy, but to the devil; not with a member of your own body.

St John Chrysostom, in Toal, vol. 3, p. 238.

1302. *Why God Armed Us with Anger*

It was for this that God armed us with anger; not to drive a sword into our own bodies, but to plunge it into the heart of the devil.

St John Chrysostom, in *ibid.*

1303. *Rightful Uses of Anger, Hatred, and Rage*

Anger and rage and hatred should be aroused, like dogs guarding the gates, only for resistance to sin, and used against the thief or enemy who enters to defile the divine treasury and comes to steal, to storm and to destroy. Instead of a weapon in the hand, one should have courage and bravery so there would be no need to be afraid and one could withstand the onslaughts of the impious.

St Gregory of Nyssa, in *The Fathers of the Church*, vol. 58, p. 57.

1304. *The Right Kind of Anger Helps Virtue*

The irascible part of the soul is serviceable to us in many acts of virtue. . . . Unless your anger has been aroused against the Evil One, it is impossible to hate him as fiercely as he deserves. For, our hatred of sin should be as intense, I believe, as our love of virtue. . . .

Anger, aroused at the proper time and in the proper manner, produces courage, endurance and continency; acting contrary to right reason, however, it becomes madness. The Psalmist admonishes us: 'Be ye angry and sin not' (ps 4:5).

St Basil, in *The Fathers of the Church*, vol. 9, pp. 456-457.

1305. *Anger Arising from Zeal*

When the spirit is aroused by zeal, we should take great care that the same anger that is used in the service of virtue does not come to dominate the mind, nor rule it as mistress, but like a handmaid ever at hand to render service; let it never depart from its place behind reason. For it is then uplifted the more strongly against evil when its service is rendered subject to reason. . . .

Because of this it is above all necessary that he who is moved by zeal for justice . . . should . . . restrain his indignation and subject the warmth of his own feelings to the rule of moderation and courtesy, so that the more he is master of himself, the more he is fit to judge of another's chastisement.

St Gregory the Great, in Toal, vol. 3, p. 247.

1306. *Anger Born of Zeal Is a Duty*

Anger born of zeal for God's honor is not only laudable; it is a duty. Christ was angry when he expelled the sellers from the temple. '*Zelus domus tuae comedit me*: The zeal of Thy house hath eaten me up' (Jn 2:17). He was angry with the Apostles who wished to drive away the children. He was angry with Peter when he said: 'Go behind Me, Satan' (Mk 8:33). Moses was angry when he broke the tablets of the law. . . . And this holy anger should be felt today by Christians, followers of Christ, who hear him, his Church and his principles blasphemed, rather than the easy tolerance which so many show. While preserving the moderation of meekness, the upright man grieves over iniquity and is ready to oppose it if it can effectively be done (cf. James 3:13-17).

Brosnahan, *Searchlighting Ourselves*, pp. 249-250.

1307. *When Anger Is Obligatory*
He who, with due cause, is not roused to anger sins by this: for patience with things that are against reason breeds evil, fosters neglect, and becomes an invitation to wrongdoing, not alone to the wicked, but also to the good.
St John Chrysostom, quoted by St Thomas Aquinas, in Toal, vol. 3, p. 229.

1308. *Lack of Zealous Anger Is a Fault*
Because Heli was wanting in this anger (which arises from zeal), he aroused against himself the force of divine vengeance (1 Kings 3:11). For the more he was neglectful of the evil of those under his charge, the more severely the justice of the Eternal Ruler burned against himself. Of this anger the Psalmist says: 'Be ye angry and sin not' (4:5).
St Gregory the Great, in Toal, vol. 3, p. 246.

1309. *When God's Anger Is Worst*
St Bernard says: 'God's anger is greatest when He is not angry. I wish, O Father of mercies, that thou mayest be angry with me.'. . . God's wrath is greatest when he is not angry with them, and abstains from chastising them.
St Alphonsus Liguori, *The True Spouse of Jesus Christ*, p. 383.

1310. *Punishment Not to Be Meted Out in Anger*
After having forbidden the Emperor the Church, in punishment of the cruel and sanguinary massacre perpetrated by his orders at Thessalonica, and having reconciled him with God and Holy Church by means of a public penance, the great Archbishop [St Ambrose] advised him to pass a law, ordering that, for the future, no sentence of death pronounced by the Emperor should be executed until the expiration of thirty days; to the end that, the ebullitions of anger having calmed down, he might have time to weigh in the balance of uprightness and justice the command which he had given and might never again, through over-haste, give cruel orders such as had been so fatal to the citizens of Thessalonica.
Scaramelli, *Directorium Asceticum*, vol. 3, p. 367.

1311. *Punishment Not to Be Meted Out in Anger*
. . . In a letter . . . to the Consul Leontius, [St Gregory wrote:] 'When you are irritated, check your anger, and delay to another time the infliction of punishment, however justly deserved it may seem to you; lest anger, anticipating reason, hurry it in its wake to some rash determination. On the contrary, reason should take the lead, and anger follow, as her servant and

the instrument of her just resolves.'
Scaramelli, *ibid.*, p. 368.

1312. *Avarice Feeds on Gain*
St Augustine says: 'The accumulation of money does not close, but widens the jaws of avarice.'
Quoted by St Alphonsus Liguori, in *Preparation for Death*, p. 18.

1313. *Cure for Avarice*
'How can avarice be healed except by the poverty of Christ?'
St Augustine, quoted by St Alphonsus Liguori, in *The Passion of Christ*, p. 208.

1314. *Avarice Called 'Dropsy'*
You have gold, you have silver, yet you are craving for gold and silver. You have them, and you are craving them. You are full, yet you crave for more. That is not wealth, it is a disease. Men suffer from a disease in which they are full of fluid, and yet are thirsty. How can you be happy with riches when you have a dropsical craving?
St Augustine, in *The Fathers of the Church*, vol. 11, p. 277.

1315. *Covetousness, a Terrible Vice*
A terrible vice is covetousness, a terrible vice. . . .
This vice made Giezi a leper instead of a disciple and prophet (4 Kings 4, 20-27); it destroyed Ananias and his followers (Acts 5: 1-11); it made Judas a traitor; it corrupted the rulers of the Jews, who accepted gifts and became partners of thieves. It has brought on innumerable wars and filled the roads with bloodshed, and the cities with mourning and weeping.
St John Chrysostom, in *The Fathers of the Church*, vol. 41, pp. 211-212.

1316. *Avarice, Injustice, Slander Harm the Unjust*
Not those who are wronged, but those who do wrong deserve our tears. For the covetous man and the slanderer, and the man guilty of any other wrongdoing injure themselves most of all, while they are of benefit to us, if we do not avenge ourselves.
St John Chrysostom, *ibid.*, p. 264.

1317. *Backbiter Poisons Three Persons at a Time*
St Bernard, treating of this subject, says that the tongue of a backbiter is a viper which poisons three persons with a single bite; a lance which pierces three men with one thrust; a three-pointed sword which makes three wounds with one blow. Then, explaining what he means by the three

wounds inflicted by the backbiter's tongue in every murmur it utters, he says that the first wound is received by him against whom the remark is directed, piercing him to the quick in his good name; the second is received in the ears of the listener, who is scandalized at the remark and brought into the occasion of sin; the third wound, more deadly than the others, is inflicted on the speaker striking his own soul with a mortal blow, that it makes it hateful and abominable in God's eyes, as the Apostle declares (Rom 1:30). . . . True, the backbiter's word flies quickly, but it wounds grievously; true, it passes quickly, but it burns cruelly.

Scaramelli, *Directorium Asceticum*, vol. 2, pp. 124-125.

1318. *Inconceivable that a Man Should Have the Right to Blaspheme God*

Do not forget that the natural law is something essential in the order of religion. God need not have created me; but since I have been created, I am and remain a creature, and the relations resulting from this fact are unchangeable. One cannot, for example, conceive that a man could be created for whom it would be lawful to blaspheme his Creator.

Marmion, *Growth in Christ*, p. 114.

1319. *The Malice of Detraction*

. . . A greater damage is done, and a more grevous fault is committed by him whose detraction deprives a neighbor of the good character which he had before enjoyed among men, than by a thief who would rob him of his money, or his wealth, or of any other worldly possession.

Scaramelli, *Directorium Asceticum*, vol. 2, p. 126.

1320. *We Should Not Listen to Detraction*

St Jerome says . . . 'If you hear a detractor, fly from him as from a serpent and leave him.' 'But, oh, how he will be hurt!' 'Do it all the more on that account,' says St Jerome, 'that the hurt may teach him to hold his tongue about other people's lives.'

Rodriguez, *Practice of Perfection and Christian Virtues*, vol. 2, pp. 144-145.

1321. *Detraction Hurts Both Detractor and Listener*

A well-known saying of St Bernard is this: 'I know not who does the greater harm, the detractor, or he who listens with pleasure to detraction.' . . . [For, as the saint says elsewhere:] 'One has the devil in his tongue, urging him to speak; the other in his ears, making him eager to listen.'

Scaramelli, *Directorium Asceticum*, vol. 2, p. 130.

1322. *How Disobedient Religious Should Be Treated*
All should certainly be compassionate toward one who obeys the Lord's commands reluctantly, as toward an ailing member of their body. The superior also should endeavor by private exhortation to cure his weakness; but if he persists in disobedience and is not amenable to correction, he should be severely reprimanded in the presence of the whole community and a remedy, together with every form of exhortation, should be administered. If he is neither converted after much admonition nor cures himself by his own actions with tears and lamentations, being, as the proverb has it, 'his own destroyer,' we should, as physicians do, cut him off from the body. . . . Benevolence to such persons is like that mistaken kindness of Heli, which he was accused of showing his sons, contrary to the good pleasure of God. A feigned kindness to the wicked is a betrayal of the truth, an act of treachery to the community, and a means of habituating oneself to indifference to evil. . . .

St Basil, in *The Fathers of the Church*, vol. 9, pp. 289-290.

1323. *Horses Do Not Drink to Excess*
Notice that when horses or other animals are brought to water, even if they are kept there for a long time, they refuse to drink any more after their thirst has been satisfied; in fact, they cannot do so. Now, the drunkards should stop to think whether they are to be considered worse than animals. Although animals refuse to drink more than is necessary, men take three or four times as much as they should.

St Caesarius of Arles, in *The Fathers of the Church*, vol. 32, p. 234.

1324. *By Envy and Jealousy Death Came into the World*
Nothing is worse than jealousy and envy; by them death came into the world. When the Devil saw man being held in honor, since he could not endure the sight of his wellbeing, he did everything to cause him to lose it (see Wis 2:24).

St John Chrysostom, in *The Fathers of the Church*, vol. 41, p. 3.

1325. *No Vice More Pernicious than Envy*
If the proud man is subject to the judgment pronounced upon the Devil, how will the envious man escape the punishment that was prepared for the Devil? . . .

Envy is the most savage form of hatred. . . .

With this weapon alone, the Devil, the destroyer of our life, has been inflicting wounds upon all men and striking them down from the foundation of the world, and he will continue to do so until its consummation. . . .

[Envy is] an invention of the demons, the seed of discord, a pledge of punishment, a barrier to holiness, a path to hell, and a cause of losing heaven.

St Basil, in *Ascetical Works*, pp. 463, 467-468, 470.

1326. *Envy Is a Blow at God*

. . . Let us pull [envy] up by the roots, keeping in mind that just as we aim a blow at God when we are consumed with envy at the good fortune of others, so we are pleasing to him when we rejoice with them, and we make ourselves sharers in the blessings which lie in store for the upright man.

St John Chrysostom, in *The Fathers of the Church*, vol. 33, p. 367.

1327. *Envy Consumes the Soul in Which It Dwells*

As rust consumes iron, so does envy wholly consume the soul it dwells in. . . .

What urged the devil, the beginner of evil, to wage fierce war against man? Was it not envy? . . .

Saul was of such a nature, for whom the greatness of the things David did for him was the reason for his war against him. . . .

Envy is the most implacable form of hatred. . . . What caused the high-minded Joseph to be sold as a slave? What but the envy of his brethren? . . .

Turn now in your mind to the greatest envy, linked to the greatest of all happenings, which burst forth from the rage of the Jews against Christ. For what cause was he envied; Because of his miracles.

St Basil, in Toal, vol. 4, pp. 142-144.

1328. *Envy – One of the Greatest Evils in Our Nature*

Let us consider here the effects of jealousy: it is one of the greatest evils of our nature. Jesus Christ, who had come to cure it, was to feel the malice of it, and the sufferings which envy was to cause him were to serve as a remedy to its poison. Envy is the black and secret effect of a feeble pride, which feels itself either diminished or completely effaced by the simplest luster in others, and which cannot endure the least light. . . . Disguised detractions, calumnies, betrayals, all evil crafts are its work. When, through these sad and dark tricks, it has gained the upper hand, it bursts forth and joins together against the just man, whose glory defeats it, insult and scorn, with all the bitterness of hatred, and the last excesses of cruelty.

Bossuet, in *Selections from Meditations on the Gospel*, vol. 1, pp. 136-137.

1329. *Envy Is Like a Spear*

Savage envy wounds as cruelly as a spear.

St Ephraim, in Toal, vol. 4, p. 16.

1330. *Envy a Diabolic Vice*
Envy is a diabolical vice, for 'by the envy of the devil, death came into the world' (Wis 2:24). The envious person does what the devil does: he is saddened by the good and rejoices over evil; he strives to hinder the good and bring about evil.

Bandas, *The Catholic Layman and Holiness*, p. 151.

1331. *Envy Opens the Door to the Evil One*
Through envy and discord brothers are separated from brothers. . . .

By it one man slays another with his tongue, and with his mouth drives another mercilessly to ruin. Day by day envy brings sorrow among men. . . .

[The nature of the envious man] is dark, his mind clouded, his intellect is blind; he gropes and stumbles. Then the Evil One takes his hand and hurries him along his way, the pathless way of deceit. He takes away from him and casts out whatsoever worthy thoughts are within him, and leads in his own shameful ones. . . .

St Aphraates, in Toal, vol. 1, pp. 347-348.

1332. *Envy More Damaging to the Envious*
Take away the font of envy, and you have taken away the river of all evil things. Cut off the root, and you cut off the fruit with it at the same time.

I have spoken these words to you because I am more concerned with those who envy than with those who are envied. For it is they above all who suffer most; bringing disaster upon themselves. For those who suffer through envy it is a beginning of the crown of glory, if they will it.

St John Chrysostom, in Toal, vol. 3, p. 21.

1333. *Envy a sign of a Small Man*
. . . He [who] is envious, proves that he is a child and a minor, for while he envies another, he shows that the one at whose prosperity he is vexed is greater than he.

Cassian, in *The Nicene and Post-Nicene Fathers*, vol. 11, p. 242.

1334. *Envy Is Hard to Cure*
. . . You should know that the evil of envy is harder to be cured than other faults, for I should almost say that a man whom it has once tainted with the mischief of its poison is without remedy.

Abbot Piamun, quoted by Cassian, in *The Nicene and Post-Nicene Fathers,* vol. 11, p. 488.

1335. *Faultfinding Makes Us Similar to Buzzards*
Let the buzzard be a type of the man who uses his powers of observation

and reasoning to discover defects and scandal. If at any time we have fallen into the fault of judging our brother to be a lobster, a clam, or something worse, let us quietly say to ourselves: 'I am a buzzard.'

Brosnahan, *Searchlighting Ourselves*, p. 219.

1336. *Faultfinding Endangers Forgiveness for Ourselves*

. . . They who search sharply into the faults of others will never merit forgiveness of their own.

St John Chrysostom, quoted by St Thomas Aquinas, in Toal, vol. 3, p. 85.

1337. *Study Your Own Faults*

Beware of spending your time in scrutinizing another's weakness. 'Give heed to thyself,' that is, turn the gaze of your soul toward self-scrutiny. Many there are, indeed, who, according to the Lord's words, see the mote in their brother's eye and see not the beam in their own (Mt 7:3). You should, therefore, be constantly examining whether your life conforms to this teaching. But do not look around outside yourself to see whether you can discover some blemish as did that stern and boastful Pharisee who stood justifying himself and despising the Publican. . . . If you find many defects in your way of living, (as, being human, you surely will), say with the Publican: 'O God, be merciful to me a sinner' (Lk 18:11-13).

St Basil, in *The Fathers of the Church*, vol. 9, pp. 439-440.

1338. *Evil Effects of Gluttony*

. . . We may say, in a few words, with St Gregory, that gluttony gives birth to an obtuseness of mind with regard to the understanding of heavenly things, to foolish joy, buffoonery, loquacity and impurity.

Scaramelli, *Directorium Asceticum*, vol. 2, p. 62.

1339. *How Jesus Hated Evil*

With all the strength of a perfect soul and of a humanity which was the sacrament of truth, Jesus hated evil. He had no alternative but to unmask and condemn it. When we ponder over these considerations, we realize that the flame of his anger which burst forth on these occasions was lighted by a furnace of love; of love for men which was stronger than death; of a love for mankind, whose destiny he knew to be God himself.

O'Mahoney, *The Person of Jesus*, p. 80.

1340. *By Hatred Man Nurtures the Devil Within Himself*

. . . If, as John says, 'God is charity' (1 Jn 4:16), the Devil is necessarily hatred. As he who has love, consequently, has God, so he who has hate

nurtures the Devil within himself.
St Basil, in *The Fathers of the Church*, vol. 9, p. 220.

1341. *Hatred Destroys the Hater*
The Scripture which said to us: whosoever hateth his brother is a murderer, also tells us plainly that he that hateth his brother is in darkness even until now (1 Jn 2:9).

Hatred then is darkness. And it cannot happen that one who hates another will not first injure himself.
St Augustine, in Toal, vol. 3, p. 95.

1342. *By Hatred We Give Place to the Devil*
. . . To be at war with each other is to give place to the devil. . . .

So therefore, let us, I beseech you, do all we can before the sun goes down to put an end to enmity and anger. For if you fail to overcome it on the first day, or on the second day, often you will keep it going for a year, and by then the enmity will nourish itself, and need no help to keep it going; making us suspect of one meaning words spoken in a wholly differend sense. . . .
St John Chrysostom, in Toal, vol. 3, pp. 237-238.

1343. *Hatred for Even One Person Endangers Salvation*
Let no one keep in his heart hatred for his neighbor, but love instead, for if a man feels hatred toward even one person, he cannot be at peace with God. A man's prayer is not heard by God as long as anger is stored up in his soul.
St Caesarius of Arles, in *The Fathers of the Church*, vol. 31, p. 81.

1344. *Hatred That Can Be Used Praiseworthily*
It is possible at times to use hatred even praiseworthily. 'Have I not hated them, O Lord, that hated thee: and pined away because of thy enemies? I have hated them with a perfect hatred' (Ps 138:21-22).
St Basil, in *The Fathers of the Church,* vol. 46, p. 289.

1345. *Hatred of Parents for Christ's Sake*
'If any man come to Me and hate not his father, and mother . . . he cannot be my disciple, (Lk 14:26-27, 33). When we remember that these are the words of him who commanded us to love even our enemies and to honor our father and mother, it is obvious that here is a Hebrew figure of speech in the use of the word *hate*. The meaning here, of course, is that we must love God above all else and let no creature interfere with the love of the Creator and all that He asks of us.
Boylan, *This Tremendous Lover*, pp. 245-246.

1346. *Impurity Gains More Souls for Hell than All Other Sins*
. . . Father Paul Segneri says that as pride has filled hell with angels, so impurity has filled it with men. In other vices the devil fishes with the hook, in this he fishes with the net; so that by incontinence he gains more for hell than by all other sins.
St Alphonsus Liguori, *Dignity and Duties of the Priest*, p. 107.

1347. *Devil Takes Delight in Impurity*
. . . According to St Thomas, there is no sin in which the devil takes so much delight as in impurity; because the flesh is strongly inclined to that vice, and he that falls into it can be rescued from it only with difficulty. Hence the vice of incontinence has been called by Clement of Alexandria 'a malady without remedy,' . . . and by Tertullian, 'an incurable vice'. Hence St Cyprian calls it 'the mother of impenitence'.
St Alphonsus, *ibid.,* p. 117.

1348. *Effects of Impurity*
. . . The first effect of the vice of impurity is, according to St Thomas, blindness of the understanding . . . : 'The effects of this impure vice are: blindness of the mind, hatred of God, attachment to the present life, horror of the future life.' . . . St Augustine says that impurity takes away the thought of eternity.
St Alphonsis, *ibid.,* p. 113.

1349. *No Venial Matter in the Vice of Impurity*
. . . There is no more slippery vice than impurity, no passion more unruly than that of carnal lust. If, then, the director does not hold his penitents in check by means of the strictest and safest opinions and of the most rigid counsels, he will soon see them stumble and bemire themselves in the filth of some grievous fall. Hence he must ever bear in mind and inculcate on his penitents the opinion which is the most common among theologians . . . that in this vice there is no venial matter; that every transgression is grievous and every fall mortal. . . .
Scaramelli, *Directorium Asceticum*, vol. 3, p. 329.

1350. *How to Avoid Impurity*
The first means [to void impurity] is to avoid the occasions of sins against purity. 'We must,' says St Jerome, 'be far from those whose presence may entice us to evil.' St Philip Neri used to say that in this warfare, cowards, that is, they that fly from the occasions, are victorious.

The divine aid alone can enable a man to preserve chastity; but this aid God gives not to those who voluntarily expose themselves to the occasion

of sin, or remain in it. 'He that loveth danger shall perish in it'.
St Alphonsus Liguori, *Dignity and Duties of the Priest*, pp. 248-249.

1351. *Flight from Temptation Urged*
St Augustine . . . in a homily to his people . . . says that we should betake ourselves to flight if we really wish to win the victory in temptations to impurity; that in such encounters, flight is not to be thought shameful if we are to earn the glorius palm of chastity.
Scaramelli, *Directorium Asceticum*, vol. 3, p. 313.

1352. *Humility Needed to Avoid Impurity*
[To observe chastity] it is necessary to practice humility. Cassian says that he who is not humble cannot be chaste. . . . It happens, not infrequently, that God chastises the proud by permitting them to fall into some sin against purity. This, as David himself confessed, was the cause of his fall. 'Before I was humbled, I offended' (Ps 118:67).
St Alphonsus Liguori, *Dignity and Duties of the Priest*, p. 260.

1353. *How to Combat Impure Thoughts*
St Jerome gives this advice: 'You must not permit bad thoughts to grow in your mind; no, kill the enemy when he is small.'. . . It is easy to kill a lion when he is small but not when he has grown to full size.

Let us guard against reasoning with temptations contrary to chastity: let us endeavour to banish them instantly. And, as the spiritual masters teach, the best means of banishing such temptations is not to combat them directly face to face by making contrary acts of the will, but to get rid of them indirectly by acts of the love of God, or of contrition, or at least by turning the mind to other things.

But the means in which we should place the greatest confidence is prayer, and recommending ourselves to God.
St Alphonsus, *ibid.*, pp. 262-263.

1354. *How to Combat Temptations to Impurity*
. . . Prayer is one of the chief remedies that Holy Writ and the saints prescribe for all temptations. . . .

Some help themselves in these temptations by the memory and consideration of the last things, according to that saying of the Wise Man: 'In all thy works remember thy last end, and thou shalt never sin' (Ecclus 7:40). . . . Others help themselves by the consideration of heaven, thinking what folly it is, as indeed it is, to give up God in exchange for a passing pleasure, and so lose everlasting glory. . . . Devotion to our Lady is a help everywhere. . . . She is the Mother of Mercy and Advocate of Sinners, whom she loves because she sees how much her Son loves them and at what price he has bought them. And above all, she sees that sinners were the occasion of the Eternal Word's taking of her flesh, and her becoming the Mother of God.

Rodriguez, *Practice of Perfection and Christian Virtues*, vol. 3, pp. 244-246.

1355. *To avoid Impurity, Avoid Idleness*

To preserve chastity, it is necessary to avoid idleness. 'Idleness', says the Holy Ghost, 'has taught much evil' (Ecclus 33:29). Ezekial says that it was the cause of all the wickedness of the inhabitants of Sodom and of their total destruction. 'Behold! This was the iniquity of Sodom . . . the idleness of her and her daughters' (Ez 16:49).

St Alphonsus, *Dignity and Duties of the Priest*, p. 258.

1356. *Breaking the Habit of Impurity a Greater Miracle than Exorcising the Devil*

In truth it is a greater miracle to root out from one's flesh the incentives of wantonness than to cast out unclean spirits from the bodies of others.

Nesteros, quoted by Cassian, in *The Nicene and Post-Nicene Fathers*, vol. 11, p. 448.

1357. *The Hail Mary a Remedy for Impurity*

Father Segneri . . . relates that a sinner addicted to the grossest impurities one day went to confession to [Father Nicholas Zucchi of the Society of Jesus, who] prescribed as a remedy for his wicked habits that he should recommend himself morning and evening to the purity of Mary, by saying three Hail Marys. After the lapse of several years, the sinner returned to Fr Zucchi, and by his confession showed that all his vices were perfectly corrected. Father asked him how such a changed had been wrought. He answered that through the little devotion of saying the three Hail Marys, he had obtained the grace to change his life.

With the permission of the penitent, Father mentioned the fact from the pulpit.

St Alphonsus Liguori, *Dignity and Duties of the Priest*, pp. 263-264.

1358. *Ingratitude Vs Gratitude Towards God*

St Bernard says . . . 'Ingratitude is a burning wind that dries up and consumes everything, and blocks and closes the fountain of God's mercy.'. . . So, gratitude and giving thanks to God for his benefits move God to preserve and increase them.

Rodriguez, *Practice of Perfection and Christian Virtues*, vol. 2, p. 517.

1359. *Pride Wounds God*
Nothing wounds God so much as pride.
Chautard, *The Soul of the Apostolate*, p. 102.

1360. *Pride Drives God Away*
St Augustine warns us: 'Lift yourself up and God will depart from you; humble yourself and God will come to you.'
St Alphonsus Liguori, *The Incarnation, Birth and Infancy of Jesus Christ*, p. 137.

1361. *Pride Vs Humility*
St John Climacus says that, as the devil endeavors to put before us our virtues and good works to make us proud, since he wishes evil to us, so God our Lord, wishing our greater good, is wont to give special light to his servants to know their faults and imperfections, and to throw a veil over and disguise his gifts so that the recipient himself does not recognize them.
Rodriguez, *Practice of Perfection and Christian Virtues*, vol. 2, p. 320.

1362. *The Devil Tries to Ensnare Good People with Pride*
To this end the devil is arming the force of his malice, in order to make your very piety its own snare, and endeavoring to overcome by boastfulness those whom he could not defeat by distrustfulness. For the vice of pride is near neighbor to good deeds, and arrogance ever lies in wait hard by virtue: because it is hard for him who lives praiseworthily, not to be caught by man's praise unless, as it is written, 'he that glorieth, glorieth in the Lord' (1 Cor 10:17). Whose intentions would that most naughty enemy not dare to attack?
St Leo the Great, in *The Nicene and Post-Nicene Fathers,* vol. 12, p.157.

1363. *The Sin of Adam and Eve*
Our first parents only fell openly into the sin of disobedience because, secretly, they had begun to be guilty. Actually, their bad deed could not have been done had not bad will preceded it; what is more, the root of their bad will was nothing else than pride. For 'pride is the beginning of all sin.'... And what is pride but an appetite for inordinate exaltation? Now, exaltation is inordinate when the soul cuts itself off from the very Source to which it should keep close and somehow makes itself become an end to itself.
St Augustine, *City of God*, bk. 14, chap. 13.

1364. *How Bad Pride Is and How to Correct It*
... The wise man has said: 'Pride is the beginning of sin.'... 'Every proud

man,' Scripture says, 'is an abomination to the Lord' (Prv 16:5). . . .

How, then, may one escape from this terrible fate, do you ask? If he ponder his own nature, and the multitude of his sins, and the greatness of the punishment in the next world, the transitoriness of things which seem beautiful here but are just grass and die more readily than the flowers of spring – if we continually revolve these reflections within ourselves and keep remembering those who lived the most virtuously, the Devil will not be able to overcome us easily. . . .

St John Chrysostom, in *The Fathers of the Church*, vol. 33, pp. 94-95.

1365. *Pride Destructive of All Virtues*

There is . . . no other fault which is so destructive of all virtues, and robs and despoils a man of all righteousness and holiness, as this evil of pride. . . .

Cassian, in *The Nicene and Post-Nicene Fathers,* vol. 11, p. 280.

1365. *The Beginning of Sin and a Gate to Hell*

The beginning of sin is a gate to hell: 'For the wages of sin is death' (Rom 6:23), and death here beyond doubt leads to hell. And what is the beginning of sin? Let us ask the Scriptures. Pride, they say, is the beginning of all sin. . . . And if pride is the beginning of sin, pride is a gate to hell.

St Augustine, in Toal, vol. 4, p. 405.

1366. *Pride Shown in Criticism of Superiors and God Himself*

Pride manifests itself in the criticism leveled against God himself, in the person of those bearing his authority.

James Leen, *By Jacob's Well*, p. 4.

1368. *Pride Leads to Disobedience*

[God said:] 'There, where pride is, can be no obedience.'

Dialogue of St Catherine of Siena, p. 299.

1369. *Pride the Beginning of All Heresies*

It is the common doctrine of doctors and saints that pride is the beginning of all heresies. A man gets such a conceit of his own opinion and judgment that he prefers it to the common sentiment of saints and of the Church, and thence he comes to plunge into heresy.

Rodriguez, *Practice of Perfection and Christian Virtues*, vol. 2, p. 171.

1370. *The Seminary of Impurity*

St Gregory calls pride the seminary of impurity; because some, while they are exalted by the spirit of pride, are precipitated into hell by the flesh.

St Alphonsus Liguori, *Dignity and Duties of the Priest*, p. 310.

1371. *All Sin Rooted in Pride*

All sin has its roots in pride. How we should hate pride, that caused Christ so much suffering! Christ's sufferings were for pride. Hence it is that degradation, insult, shame, ignominy, mockery marked every stage of the Passion. Ignominy was its note.

Edward Leen, *Retreat Notes for Religious*, p. 120.

1372. *Pride, Not Weakness of Nature, Is Source of Failures*

Men are wont to blame their moral failures on the weakness of their nature. They would be nearer the truth if they laid the blame on the strength of their pride.

Edward Leen, *The True Vine and Its Branches*, p. 229.

1373. *Pride Falsifies Man*

Pride falsifies man; humility makes him true to his real self.

James Leen, *By Jacob's Well*, p. 91.

1374. *Pride and Self-Deception*

Do not justify yourself above some other man, for fear that though justified by your own sentence, you shall be condemned by the just sentence of God.

If you think that you have done something good, then give thanks to God; do not place yourself above your neighbor.

St Basil, in Toal, vol. 4, p. 140.

1375. *Self-Excuser Like a Hedgehog*

[St Peter Damian] compares those who excuse themselves to a hedgehog, that when it feels that people want to catch or touch it, with the greatest nimbleness tucks in its head and feet and makes itself into a ball surrounded on all sides with pricks, so that you cannot seize or touch it without first pricking yourself. . . . All this springs from our excessive pride, in that we are unwilling to have our faults known or to be taken for men who have their defects.

Rodriguez, *Practice of Perfection and Christian Virtues*, vol. 2, p. 288.

1376. *Pride's Reaction to Criticism*

Fr Rodriguez says that some religious resemble the hedgehog: when touched, they become all thorns and instantly break out into words of impatience, of reproach, and even of murmuring. 'We have known many,' says St Gregory, 'who, when no one accuses them, confess themselves sinners, but when they have been corrected for a fault, they endeavor with all their might to defend themselves, as to remove the imputation of guilt.'

St Alphonsus Liguori, *The True Spouse of Jesus Christ*, p. 331.

1377. *The Pride of Those Who Resent Correction*
One of the things in which man's great pride is best seen is the great difficulty with which he takes correction and warning of his faults, a difficulty so great that you will hardly find anyone willing to accept such correction and warning. St Augustine says very well: 'Who shall easily find a man willing to be reproved?'. . . St Gregory says: 'We are so full of pride, and it is so rooted in our hearts that we cannot bear to hear our faults told, nor brook reprehension, because we take it to be an injury to our character and a disparagement of what we are worth. That touches us to the quick as a thing affecting our honor, and we at once resent it; instead of being grateful, we make a grievance of it, and fancy we are being wronged and persecuted.
Rodriguez, *Practice of Perfection and Christian Virtues,* vol. 3, p. 478.

1378. *The Pride of Those Who Resent Correction*
This pride and folly goes so far that now scarcely anyone is found to venture to correct and advise another of his faults, since no one is willing to undertake a bad job or, as they say, to provoke an uproar at his own expense. And the man gets what he deserves for this. For what does a sick man deserve who will not let himself to be attended to: He deserves to go unattended and be left to die. Now that is what he deserves who will not be corrected and takes amiss any admonition given him.
Rodriguez, *ibid.,* p. 480.

1379. *The Proud Do Not Find God*
. . . Thou art great, O Lord, and thou dost look upon the lowly, and thou knowest the proud from afar off; nor dost thou draw near except to the contrite of heart. Nor art thou found by the proud, not even if, by their curious skill, they could number the stars and the sands and measure the starry regions and trace the paths of the stars.
St Augustine, *Confessions*, bk. 5, chap. 3.

1380. *Abstinence Useless If Pride Prevails*
'Of what use is it,' says St Jerome, 'to reduce the body by abstinence, if the soul is swelled with pride?'
St Alphonsus Liguori, *The True Spouse of Jesus Christ*, p. 134.

1381. *If We Are Not Humble, We Are Not Christians*
He who is not humble, and who does not seek to imitate the humility of Jesus Christ, is not worthy of the name of Christian; for Jesus Christ, as St Augustine says, came into the world in an humble way to put down pride.

The pride of man was the disease which drew from heaven this divine physician, which loaded him with ignominies, and caused him to die on the cross. Let the proud man, then, be ashamed when he sees that a God so humbled himself in order to cure him of pride: 'Because of this very vice of pride, God came in humility. This disease drew him down from heaven, humbled him even to the form of a servant, overwhelmed him with calumnies, hung him on the Cross. Blush, then, O man, to be proud, for whom God has become humble.'

St Alphonsus Liguori, *Incarnation, Birth and Infancy of Jesus Christ*, p. 135.

1382. *Knowledge Without Charity Leads to Pride*

The Apostle, speaking under the inspiration of the Holy Spirit, says: 'Knowledge puffs up, but charity edifies' (2 Cor 8:1). He can only mean that knowledge does good only in company with charity; otherwise, it merely puffs a man with pride, swelling him, like a balloon, with a valueless volume of air.

St Augustine, *City of God*, bk. 9, chap. 20.

1383. *Pride in Personal Qualities Causes Fall of Many*

How many there are whose ruin has been occasioned by their talents and learning, of which they have grown proud, and in consequence of which they have looked down upon others with contempt – a danger which is easily incurred by those who excel others in learning and ability! How many others there are whose personal beauty or bodily strength have furnished the occasions of plunging them into innumerable acts of wickedness.

St Alphonsus Liguori, *The Way of Salvation and of Perfection*, pp. 372-373.

1384. *Pride Fed by Singularity*

[St Philip Neri] was most earnest in exhorting all to avoid the slightest singularity as being the source of pride of spirit and of all kinds of pride, and the fuel which feeds their fire.

Scaramelli, *Directorium Asceticum*, vol. 2, p. 84.

1385. *Pride over Spiritual Gifts*

When a man is proud of a happy disposition, of a nobility, of a healthy and well-formed body, a good understanding, letters and other abilities, he is a thief; but the theft is not so great, for while it is true that all these goods are of God, yet they are but the chaff and bran of his house; but he who is proud of spiritual gifts, of sanctity, of the fruit of gains in souls, is a great thief and robber of the honor of God – robber of the first magnitude, who steals the richest and most precious jewels, jewels of the greatest value in the sight of God, who sets such store by them that for them he gave his Blood and Life and thought it a good bargain.

Rodriguez, *Practice of Perfection and Christian Virtues*, vol. 2, p. 178.

1386. *Pride Is Hard to Cure*

There is no lesson harder to learn than to accept sweetly what by nature stings our innate pride. But to do this is to unite oneself intimately with Jesus, who begged forgiveness for the very men who crucified him and at the very moment when they were taunting him. . . .

Jesus told us to pray for those who persecute and calumniate us. They are only the sharp instruments in the hands of the Sculptor, who has the genius and the will to hew out of the crude block of marble a statue that will be perfect. . . .

Humility is the touchstone of sanctity, and . . . there is no way to humility except the hard way of humiliations lovingly accepted.

Nash, *The Nun at Her Prie-Dieu*, pp. 92-93.

1387. *How to Combat Pride*

Keep close to you the Lord's words: 'Everyone that exalteth himself shall be humbled, and he that humbleth himself shall be exalted' (Lk 14:11). . . . Do not take pride in today's good actions, whilst giving yourself full pardon for past or recent wicked ones. Rather, should you be pleased and satisfied with some present action, bring before your mind another kind of action from the past, and then your foolish pride will cease.

St Basil, in Toal, vol. 4, p. 140.

1388. *Cure for Pride*

'How can any pride,' asks St Augustine, 'be healed except by the humility of the Son of God?'

St Alphonsus Liguori, *The Passion of Jesus Christ*, p. 208.

1389. *Because of Pride, God Allows Us to Fall*

St Gregory says: 'Do you know how much God loves humility and how much He abhors pride and presumption? He abhors it so much that he permits us, to begin with, to fall into venial sins and many small faults, thereby to teach us that, as we cannot keep ourselves from small sins and temptations, but see ourselves stumbling and falling every day in things trifling and easy to overcome, we may be sure that we have not strength to avoid greater sins, and thus we may not become proud over these greater things, nor attribute anything to ourselves, but ever live in fear and humility, begging the Lord's grace and favor.'

Rodriguez, *Practice of Perfection and Christian Virtues*, vol. 2, p. 344.

1390. *Pride Can Be Cured by Sin*

. . . I am willing to say that it is advantageous for the proud to fall into some open and manifest sin, and so become displeasing to themselves after they had already fallen by pleasing themselves. For, when Peter wept and reproached himself, he was in a far healthier condition than when he boasted and was satisfied with himself.

St Augustine, *City of God*, bk. 14, chap. 13.

1391. *The Pride of King Saul*

[The Lord says:] 'When thou wast little in thine own sight, did I not make thee the head of the tribes of Israel?' (1 Sam 15:17). He had before seen himself little in his own eyes, but, propped up by temporal power, he no longer saw himself as little. For, preferring himself in comparison with others because he had more power than all, he esteemed himself great above all. Yet in a wonderful way, when he was little with himself, he was great with God; but when he appeared great with himself, he was little with God.

St Gregory the Great, in *The Nicene and Post-Nicene Fathers,* vol. 12, p. 15.

1392. *Quarrelsomeness and Discord Render Prayer Ineffective*

. . . To me it seems that if anyone is involved in contentions and in quarrels, his prayers are not acceptable, his supplications are not answered, his gift rises not upward from the earth; and neither does the giving of alms avail him for the forgiveness of sins. And wheresoever there is no peace and tranquility, the door is left open to the Evil One. . . .

Such a man, given to envy and discord, will stand and pray as is his daily habit; he will begin his prayer, continue on with it and bring it to an end. But his heart takes no heed of what his lips are saying, his mouth fulfills its usual office, but his heart is empty of every good work.

St Aphraates, in Toal, vol. 1, pp. 346-347.

1393. *Whole Community Blamed for Not Avenging Scandal*

The man in Corinth who had his father's wife, although he was charged with no other crime except this, was not only himself delivered over to Satan for destruction of his flesh until he made amends for his sin by fruits worthy of penance (1 Cor 5:1-5; Lk 3:8), but Paul includes the whole church likewise in his reproaches, since it did not exact vengeance for the crime of this man.

St Basil, in *The Fathers of the Church*, vol. 9, p. 50.

1394. *The Devil Uses Scandal to Catch Souls*
The sportsman employs decoys, that is, birds that are bound so that they cannot fly away, and the devil employs the authors of scandal in order to catch souls in his net. . . . But, says Caesar of Arles, the devil seeks in a special manner to employ for his decoys scandalous priests; hence this author calls them decoy birds whom the devils usually incite to catch others.
St Alphonsus Liguori, *Dignity and Duties of the Priest*, p. 147.

1395. *Scandal-givers to Be Avoided*
The Apostle says: 'And we charge you, brethren, that you withdraw yourselves from every brother walking disorderly and not according to the tradition which they have received of us' (2 Thes 3:6).
St Basil, in *The Fathers of the Church*, vol. 9, p. 368.

1396. *Harm done by Church People Through Scandal*
. . . Certainly no one does more harm in the Church than one who has the name and rank of sanctity, while he acts perversely.
St Gregory the Great, *Pastoral Rule*, in *The Nicene and Post-Nicene Fathers,* vol. 12, p. 2.

1397. *Slander by Exaggeration or Misinterpretation*
Do not say that so and so is a drunkard even though you have seen him intoxicated. . . . Because St Peter once shed blood does not mean that he was bloodthirsty, nor was he blasphemous because he once blasphemed. . . . Simon the leper called Mary Magdalen a sinner, because she had been one not long before, but he spoke untruly since she was no longer a sinner but a most sincere penitent. Hence our Savior took her under his protection. The foolish Pharisee took the Publican for a great sinner, perhaps even an unjust man, an adulterer and an extortioner. He was much deceived, for at that very hour the Publican was justified.
St Francis de Sales, *Introduction to the Devout Life*, p. 166.

1398. *Slander Is a Form of Murder*
The man who could free the world of slander would free it of a large share of its sins and iniquity.

Whoever robs his neighbor of his good name, in addition to committing sin, has the obligation of making reparation, although this must be done in different ways according to the different types of slander. No man can enter heaven in possession of another man's property, and of all external goods, a good name is the best. Slander is a form of murder. We have three kinds of life: spiritual, which consists in the grace of God; corporeal, which depends on the body soul, and social, which consists of our good name. Sin deprives us of the first kind of life, death takes away the second and slander the third. By a single stroke of his tongue, the slanderer usually commits three murders. He kills his own soul and the soul of anyone who hears him by an act of spiritual homicide, and takes away the social life of the man he slanders. As St Bernard says, the one who slanders and the one who listens to a slanderer have the devil in their company – one man has Satan on his tongue, and the other in his ear.

St Francis de Sales, *ibid.,* p. 165.

1399. *Vainglory – Destroyer of Virtuous Actions*

To kill a man is nothing more nor less than to separate his soul from his body by some violent action, the result of which is that what was a man becomes a corpse, retaining the semblance of a human being, though it is a man no longer. Now this is what vainglory does to every virtuous action to which it attaches itself; it robs each of our good deeds of whatever is good, supernatural, meritorious and holy in it; and changes it into a corpse, which bears the semblance of virtue to the eyes of man, but in the sight of God is made hideous and a mere deformity by this vainglory; it, in a word, kills all our good actions by the alluring poison of self-complacency. One man gives an alms, and while he is in the very act of bestowing it, vainglory steps in and mars the virtuous deed. . . . [Christ] said that for such there would be no reward in the world to come.

Scaramelli, *Directorium Asceticum*, vol. 2, p. 238-239.

1400. *Vainglory an Almost Unconquerable Foe*

Vainglory . . . is an almost unconquerable foe, because it is so treacherous that not only is it impossible completely to crush it by the acts of a perfect life, but it finds its nourishment in our good actions themselves, and from these strengthens itself for the fight. There is no evil, as St Chrysostom aptly observes, which has not some opposite virtue by which it may be overcome and which may not be finally destroyed by repeated acts of resistance. . . . Vainglory alone has no opposite virtue by which it may be surely overcome, for it takes occasion to raise its head from whatever good a man may do in order to keep it in check; and even the humiliations which would seem most fitted for its destruction find matter for vain self-complacency. The holy Doctor alleges an excellent reason for this saying: 'All evil springs from some vice; vainglory alone has its origin from what is good; so that, far from being extirpated by good deeds, these are its food.'

Scaramelli, *ibid.,* 244-245.

1401. *Virtues Harmful If They Cause Vanity*
. . . St Gregory the Great says in his book on morals: 'The virtues we have acquired become more injurious than their absence would be, if they beget within us a vain reliance on self; for then virtue pierces the unwary soul with the sword of vanity, and though on the one hand they strengthen and give it life, on the other they cause its ruin by unduly puffing it up.' . . . Hence, no means can be found so effectual to obtain special aid in temptation, as recourse to God, full of confidence in his help and of distrust in our own powers.

Scaramelli, *ibid.,* pp. 315-316.

1402. *Vainglory Is a Robber*
All the saints admonish us to be much on our guard against vainglory because, say they, it is a cunning thief which often steals from us even our best actions, and which insinuates itself so secretly that it has even robbed and despoiled us before we perceive it. St Gregory says that vainglory is like a robber in disguise who insinuates himself into the company of a traveler, pretending to go the same way that he goes, and afterwards robs and murders him when he is least upon his guard and thinks himself in perfect security. . . .

St Augustine says: 'Lord, he who would be praised for thy gifts and seeks not thy glory but his own in the good he does is a robber; he is like the devil himself, who endeavored to rob thee of thy glory.'

Rodriguez, *Practice of Perfection and Christian Virtues*, vol. 1, pp. 132-134.

1403. *Vainglory Based on One's Virtues*
[Vainglory] tries to lift up with pride one man because of his great endurance of work and labor, another because of his readiness to obey, another because he outstrips other men in humility. One man is tempted through the extent of his knowledge, another through the extent of his reading, another through the length of his vigils. Nor does this malady endeavor to wound a man except through his virtues. . . . And so it results that those of us who could not be vanquished in the conflict with the foe, are overcome by the very greatness of our triumph. . . .

Cassian, in *The Nicene and Post-Nicene Fathers*, vol. 11, p. 276.

1404. *St Augustine's Estimate of Vainglory*
St Augustine says: 'Vanity glides into the very contempt of vanity, and renders us vain because we are superior to vanity' (*Confessions*, bk. 10, chap. 38).

Quoted by Scaramelli, in *Directorium Asceticum*, vol. 4, p. 107.

1405. *Prayer Is the Remedy for Vainglory*
. . . St Chrysostom goes so far as to say that prayer is the only remedy against these two vices [ambition and vainglory.] 'There can be no other remedy,' he truly remarks, 'against vainglory but prayer; and prayer itself, unless you take heed, will become the parent of vainglory.'. . . No other than the Almighty Hand of God has power to uproot it when once it has established its dwelling in our hearts. But this effectual help is vouchsafed only to long, earnes and fervent prayer.
Scaramelli, *ibid.*, vol. 2, pp. 245-250.

1406. *Vainglory Used by the devil to Cheat People*
How many who were devout and eager in paying by good works the spiritual debts of religion has [the devil] not cheated out of their heavenly reward by infecting them with the desire for human glory, so that they may not receive the rewards promised to those on the right hand: for in their good works they now seek the good opinion of men rather than the praise and glory of God. And for this reason the Lord Christ, the Son of God, warning his desciples to be careful not to make known to men their uprightness, their alms, their fasting and praying, lest through the vain glory of the left-hand side they may not have the reward of the right hand, says to them: 'Let not thy left hand know what thy right hand doth' (Mt 6:3).
St Gaudentius, in Toal, vol. 3, pp. 338-339.

SINNERS

1407. *Sinners Belong to the Devil*
. . . The soul that abides in sin no longer belongs to Christ, but to the devil. Satan takes the place of Christ in the soul.
Marmion, *Growth in Christ*, p. 67.

1408. *Sinners Insane?*
With good reason did Fr Avila say that Christians who believe eternal life and live at a distance from God ought to be shut up within an asylum as insane.
St Alphonsus Liguori, *Great Means of Salvation and of Perfection*, p. 320.

1409. *Sinner, in the Formal Sense, Not Loved by God*
[After quoting Christ's words:] 'Woe to you, scribes and Pharisees' . . . and 'He that scandalizes one of these little ones . . . it were better for him that a millstone be hanged about his neck and that he should be drowned in the depth of the sea' (Mt 18:6). [Archbishop Leen says;] It is vain to

evade this conclusion by the seemingly happy distinction made in saying that Jesus hates sin but loves the sinner. This statement is simply not true if the term sinner is taken in its formal sense – to use a philosophic term. It is true only taken in its material or non-logical sense. Jesus cannot love the sinner as such; He can love a man in spite of his being a sinner.

James Leen, *By Jacob's Well*, pp. 11-12.

1410. *How Sinners' Hearts Become Hardened*

[St Paul says:] 'The Lord hath mercy on whom he will; and whom he will he hardeneth' (Rom 9:18). St Augustine explains it thus: It is not that God hardens the habitual sinner; but he withdraws his grace in punishment of his ingratitude for past graces and thus the heart becomes as hard as a stone. . . . Says St Thomas of Villanova: 'Hardness of heart is the sign of damnation.'. . . As long as your conscience smites you, rejoice: for it is a sign that God has not yet abandoned you. But amend, and leave it quickly; for if not, the wound will become gangrenous, and you will be lost.

St Alphonsus Liguori, *Preparation for Death*, pp. 28-29.

1411. *How Sinners Delude Themselves*

First Delusion: I do not wish to condemn myself, I wish to be saved. If I commit this sin, I will afterwards confess it. *Second Delusion*: At present I do not feel strength to resist this temptation. *Third Delusion*: God is merciful. . . . St Augustine says that he who sins with the intention of repenting afterwards, is not a penitent, but a mocker of God. *Fourth Delusion*: But God has hitherto shown me so many mercies, and has not punished me, so I hope he will show me mercy in the future. . . . St Gregory says that 'Those whom God waits for the longest, he punishes the most severely.' *Fifth Delusion*: I am young. God compassionates youth. Hereafter I will give myself to God. *Last Delusion*: You say, It is true that by this sin I lose the grace of God, and I have condemned myself to hell; it may be that for this sin I shall be damned; but it may also be that I shall afterwards confess it and be saved.

St Alphonsus, *ibid.*, pp. 33-34, and 36-30.

1412. *Sinners Should Be Grateful for Not Being in Hell as Yet*

[The sinner] should be most grateful to God for not having suffered him to die in his sins, and be most careful not to offend him saying . . . Ungrateful soul! if thou hadst committed the same offences against man, who is viler than the earth, verily he would not have borne with thee. And how great mercies have I exercised toward thee! How many times have I called thee, and enlightened thee, and pardoned thee? The time of punishment is at hand; the time of forgiveness is past. Thus God has spoken to many who are now suffering in hell; where one of their greatest torments is the remembrance of the mercies which they formerly received from God.

St Alphonsus Liguori, *The Way of Salvation and of Perfection*, p. 48.

1413. *Sinners Deserve Our Pity*

No one has such a claim upon our pity as the sinner; for without the grace of God, he cannot even repent of his sin, yet he has condemned himself to an eternal fate that is too appalling to consider. This need for our help should ever be present to us; there are few dispositions which put us so completely in harmony with Christ, who lived and suffered and died for sinners. . . . This is the purpose of true Christian charity, to save men from sin and to unite them to God.

Boylan, *This Tremendous Lover*, p. 212.

1414. *Better to Pity Sinners than to Judge Them*

It is a clear sign of a soul that is not yet thoroughly purged from the dregs of sin, not to sorrow with a feeling of pity at the offenses of others, but to keep to the rigid censure of the judge. . . .

Abbot Chaeremon, quoted by Cassian, in *The Nicene and Post-Nicene Fathers,* vol. 9, p. 419.

1415. *Sinners Should Be Criticized under Certain Circumstances*

It is true that we can speak openly of infamous, public, notorious sinners, provided it is in a spirit of charity and compassion and not arrogantly or presumptuously. Nor should we take any pleasures from the evils of others, for this last is always the act of a mean, debased heart. However, I exclude the declared enemies of God and his Church. It is our duty to denounce as strongly as we can heretical and schismatic sects and their leaders. It is an act of charity to cry out against the wolf when he is among the sheep, wherever he is.

St Francis de Sales, *Introduction to the Devout Life*, p. 168.

1416. *The Sinner Should Never Despair*

. . . No sinner should ever despair of God's mercy as long as he lives. For there is hardly a tree so thorny and knotted that men cannot make it smoother and beautiful. So, likewise, there is no sinner in this world so bad that God cannot adorn him with grace and many virtues.

Sayings of Brother Giles, in *Little Flowers of St Francis*, pp. 263-264.

1417. *Sinners Can Have Confidence in Christ*

The enemies of Christ unwittingly made clear to the sinners of all future ages what confidence and courage his familiar life with men had poured into the human hearts of his time by accusing him of surrounding himself with sinners and publicans.

Farrell, *A Companion, to the Summa*, vol. 4, p. 185.

1418. *How Christ Can Love Sinners*
It is true that Christ cannot love us in so far as we are sinners. But he can and does love us for any little good that remains in us, and above all he loves us for what we can possibly become if we respond to the pressing appeals of His grace. He does not love sin, but he does love those who are sinners, and he never shrinks from contact with us, or from our contact with him, as long as there remains the possibility of our rejecting that which is displeasing to his sight.

Edward Leen, *In the Likeness of Christ*, p. 202.

1419. *Christ Is a 'Specialist' in Saving Sinners*
If there is any one thing in which Christ "specializes", it is in saving sinners. 'I am not come', he said, 'to call the just but sinners.'. . . But perhaps the most appealing testimony of all is found in St Matthew's description of the Angel's message to St Joseph concerning our Lady: 'And she shall bring forth a Son and thou shalt call his name Jesus. For he shall save his people from their sins'. Our Lord's name then, signifying Savior, is more than a name; it is characteristic office, the work appointed for him by God. His very name constitutes the sinner's claim upon his goodness, his power and his mercy.

Boylan, *This Tremendous Lover*, pp. 140-141.

1420. *Christ Is the Sinner's Advocate in Heaven*
'But if any man sin, we have an Advocate with the Father, Jesus Christ, the Just, and he is the propitiation for our sins' (1 Jn 2:1).

Oh, what great confidence do these words give to penitent sinners! Jesus Christ is in heaven, advocating their cause, and he is certain to obtain pardon for them. The devil, when a sinner has escaped from his chains, tempts him to be diffident of obtaining pardon. But St Paul encourages him, saying: 'Who is He that shall condemn? Jesus Christ that died . . . also maketh intercession for us' (Rom 8:34). The Apostle means to say, if we detest the sins that we have committed, why do we fear? Who is He who will condemn us? It is Jesus Christ, the same who died, that we might not be condemned, and who is now in heaven advocating our cause.

St Alphonsus Liguori, *The Incarnation, Birth and Infancy of Jesus Christ*, p. 402.

1421. *Correction of Sinners, a Duty of Priests*
[The first of the works of a zealous priest mentioned by St Alphonsus is] the correction of sinners. Priests who see insults offered to God and remain silent are called by Isaias 'mute dogs' (Is 56:10). But to these mute dogs shall be imputed all the sins that they could have but have not prevented. 'Do not be silent,' says Alcuin, 'lest the sins of the people be ascribed to you.'...

Hence, St Leo adds: 'The priest who does not withdraw another from error proves that he is himself involved in it.'... St Gregory writes that we kill as many souls as we see committing sin without endeavouring to apply a remedy.

St Alphonsus Liguori, *Dignity and Duties of The Priest*, p. 180.

1422. *Work for the Conversion of Sinners Gives Glory to God*
After reading the lives of the holy martyrs and of the holy workmen in God's vineyard, St Teresa ... said that she envied the latter more than the former, on account of the great glory which their labor for the conversion of sinners gives to God.

St Alphonsus, *ibid.*, p. 170.

1423. *One Just Soul Can Save Thousands*
Though it is not always given to us to see the fruit of genuine zeal, yet our Lord's words to St Margaret Mary still hold good; 'One just soul shall obtain pardon for a thousand sinners.'

Gabriel, *Ascetical Conferences for Religious*, p. 35.

1424. *Sinners Converted Through St Catherine of Siena*
The Sovereign Pontiff, Gregory XI, consoled and delighted with the good effected in souls, granted to me and two companions, the powers reserved to bishops, for absolving all those who went to Catherine and confessed. We, therefore, heard men and women of heinous guilt, soiled with every variety of crime, who had either never confessed, or who had not done it in suitable dispositions. We sometimes remained fasting until the evening, and yet we could not suffice to all who presented themselves. I acknowledge to my shame and Catherine's honor, that the multitude was frequently so considerable that I was fatigued and discouraged.

Blessed Raymond of Capua, *Life of St Catherine of Siena*, p. 173.

1425. *Sinner Converted by Looking at a Crucifix*
St Vincent de Paul was trying, without success, to bring back to God a notorious sinner. His pleadings and warnings alike fell upon deaf ears till

he bethought him of a new way of approach. He came with a large crucifix and made a bet with the sinner. He challenged him to place the crucifix on the mantelpiece, look at it steadily three times a day, and say to himself slowly while looking: 'I don't care'. Yes, to be sure, the sinner would take on the bet – and win. But he lost! In less than a week, he returned to St Vincent. 'Father, you win. I cannot do it. I *do* care. I never realized before what my sins meant. Beg him to have mercy on my soul.'

Nash, *Living Your Faith*, p. 83.

1426. *Prayer for Sinners Is a Work of Charity*
The most destitute man in the world is the man in the state of mortal sin. He cannot rise out of his sin without the help of grace, which he cannot merit strictly for himself. The greatest work, then, of fraternal charity is that by which grace is obtained from God for those in mortal sin.

Boylan, *This Tremendous Lover*, p. 202.

1427. *Prayer for Salvation of Sinners a Duty*
To Mary Magdalene de Pazzi, Jesus said: 'See, Magdalene, how Christians are in the hands of the devil; unless my elect by their prayers deliver them, they shall be devoured.' Hence the saint used to say to her religious: 'My sisters, God has not separated us from the world only for our own good, but also for the benefit of sinners.' And on another occasion she said: 'My sisters, we have to render an account to God of so many lost souls: Had we recommended them to God with fervor, perhaps they would not be damned.'

St Alphonsus Liguori, *The True Spouse of Jesus Christ*, p. 371.

1428. *At Fatima, Mary Asks Prayers for the Conversion of Sinners*
[In the apparition of 13 May 1917, our Lady asked the following favor:] 'Would you like to offer yourselves to God to make sacrifices and to accept willingly all the sufferings it may please him to send you in order to make reparation for so many sins, which offend the Divine Majesty, to obtain the conversion of sinners and to make amends for all the blasphemies and offenses committed against the Immaculate Heart of Mary?'

'Yes, we should like that very much,' answered Lucy in the name of all three. With a gesture, the Lady shows how much their generosity pleases her. Then she adds: 'You will have much to suffer, but the grace of God will help you and give you the strength you need.'

De Oca, *More About Fatima and the Immaculate Heart of Mary*, p.3.

1429. *Prayer for Sinners Taught at Fatima by the Blessed Mother*
At Fatima the Blessed Mother taught the children to add the following

prayer to each decade of the Rosary: 'O my Jesus, pardon us, save us from the fire of hell, draw all souls to heaven, especially those most in need.'

Walsh, *Our Lady of Fatima*, p. 90.

1430. *Justification Is a Greater Work than Creation*

St Augustine says that to sanctify a sinner is a greater work than to create heaven and earth.

St Alphonsus Liguori, *Dignity and Duties of the Priest*, p. 35.

1431. *Restoration of Spiritual Life Greater Work than Bodily Resurrection*

It is a far greater miracle to raise to life one who will live forever, than to raise someone who must die again.

The widowed mother [at Naim] rejoiced over the young man restored to life. Mother Church rejoices daily over men restored to life in the spirit. He was dead in his body: they in the soul. His visible death was mourned before all; their invisible death is neither seen nor thought of. He sought them who had known they were dead. And he alone had known they were dead who had power to make them live. . . . No one can so easily waken one who sleeps in his bed as Christ can waken him from the grave.

St Augustine, in Toal, vol. 4, p. 116.

1432. *Forgiven Sinners Like Cured Lepers*

St John Chrysostom asks us to picture a poor leper, all covered with wounds and disfigured. Suppose anyone were to heal his body of leprosy and make him handsome and rich besides. How grateful this leper would be to his benefactor! How much more grateful should we be to God, for when our souls were hateful and disfigured by sins, he not only delivered us from our sins but made us beautiful and lovable too. . . .

St Alphonsus Liguori, *The Passion of Jesus Christ*, p. 79.

SONS OF GOD

1433. *Sons of God*

Why do we appropriate our sonship to the First Person? Because that Person in the Trinity engenders, generates the Son by communicating to him numerically the same nature. The First Person, in fact, bears within the august Trinity, the sweet glorious name of Father. In our adoptive sonship we receive communication of divine life, and hence what is more natural than to refer this participation in divine life to the First Person?

Our Lord makes it clear that he is the natural Son of God, we the adopted sons: 'Go to my brethren, and say to them: I ascend to my Father and to your Father, to my God and your God' (Jn 20:17). St Paul tells us that our sonship is patterned after the sonship of Christ... (see Rom 8:28-29).

Bandas, *The Catholic Layman and Holiness,* pp. 314-315.

SOULS

1434. *The Dignity and Worth of the Soul*
Be fully aware, O beautiful soul, of the fact that you are the image of God. And man, be aware that you are the glory of God. . . .

Know then, man, your greatness, and see to it that you never on any occasion become entrapped in the snares of the Devil.

St Ambrose, in *The Fathers of the Church*, vol. 42, p. 263.

1435. *How Highly God Values Each Soul*
The Lord is infinite in his mercy and his love has no limit, and thus he attends and esteems and assists every soul who receives him, and he rejoices in it, as if he had created it alone, and as if he had been made Man for it alone.

The Blessed Virgin to Mary of Agreda, in *City of God: Words of Wisdom,* p. 124.

1436. *The Soul's Nature Reveals God's Love for Us*
If anyone withdraws his attention for a moment from his body, and, emerging from the slavery of his passions and his carelessness, looks at his own soul with honest and sincere reason, he will see clearly how its nature reveals God's love for us and his intention in creating us.

St Gregory of Nyssa, in *The Fathers of the Church*, vol. 58, p. 127.

1437. *The Soul Can Be Satisfied By God Alone*
St Augustine, speaking of the rational soul, says: 'Thou hast made the rational soul, O Lord, capable of thy majesty, in such a way that nothing else can satisfy or sate it but Thyself.'

Rodriguez, *Practice of Perfection and Christian Virtues*, vol. 1, p. 487.

1438. *The Soul's Value Shown*
St Jerome says: 'Great is the dignity of souls, and great the value God sets on them, since at the birth of a man he at once deputes and appoints an angel to guard and take care of him.' As a princely Father gives a well-beloved son a tutor to watch over him in body and teach him good manners, so God cherishes and values us so much that he gives to each of us an angel for tutor.
Rodriguez, *ibid.*, vol. 2, p. 410.

1439. *Why God Created My Soul*
[Out of an infinite number of other souls that God might have created, he chose mine.] Back there in eternity I see him today, very deliberately placing his finger on one such possible creature, and I hear the Blessed Trinity declare that this is the creature whom they prefer. To be preferred by God, and preferred before an infinite number of others who are rejected, who never will share in the divine life – to whom is this stupendous privilege accorded? If the plan is astonishing to contemplate, the answer to my query is overpowering. I am God's choice. In eternity he prefers *me*. From eternity the thought of my soul is in his mind; there never was a moment that he did not remember me. From eternity he decides to give me this wonderful gift of life with the possibilities of growth according to his plan.
Nash, *Living Your Faith*, p. 31.

1440. *Why God Created My Soul*
The reason God plans to create this soul of mine is that he may pour into it a share of [his] marvelous perfections. My soul will be a capacity to contain some of God's life, some of God's love, of God's knowledge, of God's power and strength and wisdom. This is his plan devised in eternity, and the reason he makes it is that God is love, and love longs to give of its goodness to others.
Nash, *ibid.*, p. 30.

1441. *The Soul Is Dead Through Pride, Lust*
. . . The arrogance of pride, the pleasure of lust and the poison of curiosity are the movements of a dead soul; not that it is dead in such a way as to lack movement, but, since it dies by 'abandoning the fountain of life' (cf. Jer 2:13), and thus is taken up by the transitory world and is conformed to it.

'But, thy word, O God, is the fountain of eternal life and it does not pass away' (cf. Jn. 4:14).
St Augustine, *Confessions*, bk. 13, chap. 21.

IMMORTALITY OF THE SOUL

1442. *The Soul Is Immortal*
It is of faith that my soul is immortal, and that one day, when I least think of it, I must leave this world. I ought, therefore, to make provision for myself, which will not fail with this life, but will be eternal even as I am eternal.

. . . What folly it is, to know I must die, and that an eternity either of happiness or misery awaits me after death, and that upon dying ill or well depends my being miserable or happy forever, and yet, not to adopt every means in my power to secure a good death!

St Alphonsus Liguori, *The Way of Salvation and Perfection*, p. 49.

1443. *The Soul's Immortality Easily Proven*
. . . Consider those who laid down their lives willingly because of their faith in a life hereafter, and see how renowned they have become through their miracles. The sick approach the lifeless remains of these martyrs and are healed; perjurors come and find themselves tormented by Satan; the possessed come and are delivered from the power of the Devil; lepers approach and are cleansed; the dead are brought and are restored to life. Consider what a fullness of life they must enjoy where they now live if even their dead bodies here on earth are alive with such miraculous powers. So, if you accept the presence of a soul in the body because of the body's physical activities, why do you not also recognize the continued life of the soul after death from the miracles performed through the lifeless body?

St Gregory the Great, in *The Fathers of the Church*, vol. 39, pp. 199-200.

1444. *Saving Souls Was the Main Reason Christ Chose to Suffer*
[Christ] labored incessantly for souls. He prayed for souls, he worked miracles in order to win men's love and trust, for well did he know that love of Him would be their passport to heaven. All this He did, but for the work of redeeming souls from sin, he relied more on suffering than upon anything else. So true is this that St Paul writes: 'He loved me and delivered himself up for me.'

Nash, *Living Your Faith*, p. 247.

1445. *God's Work for Souls*
Our Heavenly Father . . . 'devotes himself more to the direction of a soul in which he reigns than to the natural government of the whole universe, and to the civil government of all empires.'
Fr P. Lallamant, quoted in Chautard, *The Soul of the Apostolate*, p.44.

1446. *The Soul Is More Valuable than the World*
St Bernard says that in the eyes of God a soul is more valuable than the whole world.
St Alphonsus Liguori, *Dignity and Duties of the Priest*, p. 167.

1447. *It is Congruous that God Heed Our Desire to Save Souls*
St Thomas goes so far as to say: 'Because a man in grace fulfills God's will, it is congruous and in harmony with friendship that God should fulfill man's desire for the salvation of another.'
Goichon, *Contemplative Life in the World*, p. 162.

1448. *The Beauty of a Soul in the State of Grace*
Our Lord one day showed St Catherine of Siena a soul for which she had obtained salvation by her prayer and patience. 'The beauty of this soul was such,' the Saint told Blessed Raymond, her confessor, 'that no words could express it.' And yet this soul was not yet clad in the glory of the Beatific Vision; it had only the beauty given by the grace of baptism. 'Behold,' said our Lord to the saint, 'it is through thee that I have regained this soul which was already lost.' Then he added: 'Does it not appear to thee resplendent and beautiful? Who, then would not accept any pain in order to win so wonderful a creature? If I have shown thee this soul, it is to make thee more ardent to procure the salvation of all, and in order that thou mayest lead others to this work according to the grace that shall be given thee.'
Quoted from *Life of St Catherine of Siena*, by Blessed Raymond of Capua, in Marmion, *Christ, the Life of the Soul*, pp. 225-226.

1449. *Giving Souls to God Is the Best Gift*
St Thomas says that it is more meritorious to offer God one's own soul and the souls of others than any other external gift.
Goichon, *Contemplative Life in the World*, p. 66.

1450. *Saving Souls Is the Greatest Work*
[St John Chrysostom says] that nothing is more agreeable to God than to labor for the salvation of souls. . . . 'St Gregory the Great could truly say that no sacrifice can be more acceptable to God than to labor with

genuine zeal for the saving of souls.' . . . Since in very deed one single soul has cost the Son of God more than the whole universe. He had but to elicit an act of his will, and the heavens, the earth, the mountains, the planets, the sun, the stars were created. But the salvation of even one soul has cost him bloodshedding, stripes, anguish, torments and a most cruel death.

Scaramelli, *Directorium Asceticum*, vol. 4, pp. 242-243.

1451. *Work for the Salvation of Souls Is Most Pleasing to God*
For God, the salvation and sanctification of souls is a work of predilection to which everything else in the universe is secondary. The Fathers of the Church call it the most divine of all divine works. But, having raised us by sanctifying grace to the dignity of his adopted children, God has lovingly assigned to each of us a part in the plan of redemption, so much so that the success of this plan is in a true sense dependent on our cooperation. . . . What a privilege, to share with Jesus for all eternity the glory and happiness of having snatched souls from damnation and led them to unspeakable bliss.

Gabriel, *Ascetical Conferences for Religious*, p. 27.

1452. *Zeal for the Salvation of Souls Is a Sacrifice Pleasing to God*
. . . Says St Gregory: 'There is no sacrifice so pleasing to God as zeal for the salvation of souls.' . . . Now this zeal is a great and excellent love of God, for, not content with itself loving and serving God all it can, it desires that all men should be taken up with his love and serve him, and that his Holy Name be known, reverenced, glorified and exalted by all, and the Kingdom of God be extended and amplified.

Rodriguez, *Practice of Perfection and Christian Virtues*, vol. 3, pp. 68-69.

1453. *Work for Souls Pleases God*
To love is to 'wish good' to another, says St Thomas . . . but all individual good is subordinated to the supreme good. That is why to give God, the Infinite Good, to the ignorant by instructing them is so pleasing to God; and so is it to pray for the conversion of infidels and sinners that they may receive faith and recover divine grace.

Marmion, *Christ, the Life of the Soul*, p. 364.

1454. *Nothing More Noble than Work for Souls*
St Denis said that there is nothing more noble and more pleasing to God than to cooperate in the work of saving souls and to frustrate the devil's plans for ruining them. The Son of God came to earth for no other reason

than to save souls.
St Louis de Montfort, *The Secret of the Rosary*, p. 69.

1455. *Souls Valued by Christ*
I think Jesus prizes one soul which by his mercy, and through our diligence and prayer, we may have gained for him, more than all the other services we can render him.
St Teresa of Avila, *Foundations*, p. 4, in Peers *Complete Works of St Teresa*.

1456. *Saving One Soul*
. . . In the terms of the Angelic Doctor, 'To offer sacrifice spiritually to God is to offer him something that gives him glory. Now of all goods, the most pleasing that man can offer to God is, undeniably, the salvation of a soul.'
Quoted by Chautard, in *The Soul of the Apostolate*, p. 40.

1457. *Prayer for the Salvation of Souls*
A short but fervent prayer will usually do more to bring about a conversion than long discussions or fine speeches. . . . A single burning prayer of the seraphic St Teresa (as was learned through a highly creditable revelation) converted ten thousand heretics. And her soul, all on fire for Christ, could not conceive of a contemplative life, an interior life, which would take no interest in the Savior's intense anxiety for the redemption of souls. 'I would accept Purgatory until the Last Judgment,' she said, 'to deliver but one of them. And what do I care how long I suffer, if I set free a single soul, let alone many souls for the greater glory of God?'
Chautard, *ibid.*, pp. 35-36.

1458. *Salvation of Souls Sought by All Who Love God*
St Augustine exhorts all those who love God, 'If you love God, draw all men to his love.'. . .
A good ground to hope for his own salvation has he who with true zeal labors for the salvation of souls. 'Have you saved a soul?' says St Augustine, 'Then you have predestined your own.'
St Alphonsus Liguori, *Great Means of Salvation and of Perfection*, p. 453.

1459. *St Francis of Assisi on Salvation of Souls*
St Francis of Assisi did not believe he could be a friend of Christ unless his charity devoted itself to the salvation of souls.
Chautard, *The Soul of the Apostolate*, p. 71.

1460. *Consecration to the Work of Saving Souls*
[St Dominic's] one constant petition to God was for the gift of true charity; for he was persuaded that he could not be truly a member of Christ unless he consecrated himself wholly to the work of gaining souls, following the example of him who sacrificed himself without reserve for our redemption.
Dorcy, *Saint Dominic*, p. 7.

1461. *Help Save Souls by Instructing Them*
. . . I beg you, dearly beloved, that what you gladly hear in this preaching under the Lord's inspiration, wherever you are, zealously carry all that you have heard to your neighbors or relatives who either cannot come to Church with you or, what is worse, will not, as well as to those who, though they come, leave quickly. Then, just as I will be guilty if I neglect to speak to you, so you, also, if you do not retain in your memory what you have heard in order to teach it to others, ought to fear that you will have to give an account for them. Therefore, with the Lord inspiring you, strive to fulfill what the Apostle says: 'If a person is caught doing something wrong, you who are spiritual, instruct such a one in a spirit of meekness' (Gal 6:1). . . . Provided that you are willing to rebuke one another in charity in case of sin, the Enemy will be able to take you by surprise only with difficulty or not at all.
St Caesarius of Arles, in *The Fathers of the Church*, vol. 31, pp. 348-349.

1462. *Zeal for Saving Souls*
. . . Since the devil is so diligent in the ruin of souls, it is only right that we should be the like to save them.
Rodriguez, *Practice of Perfection and Christian Virtue*, vol. 3, p. 72.

1463. *Saving Souls a Principal Duty of Priests*
Before you were ordained priest, says St Athanasius, you might devote yourself to any occupation you wished, but now that you are a priest, you must be employed in the fulfillment of the office for which you are destined. . . . And what is the nature of this office? One of its principal duties is, as we have shown, to labor for the salvation of souls. This doctrine is confirmed by St Prosper, who says: 'To priests properly belongs the care of saving souls.'
St Alphonsus Liguori, *Dignity and Duties of the Priest*, p. 184.

1464. *Means to Be Used by Priests in Saving Souls*
The priest must above all attend to the perfection of his own soul. The

sanctity of the priest is the principal means of converting sinners. . . . The priest, as mediator, is charged with the office of making peace between God and man, says St Thomas. . . . But he who is a mediator must not be hateful to the person before whom he has to intercede; otherwise he will increase his wrath, says St Gregory. . . . Hence the saint adds: 'Pure must be the hand of the one that wishes to cleanse others of their stains.'. . . Hence St Bernard concludes that a priest, in order to be fit to convert sinners, must first purify his own conscience and afterwards the conscience of others. . . . St Philip Neri used to say, give me ten zealous priests and I will convert the whole world. . . . A single priest of moderate learning, who loves God ardently, will convert more souls to God than a hundred priests of great learning and little zeal. . . . It is necessary, says St Bernard, first to be a reservoir and then a canal.

St Alphonsus, *ibid.,* p. 178-180.

1465. *Saving Souls Is the Greatest Proof of a Priest's Love*

A priest . . . may do what he will; he may wear himself out in watchings, fastings, in long and wearisome pilgrimages; he may score his flesh with scourges, flag it with hair shirts, torture it with all kinds of austerities; he will never give his Lord so great a proof of love as by laboring unceasingly with Christ in saving his beloved sheep.

But though there be many pastures by which the spiritual life of Christ's sheep is sustained, all may be in the main reduced to these two: the food of the Divine Word, and the food of the holy sacraments.

Scaramelli, *Directorium Asceticum*, vol. 4, p. 259.

1466. *St Ignatius's Zeal for Salvation of Souls*

The reader may understand the import of those words of St Ignatius of Loyola, that if it were given him to choose whether he would forthwith mount up to heaven, or remain on earth serving God and laboring for the salvation of souls, he would choose to live on, even with the uncertainty of his everlasting salvation.

Scaramelli, *ibid.,* p. 244.

1467. *Willingness to Stay in Purgatory if One Soul Could Be Saved*

St Teresa (of Spain) said to her daughters, when they wanted to pray for themselves: 'What care I if I stay in Purgatory till the end of the world, if I save a single soul by my prayers.'

In *Collected Letters of St Thérèse of Lisieux*, p. 319, letter to *Père Roulland,* March 1897.

1468. *The Curé of Ars Suffered Lovingly to Save Souls*
Like every friend of Christ, St John Vianney suffered lovingly, urged to it by his grasp of the enormity and prevalence of sin that surrounded him, and by his understanding that only in this way could he grapple with sin and expel it from men's souls.
Nash, *Living Your Faith*, p. 248.

1469. *Pius XI Willing to Make Concordat with the Devil*
To those who are critical of some of the concordats signed by Pope Pius XI, the Pope was quoted as saying that if he could thereby save souls, he would be willing to make a concordat with the devil.
Personal recollections of press reports.

1470. *Don Bosco's Zeal for Souls*
'If, in order to reach a soul, I had to take my hat off to the devil, I would do so at once,' [said St John Bosco].
Forbes, *Saint John Bosco: The Friend of Youth*, p. 143.

1471. *Salvation of Souls is Goal of Redemptorist Institute*
He who is called to the Congregation of the Most Holy Redeemer will never be a true follower of Jesus Christ, and will never become a saint if he fulfills not the end of his vocation, and has not the spirit of the Institute, which is the salvation of souls, and of those souls that are most destitute of spiritual succor, such as the poor people in the country. [A footnote added by editors applies this principle to all religious of both sexes.]
St Alphonsus Liguori, *Great Means of Salvation and of Perfection*, p. 451.

1472. *St Thérèse Promised to Work for Souls after Death*
I am perfectly sure that I shall not stay inactive in heaven; my desire is to go on working for the Church and for souls, that is what I keep asking God, and I am certain he will say yes. After all, the angels are continually occupied with us, while they never cease to see the Face of God, and are rapt forever in the shoreless ocean of love. Why should not Jesus permit me to do as they do? . . .

What attracts me to the homeland of heaven is the call of Jesus, the hope that I may at least love him as I have longed to love him, and the thought that I shall bring a multitude of souls to love him, who will bless him for all eternity.
In *Collected Letters of St Thérèse of Lisieux*, p. 353.

1473. *St Thérèse Expected to Work for Souls Even in Heaven*
Yes, I will spend my heaven doing good upon earth. That is not impossible, since from the midst of the Beatific Vision itself the angels watch over us.

No, I shall not be able to take my rest until the end of the world as long as there are souls to be saved. But when the angel shall declare: 'Time shall be no longer,' then shall I take my rest, because the number of the elect will be complete.

St Thérèse of Lisieux, in Novissima Verba, p. 56.

1474. *Jesus Wants Us to Give Him Souls*
Ah! Celine, I feel that Jesus is asking us too to slake his thirst by giving him souls, souls of priests above all. . . . We are so small a matter . . . yet Jesus wills that the salvation of souls should depend on our sacrifices, our love; he is a beggar begging us for souls. . . .

In *Collected Letters of St Thérèse of Lisieux,* p. 113.

1475. *Eternal Welfare of the Soul to Be Preferred*
Know your nature – that your body is mortal, but your soul immortal; that our life has two denotations, so to speak; one relating to the flesh, and this life is quickly over; the other, referring to the soul, life without limit. 'Give heed to thyself' – cling not to the mortal as if it were eternal, disdain not that which is eternal as if it were temporal. Despise the flesh, for it passes away; be solicitous for your soul, which will never die.

St Basil, in *The Fathers of the Church*, vol. 9, p. 435.

1476. *By Saving Souls, One Saves His Own*
This is the doctrine of St Augustine: 'In saving a soul, thou hast predestined your own,' says the holy Doctor. And long before, the Apostle St James said: 'He must know that he who causeth a sinner to be converted from the error of his way shall save his soul [that is, his own soul, as appears from the Greek text] from death and shall cover a multitude of sins' (Jas 5:20).

St Alphonsus Liguori, *Dignity and Duties of the Priest*, p. 172.

1477. *Saving Souls Brings Great Reward*
If, says St Gregory, he that rescues a man from temporal death deserves a great reward, how much greater shall be the recompense of a priest who delivers a soul from eternal death, and brings her to eternal life!

St Alphonsus, *ibid.,* p. 174.

1478. *Soul of a Suicide Saved*
A weeping woman told the Curé of Ars that her husband had flung him-

self into the river. The saint, enlightened from on high, assured her the suicide had saved his soul. Between the time he leaped from the bridge and reached the water, he had made an act of perfect contrition!

Nash, *The Nun at Her Prie-Dieu*, p. 152.

Note Added to the Suicide Story Above
A more detailed version of this incident was published in the Catholic press several years ago. According to that version, a fairly large group of pilgrims were lined up before the church door when the saint emerged from the rectory. Instead of going to the church door, the Curé approached a certain woman and said: 'He has been saved.' Perplexed, the woman asked what the priest meant by these words. So he explained that since her husband had consented to attend the previous May Devotions under the urging of his wife, the Blessed Mother herself intervened to procure the grace of contrition for the man between the time he jumped off the bridge and the time when he lost conciousness in the watery deep. Whether this version is authentic cannot now be verified.

SOULS IN PURGATORY

1479. *Duty of Praying for Souls in Purgatory*
St Thomas teaches that Christian charity extends not only to the living but also to all who have died in the state of grace. Hence, as we are bound to relieve our living neighbors who require our aid, so we are obliged to succor these holy prisoners. According to St Thomas, their sufferings surpass all the pains of this life.

St Alphonsus Liguori, *The True Spouse of Jesus Christ*, p. 372.

1480. *Prayers to and for the Souls in Purgatory*
. . . The souls in Purgatory, being beloved by God and confirmed in grace, have absolutely no impediment to prevent them from praying for us. Still, the Church does not invoke them or implore their intercession, because ordinarily they have no cognizance of our prayers. But we may piously believe that God makes our prayers known to them; and then they, full of charity as they are, most assuredly do not omit to pray for us. St Catherine of Bologna, whenever she desired a favor, had recourse to the souls in Purgatory, and was immediately heard. She even testified that by the intercession of the souls in Purgatory, she obtained many graces which she had been unable to obtain by the intercession of the Saints. . . .

If we desire the aid of their prayers, it is but fair that we should mind to aid them with our prayers and good works. I said it is fair, but I should have said it is our Christian duty; for charity obliges us to succor our neighbor when he requires aid and we can help him without grevous inconvenience.

If a sense of duty will not persuade us to succor them, let us think of the pleasure it will give Jesus Christ to see us endeavouring to deliver his beloved spouses from prison in order that he may have them with him in paradise.

. . . St Augustine says that God will cause those who in this life have most succored those holy souls, when they come to Purgatory themselves, to be most succored by others.

St Alphonsus Liguori, *Great Means of Salvation and of Perfection*, pp. 36-37, 40-41.

SPIRITUAL CHILDHOOD

1481. *Taught by Christ in the Our Father*

When Jesus, requested by His Apostles to teach them how to pray, answered by the 'Our Father who art in Heaven,' He gave them a clear insight into what should be the ordinary relations between the regenerated soul and God. God deigns to be, and to have the heart of a father toward all the baptized. . . . The finest expression of Christianity consists in this, in trusting God as a loving Father and in behaving, in his regard, as an utterly dependent child. This is the ideal of perfection to which Jesus directs the minds of the Apostles.

Edward Leen, *The True Vine and Its Branches*, p. 225-226.

1482. *Indispensable for Gaining Eternal Life*

Spiritual childhood . . . according to [Pope Benedict XV], is not an optional means, a better, a shorter or an easier way to holiness; it constitutes 'the indispensable condition for gaining eternal life'; hence, the 'faithful of all nations should enter courageously upon this way by which Teresa of the Child Jesus attained heroic virtue.'

Gabriel, *Ascetical Conferences for Religious*, p. 109.

1483. *Spiritual Childhood Kills Pride*

'Holy spiritual childhood is a more perfect state than the love of suffering, for nothing immolates a man to such a degree as to be *sincerely* and *peacefully* lowly. The childlike spirit kills pride more surely than the spirit of penance' (Msgr. Gay).

Quoted by Boylan, in *This Tremendous Lover*, p. 247.

1484. *Spiritual Childhood Vs. Spirit of Independence*
The chief cause of man's conflict with God, whether it be a question of man fallen or unfallen, is a *certain thirst for independence....* He wants to stand on his own feet. . . .

Christ's teaching strikes at the very root of this disorderly tendency in rational creatures. He warns men that their entry into the kingdom of God, their return to the paradise from which they had been expelled (in so far as such a return is possible under the actual condition of things) can be effected only through the abandonment of this independent attitude of soul. He tells them that they must shed the 'grown up' or 'adult' attitude in their dealings with God and become as little children with their heavenly Father.

Edward Leen, *The True Vine and Its Branches*, p. 203-205.

1485. *Spiritual Childhood – How to Develop It*
To commit ourselves wholly to God's paternal love, to put fearless, child-like trust in his goodness, and to base all one's hopes of being in the divine favor, in life and in death, in his fatherly loving kindness and mercy, is to have attained to a lofty degree of spiritual childhood.

Edward Leen, *ibid.*, p. 228.

1486. *The 'Little Way' of St Thérèse*
[Pauline (Mother Agnes of Jesus) asked St Thérèse]. What is the *little way* that you will teach? The saint answered: It is the way of spiritual childhood, the way of trust and absolute self-surrender. I want to point out to souls the means that I have always found so completely successful, to tell them there is only one thing to do here below – to offer our Lord the flowers of *little sacrifices* and win him by our caresses. That is how I have won him, and that is why I shall be made so welcome. . . . We can never have too much confidence in our God who is so mighty and merciful. As we hope in him, so shall we receive.

In *St Thérèse of Lisieux,* Autobiography and Letters, p. 232.

1487. *Comments of Benedict XV on St Thérèse*
It will not be out of place to enumerate the qualities of this spiritual childhood, both as regards what it omits and what it includes. It knows nothing of self-pride, or the thought of being able to obtain by purely natural means a supernatural end, or those spurious notions of self-reliance in the hour of danger and temptation. On the other hand, it presupposes a lively faith in the existence of God, a practical homage to his power and mercy, a confident recourse to the Providence of him who alone can give us grace to avoid evil and seek good. Thus, whether regarded from the negative or

the positive point of view, the *qualities which comprise spiritual childhood* evoke our admiration and enable us to realize why our Lord Jesus Christ pointed to it as a necessary condition for obtaining eternal life.... The Son of God was not content with merely stating that the kingdom of heaven was for children ... 'For of such is the kingdom of heaven', or that whosoever should become like a little child would be the greatest in the kingdom of heaven. He went so far as to exclude from his kingdom those who did not become as little children. ... There are some who try to persuade themselves that the way of trust and abandonment to God is the exclusive privilege of those whose baptismal robe is unsullied by sin. They are unable to reconcile the idea of spiritual childhood with the loss of their innocence. But do not the words of the Divine Master, 'Unless you be converted and become as little children,' indicate the necessity of change? 'Unless ye become converted' suggests a transformation which the disciples of Jesus had to undergo in order to become children again; and who should become a child if not he who is no longer one?

Quoted from the allocution of Pope Benedict XV on the occasion of the promulgation of the decree concerning the virtues of St Thérèse of Lisieux, in St Thérèse of Lisieux, *Autobiography and Letters*, pp. 257-258, 259-260.

1488. *Pius XII on St Thérèse's Doctrine*
The way of spiritual childhood, which, like so many other saints, St Thérèse has recalled to us, is the way recommended in these words of the Savior to the Apostles: 'Amen, I say to you, unless you be converted and become as little children you shall not enter into the kingdom of heaven' (Mt 18:3).

Some there are who believe that this is a special way, reserved to the innocent souls of young novices, to guide them in their first steps only, and that it does not suit persons already mature, who because of the great responsibilities imposed on them, must exercise much prudence. This is to forget that our Lord has recommended this way to *ALL Children of God*, even to those who, like the Apostles he trained, have the greatest responsibility: that of souls.

In St Thérèse of Lisieux, *Novissima Verba*, p. 144, quoting a letter of Pius XII.

SPIRITUAL DIRECTION

1489. *Without Spiritual Direction the Devil Has an Easy Time*
'There is no vice,' says Cassian, 'which makes it so easy for the devil to drag down to death and eternal ruin souls consecrated to God as this

desire to shape our own course independently and to dispense with the counsels of enlightened men'.

Scaramelli, *Directorium Asceticum*, vol. 1, p. 105.

1490. *Spiritual Direction Needed*
St Bernard says: 'Whoever makes himself his own master in the spiritual life, makes himself the scholar of a fool.'

Bandas, *The Catholic Layman and Holiness,* p. 75.

SPIRITUAL READING

1491. *Spiritual Reading Necessary for Holiness*
Holiness is the fruit of prayer, and mental prayer is extremely difficult without the reading of spiritual books. Such reading provides the foundation on which the work of meditation is to be built up; it affords an immediate preparation for the exercise and ministers the element by which it is sustained. It is to the exercise of prayer what oil is to the lamp; it supplies the material from which the flame of fervor derives its nourishment and by which it is kept bright and burning.

[A footnote says that St Bernard] in his explanation of the words, 'Seek and you shall find,' says: 'Seek in reading and you shall find in meditation. Strike by your prayers and the door of contemplation shall be flung open.'

Edward Leen, *Progress Through Mental Prayer,* p. 212.

1492. *Spiritual Reading as Necessary*
We consider that a firm resolution to [do spiritual reading] is of capital importance for everyone who wishes to live in Christ. In fact, unless some sufficient substitute for it is provided, we would say that there is as little chance of living spiritually without reading as there is of living corporally without eating!

This reading has for its purpose, first of all, to make us know what we really have to do and how it is to be done, and afterwards to make us remember and think of what we are really doing and why it is to be done. It is so easy to forget the supernatural or to keep it all for Sunday morning, that one must do something to preserve its remembrance on weekdays. Reading is a most important means to that end. And to reading one should join reflection.

Boylan, *This Tremendous Lover*, pp. 110-111.

1493. *How Spiritual Reading Should Be Done*
As the body is not nourished by much eating, but by good digestion of what one does eat; so neither is the soul nourished by reading much, but by ruminating and well digesting what is read.
Rodriguez, *Practice of Perfection and Christian Virtues,* vol. 1, p. 393.

1494. *Importance of Spiritual Reading*
St Athanasius says in an exhortation to his religious: 'You will find none in earnest about his spiritual progress who does not give time to spiritual reading.'
Rodriguez, *ibid.,* p. 388.

1495. *How Spiritual Reading Is to Be Done*
For this spiritual reading to be profitable, it must not be done hastily, or at a gallop, as when one reads stories, but very leisurely and attentively; for an impetuous flow of water [or] a heavy shower does not penetrate or fertilize the earth, but small, gentle rain; so for reading to enter and be drunk in by the heart, the reading must be done with pausing and pondering.
Rodriguez, *ibid.,* p. 391.

1496. *Spiritual Reading as Useful as Mental Prayer*
To a spiritual life, the reading of holy books is perhaps not less useful than mental prayer. St Bernard says reading instructs us at once in prayer, and in the practice of virtue. Hence he concludes that spiritual reading and prayer are the arms by which hell is conquered and paradise won.
St Alphonsus Liguori, *The True Spouse of Jesus Christ*, p. 513.

1497. *Spiritual Reading Not for Knowledge Only*
Directors must bear in mind that to make a study of spiritual books is one thing, and to read holy books spiritually is an entirely different thing. When we study, our object is to gain a knowledge of the truths we read; in our spiritual reading we aim at gaining a love for those same truths, and penetrating ourselves thoroughly with them, in order, afterwards, to reduce them to practice. Study aims at enlightening the mind, spiritual reading is intended to give perfection to the will by pious affections, and to spur it on to put these affections into practical shape.
Scaramelli, *Directorium Asceticum*, vol. 1, p. 146.

1498. *Spiritual Reading and Prayer*
St Augustine, addressing himself to souls that are aiming at perfection and constant union with God, tells them that they must frequently betake

themselves either to prayer or to reading; and he gives them, moreover, the reason . . . 'When we pray we speak to God, and when we read good books, God speaks to us.' St Ambrose, instructing ecclesiastics already set apart for the service of God, insists on the same thing, and bids them, when they have ended their prayers in church, give themselves to spiritual reading; because 'in prayer we discourse with Jesus Christ, and while we read, we listen to Jesus Christ speaking to our heart'.

Scaramelli, *ibid.*, p. 143.

1499. *Spiritual Reading Urged by St Augustine*

[St Augustine] says that pious books are so many letters addressed to us from our heavenly country by Almighty God, our tender Father, and by the saints, our loving brethren. In them they warn us of the perils we have to encounter on our mournful pilgrimage; they point out to us the lurking places in which our enemies are awaiting us, the snares set for our feet in order to deprive us of the life of our souls and despoil us of the priceless treasure of the divine grace; they tell us what provision of virtue we shall require that we may not faint by the roadside; they animate us to support the labors, trials and sufferings of this toilsome journey; and they show us the direct and secure road to that happy country which others like ourselves have reached. Whoever wishes to arrive at that blessed land and to win a place of honor there, let him often read these letters from Paradise.

Scaramelli, *ibid.*, p. 137.

1500. *How to Read the Bible*

'Do you know,' says St Augustine, 'how we should read holy Scripture? As when a person reads letters that have come from his native country, to see what news we have of heaven. We should read to see what the Scriptures have to tell us of our native land, where we have our parents and brethren, our friends and fellow citizens, and where we are desiring and sighing ourselves to be.'

In Rodriguez, *Practice of Perfection and Christian Virtues*, vol. 1, p. 390.

1501. *Lives of Saints Recommended*

It is a great help to read much and hear read the lives of the saints, and consider their excellent and heroic virtues; it being the intention of Holy Church, in proposing to us their heroic deeds, to invite us at least to get out of our sloth. And there is this other advantage in such reading, that it confounds and humbles us to consider the purity of life of these saints, and how far we come short of it.

Rodriguez, *ibid.*, p. 45.

1502. *Benefits derived from Spiritual Reading*
... In reading holy books, we receive many lights and divine calls. St Jerome says that when we pray we speak to God; but when we read, God speaks to us.... St Ambrose says the same: 'We address him when we pray; we hear him when we read.... St Augustine writes ... that good books are, as it were, so many letters of love that the Lord sends us; in them he warns us of our dangers, teaches us the way of salvation, animates us to suffer adversity, enlightens us and inflames us with divine love. Whoever, then, desires to be saved and to acquire divine love, should often read these letters of paradise.
St Alphonsus Liguori, *The True Spouse of Jesus Christ*, pp. 518-519.

1503. *Caution Against Reading Mystical Theology*
To some, the reading of books on Mystic Theology may be pernicious; for it may incline them to seek after supernatural prayer, and to abandon the ordinary method of mental prayer by considerations and affections; thus they may be left without one or the other. For no one should seek to attain the prayer of contemplation unless God clearly calls him to it. Hence, St Teresa after death appeared to one of her nuns and directed that the Superiors should forbid the religious to read her books of visions and revelations, saying that she had become a saint not by visions and revelations, but by the practice of virtue.
St Alphonsus, *ibid.*, p. 516.

STORM ON THE LAKE

1504. *Teaching Courage*
When there was a manifestation of miracles, Jesus allowed the people to be present, but when terror and dangers are approaching, he takes with him only his Disciples, they who had to combat the world, whom he now wishes to exercise in fortitude.
St John Chrysostom, quoted by St Thomas, in Toal, vol. 1, p. 315.

1505. *Why Christ Slept Until Storm Was at Its Height*
It seems to me that all this was arranged with profoundest wisdom, so that they might not ask his aid as soon as the storm had begun to beat against the ship, but only when the danger would be at its highest, that the might of the divine power might thus be more evident.
St Cyril, in Toal, vol. 1, p. 324.

1506. *Storm Caused by Jesus While Asleep*
In his human Body he sleeps, but in his Godhead he keeps watch. He sleeps in this body of flesh, yet he causes this storm to arise on the sea, and the waves to mount up, and fear to come upon the disciples, so that he may reveal to them His power.
Origen, quoted in Toal, vol. 1, p. 319.

SUCCESS

1507. *Aiming at False Success Destroys True Success*
If you make success in your tasks and appointments – as men judge success – to be an objective, you are ruining your work at the very base. As in all other cases, you find the devil very subtle to produce something very like what God demands, but which is utterly different. Satan is called by the French very aptly 'Le singe de Dieu,' for he imitates God as a monkey imitates a man – an imitation which is a caricature and a perversion, but which can be very misleading. God tells us we should be successful, He obliges us to aim at success. 'Be ye perfect as your heavenly Father is perfect' (Mt 5:48). If you ambition this perfection, you are a success, but this perfection is not identical with success in your enterprises.
Edward Leen, *Retreat Notes for Religious*, p. 84.

SUFFERING

1508. *Part of the Father's Plan for His Son and the Apostles*
The Father sends the Son; ordaining He shall become Incarnate for the redemption of all mankind. He willed that he should come into this world to suffer; yet he loves the Son whom He destined to suffering. And the Lord, choosing his Apostles, sends them into the world; not to taste the joys of the world, but for the same end as he was sent: that they might suffer.
St Gregory the Great, in Toal, vol. 2, p. 282.

1509. *Suffering of Christ and the Saints*
. . . Our Lord need not have selected the way of suffering. . . . He could have offered to his Father, in reparation of our sins, one single sigh. . . . Such an offering, made as it would be by one infinite in dignity, would

have been more than sufficient to redeem . . . countless worlds. . . .

When you study the lives of his best friends, you find that to them, too, he invariably sends a large measure of suffering and a large share of the cross. . . . He did not spare [his Mother]. . . . There was no one person, except himself, to whom He measured a fuller portion from the cup of sorrow. . . . The saints . . . too were subjected to trials and persecution, the most diverse and the most painful and humiliating. . . . A strange way this, it would seem, to treat men and women whom he loved. . . . This much . . . we can deduce . . . that there must be in suffering lovingly borne some hidden value and power. . . .

Nash, *Living Your Faith*, pp. 241-243.

1510. *The Severity of Christ's Sufferings*
We may get a sufficient inkling of the greatness of Christ's sufferings from the fact that the mere imagination and thought of them in the garden made him sweat a sweat of blood so copious that it ran down on the earth. . . . So great and so severe were his pains and sufferings that the saints say that no mortal man could live under them without his life's being miraculously preserved, and so it was necessary for Christ to avail himself of his Divinity not to die under them. But this is what the Divinity did there, not to prevent his feeling his suffering, but to prevent the excessive pain that he felt from putting an end to his life, so that he could suffer more.

Rodriguez, *Practice of Perfection and Christian Virtues,* vol. 2, pp. 504-505.

1511. *The Meaning of the Cross*
The Cross is the compendium of Christ's philosophy. But the Cross must be interpreted accurately. . . . There was not in Jesus any morbid love of suffering for its own sake, or for hardship or want. . . . Christ, in a sense did not choose the Cross. He bore it willingly. It was God the Father that chose and decreed the way of the Cross as the way of man's salvation.

Edward Leen, *The True Vine and Its Branches*, pp. 155-156.

1512. *Suffering in Christ and in Us*
On the way to Emmaus, Christ says in reproach, 'Ought not Christ to have suffered these things and so enter into his glory? . . . It is the same for us; we must share in Christ's sufferings if we are to share in his glory.

Marmion, *Christ, the Life of the Soul*, p. 210.

1513. *Cross of Christ – Our Protection, Our Teacher*
St Thomas writes: 'In every temptation, the Cross is our protection. There we find obedience to God, love for our neighbor, patience in adversity.' St

Augustine says: 'The Cross was not only the gallows of the sufferer, but the throne of his teaching.'

St Alphonsus Liguori, *The Passion of Jesus Christ*, p. 133.

1514. *His Death bed and His Teacher's Chair*

St Augustine says: 'The Cross is not only the bed on which Christ died, but also the chair from which He taught us by His example what we are to do and imitate.'

In Rodriguez, *Practice of Perfection and Christian Virtue*, vol. 2, p. 523.

1515. *Carrying Our Cross Voluntarily*

'If anyone will come after Me, let him deny himself, and take up his cross daily, and follow Me' (Lk 9:23). It will be useful to make a few reflections on these words of Jesus Christ. He says: 'If anyone will come after Me'; he does not say 'to me' but 'after me.' The Lord desires that we should come close after him; we must therefore walk in the same road of thorns and sufferings in which he walked. He goes before and does not rest until he reaches Calvary, where he dies; therefore, if we love him we must follow him even to death. And thus it is necessary that every one should deny himself; that is, that he should deny everything that self-love demands, but that is not pleasing to Jesus Christ.

. . . *Let him take up*; it avails little to carry the cross by compulsion; all sinners bear it, but without merit; to bear it with merit, we must embrace it voluntarily.

St Alphonsus Liguori, *The Way of Salvation and of Perfection*, pp. 208-209.

1516. *Filling Up What Is Wanting in the Sufferings of Christ*

In speaking of his sufferings, St Paul wrote those words that appear so strange and are of such profound depth: 'I . . . fill up those things that are wanting of the sufferings of Christ in my flesh, for his body, which is the Church' (Col 1:24). Is there, then, something wanting to the sufferings, to the satisfactions of Christ? Certainly not. Their value is infinite. . . . St Augustine gives us the reply: The whole Christ, he says, is formed by the Church united to her Chief, and by the members (which we are) united to the Head (which is Christ). Christ, the Head of this mystical Body, has suffered; the great expiation was that of Jesus; the members, if they wish to remain worthy of the Head, must in their turn bring their share of sufferings and renunciation.

Marmion, *Christ, the Life of the Soul*, pp. 203-204.

1517. *The Sufferings of Christ to Be Filled Up*

In the words of St Augustine, 'Christ suffered all that he had to suffer;

nothing whatever is lacking to the number and intensity of his sufferings. Hence these sufferings are complete in Christ as in the Head, but there still remain the sufferings to be endured in the body.... In fact, Our Lord Himself declared this truth when he said to Saul who was 'breathing out threats and slaughter against the disciples' (Acts 9:1): 'I am Jesus whom thou persecutest' (Acts 9:5). By this statement Christ plainly affirmed that persecutions visited upon the Church are in reality directed against himself, the Head of the Church. Therefore, since Christ is still afflicted in his mystical Body, with good reason he desires to have us as companions in his own acts of expiation.

Gabriel, *Ascetical Conferences for Religious*, p. 344.

1518. *Christ Suffers in Members of the Mystical Body*

It is true that Christ cannot now suffer in his own Person. He retains contact, however, with passibility, through his Mystical Members. He can suffer in, and through, their sacrifice. He cannot suffer in his physical body; he can suffer in his Mystic Body. 'Christ suffers still on the earth, not in his own flesh, but in mine, which endures pain still in this world.... If, in fact, Christ himself did not suffer in his members, that is in the faithful, he could not have said: "Saul, why persecutest thou me?"' (St Augustine).

Edward Leen, *The True Vine and Its Branches*, p. 75.

1519. *Through Suffering, We Cooperate in the Work of Redemption*

Through this intercommunication of the sufferings of Christ and the Christian, all that the latter is called upon to endure, through his carrying God's will into effect becomes endowed with a marvellous efficacy in expiating personal sin, in meriting actual and habitual grace, and above all in producing a profoundly purifying effect in the soul. The daily passion of the Christian, who is united to Christ by faith and charity, wears to God the aspect of a new light on the baffling problem of human pain. The holy souls who recognize Christ suffering in and through themselves, learn to attach positive value to what human nature shrinks from as a great evil.... They take an effective part in redeeming the human race. They cooperate, subordinately to Christ, in the work of Redemption. St Paul was a Christian of this stamp. Hence he cried out: 'I, Paul, who now rejoice in my suffering *for you,* and *fill up those things that are wanting* of the sufferings of Christ, *in my flesh, for his body, which is the Church* (Col. 1:23-24).

Edward Leen, *ibid.*, pp. 76-77.

1520. *Suffering with Christ*
[Jesus said to them] 'Ought not Christ to have suffered these things and so to enter His glory?' (Lk 24:26). The members must, perforce, share the passibility of the Head. It would be an utter incongruity were this not so. As it was fitting, in accordance with the plan of God's wisdom, that he should reach his glory through pain, so it is fitting that his members should tread the same path in order to be glorified with him. 'The Spirit himself giveth testimony to our spirit that we are the sons of God, and if sons, heirs also; Yet so, if we suffer with him, that we may also be glorified with him' (Rom 8:16-17).
Edward Leen, *ibid.,* p. 43.

1521. *A Means of Sharing in Christ's Victory*
Be not fainthearted in the face of . . . sufferings. Keep before your eyes him who for your sake was afflicted by them, knowing that for the sake of Christ you also must be tried therein, and you will be victorious over them; for you follow a King who is a Victor, and who wishes you to share in his Victory.
St Basil, in *The Fathers of the Church*, vol. 9, p. 11.

1522. *Suffering with Jesus Is Solution of Life's Problems*
The Savior does not mitigate but he compensates for the sufferings which his friends are called on to endure on his behalf. To have Jesus with one in the struggles of life is the solution of life's problems. If a man has to meet them alone, he is overcome by them: if he faces them in company with Jesus, he is formed, purified and perfected by them. Trials yield him virtue in this life and glory in the next.
Edward Leen, *In the Likeness of Christ*, p. 102.

1523. *Suffering in Union with Christ Has Marvelous Efficacy*
Suffering of itself does not purify. But suffering borne in union with Christ is endowed with a marvellous efficacy to burn away the anti-divine in man.
Edward Leen, *The True Vine and Its Branches*, p. 162.

1524. *Willingness to Endure the Cross a Great Gift*
Above all the graces and gifts of the Holy Spirit which Christ gives to his friends is that of conquering oneself and willingly enduring sufferings, insults, humiliations, and hardships for the love of Christ. For we cannot glory in all those other marvellous gifts of God, as they are not ours but God's, as the Apostle says: 'What have you that you have not received?'

But we can glory in the cross of tribulations because that is ours, and so the Apostle says: 'I will not glory save in the Cross of our Lord Jesus Christ!'

St Francis of Assisi to Brother Leo, quoted in *The Little Flowers of St Francis,* p. 60.

1525. *A Greater Gift than Power to Raise the Dead*
If God were to give you the gift of raising the dead, he would be giving you much less than when he permits you to suffer. In fact, with the gift of miracles, he makes you his debtor, but with sufferings he makes himself your debtor.

St John Chrysostom, in *Spiritual Diary*, p. 82.

1526. *Suffering Endured Patiently Is a Jewel*
. . . The brightest jewels in the diadems of the saints are the sufferings which they endured in this life with patience and resignation.

St Alphonsus Liguori, *The True Spouse of Jesus Christ*, p. 51.

1527. *How to Carry the Cross Meritoriously*
There is no other way to enter heaven but to resign ourselves to tribulations until death. And thus may we find peace even in suffering. When the Cross comes, what means is there for loving peace except the uniting of ourselves to the divine will? If we do not take this means, let us go where we will, let us do what we may, we shall never fly from the weight of the cross. On the other hand, if we carry it with good will, it will bear us up to heaven and give us peace on earth.

What does he gain who refuses the cross? He increases its weight. But he who embraces it, and bears it with patience, lightens its weight, and the weight itself becomes a consolation; for God abounds with grace to all those who carry the cross with good will in order to please him. By the law of nature there is no pleasure in suffering; but divine love, when it reigns in the heart, makes it take delight in its suffering.

St Alphonsus Liguori, *The Way of Salvation and of Perfection*, p. 205.

1528. *Suffering to Be Borne Patiently*
St Augustine warns us, 'If we wish to be spared the blows which the loving hand of our heavenly Father inflicts upon us, let us understand clearly that at the same time we should be rejected from the number of his sons'.

Scaramelli, *Directorium Asceticum*, vol. 3, p. 257.

1529. *Our Security Consists in Suffering with Resignation*
In this consists all our security and perfection: in suffering with resignation all things that are contrary to our inclinations, as they happen to us day

by day, whether they are small or great. And we must suffer them for those purposes for which the Lord desires that we should endure them: (a) to purify ourselves from the sins we have committed; (b) to merit eternal life; (c) to please God, which is the chief and most noble and at which we can aim in all our doings.

St Alphonsus Liguori, *The Way of Salvation and of Perfection*, pp. 206-207.

1530. *Sufferings Rightly Endured Bring Peace and Victory*

He who knows how to suffer will enjoy much peace. Such a one is a conquerer of himself and lord of the world, a friend of Christ and an heir of heaven.

Thomas à Kempis, *Imitation of Christ*, bk. II, chap. 3.

1531. *Learning How to Suffer with Joy*

... I entreat you to practice every day the beautiful advice of Fr Torres given to his penitents: 'Say every day an Our Father and a Hail Mary, in honor of the life of ignominy of Jesus; and offer yourself to suffer not only in peace but even with joy for the love of him all the contradictions and reproaches that he will send you; begging always his assistance to be faithful to him in bearing patiently all injuries and humiliations.

St Alphonsus Liguori, *The True Spouse of Jesus Christ*, p. 345.

1532. *Suffering in Peace*

The other day I hit upon the secret of suffering in peace. The word *peace* does not mean joy, at least not *felt joy*; to suffer in peace, it is enough to will whatever Jesus wills.

In *Collected Letters of St Thérèse of Lisieux*, p. 98.

1533. *Suffering with Joy Can Save Souls*

When I realize that one will love the good God better for all eternity because of suffering borne with joy – And, by suffering, one can save souls. Ah, Pauline, if at the moment of my death I could have a soul to offer to Jesus, how happy I should be! There would be a soul snatched from the fire of hell and blessing God for all eternity.

St Thérèse of Lisieux, *ibid.*, p. 45.

1534. *We Must Pray When the Cross is Heavy*

... Whenever the weight of any cross seems very heavy, let us immediately have recourse to prayer, and God will give us strength to endure it meritoriously. And let us then recollect what St Paul said, that no tribulation of this world, however grievous it may be, can be compared with the glory which God prepares for us in the world to come (Rom 8:18).

St Alphonsus Liguori, *The Way of Salvation and of Perfection*, p. 207.

1535. *The Value of Vicarious Suffering*

Gerlich, in his work on Theresa Neumann, offers the following explanation of reparatory suffering as presented by Theresa Neumann: 'I once felt the need to discuss this phenomenon with her in the state of elevated calm; it was something completely new to me and difficult to grasp. I openly admitted that I did not understand the whole affair. Then she gave me the following answer (equivalently): 'You see, our Savior is just. And so he's got to punish. But he's kind too, and he wants to help. The sins that have been committed he's got to punish; if someone else takes over the suffering and punishment, then God's justice is satisfied, and our Savior is free to exercise his kindness.'

Steiner, *Thérèse Neumann: A Portrait Based on Authentic Accounts, Journals, and Documents,* p. 185.

1536. *Value of the Cross Depends on our Attitude*

The Cross is inevitable. Our attitude toward it can vary. It is on this attitude toward it that its value for each one depends. 'All the crosses that God sends us,' writes St Augustine, 'can change their nature according to the manner in which we receive them.'. . .

Calvary itself is an awesome illustration of this truth. 'There we see,' again quoting St Augustine, 'three men crucified: of these three one gives salvation, one receives it and one rejects it. A just man suffers voluntarily and by his sufferings he merits salvation for all his guilty fellows. A sinner suffers in humble submission, is converted, and by his sufferings so accepted wins eternal life. Another sinner suffers the same tortures, but he does so in a spirit of revolt; his sufferings merit nothing for him; they are but the prelude of everlasting torment.'

James Leen, *By Jacob's Well*, p. 185-186.

1537. *How to Profit from Suffering*

When we are going to suffer anything unpleasant we ought to think, not of the hardships involved, but of the crown to come. Just as traders consider not merely the seas, but also the profits they will obtain, so we also ought to reflect on heaven and confidence in God.

St John Chrysostom, in *The Fathers of the Church*, vol. 41, p. 333.

1538. *For the Sake of Eternity*

St Augustine says: 'Here burn, here cut, here spare me nothing, that thou mayest spare me for eternity.'

Rodriguez, *Practice of Perfection and Christian Virtues*, vol. 1, p. 583.

1539. *The Advantage of Suffering*
The fire of present problems should be endured because it toughens us. Just as actual fire in the kiln toughens the earthenware vessels but does not destroy them, so, too, the fire of problems toughens spiritual vessels. . . . This is not surprising. Just as problems sting from the outside, so divine encouragement soothes from the inside. Indeed, as the sufferings of Christ overflow to us, so, through Christ, does our consolation overflow.
St Bonaventure, *Rooted in Faith*, p. 34.

1540. *Satisfaction for Sin*
The Council of Trent teaches on this subject a very consoling truth. It tells us that God is so munificent in his mercy that, not only the works of expiation that the priest imposes on us, or that we ourselves choose, but even all the sufferings inherent in our condition here below, all the temporal adversities which God sends or permits and we patiently support, serve, through Christ's merits, as satisfaction with the Eternal Father.
Marmion, *Christ, the Life of the Soul*, p. 208.

1541. *Suffering Seen as a Great Grace*
St Francis [de Sales] recommends his religious to consider illness as great a grace as health, and to love, to desire, to seek poverty, suffering and scorn with the same passion which worldly people devote to the pursuit of riches and honors. This indifference and this preference provide the key for us to escape our desolation.
Charmot, *Ignatius and Francis de Sales*, pp. 86-87.

1542. *Even Little Sufferings Are Meritorious*
. . . Nothing, how little soever, that is suffered for God's sake, can pass without merit in the sight of God.
Thomas à Kempis, *Imitation of Christ*, bk. III, chap. 19.

1543. *The Cross Makes Saints*
To quote Fr Faber: 'It is affliction which makes saints.'
Boylan, *This Tremendous Lover*, p. 240.

1544. *Suffering Breaks Down Obstacles to Divine Life*
For the soul that is faithful, sufferings break down the obstacles to the growth of divine life. Sufferings, rightly borne, win great graces for action and foster fidelity to the promptings of the Divine Spirit.
Edward Leen, *The True Vine and Its Branches*, p. 106.

1545. *Suffering Permitted by God Is Valuable*
[It is true] that people may say sharp things to me, that I may be misunderstood, or laughed at, or that sickness or failure may pursue me relentlessly. But God permits these things. They emanate from him. And God loves me with an eternal love. If these 'misfortunes' seem hard and difficult to understand, I have only to remember that never would a loving Father allow them to come my way unless he saw very clearly what an immense blessing would accrue from them to me, whom he loves. And this attitude toward them must necessarily bring joy into my life.
Nash, *Living Your Faith*, p. 64.

1546. *Suffering Sent by the Lord Is a Remedy*
Be persuaded . . . says St Augustine, that when the Lord sends you suffering, He acts as a physician; and that the tribulation that he sends you is not the punishment of your condemnation, but a remedy for your salvation. 'Let man understand,' says the holy Doctor, 'that God is a physician, and that tribulation is a medicine for salvation, not a punishment for damnation.'
St Alphonsus Liguori, *The True Spouse of Jesus Christ*, p. 381.

1547. *Suffering as Part of God's Plan*
. . . It is the way of Providence to test by . . . afflictions men of virtuous and exemplary life, to call them, once tried, to a better world, or to keep them for a while on earth for the accomplishment of other purposes.
St Augustine, *City of God*, bk. 1, chap. 1.

1548. *Suffering – Why and Wherefore*
. . . Everybody knows that wherever there is great love, there is always present also the urge to do more, much more, than is strictly necessary. . . . True love would bear "all things" for the sake of the person loved. . . . 'Love,' writes St Ignatius, 'is shown by deeds rather than by words.' But there is no proof of love more searching than willingness to suffer for the person loved. A mother will rush blindly into a burning house . . . because she sees the child she loves standing at the window by flames . . . 'Suffering is the badge of those who love' is a saying dear to St John of the Cross.
Nash, *Living Your Faith*, pp. 243-244.

1549. *Suffering Borne with the Right Spirit Shows the True Christian*
There is no better means of distinguishing the chaff from the wheat in the Church of God than the suffering of contradictions, trials and contempt. He who stands firm through these is the grain. He who recoils from them is the chaff. The further he recoils, that is, the more upset and arrogant he

becomes, the more worthless he is.
St Augustine, in *Spiritual Diary*, p. 86.

1550. *Suffering Can Be a Blessing or a Curse*
The worship of sorrow, is not the 'core' of the religion of Jesus Christ. . . . It is the loving and reverential worship of God the Father that is the center of the religion of Jesus Christ. . . . Calvary offers a most striking illustration of the truth of this statement. There was one there whose wicked nature, so far from being changed for the better by crucifixion, was made, on the contrary, more vicious, vile and perverse. . . . There was a second malefactor crucified by the side of Christ. He endured the same horrible agonies as his companion. But in his case, his soul found greatness and astonishing elevation through patient endurance of his bitter lot.

The truth is that suffering can prove either a blessing or a curse.
Edward Leen, *The True Vine and Its Branches*, pp. 151-152.

1551. *Sufferings from Perversity of Others*
. . . The iron of our soul will not come to fineness of understanding so long as it has not been burnished by the file of another's perversity.
St Gregory the Great, in Toal, vol. 4, p. 230.

1552. *Opportunity to Expiate Our Faults*
When sufferings come to us from the hands of others, when, for example, we are the objects of malevolence, jealousy, treachery, contempt and abuse, what is the attitude to take? Experiences of this kind are extremely painful and are a fertile source of sharp mortification. . . . It behoves us to see the justice of God toward us working itself out in the injustice of our neighbor. God permits this suffering to fall on us in order to offer us an occasion of expiating faults of which not our neighbor but our conscience accuses us. Experience proves, too, that trials of this kind have a wonderful efficacy in detaching us from creatures, in delivering us from disorderly affections, in revealing to us the vanity of man's evaluations, and, by contrast, in bringing home to us the fairness and loyalty of God.
James Leen, *By Jacob's Well*, p. 197.

1553. *Saints Who Embraced Suffering*
St Teresa said, 'Either to suffer or to die'; St Mary Magdalen de Pazzi, 'To suffer, and not to die'; St John of the Cross: 'To suffer and to be silent.'
St Alphonsus Liguori, *The Way of Salvation and of Perfection*, p. 495.

1554. *St John Vianney on Bearing the Cross*
[The Curé of Ars declared:] 'The heart of an interior soul stands in the

middle of humiliations and sufferings like a rock in the midst of the sea.'
Quoted by Chautard, in *The Soul of the Apostolate*, p. 104.

1555. *Becoming the Wheat of God*
[As St Ignatius of Antioch said:] 'I am the wheat of Christ; may I be ground by the teeth of beasts that I may become pure bread.' In our case, it is other men who take on this task of grinding us. But we must acquiesce to this less violent form and receive with great love every blow coming from them or from circumstances. St Thérèse of Lisieux understood this very well: I am thinking of the word of St Ignatius of Antioch. I, too, must be pulverized by suffering, in order to become the wheat of God.'
In Goichon, *Contemplative Life in the World*, p. 167.

1556. *Some Who Willingly Accepted Suffering*
Gerlich in his book on Thérèse Neumann wrote: 'I also asked her what her inner attitude toward suffering was. I felt that I had noticed that she was afraid of suffering and did her best to bear up under it with great will power and only out of obedience to the will of God, who laid these crosses on her shoulders. This was her answer: 'No one can really like to suffer. I don't like it either. No man likes pain and I'm just as human as anyone else. But I also love our Savior's will, and when he sends me some suffering I'm happy to accept it because he wills it so. But suffering itself, I don't like".
Quoted by Steiner, in *Theresa Neumann: A Portrait Based on Authentic Accounts, Journals, and Documents*, pp. 185-186.

SUPERIORS

1557. *Superiors Must Give Good Example*
The Superior, mindful of the Apostle's precept: 'Be thou an example to the faithful' (1 Tm 4:12), should make his life a shining model for the observance of every commandment of the Lord so that there may be no excuse for those under his guidance to think the Lord's commands impossible or readily to be set aside.
St Basil, in *The Fathers of the Church*, vol. 9, p. 319.

1558. *Superiors Should Try to Be Loved so as to be Heard*
. . . It is indeed difficult for a preacher who is not loved, however well he may preach, to be willingly listened to. He, then, who is over others ought to study to be loved, to the end that he may be listened to, and still not

seek love for its own sake, lest he be found in the hidden usurpation of his thought to rebel in his office against him whom in his office he appears to serve.

St Gregory the Great, in *The Nicene and Post-Nicene Fathers*, vol. 12, p. 20.

1559. *The Dangers Facing Superiors*

There is danger that certain persons, knowing that they are in charge of others and directing them to the celestial city, may destroy themselves without realizing it. It is necessary for those in charge of supervision to work harder than the rest, to think humbler thoughts than those under them, and to furnish their own life as an example of servitude to the brothers, looking upon those entrusted to them as a deposit of God.

St Gregory of Nyssa, in *The Fathers of the Church,* vol. 58, p. 146.

1560. *Faults That Are Light in Others May Be Mortal Sins in Superiors*

. . . According to the common opinion of theologians, many violations of rule, which in subjects are but light faults, will be grievous sins in the Superior if, when they are frequent and apt to produce general relaxation of discipline, she does not correct them according to the best of her ability, and insist on the reparation necessary to preserve exact observance.

St Alphonsus Liguori, *The True Spouse of Jesus Christ*, p. 108.

1561. *Superiors Must not Place Secular Affairs over Souls*

It is often the case that some, as if forgetting that they have been put over their brethren for their souls' sake, devote themselves with the whole effort of their heart to secular concerns. . . . And so it comes to pass that while they delight in being hustled by worldly tumults, they are ignorant of the things that are within, which they ought to have taught others. And from this cause, undoubtedly, the life also of their subjects is benumbed; because, while desirous of advancing spiritually, it meets a stumbling block on the way in the example of him who is set over it. For when the head languishes, the members fail to thrive. . . .

St Gregory the Great, in *The Nicene and Post-Nicene Fathers*, vol. 12, p. 17.

1562. *Superiors Warned – Vices Can Pass as Virtues*

The ruler also ought to understand how commonly vices pass themselves off as virtues. For often niggardliness palliates itself under the name of frugality, and on the other hand, prodigality hides itself under the appelation of liberality. Often inordinate laxity is believed to be loving kindness, and unbridled wrath is accounted the virtue of spiritual zeal.

Often precipitate action is taken for the efficiency of promptness, and tardiness for the deliberation of seriousness.

St Gregory the Great, in *The Nicene and Post-Nicene Fathers*, vol. 12, p. 20.

1563 *Relaxation in Communities Blamed on Superiors*

That great religious, Fr Doria, a Discalced Carmelite, used to say that religious Orders are relaxed more by headaches than by the gout; that is, by diseases of the head than of the feet. He meant that the relaxation does not proceed from the inferiors so much as from the superiors who shut their eyes to the neglect of the rule and to abuses, the removal of which, if they be once introduced into the monastery, will be morally impossible.

St Alphonsus Liguori, *The True Spouse of Jesus Christ*, pp. 668-669.

1564. *Superiors to Lord It Over Vices, Not the Brethren*

Supreme rule, then, is ordered well when he who presides lords it over vices, rather than over his brethren. But, when superiors correct their delinquent subordinates, it remains for them anxiously to take heed how far, while in right of their authority they smite faults with due discipline, they still, through custody of humility, acknowledge themselves to be on a par with the very brethren who are corrected; although for the most part it is becoming that in our silent thought we even prefer the brethren whom we correct to ourselves.

St Gregory the Great, in *The Nicene and Post-Nicene Fathers,* vol. 12, p. 15.

1565. *Superiors Suffer When Subjects Cause Difficulties*

Anyone may see the pain that the superior feels and the affliction he suffers when the subject makes a difficulty of obeying orders. These people make their superior go groaning and ready to burst with grief over the burden of his office, and wishing it were possible to do everything by himself rather than command others.

Rodriguez, *Practice of Perfection and Christian Virtues*, vol. 3, p. 333.

1566. *Authority – Its Relation to Humility*

[Commenting on Christ's words: 'He that will be first among you shall be your servant' (Mt 20:26), Bourdalous asks:] But would that not take away the power of authority? There will always be enough authority among you if there is enough humility, and if humility is lost, authority will become an intolerable burden.

Chautard, *The Soul of the Apostolate*, p. 133.

1567. *Superiors Must Maintain Humility in Heart, Discipline in Action*
In the heart humility should be maintained, and in action, discipline. And all the time there is need of sagacious insight, lest through excessive custody of the virtue of humility, the just claims of government be relaxed, and lest, while any superior lowers himself more than fit, he be unable to restrain the lives of his subordinates under the bonds of discipline.

St Gregory the Great, in *The Nicene and Post-Nicene Fathers*, vol. 12, p. 15.

1568. *Equality Not to Be Stressed above Discipline*
Sometimes there is more grievous delinquency if among perverse persons equality is kept more than discipline. For Eli, because overcome with false affection, would not punish delinquent sons, smote himself along with his sons before the strict judge with a cruel doom (1 Sm 4:17-18). . . . Care should be taken that a ruler show himself to his subjects as a mother in loving kindness, as a father in discipline. And all the time it should be seen to with anxious circumspection, that neither discipline be rigid, nor loving kindness lax.

St Gregory the Great, *ibid.,* p. 16.

1569. *Fraternal Correction a Duty for Superiors*
There is no doubt, dearly beloved priest, says St Bernard, that to become the judge of conscience is attended with much danger if through sloth or excessive fear, you neglect to fulfill this office when God calls you to do it. 'Woe to you,' says this same saint, 'if you are a superior. But greater woe to you if through fear of commanding you shrink from doing good.'

St Alphonsus Liguori, *Dignity and Duties of the Priest*, p. 182.

1570. *Superiors Especially Must Give Fraternal Correction*
With St Augustine, let me observe that 'He is not exempt from fault who, though not set over the delinquent, neglects, out of human respect and fear of giving offense, to admonish him when occasion arises.'. . . The reason is given in the book of Ecclesiasticus: To every man God has given charge of his neighbor (cf. Ecclus 17:12). It belongs, consequently, not alone to superiors, but to all men indiscriminately, to make efforts for the amendment of our neighbor. 'True it is,' adds this great Doctor, 'that Superiors are more strictly bound to such correction, seeing that they are held to it, in reason of their charge, by the twofold title of charity and justice; and that if they fail in this duty, they will have to render a most strict and rigorous account of the sins of others. This results plainly from those words of God, uttered by the Prophet Ezechiel: If the watchman see the sword come and blow not the trumpet, and the people are not warned;

if the sword come and take any person from among them, he is taken away in his iniquity; but his blood will I require at the watchman's hand (Ez 33:6). 'By the watchman', continues the saint, 'we are to understand the Superiors, especially of ecclesiastics, to whom it belongs to watch over the behavior of their subjects with a view to their correction. If from their not rebuking the sins of their people, any loss of souls occurs, God will exact of them a most rigid account'.

Scaramelli, *Practice of Perfection and Christian Virtues*, vol. 4, pp. 248-249.

1571. *Superiors Will Be Blamed for Not Correcting Faults*

He who is charged with the general supervision should feel as if he is liable to an account for each individual under his care. He should bear in mind that if one of the brethren falls into sin . . . or if, having fallen, he remain in that state uninstructed as to the manner of making amends, the blood of that one will be required at his hands, as it is written (Ez 3:20) – especially if he neglect that which is pleasing to God, not through ignorance, but for flattery's sake, accomodating himself to each one's vices and relaxing strict discipline.

. . . No father abandons his child when he is about to fall into a pit or leaves him to his fate after he has fallen therein. Needless to say, it is far more dreadful to allow the soul to be destroyed after it has fallen into the pit of evils. The superior is obliged, therefore, to be vigilant on behalf of the souls of the brethren and as seriously concerned for the salvation of each one as if he himself were to render an account for him.

St Basil, in *The Fathers of the Church*, vol. 9, pp. 287-288.

1572. *Superiors Have a Grave Duty of Correcting Subjects*

. . . Were the prelate, or any other lord having subjects, on seeing one putrefying from the corruption of mortal sin, to apply to him the ointment of encouragement alone, without reproof, he would never cure him, but the putrefaction would rather spread to the other members who, with him, form one body under the same pastor. But if he were a physician, good and true to those souls as were those glorious pastors of old, he would not give salving ointment without the fire of reproof. And were the member still to remain obstinate in his evildoing, he would cut him off from the congregation in order that he corrupt not the other members with the putrefaction of mortal sin. But they act not so today, but in cases of evildoing they even pretend not to see. And knowest thou wherefore? The root of self-love is alive in them, wherefore they bear perverted and servile fear. Because they fear to lose their position or their temporal goods or their prelacy, they do not correct but act like blind ones in that they

see not the real way by which their position is to be kept.
Dialogue of St Catherine of Siena, p. 247.

1573. *Superiors Should Not Be Dumb Dogs*
. . . As incautious speaking leads into error, so indiscreet silence leaves in error those who might have been instructed. For often improvident rulers, fearing to lose human favor, shrink timidly from speaking freely the things that are right; and according to the voice of truth (Jn 10:12), serve unto the custody of the flock by no means with the zeal of shepherds, but in the way of hirelings; since they fly when the wolf cometh if they hide themselves under silence. For hence it is that the Lord, through the Prophet, upbraids them, saying, 'Dumb dogs that cannot bark' (Is 56:10).
St Gregory the Great, in *The Nicene and Post-Nicene Fathers*, vol. 12, p. 11.

1574. *St Thérèse Preferred to Be Rebuked*
I would prefer to receive a thousand reproofs rather than inflict one, yet I feel it necessary that the task should cause me pain, for if I spoke through natural impulse only, the soul in fault would not understand she was in the wrong and would simply think: 'The sister in charge of me is annoyed about something and vents her displeasure upon me, although I am full of the best intentions.'
St Thérèse of Liseux, in *Autobiography and Letters,* pp. 176-177.

1575. *How Superiors Are to Be Admonished*
Just as it is the superior's duty to be the leader of the brethren in everything, so, in turn, if ever he is himself suspected of being guilty of a fault, it devolves upon the rest to call it to his attention. That good order may not be disturbed, however, those who are eminent by reason of age and sagacity should be assigned the task of giving the admonition.
St Basil, in *The Fathers of the Church*, vol. 9, p. 289.

1576. *Why God Permits Superiors to Have Defects*
Blosius relates something like this of [St Gertrude], that one day as she was praying for a defect of a certain person who was superior of a congregation, the Lord appeared to her and said: 'I, for the abundance of my loving kindness, gentleness and divine love, wherewith I have cherished this congregation, permit the existence of some defects even in those who govern it, that in that way the merit of the congregation be increased; for there is much more virtue in subjecting oneself to another whose faults are known than to one whose actions seem perfect. I permit superiors to have some defects, and sometimes to forget themselves for the numerous occu-

pations and variety of cares that they have, that they may humble themselves more. The merit of subjects grows and is augmented as well by the defects as by the virtues of those who govern them; and on the same principle, the merit of those who govern and direct them grows, as is reasonable, as well by the progress and virtues as by the defects of their subjects.' By these words of the Lord, St Gertrude understood the exuberant loving kindness of the Divine Wisdom.

Rodriguez, *Practice of Perfection and Christian Virtues*, vol. 3, pp. 314-315.

TABERNACLE

1577. *Three Tabernacles Seen by Faith*
For the soul that lives in the spirit of faith, this whole world is God's tabernacle. . . . [There is a special tabernacle containing the Blessed Sacrament] 'If I believed,' said a Protestant, 'what you Catholics believe about the Blessed Eucharist, I think I should never be off my knees.'. . . The third tabernacle containing the Presence is the very soul itself.

Nash, *The Nun at Her Prie-Dieu*, pp. 178-180.

TEMPTATION

1578. *Temptation – What It Is and What It Is Not*
A temptation is an exterior or interior incitement to sin. Therefore, merely to think, see, hear or feel something that is forbidden is not a temptation if it does not stimulate our will to consent.

Wallenstein, *Guide to Perfect Christian Living*, p. 9.

1579. *Temptation of Christ by the Devil*
[The devil] seeks by guile to find out, first, whether or not our Lord was himself the Creator of all things, and could therefore change the earthly things into what he willed. Secondly, whether under the appearance of human flesh the divinity lay concealed: to whom it would be a simple thing to pass through the air and bear His earthly members through the void. But since it was the Lord's desire to defeat him by the justice of a true man rather than by the power of his Divinity, [Christ did not act as the devil suggested]. 'The wisdom of God makes folly of the artifices of the devil.'

St Leo the Great, in Toal, vol. 2, pp. 30-31.

1580. *Why Christ Answered the Devil by Scriptures*
. . . The Lord when tempted by the devil, answers in words from Holy Scripture; that he who by the Word, which he is, could have cast the tempter into the pit, does not reveal his majesty, but only answers according to the precept of the divine words. He did this to give us an example of patience, that we also, as often as we suffer anything from an evil person, may be moved to remembrance of what he taught us rather than to desire revenge.
St Gregory the Great, in Toal, vol. 2, p. 34.

1581. *Christ Conquered the Devil Not as God but as Man*
[Christ inflicted greater punishment on] the adversary by conquering the enemy of the human race not now as God but as man. He fought then, therefore, that we too might fight thereafter: He conquered that we too might likewise conquer. For there are no works of power, dearly beloved, without the trials of temptations, there is no faith without proof, no contest without a foe, no victory without conflict. This life of ours is in the midst of snares, in the midst of battles; if we do not wish to be deceived, we must watch: if we want to overcome, we must fight.
St Leo the Great, in *The Nicene and Post-Nicene Fathers*, vol. 12, p. 153.

1582. *The Devil Tempts Us, Christ Helps Us*
. . . The more zealous we are for our salvation, the more determined must be the assaults of our opponents. But 'Stronger is he that is in us than he that is against us, and through him are we powerful in whose strength we rely: because it was for this that the Lord allowed himself to be tempted by the tempter, that we might be taught by his example as well as fortified by his aid.
St Leo the Great, in *ibid.*, pp. 152-153.

1583. *Temptation to Be Recognized as Such*
Against all temptations, it is a great remedy to understand that it is a temptation; therefore, when the devil tempts us, he labors all he can that his temptation may not appear as a temptation but as right reason, so that we may fall into it.
Rodriguez, *Practice of Perfection and Christian Virtues*, vol. 3, p. 322.

1584. *Three States of Temptation*
There are three states in a temptation:
(1) *Suggestion*: At this stage the mind or the imagination represents to us the forbidden fruit in a vivid and sometimes attractive manner. Occasion-

ally the representation becomes almost an obsession and will not leave despite our efforts and protests. At this stage there is no sin unless we have deliberately provoked the image.

(2) *Pleasure*: Our soul is substantially united to the body. It is a law of nature that every idea and image react upon the body. Hence the evil suggestion immediately and spontaneously produces a certain pleasure in our fleshly nature. There is still no sin as long as we do not consent. Yet this pleasure constitutes a danger.

(3) *Consent*: Now comes the critical moment. If we repel and reject the temptation, we not only have not sinned, but have performed a meritorious act. If, on the other hand, we enjoy and delight in the pleasure and consent to it, we commit a sin. Sometimes one finds it difficult to decide whether he has consented or not. In that case he will be helped to make a decision with the aid of the following rules:

(a) If he experienced disgust and annoyance at being tempted in this way, if he struggled not to give in; if he prayed to God for help, then – despite the instinctive pleasure that he might have experienced – he can conclude that he has not consented;

(b) If one freely performs an action from which a temptation arises, he is guilty in the measure in which he foresaw that the temptation would arise.

(c) If he did not repel the temptation at once, if he hesitated a moment, if he resisted in a halfhearted way, he is guilty of venial sin.

(d) If despite the protests of conscience he freely embraced a pleasure which he knew to be gravely sinful, he has committed a mortal sin.

Bandas, *The Catholic Layman and Holiness*, pp. 95-96.

1585. *What God and the Devil Aim at Through Temptation*

St Gregory says: 'The aim of the devil in temptation is evil, but that of the Lord is good.'. . . Thus, the aim of the devil in temptation is to ruin our virtue, merit and glory; but the Lord's aim is otherwise, and he marvelously works the exact contrary effect by the same means.

Rodriguez, *Practice of Perfection and Christian Virtues*, vol. 2, pp. 379-380.

1586. *Temptations Not Harmful if We Do Not Consent*

You must have great courage in the midst of temptation, Philothea. Never think yourself overcome as long as they are displeasing to you, keeping clearly in mind the difference between feeling temptation and consenting to it. That is, we may feel temptations even though they displease us, but we can never consent to them unless they please us, since to be pleased by them usually is a step toward consent to them. . . . As long as we remain steadfast in our resolution not to take pleasure in temptation, it is utterly impossible for us to offend God.

St Francis de Sales, *Introduction to the Devout Life*, p. 197.

1587. *The Meaning of 'Lead Us Not into Temptation'*

In place of the word *bring* [us not into temptation], many codices have the word *lead*. I regard these words as exactly equivalent; for they are both translated from the same Greek word, which is *eisenégkes*. But in making application, many persons say: 'Suffer us not to be lead into temptation,' and in this way they clearly show the intended meaning of the word *lead*. God does not of himself lead a man into temptation when – through one's just deserts and in accordance with a most hidden disposition – he leaves him bereft of divine aid. Often, for reasons that are quite evident, He adjudges a man deserving of being abandoned and lead into temptation.

Note: Blessed Cyprian ... has written in this way ... 'Suffer us not to be led into temptation.'

St Augustine, in *The Fathers of the Church*, vol. 11, p. 138.

1588. *The Meaning of 'Lead Us Not into Temptation'*

Do not wait for the temptation, for then the trouble and the agitation will prevent you from praying. Pray before temptation, and forestall the enemy. 'God tempts no one', says St James (Js 1:13). Thus, when we say to him, 'Lead us not into temptation,' obviously we must understand: Do not permit us to enter there. Also, as St Paul says, 'God is faithful to his promises' (1 Cor 10:13) and he will not suffer you to be tempted beyond your strength. We must remember, however, that our strength consists principally in our prayers.

Bossuet, in *Selections from Meditations on the Gospel*, vol. 1, p. 57.

1589. *Why God Permits Us to Be Tempted*

... Why does God permit us to be tempted? The reward of heaven is destined for those who have fought and struggled; now it is by overcoming many temptations that we merit our heavenly reward; and the harder we have fought, the greater will be our joy. Every temptation is, in fact, a test of our love of God; when we overcome a temptation, we equivalently proclaim that we prefer God to any created thing. Temptation thus becomes a source of merit. Temptation also makes us realize our weakness ... makes us more humble, more vigilant, more distrustful of our own powers, more reliant on God's grace. Temptations also acquaint us with the technique of the devil and thus prepare us for his onslaughts in the future.

Bandas, *The Catholic Layman and Holiness*, p. 95.

1590. *Why God Permits Us to Be Tempted*
. . . [An] end which God has in thus allowing his servants to be tempted is to ground them in virtue. Virtue is not won except by conflict. . . . But how shall virtuous actions be frequently repeated if attacks of temptation be altogether wanting? How shall he who is never crossed make acts of patience? . . . Cassian concludes from this, that our most loving Savior has done us a greater favor in exposing us to the conflict with temptations than if he had wholly freed us from them, because if amid those combats we but remain steadfast in well-doing, we shall attain to an eminent and sublime degree of virtue, according to those words which God spoke to St Paul: 'Virtue is made perfect in infirmity'.
Scaramelli, *Directorium Asceticum*, vol. 2, p. 299-300.

1591. *Why God Permits Temptations*
A little consideration will prove that temptation, too, is permitted to befall simply because God loves. We are at times inclined to argue the other way round and affirm that if he did indeed love, He would shield our souls from the blasts of temptation. This is not so. . . . Serious temptation destroys the proud man's belief in his own superiority. It teaches in a deadly practical way what no amount of theorizing could accomplish, that there is no depth of depravity so deep but the soul is capable of sinking into it.
Nash, *Living Your Faith*, p. 139.

1592. *Temptations Are an Opportunity for Us to Gain Greater Glory*
The saints say that God does us a greater favor in sending us temptations, giving us at the same time grace to overcome them, than if He were entirely to deliver us from them, because at that rate we should miss the reward and glory that we merit thereby.
Rodriguez, *Practice of Perfection and Christian Virtues*, vol. 2, p. 367.

1593. *Temptations Are Useful for Us*
[St Bonaventure says] that the Lord, loving us so much, is not satisfied with our gaining glory, and great glory, but wishes us to gain it quickly, and not to have to detain us in purgatory; and therefore He sends us here afflictions and temptations, which are his hammer and forge whereby the rust and dross is cleared off our soul and it is cleansed and purified so as to be able to enter at once into enjoyment of God.
Rodriguez, *ibid.*, p. 368.

1594. *Why God Permits Us to Be Tempted*
. . . The Divine Dispensation so deals with us that while making progress

we shall not forget our weakness; and that tempted, we recall it, so that in our progress we may understand what we are from divine favor, and in temptation, what we are of our own strength. And such temptation would indeed lead us wholly astray were we not protected from above.

St Gregory the Great, in Toal, vol. 4, p. 198.

1595. *Why God Permits the Baptized to Be Tempted*

Who therefore among you is even more tempted after baptism should not be troubled. It is for this you have received arms: not to stand at ease, but to fight. God will not then ward you off from temptations; and this He does for many reasons. First, that you may learn that you are now stronger. Then, lest you be exalted by the greatness of his gifts. Third, that the devil may receive proof you have wholly renounced him. Fourth, that by this trial you may become yet stronger. Fifth, that you may receive an indication of the treasure you have received: for the devil would not so pursue you, to tempt you, did he not see that you had now come to a higher dignity.

St John Chrysostom, in Toal, vol. 2, pp. 2-3.

1596. *Temptations Are to Make Us Humble, Induce Us to Pray*

God knows how useful it is to us to be obliged to pray, in order to keep us humble, and to exercise our confidence; and he therefore permits us to be assaulted by enemies too powerful to be overcome by our own strength, that by prayer we may obtain from his mercy aid to resist them; and it is especially to be remarked, that no one can resist the impure temptations of the flesh without recommending himself to God when he is tempted. This foe is so terrible that, when he fights with us, he, as it were, takes away all light; he makes us forget all our meditations, all our good resolutions; he makes us also disregard the truths of faith and even almost lose the fear of divine punishments. For he conspires with our natural inclinations, which drive us with the greatest violence to the indulgence of sensual pleasures. He who in such a moment does not have recourse to God is lost. The only defence against this temptation is prayer, as St Gregory of Nyssa says: 'Prayer is the bulwark of chastity'; and before him, Solomon: 'And as I knew that I could not otherwise be continent except God gave it, I went to the Lord and besought him.' Chastity is a virtue which we have not strength to practice unless God gives it to us; and God does not give strength except to him who asks for it. But whoever prays for it will certainly obtain it.

St Alphonsus Liguori, *Great Means of Salvation and of Perfection*, p. 32.

1597. *Temptation Useful for Two Reasons*
Normally we shall all be subject to temptations. And for two reasons it is not desirable that we should be free from them. First, because they help to keep us humble. . . . Second, because virtue is perfected by temptation. Every temptation conquered makes us stronger and freer, as every one yielded to makes us weaker in will.

Brosnahan, *Searchlighting Ourselves*, p. 207.

1598. *Reason for Temptations and Trials*
St Augustine . . . says that temptations and trials go to show the misery of this life that we may more ardently long for that life of heavenly bliss and seek after it with greater diligence and fervor.

Rodriguez, *Practice of Perfection and Christian Virtues*, vol. 2, p. 365.

1599. *Faith and Charity Help Overcome Temptation*
God will allow temptations to assault us so that we can make greater acts of charity in resisting them, be victorious in the battle, and win a reward for our victory. If we feel pleasantly attracted by temptation, that is only natural. We are made in such a way that anything good irresistably attracts us, be its goodness real or only apparent; so temptation always uses something of the sort for bait. . . .

Faith, if kept on the alert, is charity's surest safeguard: it can separate truth from falsehood; it can show what things to make for, what to avoid. Faith would raise the alarm at the approach of evil under the pretense of good; then charity could immediately drive it back. But, because our faith is usually dormant, or not sufficiently on the alert to safeguard charity, temptation often takes us by surprise; it seduces our senses, and they in their turn incite the lower part of the soul to rebellion.

St Francis de Sales, *The Love of God*, p. 157.

1600. *Temptation Often Profitable*
. . . Temptations are often very profitable to a man, although they be troublesome and grievous; for in them a man is humbled, purified and instructed.

Thomas à Kempis, *Imitation of Christ*, bk. I, chap. 13.

1601. *Not to Resist Temptation Is Dangerous*
By flight alone we cannot overcome; but by patience and true humility we are made stronger than our enemies. . . .

Fire tries iron, and temptation tries a just man. . . .

The longer a man is negligent in resisting, so much the weaker does he daily become in himself; and the enemy becomes stronger against him.

Thomas à Kempis, *ibid.*,

1602. *Every Victory over Temptation Brings Added Grace and Glory*

Every time the soul conquers a temptation she gains a degree of grace, for which she shall afterwards be rewarded with a degree of glory in heaven. Hence, we shall receive as many crowns as we resist temptations. 'As often,' says St Bernard, 'as we conquer, we are crowned.'

St Alphonsus Liguori, *The True Spouse of Jesus Christ*, p. 410.

1603. *Temptation Conquered Brings Rewards*

When the struggle commenced, the man had a certain amount of sanctifying grace in his soul; now that the fight is over – at least for a while – he has increased his stock of grace in a manner and measure that would amaze him if he could look into his own soul and see the difference....

But even in this life there is a reward too. The fact that he has been tempted and won through will make the next struggle easier. There may indeed be many another fight before complete victory is won, but each time he overcomes he is in a stronger position for the next attack. It is not so difficult, he learns, to stand his ground. He has done it before – ten, twenty or thirty times. Why not do it again? The good habit is strengthened.

Nash, *Living Your Faith*, pp. 142-143.

1604. *Benefits Derived from Conquering Temptations*

It is not temptations, but the consenting to temptations, that is the cause of our loss of divine grace. Temptations, when we overcome them, keep us more humble, gain for us greater merits, make us have recourse to God more frequently; and thus keep us further from offending him, and unite us more closely to his holy love.

St Alphonsus Liguori, *The Way of Salvation and of Perfection*, p. 382.

1605. *Temptation Conquered Is Fruitful*

... The fortitude of any good man would not ... be worthy of praise, if his victory was gained without his being tempted, as most certainly there is no room for victory where there is no struggle or conflict: for 'Blessed is the man that endureth temptation, for when he has been proved he shall receive the crown of life which God hath promised to them that love Him' (Js 1:12).

Abbot Piamun, quoted by Cassian, in *The Nicene and Post-Nicene Fathers*, vol. 11, p. 485.

1606. *Victories over Little Temptations*
While we must resist great temptations with unconquerable courage and while the victory we gain over them is in the highest degree helpful to us, it may be that we will profit more by resisting small temptations. Although great temptations exceed in quality, small ones immeasurably exceed in number so that victory gained over them may be comparable to that gained over greater temptations. Wolves and bears are certainly more dangerous than flies but don't give us as much trouble or try our patience as much. It is easy enough to refrain from murder, but it is extremely difficult to restrain all the little angry feelings for which occasions are offered at every moment.
St Francis de Sales, *Introduction to the Devout Life*, pp. 203-204.

1607. *Victories over Small Temptations Are Precious*
These little temptations to anger, suspicion, jealousy, envy, fond love, frivolity, vanity, affection, craftiness and evil thoughts continually attack even the most devout and resolute. For this reason . . . we must carefully prepare ourselves for such combat. Let us rest assured that for as many victories as we gain over these trifling enemies, so many more precious stones will be added to the crown of glory that God prepares for us in paradise.
St Francis de Sales, *ibid.,* p. 204.

1608. *How to Conquer or Avoid Temptations*
Were you to ask what are the means of overcoming temptations, I would answer: The first means is prayer; the second is prayer; the third is prayer; and should you ask me a thousand times, I would repeat the same.
St Alphonsus Liguori, *The True Spouse of Jesus Christ*, p. 413.

1609. *Prayer Needed to Overcome Carnal Appetites*
Let us rest assured that we can never overcome our carnal appetites if God does not give us help, and this help we cannot have without prayer; but if we pray, we shall assuredly have power to resist the devil in everything, and the strength of God Who strengthens us; as St Paul says: 'I can do all things, through God Who strengthens me' (Phil 4:13).
St Alphonsus Liguori, *The Way of Salvation and of Perfection*, p. 193.

1610. *Prayer for Help Against Devil and Self*
When we ask for strength against temptation, it isn't only against the devil, but also against ourselves. As St James says: 'Each one is deceived by his own concupiscence, which attracts him and which carries him away' (Jas 1:14). This is the greatest temptation, and the devil himself cannot en-

snare us except by recourse to it.

Bossuet, in *Selections from Meditations on the Gospel*, vol. 1, p. 58.

1611. *To Conquer Temptations Never Be Idle*
It is also a great remedy against temptations never to be idle. Cassian says that the Fathers of Egypt took this for a first principle, and kept it as an ancient tradition received from their elders, and recommended it to their disciples for a singularly good remedy.

Rodriguez, *Practice of Perfection and Christian Virtues*, vol. 2, p. 407.

1612. *Temptation to be Fought Off When It Begins*
Of resisting first beginnings, St Jerome says: 'slay your enemy while he is small, strangle him at the commencement, root him out before he grows, because afterwards you will not be able.' Temptation is like a spark, which, if once it catches on, causes a conflagration.

Rodriguez, *ibid.*, vol. 2, p. 405.

1613. *Practical Way of Escaping from Temptation*
With temptation, if you keep violently repelling the evil suggestion, protesting that you do not want it, you *may* at times be only injuring yourself because you are driving in by such tactics the very thing you want to drive out. Of course we are taught to pray, and very earnestly, in time of temptation, but our prayer should not be inspired by terror or panic, but by confidence and love. Having said a short fervent prayer, perhaps a favorite ejaculation to our Lady, I now take my troublesome imagination and wrench from its hands the dangerous object, and give it a harmless toy instead. How can this be done?

Instead of saying that I am *not* going to think of *this* let me fall back on this simple device of saying that I *am* going to think of *this other* . . . [The penitent] begins at once to recall all that happened to him since he got up in the morning . . . what his daughter said at breakfast, what a scene there was when little Jackie spilt the hot tea on his thumb . . . the accident he witnessed, the exciting item in the evening paper. What has become of the bad thought? The chances are that it has gone; it has been banished more effectively than if the man was to keep on 'resisting' all the time.

Nash, *Living Your Faith*, pp. 128-129.

1614. *Methods of Resisting Temptation*
When the flesh would lure me to shameful pleasures, I will make this answer: I am a child of God; I am called to too high a destiny to make myself the slave of vile passions. When the world solicits me, I will answer thus: I am a child of God; heaven's riches are laid up for me; it is beneath

my honor to set value on a clod of earth. When the demon should offer me the high places of this world, I will answer him: Begone Satan, cease to defile with thy suggestions a child of God.

St Cyprian, quoted in Bandas, *The Catholic Layman and Holiness*, p. 313.

1615. *How to Resist Temptation*

When temptation comes, I will recall the words of St Gregory [Nazanzen]: 'If the devil attacks you, if he shows you, as he did to our Lord Jesus Christ, the pomp of riches and grandeurs in order to obtain your adoration, despise him as a miserable creature. Armed with the sign of the Cross, reply to him: "I, too, am the image of God, but pride did not make me fall from the heights of glory as it did to you. I am clothed with Christ. By Baptism, Christ became my property. It is you who should adore me."'

Bandas, *ibid.*, p. 317.

1616. *Temptation to Offer Insults*

Whenever the temptation to offer insult seizes you, think to yourself that you are being tested: to see whether in patience you turn to God, or yield in anger to the Adversary.

St Basil, in Toal, vol. 4, p. 273.

1617. *Thoughts of St Ambrose and St Teresa*

'We walk among snares,' says St Ambrose, 'amidst the deceits of enemies who seek to cause us to lose the divine grace.' Therefore, St Teresa, every time that the clock struck, gave thanks to God that another hour of struggle and peril had passed without sin; and therefore she was rejoiced at the tidings of her coming death.

St Alphonsus Liguori, *The Way of Salvation and of Perfection,* p. 296.

1618. *Temptations and Scruples Suffered by Saint*

For forty-one years, St Jane Frances de Chantal suffered these internal pains, accompanied by terrible temptations, and by fears that she was in a state of sin, and was abandoned by God. Her pangs were so great that she was accustomed to say that the thought of death was the only thing that gave her relief. . . .

St Francis de Sales used to say to her that the blessed soul was like a deaf musician who could sing most admirably but had no pleasure in his voice, because he could not hear it.

St Alphonsus, *ibid.*, pp. 288-289.

1619. *St Catherine Saved from Temptation*

[After St Catherine had suffered from some horrible temptations, Christ appeared to her and she asked him:] 'Lord, where wast Thou, when my heart was so tormented?' 'I was in the midst of thy heart.' 'Ah, Lord, thou art the everlasting truth and I humbly bow before thy Majesty; but how can I believe that thou wert in my heart, when it was filled with such detestable thoughts?' 'Did those thoughts and temptations give thee pleasure or pain?' 'An excessive pain and sadness.' 'Thou were sad and in suffering because I was hidden in the midst of thy heart. Had I been absent, these thoughts would have penetrated thy heart and would have filled thee with joy; but my presence rendered them insupportable to thee; thou didst wish to repel them because thou didst hold them in horror, and it was because thou didst not succeed that thou wert borne down with sadness. I acted in thy soul, I defended thee against thy enemy; I was in the interior, and I only permitted these attacks from without, inasmuch as they could prove useful to thy salvation; when the period which I had determined for the combat had elapsed, I sent my beams of light and the shadow of hell was dissipated because they could not resist the light. Is it not I, in fine, who giveth thee to comprehend that these trials are serviceable to thee for the acquisition of strength, and that it was thy duty to support them cordially according to my good pleasure? Because thou hast accepted them with thy whole heart, thou art delivered from them by my presence; what pleases me is not *trouble*, but the *will* that supports it courageously.'

Blessed Raymond of Capua, *Life of St Catherine of Siena*, pp. 71-72.

1620. *A Sign that God Takes Care of Us*

[St John Chrysostom says:] 'No one should consider that he is overlooked or forsaken by God, on beholding himself exposed to the onslaught of temptations; for this is the surest token he can have that God takes special care of him.'

Scaramelli, *Directorium Asceticum*, vol. 2, p. 307.

1621. *How To Remain Calm Though Temptation Continues*

'It is a very good sign,' says St Francis de Sales, 'when the enemy strikes and makes a commotion at your door, for it indicates that he does not have what he wants. If he had it, he would not be shouting; he would enter and stay there. Take note of this, so as not to become scrupulous.'

Quoted by Charmot, *Ignatius Loyola and Francis de Sales*, p. 98.

TEPIDITY

1622. *Two Kinds of Tepidity*

There are two kinds of lukewarmness; one that can be avoided, and the other that cannot. We cannot avoid that kind which, in the present state of our being, is suffered even by spiritual souls, who, through their natural weakness, cannot avoid falling, but who, from time to time, without the full consent of their will, fall into some light fault; from which defects no one is free, because of the corruption of our nature, without a most special grace, which was granted to none but the Mother of God. . . .

There is true lukewarmness to be mourned over, when the soul falls into venial sins with a full will, and grieves but little over them, and takes little care to avoid them, asserting that they are trifles of no moment. What! is it nothing to displease God; St Teresa said to her nuns: 'My daughters, may God deliver us from known sins, however small.'

St Alphonsus Liguori, *The Way of Salvation and of Perfection*, p. 297-298.

1623. *The Hallmark of Tepidity*

As long as we are dissatisfied with ourselves and try to do better, all will be well; it is satisfaction with our state that is the hallmark of tepidity.

Fr Bruno St James, in Nash, *How to Pray and Other Conferences,* p. 33.

1624. *Lack of Desire for Perfection is Disastrous*

[St Augustine says:] 'If you have said, "It is sufficient", you have perished.'. . . If you have said that you have already attained sufficient perfection, you are lost; for not to advance in the way of God is to retrograde. And, as St Bernard says: 'Not to wish to go forward, is certainly to fail.'. . . Hence St John Chrysostom exhorts us to think continually on the virtues which we do not possess, and never to reflect on the little good which we have done; for the thought of our good works 'generates indolence and inspires arrogance.'

St Alphonsus Liguori, *The True Spouse of Jesus Christ*, p. 92.

1625. *How Tepidity Differs from Aridity*

It is voluntary aridity when a person commits voluntary and deliberate faults and takes no pains to amend. This is not, properly speaking, to be called aridity, but tepidity, from which if the soul does not exert itself to get free, it will ever be going on from bad to worse. . . .

St Alphonsus Liguori, *The Way of Salvation and of Perfection*, pp. 460-461.

1626. *The Danger Involved in Tepidity*

St Teresa never fell into any grievous sin, as is related in the Bull of her canonization; yet it was revealed to her that a place was prepared for her in hell if she did not shake off her tepidity. How was this? since it is only mortal sin that is punished in hell. The Holy Spirit supplies the answer when he says, 'He that despiseth small things shall fall by little and little' (Ecclus 19:1). He who makes no account of deliberate venial sins will easily fall into those which are mortal; because by habitually offending God in small things he will not have much dread of sometimes offending him in great things; and because by continually withdrawing himself from God, he provokes God not to afford him those special helps without which he will easily be overcome by powerful temptations.

St Alphonsus, *ibid.*, p. 150.

1627. *Dangers Involved in Tepidity*

'I would thou wert cold or hot, but because thou are lukewarm, I will begin to vomit thee out of my mouth.'. . . 'Although he that is cold,' says Cornelius à Lapide, 'is worse than he that is tepid, yet the condition of the tepid is worse, since the danger of falling is greater, without any hope of recovery.'

St Alphonsus Liguori, *Dignity and Duties of The Priest*, pp. 92-93.

1628. *God Ordinarily Abandons Tepid Souls*

St Augustine says that God ordinarily abandons tepid souls who, reckless of consequences, wilfully neglect their duties and disregard their defects: 'God is accustomed to desert the negligent.'

St Alphonsus Liguori, *The True Spouse of Jesus Christ*, p. 107.

1629. *Danger Growing from Tepidity*

'He that despiseth little things, by little degrees shall he fall.' He that takes no account of trifling falls, will one day find himself upon a precipice. The Lord said: 'Because thou art lukewarm, I am about to vomit thee out of my mouth.' This signifies that the soul would be abandoned by God, or at least deprived of those special divine aids which are necessary to preserve us in a state of grace.

St Alphonsus Liguori, *The Way of Salvation and of Perfection*, p. 298-299.

1630. *Tepidity Makes One Lose The Fear of God*
'It is necessary to understand what St Gregory teaches, that the habit of committing light faults without remorse, and without an effort to correct them, gradually deprives us of the fear of God; and when the fear of God is lost, it is easy to pass from venial to mortal sin.'
St Alphonsus, *Dignity and Duties of The Priest*, p. 90.

1631. *Tepidity a Gradual Process Toward Serious Sin*
'Do not imagine,' says Cassian, 'that any one falls at once into ruin.'... That is, when you hear of the fall of a spiritual soul, do not imagine that the devil has suddenly precipitated her into sin; for he first brought her into tepidity and then has cast her into the precipice of enmity with God.
St Alphonsus, *Dignity and Duties of The Priest*, pp. 90-91.

1632. *Tepidity in a Priest Leads Him From Bad to Worse*
The tepid priest, weighed down by so many venial sins and by so many inordinate attachments, remains, as it were, in a state of insensibility. Hence the graces received and the obligations of the priesthood make but little impression on him, and therefore the Lord shall justly withold the abundant helps that are morally necessary for the fulfillment of the obligations of his state; thus he shall go from bad to worse, and with his defects, his blindness shall increase. Perhaps God is bound to make his grace abound in those that are parsimonious and ungenerous to him? No, says the Apostle, he who sows little shall reap but little (2 Cor 9:6).
St Alphonsus, *ibid.*, p. 98.

1633. *Tepidity in a Priest Is Hard to Cure*
St Bernard says that it is easier to convert a wicked layman than a tepid ecclesiastic.
St Alphonsus, *ibid.*, p. 93.

1634. *Cure of Tepidity in a Priest*
It is impossible for the tepid priest to rise, but to raise him up is not impossible to God. However, a desire, at least, is necessary on our part. How can he that does not even desire to rise hope for the divine aid? Let him that has not even this desire ask it of God.
St Alphonsus, *ibid.*, p. 105.

1635. *Tepidity in Religious*
A lukewarm religious will be contented with what little he does for God; but God, who called him to a perfect life, will not be contented, and in

punishment for his ingratitude, will not only deprive him of his special favors, but will sometimes permit his fall. 'When you said, "It is enough, then you have perished," ' says St Augustine.

St Alphonsus Liguori, *Great Means of Salvation and of Perfection*, p. 435.

1636. *Tepidity in Religious Makes Good Works Valueless*

If the tepid religious should continue her Communions, meditations, and visits to the Blessed Sacrament, she will draw but little fruit from them. In her will be verified the words of the Holy Ghost: *You have sowed much and brought in little . . . and he that hath earned wages, put them in a bag with holes*. . . . All her spiritual exercises are laid up in a bag with holes; for them no reward remains. Being performed with so much tepidity, they render her always more deserving of chastisement, and deprive her of those abundant helps which God had prepared for her, had she corresponded to his holy inspirations.

St Alphonsus Liguori, *The True Spouse of Jesus Christ*, pp. 110-111.

1637. *Tepid Souls Hard to Convert*

Speaking of a sinner not yet converted, St Gregory holds out hopes of repentance, but speaking of a tepid soul who is not afraid of her imperfections, he despairs of her amendment. 'Warmth which has failed from fervor is in despair.'. . . The Son of God says: 'Because thou art lukewarm, I will begin to vomit thee out of my mouth.'. . . By the words 'I will begin to vomit thee out of my mouth', the Redeemer signified that he was ready to abandon the tepid soul, for what is vomited is taken back only with horror.

St Alphonsus, *The True Spouse of Jesus Christ*, pp. 119-120.

1638. *Tepidity Harder to Remedy than Gross Worldliness*

Cassian is of the opinion that a thorough worldling will be converted and mount to the loftiest heights of perfection more easily than a monk or anyone else who has fallen from fervor into tepidity. . . . The reason [is that] . . . the sinner at the sight of his wickedness is more easily moved to compunction . . . [while the one who is lukewarm] can never bring himself to see that he is blind and wretched and in need of guidance, for he thinks himself an enlightened man.

Scaramelli, *Directorium Asceticum*, vol. 1, pp. 89-90.

1639. *How to Overcome Tepidity*

Though it is very difficult for a lukewarm person to amend, yet there are remedies if only he desires amendment. The remedies are: (a) resolution to escape at all costs from his miserable state; (b) the removal of the occasions of falling, without which there is no hope for amendment; and (c) the constant recommendation of himself to God, with fervent prayer that he would give him strength to escape from this deplorable condition, continued until he finds himself free.

St Alphonsus Liguori, *The Way of Salvation and of Perfection*, p. 299.

TIME

1640. *Time That Is Not Spent for God*

St Augustine says that all the time that is not spent for God is lost time.

St Alphonsus Liguori, *The True Spouse of Jesus Christ*, p. 666.

TONGUE

1641. *Even Tongues of Priests and Religious Sting Like Wasps*

In every walk of life we find good and bad people, and so in the Church of Christ, which is now compared to a threshing floor where chaff as well as the wheat is found. What is worse, we find there, not only lay people, but even clerics and monks and religious who are so careless and lukewarm that they do not produce the sweet honey of souls like spiritual bees, but like most cruel wasps, they pierce the hearts of their brothers and sisters with the poisoned darts of their tongue. People like these are not helpers of Christ, but they are shown to be defenders of the devil.

St Caesarius of Arles, in *The Fathers of the Church*, vol. 47, p. 351.

1642. *Talebearing Is the Devil's Work*

'Never give occasion to anyone,' says Ecclesiasticus (5:16), 'to be able to say that you are a talebearer.' What can be a more pernicious and prejudicial thing in community than to be a scandalmonger and to go about making your brethren fall foul of one another; This is doing the devil's work, for that is his office.

Rodriguez, *Practice of Perfection and Christian Virtues*, vol. 1, pp. 218-219.

1643. *Why Sins of the Tongues Are So Common*

It is surprising, but nevertheless true, that we more easily fail in speech than in any other form of doing. . . . To carry on a conversation and maintain oneself in one's words in a spirit of faith for a considerable length of

time is within the power of comparatively few.
Edward Leen, *Progress Through Mental Prayer*, pp. 257-258.

1644. *How to Avoid Idle Talk*
. . . We read of our father [St Ignatius], that, if he received a visit from any idle man with whom he was likely to waste much time and do no good, after having given him a pleasant reception once or twice, if he continued his visits without profit, our father would begin to speak to him about death, judgment, and hell; for, he said, if the man had no liking for such conversation, he would get tired and not return anymore; while if he had a liking for them, he would gather some spiritual fruit for his soul.
Rodriguez, *Practice of Perfection and Christian Virtues*, vol. 2, p. 160.

1645. *Sins of the Tongue*
This is the difference which Ecclesiasticus puts between the wise man and the fool: 'Fools keep their heart in their tongue' (21:29), because they give themselves over without restraint to their tongue and its disorderly craving for talking, and say whatever comes into their mouth, the heart consenting at once as though heart and tongue were one. But the wise and prudent keep their tongue in their heart because all they have to say comes forth from it according to the counsel of reason. They keep their tongue submissive to their heart, and not their heart to their tongue as fools do.
Rodriguez, *ibid.*, vol. 2, pp. 130-131.

1646. *How the Tongue Is to Be Governed*
St Cyprian says that as a sober and temperate man takes nothing into his stomach without first having masticated it thoroughly, so a prudent and discreet man utters no word from his mouth without first having ruminated it right well in his heart, for from words not well weighed or thought over, disputes commonly arise.
Rodriguez, *ibid.*, vol. 2, p. 131.

1647. *Good Uses of the Tongue*
It is the words of wisdom that fell from our Divine Lord's lips that have reformed the world. What would this world be like if He had not spoken? . . . It is by words pronounced by human lips that the substance of bread is changed into the Body of our Lord, and Jesus is made present with us. The priest speaks and as his voice dies away, the tide of absolution flows on the sinner's soul, washing away the darkest stains; and when God's minister pronounces the formula of baptism, the slave of Satan is elevated

from his servile state to the exalted condition of a child of God.
Edward Leen, *Progress Through Mental Prayer*, pp. 261-262.

1648. *Right Use of the Tongue*
[A good rule] is never to speak merely for one's own sake or for one's own gratification or to satisfy some impulse, but solely for the glory of God, for the right accomplishment of duty, for the promotion of truth, for the exercise of charity, for the comfort of the sorrowful and for the purpose of brightening the life of one's fellows.
Edward Leen, *ibid.*, p. 274.

TRADITION

1649. *Canonical Tradition Defended by St Basil*
The common aim of all our adversaries and of all 'who are contrary to sound doctrine' (1 Tm 1:10), is to overthrow the foundations of the faith of Christ, by leveling the apostolic traditions to the earth and wholly destroying them, So, like debtors, good debtors of course, they demand proof, written proof, from the Sacred Writings, and dismiss, as wholly unworthy of belief, the unwritten witness of the Fathers.
St Basil, in Toal, vol. 3, pp. 9-10.

1650. *Canonical Tradition Defended by St Basil*
. . . Were we to attempt to reject the unwritten practices of the Church as being without great importance, we would unknowingly inflict mortal wounds on the Gospel, or rather, we would make our public teaching a mere pretense. . . . For we are not content with the words both the the Gospel and the Apostle have recorded, but have added some others, both before these and after them, as having great significance in relation to the *mystery* and which have been received from unwritten tradition. . . .

[For the Fathers] had learned to guard the sacredness of the mysteries in silence. For doctrine that was witheld even from the uninitiated [catechumens] were not to be made known to all and sundry in writing. . . .

If the greater number of our mystical truths have come down to us through unwritten tradition, then let us receive this together with these so many others. . . . 'Hold the traditions which you have learned, whether by word or by our epistle' (2 Thes 2:14).
St Basil in Toal, vol. 3, pp. 62-64.

TREASURES

1651. *Temporal Treasures Eternal*
We must cling inseparably to eternal treasures, but things temporal we must use like passersby, that as we are sojourners hastening to return to our own land, all the good things of this world which meet us may be as aids on the way, not snares to detain us.

St Leo the Great, in *The Nicene and Post-Nicene Fathers*, vol. 12, p. 200.

1652. *Treasures of the Heart May Be Good or Bad*
. . . Let us examine our own consciences. Let us consider the inner compartments of our soul and see whose treasures we have hidden there. Then we will truly be able to know to whose domain both we and our treasures belong. If, with God's help, we always have good thoughts and perform honorable deeds, we not only keep Christ's treasures in our hearts, but we ourselves are the treasure of Christ. But if our soul is often occupied with unclean or wicked thoughts, there is no need to say to whom the treasure of our heart belongs.

St Caesarius of Arles, in *The Fathers of the Church*, vol. 47, p. 370.

TRIALS

1653. *Trials and Tribulations Can Be Useful*
It is good for us to have sometimes troubles and adversities; for they make a man enter into himself, that he may know that he is in a state of banishment and may not place his hopes in anything in this world. It is good that we sometimes suffer contradictions and that men have an evil or imperfect opinion of us when we do and intend well. These things are often helps to humility and defend us from vainglory. For then we better run to God, our inward Witness, when outwardly we are despised by men and little credit is given to us.

Thomas à Kempis, *Imitation of Christ*, bk. I, chap. 12.

1654. *Trials, Pains, and Labors Come to Us for Our Good*
. . . As for the pains and labors that God sends men in this life, whether they be just or sinners, we must always so trust in His infinite goodness and mercy as to believe that he sends them for our good and because that is what makes better for our salvation. So said holy Judith to her townsmen when they were in that affliction and so grave a crisis, surrounded by their enemies: 'Let us believe that God hath sent us these troubles, not for our ruin, but for our amendment and profit' (Jdt 8:27). Of a will so good as that of God, a will that loves us so much, we may rest assured that He seeks only what is good, and what is better and more suited to our condition.

Rodriguez, *Practice of Perfection and Christian Virtues*, vol. 1, p. 503.

1655. *Trials Willed for Us by God*
. . . God certainly does not will the injustice or the bad habits of your neighbors, but he does will to afflict you, to try you by the crosses which come to you from the perversity of your fellows; and he seeks herein the salvation and perfection of your soul. For which reason, abstracting from the faults of others, you must in every cross that falls to your lot, be wholly resigned to the divine will.

Scaramelli, *Directorium Asceticum*, vol. 4, p. 158.

1656. *Whom God Loves, He Chastises*
. . . Tribulations are, for those well prepared, like certain foods and exercises for athletes which lead the contestant on to the hereditary glory, if, when we are reviled, we bless; maligned, we entreat; ill-treated, we give thanks; afflicted, we glory in our afflictions. It is indeed shameful for us to bless on propitious occasions, but to be silent on dark and difficult ones. On the contrary, we must bless more at that time, knowing that 'Whom the Lord loves, he chastises, and he scourges every son whom he receives.'

St Basil, in *The Fathers of the Church*, vol. 46, pp. 249-250.

1657. *Trials Are a Measure of God's Love*
[Christ once said to St Theresa:] 'Believe me, my daughter, his trials are the heaviest whom my Father loves most; trials are the measure of his love.'

The Life of St Teresa of Jesus, Written by Herself, p. 452.

1658. *Trials Sent by God More Valuable than Those We Choose Ourselves*
Be it known that, in the eyes of God, one gains more merits in a single day through trials given us by God and neighbor than in ten years of penances

and other practices chosen by us.
St Teresa of Avila, in *Spiritual Diary*, p. 91.

1659. *Trials Enable Us to Pay Our Debts to God*
God sends us trials and infirmities to give us the means of paying the enormous debts we owe him. Hence, the wise . . . receive them with joy, thinking more of the good they derive from them, than of the sufferings they are undergoing.
St Vincent de Paul, in *Spiritual Diary*, p. 92.

1660. *How to React to Trials, Persecutions*
'If the rational creatures persecute thee, love them with all thy heart and regard them as the instruments of divine justice which afford thee some opportunity of rendering satisfaction for thy deficiency. Rather, strengthen and console thyself in labors, adversities and tribulations, not only considering them as fully deserved by the faults committed, but deeming them ornaments of the soul and most rich jewels given thee by thy Spouse.'
Advice of the Blessed Virgin Mary to Mary of Agreda, in *City of God: Words of Wisdom*, p. 23.

1661. *Tribulations Are Evil Because We Make Them So*
We call tribulations evils and misfortunes; and we make them so by suffering them with impatience; but if we received them with resignation, they would become graces and jewels to enrich our crown in heaven. In a word, he who is always united with the will of God becomes a saint and enjoys even here on earth a perpetual peace: 'Whatever shall befall the just man, it will not make him sad' (Prv 12:21).
St Alphonsus Liguori, *Great Means of Salvation and of Perfection*, p. 367.

UNION WITH GOD

1662. *In What Union Consists*
The purpose of all virtue is to lead us to union with God, in which alone is to be found all the happiness possible in this world. Now, in what precisely does this union consist? In nothing else than the perfect conformity and similarity of our will with the will of God. These two wills are to be in complete conformity with one another, so that there is nothing in one which is repugnant to the other; whatever one desires and loves; whatever one likes or dislikes, the other likes or dislikes.
St John of the Cross, in *Spiritual Diary*, p. 245.

1663. *Union with God Through Understanding, Memory and Will*
Union with God is effected by the action of the three faculties of understanding, memory and will, operating through the divine infused virtues of faith, hope and charity. It is the activity of those virtues that attaches the soul to its Creator as its final end.
Edward Leen, *Progress Through Mental Prayer*, p. 119.

1664. *It was for This Union that Man was Created*
The union with God, which results from the indwelling of His Holy Spirit in us, is the unique object of our existence. It is for this alone that we have been created and have been redeemed. No other purpose whatever can be assigned to our life's effort.
James Leen, *By Jacob's Well*, p. 66.

1665. *Union with the Trinity*
I belong to *God the Father* because he has created me. I am a thing fashioned, and I depend on him who fashioned me, not merely for my existence in the first instance, but for its continuation from one second to the next....

I belong to God, to *God the Son*. For with a great price has he bought me back when sin had made havoc of the plan devised for my soul by the Father....

I belong to the *Holy Ghost*. Through him the infinite merits of Christ are applied to my soul.... He has taken possession and therefore I am his property....

God belongs to me. On every page of Holy Scripture we are met with the phrase: '*My* God,' '*Our* God and Lord!... We are taught to pray to him as '*Our* Father.' ...

Jesus Christ belongs to me. 'God so loved the world as to give his only-begotten Son' ... The Holy Ghost belongs to me. 'Receive the Holy Ghost.'
Nash, *The Nun at Her Prie-Dieu*, pp. 59-61, 63.

1666. *Union with God Demands Total Conformity*
If we wish nothing to interpose between us and God, nothing to hinder our union with him, if we wish divine blessing to flow in upon our souls, we must not only renounce sin and imperfection, but moreover despoil ourselves of our personality *insofar as it constitutes an obstacle to perfect union with God*. It constitutes an obstacle to perfect union when our judgment, our self-will, our self-love, our susceptibilities make us think and act otherwise than according to the desires of our Heavenly Father. Believe me, our faults of frailty, our miseries, our human limitations hinder our union with God infinitely less than that habitual attitude of the soul

which, so to speak, wills to keep in everything the proprietorship of its activities. We must therefore not annihilate our personality – which is neither possible nor willed by God – but bring it to an entire capitulation before God. We must lay it down at God's feet and ask him to be by his Spirit – as he is for the humanity of Christ – the Supreme Mover of all our thoughts, of all our feelings, of all our words, of all our actions, of all our life.

Marmion, *Christ, the Life of the Soul*, pp. 42-43.

1667. *Union with God by Resignation to His Will*

They who are little faithful in loving God will desire that he should agree with them, that he should conform himself to their pleasure, and do whatever they desire; but they who love God agree with him and unite their wills to his will and are satisfied with everything that God does with them . . . they ever have on their lips and in their hearts these words: 'Thy will be done.' . . .

God only desires that which is best for us, which is our sanctification (1 Thes 4:3). Let us take care, therefore, to quiet our own will, uniting it ever to the will of God; thus we shall be able, also, to quiet our intellect, recollecting that everything that God does is the best thing that can befall us. Whoever does not this, will never find true peace.

St Alphonsus Liguori, *The Way of Salvation and of Perfection*, pp. 232-233.

1668. *For Perfect Union, Three Things Are Necessary*

That a soul may give itself wholly to God, three things are especially necessary: (a) the avoidance of all defects, even the very least, accompanied with conquests over every inordinate desire, such as abstinence from observing such and such an object of sight or hearing, from certain pleasures of sense, from certain witty or unnecessary conversations, and suchlike; (b) among many things which are good, the constant choice of those that are the best and the most pleasing to God; and (c) the receiving with peace of mind and thanksgiving, from the divine hands, all things that are displeasing to our self-love.

St Alphonsus, *ibid.*, p. 183.

1669. *Union with God Gives Us Value and Strength*

[Speaking of herself, St Teresa of Avila says:] Teresa is nothing; four pennies are nothing; but Teresa, four pennies *and God Almighty* are much indeed.

Nash, *The Nun at Her Prie-Dieu*, p. 201.

1670. *Union with God, Special Duty of Religious*
Religious . . . must by long and planned effort make union with God so beautiful and inspiring that men of the world will want to imitate it from afar even in their own limited sphere of daily life. Holiness must be the first concern of religious. External activity, even in the service of souls, must come second.

Hoeger, *The Convent Mirror*, p. 3.

1671. *How We Priests Come to Belong to Him*
Let us now see what a priest must do in order to belong entirely to God. First of all, he must have a great desire of sanctity. . . .

Miserable, then, is the man who is content with his conduct and seeks not to advance. 'Not to advance is to go backward,' says St Augustine. . . . And St Gregory has said . . . 'He who remains in a river without making effort to make way against the current, shall be carried back by it.'

St Alphonsus Liguori, *Dignity and Duties of The Priest*, pp. 391-392.

1672. *Union Through Love – Our Goal, Our Final Good*
Our goal [our end or good] is nothing else than union with [God], whose spiritual embrace, if I may so speak, can alone fecundate the intellectual soul and fill it with true virtue. . . .

It is toward this Good that we should be led by those who love us, and toward this Good that we should lead those whom we love. In this way, we fulfill the commandments on which depend the whole law and the Prophets: 'Thou shalt love the Lord thy God with thy whole heart, and thy whole soul, and with thy whole mind'; and 'Thou shalt love thy neighbor as thyself' (Mt 22:37-39).

For, in order that a man might learn how to love himself, a standard was set up to regulate all his actions on which his happiness depends. For, to love one's self is nothing but to wish to be happy, and the standard is union with God. When, therefore, a person who knows how to love himself is bidden to love his neighbor as himself, is he not, in effect, commanded to persuade others, as far as he can, to love God?

St Augustine, *City of God*, bk. 10, chap. 3.

1673. *Happiness Vs. Unhappiness*
Since the happiness of all angels consists in union with God, it follows that their unhappiness must be found in the very contrary, in not adhering to God. To the question: 'Why are the good angels happy?' the right answer is: 'Because they adhere to God.' To the question: 'Why are the others unhappy?' the answer is: 'Because they do not adhere to God.' In fact, there is no other good which can make any rational or intellectual

creature happy except God. Not every creature has the potentialities for happiness. Beasts, trees, stones and such things neither acquire nor have the capacity for this gift. However, every creature which has this capacity receives it, not from itself, since it has been created out of nothing, but from its Creator. To possess him is to be happy; to lose him is to be in misery.

St. Augustine, *City of God*, bk. 12, chap. 1.

1674. *Obstacles Opposed to Union with God*
. . . Why do so few here in this life ever achieve this union of love? For Three very simple reasons: sin, excessive self-love, and mental dissipation.

Sin attacks the union itself. If it is mortal, it utterly destroys union with God. If it is venial, either it weakens God's influence on the soul as mud on auto headlights lessens their radiating power, or it ultimately leads to the dissolution of the union. . . . Man sins because he loves himself too much. Sin stems from loving more than God anything which is less than God – like self, wealth, pleasure. Sin is but the preferring of one's own will to God's. It is simply self-love gone out of control. Man gets that way – gets to love himself too much – because he doesn't think: 'With desolation is the whole land made desolate because no man thinketh in his heart.' We become estranged from God when we sin; we sin because we love wrongly; and we love wrongly because we do not stop to think rightly.

Shamon, *The Only Life*, p. 59.

1675. *Union with God Achieved Only Through God's Action*
In whatever way union of soul with God is achieved – consciously or unconsciously – God is always responsible for it. No one can become one with God without going out toward him; nor can anyone go out toward God unless attracted by him. The Divine Bridegroom made this clear when he said: 'Nobody can come to me without being attracted toward me by the Father who sent me.'

St Francis de Sales, *The Love of God*, p. 277.

UNION WITH CHRIST

1676. *Union with Christ*
The perfect union with Christ is to do the will of God for the love of God. There is nothing higher than that.

Boylan, *This Tremendous Lover*, p. 175.

1677. *What Union with Christ Means*
Active union with Christ means an endeavor to practice, in one's conduct, the virtues of Christ. It means a constant effort to be pure like Him, to be spiritual like him, to love God like him, and to be kind and unselfish after his example.

Edward Leen, *The True Vine and Its Branches*, p. 96.

1678. *Abiding in Christ*
There is no greater union than that of the Father and the Son in the Holy Trinity, since, with the Holy Ghost, they both possess one and the same divine nature; St John says that the Father *abideth* in the Son.

To abide in Christ, is, first of all, to share, by grace, in his divine Sonship; it is to be one with him by being, as he is, although in a different manner, a child of God. That is the essential and fundamental union, which Christ himself points out in the parable of the vine; 'I am the Vine; you the branches; he that abideth in me, and I in him, the same beareth much fruit.'

Marmion, *Christ, the Life of the Soul*, p. 283.

1679. *Union With Christ in Mind, Heart, and Desire*
To abide in Christ is to be identified with him in all that relates to our intelligence, our will, our activity. We abide in Christ *through our intelligence* when we accept with a simple, pure, and integral act of faith all that Christ tells us. . . .

To abide in Him is also to *submit our will* to his, it is to make all our supernatural activity dependent on his grace. That is to say, we must abide in his love by accepting to *do His will*. . . . It is to prefer his desires to our own, it is to espouse his interests, it is to yield ourselves to him entirely without counting the cost, reserving nothing and taking nothing back. . . .

Marmion, *ibid.*, pp. 283-284.

1680. *Christ Abiding in Us*
Not only do we abide in our Lord, but he also abides in us. . . .

Without establishing a union as close as that of the Word with his Sacred Humanity, Christ in giving himself to us, wills to be in us by his grace and in the action of the Holy Spirit the principle of all our inner activity . . . ; he is in the soul, he abides in it, but he is not idle. He wills to work in it, and when the soul remains given up to him, to his every will, then Christ's action will become so powerful that this soul will be carried to the highest perfection, according to God's designs.

Marmion, *ibid.*, pp. 284-285.

1681. *The Result of Christ's Coming to Us*
. . . The coming of Christ in us, of its nature, tends to establish between his thought and ours, between his sentiments and our sentiments, between his will and our will, such an exchange, such a correspondence and similitude that we have no other thoughts, no other sentiments, no other will than those of Christ.
Marmion, *ibid.,* p. 286.

1682. *God Cannot Separate Us from Christ*
'Christ prays for us as our High Priest. He prays in us as our Head,' says St Augustine. . . . That is why, he adds, the Eternal Father cannot separate us from Christ, any more than the head is separated from the body. In seeing us, he sees his Son, for we only make one with him.
Marmion, *ibid.,* p. 350.

VALUES

1683. *Eternal Values Alone Worthwhile*
Let nothing appear great, nothing valuable or admirable, nothing worthy of esteem, nothing high, nothing truly praiseworthy or desirable, but what is eternal.
Thomas à Kempis, *Imitation of Christ,* bk. III, chap. 4.

1684. *Eternal Vs. Temporal Values*
If thou didst know the whole Bible by heart, and the sayings of all the philosophers, what would it all profit thee without the love of God and his grace. . . . It is vanity, therefore, to seek after riches which must perish and to trust in them. . . . It is vanity to follow the lusts of the flesh and to desire that for which thou must afterwards be grievously punished. It is vanity to wish for a long life and take little care of leading a good life. It is vanity also to mind this present life and not to look forward unto those things which are to come. It is vanity to love that which passeth away with all speed and not to hasten thither where everlasting joy remaineth.
Thomas à Kempis, *ibid.,* bk. I, chap. 1.

1685. *True Values to be Preferred*
. . . No one will choose to scorn these things as of little worth – silver, gold, and the rest of the array – unless he has a desire for things of greater worth, just as no one scorns the lead coin unless he is in possession of a gold one. . . .

Therefore, I beg and beseech, do not punish yourselves, and do not deprive yourselves of the treasures from above by holding on to mud or by bringing your ship into the harbor laden only with straw and chaff.

St John Chrysostom, in *The Fathers of the Church*, vol. 41, pp. 384-385.

1686. *Values for Life*

. . . He weeps as though he wept not, who so grieves over his temporal losses, that his soul will still draw comfort from the thought of his eternal gain. He rejoices as if he rejoiced not, who is happy in his temporal possessions, while still mindful of the torments that do not end; and when his mind is uplifted through joy, he will restrain it with the counterweight of prudent fear. He buys as though he possessed not, who provides what is needed, and yet with wise reflection is aware that soon these too will be left behind. And he uses the world as if he used it not, who gathers what is needed for his daily needs in this world, yet not permitting that such things shall rule his life; that as subject to him, they may serve him outwardly, never hindering the end of his soul, in its striving toward the things that are above. Whoever, therefore, are of such mind, they do indeed possess all things, not for their desires, but for their daily use; for they use what is needed, and desire not to possess anything through sin. They also gain a reward daily from the things they possess; but they rejoice more in a good work than in good property.

St Gregory the Great, in Toal, vol. 3, p. 188.

1687. *The Value of Our Works*

[Pauline, Mother Agnes of Jesus, a sister of St Thérèse of Lisieux, had told the saint that later her virtues would be recognized at their true value. St Thérèse replied:] 'It is to God alone all value must be attributed, because there is nothing of value in my little nothingness.'

St Thérèse of Lisieux, in *Novissima Verba*, p. 91.

VANITY

1688. *Vanity, a Deadly Poison*

It is the glory of vain men never to yield to truth. Such vainglory is a deadly poison for those it dominates. It is a disease that, in spite of every effort, is never cured – not because the doctor is inept, but because the patient is incurable.

St Augustine, *City of God*, bk. 6, preface.

VICTIM SOULS

1689. *Why Desire to Become a Victim Soul?*
There are many reasons why I should desire to become a victom soul. (1) The boundless love of the Savior impels me. . . . (2) Conditions in the world demand that I consecrate my whole life to reparation. Many men hate God. . . . They insult and profane the Holy Eucharist. (3) Even chosen souls, and I myself, often treat God and the Eucharistic Christ with coldness, neglect and even irreverence. (4) Sacrifice is the shortest and best way to heaven. It is the most meritorious of works because it is most difficult. It offers the opportunity for the exercise of many virtues. It merits an abundance of graces and produces in us a marvelous peace of soul. To those who sacrifice themselves and give themselves without reserve to God, he gives unsparingly his reward. Should I not, then, become a co-victim with Christ?

Bandas, *The Catholic Layman and Holiness,* pp. 112-13.

VICTORY

1690. *Victory over sin and Temptation Must Be Attributed to God*
The battle of self-conquest is filled with perils and temptations. The flesh never ceases to lust against the spirit, nor the spirit against the flesh. . . . Above all, in this war so full of toil and trouble, we have to strive to supress the vain hope that our efforts can bring us victory, and also the illusion that, when victory comes, our efforts were the important factor. On the contrary, we owe all victories to God, and we must say with St Paul: 'Thanks be to God, who has given us the victory through our Lord Jesus Christ' (1 Cor 15:57). And we must remember those other words: 'In all these things we overcome because of him who has loved us' (Rom 8:37).

St Augustine, *City of God*, bk. 22, chap. 23.

1691. *Violence in Attaining to Kingdom of Heaven*
The Gospel lesson says: 'and the violent bear it away'. We do violence, I say, against the Lord, not by compelling, but by weeping; not by provoking him by insults, but by pleading with tears of repentance; not by blaspheming in pride, but by grieving in humility. . . .

These are the weapons of our Faith, by means of which we wage war. That we may use these weapons we must, however, do violence to ourselves. We must drive out vice from our members, that we may attain to the rewards of virtue. For we must first rule in our own hearts, before we can seize the kingdom of heaven.

St Maximus, in Toal, vol. 1, pp. 64-65.

VIRGINITY

1692. *Virginity Not Merely a Matter of the Body*

[Achieving virginity] is not as simple as one might think, nor is it confined to the body; it pertains to all things and extends even to thought, which is considered one of the achievements of the soul: the soul, adhering to its true Bridegroom through virginity, not only keeps itself away from bodily defilements, but begins its purity there, and proceeds to all things in the same way with steadfastness. . . . The soul, clinging to the Lord for the purpose of becoming 'one spirit' (1 Cor 6:18) with him, and having entered into a kind of symbiotic agreement to love him alone with its whole heart and power, must not become involved . . . in anything else that is opposed to salvation.

St Gregory of Nyssa, in *The Fathers of the Church*, vol. 58, p. 51.

VIRTUES

1693. *Virtue Makes Man's Spirit Strong*

The name virtue is derived from the Latin word *vir*, which means 'man.' Virtue makes man's spirit strong. It builds up morale in the sense of spiritual manhood.

Garrigou-Lagrange, *The Theological Virtues*, vol. 1, p. 11.

1694. *Virtue Practiced Not for Its Own Sake*

Jesus did not exercise virtue for virtue's sake, but because he apprehended it as God's will. Through and in the act of virtue, he, as Man, kept united with God, his Supreme Good.

Edward Leen, *Progress Through Mental Prayer*, p. 8.

1695. *A Christian Must Practice Christ's Virtues*

If . . . someone puts on the name of Christ, but does not exhibit in his life what is indicated by that term, such a person belies the name and puts on a lifeless mask in accordance with the model proposed to us. For it is impossible for Christ not to be justice and purity and truth and estrangement from all evil, nor is it possible to be a Christian, (that is, truly a Christian) without displaying . . . a participation in those virtues. If one can give a definition of Christianity, we shall define it as follows: Christianity is an imitation of the divine nature.

St Gregory of Nyssa, in *The Fathers of the Church*, vol. 58, p. 85.

1696. *Virtue Must be Tested by Trials*

. . . A man does not acquire virtue without being afflicted by those things which go against the grain. We shall never get anywhere simply by thinking a lot about humility without ever being humiliated, thinking about patience without ever having our patience tried, and soon. Virtue of this kind comes to nothing because it is not real. It is an artificial thing with no foundation. . . .

When other people humiliate and hurt us by their words or behavior, we should lose no time in repaying them with some charitable service, gently and lovingly done.

Tauler, *Spiritual Conferences*, p. 105.

1697. *Virtue Can Have No Life Without Charity and Humility*

God as Supreme Truth says: 'No virtue, my daughter, can have life in itself except through charity, and humility, which is the foster mother and nurse of charity.'

Dialogue of St Catherine of Siena, p. 32.

1698. *Virtues Grow Out of One Another*

Simplicity gives way to obedience, obedience to faith, faith to hope, hope to justice, justice to service, service to humility. From this comes gentleness, which leads to grace, grace to love, and love to prayer.

St Gregory of Nyssa, in *The Fathers of the Church*, vol. 58, p. 151.

1699. *What Virtue Implies in Actual Life*

. . . In this world, [this] is the life of virtue. When God commands, man obeys; when the soul commands, the body obeys; when reason rules, our passions, even when they fight back, must be conquered or resisted; man must beg God's grace to win merit and the remission of his sins and must thank God for the blessings he receives.

St Augustine, *City of God*, bk. 19, chap. 27.

1700. *Virtue Not to Struggle*

. . . St Gregory the Great . . . likens our soul to a little boat in the midstream of a rapid river, which, if every effort is not put forth to make headway against the force of the water, can never stand still in the middle, but is perforce carried back by the violence of the current. And thus if the soul, says the Saint, does not exert itself to advance in virtue, resisting bravely the impetus of its own bad propensities and the shock of the devil's attacks, it can never stand still on the voyage to perfection, but will have to go back in spite of itself, and to lose all the way it had made in the whole course of its spiritual voyage.

Scaramelli, *Directorium Asceticum*, vol. 1, pp. 87-88.

1701. *Infused Virtues, Moral and Theological*

In treating of sanctifying grace, the Roman Catechism observes: 'It is followed by a most noble retinue of all the virtues which, with grace, are alike poured into the soul divinely.'...

Aquinas offers theological proof for the existence of moral virtues *per se* infused. 'Effects are necessarily proportioned to their causes and principles. God directly confers on us the theological virtues as our equipment for a supernatural end. But in the same way that nature's pre-existent principles of virtues develop the acquisition of intellectual and moral habits that are distinct virtues, so the divine infusion of theological virtues would not be complete for human needs without a parallel accompaniment of intellectual and moral virtues, also infused.' (Therefore, there are two sets of moral virtues; one, natural and acquired; the other, supernatural and divinely infused.) . . .

The disproportion between the virtues of the natural, contrasted with the supernatural order, is such that God himself must supply what nature cannot provide; namely an independent equipment of intellectual and moral virtues, proportioned to the theological group, in which case the moral virtues, like the theological, would have to be infused.

The power of natural virtues cannot reach above the capacity of nature itself. But man's goal is formally supernatural, which entails the necessity of a perfection on man's part that can come only from special moral virtues, supernatural in themselves, and not attainable except through an additional infusion on God's part.

Garrigou-Lagrange, *The Theological Virtues*, vol. 1, pp. 26-27.

1702. *Infused Virtues Are Absolutely Necessary*

The infused virtues do not presuppose the power of acting divinely, they bestow it. Suppress them, and supernatural action becomes an utter impossibility. They do not give a certain definite inclination to faculties already existing and which might be inclined in a contrary direction. Faith does not modify in one sense rather than another an already existing power to know God in a supernatural manner. It imparts that very power. Without faith, the intellect would not in any degree know God as he is known supernaturally. Charity does not take and give a certain fixed disposition to an already existing faculty of loving God. It gives to the will an aptitude to love God. The will can love the good. It could love God as revealed by reason. It is utterly powerless of itself to give itself the slightest movement toward God as an object of *supernatural affection*. The will of its own natural resources can love God naturally; it cannot love him supernaturally.

Edward Leen, *The Holy Ghost*, pp. 300-301.

1703. *Infused Supernatural Virtues*

Sanctifying grace animates our souls, and giving us a like-new being, *nova creatura*, makes us children of God. But to this being, God, who does all things with wisdom and scatters his gifts munificently, has given some faculties, which proportioned to this new condition, give him the capacity of acting according to the supernatural end to be attained, that is to say, as a child of God awaiting the inheritance of Christ in eternal beatitude: these are the infused supernatural virtues.

These faculties are called *virtues* (from the Latin word *virtus*, 'strength' because they are the capacities of action, principles of operation, and energies that remain in us as stable habits, and, being exercised at the fitting moment, cause us to produce with promptitude, ease and joy, works pleasing to God. . . .

'By grace, we *are* children of God; by the infused supernatural virtues, we can *act* as children of God and produce acts worthy of our supernatural end.

Marmion, *Christ, the Life of the Soul*, pp. 231-232.

1704. *Why Infused Virtues are Absolutely Necessary*

No natural virtue, however powerful it may be, can be raised of itself to a supernatural level; that only belongs to the infused virtues, and this constitutes their superiority and preeminence.

Marmion, *Growth in Christ*, p. 143.

FAITH

1705. *Faith, Its Nature and Genesis*

To believe, says St Thomas, is to give, under the empire of the will, moved by grace, the assent and adhesion of our intelligence to the Divine Truth. . . . It is the mind that believes, but the heart is not absent from believing;

and so that we can make this act of faith, God places in us at baptism, a power, a force, a 'habitude,' namely the virtue of faith, whereby our intelligence is inclined to admit the testimony of God out of love for his truth.

Marmion, *Christ, the Life of the Soul*, p. 137.

1706. *Faith Is Necessary*

Faith is necessary; for if faith had not assured us of it, who could ever believe what God has actually done for us? 'He emptied himself, taking the nature of a slave' (Phil 2:7). Unless a person had the infallible assurance of faith, could he ever believe that Jesus, born in a stable, is the God adored by the angels in heaven? How, without the aid of faith, can anyone who sees the Savior fleeting into Egypt to escape the hands of Herod believe that he is omnipotent? How could we, without the assurance of faith, believe that the Man in the Garden, sorrowful unto death, is infinitely happy, or that he who was bound to a pillar and hung on the Cross is the Lord of the universe?

St Alphonsus Liguori, *The Passion of Jesus Christ*, p. 88.

1707. *Why Is Faith Necessary?*

The virtue of faith is necessary: (a) to avoid sin; (b) to practice all virtues, especially obedience, patience in suffering and charity; (c) to perform our prayer well and receive the Sacraments worthily; (d) to attain to eternal salvation.

Faith is the 'beginning of the salvation of man, the foundation and root of all justification,' says the Council of Trent. . . .

It is impossible to please God without faith. Nobody reaches God's presence until he has learned to believe that God exists, and that he rewards those who try to find him.

Wallenstein, *Guide to Perfect Christian Living*, p. 169.

1708. *The Nature and Necessity of the Spirit of Faith*

The spirit of faith is the spirit of basing one's actions on considerations that embrace in their ambit the world of eternity as well as the world of time. . . .

All actions are wasted if they have not God for their end, the spirit of Jesus for their principle, and the light of faith for their direction.

Edward Leen, *The True Vine and Its Branches*, pp. 144-145.

1709. *The Function of Faith Is to Make Us Know God*

The exercise of faith is not a mere knowledge about God; it is a knowing of God. It is impossible to love what we do not know. If we are not aware

of, and alive to, an attraction, it can exercise no appeal on us.
James Leen, *By Jacob's Well*, p. 72.

1710. *Faith Pleases God*
. . . The scope of this theological virtue of faith is to unite our feeble intellects to the Infallible Intelligence and to conform our finite minds to the Infinite Mind, so that we may think as God thinks and may judge as God judges. The primary function of divine revelation is to teach us the ineffable truths that exist from all eternity in the Divine Being. By believing in this revelation, we are endowed with God's own wisdom and participate in God's own knowledge.

. . . We may observe here that faith is eminently pleasing to God, both because it does homage to his truth and because it fosters reliance on his power.
Gabriel, *Ascetical Conferences for Religious*, pp. 53-54.

1711. *Motives for Believing*
The motives which determine our belief are solely the revelation of them to Holy Church by the God of infinite wisdom and truth. These motives impart to the act of faith two most precious qualities. First, they render it certain and infallible; for, as the utterances of God, who cannot misapprehend what he conceives in his mind, on account of his wisdom, and, since he is very truth, cannot depart in his sayings from that which he has in his mind, must surely be infallibly true, so that faith of one who assents to such sayings must be equally true and infallible. Second, these motives render our belief most meritorious, inasmuch as by blindly submitting our understanding to the word of a God infinitely wise and truthful, we acknowledge him for what he is, to wit, the first and infallible Truth, and make him an offering of the noblest of our faculties, I mean the mind, sacrificing in his honor our own private judgment.
Scaramelli, *Directorium Asceticum*, vol. 4, pp. 9-10.

1712. *Three Properties of Faith*
The first quality of faith is simplicity. . . . As St Augustine aptly observes, the stability of our faith comes not from the acuteness of our own understanding, but from the simplicity of our adhesion to God's utterances. . . .

The second property of faith is that it be stable and waver not, but remain forever firm and constant in believing. This property results from the former. . . .

The third property of faith is the fortitude wherewith it enables us to bear all manner of inconvenience, and of torments even, rather than swerve

a hair-breadth from our belief in any article of faith.
Scaramelli, *Directorium Asceticum*, vol. 4, pp. 13, 15, 17.

1713. *The Fiber of Our Intellectual Life*
. . . We have received the gift of faith; but it remains for us to merit its development until it becomes the very fiber of our intellectual life. We must aim at acquiring that condition of soul in which we shall, instinctively, view all things with the eyes of faith and judge everything under its light. To judge events by appearances and palpable effects; to regard them only in relation to their proximate and secondary causes is to put oneself in the impossibility of understanding anything of the ways of God. For behind the tapestry of events are the knowledge, the wisdom and the omnipotence of God. There, presiding over all, is his infinite love, whence proceeds his merciful design of sanctifying and unifying all creatures in Christ.
James Leen, *By Jacob's Well*, p. 44.

1714. *The Spirit of Faith Must Guide Our Lives*
The integral Christian is the man who not only submits his judgment to the truths of faith, but strives, in addition, to have his whole life guided by the spirit of faith. . . .

We are Christians to the exact degree in which 'faith' is the controlling motive in our thoughts, views, decisions and actions.
Edward Leen, *The True Vine and Its Branches*, pp. 131 and 134.

1715. *Believing Christ Vs. Believing in Christ*
. . . There is a great difference between a man believing he is Christ, and believing in Christ. For that he is Christ, even the demons believed; but the demons did not believe in Christ. For he believes in Christ who hopes in Christ and loves Christ. Should he have faith, but be without hope and without love, he believes that Christ is, but he does not believe in Christ. He, therefore, who believes in Christ, believing in Christ, Christ comes to him, and he is in a certain manner united to Christ, and made a member of his Body. This cannot be unless hope is added and likewise charity.
St Augustine, in Toal, vol. 2, p. 366.

1716. *Our Faith Must Not Be the Same as the Devils'*
Our faith must not be the same as that of devils. Our faith makes the heart pure, while their faith makes them guilty. Their works are evil; therefore they say to the Lord: 'What have we to do with thee?' (Lk 4:34). When you hear the devils say this, do you think they do not acknowledge Him? 'We know who thou art,' they say: 'Thou art the Son of God' (Mt 16:16). Peter says this, and he is commended; the devil says it and is condemned.

What is the reason except that the heart is different, while the voice is the same? Let us, therefore, analyze our faith; let not belief suffice. That is not the kind of faith that makes the heart pure. There is the saying: 'cleansing their hearts by faith' (Acts 15:9). But by what faith? By what kind of faith except the kind that the Apostle Paul defines when he says: 'Faith which works by charity' (Gal. 5:6). That faith differs from the faith of devils, and it differs from the shameful and profligate morals of men.

St Augustine, in *The Fathers of the Church*, vol. 11, pp. 219-220.

1717. *Three Means for Acquiring Perfect Faith*

The first means is to ask it earnestly and unceasingly of God. . . . Faith is a gift of God, for it depends on a supernatural light illuminating the mind in order to the knowledge of divine truth. . . .

A second means is to make frequent acts of faith. Every virtue is acquired by exercise. . . .

The third means is the practice of good works and the performance of pious exercises, since with these faith is quickened, while without them it fails and becomes extinct. St James teaches this doctrine when he writes that, as a body deprived of life is not living but a corpse, so faith, if devoid of good works, languishes and dies (Jas 2:26).

Scaramelli, *Directorium Asceticum*, vol. 4, pp. 26, 27, 29.

1718. *How Must We Foster the Virtue of Faith?*

We must foster the virtue of faith by: (a) making frequent, lively acts of faith; (b) thoroughly studying the truths of faith and meditating on them; (c) regulating our lives according to faith; (d) accepting trials and sufferings as well as the orders of superiors, and all other eventualities, in the spirit of faith; (e) avoiding dangers to faith and combating doubts of faith.

It is advisable to begin all (and especially long) prayers with an act of faith in God's presence and goodness. The Creed should be one of our favourite prayers: It is the best beacon for our intellect and contains the most powerful motives for good conduct.

Wallenstein, *Guide to Perfect Christian Living*, p. 170.

1719. *Genuine Faith a Great Blessing*

Faith is a great blessing, then, when it proceeds from a fervent mind, from great love, and a zealous soul. It shows that we are practical Christians, it conceals human worthlessness and, despising earthly reasoning, seeks after the knowledge of heavenly things. . . .

Both Christ and Paul, who were particularly concerned with regard to this matter, made it clear that orthodoxy of faith is of no profit if one's life is a corrupt. Christ taught: 'Not everyone who says to Me, Lord, Lord, shall enter the kingdom of heaven.'

St John Chrysostom, in *The Fathers of the Church*, vol. 41, pp. 185 and 187.

1720. *Faith Without Works Is Dead*

. . . Even if a man says verbally and with many oaths that he possesses faith, if he is unwilling to fulfill in deed what he says verbally that he believes, that is not faith. . . .

If you claim to believe in the reward which God promises and the punishment which he threatens and still, as was said, refuse to act in such a way as to escape endless punishment and obtain eternal rewards, there is no faith at all in you. . . . The Holy Spirit proclaims to you through St James: 'Faith without works is dead' (Jas 2:26).

St Caesarius of Arles, in *The Fathers of the Church*, vol. 31, pp. 68-69.

1721. *Presumption and Lack of Confidence*

. . . We must fear lest someone believes so strongly that he will receive God's mercy that he does not dread his justice. If a man does this, he has no faith. Likewise, if he dreads God's justice so much that he despairs of his mercy, there is no faith. Since God is not only merciful but also just, let us believe in both. Let us not despair of his mercy because we fear his justice, nor love his mercy so much that we disregard his justice.

St Caesarius, *ibid.*, p. 72.

1722. *In Scripture, 'Faith' Has Wide Significance*

In the Scriptures, *faith* is not often used in the isolated sense of a mere intellectual assent to truth; 'There is nearly always added to it a sentiment of security, confidence, abandonment, obedience, and filial love; the adhesion of the mind produces a thrill of the heart' (Prat, *Theology of St Paul*, vol. 2, p. 236). In St Paul's writings, some such complex meaning of the word is common; in particular when he uses the phrase to believe *in* God, it means not only to 'believe in his existence,' but variously, 'to rest upon him as on an immovable support, to take refuge in him as in a sure place of shelter, to tend toward him as to one's supreme end.'

Boylan, *This Tremendous Lover*, p. 53.

1723. *Faith of the Blessed Virgin*

Just as Mary is the mother of love and hope, so she is also the mother of faith. St Irenaeus says that this is so for a very good reason, for 'The evil done by Eve's unfaithfulness was remedied by Mary's faith.' Tertullian confirms this by saying that because Eve believed the serpent against the warning she had received from God, she brought death into the world; but because Mary believed the angel at the Annunciation, she brought salvation into the world. He puts it this way: 'Eve believed the serpent; Mary believed Gabriel. What Eve demolished by her foolish credulity, Mary restored by her genuine faith.' St Augustine says: 'It was Mary's faith that opened heaven to men when she agreed to cooperate in the Incarnation of the eternal Word.'

St Alphonsus Liguori, *The Glories of Mary*, vol. 2, p. 160.

1724. *The Faith and Confidence of the Good Thief*
. . . As he drew near his end, the Lord himself says to the thief, then hanging on his cross . . . whose faith neither Christ's torment nor his own had weakened: 'Amen, I say to you, this day thou shalt be with Me in paradise'. For the thief had said to him: 'Lord, remember me when Thou shalt come into thy kingdom' (Lk 23). How admirable this faith, brethren; that a thief who had been judged unworthy of this life, should amid his torments nourish the hope of life eternal, and believe that this could be given to him by one who also was being crucified? And how justly does the believing thief receive the favor of such a promise: he who, in that hour when the apostles scattered in fear, had confessed the Kingdom of God? And the merit of one confession wipes away all his past sins; in that brief moment, whatever crimes he had committed, throughout all the years of his life were now forgiven. . . .

Who can despair of God's grace when the thief was forgiven. . . ?

St Maximus, in Toal, vol. 22, p. 240.

HOPE

1725. *Grace Needed for the Act of Hope*
Hope . . . is a theological virtue which raises our will to a steadfast expectation of everlasting bliss as well as of the means of attaining it, grounded on the promises of a God at once infinitely powerful and supremely faithful in keeping his word. . . . Neither may we doubt the utter impotence of our will to produce such an act, to conceive such hope, unless God, raising our will by his grace, makes it capable of putting forth an act which wholly transcends our natural powers.

Scaramelli, *Directorium Asceticum*, vol. 4, pp. 44.

1726. *By Commanding Us to Hope, God Obliges Himself to Give us Grace*
The virtue of hope is so pleasing to God that He has declared that He feels delight in those who trust in Him: 'The Lord taketh pleasure in them that hope in His Mercy' (Ps 46:11). And He promises victory over his enemies,

perseverance in grace, and eternal glory to the man who hopes: 'Because he hoped in Me, I will deliver him; I will protect him. . . . I will deliver him and I will glorify him' (Ps 90:14). 'Preserve me, for I have put my trust in thee' (Ps 15:1). 'No one hath hoped in the Lord and been confounded' (Ecclus 2:11). And let us be sure that the heaven and the earth will fail, but the promises of God cannot fail: 'Heaven and earth shall pass away, but my words shall not pass away' (Mt 24:35). St Bernard, therefore, says that all our merit consists in reposing all our confidence in God: 'This is the whole merit of man, if he places all his hope in him.'. . . The reason is that he who hopes in God honors him much: 'Call upon Me in the day of trouble; I will deliver thee and thou shalt glorify me' (Ps 49:15). He honors the power, the mercy, the faithfulness of God; since he believes that God can and will save him; and that he cannot fail in his promises to save the man who trusts in him.

St Alphonsus Liguori, *Great Means of Salvation and of Perfection*, pp. 228-229.

1727. *Why God Imposed Upon Us the Precept of Hope*
. . . As this virtue of hope is so pleasing to God, he has willed to impose it upon us by a precept that binds under pain of mortal sin, as all theologians agree, and as is evident from many texts of Scripture. 'Trust in Him, ye congregations of people' (Ps. 61). 'Ye that fear the Lord, hope in him' (Ecclus 2:9). . . . 'Hope perfectly for that grace which is offered to you' (1 Pet 1:13). Then this hope of eternal life ought to be sure and firm in us, according to the definition of St Thomas: 'Hope is the certain expectation of beatitude' (ST II IIae q.18 a.4). And the Sacred Council of Trent has expressly declared: 'All men ought to place and repose a most firm hope in the help of God; for God, unless they fail to correspond to his grace, as he has begun the good work, so he will finish it, working in them both to will and to perform.' . . . And long before, St Paul said of himself: 'I know whom I have believed, and I am certain that he is able to keep what I have committed to him' (2 Tm 1:12). And herein is the difference between Christian and worldly hope.

St Alphonsus, *ibid.,* p. 229.

1728. *Hope in the Mind of St Thomas*
St Thomas sums up the theology of Christian hope in his usual laconic style. 'Hope,' he says, 'reaches out to God, relying upon his help to acquire the good hoped for.'. . . 'Hope,' he writes, 'is not based on grace already possessed, but on the divine omnipotence and mercy, by which even he who has not grace can obtain it that so he may reach eternal life. Anyone who believes in God can be certain of the omnipotence of God and of

his mercy.'
Boylan, *This Tremendous Lover*, p. 55.

1729. *Hope of Salvation Based on God's Conditional Promise*
Our hope of salvation, and of receiving the means necessary for its attainment, must be certain on God's part. The motives on which this certainty is founded, as we have seen, are the power, the mercy and the truth of God; and of these the strongest and most certain motive is God's infallible faithfulness to the promise he has made to us, through the merits of Jesus Christ, to save us, and to give us the graces necessary for our salvation; because, though we may believe God to be infinite in power and mercy, nevertheless, as Giovenino well observes, we could not feel confident expectation of God's saving us, unless he had surely promised to do so. But this promise is conditional, if we actively correspond to God's grace and pray, as is clear from the Scriptures: 'Ask, and ye shall receive; if ye ask the Father anything in my name, he will give it to you. He will give good things to those that ask him. We ought always to pray. Ye have not, because ye ask not'.
St Alphonsus Liguori, *Great Means of Salvation and of Perfection*, pp. 232-233.

1730. *Hope Involves Free Will, Distrust of Self, Confidence in God*
Reasonably . . . did the Council of Trent condemn the innovators who, because they entirely deprive man of free will, are obliged to make every believer have an infallible certitude of perseverance and salvation. This error was condemned by the Council because, as we have said, in order to obtain salvation, it is necessary for us to correspond; and this correspondence of ours is uncertain and fallible. Hence God wills that we should, on the one hand, always fear for ourselves, lest we fall into presumption in trusting to our strength; but, on the other, that we should always be certain of his good will, and of his assistance to save us; provided always that we ask him for it. In other words, that we might always have a secure confidence in his goodness. St Thomas says that we ought to look with certainty to receive from God eternal happiness, confiding in his power and mercy, and believing that he can and will save us. 'Whoever has faith is certain of God's power and mercy.'
St Alphonsus, *ibid.*, p. 230.

1731. *Properties of Theological Hope*
The first property of theological hope is that its reliance be on God alone, for God alone is the giver of every best gift. . . The Angelic Doctor says . . . that it is not lawful to expect great goods at the hands of men, con-

sidered as primary causes, but that we may place our hopes in them as instrumental causes, in other words, as the instruments God makes use of to lead us to everlasting blessedness. . . . 'The second property of true hope is the certain and established expectation of unfailing bliss, as well as of the means necessary for its attainment.

Scaramelli, *Directorium Asceticum*, vol. 4, pp. 55 and 59.

1732. *Hope – and Healthy Fear*

The third property of hope consists in the union of a wholesome fear with the assured expectation of supernatural blessings. . . . Hope is stirred up in us by God's infallible promises and by his goodness. . . .

Fear, on the other hand, is produced by the consideration of our own nothingness, insufficiency, weakness, faults. . . . 'He that hopes without fearing,' says St Augustine, 'will grow heedless on account of excessive security; he that fears, but hopes not, falls into discouragement. . . .

St Bernard inculcates the same spiritual lesson when treating of these two affections. He observes that 'fear of God's judgments, apart from hope, casts us down into the pit of despair; while indiscreet hope, unmixed with a reasonable fear, engenders a hurtful security'.

Scaramelli, *ibid.,* vol. 4, pp. 62-63.

1733. *Hope Pleases God*

. . . Perfect hope is undoubtedly pleasing to God. He cannot but love those who aspire only to possess him and who for his sake despise all earthly goods. He cannot but bless those who in the face of severe trials and violent temptations expect all things from his goodness. 'The more we hope for from God, the more we obtain,' says St John of the Cross. 'and our hope grows in proportion as we renounce self.' Indeed, invincible confidence conquers the heart of God.

Gabriel, *Ascetical Conferences for Religious*, p. 179.

1734. *Hope Brings Peace of Soul*

[God's promises concerning eternal life] bring us peace of soul – a peace which is the root of the virtue of hope. When faith assures the will that it can enjoy the possession of God by using the means provided, we make two great acts of virtue: we look forward to the fulfillment of God's promise, and we set our hearts on the possession of him.

St Francis de Sales, *The Love of God*, pp. 91-92.

1735. *Two Effects of Hope*

The first effect of hope is to enlarge the heart, to inspire it with a readiness to keep all the commandments of God and make us strive after Christian perfection. . . .

The second effect of hope is the consolation and gladness which accrue from it to him that hopes. The Apostle exhorts the Romans to 'rejoice in hope' (Rom 12:12). And in the Epistle to the Hebrews (6:18), he says: 'We have a strong consolation, who have fled for refuge to lay hold on the hope set before us'.

Scaramelli, *Directorium Asceticum*, vol. 4, pp. 64 and 67.

1736. *Hope as Related to Love for God*

We love God because, on account of his perfections, he deserves to be loved, and we should love him though there were no reward for loving him; but since he wishes to give us a reward, and even commands us to hope for it, we are bound to hope for it and to desire it. Besides, to desire paradise in order to possess God, and to love him better, is true and perfect charity. For eternal glory is the consummation of love.

St Alphonsus Liguori, *The True Spouse of Jesus Christ*, pp. 642-643.

1737. *Our Hope Is in God's Mercy*

My whole hope is nowhere but in thy exceeding great mercy.

St Augustine, *Confessions*, bk. 10, chap. 29.

1738. *Hope and Suffering*

Christ taught us by his Passion what we should suffer for the truth, and by his resurrection what we should hope for in eternity.

St Augustine, *City of God*, bk. 18, chap. 49.

1739. *Temporal Blessings Can Be Object of Theological Hope*

. . . Health, bodily strength, prosperity, honors, office, wealth, riches and the like – are an object of supernatural and theological hope . . . if we look for these frail goods as means necessary or suited to our successful attainment of everlasting blessings, that is, inasmuch as they help us to recover or to obtain God's grace, to avoid sin or to rise out of it, to acquire virtue . . . or to procure God's glory. . . . St Augustine expressly says as much. His words are: 'Those blessings alone are objects of the theological virtue of hope which are contained in the Lord's Prayer.' He then adds that this prayer comprises seven petitions, three of which regard eternal blessings, and the remaining four such as are temporal; but that the goods of this world are objects of godly hope only in so far as they are sought as means to the attainment of everlasting blessings. . . .

Scaramelli, *Directorium Asceticum*, vol. 4, p. 49.

LOVE

1740. *Love as Related to Other Emotions*
Love . . . is the first feeling of satisfaction at the awareness of good; so, obviously it comes before desire – in fact we only desire things when we love them. It comes before pleasure; for would we find pleasure or joy in anything if we did not love it? It comes before hope, because hope reaches out only to a future good that we love. It comes before hatred, for we only hate evil because we love good; evil is evil only because it is opposed to good. It is the same with the other passions or emotions; they come from love – their root, the source of all their activity.
St Francis de Sales, *The Love of God*, p. 10.

1741. *Love in Relation to Free Will*
. . . Love determines the will to such an extent as to turn that faculty into something like itself. . . .
For all that, however, it does not follow that the will has no mastery over love. Only by deliberate choice does the will love; it can cling to the one love (out of many before it) which it approves – otherwise love could never be forbidden or commanded.
St Francis de Sales, *ibid.*, p. 11.

1742. *Charity as Mother of All Other Virtues*
St Thomas accounts as follows for this close dependence of the other virtues on charity: 'It is,' he writes, 'the mother, the root, the fountainhead whence the other virtues have their origin; inasmuch as it stamps them all with that divine character which renders them worthy of an everlasting reward.'
Scaramelli, *Directorium Asceticum*, vol. 4, p. 100.

1743. *Love in the Life of the Church*
Love, and love alone, is heritage and heart, motive and mainspring in the life of the Church.
St Francis de Sales, preface to *The Love of God*, p. xxvii.

1744. *Love Must Be Fiery to Set the World on Fire*
. . . St Gregory says: 'He who is not on fire himself, will never set fire to

others. . . . ' That holy Friar, Thomas of Villanova, Archbishop of Valentia, used often to repeat these words: 'How can burning words issue from a cold breast?'

Rodriguez, *Practice of Perfection and Christian Virtues,* vol. 3, p. 55.

1745. *Love as a Dangerous Passion*

One of the things most to be feared is the passion of love. Love is the chiefest and strongest of the passions, and the passion most difficult to withstand. . . . The blessed St Augustine well sets forth the force and violence of this passion and the reason we have to fear it, by two grave examples from Holy Writ. The first of these is that of our father Adam. . . . When God asked Eve: 'Why hast thou done this?' she answered: 'The serpent deceived me.'. . . Adam answered: 'The woman that thou gavest me for a companion gave me that fruit and I ate it' (Gn 3:12-13). . . .

The second example is that of Solomon. . . . He loved with a most passionate love idolatrous women . . . [built temples for idolatrous wives] . . . and King Solomon . . . adored [their idols also].

Rodriguez, *Practice of Perfection and Christian Virtues,* vol. 3, pp. 240-242.

1746. *Danger of Being Loved in Place of God*

Because it is necessary to be loved and feared by men, on account of certain functions in human society, the Adversary of our true happiness keeps urging and spreading: 'Well done, well done,' among his snares for us. The purpose is that, while we greedily gather them in, we may be caught in our carelessness and put our joy far from thy truth and in the fallacies of men; that we may be pleased at being loved and feared, not on account of thee, but in place of thee. In this way the Devil would possess those who have been made like unto him, not for concord in charity, but for companionship in chastisement.

St Augustine, *Confessions,* bk. 10, chap. 36.

1747. *Love for God the One Purpose of Our Existence*

It is for this one only end, that of loving God, that we have been created and put into this world by him.

St Alphonsus Liguori, *The Way of Salvation and of Perfection*, p. 498.

1748. *Love for God the One Road to Salvation*

. . . Love . . . is the universal means of salvation. It is the warp and woof of all creation; without it, nothing can be saved. . . . For this reason our good Jesus, whose Blood paid our ransom, has an infinite longing for us to love him, so that we may be saved forever; he has a longing, too, for our salvation, so that we may love him forever. . . . His love urges him to save us; our salvation urges us to love him.

To provide a more vigorous expression of this desire, he compels our love in wondrous terms: 'Thou shalt love the Lord thy God with thy whole heart and thy whole soul and thy whole mind. This is the greatest of the commandments and the first'. Heaven above, Theotimus, how desperately the Heart of Christ longs for us to love Him. . . . No reflection on the great gulf that separates majesty from misery, God from us, nor any other excuse whatever, should deter us from loving Him. . . . To make it possible for his command to be carried out, God sees to it that no man alive lacks what he needs to practice it.

St Francis de Sales, *The Love of God*, pp. 68-69.

1749. *In What True Love for God Consists*

The ordinary mark of true love is that the love espouses the interests of the beloved. These interests he makes his own. What is an object of desire to the beloved becomes such to the lover. . . . So it is between God and the soul. The soul loves God when it wills what God wills and pursues the objects of that Divine will. God, in regard to his creatures, desires and wills that creature's happiness and the perfection which is a means to that happiness. In this is involved the willing of all that makes for the creature's perfection. . . . Love of God lies in making God's interests and objective the soul's own interests and objective. . . . To act for the sole motive of contenting God by our actions is to act in the spirit of love of God. This love of God is not dependent on feeling or emotion but on the firmness of the act of will and its freedom from a mixture of any other motives but the motive of the fulfillment of God's will.

Edward Leen, *In The Likeness of Christ*, pp. 329-330.

1750. *In What Love of God Consists*

. . . Love consists not in the extent of our happiness, but in the firmness of our determination to try to please God in everything, and to endeavor in all possible ways not to offend him, and to pray him ever to advance the honor and glory of his Son and the growth of the Catholic Church.

St Teresa, *Interior Castle*, in Peers, *Complete Works of St Teresa*, vol. 2, p. 233.

1751. *Love of God Not a Matter of Emotion*

. . . Love of God is not at all a matter of emotions or feelings, rather does it concern the will. Feelings represent merely the satisfaction that we get out of love, and if a strong will is not ready to follow them up, they are worse than useless. So far are they from being characteristic of it, that we can say that the love of God is never more pure than when the soul keeps on blindly serving and seeking him while experiencing no satisfaction whatsoever. The love of God consists in that supreme and sustained act of the will whereby we direct our whole heart and our whole mind to Him alone.

Fr Bruno St James, in Nash, *How To Pray and Other Conferences*, pp. 27-28.

1752. *God Wants Our Love*

God, who has enriched us with spiritual and temporal gifts, does not disdain to ask of us our love. He exhorts and commands us to love Him.... 'It is as if,' says St Thomas, 'He could not be happy without thee.'

St Alphonsus Liguori, *The Way of Salvation and of Perfection*, p. 312.

1753. *God Wants Our Love*

'My delights are to be with the children of men' (Prv 8:31). The paradise of God, so to speak, is the heart of man. Does God love you? Love him. His delights are to be with you; let yours be to be with him, to pass all your life with him, in the delight of whose company you hope to spend a blissful eternity. Accustom yourself to speak with him alone, familiarly, with confidence and love, as to the dearest friend you have, and who loves you best.

St Alphonsus, *ibid.*, p. 395.

1754. *God Seeks Even the Love of Sinners*

Man, by despising God, says St Fulgentius, separated himself from God; but God, through his love for man, came from heaven to seek him. And why did he come? He came in order that man might know how much God loved him, and that thus, out of gratitude at least, he might love him in return.

St Alphonsus Liguori, *Incarnation, Birth and Infancy of Jesus Christ*, p. 302.

1755. *How Greatly Christ Desires Our Love*

... With the same vehemence with which [Christ] loves us, he also desires our return of love, so much so that the least act of love from the most worthless sinner charms him more than all the munificence of the physical universe.

Gabriel, *Ascetical Conferences for Religious*, p. 247.

1756. *Jesus Suffered All Things to Win Our Love*

Jesus could have saved us without suffering; but he chose rather to embrace a life of sorrow and contempt, deprived of every earthly consolation, and a death of bitterness and desolation, only to make us understand the love which he bore us and the desire which he had that we should love him. He passed his whole life in sighing for the hour of his death, which he desired to offer to God to obtain for us eternal salvation. And it was this desire which made him exclaim: 'I have a baptism wherewith I am to be baptized, and how am I straightened until it be accomplished?'

St Alphonsus Liguori, *Incarnation, Birth and Infancy of Jesus Christ*, p. 296.

1757. *Love's Summit Must Be Reached by All*

The summit of . . . love . . . must be reached either here or hereafter. There is no choice finally except heaven or hell. Heaven supposes perfect love of God, which must either be reached in this life, or else, with far more suffering, in the next life through the fires of Purgatory. The easier way is to be sanctified here and now.

Boylan, *This Tremendous Lover*, Preface p. X.

1758. *When Love for God Is Imperfect*

We love God imperfectly when we love him more for our own sake than his; that is, because he makes us happy and insofar as he makes us happy.

This kind of love belongs more to the virtue of hope. It is lawful and good, but is far behind perfect charity in value and effect.

Wallenstein, *Guide to Perfect Christian Living*, p. 172.

1759. *When Love for God Is Perfect*

We love God perfectly when we perseveringly love him above all else because he is so infinitely good and perfect and is our most amiable Father and greatest benefactor.

Three things belong to perfect love:

a) The right mental attitude: we must love God, in that we find complacency in him, are kindly disposed toward him, and prefer him above all creatures.

b) The right motive: we must love God because in himself he is infinitely perfect and so infinitely good to us.

c) The right strength: We must love God more than anything else; i.e., we must be ready to lose everything rather than separate ourselves from him by one mortal sin.

Perfect love has many steps. He who will avoid mortal sin only, but not venial sin, is on a low step. We must strive to grow steadily in perfect love for God and free ourselves even of venial sins and imperfections.

Wallenstein, *ibid.*, pp. 172-173.

1760. *How to Practice Love for Christ*
Above all, to love Jesus Christ with our whole heart it is necessary to deny ourselves, by embracing what is painful to self-love, and by abstaining from what self-love seeks. St Teresa once refused to taste a dish that was brought to her in sickness. The infirmarian entreated her to eat it saying that it was well dressed. The saint replied: 'It is because it is well dressed that I do not wish to taste it.' Hence we ought to abstain from things that are agreeable because they please us.

St Alphonsus Liguori, *The True Spouse of Jesus Christ*, p. 655.

1761. *We Should Rejoice with God in His Happiness*
If we love God more than ourselves, as we are bound to love him, we ought to rejoice more at God's happiness than at our own.

St Alphonsus Liguori, *Great Means of Salvation and of Perfection*, p. 362.

1762. *The Right Kind of Love for God*
We possess the right love for God when we: (a) live in the state of sanctifying grace; (b) love God not only with our heart but in our actions and sacrifices; (c) make acts of love frequently, gladly and perseveringly; (d) practice diligently the other Christian virtues as well, especially love of our neighbor; (e) commit no voluntarily venial sin, at least not habitually.

Genuine love of God does not consist in sweet feelings and emotions but in the exercise of the will. It may have different degrees. It is greatest when we suffer or act not only from pure love of God, but in the way we recognize to be the most perfect. Our most exalted model is the Divine Humanity, Jesus Christ.

Wallenstein, *Guide to Perfect Christian Living*, pp. 2-3.

1763. *Love for God as Virtue, Gift, Fruit and Beatitude*
So charity, after all, is a virtue, a gift, a fruit and a beatitude. *As a virtue*, it makes us obedient to the inspirations which come to us from outside, which God affords us through his commandments, his counsels; in keeping them we practice all the virtues – this renders charity queen of virtues. *As a gift*, charity makes us docile, responsive to inspirations from within, to God's secret commands and counsels; in keeping them we use the gifts of the Holy Spirit – this makes charity queen of gifts. *As a fruit*, charity gives us a liking for, an enjoyment in practicing devotion; we experience this through the twelve fruits of the Holy Spirit – therefore charity is queen of the fruits. As a *beatitude*, charity causes us to count insults, misrepresentations, abuse and discredit of this world as supreme favors, signal honors; it inspires us to refrain from making a display of anything but the Cross of

Christ – this leads us to make our display by self-abasement self-renouncement, self-obliteration. No badge of royalty we seek but the thorns which crowned the Crucified, the reed that was his sceptre, the cloak of mockery in which he was arrayed, and the Cross that was his throne. Never did Solomon on his throne of ivory know such satisfaction, joy, glory and bliss as God's lovers on the throne of Calvary.

St Francis de Sales, *The Love of God*, pp. 514-515.

1764. *Love for God Produced in Us Only by the Holy Spirit*
Divine love . . . is a wonder-child; no human will can give it life, only the Holy Ghost can pour it into our hearts; and supernatural as it is, it must take first place, reign over all the emotions – even over intellect and will.

Of course, there are other supernatural movements in the soul – fear, piety, fortitude and hope . . . but the love of God is master, heir and superior . . . it is the reason why heaven is promised to man.

St Francis de Sales, *ibid.,* p. 15.

1765. *Love for God Is God's Gift to Us*
Man's love for God owes its origin, growth and perfection to God's eternal love for man. . . . Everything we have is God's gift to us – above all, the supernatural blessings of charity. If they are ours by gift, why boast about them?

St Francis de Sales, *ibid.,* p. 163.

1766. *Conditions for Loving God with One's Whole Heart*
To love God with our whole heart implies two things: the first is to drive from it every affection that is not for God, or not according to the will of God. 'If I knew,' said St Francis de Sales, 'that I had one fiber in my heart which did not belong to God, I would instantly tear it out.' The second is prayer, by which holy love introduces itself into the heart.

St Alphonsus Liguori, *The Way of Salvation and of Perfection*, p. 292.

1767. *Love for God Is Impossible Without God's Help*
. . . The good will by which we love God cannot exist in man unless God works in him so to will. This, then, is good will, that is, a will faithfully subjected to God, a will inflamed by the holiness of divine ardor, a will which loves God and its neighbor for God's sake.

St Augustine in *The Fathers of the Church*, vol. 16, p. 259.

1768. *Means for Acquiring Love for God*
The first means to love Jesus Christ is mental prayer. Mental prayer is that blessed furnace in which the soul is inflamed with divine love. . . .

The second means is Holy Communion. . . .
The third means is mortification. . . .
The fourth means is retirement.
St Alphonsus Liguori, *The True Spouse of Jesus Christ*, pp. 28-30.

1769. *Means for Preserving Love for God*
Acts of love, says St Teresa, are the fuel with which the fire of divine love is kept burning in our hearts.
St Alphonsus Liguori, *Great Means of Salvation and of Perfection*, p. 361.

1770. *Love for God, the Greatest Grace That God Gives Us*
[In answer to a comment made by Brother Giles,] St Bonaventure answered: 'If our Lord gave no other grace to a man but that of being able to love Him, that would be enough for him to do God greater services than all other graces put together.' Brother Giles said: 'Can an unlettered man love our Lord Jesus as much as a doctor?' 'One little simple old woman,' said St Bonaventure, 'can love our Lord more than any master of theology.'
Rodriguez, *Practice of Perfection and Christian Virtues*, vol. 1, p. 322.

1771. *Love Is the Best Service We Can Offer to God*
God himself esteems our love of him the best form of our service to him. . . .
God does not attach value to the task that is done without charity. The things done can be excellent in themselves; they may even promote the cause of God; they may be useful to mankind. But if these activities do not have their inspiration in a regard for God, the divine purpose is frustrated as regards the supernatural development of those who act in this loveless manner.
James Leen, *By Jacob's Well*, p. 37.

1772. *Love for God, the Best Motive for Action*
God regards the heart rather than the gift. Thus, one with fewer works may please God better than another with more if he does it with greater love. . . . [We see this literally laid down in the matter of the two mites which that widow in the Gospel offered.]
Rodriguez, *Practice of Perfection and Christian Virtues*, vol. 1, p. 166.

1773. *Love for God Because He Reserves Himself for Us*
It is a true and chaste love which loves [God], not because he gives us some earthly good, but because he reserves himself for us.
St Caesarius of Arles, in *The Fathers of the Church*, vol. 47, p. 271.

1774. *Love Must Be shown in Action*
The true measure of charity is not to feel much, but to do and suffer much for God. . . . [In the words of St Gregory,] 'The love of God cannot stand idle: if it be real, it does great things, if it refuse to work, it is not true love.'. . . [In the words of St Augustine:] 'To him that loves, labor is not burdensome but pleasant. . . . Labors undertaken in love are either not labors, or are labors loved.'
Scaramelli, *Directorium Asceticum*, vol. 4, pp. 143-144.

1775. *Love Increased by Good Intentions*
Charity is maintained and its intensity increased above all by the renewal of the intention in view of which we act. . . .

Is it necessary that this intention of acting for love of God, that is to say, to procure his glory by doing his will, should be always actual? No, that is not required nor even possible, but experience and the science of the saints have shown how well founded and helpful is the practice of frequently renewing our intention so as to advance, to progress in the love of God and the divine life. Why is this? Because purity of intention keeps our soul in the presence of God and urges us on to seek him alone in all things; it prevents our curiosity, levity, vanity, self-love, pride and ambition from insinuating and diffusing themselves into our actions so as to diminish their merit. A pure intention, frequently renewed, surrenders the soul to God in its being and its activity; it unceasingly reanimates and maintains in the soul the fire of Divine Love, and thus by each good work it causes to be done and referred to God, it increases the life of the soul.
Marmion, *Growth in Christ*, pp. 147-148.

1776. *What Perfect Love Achieves in Us*
Perfect love wipes away all mortal sins, no matter how grave or numerous they may be, and the eternal punishment due them as well.
Wallenstein, *Guide to Perfect Christian Living*, p. 173.

1777. *Effectiveness of Great Charity*
A little good done with great charity is much more valuable in the eyes of God, than a great achievement carried through with less love.
Edward Leen, *The True Vine and Its Branches*, p. 105.

1778. *Love for God Enables Us to Know Him*
In human sciences, knowledge excites love; but in the science of the saints, love produces knowledge. He that loves God most knows him best. Besides, it is not lofty and fruitless conceptions, but works that unite the

soul to God and make it rich in merits before the Lord.
St Alphonsus Liguori, *The True Spouse of Jesus Christ*, p. 12.

1779. *Love for God Brings All Other Virtues*
The grace of divine love is that grace, says St Francis de Sales, which contains in itself every grace, because the virtue of charity toward God is humble, chaste, obedient, mortified, and, in fine, possesses all virtue. St Augustine says: 'Love God, and do what thou wilt'; yes, because he who loves God will endeavor to avoid everything that is displeasing to him, and will seek solely to please Him in all things.
St Alphonsus Liguori, *Preparation for Death*, p. 6.

1780. *Best Remedy Against Temptations*
As the love of God contains in itself every perfection of every virtue and more excellently than the virtues themselves, so also is it the sovereign antidote against vice of every kind. By accustoming your mind to turn to this remedy, you do not need to consider and examine the kind of temptation by which it has been disturbed. At the bare perception of trouble, this great remedy will set your mind at rest. Moreover, this is so terrifying to the evil spirit that as soon as he sees that his temptations urge us on to God's love he ceases to tempt us.
St Francis de Sales, *Introduction to the Devout Life*, p. 205.

1781. *Love for God is Operative*
Love is, above all things, operative. Supernatural love shows itself in an enthusiastic and affectionate submission to the holy will of God in all things. It proves itself in a brave acceptance of the cross as coming from the kind hands of our Heavenly Father.
Edward Leen, *The True Vine and Its Branches*, p. 100.

1782. *Effects of Love for God*
'If I would become a friend of Caesar,' said a certain courtier, as St Augustine relates, 'I should have great difficulty in becoming such; but if I would become the friend of God, I am already his friend.'. . .

An act of contrition and of love makes us friends of God. St Peter of Alcantara said: 'No tongue can express the greatness of the love of Jesus for a soul in the state of his grace.'
St Alphonsus Liguori, *The Way of Salvation and of Perfection*, p. 167.

1783. *Love as a Guide and as Meriting a Reward*
. . . Augustine says: 'Love and do what you wish!'. . . That command 'to love' in relation to activities offers pleasurable acceptance of 'reward.'

Thus he grants to activity a measure of repayment. In proportion as we love in this life, we will be given shares in the glory of heaven. Where there is more love, there will be a closer approach to God. The greatness of our future reward depends not on exterior actions but on interior love. This is why martyrdom, which is of the greatest reward of all the actions which a person performs, is said to be an activity of greater love. A man can have no greater love than to lay down his life for his friends.

St Bonaventure, *Rooted in Faith*, p. 47.

1784. *The Greatest Commandment: Four Conditions Needed*
[Asked by masters of the law concerning the greatest commandment, Jesus said:] 'Thou shalt love the Lord thy God with thy whole heart, and with thy whole soul, and with all thy mind. . . . '

But to fulfill this commandment four conditions are required: First of all, to remember the divine benefits. We have nothing, body, soul, goods, which we do not have from God. . . .

Secondly, we must consider the sovereign greatness of God: He is 'greater than our heart' (1 Jn 3:20). . . . The third condition is the renouncement of worldly attachments: It is a great injury done to God to equate anything with him. . . .

Finally, it will be a question of avoiding every kind of sin. . . . 'You cannot serve God and Mammon' (Mt 6:24).

Mennessier, *Pattern for a Christian, According to St Thomas Aquinas*, pp. 195-196.

1785. *Love Embraces All Commandments*
Since all the Sacred Writings are filled with commandments of the Lord, why does he say of charity, as if it were some singular commandment: 'This is my commandment, that you love one another'? if not for the reason that every commandment is a commandment solely of love and that all of them are one single precept; because, whatever is commanded, is based solely on love. For as the many branches of a tree derive from one root, so the multitude of virtues derive from one charity. And a branch of good work has no freshness unless it remain rooted in charity.

The commandments of the Lord, therefore, are many, and one: many in the diversity of their works, one in their root of love.

St Gregory the Great, in Toal, vol. 4, pp. 170-171.

1786. *Obeying Commandments for Love of God Is a Sign of Grace*
Suppose you have an opportunity of making such and such profit, but it is dishonest to do so; or an opportunity occurs for you to indulge yourself in some pleasure, but that pleasure is unlawful; the duties of your state

trouble you, or the labors of your employment wear you; and for the sake of your God you do not care to make that profit, you renounce that pleasure, do your duty, and continue your work, – then you have the holy love for God, your love is fire which operates; otherwise you have it not. . . .

St Alphonsus Liguori, *The Way of Salvation and of Perfection*, pp. 493-494.

1787. *Love for God Vs. Self-Love*

. . . When we want God's love to live and reign in us, we deaden self-love. If we cannot suppress self-love altogether, we at least weaken it; still alive it may be, but it has ceased to reign. Similarly, we can do the opposite. We can forego charity and cling to creature loves – the despicable adultery with which the heavenly bridegroom so frequently upbraids sinners.

St Francis de Sales, *The Love of God*, pp. 11-12.

1788. *Love for God Must Be Single-Hearted*

'Woe to them that are of a double heart' (Ecclus 2:14). 'Woe,' says St Augustine in his comments on these words, 'to them who divide their heart, giving it partly to God and partly to the devil.'. . . 'God is angry because in the affections of a double heart He is associated with the devil: He departs and the devil possesses the whole.'

St Alphonsus Liguori, *The True Spouse of Jesus Christ*, p. 64.

1789. *How to Obtain Love for God*

[The foremost means to obtain divine love is] to desire it earnestly and to ask for it without ceasing. . . . A second means is to subdue, by continual mortification, the enemy of divine love, which is self-love. . . . Now, by self-love I do not mean that reasonable and well-regulated affection whereby we love ourselves, our kinsfolk, and neighbors, for the Apostle says the express contrary; but I mean that inordinate love which makes us seek our own convenience, our own satisfaction, our own honor and interest, without any regard for God and right reason (Eph 5:29). This kind of self-love is the sworn foe of charity, which it banishes from our hearts. Hence it must be kept under by unwearying mortification. St Augustine [says that] the 'two loves establish within us two hostile cities. Self-love erects a city of clay, which comes at length to openly set God at defiance; the love of God founds a heavenly city, which reaches even to the contempt of self. The former gives glory to itself, the latter glorifies God . . . so that it is impossible that the soul can harbor at the same time tendencies so opposite to each other.'

Scaramelli, *Directorium Asceticum*, vol. 4, pp. 104-105.

1790. *Love for God Vs. Self-Love*
St Augustine says that the love of God increases in proportion as self-love is diminished; and that the destruction of the latter is the perfection of the former. 'The diminution of cupidity,' says the holy Doctor, 'is the nutriment of charity; but its total absence is the perfection of charity.'
St Alphonsus Liguori, *The True Spouse of Jesus Christ*, p. 72.

1791. *Divine Love Needed in a Priest*
Peter de Blois says that a priest without divine love 'may be called a priest but is not a priest. . . . From the day of his ordination, a priest is no longer his own, but belongs to God.' St Ambrose says that 'a true minister of the altar is in the world for God and not for himself.'
St Alphonsus Liguori, *Dignity and Duties of the Priest*, p. 384.

1792. *Love for God is Torture for the Devil*
. . . Chaff would endure fire better than the devil the flame of charity. So does the constancy of love overcome all things.
St John Chrysostom, quoted in Toal, vol. 4, p. 25.

1793. *Love of Aspiration for God*
He that loves always remembers his beloved. Thus the soul that loves God thinks of him, and always endeavors to show him its affection by ardent signs and ejaculations of love. This is called 'the love of aspiration'.
St Alphonsus Liguori, *The True Spouse of Jesus Christ*, p. 661.

1794. *Love of Benevolence Toward Jesus Christ*
He that loves desires to see his beloved loved by all: such love is called the love of 'benevolence', which you should practice by desiring to see Jesus Christ ardently loved by all men. Hence you would do well to speak frequently to others of his love in order to kindle it in the hearts of all those with whom you converse.
St Alphonsus, *ibid.*, pp. 658-659.

1795. *Love of Benevolence in the Life of St Augustine*
[Writing about the love of benevolence toward God practiced by St Augustine, St Francis de Sales says that Augustine often spoke to God as follows:] 'I am Augustine, Lord, and you are God. Yet were the impossible possible, that I were God and you Augustine, I should want to change places with you so that You could be God.'
St Francis de Sales, *The Love of God*, pp. 196-197.

1796. *Love of Complacency*
He that loves, in the first place, rejoices at the welfare and the happiness of his beloved; this is called love of 'complacency'. Rejoice then . . . in the infinite felicity of your God, and delight in it more than if it were your own. . . . Hence you ought to feel consolation in knowing that so many millions of angels and saints love him perfectly in heaven.
St Alphonsus Liguori, *The True Spouse of Jesus Christ*, p. 658.

1797. *Love Is Compliant with God's Inspirations*
The sun's rays give both light and warmth together. Inspiration is a ray of grace bringing light and warmth to our hearts; light to show us what is good; warmth to give us energy to go after it. All living things in this world are numbed by winter's cold; with the return of spring's warmth they come to life again – animals move more swiftly, birds fly higher with livelier song, plants gaily bud and blossom. Without inspiration, the life of the soul is sluggish, impotent, useless. Once the rays of God's inspiration strike it, however, we are aware of light and life . . . our minds are enlightened, ed, our wills inflamed and quickened with strength to intend and fulfill whatever may lead to our salvation. . . .

The ways God has of inspiring us are past all counting. . . . Saint Mary of Egypt was inspired by seeing a picture of Our Lady; St Anthony by hearing the Gospel read at Mass; St Augustine by listening to the life of St Anthony; the Duke of Gandia by the sight of the empress's corpse; St Pachomius by noticing an act of charity; the saintly Ignatius of Loyola by reading the lives of the saints.

Blessed are those whose hearts are ever open to God's inspiration; they will never lack what they need to live good, holy lives, or to perform properly the duties of their state.

The first inspiration God ever sends to a man is that of obedience. Was there ever a finer, more unmistakable inspiration than St Paul's: 'Rise up, and go into the city; there thou shalt be told what thy work is'. He was to obey Ananias, the well-known bishop of Damascus (according to St Dorotheus). A man who claims to be inspired, but refuses to obey his superiors or to follow their advice is an imposter.

. . . The three finest, surest proofs of the genuine character of inspirations are: perseverance in contrast to fickleness, peace of soul in contrast to impulsive anxiety; humble obedience in contrast to stubborn wilfulness.
St Francis de Sales, *The Love of God*, pp. 340-341, 343, 350-351.

1798. *Love of God's Will in Misfortune*
[St John Climacus says:] 'If you thank God for good things, you pay a

debt; if you thank him for evil things, you make him your debtor.'

Quoted by St Alphonsus Liguori, in *Incarnation, Birth and Infancy of Jesus Christ*, p. 107.

1799. *Conformity to the Will of God*

'It is fairer,' says St Augustine, 'that we should follow God's will than that He should follow ours.'

Quoted by Rodriguez, in *Practice of Perfection and Christian Virtues*, vol. 1, p. 548.

1800. *Conformity to the Will of God*

This entire resignation and conformity to the will of God is the greatest and most acceptable and agreeable sacrifice that a man can offer of himself to God. In other sacrifices he offers of his goods, but in this he offers himself. In other sacrifices and mortifications he mortifies himself in part – as in temperance or modesty, in silence or in patience, he offers a part of himself to God; but this is a holocaust in which man offers himself entirely and wholly to God to do all that he wills and when he wills without exception of anything or reservations of anything for himself.

Rodriguez, *ibid.,* vol. 1, p. 477.

1801. *Conformity with God's Will Makes a Man a Saint*

A single act of perfect conformity to the divine will is sufficient to make one a saint. . . . Yes, for he who gives his will to God gives him everything: he who gives him his goods in alms, his blood by disciplines, his food by fasting, gives God a part of what he possesses; but he who gives him his will gives Him the whole; so that he can say to him: Lord, I am poor, but I give thee all that is in my power; in giving thee my will, there remains nothing for me to give thee. But this is precisely all that God claims for us: 'My son, give Me thy heart' (Prv 23:26). My son, says the Lord to each of us, – My son, give me thy heart; that is to say, thy will.

St Alphonsus Liguori, *The Way of Salvation and of Perfection*, pp. 356-357.

1802. *For Our Conformity with Christ, God Loves Us More*

The more we are conformed to his Son, the more the Father loves us because we are more closely connected with him. . . . When he sees a soul fully transformed in his Son, he surrounds it with his special protection, the most tender care of his Providence; he showers his blessings upon it, he places no limit to the communication of his graces; that is the secret of God's extraordinary gifts.

Marmion, *Christ, the Life of the Soul*, p. 43.

1803. *Submission to God's Permissive Will*
Beyond compare is St Paul: his disinterestedness surpasses the heroic. I am hemmed in on both sides, he tells the Philippians. 'I long to have done with this life, and be with Christ, a better thing, much more than a better thing; and yet, for your sakes, that I should wait in the body is more urgent still'. That great Bishop, St Martin, followed the Apostle's example. At the close of his life he longed to go home to God . . . yet he [exclaimed:] 'Nevertheless, Lord, if I am still needed here for the salvation of souls, it is not for me to lay down the burden; Thy will be done.'
St Francis de Sales, *The Love of God*, p. 365.

1804. *God Wills that We Suffer with Patience*
[Souls that really love God] know that everything that happens in the world is either ordered or permitted by God; consequently, in all that comes to pass they humbly bow their head and live contented with what God assigns. And although it be frequently the case that he does not will that those who persecute and injure us should do so, yet he nevertheless wills for wise reasons that we should suffer patiently the persecution or injury by which we are afflicted.
St Alphonsus Liguori, *The Way of Salvation and of Perfection*, pp. 323-324.

1805. *Love for God*
All good consists in loving God. And loving God consists in doing his will.
St Alphonsus Liguori, *Great Means of Salvation and of Perfection*, p. 358.

1806. *Love of Conformity Gives Value to Our Simplest Actions*
Everything we do derives its value from our conformity to the will of God. Hence, even eating, if done because such is the will of God, is more meritorious than death would be without that intention.
St Francis de Sales, in *Spiritual Diary*, p. 183.

1807. *The Most Perfect Act*
The most perfect act of love which a soul can perform toward God is that of St Paul, when, on his conversion, he said: 'Lord, what wilt Thou have me to do? Lord, tell me what thou dost desire of me, for I am ready to do it.' This act is worth more than a thousand fasts and a thousand disciplines.
St Alphonsus Liguori, *The Way of Salvation and of Perfection*, p. 324.

1808. *Love of Conformity – in Union with the Divine Permissive Will*
Sin excepted, nothing happens but by God's will – by a positive or per-

missive will, which no one can obstruct, which is known only by its results. These events, when they occur, show that God has willed and planned them.

Trials are the chief source of union between the human will and God's permissive will. There is nothing attractive about trials in themselves; only when seen as coming from Providence, enjoined by God's will, are they infinitely lovable. On the ground Moses's staff was a frightful serpent; in his hand it was a miraculous wand. Trials, in themselves, are dreadful; seen as part of God's will, they are attractive, delightful.

To love suffering and distress out of love for God is charity's highest degree. There is nothing, then, to attract us but God's will; it goes very much against the grain of our nature; it leads to more than giving up pleasure – we actually choose toil and trouble. . . .

St Francis de Sales, *The Love of God*, pp. 357. 359-360.

1809. *Love of Conformity According to God's Will and Commandments*

'If you love Me, says the Redeemer, keep My commandments. . . . He that has My commandments and keeps them, he it is that loves Me' (Jn 14:15). . . . St Gregory says well: 'Let each one enter into himself, and prove whether he loves God in very deed. Yet he should not believe his heart, whatever be its answer, unless that answer is authenticated by the witness of his works. Let him, therefore, examine how his tongue speaks, what are the thoughts in his mind, how he keeps in check the affections of his heart, whether or not his life is in conformity with the Savior's teaching. These alone are the unexceptional witnesses to his love.'

Scaramelli, *Practice of Perfection and Christian Virtues*, vol. 4, pp. 150-151.

1810. *Conformity with God's Will More Valuable than Desire to Suffer for Him*

The masters of the spiritual life teach that, though the desire which certain souls have of suffering to give him pleasure is acceptable to him, he is yet more pleased with the conformity of those who wish for neither joy nor pain, but in perfect resignation to his holy will, have no other desire than to fulfill whatever that will may be.

St Alphonsus Liguori, *The Way of Salvation and of Perfection*, p. 369.

1811. *The Sum and Substance of Perfection*

If, then, we would give full satisfaction to the heart of God, we must bring our own will in everything into conformity with his; and not only into confirmity, but into uniformity, too, as regards all that God ordains. Conformity signifies the conjoining of our own will to the will of God; but uniformity, signifies, further, our making of the divine will and our own will one will only, so that we desire nothing but what God desires, and His sole will become ours. This is the sum and substance of that perfection to which we ought to be ever aspiring; this is what must be the aim of all our works, and of all our desires, meditations and prayers.

St Alphonsus, *ibid.*, pp. 357-358.

1812. *The Essence of Love for God*

The love of God consists above all in conformity to his holy will, especially in regard to things that are mostly contrary to self-love, such as sickness, poverty, contempt, persecutions, spiritual aridities. We should be persuaded that all that comes from God is useful to us, since all that he does, he does for our own good; for there is no one that loves us more than God. If we wish to sanctify ourselves, let us say in all that happens to us; May thy will be done.

St Alphonsus Liguori, *Dignity and Duties of the Priest*, p. 441.

1813. *Love of Conformity with God's Will*

This is the great object of all those who love God, to conform themselves at all times to his divine will. And this is what Jesus taught us to pray for, that we may be able to fulfill the will of God here upon earth with as much perfection as the blessed do in heaven. 'Thy will be done on earth as it is in heaven. . . . '

Ah, how effectually does one perfect act of conformity to the will of God change the sinner into a saint, as it happened to St Paul, who by only saying to God, 'Lord, what wilt Thou have me to do?' from a persecutor of the Church was changed into an apostle and vessel of election.

St Alphonsus Liguori, *The Way of Salvation and of Perfection*, p. 168.

1814. *How to Achieve Love of Conformity with Christ*

St Paul exhorts his disciples, saying: 'Put ye on the Lord Jesus Christ; and make not provision for the flesh in its concupiscences.'

This putting on of Christ is a work that cannot be accomplished in a day. Before the iron can be wrought to the required design, it must be made malleable in the fire. So, too, the soul of fallen man must be submitted to a long process before it can receive, under the action of the Holy Spirit, the form of Jesus. It must, in the fire of effort and suffering, lose the hard resistance of its inveterate egoism.

Edward Leen, *The True Vine and Its Branches*, p. 20.

1815. *God's Right to Our Submission*

. . . He that builds a house, fashions a statue, or paints a picture, is the master of his own work; and so too the person who buys them is the master of his purchase. Now it is precisely on these two titles that God's claim to an absolute dominion over ourselves and our acts, especially over those of our will – the principal and most noble – is based. His almighty hands have made us, and he has bought us at the price of his own Blood.

Scaramelli, *Directorium Asceticum*, vol. 4, p. 161.

1816. *Example of a Beggar*

Blosius relates that a poor beggar man of very perfect life, being asked by a theologian how he had attained to perfection, answered in this manner. 'I have determined to give myself over to God's will alone, to which I have so conformed my own that whatever God wills, I will also. When hunger exhausts me, when cold pinches me, I praise God. Be the weather fair, or foul and stormy, I likewise praise God. Whatever lot he gives me or permits to come upon me – be it prosperous or unfortunate; be it sweet or bitter and disagreeable – I receive it at his hand with great alacrity as a very good thing, resigning myself to it in all humility. Never have I been able to find repose in anything that was not God; and now I have found unto myself God, in whom I enjoy repose and peace everlasting.'

Rodriguez, *Practice of Perfection and Christian Virtues*, vol. 1, p. 499.

1817. *Love of Conformity According to St Thérèse*

[Mother Agnes of Jesus (Pauline Martin) asked her sister, St Thérèse:] 'Would you rather die than live?'

'Oh, little Mother,' [St Thérèse answered] 'I tell you again I do not prefer one thing more than another. That which God loves best and chooses for me, that is the thing which pleases me most!'

St Thérèse of Lisieux, *Novissima Verba*, p. 122.

1818. *Love of Contrition Directed to God*

A man who loves God and takes delight in the infinite perfections wherewith he is endowed . . . cannot but feel greatly grieved and pierced to the heart with sorrow at the thought that whims and caprices have many a time been preferred to God. . . . St Thomas, speaking of interior repentance of heart which is none other than the sorrowing love which we are now considering, says that it should cease only with life, because one who loves should ever grieve at having offended the object of his love. . . . St Augustine is of a like opinion, saying that 'We should always do penance as long as we abide in this mortal flesh.' . . . He moreover adds, that if one had never defiled his conscience with mortal sin, still he should daily do penance on account of the dust of venial faults, which is ever accumulating on the soul that lives in this wretched exile. And his reason is that although these slight faults do not inflict a fatal wound on the soul (as in the case of grievous sin), yet, taken together, they form an eruption and a leprosy that mar the beauty of the soul, and debar it from the chaste and delightful embraces of the heavenly Bridegroom unless they be healed by the remedy of daily penance.'

Scaramelli, *Directorium Asceticum*, vol. 4, pp. 136-137.

1819. *Love of Friendship with God*

Charity, in a word, is the unselfish love of friendship, by which we love God for his own sake because his goodness is supremely lovable. It is a true friendship, for it is mutual: God has loved from all eternity anyone who has loved, is loving, or will love him in time. There is also mutual knowledge and expression of that love: God is not unaware of our love for him, since it is his gift to us; nor can we be unaware of his love for us, since he has proclaimed it so widely; we also recognize that all the good things we possess are due to his benevolence. Finally, we are in constant communication with him; he is ever talking to us by his inspirations and impulses of grace; he never fails to do good to us, to give every indication of his love for us. . . . As for ourselves, we can call on Him at all times in prayer, at our pleasure: for 'it is in him that we live, and move and have our being.'

This love 'can have no source in nature, human or angelic; 'it is poured out in our hearts by the Holy Spirit.'

St Francis de Sales, *The Love of God*, p. 108.

1820. *Love of Preference for God*

He that loves prefers his beloved to all other objects, and this is the love of *preference*, with which God principally wishes us to love him. The first degree of this love consists in being prepared to lose all things rather than forfeit the grace of God.

St Alphonsus Liguori, *The True Spouse of Jesus Christ*, pp. 658-659.

1821. *Love of Preference for God Practiced by St Thomas More*

[The wife of St Thomas More visiting him in prison asked:] 'How long then, Thomas, will you bear to behold your wife and children reduced to this wretched plight, deprived of their income, which the king has confiscated, rendered homeless by the law's award, without bread, without shelter? . . . Children, plead your cause; fall at the feet of your father; ask whether he would have you rich or poor. Your lot is in your own hands.'

On hearing these words, Thomas felt himself moved to the very depths of his heart, for he had a tender, and not a flinty heart; and then turning to his wife, whose name was Alice, he replied: 'If, to gratify my king, I should displease my God, for how long, think you, should we enjoy the honors of our country, the wealth of our establishment, the favor of our king?' She answered, that the time of life to which they had both attained would justify them in looking forward to at least twenty years more.

'Twenty years more!' replied he in astonishment. 'Must I, then, for the sake of this brief span, offend my God, lose his friendship, forego the never-ending bliss promised me above if faithful to my duty? You are mad, my good wife, to press so unfair a bargain upon me.'

Scaramelli, *Directorium Asceticum*, vol. 4, pp. 123-124.

1822. *Love of Neighbor Based on God's Will*

'This commandment we have from God, that he who loveth God loves also his brother' (1 Jn 4:21). Hence St Thomas teaches . . . that the love of God and the love of our neighbor proceed alike from charity; for charity makes us love God and our neighbor, because such is the will of God.

St Alphonsus Liguori, *The True Spouse of Jesus Christ*, p. 346.

1823. *Love of God, Self, and Neighbor*

. . . If a man loves his neighbor, then he will also love God: for it is from one and the same love that we love God and our neighbor; God, however, for his own sake, ourselves and our neighbor, for God's sake.

St Augustine, quoted in Toal, vol. 4, p. 157.

1824. *Love of God and Neighbor*

'By this shall men know that you are my disciples, if you have love for one another' (Jn 13:35). Further, he establishes so close a connection between the two great commandments that benefit conferred upon the neighbor is transferred to himself: 'For I was hungry', he says, 'and you gave me to eat,' and so on, adding: 'As long as you did it for one of these my least brethren you did it to me' (Mt 25:40).

It is, accordingly, possible to keep the second commandment by observing the first, and by means of the second we are led back to the first.

He who loves the Lord, loves his neighbor in consequence. 'If anyone love me,' said the Lord, 'he will keep my commandments' (Jn 14:23). And again, he says: 'This is my commandment, that you love one another as I have loved you' (Jn 15:12). On the other hand, he who loves his neighbor fulfills the love he owes to God, for he accepts this favor as shown to Himself.

St Basil, in *The Fathers of the Church*, vol. 9, p. 240.

1825. *Love for God, Self and Neighbor*

The Lord himself has told us in the Gospel and clearly showed us in what order we have true love and charity. For he spoke thus: 'thou shalt love the Lord thy God with thy whole heart, and with thy whole soul and with thy whole strength; and thy neighbor as thyself' (Lk 10:27). Therefore, first love God and then yourself; after these love your neighbor as yourself. First learn how to love yourself, and then love your neighbor as yourself; for if you do not know how to love yourself, how will you be able to love your neighbor in truth?

St Caesarius of Arles, quoting St Augustine, in *The Fathers of the Church*, vol. 47, pp. 431-432.

1826. *Love of Neighbor Takes Its Rise in Love for God*

Charity is that love of our neighbor which takes its rise in the love of God, as by means of this virtue we love our neighbor, not for his own sake, nor for his natural excellence, but solely with reference to God. 'Let no one,' says St Gregory, 'who loves another jump to the conclusion that he has charity; for if he love not his neighbor for the sake of God, he may imagine himself possessed of charity, while in reality he is without it.'... St Bernard, in like manner, dealing with this subject, says that for love of neighbor to be perfect, that is supernatural, it must spring from the love of God; in other words, we must love our neighbor in God. But this we cannot do unless we first love God, and then love our neighbor for the love of God.

Scaramelli, *Directorium Asceticum*, vol. 4, p. 196.

1827. *Measure of God's and Mary's Charity Toward Us*

Love of God and love of neighbor are commanded by God in the same precept: 'And this commandment we have from Him, that he who loves God loves his brother' also (1 Jn 4:21). St Thomas says that the reason for this is that the person who loves God loves all that God loves.

St Bonaventure says: 'Mary so loved the world as to give her only-begotten Son....'

St Gregory Nazianzen assures us that there is no better way to make Mary love us than by practicing charity toward our neighbor.

We may take it for granted that our charity toward our neighbor will be the measure by which God and Mary will show charity towards us: 'Give and it shall be given to you. For with what measure you measure it shall be measured to you.'

St Alphonsus Liguori, *The Glories of Mary*, vol. 2, pp. 158-159.

1828. *Love of Neighbor and Love for God*

St Catherine of Genoa once said to the Lord: 'My God, thou dost command me to love my neighbor; and I can love nothing but thee.' 'My child,' answered Jesus, 'he that loves me loves whatever I love.'... Why do we love our neighbor? It is because God loves him. Hence St John says that 'if any man say I love God and hateth his brother, he is a liar. . . .' St Catherine of Genoa used to say that our love of God is to be measured by our love for our neighbor.

St Alphonsus Liguori, *The True Spouse of Jesus Christ*, pp. 346-347.

1829. *Love of God and Neighbor Are Inseparable*
We cannot love God without loving our neighbor and we cannot love our neighbor with a love of charity without loving God at the same time, since God is our reason for loving our neighbor.

Rodriguez, *Practice of Perfection and Christian Virtues*, vol. 1, p. 201.

1830. *Love for God and for Neighbor*
Be as God to the unfortunate, by imitating the mercy of God.

For in nothing do we draw so close to God as in doing good to man.

St Gregory Nazianzen, in Toal, vol. 4, p. 56.

1831. *Love for God and Neighbor*
Love for God finds its motive in God's goodness, and its affections terminate in God alone. Love of our neighbor proceeds from the same motive, but its acts terminate in our neighbor. The perfection of the Christian is in the combination of both the one and the other, but it consists, primarily, in the love of God, and, secondarily in the love of our neighbor.

Scaramelli, *Directorium Asceticum*, vol. 4, p. 90.

1832. *Happy Those Who Love God, Friends, Enemies*
'Happy is he who loves thee' (Tb 13:18), 'and his friend in thee, and his enemy because of thee' (Mt 5:44).

St Augustine, *Confessions*, bk. 4, chap. 9.

1833. *Love of Neighbor Must Come Through Love for God*
The only right love for our neighbor is that which is extended to him through love for God. If a man incorporated in Christ practices the supernatural love of God and of his neighbor, the process of divinization goes on apace.

Edward Leen, *The True Vine and Its Branches*, p. 174.

1834. *Love for God Does Not Forbid Proper Love of Others*
It is most important to aim at loving only God and severing every tie of which the Divine Master is not the beginning and the end. Our lord, who has created our human hearts, does not discountenance the natural affec-

tions of those hearts; on the contrary, He concentrates and blesses all. It is only when they become disorderly and usurp the place of God in our souls that they are displeasing to him. The soul desirous of making progress must aim then, not at destroying its natural affections, but rather at purifying them. It must make its object be to love only according to God, and in the manner in which he approves.

Edward Leen, *Progress Through Mental Prayer*, p. 204.

1835. *Love for God Benefits Humanity*

A man has charity, that is, he loves God, when he pursues the interests of God with the same eagerness as the self-lover, that is the egoist, pursues his own. One cannot love God with any intensity without being driven by that love to make God's purposes on earth to be realized. God is charity, his purpose is to achieve the welfare, the peace and happiness of mankind. . . . The truly interior soul is always energetic with the energy of God. The saints are always 'doers!' Efficiency stamps their work. They have been the great benefactors of mankind. Enduring works of charity mark their passage on earth. They, too, pass doing good (see Acts 10:38). Without seeking success in the sense of making it a motive of action, none have been so successful as they. Charity is essentially energetic. The love of God necessarily expresses itself in devotedness to one's fellowman.

Edward Leen, *In the Likeness of Christ*, pp. 340-341.

1836. *Love for God and Man Brings All Virtues*

The man who has charity . . . possesses a single perfection which embodies the virtue of every perfection, the perfection of every virtue. With the result that charity is patient, is kind; charity feels no envy, for it is good-natured; charity is never perverse, for it is prudent, or proud, for it is humble; charity is never insolent or ambitious, for it is friendly, courteous; charity does not claim its rights, for it is unselfish, gracious; charity cannot be provoked, for it is placid; charity does not brood over an injury, for it is magnanimous; charity takes no pleasure in wrongdoing, but rejoices at the victory of truth, revels in truth; to the last charity sustains, believes readily all the good it hears, without stubbornness, discussion, distrust; to the last, charity hopes for good in those around, never despairing of their salvation; to the last charity endures, patiently awaiting the fulfillment of promises.

Charity, to sum up, is that gold, proved in the fire, which our Lord counseled the Bishop of Laodicea to come and buy, it is the value of all things, which it can and does provide.

St Francis de Sales, *The Love of God*, p. 480.

1837. *Love for God and Love for Neighbor*
. . . The Lord asks only two things of us: love for his Majesty and love for our neighbor. It is for these two virtues that we must strive, and if we attain them perfectly, we are doing his will and so shall be united with him. But, as I have said, how far we are from doing those two things in the way we ought for a God who is so great! May his Majesty be pleased to give us grace, so that we may deserve to reach this state, as it is in our power to do if we wish.

The surest sign that we are keeping these two commandments is, I think, that we should really be loving our neighbor; for we cannot be sure if we are loving God, although we may have good reasons for believing that we are, but we can know quite well if we are loving our neighbor. And be certain that the farther advanced you are in this, the greater love you will have for God; for so dearly does his Majesty love us that he will reward our love for our neighbor by increasing the love which we bear to himself, and that in a thousand ways: this I cannot doubt. . . . Our nature being so evil, I do not believe we could ever attain perfect love for our neighbor unless it had its roots in the love of God.

St Teresa, *The Interior Castle,* in Peers edition, pp. 261-262.

1838. *Sign that God Gives Us His Friendship*
'Would you know,' says St Augustine, 'if you are living the life of grace, if God is giving you his friendship, if you are numbered among Christ's disciples, if you are living in his spirit? Question yourselves; see if you love men, your brethren, all men; if you love them for God, you will have the answer. And this answer does not deceive' (in Epistol. Joan. Tract. VI, c. 3).

Quoted in Marmion, *Christ, the Life of the Soul*, p. 355.

1839. *Love of Neighbor as Love for Christ*
St Augustine writes: 'Do not regret . . . that you were not born in the happy age when Christ was dwelling on earth, clad in our mortal flesh; complain not that you have been debarred from seeing Him with your eyes, from receiving him into your house, from waiting upon him in your abode, and from conversing familiarly with him; for he has not deprived you of the dignity and honor of rendering him all the services and love you desire by doing to your neighbor whatever you would have wished to do to Him.'

Scaramelli, *Directorium Asceticum*, vol. 4, p. 201.

1840. *Love for Christ and for Neighbor*
. . . What of the man who puts his human loves above the love of Christ? . . . He will not be saved at all because he has no way to become one with

the Savior, who has told us so clearly in this connection: 'He who loves father or mother more than me is not worthy of me; and he who loves son or daughter more than me is not worthy of me'.

On the other hand, there is the man who loves his human relations with the fullest human affection, yet who keeps the first place in his heart for Christ, the man who would choose to give up all his friends rather than lose Christ, if he were faced with such a hard choice in some great crisis. This man will be saved through fire, because it burns like fire to lose one's friends. . . .

Finally there is the love of the man who has loved his father and his mother, his sons and daughters as Christ would have them loved, loving them in a way that leads them to the kingdom of Christ's faith and love, or loving them because they are already one with Christ, members of his Body. Love like this has Christ for its foundation and builds no superstructure of perishable wood and hay and straw; it builds with lasting silver, gold and precious stones. For how can one love more than Christ those who are loved on account of Christ?

St Augustine, *City of God*, bk. 21, chap. 26.

1841. *Motive Is the Criterion*

No one should think that he observes this law [of charity] because he loves his neighbor. For he who loves others, but not for God's sake, has not charity, even though he may think he has. True charity lies in loving our friend with and in God, and our enemy for God's sake. He loves for God's sake who loves even those by whom he is not loved.

St Gregory the Great, *Parables of the Gospel*, pp. 44-45.

1842. *Love of Christ in Neighbor*

I am sure that many souls will here find the reason of the difficulties, the sadness, the want of expansion in their inner life; they do not give themselves enough to Christ in the person of his members; they hold themselves back too much. If they would but give, it would be given to them and given abundantly; for Jesus Christ will not let himself be outdone in love; if they would overcome their selfishness, and give themselves generously to their neighbor for God's sake, Christ would give himself to them in His fullness. . . .

Marmion, *Christ, the Life of the Soul*, p. 360.

1843. *Even Little Acts Bring Increase of Love*

. . . In a soul possessing charity, not only extraordinary actions, but little tasks also, feel the effects of charity's influence; and their fragrance draws down from God an increase of charity. From God, I say, because charity does not increase itself like a tree, putting forth branches. Faith, hope and charity are virtues which the goodness of God brings to birth in our hearts; so also is he the source of their increase and perfection.

St Francis de Sales, *The Love of God*, p. 115.

1844. *The New Commandment*

'A new commandment I give unto you, that you love one another as I have loved you' (Jn 13:34). Christ's commandment of love is new by reason of the principle: It is enjoined by the founder of the New Covenant and is to be fulfilled not by natural means but with the help of grace, merited for us by Christ's passion and death.

It is new by reason of the motives: We are to love our neighbors as sons of God, as our brothers, as members of the Mystical Body. Christ promised that whatever we do for our neighbor will be accepted as done for him personally and will be rewarded by him accordingly on the Day of Judgment.

It is new by reason of Christ's example, who not only loved us 'as Himself' and procured for us the necessary graces but bestowed upon us superabundant merits, even more, gave us the gift of himself.

It is new by reason of its extension, since we are bound to love not only our friends, relatives, countrymen, and benefactors, but also strangers, heretics and enemies.

It is new by reason of the effects because the observance of this commandment makes new men of us, like unto God, and disciples of Christ. It spurred countless Christians to heroic endeavors and inspired charitable institutions and enterprises such as were wholly unknown in pre-Christian times.

Bandas, *The Catholic Layman and Holiness*, pp. 238-239.

1845. *Love of Neighbor as Christ Loved Us*

'We must love our neighbor even as Jesus Christ loved us' (see Jn 13:34). And how did Christ love us? He loved us without our having any claim to his love. He loved us when we were sinners and his enemies. He loves us without any self-interest, for God has no need of our love or our goods. He loved us, in a sense, more than himself, for he gave his life, his Blood, his All – for us. Hence we too must love our neighbor even when he has no claim to our love and even when we have no inclination to love him. We must love him without any self-interest. And we must be ready when the salvation of our neighbor demands it, to sacrifice everything, even life itself, for him. 'In this we have known the charity of God because he hath laid down his life for us, and we ought to lay down our lives for our breth-

ren' (1 Jn 3:16).
Bandas, *ibid.*, pp. 239-240.

1846. *St Paul's Teaching on Charity*
[St Paul says:] 'Charity is patient, is kind; charity does not envy, is not pretentious, is not puffed up, is not ambitious, is not self-seeking, is not provoked; thinks no evil; does not rejoice over wickedness but rejoices with the truth; bears all things, believes all things, hopes all things, endures all things' (1 Cor 13:4-7). This text shows how charity should enter into every contact with our fellowman. It must take from our relations with him all that is harsh. Patience makes us tolerant of characteristics, the *kindness* of our charity should make our relations with him gracious. Charity should go further than that. It should take all bitterness of thought and action out of our mutual relations. Hence the Apostle says charity is neither *envious* nor *pretentious*. Charity demands that we conquer superiority complexes. Hence St Paul tells us that charity is *not puffed up*. It is not *ambitious* or *self-seeking*. Charity allows no intolerance, *thinks no evil.* It does *not rejoice over wickedness* and is, therefore, not elated when it discovers evil in another. It consistently takes the stand that God alone has the right to judge. Hence it *bears all things, hopes all things, endures all things.*
Hoeger, *The Convent Mirror*, pp. 80-81.

1847. *Love of Neighbor – Three Degrees*
There are three degrees of [fraternal] charity. The first degree consists in ministering to the bodily wants of our brethren by clothing the naked, feeding the hungry, tending the sick, and the like. Our Lord promises to consider as done to himself everything of this nature that we do for others. The second degree of charity consists in bestowing upon our neighbor such spiritual benefits as do not exceed the capability of human nature. Among such benefits, we may mention the instruction of the ignorant. . . . The third degree of charity consists in enriching our neighbor with such spiritual benefits as are supernatural and exceed human reason. Such benefits are instruction in divine truth, direction to God and the spiritual communication of the sacraments.
Mennessier, *Pattern for a Christian*, p. 221.

1848. *Love of Neighbor Must be Supernatural*
This love of charity must be supernatural. We do not satisfy our Lord's commandment by a natural love. It must be supernatural in its principle and in its nature. We must love our neighbor for God and according to God.
Boylan, *This Tremendous Lover*, p. 198.

1849. *Love of God and Neighbor*
. . . We cannot love God unless we love our neighbor; nor love our neighbor without loving God.

St Gregory the Great, in Toal, vol. 3, p. 56.

1850. *The True Disciple of Christ*
Christ said: 'By this shall all men know that you are my disciples, if you have love for one another' (Jn 13:34-45). He says not: 'If you do signs and miracles in the same way,' but 'if you have love for one another.'

Abbott Nesteros, quoted by Cassian, in *The Nicene and Post-Nicene Fathers*, vol. 11, p. 448.

1851. *Love of Neighbor Rooted in a Living Faith*
A living faith alone will enable us to regard our fellowmen as dear children of our heavenly Father, as beloved brothers of our adorable Savior, as members of the very family of God. Left to ourselves, we are inclined to notice only the shortcomings of poor human nature, and to lose sight of the sanctifying grace which lies hidden under these flaws like a diamond embedded in a lump of clay.

Gabriel, *Ascetical Conferences for Religious*, p. 32.

1852. *Love for God Demands Zeal for Souls*
'If,' says St Gregory, 'you go to God, take care not to come alone to him.' . . . And St Augustine says: 'If you love God, draw all to the love of God.' . . . If you love God, you should take care not to be alone in loving him, but should labor to bring to his love all your relatives, and all those with whom you have intercourse, particularly your sisters in religion.

St Alphonsus Liguori, *The True Spouse of Jesus Christ*, p. 370.

1853. *Love for Self a Standard*
. . . What does the Lord say through the Scriptures? 'Thou shalt love thy neighbor as thyself' (Mt 22:39). Therefore if you do not love yourself, how do you love your neighbor? You have taken the measure of love for your neighbor from yourself.

St Caesarius of Arles, in *The Fathers of the Church*, vol. 47, p. 306.

1854. *Kindness*
'Kindness,' says Fr Faber, 'is the overflow of self on others. To be kind is to put others in one's place. Kindness has convinced more sinners than zeal, eloquence, or learning, and these three things have never converted anybody without kindness having something to do with it. In a word, kindness makes us as gods towards one another. It is the manifestation of

this feeling in apostolic men which draws sinners to them and brings them thus to their conversion' (Spiritual Conferences).

And he adds: 'Without doubt the fear of the Lord is frequently the beginning of that wisdom which we call conversion: but we must frighten men kindly, for otherwise fear will only make infidels.'

Chautard, *The Soul of the Apostle*, p. 128.

1855. *Love and Courtesy*
Courtesy is a sister of charity. It extinguishes hatred and keeps love alive.
St Francis of Assisi, quoted in *The Little Flowers of St Francis*, p. 126.

1856. *The Cheerfulness of St Thérèse*
[We read in the *summarium* of her Cause that she said on one occasion:] I am always gay and content even when I suffer. It is told of certain saints that even in recreation they were grave and austere. They attract me less than does Theophane Venard, who was gay everywhere and at all times'. [Indeed, her extraordinary charity had rendered her so bright and cheerful that when she was not at recreation, the nuns expressed their disappointment:] 'There will be no laughing today – Soeur Thérèse is not here.'
St Thérèse of Lisieux, in *Autobiography and Letters*, p. 326.

1857. *Love Nourished by Compassion*
. . . Nothing so nourishes love as to be compassionate toward others.
St John Chrysostom, in Toal, vol. 3, p. 311.

1858. *Little Acts Give Pleasure to Jesus*
. . . When I *feel nothing*, when I am incapable of praying or practicing virtue, then is the moment to look for small occasions, *nothings*, that give Jesus more pleasure than the empire of the world, more even than martyrdom generously suffered. For example, a smile, a friendly word, when I would much prefer to say nothing at all or look bored, etc.
Collected Letters of St Thérèse of Lisieus, p. 193.

1859. *Love of Neighbor by Good Will and Prayer*
Let each one keep a good will and love for all men as himself. Moreover, he should want others to be treated as he himself wishes to be treated by them. He should pray for the good, that they may be protected by the lord; for the mediocre, that they may become better; for the wicked, that they may quickly be corrected. In all sinners, he should hate their vices rather than the men themselves, and, like good doctors, hate the disease but not the sick person.
St Caesarius of Arles, in *The Fathers of the Church*, vol. 31, p. 119.

1860. *How to Test our Progress*
One test by which we may ascertain whether we are advancing in the love of our neighbor is our willingness to excuse his faults. Even on the Cross, Jesus prayed for his bitter enemies and cruel persecutors. There was apparently nothing lovable in them; they did not seem to be deserving of anything but execration. Yet the love of Our Savior found an excuse for them in their imperfect realization of the heinousness of their crime: 'Father, forgive them, for they know not what they do.'
Gabriel, *Ascetical Conferences for Religious*, p. 76.

1861. *Seeing Good in our Neighbor*
We have to train ourselves to see the good in others. Take it from me – and this is based on years of experience – people are always better than they appear; they seem worse than they really are. There are some hypocrites who seem better, but they are few. Especially, religious are better than they appear. It is the evil in us that shows. If a person gives way to a fit of bad temper, everyone sees it, but no one sees the number of times that that person has conquered temper. One failure perhaps for twenty successes. A priest knows that there will be twenty to fifty successes for one defeat. We see only the defeat and we mark it: 'That's temper!'
Edward Leen, *Retreat Notes for Religious*, p. 131.

1862. *Love of Neighbor in Thought*
Should you see your neighbor commit a sin, see that you think not only of his sin, but that you also think of what he does, and has done well, and doing this, you will often find that he is better than you are.
St Basil, in Toal, vol. 4, p. 140.

1863. *A Maxim of St Teresa*
Listen to ill of no one and speak ill of no one save of yourself; when you begin to like doing this, you are making progress.
Complete Works of St Teresa, vol. 3, p. 257.

1864. *Liking One's Neighbor Is Not Obligatory*
Let it be noted here that charity does not compel us to *like* people, but to *love* them. And love is an act of the will wishing one well.
Boylan, *This Tremendous Lover*, p. 62.

1865. *Loving Neighbor Vs. Liking Him*
We should note that though we are bound to *love* all, we are not bound to like anyone. It is true our likes and dislikes can be offenses against charity, insofar as they are wilful and inordinate; but there are many natural causes

which produce sympathy or an antipathy for which we are not responsible. What we are responsible for is to see that these natural likes and dislikes do not interfere with the discharge of the obligations that justice and charity impose upon us in regard to our neighbor.

Boylan, *ibid.*, p. 197.

1866. *Union in Charity*

. . . Plato comes to say that there is nothing in a commonwealth more pernicious than discord and disunion, nor anything more useful and profitable than peace and mutual union. St Jerome says this of religious life, and says it more forcefully. It is this unity and charity, he says, that makes religious to be religious; without it, a monastery is a hell and its inmates, devils.

Rodriguez, *Practice of Perfection and Christian Virtues*, vol. 1, p. 192-193.

1867. *Love of Neighbor in Religious Community*

Happy the religious house in which all are united in holy charity; but miserable is the monastery in which disunion and party spirit prevail. 'Yes,' says St Jerome, 'such a monastery is not the tabernacle of the Lord, but the abode of Lucifer; it is a house, not of salvation, but of perdition.'

St Alphonsus Liguori, *The True Spouse of Jesus Christ*, p. 349.

1868. *The Test of True Charity*

. . . Let no one, when he loves someone, think to himself that he now begins to possess charity, until he has first examined the motives of his love. For if one loves another, but does not love him for God's sake, he has not charity, but thinks he has. But when we love our friend in God, and our enemy because of God, this is true charity. He loves for God's sake who loves those whom he knows do not love him. Charity is proved true solely by means of its opposite, hate. And so because of this the Lord himself says to us: 'Love your enemies. Do good to them that hate you' (Lk 6:27).

St Gregory the Great, in Toal, vol. 4, p. 233.

1869. *Love for Enemies*

[St Gregory of Nyssa asks:] 'What is the conduct of the man whose heart is kindly and lovingly disposed toward his enemies? It is like unto God; for in forgiving his enemies and doing good to those that persecute him, he does that which belongs peculiarly to God himself.'. . . . 'Wherefore,' observes St Augustine, 'It is in our power to make ourselves like unto God; for by loving our enemies we shall be raised, not only to the honor of being friends of the Almighty, but to the still more eminent dignity of being his true sons; according to the assurance of Christ, that by loving them who hate us, we become the children of our Father, who is in heaven.'

Scaramelli, *Directorium Asceticum*, vol. 4, p. 211.

1870. *Love for Enemies*

. . . Love your enemy: for so you are doing good, not to him, but to yourself. How is this? Doing this you become like to God.

St John Chrysostom, in Toal, vol. 3, p. 243.

1871. *Love Your Enemies*

. . . Dearly beloved, let us love our enemies. . . . Your enemy may be converted to repentance in such a way that he merits to be your fellow citizen in that heavenly Jerusalem; in fact, he might even become greater than you. . . . At first the Apostle Paul was a wicked enemy of the Christians. . . . At one word of the Lord he became a preacher instead of a persecutor. He surpassed those whom he hated, for not all the Christians he persecuted were such as he became.

St Caesarius of Arles, in *The Fathers of the Church*, vol. 31, p. 191.

1872. *Loving Enemies Possible with God's Help*

. . . You have enemies. Indeed, who could live on this earth without having them? See to it that you love them. In no way can a raging enemy injure you as much as you injure yourself unless you love your enemy. He can damage your farm or your flock, he can injure your household – your manservant or maidservant, your son or your wife, or at most, he can injure your body if he has been given the power. But – unlike you – can he injure the soul?. . .

You will not even try to love your enemy if you think it is impossible, and then pray that the will of God be done in you. If your enemy had no wickedness, he would not be an enemy. But how profitable his wickedness can be for you! Wish him well: let him put an end to his evils and he will no longer be your enemy. It is not the man's nature that is your enemy; it is his vice.

St Augustine, in *The Fathers of the Church*, vol. 11, p. 252.

1873. *Correct Enemies and Be Their Friends in Heaven*

Anyone whose virtues are from the Spirit of God will be so in love with righteousness as to love his very enemies, and he will so love those who hate him or slander him that he will want to correct them and have them for his friends in heaven.

St Augustine, *City of God*, bk. 5, chap. 19.

1874. *Who Practices Love of Neighbor?*

They practice the love of neighbor who love their neighbor as they love themselves, for the love of God. . . . 'For the love of God' means: because God has commanded it, and because all men stand in such close relationship with God.

Anyone who loves his neighbor only for his natural superiorities of body, mind and character, does not practice Christian charity.

Anyone who loves him from self-interest, or from lower sensuality actually commits sin.

'As thyself,' that is: according to the saying: Do unto others as you would have others do unto you. If we don't want something done to us, we should not do it to others: what we want others to do to us, we should do to them.

Wallenstein, *Guide to Perfect Christian Living*, p. 175.

1875. *Uncharitableness to Neighbor Is Injury to Christ*

Let us remember that every word we utter or every insinuation we make to the detriment of our neighbor is an injury done to Christ. There are occasions when one must speak unpleasant truths about one's neighbor – for example, in a law court, or to avoid greater evil – but, normally we are not allowed to speak evil of him, even when what we say is true. The Christian man does his best to hide the faults of others and will not listen to detraction.

Boylan, *The Tremendous Lover*, p. 199.

1876. *Suspicions and Judgments*

St Augustine advises us: 'If you wish to maintain yourself in love and charity with your brethren, before all things it is necessary to be greatly on your guard against judgments and suspicions, which are the poison of charity'.

Rodriguez, *Practice of Perfection and Christian Virtues,* vol. 1, p. 243.

1877. *Fraternal Charity Needed*

. . . With the Father on high, he that is not in charity with the brethren, will not be reckoned in the number of His sons.

St Leo the Great, in *The Nicene and Post–Nicene Fathers,* vol. 12, p. 162.

1878. *Love of Neighbor – Penalty for Lack of It*
If you, as man, deny humanity to man, God will deny you divinity. . . .
St Augustine, in Toal, vol. 2, p. 278.

1879. *Feeding the Poor More Meritiorious than Feeding Christ*
[St John Chrysostom says that] to tend and feed Christ in his poor is a far nobler and more meritorious act than to tend and feed Christ in person; for were our Lord to appear to you, his very presence would sweetly compel you to do such acts of service. What heart so strong as to be able to withstand the ravishing aspect of our most loving Redeemer? While, on the other hand, when you assist and feed Jesus Christ in the persons of the needy, you do it with a more effectual love, and with greater purity of intention, since you serve the wretched for the sake of Christ, but without the consolation of the sweet attractions of love. You serve our Lord with greater faith when you serve him in the person of a poor man; for the very reason that you see him not with the eyes of the body. . . . Greater honor is shown to a prince by doing homage and service to one of his menials for his sake, than if homage were done to him in person.
Scaramelli, *Directorium Asceticum*, vol. 4, pp. 232-233.

1880. *Charity Toward the Poor Makes Us Comrades of Christ*
. . . He who ministers zealously to the poor man becomes a comrade of Christ – not only if he is rich and shares great possessions, but even if he offers to the needy the little that he has, although it is merely a cup of cold water which he gives a disciple to drink in the name of a disciple (Mt 10:42). The neediness of the disciple, which to the worldling is poverty, is a source of true riches to you, O man of wealth, for you become thereby a co-worker with Christ.
St Basil, in *The Fathers of the Church*, vol. 9, p. 512.

1881. *Love of Neighbor*
St John Chrysostom, commenting on these words of Proverbs: 'He that hath mercy on the poor lendeth to the Lord' (Prv 19:17), says: 'Whoever helps the needy makes God his debtor.'
St Alphonsus Liguori, *The Glories of Mary*, vol. 2, p. 160.

1882. *The Value of Love of Neighbor*
. . . St John Chrysostom says that the practice of charity is a powerful means of obtaining great graces from God. 'Alms,' says the saint 'is the most lucrative of arts.'. . . Saint Mary Magdalene de Pazzi used to say that she felt more happy during the time she assisted her neighbor than when she was rapt in contemplation. 'Because,' says the saint, 'when I am rapt

in contemplation, God assists me; but when I relieve a neighbor, I assist God.'

St Alphonsus Liguori, *The True Spouse of Jesus Christ*, pp. 367-368.

1883. *Service to the Poor*

Don't be satisfied merely with being poor like the poor, but be poorer than the poor themselves. How may this be brought about? The servant is less than the master; therefore make yourself a servant of the poor. Go and wait on them when they are sick in bed, wait on them, I say, with your own hands. Prepare their food for them yourself and at your own expense. Be their seamstress and laundress. Philothea, such service is more glorious than that of a king.

St Francis de Sales, *Introduction to the Devout Life*, p. 135.

1884. *God Will Reward the Giver of Alms*

. . . That part of [a man's] material possessions with which he ministers to the needy is transformed into eternal riches, and such wealth is begotten of this bountifulness as can never be diminished or in any way destroyed, for 'Blessed are the merciful, for God shall have mercy on them', and he himself shall be their chief reward who is the Model of his own command.

St Leo the Great, in *The Nicene and Post-Nicene Fathers*, vol. 12, p. 124.

1885. *Christ Appears as a Leper*

Pope Gregory the Great quotes the deacon, Epiphanius, then present in the audience, as telling the story of a pious monk named Martyrius, who saw a helpless leper by the roadside. Martyrius spread his own cloak on the ground, laid the leper on it and then carried him to the monastery. Arrived there, the leper leaped down from the shoulder of Martyrius and was immediately recognized as Christ in Person. Before returning to heaven, He said: 'Martyrius, you were not ashamed of me on earth; I shall not be ashamed of you in heaven.

St Gregory the Great, in Toal, vol. 3, p. 354.

1886. *Charity of Nun Wins Communist Back to the Faith*

A nun was asked by a priest to nurse a sick mother in her home. The family was poor and the father a rabid Communist. He had taught his children to ridicule the notion of God and when the nun came he encouraged them to laugh at her religious garb, and to poke fun at her when she knelt down to pray. Over the bed where the sick woman lay there hung a picture of Lenin, and the house was plentifully stocked with Communist literature. Before the nun left, the man had, with his own hands, torn down the picture of Lenin; of his own accord he had given up his supply of literature, sent his children to a Catholic school and himself received the sacraments. How did all this happy change come about? Through the sincere, disinterested love for the poor, which he saw in that nun. . . . This . . . is a true account of an incident from the life of a nun who works for the poor in Catholic Dublin.

Nash, *The Nun at Her Prie-Dieu*, pp. 66-67.

1887. *Love of Neighbor Could Make the Church Indispensable*

An eminent but unbelieving statesman once said to us: 'If the Church could find a way to impress more deeply on the hearts of men the testament of her Founder: "Love one another", she would become the one great power *indispensable* to all nations'. Might we not also apply this same thought to several other virtues?

Chautard, *The Soul of the Apostolate*, pp. 164-165.

1888. *Fraternal Correction an Act of Perfect Charity*

. . . If we rely on the word of the Angelic Doctor St Thomas Aquinas, [fraternal correction] is an act of such perfect charity, that it is to be preferred to relief of the poor in his bodily needs, and to the care given to the sick in their bodily ailments. . . . St Augustine, most certainly, will not be the person to deny this, since he teaches that by omitting such correction we become worse than the delinquents, and that our silence is more blameworthy than their sin. The saint grounds his opinion in the strict command laid down upon us by our Savior himself.

Scaramelli, *Directorium Asceticum*, vol. 4, p. 246.

1889. *Fraternal Correction a Serious Duty*

St Augustine says that he who sees a brother destroying his soul, by giving way to anger against a neighbor, or by insulting him, and neglects to correct him, sins more grievously by his silence than the other by his insults and contumely. 'You', says that saint, 'see him perish, and care not; your silence is more criminal than his reproachful language.' Do not excuse yourself by saying that you know not how to correct him. St John Chrysostom tells you that for correcting the faults of others charity is more necessary than wisdom.

St Alphonsus, *The True Spouse of Jesus Christ*, pp. 368-369.

1890. *Necessity of Fraternal Correction*

If anyone passing by saw an animal of yours endangered by an attack of wolves and kept silence without offering any defense, I think you would blame him and say he is not your friend. However, we very frequently see the sheep of our Lord struck by the poison of envy, suffocated in the slough of dissipation, or immersed in the sewer of drunkenness, or guilty of any of the other crimes. Now, how will we stand in the Lord's sight if we do not shout or stop them, if we do not to the best of our ability strive to recall them from the pit of perdition and the abyss of vices by rebuke, punishment if necessary, or censure?

St Caesarius of Arles, in *The Fathers of the Church*, vol. 31, p. 15.

1891. *Evil Must Be Condemned Under Certain Circumstances*

To speak rightly against another's vices, it must be for the profit of either the person spoken about or the person spoken to. Someone talks in the presence of young girls of the imprudent and manifestly dangerous familiarities of such and such persons, or about dissolute conduct of such and such a man or woman, either with words or gestures that are clearly lascivious. If I do not boldly condemn such evil or even wish to excuse it, the tender minds that hear all this will take occasion to yield to similar things. For their good I must boldly rebuke such liberties on the spot, unless I can postpone this duty to a later date when it can be done better with less disadvantage to the persons spoken of.

St Francis de Sales, *Introduction to the Devout Life*, p. 167.

1892. *Fraternal Correction for His Sake*

'If thy brother offend thee, rebuke him between thee and him alone'. And why do you rebuke him? Is it because you suffer through his injury against you? Far from it. If you do this from self-love, you do nothing. If you do it out of love for him, then you have done well. See in the words themselves, for love of whom you should do it: for love of him or love of yourself? 'If he shall hear thee, he says, 'thou shalt gain thy brother'. Therefore, do it for his sake: to gain him. Doing it, you gain him who would have been lost had you not done it. Why is it then that many men take little notice of these sins and say of them: '‘What great harm have I been doing? I only sinned against a man'? Do not take these sins lightly. You have sinned against a man. Do you know that in sinning against a man you are lost? If he against whom you have offended rebuked you, between him and you alone, and you listen to him, 'he has gained you'. And what does this mean, 'he has gained you,' if not that you were lost had he not gained you? For unless you were lost, how could he have gained you? Let no man therefore regard as a small thing to sin against a brother.

St Augustine, in Toal, vol. 3, p. 96.

1893. *Fraternal Correction – in Secret or in Public*

What sayest thou, O Lord? 'If thy brother shall offend against thee, go, and rebuke him between thee and him alone.' What sayest thou, O Apostle? 'Them that sin reprove before all; that the rest also may have fear.'

When it is not known that he sinned against you, seek for a secret place when you correct him who sinned against you. For if you alone know he has offended you, and you wish to reprove him before all, you are not his corrector, but his betrayer. . . .

And so those faults should be corrected before all, which have been committed before all; and those must be corrected in secret which were committed in secret. Choose the times, and the Scripture will then be in agreement.

St Augustine, *ibid.,* pp. 98-100.

1894. *When and How to Administer Fraternal Correction*

Fraternal correction is an act of charity, an act of love. This means that it will be used always with prudence. It will be used only when, where, and how it ought to be done. Fraternal correction will be used only when it is necessary to lead the sinner to repentance. It will be used with discretion. If a private word of warning is sufficient, that is all that is required. A public denunciation of the sinner is allowable only when his sins are harmful to the community or to other men and when no other means will reform him. And in all cases charity demands that the correction be administered with and through love. This means that we may correct our superiors only with respect and reverence, and our equals and inferiors with kindness and mercy. Above all, correction is never allowable unless the facts are clear and certain.

Farrell and Healy, *My Way of Life,* p. 357.

1895. *How and How Not to Correct*

. . . As St Ambrose teaches: 'A loving admonition is usually of greater avail than an angry rebuke . . . because the former moves to humble shame, while the latter provokes indignation.'

Scaramelli, *Directorium Asceticum*, vol. 4, p. 250.

1896. *How and How Not to Correct*

. . . Just as medicine, dispensed in fitting doses and in due time, works recovery, so, if it is to be administered without measure and out of season, it causes death. In like manner, correction duly and seasonably given communicates life to the soul; while, if fitting time and manner be not observed, it causes death. How many have been rescued from their ruin by a timely warning, but what numbers has an indiscreet reproof hardened in

their headlong course?
Scaramelli, *ibid.*, p. 249.

1897. *Fraternal Correction – St Thérèse*
My whole strength lies in prayer and sacrifice: These are my invincible weapons, and experience has taught me that the heart is won by them rather than by words.
St Thérèse of Lisieux, *Autobiography and Letters*, p. 179.

1898. *Fraternal Correction Urged by Philosopher Galen*
. . . Galen, who not content with writing maxims for the cure of bodies, has also written a book on how to know and cure the ailments of the soul. There this philosopher says: Anyone who wishes to amend his faults and make progress in virtue should seek out a good and prudent man to warn him of them; and if he finds a proper person for that purpose, he should call him aside and ask him very earnestly to do him the favor of admonishing him of all the faults that he observes in him, offering and promising to be very grateful for it and to take him as a true friend; telling him that hereby he will do him a greater favor and benefit than if he cured him of some ailment of the body, inasmuch as the soul is more than the body.
Rodriguez, *Practice of Perfection and Christian Virtues*, vol. 3, p. 482.

1899. *Fear of Undertaking Fraternal Correction Is Reprehensible*
What is reprehensible . . . is that, while leading good lives themselves, and abhorring those of wicked men, some fearing to offend, shut their eyes to evil deeds instead of condemning them and pointing out their malice. To be sure, the motive behind their tolerance is that they may suffer no hurt in the possession of those temporal goods which virtuous and blameless men may lawfully enjoy; still, there is more self-seeking here than becomes men who are mere sojourners in this world and who profess the hope of a home in heaven.
St Augustine, *City of God*, bk. 1, chap. 9.

1900. *Those Who Refuse the Duty of Fraternal Correction are Hirelings*
[When the hireling] sees a man perishing in sin, sees the wolf close upon him, sees him held fast by the throat, dragged to torment, he does not tell him: 'You are committing sins'; he does not correct him for fear he may lose his own advantages. This then is 'when he sees the wolf coming and flieth'; when he does not tell him: 'You are acting wickedly.' This is flight, not of the body, but of the soul; he, though standing there in body, flies in his soul; since he sees a sinner and does not say to him: 'You are com-

mitting sin'; since he is even aiding and abetting him.
St Augustine, in Toal, vol. 2, p. 305.

CARDINAL VIRTUES

1901. *No Virtue Without Prudence*
How important prudence is for acquiring Christian perfection may be deduced from the fact that, without this virtue, there cannot be any virtue at all; because prudence must necessarily cooperate with and assist all other virtues in their proper acts. . . . Hence, [as St Thomas remarks,] we may say that prudence is the full complement and perfection of all the virtues and, so to speak, a light that imparts to each of them its own peculiar luster and beauty. . . .
Scaramelli, *Directorium Asceticum*, vol. 3, p. 19.

1902. *A Ship without a Pilot*
St Basil says truly that a man devoid of prudence is like a ship without a pilot; because as a ship without a pilot cannot sail direct for the wished-for port, but is driven hither and thither by the fury of the winds, and is borne helplessly along to be at length dashed against the rocks, so too a soul devoid of prudence knows not how to keep to the middle courses . . . but is carried by indiscretion now to one extreme, now to another, and is at length dashed against the rock of some vice. . . . There is no action so good as not to become vicious when performed imprudently, that is at an improper time or without moderation.
Scaramelli, *ibid.*, pp. 20-21.

1903. *Prudence Regulates All the Virtues*
Speaking of discretion, otherwise called prudence, St Bernard says: 'This virtue regulates all the virtues; it imparts to them moderation, brightness and stability. Prudence is not so much a single virtue as a director and guide of all the virtues; it regulates the affections and is the master of habits. Deprive a man of prudence and all his virtues will forthwith become so many vices' (in Gant. Serm. 49).
Scaramelli, *ibid.*, p. 23.

1904. *What the Virtue of Prudence Does in Us*
The infused virtue of prudence disposes us to refer all our judgments, decisions, and actions to our ultimate supernatural end – the beatific vision of God. It helps us to judge everything from the viewpoint of eternal salvation. It tries in each instance to answer such questions as the follow-

ing: 'What does this matter for eternity?' 'Is anything that is not eternal of any account?' 'What does it profit a man if he gain the whole world and suffer the loss of his own soul?' Prudence trains the mind to think before acting, to consult God's thinking, to take counsel with those who represent him. It makes us ask the question: 'What would Christ have done in my place?'

Bandas, *The Catholic Layman and Holiness*, p. 243.

1905. *How to Learn to Judge Justly*
Be just and equitable in all your actions, Philothea. Always put yourself in your neighbor's place and him in yours, and then you will judge rightly. Imagine yourself the seller when you buy, and the buyer when you sell, and you will sell and buy justly.

St Francis de Sales, *Introduction to the Devout Life*, p. 177.

1906. *Fortitude Represses Fear, Controls Daring*
Fortitude represses excessive fear, but it also controls blind daring. St Thomas Aquinas says: 'It is a greater act of fortitude to hold out under danger than to be unreasonably aggressive in danger.'

Hoeger, *The Convent Mirror*, p. 121.

1907. *St Basil Defies the Prefect*
'... In other respects, Prefect,' (said Basil), 'we are reasonable and more submissive than anyone else, for so our law prescribes. We do not show ourselves supercilious to such high authority or even to any ordinary person. But when God's interests are endangered or at stake, we count the rest as nothing, and look to these alone. Fire and sword and wild beasts and tongs that tear the flesh are a source of delight to us rather than of terror. Therefore, go on with your insults and threats, do whatever you will, make the most of your authority. Let the Emperor hear this also, that you will never prevail on us or persuade us to make a covenant with impiety, even though you utter threats still more violent.'

Quoted by St Gregory Nazianzen, in *The Fathers of the Church*, vol. 22, pp. 67-69.

1908. *Facing Life Takes More Courage than Does Suicide*
Those who put an end to themselves may possibly impress people with their courage, but are not to be commended for sound judgment.... There is more courage in a man who faces rather than flees from the storms of life, and who holds cheap the opinions of men, especially that of the rabble. For what is public opinion but a cloud of error compared with the

light and purity of one's conscience.

St Augustine, *City of God*, bk. 1, chap. 22.

1909. *Courage and Resoluteness in Serving God*

Resolve, then, resolve! says St Teresa. . . . 'The devil is afraid of resolute souls.' St Bernard teaches that many souls are lost through want of fortitude. Take courage, then, and trust in the power and goodness of God; strong resolutions overcome difficulties.

St Alphonsus Liguori, *The True Spouse of Jesus Christ*, p. 76.

1910. *Fortitude's First Degree*

The first degree of fortitude is to mortify every passion, to keep under all our vices. . . . [Cicero says that] to conquer one's self, to control our anger (which Hercules did not do) belongs only to a man of eminent fortitude. . . . St Ambrose teaches the same doctrine. 'And in every deed,' he writes, 'think that alone is fortitude whereby a man overcomes himself, checks anger, yields not to the seductions of any pleasure, is not troubled by adversity, or puffed up by prosperity; whereby he does not allow himself to be tossed about by the ever-changing winds of human vicissitudes.'

Scaramelli, *Directorium Asceticum*, vol. 3, pp. 75-77.

1911. *Second and Third Degrees of Fortitude*

The [second] degree of fortitude is to risk our life for the spiritual or temporal welfare of our neighbors.

The third degree of fortitude is to expose ourselves courageously to martyrdom. If that person be brave who shrinks not from the danger of death, braver far is he who quails not at its presence but goes forward fearlessly to meet it, especially for the sublime end of witnessing to his fidelity to Christ and the holy faith of Christ. . . .

Bishop Fisher, Cardinal of the Holy Roman Church . . . coming in sight of the stern countenance of the executioner and of the glitter of his axe, far from moaning or complaining or flinching, was filled with a heavenly joy, and intoning with a loud voice the hymn of thanksgiving and triumph, the *Te Deum*, he showed thereby that he had attained the term of all his desires.

Scaramelli, *Directorium Asceticum*, vol. 3, pp. 78-80.

1912. *The Fourth Degree of Fortitude*

The fourth degree of fortitude is to bear patiently with serious evils in unlooked-for vicissitudes; for, as Aristotle says, he is truly a brave man who is undaunted in the presence of death or other serious casualties, when

happening unexpectedly.
Scaramelli, *ibid.,* p. 80.

1913. *What Is Temperance?*
[Temperance] holds in check our fiery animal nature in order that the will may not yield to the allurement of sensual pleasure, nor be immoderately attracted to it.
Scaramelli, *ibid.,* p. 95.

1914. *Temperance Makes Men Like Angels*
. . . If want of moderation in bodily pleasures makes a man like to the brutes, and even more loathsome than they, temperance, on the contrary, raises a man above himself and makes him superior to his own nature by putting him on a par with the angels of heaven. Angels take no pleasure in meat and drink, they are incapable of it. The temperate man is capable of such pleasure, and either rejects it altogether or partakes of it with perfect detachment, and no further than necessary. An angel feels no sensual gratification because his nature is incapable of it. The temperate man is capable of the feeling, but nevertheless does not experience it, or if he does become aware of any motion of it, he tramples the sensation under foot with virtuous indignation, and forces it to be still. . . . The temperate render themselves, by their moderation, like unto the angels.
Scaramelli, *ibid.,* p. 101.

1915. *Temperance in Eating*
To practice temperance, St Bonaventure says that we must avoid four things: first, eating out of the time of meals, as animals do; secondly, eating with too much avidity, like famished dogs; thirdly, eating too large a quantity of food; and fourthly, we must avoid too much delicacy.
St Alphonsus Liguori, *Dignity and Duties of the Priest*, p. 376.

VIRTUES

1916. *Moral Virtues*
[If perfection consists in love of God and neighbor, what must be said of the moral virtues?] Beyond all doubt these virtues concur powerfully in the formation of perfection, not because they constitute its substance, but, as the angelic Doctor teaches, because they are instruments by which perfection is elaborated.
Scaramelli, *Directorium Asceticum*, vol. 1, pp. 16-17.

1917. *Moral Virtues Protect Charity*
Supernatural charity is a pearl of great price, an inestimable treasure, but it is exposed to be lost by any grave fault whatsoever. That is why it is necessary to protect it on all sides, and such is the function of the *moral virtues.* These virtues are the safeguards of love; by means of them the soul is kept free from deliberate venial sins and from the grave sins which threaten charity.
Marmion, *Growth in Christ*, p. 141.

1918. *Little Acts Lead to Meanness*
When it comes to practicing the moral virtues, little deeds are never the source of an increase of the virtue from which they proceed; in fact, if they are very little, they weaken it. Insignificant giving is death to generosity; it turns to meanness.
St Francis de Sales, *The Love of God*, p. 117.

1919. *The Necessity of Chastity*
When St Gregory the Great tells us in his thirteenth homily on the Gospels that chastity without other good works does not amount to much, but that without it no other good work will prosper, he states the positive need of chastity if we would build up a life of morality and virtue. . . St Alphonsus agrees with St Jerome that more souls are damned for impurity than for any other vice.
Kirsch, *Sex Education and Training in Chastity*, p. 1.

1920. *Chastity Held in Higher Esteem in Men than in Angels*
St John Chrysostom examined closely the reason why chastity is to be held in higher esteem in man than in angels. 'The angels,' he says, 'are not made up as we are of flesh and blood; they are incapable of marriage; they are not living, as we are, on this filthy earth, nor are they liable to the upheavings of passion; they have no need of food or drink, which so often add fuel to the flames of lust; their nature is not affected by a sweet sound, a dulcet song, or a beauteous form; they are impervious to all these allurements. What wonder, then, that they should be chaste? But that man, so far inferior by nature to these blessed spirits, with so many drawbacks, should yet strive to be like them in purity, this is indeed a height of virtue worthy of all admiration. . . . The fact that, being beneath the blessed spirits by their condition, they equalled them in purity, must ever rebound to their praise and glory.'
Scaramelli, *Directorium Asceticum*, vol. 3, pp. 300-301.

1921. *How to Preserve Chastity*
St Philip Neri coined the expression: 'In the war of the senses, cowards conquer.' By cowards he meant those who flee from dangerous occasions.
St Alphonsus Liguori, *The Glories of Mary*, vol. 2, p. 166.

1922. *Prayer Needed More for Chastity than for Any Other Virtue*
[Cassian admits that] the continued help of divine grace is needed in order to make progress in every virtue and for the uprooting of every vice; but the victory over the vice which tends to defile purity cannot be won without a most special gift of God; as the Fathers have taught, and as is proved by the experience of those who have possessed the virtue of chastity in its perfection. Whence it follows that prayer is more needed for this virtue than for any other virtues.
Scaramelli, *Directorium Asceticum*, vol. 3, p. 327.

1923. *The Chastity of Mary*
St Gregory of Nyssa says that the Blessed Virgin loved chastity so much, that to preserve it, she would have been willing to renounce even the dignity of the Mother of God.
St Alphonsus Liguori, *The Glories of Mary*, vol. 2, p. 165.

1924. *Chastity Demanded in a Priest*
According to St John Chrysostom, a priest should have purity which would entitle him to stand among the angels. . . .

St Athanasius, then, had reason to call chastity the house of the Holy Ghost, the life of angels, and the crown of saints.
St Alphonsus Liguori, *Dignity and Duties of the Priest*, pp. 246-247.

1925. *Chastity Changes a Man into an Angel*
Chastity, says St Ephrem, changes a man into an angel. . . . St Bernard says: 'Chastity makes an angel of man.' And according to St Ambrose, 'He who has preserved chastity is an angel; he who has lost it is a devil.'
St Alphonsus, *ibid.,* p. 243.

1926. *Keeping Young Hearts Chaste*
. . . Cardinal Newman wrote: 'It is the boast of the Catholic Church that it has the gift of making the young heart chaste; and why is this, but that it gives us Jesus Christ for our food and Mary for our nursing mother.'
Kirsch, *Sex Education and Training in Chastity*, p. 370.

1927. *Aristotle Against Indecent Pictures*
. . . Aristotle, who was a pagan, bids us not to tolerate indecent pictures,

lest children, seeing them, be corrupted. . . .
Kirsch, *ibid.,* p. 2.

1928. *Confidence in Jesus Christ*
The Lord revealed to St Gertrude that our confidence so constrains him that he cannot possibly refuse to hear us in everything we seek of him. The same was said by St Climachus: 'Prayer exerts a holy violence upon God.'. . . Every prayer offered with confidence, as it were, forces God; but this force is acceptable and pleasing to him. Therefore, St Bernard writes that the divine mercy is like a vast fountain, from which whosoever brings a larger vessel of confidence, carries away a larger abundance of graces.
St Alphonsus Liguori, *The Way of Salvation and of Perfection*, p. 226.

1929. *Confidence in God as Our Father*
Christ does not say: God knoweth, but 'Your Father knoweth', to lead them to greater confidence. For if he is our Father, it cannot be that he will abandon his children, since not even a human father could bear to do this. He says: 'that you have need of all these things,' so that since such things are necessary, all the more should we put aside solicitude.
St John Chrysostom, quoted in Toal, vol. 4, p. 96.

1930. *The Example of St Peter*
. . . Why in the world did the Evangelists all universally record this denial of St Peter? It was not to condemn the disciple for this, but in the desire to teach us how great an evil it is not to place one's confidence completely in God, but to trust to oneself. And as for you – marvel at the solicitude of the Master, and how, even though under arrest and bound, he was deeply concerned for his disciple, and by a glance raised him up from his fall, and moved him to tears (Lk 22:61).
St John Chrysostom, in *The Fathers of the Church,* vol. 41, pp. 408-409.

1931. *Confidence in God, Not in Self*
. . . It is one of the best dispositions that a workman in God's vineyard can have to understand that of himself he can do nothing that is of any good, and so to place his entire trust in God. These are the sort of men whom our sovereign Lord uses as instruments to do great things by them, and to work great and marvelous conversions. So says the Apostle St Paul: 'We have confidence through Christ in God; not that we are sufficient to do anything of ourselves, not so much as to have one good thought; but our sufficiency must come from God, who made us fit ministers' of the New

Testament (2 Cor 3:4-6).
Rodriguez, *Practice of Perfection and Christian Virtues,* vol. 3, p. 88.

1932. *Great Confidence in God Brings Great Results*
St Bernard says . . . 'If you have great confidence in God and hope great things of him, great things will he grant you and do by your means; and if little, little,' [Examples cited by the author: The ruler of the synagogue asking Christ to save his daughter . . . ; the woman suffering from a flow of blood 'If I can touch but the hem of his garment, I shall be healed'; the centurion: 'Say but the word and my servant shall be healed.']
Rodriguez, *Practice of Perfection and Christian Virtues*, vol. 3, pp. 96-97.

1933. *Devil Never Has Full Conquest Until He Has Robbed Us of Confidence in Christ*
. . . The devil has never got a fully decisive victory over a soul until he has robbed it of full confidence in the inexhaustible goodness of the Heart of Jesus to the wayward, the faithless and the sinful. And not the very gravest of our infidelities inflict so cruel a wound on that Heart, as is the wound that is inflicted on it when we doubt of its tenderness and mercy.
Edward Leen, *In the Likeness of Christ*, p. 202.

1934. *Lack of Confidence Hurts Jesus*
What offends Jesus, what wounds his heart, is want of trust!
Collected Letters of St Thérèse of Lisieux, p. 108.

1935. *Confidence in God in Spite of Our Sins*
It is not merely because I have been preserved from mortal sin that I lift up my heart to God in trust and in love. I am certain that if I had on my conscience every imaginable crime, I should lose nothing of my confidence but would throw myself, my heart broken with sorrow, into the arms of my Savior. I remember his love for the prodigal son, I have heard his words to St Mary Magdalen, to the woman taken in adultery, and to the woman of Samaria. No . . . there is no one who could frighten me, for I know too well what to believe concerning His mercy and love.
St Thérèse of Lisieux, *Autobiography and Letters*, pp. 194-195.

1936. *Confidence of St Thérèse in the Goodness of Jesus*
How happy I am that I am going to heaven soon! But when I ponder on those words of our Lord: 'Behold, I come quickly: and my reward is with me to render to everyone according to his works'; I think to myself he will

be very much embarrassed with me, because I have no works! He will be unable, then, to render me 'according to my works.'. . . Oh, well! I am confident he will render to me, therefore, according to his own works.

St Thérèse of Lisieux, *Novissima Verba,* p. 2.

1937. *Remembrance of God's Benefits Help Us*

God desires, and sets great store by it, that we should ever remember him and think of him and of the benefits and marvels that he has wrought for us – especially seeing that, if we exercise ourselves in the memory of these benefits, before long they will awaken in our hearts a desire of serving the Lord earnestly for them.

Rodriguez, *Practice of Perfection and Christian Virtues*, vol. 2, p. 501.

1938. *Three Ways of Practicing Gratitude*

St Thomas, treating of gratitude, says that thanks may be paid in three ways: first, interiorly, in the heart, recognizing and esteeming the greatness of the benefit and holding oneself much bounden to the benefactor; second, by praising and thanking him in words; third, by recompensing the benefit in deeds according to the capacity of the recipient.

Rodriguez, *ibid.,* p. 515.

HUMILITY

1939. *The Road to Humility*

'Humiliation,' says [St Bernard,] 'is the path that leads to humility, as patience leads to peace and study to knowledge. If, then, thou desirest to gain humility, do not withdraw from the way of humiliation. For if thou canst not humble thyself, thou shalt never acquire true humility.'

In Scaramelli, *Directorium Asceticum*, vol. 3, p. 402.

1940. *The Road to the Highest Degree of Humility*

[When Christ, with a cross on his shoulders, appeared to St John of the Cross, he said:] 'John, ask from me what thou wishest,' John answered: 'O Lord, to suffer and to be despised for thee.' The Doctors teach, with St Francis de Sales, that the highest degree of humility we can have is to be pleased with adjections and humiliations. And in this consists also one of the greatest merits we can have with God. One contempt suffered in peace for the love of God is of greater value in his sight than a thousand disciplines and a thousand fasts.

St Alphonsus Liguori, *Great Means of Salvation and of Perfection*, pp. 407-408.

1941. *How to Rejoice in Humiliations*
By our own strength we certainly cannot rejoice in humiliations, but by the aid of Jesus Christ we can imitate the Apostles, who 'went from the presence of the Council, rejoicing that they were accounted worthy to suffer reproach for the name of Jesus' (Acts 5:41).
St Alphonsus Liguori, *The True Spouse of Jesus Christ*, p. 343.

1942. *Humiliations as Source of Merit*
You will acquire more merit by meekly receiving an affront than by fasting ten days on bread and water.
St Alphonsus, *ibid.*, p.335.

1943. *Humiliations Prove Our Hidden Qualities*
It takes an insult to prove our hidden qualities. For while the proud rejoice in honors, the humble are usually happy to be despised.
St Gregory the Great, in *The Fathers of the Church*, vol. 39, p. 27.

1944. *The One Way to Make Saints*
What happiness it is to be humbled! It is the one way that makes saints!
In *Collected Letters of St Thérèse of Lisieux*, p. 93.

1945. *What Humility Is*
What is humility? It is a virtue that is derived from a profound reverence toward God. It lies in a recognition of our true position with respect to our Creator and fellow creatures, and in a disposition to shape our conduct in accordance with that position. Humility is the true expression in thought and conduct of what we really are. Hence, it is based on truth. It is primarily a disposition of our will to restrain that tendency which we all have to claim an esteem and consideration which is beyond our due, and to assert an independence of judgment and of will that does not belong to us as creatures. . . . To be humble, then, we must have a perfect understanding of what we are, and of the relations in which we stand with God.
Edward Leen, *In the Likeness of Christ,* pp. 177-178.

1946. *Humility as Foundation of All Virtues*
Although in point of excellence the virtue of humility does not hold the highest rank, still, according to St Thomas, because it is the foundation of all virtues, it has obtained the first place among them. Hence, as in the structure of an edifice, the foundation takes precedence over the walls, and even of the golden ornaments, so, to expel pride, which God resists, humility must, in the edification of the spiritual man, precede all other virtues. 'Humility,' says the Angelic Doctor, 'holds the first place, inasmuch

as it expells pride, which God resists.'

St Alphonsus Liguori, *The True Spouse of Jesus Christ*, p. 299.

1947. *The Humility of God in Becoming Man*
. . . Though all that the creator expends upon his creatures is part of one and the same fatherly love, yet it is less wonderful that man should advance to divine things than that God should descend to humanity.

St Leo the Great, in *The Nicene and Post-Nicene Fathers*, vol. 12, p. 135.

1948. *Humility Contrasted with Pride*
St Augustine . . . cries out, saying: 'O holy humility, how unlike thou art to pride! Pride, my brethren, hurled Lucifer from heaven, but humility brought the Son of God to make himself Man. Pride cast Adam out of paradise, but humility lifted up the good thief there.'

In Rodriguez, *Practice of Perfection and Christian Virtues,* vol. 2, p. 253.

1949. *The Gold Mine of Humility*
'If any man thinketh himself to be anything, whereas he is nothing, he deceiveth himself.' So says St Paul (Gal 6:3). Here is a great mine opened to us, whence to enrich ourselves with humility.

Rodriguez, *ibid.,* p. 191.

1950. *What We Have Is Not from Ourselves*
To assert that there is in me a single thing which comes not from God, would be the height of impiety, for it would be equivalent to saying that I have some one thing of which God is not the author. To affirm that in me there is any single thing which I have from myself, would be impious presumption, as it would be to pretend independence from God. . . .

Hence, we hold all that we have and are from God, not only because it is his gift, but because He repeats the gift at every instant, and preserves us by the working of a power which yields in nothing to that by which he created us. Wherefore I may well say with the Apostle: 'What hast thou that thou has not received' at every instant from the open and beneficient hand of God?

Scaramelli, *Directorium Asceticum*, vol. 3, pp. 378-379.

1951. *One Motive for Humility*
For an action to be deserving of life everlasting, it is necessary that it be done in the state of grace. . . .

Further, to perform a meritorious deed, besides sanctifying grace, we stand in need of the aid of actual grace. It is necessary that God enlighten our minds to know supernatural good, and stir up our will to embrace it; for, although sanctifying grace renders our acts deserving of an everlasting reward, it does not excite the will to their performance. For this purpose certain heavenly lights are needed and certain motions and pious inclinations, which sweetly draw on the will to do good. . . . You may tell me that you give, at least your cooperation to grace. . . . If God had not given you his grace, and, before that, the being and powers necessary to act, you had never been able to afford this cooperation.

Scaramelli, *ibid.,* pp. 385-386.

1952. *The Grand Science of the Christian*

This, then, we may conclude with St Augustine, is all the grand science of the Christian – to know that he is nothing, and can do nothing. 'This is the whole of the great science, to know that man is nothing.'. . . For then he will never neglect to furnish himself by prayer to God, with that strength which he has not of himself, and which he needs in order to resist temptation and to do good; and so, with the help of God, who never refuses anything to the man who prays to him in humility, he will be able to do all things.

St Alphonsus Liguori, *Great Means of Salvation and of Perfection*, pp. 75-76.

1953. *Humility Is Not Self-Depreciation*

Humility . . . has nothing to do with self-depreciation. It is not thinking little of oneself; it is rather not thinking of self at all. As long as we can feel humiliated, we are not perfectly humble.

Edward Leen, *In the Likeness of Christ*, p. 190.

1954. *What Humility Means*

To be humble means to be so submissive to God that you seek to please him – and not yourself – in all your good works, that you are displeased with yourself – and not with him – in whatever ills you justly suffer.

St Augustine, in *The Fathers of the Church*, vol. 11, p. 212.

1955. *Why God Loves Humility*

I was wondering once why Our Lord so dearly loved this virtue of humility; and all of a sudden – without, I believe, having previously thought of it – the following reason came into my mind: that it is because God is sovereign truth and to be humble is to walk in truth, for it is absolutely sure to say that we have no good in ourselves, but only misery and nothingness;

and everyone who fails to understand this is walking in falsehood.
In Peers edition, *Complete Works of St Teresa, Interior Castle,* p. 323.

1956. *Humility Based on Knowledge of Self and of God*
In the beginning of her visions, Catherine related to her confessor that Our Lord appeared to her while she was meditating and said to her: 'Know, my daughter, what thou art and what I am; if thou learnest these two things, thou shalt be truly blest: thou art what is not, and I am the great *I am*; if thy soul is deeply penetrated with this truth, the enemy cannot deceive thee, and thou wilt avoid all his snares; thou wilt never consent to do anything against My commandments, and thou wilt acquire without difficulty, grace, truth and peace.'
Blessed Raymond of Capua, *Life of St Catherine of Siena*, p. 63.

1957. *Humility in Truth*
Keep always before your eyes the great saying of St Francis of Assisi: 'What I am before God, that I am, and no more.'
St Alphonsus Liguori, *The True Spouse of Jesus Christ*, p. 323.

1958. *Humility Does not Deny God's Gifts*
'To make avowal of what I have received is not pride but devotion,' says St Augustine.
Edward Leen, *Progress Through Mental Prayer*, p. 193.

1959. *Humility of Intellect or of Judgment*
[St Alphonsus says that without humility of intellect or of judgment, humility of the will or heart cannot be acquired.]

It is necessary . . . to pray continually in the words of St Augustine: 'May I know myself; may I know thee, O my God, that thus I may love thee and despise myself.'. . . Make me O Lord, understand what I am and what thou art. Thou art the source of every good; I am misery itself. Of myself, I have nothing, I can do nothing but evil. It is only the humble that truly honor God. 'He', says the Holy Ghost, 'is honoured by the humble' (Ecclus 3:21). Yes, it is only the humble that can give glory to the Lord, for they alone acknowledge him to be the supreme and only good. If, then, you desire to honor God, keep continually in view all your miseries; confess in the sincerity of your soul, that of yourself you are nothingness and sinfulness, and that whatsoever you possess belongs to God.
St Alphonsus Liguori, *The True Spouse of Jesus Christ*, pp. 308-310.

1960. *Humility in the Mind and in the Will*
St Bernard, speaking of this virtue [humility], distinguishes a twofold humility, which partly consists in the appreciation of the mind, and partly abides in the affection of the will. Through the former component, we know our nothingness and our misery; through the latter, despising ourselves, we trample under foot the empty glory of the world and, after the example of Christ, we go forth to meet ignominy and reproach. . . . The reader must not run away with the notion that to acquire this humility of self-knowledge it is necessary to imagine evils and miseries within us which have no existence. . . . It suffices that we know ourselves as we really are and appear in the sight of God. . . .

This humble-mindedness being presupposed, it gives birth, by a sort of natural consequence, to the affection of humility in the will. . . . Now, let us suppose that a man, by means of his humility of mind, is intimately convinced that he has none of these gifts, or that if he has, they are not his own but God's; it is certain that he will no longer care to parade them and still less confirm himself in the esteem of what he perceives does not belong to him; and, hence, he will be freed from the hankering after worldly glory.

Scaramelli, *Directorium Asceticum*, vol. 3, pp. 372-373.

1961. *We Should Not Deny the Gifts God Has Given Us*
. . . It must be observed that it is in no way contrary to that humility of heart which is due to the Sovereign Lord and Maker for us to acknowledge the good that is in us, even though it be great and sublime; for, as St Paul says, 'We have received the Spirit, who is of God that we may know the things which are freely given to us of God' (1 Cor 2:12). . . . So you may also be conscious of the favors vouchsafed to you by God in prayer, of the virtues which you practice, of the progress which you are constantly making in the path of perfection, provided only that you know how to separate the precious portion, which is God's gift, from that vile share which is your own, and that you give all the glory to him who is the source of whatever good you possess; remain plunged in the abjection of your own nothingness.

Scaramelli, *ibid.*, pp. 390-391.

1962. *Degrees of Humility of the Will*
Speaking of humility of the will, St Bernard says: 'The first degree is not to wish for power; the second, to wish to be in a state of subjection to authority; the third is, in subjection, to bear injuries with equanimity.' . . . Such is the humility of heart which Jesus Christ wished to teach us by His own example. 'Learn of Me, said the Redeemer, because I am meek and

humble of heart' (Mt 11:29).
St Alphonsus Liguori, *The True Spouse of Jesus Christ*, p. 319.

1963. *Through Sin We Are Worse than Nothing*
What is deeper than nothingness? Yes, there is something a great deal deeper. What is that? The sin that you have added to your nothingness. . . . See what a wretched state you were in when before the eyes of God you were foul, displeasing, and his enemy, a child of wrath, bound over to everlasting fires; and so depreciate yourself and abase yourself to the lowest degree that you can. There is plenty room for it.
Rodriguez, *Practice of Perfection and Christian Virtues*, vol. 2, p. 193.

1964. *Reasons for Practicing Humility*
If we committed only one mortal sin, we offended God and are deserving of the scorn of men and angels and the sufferings and punishment of hell. We can do nothing of ourselves, but our sufficiency is from the grace of God. . . . If we have not fallen into all kinds of sins, it is only because God has helped us by his grace.
Bandas, *The Catholic Layman and Holiness*, pp. 277-278.

1965. *Humility Must Be Linked with Confidence*
Humility . . . is the royal road to sanctity; but it must be joined to unbounded confidence. We only forget ourselves to remember Christ, of whom we are members, and who loved us and delivered himself to death for us. Humility is the great way of repairing failures of the past.
Boylan, *This Tremendous Lover*, pp. 229-230.

1966. *Surest Salvation of Fallen Man*
The surest salvation [for fallen man], the remedy of his ills, and the means of restoration to his original state is in practicing humility, and not pretending that he may lay claim to any glory through his own efforts, but seeking it from God.
St Basil, in *The Fathers of the Church*, vol. 9, p. 475.

1967. *The Necessity of Humility*
. . . St Augustine writes: 'The highest honor should be united with the greatest humility.'. . . And before him, Jesus Christ said, 'He that is the greater among you, let him become as the younger' (Lk 22:26). Humility is truth. . . . Hence we must always pray with St Augustine: 'O Lord, may I know thee, may I know myself!'. . . St Francis of Assisi, admiring in God his greatness and goodness, and in himself his unworthiness and misery, used to say continually to the Lord: 'Who art thou, and who am I?' Hence

the saints, at the sight of the infinite perfections of God, humble themselves to the very earth. The more they know God, the better they see their own poverty and defects. The proud, because they are bereft of light, have but little knowledge of their own vileness.

St Alphonsus Liguori, *Dignity and Duties of the Priest*, pp. 305-306.

1968. *First Degree of Humility According to St Bonaventure*

The first degree of humility, according to St Bonaventure, is for a man to make little account of himself and think meanly of himself, and the one necessary means is knowledge of oneself.

Rodriguez, *Practice of Perfection and Christian Virtues*, vol. 2, pp. 188.

1969. *Second Degree of Humility*

The second degree of humility, says St Bonaventure, is a desire to be held cheap by others – love to be unknown and counted for nothing – *ama nesciri et pro nihilo reputari* – a desire that others shall neither know you nor esteem you nor make any account of you. If we are well grounded in the first degree of humility, we should have gone a long way toward gaining the second. If we really hold ourselves cheap, we should make no great difficulty about others likewise holding us cheap, rather we should be glad of it.

Rodriguez, *ibid.*, p. 216.

1970. *Third Degree of Humility*

The third degree of humility is when one endowed with great virtues and gifts of God, and standing high in the honor and esteem of men, is not proud of anything, nor attributes anything to himself, but refers and attributes everything to the same source, which is God, of whom comes 'every good and perfect gift' (Jas 1:14). This third degree of humility, says St Bonaventure, is proper to the good and perfect men, who, the greater they are, humble themselves the more in everything.

Rodriguez, *ibid.*, p. 300.

1971. *Humility of the Blessed Virgin*

[This third degree of] humility was found most perfectly in the Holy Queen of Angels, who, knowing herself to be chosen for Mother of God, with the deepest humility recognized herself for His servant and handmaid. St Bernard says: 'Being chosen for such a high dignity and great honor as to be Mother of God, she calls herself His handmaid; and being pronounced by the mouth of St Elizabeth blessed among women, she takes to herself no glory for those great endowments she has, but attributes them all to God, thanking him and magnifying him for them while herself she remains entire and firm in the deepest humility.' 'My soul doth magnify. . . ' (Lk 1:46).

Rodriguez, *ibid.,* p. 301.

1972. *A Powerful Weapon Against the Devil*

The most powerful weapon with which to overcome the devil is humility; because, not knowing how to use it, he does not even know how to defend himself against it.

St Vincent de Paul, in *Spiritual Diary*, p. 37.

1973. *Humility and Meekness – What They Achieve*

[Christ said;] 'Learn of me for I am meek and humble of heart.' Humility perfects us with respect to God, and meekness with respect to our neighbor.

St Francis de Sales, *Introduction to the Devout Life*, p. 119.

1974. *Source of Strength and Perfection*

The power of the world is manifested in riches and honors, but the power of God in humility and endurance. That is why St Augustine says that our strength lies in knowing that we are weak and humble, in confessing what we are. And St Jerome says that the only perfection of this present life consists in knowing that we are imperfect, that we distrust our own strength and abandon ourselves to God. God protects and saves those who hope in him: 'He is the protector of all who trust in him (Ps 17:31).

St Alphonsus Liguori, *The Passion of Jesus Christ*, p. 196.

1975. *Humility Brings Courage to Do Great Things*

. . . St Leo very well said: The truly humble man is the magnanimous man, courageous and strong to meet and undertake great things; nothing shall be to him arduous or difficult, since he does not trust in himself, but in God, fixing his eyes on God and resting on him.

Rodriguez, *Practice of Perfection and Christian Virtues*, vol. 2, p. 329.

1976. *Humility Obtains Strength from God*

A humble person is ordinarily very strong because he does not rely on frail human nature, but on the strength and power of God.

Bandas, *The Catholic Layman and Holiness*, p. 264.

1977. *Humility Is Not Weakness*

As a matter of fact, humility is not weakness, timidity or subservience; on the contrary, it is all energy, intrepidity and uprightness. Every virtue, as the word itself implies, is a form of manliness. Therefore, earnest religious labor constantly . . . to conform their daily conduct in every particular to the will of God, while at the same time they apply themselves to a whole-hearted acceptance of whatever lowers them in their own esteem or in that of others. In all this they are first animated chiefly by a keen sense of truth and justice.

Gabriel, *Ascetical Conferences for Religious*, p. 312.

1978. *Humility Makes All Things Possible*

'Nothing,' says St Leo, 'is difficult to the humble.'. . . No, for the humble, trusting in God, act with the strength of the divine arm, and therefore they effect whatever they wish.

St Alphonsus Liguori, *Dignity and Duties of the Priest*, p. 318.

1979. *Advantages of Humility*

Humbleness, indeed, is the spirit which frees one from the fire of gehenna and obtains that fire which is 'sent from on high'. Augustine insists that 'We are more filled with love in proportion as we are healed from the cancer of pride.'

St Bonaventure, *Rooted in Faith*, p. 36.

1980. *Ways of Combating Pride*

Whenever the present arouses pride in you, recall the past to mind and you will check the foolish swelling of conceit. If you see your neighbor committing sin, take care not to dwell exclusively on his sin, but think of the many things he has done and continues to do rightly. Many times, by examining the whole and not taking the part only into account, you will find that he is better than you.

St Basil, in *The Fathers of the Church*, vol. 9, p. 483.

1981. *Humility Causes Us to See Our Own Faults*

A truly humble person sees only his own defects and does not notice those of others. What a melancholy occupation, dear God, to waste one's time in examining the lives of others!

Blessed Claude de la Colombière, *Faithful Servant,* p. 349.

1982. *How Can We Consider Ourselves Worse than Others?*

. . . It is unquestionable that men are not all equal in merit, but that one is better than another, one superior to his fellows. How, then, is it possible that each one should believe himself worse than everybody else, with sincerity, and without danger of giving credit to a falsehood? St Thomas replies, that each person may consider in himself what he is of himself – that is, nothingness and sins, which should ever be before him – for he can call nothing else his own. He may further consider in his neighbors, what they are from God; that is to say, their virtues, their gifts of nature and grace; and he ought ever to bear this in mind, as charity dictates.

Scaramelli, *Directorium Asceticum*, vol. 3, p. 396.

1983. *The Humility of St Francis of Assisi*

Being asked by his companion how he could with truth call himself the greatest sinner in the world, seeing that he had never fallen into any of the crimes which others commit, St Francis replied: 'I believe and hold for certain that, had God dealt with the vilest assassin in the world with the same mercy which he has shown me, this man would have served him more faithfully and be more pleasing in his eyes than I am now. Further, it is my firm conviction that if God were to withdraw his holy hand from me, I should fall into enormities beyond anything that has yet been committed'.

Scaramelli, *Directorium Asceticum*, vol. 3, p. 398.

1984. *How to Obtain Humility*

If one asks: 'How am I to become humble,' the immediate answer is 'by the grace of God,' and that is indeed the truth. Only the grace of God can give us that insight into our own condition and realization of his exaltation that make for humility. But even though it be a grace, it is a grace with which we must cooperate. The first thing to do is to ask in prayer for the grace of humility, and to ask sincerely. The second thing is to accept humiliations when they come our way; but let us not forget that there is an enormous difference between being humble and being humiliated.

Boylan, *This Tremendous Lover*, p. 215.

1985. *How Humility Is to Be Acquired*

. . . We should . . . ponder with careful thoughts how holy men of God, in order to safeguard themselves in humility, when they knew many things well, endeavor to keep before their minds that which they do not know, so that on the one hand they remind themselves of their limitations and on the other, they are not raised above themselves because of those things in which their mind is accomplished. Knowledge is indeed a virtue, but humility is the guardian of virtue.

St Gregory the Great, in Toal, vol. 1, p. 69.

1986. *How to Learn Humility*

Someone asked one of those ancient Fathers how he might obtain true humility, and he answered: 'By keeping your eyes off other people's faults and fixing them on your own.'

Rodriguez, *Practice of Perfection and Christian Virtues*, vol. 2, p. 201.

1987. *Humility Helped When Others Know our Faults*

Oftentimes it is very profitable for keeping us in greater humility that others know and reprehend our faults.

When a man humbles himself for his defects he then appeases others, and quickly satisfied those that are angry with him.

Thomas à Kempis, *Imitation of Christ*, bk. 2, chap. 2.

1988. *The Value of Humility*

In the eyes of infinite wisdom, believe me, a little striving after humility and a single act thereof are worth more than all the science of the world.

The Life of St Teresa of Jesus, Written by Herself, p. 121.

1989. *Humility, Foundation for Prayer*

The whole foundation of prayer must be laid in humility. . . . The more a soul humbles itself in prayer, the more God lifts it up.

St Teresa, *ibid.*, p. 192.

1990. *What Is Needed to Practice Humility*

. . . To acquire humility, it is, above all necessary to accept humiliations that come to us from God and from men, and in the time of humiliations to say with Job: 'I have sinned, and indeed I have offended God, and I have not received what I deserved' (Jb 33:27). . . . 'He is humble,' says St Bernard, 'who converts humiliations into humility.'

St Alphonsus Liguori, *Dignity and Duties of the Priest*, pp. 319-320.

1991. *What Is Needed to Practice Humility*

Second, it is necessary to guard against glorying in any good that we may do, particularly if we are raised to the height of the priesthood. . . . We priests must pray, and say with St Paul: 'By the grace of God I am what I am' (1 Cor 15:10). For of ourselves we are incapable not only of doing good works, but even of having a good thought: 'Not that we are sufficient to think anything of ourselves' (2 Cor 3:5). . . .

Hence St Augustine remarks that unless humility go before, pride will steal from us all the good we do. . . . In another place, he says: 'Pride lays snares for good works that they may be lost.'

St Alphonsus, *ibid.*, pp. 312-315.

1992. *What Is Needed to Practice Humility*

Let us examine what we must do in order to be humble, not in name, but in reality.

In the first place it is necessary to entertain a great fear of the vice of pride; for, as has already been said, God resists the proud, and deprives them of his graces. A priest, particularly, in order to preserve chastity, stands in need of special aid from God. But how can a proud priest practice that sublime virtue if in punishment of his pride, the Lord withholds his assistance?

St Alphonsus, *ibid.*, pp. 309-310.

1993. *Humility in Speech*

The best rule is, never to speak well or ill of yourself, but to regard yourself as unworthy to be even mentioned in conversation.

St Alphonsus Liguori, *The True Spouse of Jesus Christ*, p. 322.

1994. *Humility When One Is Praised*

Whenever you hear your own praises, say in your heart, with St Augustine: 'I know myself better than they do; and God knows me better than I do myself.'

St Alphonsus, *ibid.*, p. 324.

1995. *Humility in the Face of Another's Anger*

Let man consider carefully with what great humility he should fly from the anger of his neighbor, when God, hiding himself, turned away from the fury of those who raged against him. Let no one then rise in anger against the injuries he receives; let no one give back injury for injury. For, imitating God, it is more glorious to turn away in silence from insult than to triumph over it by answering in kind.

St Gregory the Great, in Toal, vol. 2, p. 155.

1996. *Humility Should Not Seek Praise for Good Works*

The Kingdom of Heaven is compared to a treasure hidden in a field, 'which a man having found, hid it; and for joy goeth and selleth all that he hath and buyeth that field.' In all this, we should note that the treasure, once found, is hidden in order to preserve it; because the desire of celestial happiness is not sufficient shield against the evil spirits for him who does not hide it from human flattery. . . . I say this, not that our neighbor should not see our works, as it is written: 'That they may see your good works and glorify your Father who is in heaven, but so that we should not seek praise for what we do before others' (Mt 5:16).

St Gregory the Great, *Parables of the Gospel*, pp. 16-17.

1997. *True and False Humility*
Some think it humility not to believe that God is bestowing his gifts upon them. Let us clearly understand this, and that it is perfectly clear that God bestows his gifts without any merit whatever on our part; and let us be grateful to his Majesty for them; for if we do not recognize the gifts received at his hands, we shall never be moved to love him. It is a most certain truth that the richer we see ourselves to be, confessing at the same time our poverty, the greater will be our progress, and the more real our humility.

The Life of St Teresa of Jesus, Written by Herself, p. 73.

1998. *How to Acquire True Humility*
He who would gather virtue without humility, carries dust in the wind; and where he seems to possess something, from the same is he blinded and made worse. . . . Pay not heed to the things in which you are better than others, but to those in which you are worse; so that while you keep before you the example of those that are better than yourself, you may, through humility, be enabled to ascend to greater things, by the bountiful mercy of Our Lord Jesus Christ. . . .

St Gregory the Great, in Toal, vol. 1, p. 70.

1999. *Humility, True and False*
Let us be clear about what we mean by humility. It does *not* mean that we deny the good that is in us. Quite the contrary – for humility is truth. If a man who knows six languages denies his knowledge he is not telling the truth. But if he ascribes his ability to learn languages and all his other talents to himself or to his merit, he is also far from the truth. The most wonderful person that God ever created was his Mother, and she knew it. She even knew she was humble. In her great poem of praise to God – the *Magnificat* – she tells us that it was her humility that attracted God's attention and grace. But she ascribes all that she sees in herself to the mercy of God. . . .

What then is humility? Our Lady's *Magnificat* gives us the clue. Humility is a supernatural virtue by which we lovingly recognize our true value in God's eyes and are disposed to render him due recognition for all the good we find in ourselves. It and its shadow, meekness, are the only virtues that Our Lord pointed out in himself for our imitation. 'Learn of me for I am meek and humble of heart.'

Boylan, *This Tremendous Lover*, pp. 73-74.

2000. *Humility Required in Religious Life*
How can one ever be said to be dead according to that promise he made to

Jesus Christ on entering religions to die to himself, if he remains alive to resentment and disquiet when he sees himself humbled? Out of the Order with such subjects so attached to their own esteem! Out with them! It is well for them to go as soon as possible that they may not infect the rest also with their pride. In religion everyone ought to be dead, and especially to his own self-esteem, otherwise it is better for him not to enter, or, to depart again if he has already entered.

St Alphonsus Liguori, *Great Means of Salvation and of Perfection*, p. 409.

2001. *False Humility Is Hateful*

'Most hateful is that pride which lurks under the mask of humility' (St Jerome, in a letter to Celantia). St Ambrose is of the like mind. Many, he says, have the appearance but not the virtue of humility; they show it outside but contradict it in their interior. They make parade of it, but with its reality they have nothing to do.

Scaramelli, *Directorium Asceticum*, vol. 3, p. 411.

2002. *Humility Based on the Attraction Sin has for Us*

This frightful attraction which vice has for our fallen nature can be made one of the most solid props of our spiritual lives, and the realization that this attraction is so strong is taught and enforced most of all in the school of temptation. 'There goes Philip Neri,' said the saint to his companion on meeting a notorious sinner, 'only for the grace of God.' Such a deep and heartfelt conviction is another name for humility, the foundation of the edifice of true sanctity.

Nash, *Living Your Faith*, p. 140.

2003. *Humility of the Blessed Virgin*

The first effect of humility of heart is a lowly opinion of oneself. Mary always had such a humble opinion of herself that, as was revealed to St Matilda, although she saw herself enriched with more graces than all other people, she never placed herself ahead of anyone. . . . Humility is truth, as St Teresa remarks, and Mary knew that she had never offended God. She also knew that she had received more graces from God than all other creatures. A humble heart always acknowledges the special favors of the Lord in order to humble itself all the more. But the Blessed Mother, because of the greater light which made her aware of the infinite greatness and goodness of God, was also aware of her own nothingness. That is why she humbled herself more than anybody else.

St Alphonsus Liguori, *The Glories of Mary*, vol. 2, pp. 150-151.

2004. *Humility of the Blessed Virgin*

It is a most remarkable fact that [Mary's] humility is that of the child. Hers is the calm humility that does not have a passionate desire to be nothing, but finds it quite natural that she is nothing. . . . It was never recorded that she ever sought anything, not even the lowest place. Her basic disposition is one of absolute freedom of soul with regard to past and future, total forgetfulness of self in obedience and abandonment to God. Hers is a fundamental, absolute abandonment to all God's wishes.

Goichon, *Contemplative Life in the World*, pp. 48-49.

2005. *Humility of St Peter*

As St Augustine observes, before he was tempted, St Peter presumed upon himself; in temptation he came to know what he was and he learned humility.

Scaramelli, *Directorium Asceticum*, vol. 2, p. 302.

2006. *Humility of Father Lallemant*

When Father Lallemant was rector of a Jesuit college, he had a visit one morning from an irate brother, the baker, who complained loudly that he had too much work and demanded assistance. His superior, who himself was already overburdened with work, did no more than promise that the brother would certainly have his demands attended to. That evening, on entering his bakery, he found the rector before him baking the bread. The brother at once fell on his knees and begged a penance and pardon.

Nash, *The Nun at her Prie-Dieu*, pp. 231-232.

2007. *The First Virtue Needed to Acquire the Kingdom of God*

Let no one be surprised that St Benedict, writing for men seeking perfection, and St Thomas, the Doctor of the whole Church, lay down humility as the first virtue for the acquisition of the Kingdom of Heaven, for it removes the obstacles to God's action and to God's mercy. We have God's word for it.

Boylan, *This Tremendous Lover*, p. 73.

2008. *A Sure Road That Leads to God*

The sure road that leads to God, without danger of being led astray, according to what [St Augustine] says to Dioscorus, is – first, humility; next humility; lastly, humility. 'Ask me,' he writes, 'the question as often as you please, and my answer will ever be the same. Not that there are no other precepts in God's law, but because unless humility both precede and follow our good works, and also accompany them – unless we keep it ever before our eyes, unless we hold fast to it in order to repress pride and all

vain self-conceit – our good deeds will be snatched out of our hands.'
Scaramelli, *Directorium Asceticum*, vol. 3, p. 419.

2009. *Where Humility Exists, All Other Virtues Are Present*
God is said 'to resist the proud and give grace to the humble' (Jas 4:6; see also 1 Pt 5:5). In these words of the Apostle is revealed the connection, not logically immediate, between humility and spiritual perfection. Humility is not fortitude, nor temperance, nor yet charity. But where it exists, all these will exist. For the Christian, supernatural virtues, the only ones that avail for union with God in this life and in the next, are not acquired but infused. God gives them. They are communicated with grace. They grow with grace and are proportioned in their perfection to the measure of grace.
Edward Leen, *Progress Through Mental Prayer*, p. 12.

2010. *Humility Essential for Perfection*
'Humility is the foundation of all the other virtues; hence, in the soul in which this virtue does not exist, there cannot be any other virtue except in appearance. Similarly, it is the best disposition to receive celestial gifts. Finally, it is so necessary for perfection that, among all the ways to reach it, the first is humility, the second is humility and the third is humility. And if I were asked about it one hundred times, I would still give the same answer.'
St Augustine, in *Spiritual Diary*, p. 35.

2011. *Humility and Grace*
The humbler we are when God visits us, the more grace we shall receive; and the less humility we have, the less grace we shall receive. And if He finds us proud, you may be sure that He will bring us low; whereas if He finds us lowly, He will raise us up, for lowliness will bring us to Him. So be humble and abase yourselves, and you will be exalted.
Tauler, *Spiritual Conferences,* p. 41.

2012. *Humility Attracts God*
St Augustine says that humility attracts to itself the Most High God: 'God is high; if you humble yourself, he comes down to you; if you lift yourself up and are proud, he shuns you.'
Rodriguez, *Practice of Perfection and Christian Virtues*, vol. 2, p. 340.

2013. *Humility Needed to Protect Value of Good Works*
The glorious St Augustine says: 'All our works must be guarded and accompanied by humility in the beginning, in the middle, and at the end;

for if we are ever so little careless and allow vain complacency to come in, all will be carried away by the wind of pride.'

Rodriguez, *ibid.*, p. 167.

2014. *Mother of Many Virtues*

'Humility is the mother of many virtues because from it obedience, fear, reverence, patience, modesty, meekness and peace are born. He who is humble easily obeys everyone, fears to offend anyone, is at peace with everyone, is kind to all, is submissive to everyone, does not offend or displease anyone, does not resent the injuries inflicted upon him; he lives happy, contented and in great peace.'

St Thomas of Villanova, in *Spiritual Diary*, pp. 35-36.

2015. *Foundation of All Virtues*

'Humility,' says St Bernard, 'is the foundation and guardian of the virtues.' He is right, for without it, no other virtue can exist in the soul. . . .

This beautiful and necessary virtue was unknown in the world in early days. But the Son of God came to earth to teach it by His example, and He willed that we should endeavor to imitate Him in that virtue particularly: 'Learn of Me, because I am meek and humble of heart.'

St Alphonsus Liguori, *The Glories of Mary*, vol. 2, p. 150.

2016. *Foundation of all Virtues*

. . . Someone will say: 'How can you say that humility is the foundation of all virtues . . . when the saints in common say that faith is the foundation. . . . ' To this, St Thomas very aptly replies: Two things are requisite to lay a foundation well. First, it is necessary to open well the trenches and cast out all the loose earth until you arrive at firm ground to build it upon; and after having dug the trench deep and thrown out all the loose earth, they begin to lay the foundation upon stone, which, with other stones that are laid upon it, makes the main foundation of the building. So, St Thomas goes on to say, are humility and faith in the spiritual foundation and fabric of virtues. Humility is that which opens the ground; its office is to dig the trench deep and throw out all the loose stuff, that is, the weakness of human strength. You must not build on your own strength, for that is all sand: All *that* you must cast out, having no confidence in yourself; you must go on digging until you arrive at the living rock, and firm stone, which is Christ (1 Cor 10-4).

Rodriguez, *Practice of Perfection and Christian Virtues,* vol. 2, p. 169.

2017. *No Virtue Possible Without Humility*

A foundation has these two properties – first, without it no building can be erected; second, without it, no building can stand. Now, these two properties may be claimed by holy humility, for without it no virtue can be acquired, nor can any virtue be preserved or cultivated. . . . According to the saying of St James, 'God resisteth the proud, but gives his grace to the humble' (Jas 4:6). [St Gregory says] that humility opens the mind to the light from above, while pride closes it.

Scaramelli, *Directorium Asceticum*, vol. 3, pp. 414-415.

2018. *Needed for Sanctifying Ourselves or Others*

If we desire to strive successfully for personal holiness or if we desire to labor efficaciously for the salvation and sanctification of our neighbor, what we need first and foremost is humility. Through neglect of this virtue, many religious never achieve any marked progress in perfection, never arouse any genuine and lasting fervor in others, never rise to become intimate friends with Jesus, the eternal Son of God. Not a few would like to acquire humility, but do not sincerely resolve to use the obvious means. Such means are supplication, faithful observance of rules, rubrics, and customs, genuine obedience of execution, will, and judgment, loving acceptance of humiliation and affliction. Even when praying for humility, they do not implore the grace of striving courageously for its acquisition, but rather desire the smug satisfaction of possessing it without strife.

Gabriel, *Ascetical Conferences for Religious*, p. 311.

2019. *Humility Essential in Realm of Eternal Life*

In the realm of eternal life, which is a gift from God, it is not human strength or human power that matters, but humility and the sense of one's own sinfulness. Humility may be the pearl that a man can find only in the dust of his own defeat. We must find our sinfulness before we can seek the remedy.

O'Mahoney, *The Person of Jesus*, p. 86.

2020. *Humility Essential for the Spiritual Life*

To strive after a spiritual life, and not to strive after humility, is to build upon the sand.

Scaramelli, *Directorium Asceticum*, vol. 3, p. 420.

2021. *Valleys to be Filled, Mountains Brought Low*

'Every valley shall be filled and every mountain and hill brought low.' What is here meant by valleys unless the humble, and by the hills and mountains but the proud? At the coming of the Redeemer, therefore, the valleys shall be filled, the mountains and hills brought low, according to His Word: 'Every one that exalteth himself shall be humbled, and he that

humbleth himself shall be exalted.'
St Gregory the Great, in Toal, vol. 1, p. 89.

2022. *Christ Came to Heal Humanity of Pride*
Christ came on earth to redeem mankind, and, through redemption, to heal human nature of its radical diseases. The radical disease of human nature was not the concupiscence of the flesh nor the concupiscence of the eyes, but the pride of life. . . .

If Christ's humanity existed to cure this radical evil, his radical quality should be the one directly opposed to this egoism. Humility is the virtue that restrains in us the inordinate tendency to claim for ourselves a consideration beyond our merit, an autonomy that belongs to God. This virtue cannot operate unless we have a clear insight into two things – the sovereign rights of God and the duties of a creature. . . . You can have no humility without intelligence, without clarity of insight. . . .

Our Lord coming on earth had the clearest of clear insights. His grand mind penetrated the very roots of what He was as a creature. He had a deep sense of his own creaturehood and of his utter 'belongingness' to God. It was clear to him that as Man he was nothing of himself and that all his splendid qualities belonged to God, and so were consecrated to God. He knew that God was the center and that he was in the circumference. He never vacated that position. . . .

Humility demands reverence for God and God's rights. Hence, Christ's relations to God the Father were marked with profound humility. They were stamped with the deepest reverence. This reverence was the consuming passion of his life. Hence, you have in the Office of the Passion one of the inspired phrases which describes his attitude perfectly: 'The zeal of Thy house hath devoured me.'
Edward Leen, *Retreat Notes for Religious*, pp. 69-70.

2023. *How To Explain the Humility of Christ*
[Christ] saw clearly with his human intelligence that his own Humanity was something created and, therefore, absolutely nothing in itself. He realized, as we cannot realize, the absolute nothingness of that Humanity when considered in itself apart from God. He saw the full indebtedness of his sacred Humanity to the Creator for every single instant of its existence, for every vital act and for every natural and supernatural perfection of which it stood possessed.
Edward Leen, *In the Likeness of Christ*, p. 178.

2024. *Humility as Taught by Christ*
. . . Christ is our Teacher of humility: He who humbled himself, becoming

obedient unto death; even to the death of the Cross (Phil 2:8). But in teaching us humility, he did not lessen his divinity; in his divinity, he is equal to the Father, in his lowliness, he is like us. Through that in which he is equal to the Father, He created us and gave us existence; through that in which he is like us, He saved us lest we perish.

St Augustine, in Toal, vol. 4, p. 449.

2025. *Humility of Christ a Remedy for Our Pride*

Christ's humility is the remedy for man's pride. . . . Man would not have fallen had he not fallen through pride. For 'pride', as the Scripture says, 'is the beginning of all sin' (Ecclus 10:15). . . . So if pride is the beginning of sin, whence could pride's swelling be healed, had God not deigned to become lowly? Let man be ashamed to be proud; since God himself became humble.

St Augustine, in Toal, vol. 1, p. 273.

2026. *Washing the Feet of His Disciples*

The ruler of the universe, the only-begotten Son of God, humbles himself by washing the feet of his creatures! O angels, what do you say? It would have been a great favor if Jesus Christ had permitted you, as he did Magdalene, to wash his divine feet with your tears. But no; he wanted to place himself at the feet of his servants so that he could leave us at the end of his life this great example of humility, this tremendous proof of his love for men. And, O Lord, shall we continue to be so proud that we [cannot] bear a word of contempt, or the smallest slight, without instantly feeling resentment and planning revenge, we, who have deserved by our sins to be trampled on by the devils in hell?

St Alphonsus Liguori, *The Passion of Jesus Christ*, p. 94.

2027. *Washing the Feet of His Disciples*

[Not merely did Christ] perform these ablutions, but he did so after he had laid aside his garments. And he did not stop with this but girded himself with a towel. He was not satisfied with this, but He Himself filled the basin. He did not bid someone else to fill it, but did all these things himself to show that, when we do good, we must not do such things in a spirit of routine, but with enthusiastic zeal.

St John Chrysostom, in *The Fathers of the Church*, vol. 41, p. 254.

2028. *Humility of Christ Vs. Pride of the Devil*

How much better it would be to follow the humble Christ than through pride to be trodden on by the feet of the devil!

St Caesarius of Arles, in *The Fathers of the Church*, vol. 31, p. 248.

2029. *What is Meekness?*
What is meekness? Meekness is moderation and evenness of soul, which regulates the irascible passions. It is to the soul what a temperate and equable climate is to a country. A meek soul is one in which storms of anger and the passions consequent on anger – hatred, vindicativeness, jealousy – do not arise.

Brosnahan, *Searchlighting Ourselves*, p. 248.

2030. *Nature and Derivation of Meekness*
Meekness, according to Father Tanquerey, is a 'supernatural moral virtue by which we prevent and restrain anger, bear with our neighbor in spite of his defects, and treat him with kindliness.' According to the same author, it flows from several other virtues. Insofar as it implies a certain self-mastery, it is related to temperance; insofar as it involves tolerance of the failings of others, it is related to patience and fortitude; insofar as it demands forgiveness of injuries and kindliness to all, even to enemies, it includes charity.

Bandas, *The Catholic Layman and Holiness*, p. 287.

2031. *What Meekness Does*
. . . It belongs to meekness to check anger which is provoked by affronts and to hinder vengeance which this dark passion urges us to take. Such is the teaching of St Thomas. . . . St Ambrose . . . says the meek are they who have wholly overcome the passions of anger, of vengeance, of rage, and all spirit of discord.

Scaramelli, *Directorium Asceticum*, vol. 3, p. 334.

2032. *Meekness – Its Nature and Practice*
St John Chrysostom says that meekness is, of all virtues, that which renders us most like God. . . .

The virtue of meekness consists in two things: (a) in restraining the motions of passion against those that provoke us to anger; and (b) in bearing insults.

St Francis de Sales in his *Introduction to the Devout Life* . . . says that however just the reason of our anger, it is always expedient to restrain it; and that it is better for you to have it said that you are never angry than that you are wisely angry. When, says St Augustine . . . , anger has entered the soul, it is difficult to expel it.

St Alphonsus Liguori, *Dignity and Duties of the Priest*, pp. 323 and 325.

2033. *Heroic Degree of Meekness*
The heroism of Christian meekness consists in treating humbly and affectionately those who hate, outrage and persecute us, and in conciliating them

by kindness and services.

Scaramelli, *Directorium Asceticum*, vol. 3, p. 356.

2034. *Meekness in the Face of Contempt*
A soul gains more by peacefully bearing an affront than by fasting for ten days on bread and water.

St Alphonsus Liguori, *Dignity and Duties of the Priest*, p. 330.

2035. *Meekness Does Not Prevent Fraternal Correction*
... To be meek does not imply that in order to show kindness or to avoid the displeasure of another we should omit to correct him with just rigor when such correction is necessary. To omit correction in that case would not be virtue, but a culpable and abominable negligence. . . . Meekness, then, implies that when it is necessary to correct a brother, we should do it with firmness, but at the same time with sweetness.

St Alphonsus, *ibid.,* p. 326.

OBEDIENCE

2036. *The Nature and Extent of Obedience*
St Thomas defines obedience to be a moral virtue inclining the will to carry out the commands of those who are lawfully set over us. . . . The virtue of obedience concerns also the commands of other people: of parents to their offspring; of husbands to their wives; of employers to those in their employ; of captains to the soldiers under them; of priests to laymen; in a word, it extends to every reasonable order given by one who may lawfully command, provided it exceed not the sphere to which the authority giving the order is limited. . . .

Scaramelli, *Directorium Asceticum*, vol. 3, p. 193.

2037. *Christ, a model of Obedience*
'I came down from heaven,' he says. . . , 'not to do my own will, but the will of him that sent me that I may perfect his works.' . . .

'Not everyone that saith to me: "Lord, Lord," shall enter into the kingdom of heaven, but he that 'doth the will of my Father who is in heaven, he shall enter into the kingdom of heaven.' . . .

'My meat is to do the will of him that sent me.' . . .

In Gethsemani Jesus prays that the chalice might pass from him, but he is careful immediately to add: 'Nevertheless, not my will but thine be done.' In obedience to that will, he accepts the bitter chalice. . . . 'The things that are pleasing to him I always do.' His teaching and his conduct both emphasize this truth – that man has no reason for being here on earth, except alone to find out what God wants him to do, and having found that out, to bend all his energies to that one task.

Nash, *Living Your Faith*, pp. 46-48.

2038. *The Obedience of Christ*

It was not the heroic or even the virtuous that Christ set before himself to accomplish; he aimed simply at being obedient to the injunctions of his Father in heaven. Filial docility, not heroism, was for him the essential quality of all he did. His life, in its dynamic aspect, was one of obedience. . . .

The whole life of Christ on earth was one series of acts of obedience to his Father. It was under that aspect of obedience that he envisioned everything he had to do or say. He did not cultivate eloquence, or even virtue for its own sake. He was concerned only with carrying out the orders or desires of God, whatever these should entail, whether they should mean the accomplishment of ordinary simple tasks, or . . . the most arduous enterprises. He was indifferent to what was ordered; its importance for him lay in that it was a thing commanded.

James Leen, *By Jacob's Well*, p. 93.

2039. *Life of Christ – Complete Submission to God*

To make sure of our heavenly calling, it is imperative to make a close study of the human life of God made Man. This life, so exalted in worth and so rich in perfections, reveals itself as being one of surpassing simplicity. It can be resumed in one word. This word is *obedience*. . . . We must push our obedience to the fullest of its demands on us. This obedience must express itself in a complete submission to the will of God, proving its sincerity in a generous acceptance of all that it shall please God to make us undergo. And just as in the case of Jesus, his Passion was not the end, but only the gateway to a life freed from the shackles of mortality, so, too, in our case, such suffering as we shall have to experience will be but the prelude of an existence without flaw.

James Leen, *ibid.*, p. 6.

2040. *The Obedience of Christ*

. . . Our Lord's life was a lesson in docility. It was simply the fulfilment of the desires and wishes of his Father. Things of great moment and things of little moment marked his career. Things of great moment did not appeal to him for themselves alone. He worked miracles, spoke with power, exercised all the virtues, but it was not the fairness of virtue, or the splendor of courage or the beauty of chastity in themselves that appealed to him. Their only appeal was that they were things commanded by his Father. Hence the lowliest action was as great in his eyes as the sublimest act of virtue, inasmuch as the lowly one was stamped with the command of his Father as well as the other. He did not reason further.

Edward Leen, *Retreat Notes for Religious*, p. 89.

2041. *Obedience of Christ to Mary and Joseph*

Who is subject to whom? A God to men. God, I repeat, to whom the angels are subject: whom principalities and powers obey: was subject to Mary; and not alone to Mary, but to Joseph also because of Mary.

St Bernard, in Toal, vol. 1, p. 247.

2042. *Adam Disobeyed: Christ Came to Teach Obedience*

St Augustine says that after Adam had by his disobedience entailed misery on himself and the whole human race, the Son of God became man, principally to teach obedience by His own example. Jesus from his infancy began to obey Mary and Joseph: He continued to obey them during His life; and by his obedience was in the end brought to the ignominious death on the cross. He humbled himself, becoming obedient unto death – even to the death of the cross.

St Alphonsus Liguori, *The True Spouse of Jesus Christ*, p. 156.

2043. *Conforming Ourselves to God's Plan*

Obedience is the virtue through which man conforms his life to the plan of God, manifested through God's law or through his representatives. As the plan of God is the law of all life and love, obedience is a necessary and noble virtue for both salvation and religious perfection. Daily we pledge to God our service of unrestricted obedience when we pray: 'Thy will be done on earth as it is in heaven.'

Hoeger, *The Convent Mirror*, p. 113.

2044. *Doing God's Will Is the Best Thing for Us*

'The best thing for creatures is to fulfill God's will, and this is best done by the practice of obedience, which effects the annihilation of self-will and the freedom of the children of God. This is the reason good souls find such happiness and satisfaction in obedience.'

St Vincent de Paul, in *Spiritual Diary*, p. 128.

2045. *Obedience of the Blessed Virgin*

St Bede explains Our Lord's answer to the woman in the Gospel who exclaimed: 'Blessed is the womb that bore thee. . . . Rather, blessed are they who hear the word of God and keep it' (Lk 11, 28). He says that Mary was very blessed by being the Mother of God, but was even more

blessed by always loving and obeying his divine will.
St Alphonsus Liguori, *The Glories of Mary*, vol. 2, p. 170.

2046. *By Obedience We Do God's Will*
[One of the greatest advantages and consolations for religious is that in] the occupations given us by obedience we are doing what God would have us to do. This stands for a first principle in religion, drawn from the Gospel and the doctrine of the Saints. 'He that hereth you heareth me' (Lk 10:16). In obeying the superior, we obey God and do his will, for that is what God requires us to do there and then.
Rodriguez, *Practice of Perfection and Christian Virtues,* vol. 1, p. 98.

2047. *The Most Excellent of the Moral Virtues*
[The chief of our spiritual endowments] is the free use of our own will, which rules as queen over the miniature world within us, and enables us to use and enjoy all other goods whereof we are capable. Now, this same will, which is the chief good we possess, we give up to God when, for his sake, we submit to do the will of one set over us, and by thus doing we make him the greatest offering in our power, and pay him the greatest homage of which we are capable. By means of the other virtues we despoil ourselves for God's sake of goods of less price; by obedience we yield up to him our most precious endowment. . . . The saint repeats the same elsewhere, saying that man can make no offering so pleasing to God as that of his will, by subjecting it for God's sake, to the will of another. This is an offering of such value that it cannot be equalled.
Scaramelli, *Directorium Asceticum,* vol. 3, pp. 203-204.

2048. *Obedience to Man for God*
. . . St Bonaventure says: 'It is a high degree of obedience to obey what God immediately commands and ordains; but in some sort, it is a higher degree to obey man for God, and sometimes the merit and reward will be greater; for there is a greater humiliation of heart in obeying man for God, as it is more to obey a king's servant for love of the king than to obey the king himself. If God himself came in person to command you, would it be anything much if you obeyed with promptitude and resignation? But for love of him to obey a man like yourself, and submit to him with entire resignation is an act in which there is much to reward and appreciate.'
Quoted by Rodriguez, in *Practice of Perfection and Christian Virtues*, vol. 3, p. 339.

2049. *Obedience as Self-Surrender Difficult*
'It is not difficult,' says St Gregory, 'for a man to abandon his most

cherished external possessions, but it is a task of great proportions to quit oneself. One may readily give up what one has: it is not so easy to give up what one is.' The great St Teresa on her deathbed gave this last recommandation to her daughters: 'I implore you,' said the dying saint, 'for the love of God to observe your rule and to obey your superiors. If you but do this in the way you ought to do it, there will not be needed any miracles for your canonization.'

James Leen, *By Jacob's Well*, p. 120.

2050. *The Great Value of Obedience*
St Gregory the Great says: 'To submit one's will invariably to that of another is beyond compare, more sublime than to wear ourselves out by rigorous fastings, to melt in devout affections, or to immolate ourselves by inward compunction on the altar of prayer.'... According to the saints, perseverance in obedience during one's whole lifetime is a far greater achievement than a martyr's death.

Bandas, *The Catholic Layman and Holiness*, p. 260.

2051. *Obedience Impossible Without Faith*
The practice of the virtue of obedience is impossible without a strong faith. The good religious must not allow his vision to be arrested by the human qualities or defects of those who are his lawful superiors. He must see through the human veil to the authority of God revealing itself with evidence to the eyes of faith.... The unique reason for the promptitude of our will in obeying should be that the act is commanded by God.

James Leen, *By Jacob's Well*, p. 98.

2052. *Perfect Obedience*
To be perfect in obedience, a religious must obey with promptness, exactness, cheerfulness and simplicity. These are the four degrees of perfect obedience.

St Alphonsus Liguori, *The True Spouse of Jesus Christ*, p. 190.

2053. *Three Degrees of Obedience According to Ignatius*
Our Father [St Ignatius], speaking of obedience in the Third Part of the Constitutions says: 'It is very expedient for spiritual advancement, and quite necessary, that all should give themselves up to perfect obedience.' And he goes on explaining what this perfect obedience is. He says that it should not only be the exterior execution, carrying out in act the order given, which is the first degree of obedience, but it should extend also to the will and the heart, conforming our will to that of the superior, willing and not willing as he wills or does not will, which is the second degree

of obedience. And we are not to stop here, but pass on further, conforming our judgment also to that of the superior, so that you should think as the superior thinks, and judge that the order given is a good order, which is the third degree of obedience. When there is this conformity of deed, will and understanding, then the obedience will be perfect and entire....

Rodriguez, *Practice of Perfection and Christian Virtues*, vol. 3, p. 284.

2054. *Obedience as Compared with Discipline*

Obedience does not consist in just doing what one is told. That is mere discipline. While I am speaking to you, thousands and even millions of men are doing what they are told, at immense cost to themselves, and they are not obedient. A soldier does what he is told, even at risk of life, and yet he is not obeying in the virtue sense of the word. He is moved to do what he is told by the instinct of self-preservation, or by confidence in his superiors, or through esteem of military discipline. None of these motives can constitute the virtue of obedience.

Obedience consists in our willing to be told what we are to do, in our being ready to put our talents of mind or imagination and of body at the disposal of another's mind and will. We are not obedient unless we have that resolve of will and adhere to it. By it we renounce what is most intimate of us – a renunciation far deeper than the renouncement made by Poverty or Chastity.

Edward Leen, *Retreat Notes for Religious*, p. 91.

2055. *Obedience to God as Represented by Superiors*

Our father [St Ignatius] instructed us that we must not obey the superior because he is a very prudent man, or because he is a very good man, or a man highly qualified in any other gifts, but because he holds the place and authority of Our Lord. Set that aside and fix your eyes on other more human reasons, then, he said, the force of obedience is lost. . . . He goes on to say that we ought nowise to look to see whether it is the cook or the superior of the house that commands us, nor whether it be this man or that, since it is not for their sake that we obey, but for God's sake alone. We should obey subordinate officials with the same humility, readiness, and submission as the superior in chief.

Rodriguez, *Practice of Perfection and Christian Virtues*, vol. 3, p. 342.

2056. *Best Means of Practicing Obedience*

The principal and most efficacious means of practicing the obedience due to superiors, and of rendering it meritorious before God, is to consider that in obeying them, we obey God himself; and that by despising their commands we despise the authority of our Divine Master, who has said of superiors: 'He that heareth you, heareth me, and he that despiseth you, despiseth me' (Lk 10:16).

St Alphonsus Liguori, *The True Spouse of Jesus Christ*, pp. 160-161.

2057. *Necessary to see Superior as Representative of God*

He, who does not reckon that it is God whom he obeys, will not only not be perfect in obedience, but will not be a good subject at all. . . .

Rodriguez, *Practice of Perfection and Christian Virtues*, vol. 3, p. 340.

2058. *Obedience Due Even to Imperfect Superiors*

Defects in superiors, real though they be, do not exempt us from accepting them individually as representatives of God. God never promised to give us angels as superiors. Look at those he chose himself . . . St Peter, St Paul. . . . [God] has never authorized us to separate the position from the person occupying it. For if he wished us to obey only the irreproachable, he would wish us to obey no man.

Brosnahan, *Searchlighting Ourselves*, p. 106.

2059. *Obedience Even to Imperfect Superiors*

St Gregory teaches that 'the commands of superiors should be respected, though their lives be not deserving of praise.'. . . And speaking of the Scribes and Pharisees, who blasphemed His works, Jesus Christ says: 'All things whatsoever they shall say to you, observe and do, but according to their works do ye not.'

St Alphonsus Liguori, *The True Spouse of Jesus Christ*, p. 167.

2060. *Obedience to Temporal Rulers*

. . . Writing to the Ephesians (Eph 6:5), St Paul commands them to obey even temporal and heathen masters as Christ our Lord.

Rodriguez, *Practice of Perfection and Christian Virtues*, vol. 3, p. 335.

2061. *Mother of Every Virtue*

[St Augustine] calls obedience the mother and, as it were, the trusty guardian, of every virtue in the humble soul. . . . And to this St Gregory adds that it is the mother of every virtue, since it begets them all in the soul; and it is their guardian also, because it preserves them all.

Scaramelli, *Directorium Asceticum*, vol. 3, p. 204.

2062. *Obedience and the Other Virtues*

'Obedience,' says St Gregory, 'implants all the other virtues in our hearts, and preserves them when implanted.'

James Leen, *By Jacob's Well*, p. 97.

2063. *The Tomb of Self-Will and Awakener of Humility*

St John Climacus says: 'Obedience is the tomb of self-will and the awakener of humility. In entering religion we have to take account that we are burying our own will, and that henceforth we must in all things follow that of the superior.'

Quoted in Rodriguez, *Practice of Perfection and Christian Virtues*, vol. 3, p. 290.

2064. *Obedience Leads to Victory*

'An obedient man shall speak of victory' (Prv 21:28). Yes, says St Gregory, the obedient shall overcome all the temptations of hell, because by obedience they subject their will to men, and thus become superior to the devils who fell through disobedience. 'They who obey,' says the saint, 'are conquerors, because when they submit their will to others, they triumph over the angels who sinned by disobedience.'

St Alphonsus Liguori, *The True Spouse of Jesus Christ*, p. 155.

2065. *Obedience Makes the Simplest Acts Meritorious*

Eating, drinking, sleeping, walking, working, talking, recreation are actions in themselves indifferent and have no claim to be considered virtuous; but when done out of obedience, they become virtuous; they are rendered even supernatural, meritorious and deserving of an everlasting reward.

Scaramelli, *Directorium Asceticum*, vol. 3, p. 207.

2066. *The Advantage of Obedience*

The sweeping of a floor, when prescribed by rule, is a greater act and, of course, incomparably more meritorious than hours passed in prayers before the Blessed Sacrament when the rule does not permit such an employment of one's time. The menial and somewhat trivial act is dignified by the divine authority. The act of prayer would spring from self-will and a mistaken idea of the meaning and purpose of prayer. . . . It remains true that each little task or obligation, if acquitted in a spirit of obedience to the divine will, has value for eternity.

James Leen, *By Jacob's Well*, p. 117.

2067. *Obedience Gives Strength*

[When St Teresa's confessor, Fr Ripalda, SJ, who had read the saint's report concerning her first foundation, ordered her to write the story of seven other convents established by her, she felt that such a task was impossible. Jesus, however told her:] 'Daughter, obedience gives strength.'

In *Complete Works of St Teresa*, Peers edition, vol. 3, p. xxii.

2068. *Advantages of Obedience*
A soul which is not obedient in everything, just like a child, is exposed to all the tricks of the devil, who has never misled and never will mislead a soul that is truly obedient.
Blessed Claude de la Colombière, *Faithful Servant*, p. 352.

2069. *Lack of Obedient Spirit Harmful*
[St Bernard says:] 'If you receive a command with unwillingness, murmuring and complaint, you do not practice the virtue of obedience, even though you do what is enjoined. We must say rather that beneath the external action you cloak the interior malice of your heart.'
In Scaramelli, *Directorium Asceticum*, vol. 3, p. 216.

2070. *Obedience Vs. Grumbling*
A truly obedient religious is like a well-armed knight riding on a good horse who passes safely among enemies and no one can harm him. But a religious who grumbles at obeying is like an unarmed knight riding on a bad horse who, when passing among the enemy, falls and is immediately captured, chained, wounded, imprisoned and sometimes put to death. A religious who wants to live according to his own will wants to go into the fire of hell.
Brother Giles, quoted in *The Little Flowers of St Francis*, p. 288.

2071. *When We Should Disobey*
The precept of a lawful superior is an object of obedience excluding only the supposition that it is plainly at variance with the commandments of God; for if he that is in authority (as the Angelic Doctor says) commands one thing, and God commands the contrary, it is obvious that we should make no account of the command of the human superior, and obey only the law of the Most High.
Scaramelli, *Directorium Asceticum*, vol. 3, p. 198.

2072. *What Kind of Man Should the Superior be?*
No one securely governs but he who would willingly live in subjection. No man securely commands but he who has learned well to obey.
Thomas à Kempis, *Imitation of Christ*, bk. 1, chap. 20.

PATIENCE

2073. *A Virtue We Can Share with God*
. . . How can anyone be patient or truly wise who knows nothing of the wisdom or of the patience of God? . . . He is truly patient who is meek and humble. . . . [Patience] is a virtue that we may share with God. For it is from him that patience comes. . . . Though we provoke God by fre-

quent, nay, by continuous offences, he restrains his wrath and waits in patience for that destined day of retribution. . . . He says: 'I desire not the death of the wicked, but rather that he turn from his ways and live' (Ez 33:11).

St Cyprian, in Toal, vol. 2, pp. 346-347.

2074. *Patience Taught by Christ*

. . . In his unvarying forbearance, Christ showed also the patience of his heavenly Father. . . .

He suffered Judas to the end; taking food with one who was his enemy.

Even in his very Passion and Crucifixion, before they had come to the shedding of blood . . . what infamies of reproach did he not patiently endure, what revilings, what mockeries. . . . The Judge of all men was placed standing before an earthly judge. The Word of God was led wordless to be sacrificed. . . . Even he who has shed Christ's blood is through Christ's blood given life everlasting. So wondrous, so sublime is the patience of God! And had it not been so wondrous and so sublime, the Church would not have had Paul . . . as an Apostle.

St Cyprian, *ibid.,* pp. 348-350.

2075. *Patience as a Gift of Christ*

. . . As patience is the gift of Christ, so impatience is an affliction of the devil. . . . It is patience that commends us to God and keeps us close to him. It is patience that calms anger, restrains the tongue, controls the mind, safeguards peace, governs the way in which we serve God. . . .

St Cyprian, *ibid.,* pp. 352-353.

2076. *Patience and Charity*

Charity is the bond of brotherhood . . . but take patience from it, and forsaken, it will not long continue. Take from it the power to *bear* and *endure*, and it remains without root and without strength. . . . [Patience also demands] that when you receive a blow, you turn the other cheek to the smiter, that you forgive a brother who has offended you, not merely seven times but seventy times seven times, and that you forgive all offenses whatsoever, that you love your enemies, that you pray for those who injure you and persecute you.

St Cyprian, *ibid.,* p. 351.

2077. *Patience to Be Loved*

Love this virtue [of patience], O Christian, as the mother of fortitude. . . . Exercising patience you will discover hope, the source of all good; and hope confoundeth not.

St Ephraem, in Toal, vol. 1, p. 10.

2078. *Patience Facilitated by Hope*
[Labor may fatigue] the husbandman, weariness may exhaust and deject him, but he is borne up in spite of all this by the hope of seeing the fields covered with corn and his granaries full of the finest wheat. Thus, too, says St Gregory, should the hope of imperishable goods encourage us to bear patiently the trials of this life, these being the seed whence shall spring the fruit of life everlasting; for, as the Psalmist says, 'They who in this life sow in tears shall reap in joy the life to come.' . . .

What proportion does there exist between present dishonor and heavenly glory, between bodily suffering and never-ending joy? What is poverty or want compared with the unfading treasures of our home above? We have it on the word of St Paul that there is no proportion between them (Rom 8:18). Add to this that the sufferings of the present life are short, fleeting, momentary; while if we bear them patiently, the glory that is to be our reward will be immortal and will never end; as the same Apostle observes (2 Cor 4:17).

Scaramelli, *Directorium Asceticum*, vol. 3, pp. 263-264.

2079. *Three Degrees of Patience*
Do I practice the first degree of patience, that is, do I bear evils without any revolt against God's will . . . although with some difficulty and some little complaints which show my repugnance to suffering? . . .

Do I practice the second degree of patience, that is, do I submit wholly and entirely, without a murmur, to the will of God in all the trials that he may send me? Am I disposed not to commit the slightest fault to deliver myself out of these evils? . . .

Do I practice the third degree of patience, that is, do I suffer misfortunes not only with resignation but with joy and gratitude, knowing that whatever comes from the hand of the omniscient and all-good God ought never to be regarded as an evil but as a blessing?

Bandas, *The Catholic Layman and Holiness*, pp. 269-270.

2080. *A Road to Salvation*
The good and the bad thief both died on the cross and suffered the same pains; but because the one embraced them with patience, he was saved; and because the other bore them with impatience, he was damned. St Augustine says that the same affliction sends the just to glory because they accept it with peace, and the wicked to fire because they submit to it with impatience.

St Alphonsus Liguori, *The True Spouse of Jesus Christ*, p. 380.

2081. *Crosses Are Something to Be Grateful For*
'A "thanks be to God," a "blessed be God" said in times of adversity

have more value than a thousand "thank yous" in times of prosperity.'
Father M. D'Avila, in *Spiritual Diary*, p. 82.

2082. *Patience According to St Francis de Sales*
'To suffer,' says St Francis de Sales, 'is almost the only good thing we can do in this world. . . . An ounce of patience is worth a pound of action.'
Quoted by Gabriel, in *Ascetical Conferences for Religious*, p. 98.

2083. *Patience in Small Matters*
Let it be remembered . . . that it is very useful to resign ourselves in small things; for example, to suffer a painful word, an importunate fly, the barking of a dog, a trip in walking, the extinguishing of a candle, the tearing of a garment, and the like. It is of greater importance to bear these trifles than to submit to great crosses. First, because they are more frequent; second, because we thus more easily acquire a habit and facility of resigning ourselves to things that are difficult.
St Alphonsus Liguori, *The True Spouse of Jesus Christ*, p. 430.

2084. *Patience for the Sake of God, Self, and Neighbor*
'Bear with patience the offenses which your neighbor commits against you – for God's sake, for your neighbor's sake, and for your own sake.'
Sayings of Brother Giles, in *Little Flowers of St Francis*, p. 267.

2085. *Patience Makes Martyrs*
St Gregory urges us to take courage, maintaining that 'we can be martyrs without the executioner's sword, by merely preserving patience.' 'Provided, of course,' adds St Bernard, 'that we endure the trials of this life not only patiently but willingly and with joy.'
St Alphonsus Liguori, *The Glories of Mary*, vol. 2, p. 172.

2086. *Reasons for Practicing Patience*
We should be patient in trials and tribulations because of our past offenses and sins. How can we complain of any suffering, no matter how great it may be, when we have deserved eternal damnation, the greatest of all punishments, for our mortal sins? The thought of heaven should make us patient. 'For that which is at present momentary and light of tribulation worketh for us above measure exceedingly an eternal weight of glory' (2 Cor 4:17).
Bandas, *The Catholic Layman and Holiness*, p. 268.

2087. *Patience with Self*
For my part, if I made a firm resolution not to yield to the sin of vanity,

for example, and yet had seriously fallen into it, I would not reprove myself in this manner: 'Aren't you wretched and abominable, you who have so many resolutions and yet let yourself be carried away by vanity? You should die for shame. Never again lift your eyes to heaven, blind, insolent traitor that you are, a rebel against your God' I would correct it in a reasonable, compassionate way. 'Alas, my poor heart, here we have fallen into the pit we were so firmly resolved to avoid! Well, we must get up again and leave it forever. We must call on God's mercy and hope that it will help us to be steadier in the days to come. Let us start out again on the way of humility. Let us be of good heart and from this day be more on guard. God will help us; we will do better.' On the basis of such correction I would build a firm, solid resolution never again to fall into that fault, using the proper means of avoiding it under the advice of my director.

St Francis de Sales, *Introduction to the Devout Life*, p. 123.

PENANCE

2088. *Penance as a Virtue*

Even when God has forgiven us, there remain in us the remnants of sin, evil roots ever ready to spring up and bring forth evil fruits. Neither baptism nor the sacrament of Penance takes concupiscence totally away. If then we wish the divine life to develop greatly in our souls, we must labor unceasingly to diminish these remnants of sin, to weaken these evil roots that disfigure our souls in God's sight.

Besides the action of the sacrament of Penance, an efficacious means exists for removing those scars of sin that prevent God from communicating His life to us in abundance. This means is the *virtue* of penance. It is a habit which, when deeply implanted, constantly inclines us to the expiation of sin, and the destruction of what remains of it. This virtue must doubtless, as we are about to see, manifest itself by acts proper to it; but it is above all an habitual attitude of the soul – an abiding regret for having offended God, and desire to make reparation for our faults. This habitual sentiment ought to inspire our acts of penance. . . .

Then, moved with sorrow, the soul says to God: 'O my God, I detest my sin, I long to avenge thy rights by penance, I would rather die than offend thee again.' That is the *spirit* of penance that urges and inclines the soul to make *acts* of expiation.

You will understand that this attitude of soul is necessary for all who have not lived in perfect innocence. When the motive is fear of hell, it is good, says the Council of Trent . . . ; God accepts it. But when the motive is love, it is excellent and perfect; the more the love of God increases in us, the more we feel the need of offering to God the sacrifice of a 'contrite and humble heart.'

Marmion, *Growth in Christ*, pp. 93-94.

2089. *Perseverance in Grace Demands God's Special Help*
[The holy Council of Trent] teaches that, in order to gain the grace of God and to persevere in it, we must be helped by His special assistance.

Scaramelli, *Directorium Asceticum*, vol. 1, p. 210.

2090. *Perseverence Cannot Be Merited*
It is true that we cannot merit final perseverance, as the Council of Trent . . . has declared, for it is a gift that God grants us quite gratituously; nevertheless, St Augustine tells us that perseverance may, in a certain way, be merited by prayer: 'This gift of God may be merited in the way of begging; that is, it may be obtained by supplication.'. . . So that the man who asks for perseverance, though he cannot merit it, will yet, as Suarez says, infallibly obtain it. But, says Bellarmine, 'it is not enough to ask for it once, we must ask it daily, in order to obtain it daily.'

St Alphonsus Liguori, *The Way of Salvation and of Perfection*, p. 438.

2091. *Prayer Needed to Obtain Final Perseverance*
Our prayers, then, must be humble and confident; but this is not enough to obtain final perseverance and, thereby, eternal life. Individual prayers will obtain the individual graces which they ask of God; but unless they are persevering, they will not obtain final perseverance: which, as it is an accumulation of many graces, requires many prayers that are not to cease until death. The grace of salvation is not a single grace but a chain of graces, all of which are at last linked with the grace of final perseverance. Now, to this chain of graces, there should correspond another chain (as it were) of our prayers; if we, by neglecting to pray, break the chain of our prayers, the chain of graces will be broken too; and as it is by this that we have to obtain salvation, we shall not be saved.

It is true that we cannot merit final perseverance, as the Council of Trent teaches: 'It cannot be had from any other source but from him who is able to confirm the man who is standing, that he may stand with perseverance.'. . . Nevertheless, says St Augustine, this great gift of perseverance can in a manner be merited by our prayers; that is, can be obtained by praying: 'This gift, therefore, can be suppliantly merited; that is, can be obtained by supplication.'

St Alphonsus Liguori, *Great Means of Salvation and of Perfection*, pp. 94-95.

2092. *Why God Delays Granting Final Perseverance*
. . . Someone will say, since God can give and wishes to give the grace of perseverance, why does he not give it to me all at once when I ask him? The holy Fathers assign many reasons: God does not grant it at once but

delays it, first, that he may better prove our confidence. And, further, says St Augustine, that we may long for it more vehemently. Great gifts, he says, should be greatly desired; for good things soon obtained are not held in the same estimation as those long looked for: 'God wills not to give quickly that you may learn to have great desire for great things; things long desired are pleasanter to obtain, but things soon given are cheapened.' Again, the Lord does so that we may not forget him: if we were already secure of persevering and of being saved, and if we had not continual need of God's help to preserve us in his grace and to save us, we should soon forget God.

[St Chrysostom says] 'It is not because he rejects our prayers that he delays, but by this contrivance he wishes to make us careful and to draw us to himself.'... Again, he does so in order that we, by persevering in prayers, may unite ourselves closer to him with the sweet bonds of love. 'Prayer,' says St Chrysostom, 'which is accustomed to converse with God, is no slight bond of love to him.'

St Alphonsus, *ibid.*, pp. 99-100.

2093. *Perseverance Can Certainly Be Obtained by Prayer*
[Father Suarez says:] 'If anyone pray constantly for perseverance in grace, he will most assuredly obtain it.' 'This, too, though it be a gratuitous gift, which cannot be a matter of strict merit. And he continues, 'Hence we assert that a just man, by duly persevering in earnest, frequent prayer, can infallibly obtain final perseverance.'

Scaramelli, *Directorium Asceticum*, vol. 1, pp. 227-228.

2094. *Perseverance, The Gate of Heaven*
St Bonaventure says that the crown is given to perseverance alone: 'Only perseverance is crowned.' For this reason, St Lawrence Justinian calls perseverance 'the gate of heaven.'

St Alphonsus Liguori, *Preparation for Death*, p. 79.

2095. *Purity of Action*
Purity of action consists principally in purity of intention, or in a pure motive of pleasing God. Hence our actions will be agreeable to God in proportion to their conformity to his holy will, and to their freedom from the corruption of self-will.

St Alphonsus Liguori, *The True Spouse of Jesus Christ*, p. 42.

2096. *Purity of Heart*
Nowhere [in the beatitudes] has it been said that 'they shall see God.' But when we come to the pure of heart, the vision of God is promised to

them. The reason for this is the fact that the eyes by which God is seen are within the heart. Speaking of those eyes, the Apostle Paul uses the expression, 'the enlightened eyes of your heart' (Eph 1:18). At the present time, those eyes are enlightened by faith insofar as their weakness allows, but hereafter they will be enlightened by sight in accordance with their strength. For, 'as long as we are in the body we are exiled from the Lord, for we walk by faith and not by sight' (2 Cor 5:6-7). What is the saying with regard to us as long as we are in this faith? 'We see now through a mirror in an obscure manner, but then face to face' (1 Cor 8: 12).

St Augustine, in *The Fathers of the Church*. vol. 11, p. 215.

RELIGION AS A VIRTUE

2097. *The Most Excellent of Moral Virtues*

Of all the moral virtues, the most excellent is that of religion, the virtue which leads us to give God the supreme honor due to him as our first beginning and our last end. We owe him our existence; without his conservation, we could not continue to exist; without his cooperation, we could not perform a single action; without him, we can never find happiness. We are completely dependent upon him, and we owe it to him and to ourselves to acknowledge that dependence.

Boylan, *This Tremendous Lover*, p. 155.

2098. *The Virtue of Religion*

. . . Justice requires that we give everyone his due, and religion requires that we give God the worship that belongs to him. So far these two admirable virtues agree, but still they are unlike, as justice requires that our payment be fully equal to the debt; while religion can never give to God all the honor to which he has a right, as his claim is simply infinitive. . . .

Treating then of religion, the Angelic Doctor says that it is a virtue which pays God the homage due to him inasmuch as he is the First Cause and Preserver of all things. . . . Hence, to God, whose excellence is infinite, and who, by his almighty power, imparts being to all things and preserves them in it, the highest honor is due, and this we pay him by acts of worship, which in themselves are nothing but a sincere protestation of his boundless excellency. . . . Even our sins and miseries may furnish this virtue with motives for exercising acts of self-abasement and of lowly reverence.

Scaramelli, *Directorium Asceticum*, vol. 3, pp. 116-117.

RESIGNATION

2099. *Resignation to God's Will*
Those who desire nothing but that God's holy will be done in them and by them are perfectly resigned to his will.
Wallenstein, *Guide to Perfect Christian Living*, p. 179.

2100. *How to Attain to Resignation*
We attain to the virtue of resignation when we: (a) frequently meditate on the wisdom, power and goodness of God; (b) deny self, constantly, more and more; (c) exercise ourselves particularly in strict obedience.
Wallenstein, *ibid.*, p. 179.

2101. *Resignation in Sickness, Infirmity*
. . . We must be particularly resigned under the pressure of corporal infirmities; and we must embrace them willingly, both in such a manner and for such a time as God wills. Nevertheless, we ought to employ the usual remedies; for this is what the Lord wills also; but if they do no good, let us unite ourselves to the will of God, and this will do us much more good than health. . . . Certainly the virtue is greater if, in times of sickness, we do not complain of our sufferings; but when these press heavily upon us, it is not a fault to make them known to our friends, or even to pray to God to liberate us from them. . . . Even Jesus Christ, on seeing the near approach of his most bitter Passion, manifested to his disciples what he suffered: 'My soul is sorrowful even unto death' (Mt 26:38); and he prayed to the Eternal Father to liberate him from them: 'My Father, if it be possible, let this chalice pass from me.' But Jesus himself has taught us what we ought to do after praying in this manner. . . . 'Nevertheless, not as I will, but as thou wilt.'
St Alphonsus Liguori, *The Way of Salvation and of Perfection*, pp. 373-374.

2102. *Resignation Regarding Personal Limitations*
If we have any natural defect, either in mind or body – a bad memory, slowness of apprehension, mean abilities, a crippled limb, or weak health – let us not therefore make lamentation. What were our deserts, and what obligation had God to bestow upon us a mind more richly endowed

or a body more perfectly framed? Could he not have created us mere animals? or have left us in our own nothingness?
St Alphonsus, *ibid.*, p. 372.

2103. *Resignation in Times of Aridity*
We ought to be resigned in times of spiritual desolation. The Lord is accustomed, when a soul gives itself up to the spiritual life, to heap consolations upon it in order to wean it from the pleasures of the world; but afterwards, when he sees it more settled in spiritual ways, he draws back his hand, in order to make proof of its love, and to see whether it serves and loves him unrecompensed, while in this world, with spiritual joys. . . .

Let, then, the soul thank the Lord when he caresses it with sweetnesses; but not torment itself by acts of impatience, when it beholds itself left in a state of desolation. . . . These spiritual desolations and abandonments are what all the saints have suffered.
St Alphonsus, *ibid.*, p. 378-379.

2104. *The Resignation of St Ignatius*
St Ignatius said: 'If the Company [the Jesuits] were to be suppressed, without any fault on my part, a quarter of an hour alone with God would be enough to give me back my calm and peace.'
Chautard, *The Soul of the Apostolate*, p. 104.

2105. *Resignation in Sickness*
Sometimes . . . I used to think that if I recovered my health, and yet were lost forever, I was better as I was. But, for all that, I thought I might serve God much better if I were well. This is our delusion: we do not resign ourselves absolutely to the disposition of the Lord, who knows what is for our good.
The Life of St Teresa of Jesus, Written by Herself, p. 37.

ZEAL

2106. *Zeal for Souls*
To make our fellowmen happier by making them more virtuous is the object of true zeal and constitutes the most perfect exercise of fraternal charity. Such spiritual charity is as far superior to corporal charity as the soul is superior to the body; for the good that is done to the body is temporal, while the good done to the soul is eternal. . . .

The motive power of true zeal is divine love. He who really loves God will labor to make him known, obeyed and worshiped by all his creatures.

He who truly loves Our Lord will strive to bring about that for which he longed so ardently, for which he bore so many hardships, endured so much ignominy, and suffered such excruciating torments. He who sincerely loves his brethren will spend himself in ceaseless endeavors to procure for them not only temporal relief but, what is incomparably more valuable, the attainment of everlasting bliss.

Gabriel, *Ascetical Conferences for Religious*, pp. 26-27.

2107. *Zeal for Conversion of Souls*

. . . St Chrysostom says that, though you were to do great penances, fast all your life and sleep on the ground, and give all your substance to the poor, that bears no comparison with this zeal for the conversion of souls.

Rodriguez, *Practice of Perfection and Christian Virtues*, vol. 3, p. 70.

2108. *Zeal Effective for Winning Souls*

A priest of moderate learning and great zeal will bring more souls to God than a great number of tepid though learned priests. St Jerome says: 'A man inflamed with zeal is sufficient to amend an entire people.'

St Alphonsus Liguori, *Dignity and Duties of the Priest*, p. 301.

2109. *Zeal Is Suspect if God's Will Is Not the Criterion*

All zeal is suspect, be its results ever so specious in man's eyes and successful as reckoned by man's standard, unless it is built upon a determination to accept God's criterion of what is right and wrong. . . .

If God's will for a mother is to be giving breakfast to her children, she would displease him by being at Mass instead. If God's will for me is to sit in my office and type out those long lists of tiresome names and addresses, it is wrong for me to close down half an hour early in order to visit the sick or help the poor, or even reclaim a sinner. If God's will assigns me the task of breaking stones, he quite definitely wants me breaking stones rather than kneeling before him in the Blessed Sacrament.

Nash, *Living Your Faith*, pp. 304-305.

2110. *St Teresa's Zeal for Souls*

To make one step in the propagation of the faith, and to give one ray of light to heretics, I would forfeit a thousand kingdoms.

The Life of St Teresa, Written by Herself, p. 177.

2111. *Zeal for Souls Taught by Jesus to St Catherine of Siena*

For a long time Jesus often appeared to St Catherine in her own little room and encouraged her to lead a retired life there. Then, however, he urged her to rejoin her family, and she complained: 'Ah, no, no, thy infinite goodness will never command anything which can separate the soul from thee.' Christ answered: 'Calm thyself, beloved daughter, thou must accomplish all justice and cause my grace to fructify in thee and in others; far from being desirous of separating from thee, I desire to become more closely united to thee by *charity toward thy neighbor*. Thou knowest that my love has two commandments, to love me and to love thy neighbor, now I wish thee to observe these two commandments.'

St Catherine replied: 'Lord, suffer me to inquire how I shall execute thy commands – my sex presents an obstacle, for women have no authority over men and propriety interdicts frequent relations with them.'

Our Lord answered: 'I know it is humility and not a disobedient spirit that prompts thee to speak thus, and now I wish thee to know that in this age, the pride of men has become so great, especially among such as believe themselves learned and discreet, that my justice can no longer endure them and is about to confound them by a just judgment; but because my mercy is the gentle attendant of all my works, I deign at first to give them a salutary confusion, in order that they may acknowledge and humble themselves like the Jews and Gentiles when I sent them stupid persons whom I filled with divine wisdom. Yes, I will give them women ignorant and weak by their nature, but prudent and powerful through my grace, to confound their arrogance.'

Blessed Raymond of Capua, *Life of St Catherine of Siena*, pp. 79-80.

2112. *Zeal of the Devil and of Priests*
St Bernard says the solicitude of the devils for our destruction should make us solicitous in laboring for salvation. . . . Oh, how active are our enemies in seeking the perdition of a priest. They desire the fall of a priest more ardently than that of a hundred seculars; as well because the victory over a priest is a far greater triumph than a victory over a layman, as because a priest that falls brings many others with him to perdition.

St Alphonsus Liguori, *Dignity and Duties of the Priest*, p. 101.

2113. *Zeal Must be Linked with Charity*
[St Francis de Sales says:] A zeal that is not charitable comes from a charity that is not genuine.

Chautard, *The Soul of the Apostolate*, p. 126.

VOCATIONS

2114. *Principal Marks of Vocation to the Priesthood*
[St Alphonsus says there are three principal marks indicating a vocation

to the priesthood:]

(1) Purity of Intention. The first is a good intention. It is necessary to enter the sanctuary by the door, but there is no other door than Jesus Christ.... To enter, then, by the door is to become a priest, not to please relatives, not to advance the family, nor for the sake of self-interest or self-esteem, but to serve God, to propagate his glory and to save souls.

(2) The second mark is the talent and learning necessary for the fulfillment of the duties of a priest. Priests must be masters to teach the people the law of God. 'The lips of the priest shall keep knowledge, and they shall seek the law at his mouth' (Mal 2:7).

(3) The third mark of an ecclesiastical vocation is positive virtue.

St Alphonsus Liguori, *Dignity and Duties of the Priest*, pp. 192-194.

2115. *Vocation to an Institute of Exact Observance*

He who feels himself called by God to a religious institute in which reigns exact observance ought to know that the end of every regular observance is to follow as exactly as possible the footsteps and examples of the most holy life of Jesus Christ. (*Note*: I say 'in which reigns exact observance,' for it would be perhaps, better to remain in the world than to enter a religious institute in which relaxation has been introduced.)

St Alphonsus Liguori, *Great Means of Salvation and of Perfection*, p. 399.

2116. *Detachments Required for Vocation of Exact Observance*

It is... necessary that he who wishes to be admitted into an order of exact observance should enter with a mind determined to overcome himself in everything, by expelling from his heart every inclination and desire that is not from God, nor for God, so that he must detach himself from all things, and especially from the four following: (a) from his comforts; (b) from his parents; (c) from self-esteem; (d) from his own will.

St Alphonsus, *ibid.*, p. 402.

2117. *Vocation to Religious Life Demands Resolution to Become a Saint*

... Let him who wishes to enter religion not forget to resolve to become a saint, and to suffer every exterior and interior pain, in order to be faithful to God and not lose his vocation. And if he is not resolved to this, I exhort him not to deceive the superiors and himself, and not to enter at all, for this is a sign that he is not called, or, which is a still greater evil, that he wished not to correspond as he ought with the grace of his vocation.

St Alphonsus, *ibid.*, p. 416.

2118. *Way of the Lord to Be Made Straight*
The way of the Lord to the heart is made straight when his words of truth are received with humility. The way of the Lord to the heart is made straight when our life is lived in harmony with his precepts. Hence it is written: 'If anyone love me, he will keep my Word, and my Father will love him, and we will come to him and make our abode with him' (Jn 14: 23).
St Gregory the Great, in Toal, vol. 1, p. 67.

2119. *Wealth Is Not Bad, But Avarice Is*
Wealth is not an evil thing (for we can use it as we ought when we spend for those in need); but avarice is an evil thing and brings everlasting punishment.
St John Chrysostom, in *The Fathers of the Church*, vol. 41, pp. 204-205.

2120. *Whitewashing a Sinner's Conduct Is Wrong*
While we must be extremely cautious in slandering our neighbor, we must avoid another extreme into which some men fall. To avoid slander, they praise and speak well of vice. If a person is actually a slanderer, don't say in excuse of him that he speaks frankly and freely. If a person is obviously vain, don't say that he is genteel and well-mannered. Never call dangerous familiarity mere natural, simple association. Don't adorn disobedience with the name of zeal, insolence with the name of frankness, or lewd familiarity with the name of friendship. No, dear Philothea, to avoid the vice of slander we must not favor, flatter or cherish vice. We must freely and frankly speak evil of evil and condemn things that need condemnation. By doing so we glorify God, provided we observe the necessary conditions.
St Francis de Sales, *Introduction to the Devout Life*, p. 167.

WICKEDNESS

2121. *Wickedness of Men Toward Us Is the 'Axe Of God'*
St Augustine explains that 'the wickedness of these men [the Assyrians] is made to be, as it were, an axe of God. . . . God uses the iniquity of the Assyrians like an axe to chastise the Jews.' And Jesus himself said to St Peter that his Passion and Death did not come so much from men, as from his Father himself: 'The chalice which My Father has given Me, shall I not drink it?'

St Alphonsus Liguori, *The Way of Salvation and of Perfection*, p. 360.

WIDOWHOOD

2122. *The Excellence of Widowhood*
. . . Thus speaks the Apostle, the teacher of the Gentiles, and the vessel of election: 'But I say to the unmarried and to widows, it is good for them if they so remain, even as I' (1 Cor 7:8). . . . 'The unmarried woman thinks about the things of the Lord, how she may please the Lord. Whereas she who is married thinks about the things of the world, how she may please her husband. . . . '

How excellent is the faith of married women, that is to say, of pious Christian wives, can be understood from his words addressed to married persons in commanding them to avoid fornication: 'Do you not know that your bodies are members of Christ?' (1 Cor. 6:15). So great, therefore is the good of faithful marriage that the bodies of the wedded are members of Christ. From the fact that widowhood is superior to this good, it does not follow that the Catholic widow is by her profession more than a member of Christ, but that she occupies a higher place among the members of Christ than the married women.

St Augustine, in *The Fathers of the Church*, vol. 16, pp. 280-282.

THE WILL OF GOD

2123. *Who Do the Will of God Are Brothers of Christ*
[Jesus] said that he would recognize as a brother of his own him who . . . acted according to the divine will: 'Whosoever shall do the will of my Father, he is my brother' (Mt 12:50).
St Alphonsus Liguori, *The Way of Salvation and of Perfection*, p. 355.

2124. *Doing God's Will Is Safer than Working for His Glory*
. . . Let it be observed that it is better and safer to act through a motive of doing the will of God than with the intention of promoting his glory; because we shall thus escape all the delusions of self-love. Under the pretense of seeking the glory of God, we often do our own will; but on the other hand, when we endeavor to do the divine will, and what is most pleasing to God, we can never err. And let us be persuaded, that the greatest glory we can give God consists in doing His will.
St Alphonsus Liguori, *The True Spouse of Jesus Christ*, p. 604.

2125. *Perfection Of Love Consists In Resignation to God's Will*
St John Chrysostom says that all the perfection of the love of God consists in resignation to the divine will. As hatred divides the wills of enemies, so love unites the wills of lovers, so that each wishes only what the other desires.
St Alphonsus, *ibid.,* p. 421.

2126. *Doing God's Will Is the Fast Road to Perfection*
Says St Mary Magdalen of Pazzi: 'To arrive at great perfection in a short time, do everything with the deliberate intention of doing the Divine Will. This intention strips us of self-will and sanctifies all our works' (quoted in Cardinal Vaughan's *The Young Priest*, Conf. 11). . . . The least act done for the glory of God is greater in his eyes than the conquest of a kingdom. The most humble person, who acts solely for the glory of the heavenly Father, is more illustrious in his eyes than the mighty ones of this world.
Bandas, *The Catholic Layman and Holiness*, p. 214.

2127. *The Will of God, an Immense Storehouse*
The divine will . . . is an immense storehouse. The present moment lived in

a spirit of faith and love is the key of entry. When the soul enters the threshold it finds limitless treasures. To lay hold of this truth is to discover a path which leads straight to God. It is to discover, from morning until evening, in the commonplace happenings of life, numberless opportunities for accumulating supernatural treasure. These acts may be extremely ordinary and trivial in outward appearance. The constant recognition that they are God's demand on us develops that tender thoughtfulness toward God and toward one's fellows for the love of God which is characteristic of perfect charity. It might appear to the soul itself that it is offering to God the merest trifles, but it does not so appear to God. They are most precious in His eyes.

James Leen, *By Jacob's Well*, p. 194.

2128. *Value of Doing the Will of God*
One man who does the will of God is better than thousands who transgress it.

St John Chrysostom, in *The Fathers of the Church*, vol. 41, p. 121.

2129. *The Aim of All Our Prayers, Works Is to Do Will of God*
To this end should be directed all the prayers that you offer to God and to the Mother of God, to your Guardian Angel, and to all your patron saints, that they should obtain for you the grace perfectly to do the will of God; in short, let this one expression: *Fiat Voluntas tua* serve you as a remedy for all your evils, and as a means of attaining all that is good.

St Alphonsus Liguori, *The Way of Salvation and of Perfection*, p. 477.

WIVES

2130. *Can Have Good Influence on Husbands*
Nothing, – nothing, I repeat – is more potent than a good and prudent woman in molding a man and shaping his soul, in whatever way she desires. . . . When your husband sees that you are not an evil woman, or a busybody and a fashion plate, and that you do not demand an extravagant expenditure of money, but are content with what you have, then, then indeed, he will bear with you even when you give him advice. . . . When you provide him with instruction, not only by your words but also by your example, then he will both show approval of you and be the more effectively convinced.

St John Chrysostom, in *The Fathers of the Church*, vol. 41, pp. 161-162.

WORK

2131. *Good Works Increase Grace in Us*
. . . 'Every meritorious work is a source of the increase of grace within us' (St Thomas. . .). The good acts of a soul in a state of grace are not only the fruits or manifestations of our quality of children of God; they are besides, says the Council of Trent, a cause of the increase of that justification which makes us pleasing to God. . . . In the measure, then, that our good works are multiplied, grace increases, it becomes stronger, more powerful and, with it, so does charity; and with it, likewise, is increased the future glory which is only the blossoming in heaven of our degree of grace here below.

Marmion, *Christ, the Life of the Soul*, p. 231.

2132. *Spiritual Better than Corporal Works of Mercy*
St Thomas teaches that the spiritual works of mercy should be held in greater esteem than the corporal, for three reasons. First, because by them we impart to our neighbor a far higher benefit, namely, a spiritual benefit, which is unquestionably of greater value than that which concerns only the body. Second, because the subject on whom the benefit is conferred, is far more noble; for beyond all doubt the soul is more noble than the body. Third, because the act of charity by which we afford succor to the soul is far more spiritual than that by which we assist the body in its needs, and therefore has a brighter luster.

Scaramelli, *Directorium Asceticum*, vol. 4, pp. 240-241.

2133. *Spiritual Works of Mercy More Praiseworthy*
St John Chrysostom says: 'They who, by reproof, by instruction, by showing the charms of virtue and the turpitude of vice rouse the lukewarm and spur them onward in the way of perfection, are deserving of greater praise and of higher recompense than they who give money to relieve their misery; for our soul is more noble and of greater account than our vile body.'

Quoted in Scaramelli, *ibid.*, vol. 4, p. 241.

2134. *'Heresy of Good Works'*
Now, for a man, in his practical conduct, to go about his active works as if

Jesus were not his one and only life-Principle, is what Cardinal Mermillod has called 'the heresy of good works.' He uses this expression to stigmatize the apostle who so forgets himself as to overlook his secondary and subordinate role, and looks only to his own personal activity as a basis for apostolic success. Is this not, in practice, a *denial of a great part of the Tract of Grace*?

Chautard, *The Soul of the Apostolate*, p. 10.

2135. *Good Works Without Interior Life a Danger to Salvation*

. . . 'Good' works without an interior life can jeopardize one's salvation. Activity – no matter how seemingly good – can, like the thorns in Christ's parable, choke the good seed of the interior life and destroy it. It was in this sense that St Bernard, in a letter to Pope Eugenius III, dared to brand such holy works as those entailed in governing the Church of Jesus Christ as 'accursed occupations.' 'Accursed,' if they destroy the interior life. Hence he warned the apostle to be a reservoir, not a channel, for the channel conducts water to others without retaining a drop for itself; whereas a reservoir simply gives its overflow; always full, though always giving. Only when the active life overflows from the contemplative life, as the moon's light from the sun's, will activity be safe and contribute to the inner life. 'If perceiving what you wish, O Jesus, and how you wish it,' wrote Dom Chautard, 'I do it because you wish it, then my union with you, far from becoming less, will only be more intensified.'

Shamon, *The Only Life*, p. 10.

2136. *Work to Be Supported by Contemplation*

Works are carried on in the midst of the world; and yet if action is not thoroughly imbued with contemplation, it remains sterile.

[A footnote adds:] With this in mind, the Holy Father [Pius XII] has gone so far as to speak of the 'heresy of action,' and he reminded the Most Rev Father Janssens, SJ, of it on the occasion of the Congress of the Directors of the Apostolate of Prayer.

Goichon, *Contemplative Life in the World*, p. 7.

2137. *Avoidance or Evil Is Not Enough*

There are many people, dearly beloved, who think this alone is sufficient for eternal life, that they do no evil. Therefore, all who, perchance, deceive themselves with this false assurance should clearly understand that the mere avoidance of evil is not enough for any Christian unless he does as much good as he can. . . .

The Lord says: 'He who has my commandments and keeps them, he it is who loves Me,' and: 'What does it avail that you call me "Lord, Lord," and do not practice the things that I say?' (Jn 14:21; Lk 6:46). . . . [If a man] has planted a vine in his field, would he want it to be the same after ten years as it was the day he planted it? . . . Since no one is pleased with such things, just as a man grieves over a vineyard or olive tree or son that shows no growth, so he should grieve if he recognizes that he has made no progress since the time he was reborn in Christ.

St Caesarius of Arles, in *The Fathers of the Church*, vol. 31, pp. 83-86.

2138. *The Simplest Acts Can Be Meritorious*

. . . The most commonplace actions, the most ordinary incidents of our daily life, such as taking food, attending to our business or work, fulfilling our social duties, taking rest and recreation . . . all these actions that occur every day and literally weave, in their monotonous and successive routine, the thread of our entire life, can be transformed, by grace and love, into acts very pleasing to God and rich in merit. To use another simile, each is like the grain of incense which seems nothing in itself, but, when thrown into the fire, becomes a fragrant perfume.

Marmion, *Christ, the Life of the Soul*, p. 248.

2139. *The Value of Ordinary Work*

[In Christ's eyes,] preaching and working miracles were not one whit more important than washing dishes or hammering in nails or using the plane or the saw or mending a broken plowshare.

Nash, *Living Your Faith*, p. 57.

2140. *Work for God Vs Work with God*

All men must work for God in order to save their souls. But religious have the enviable assignment of working with God and of being His right hand in the saving of souls.

Hoeger, *The Convent Mirror*, p. 12.

2141. *Work with God for Salvation of Souls*

Religious and all who aspire after perfection ought to develop a spirit of cooperation with God. They are his humble partners in saving others. . . . A vocation to work for the salvation of souls is such a mark of confidence in us on the part of God, that nothing less than supreme confidence in God can be expected of such a one.

Hoeger, *ibid.*, p. 72.

2142. *Manual Work Pleasing to God*

I know a man who has loved God more dearly than most, and he has passed his whole life as a plowman. He has followed the plough for forty years, and that is what he does to this day. This man once asked Our Lord if he wanted him to stop working and go and sit in church; but the answer was: No, He did not want that. He wanted him to go on earning his bread with the sweat of his brow, to the honor of his Most Precious Blood.

Tauler, *Spiritual Conferences*, pp. 282-283.

2143. *Little Works Can Convert a Soul*

To pick up a pin through love could convert a soul! . . . Only Jesus can give such value to our acts, so let us love him with all our might.

Collected Letters of St Thérèse of Lisieux, p. 228.

2144. *How Much St Thérèse Desired to Work for God's Glory*

. . . I confess that if I could no longer work for God's glory in heaven, I should like exile better than the Homeland.

St Thérèse of Lisieux, *ibid.,* p. 313.

THE WORLD

2145. *A School for Attaining Knowledge of God*

The world was not devised at random or to no purpose . . . it is truly a training place for rational souls and a school for attaining the knowledge of God, because through the visible and perceptible objects it provides guidance to the mind for the contemplation of the invisible, as the Apostle says: 'Since the creation of the world, his invisible attributes are clearly seen . . . being understood through the things he has made' (Rom 1:20). . . .

This world is a work of art, set before all for contemplation, so that through it the wisdom of Him Who created it should be known. . . .

St Basil, in *The Fathers of the Church*, vol. 46, pp. 11-12.

2146. *The World Is More Dangerous than the Devil*

The devil is a great enemy, but the world is worse. If the devil did not make use of the world and of bad men (by which is meant *the world*), he would not gain such victories as he does. . . . Men are often worse than devils because the devils are put to flight by prayer and by invoking the holy names of Jesus and Mary; but if bad companions tempt a person to sin, and he reply by some spiritual word, they do not fly, but tempt him the more; they laugh at him and call him a miserable man of no education, and good for nothing else; they call him a hypocrite who affects sanctity. To avoid such reproaches and derision, certain weak souls unhappily associate with these ministers of Lucifer and return to the vomit.

St Alphonsus Liguori, *Preparation for Death*, pp. 81-82.

WORLDLINESS

2147. *Worldliness in Religious Is Apostasy*
'To maintain,' says St Bernard, 'a secular spirit under the habit of religion, is apostasy of the heart.'

Quoted by St Alphonsus Liguori, in *The True Spouse of Jesus Christ*, p. 53.

WORSHIP

2148. *Worship Owed to God in Justice*
In the life of all men, but professionally in the life of religious, acts of worship are a 'must.' We owe them to God more than a debtor owes dollars and cents to a creditor, because the virtue of religion demands more than a pound-for-pound justice. Religion is the supernatural virtue that is concerned with rendering to God the worship due to his supreme excellence. Its object is to render to God the worship to which he has a right. We depend on God, soul and body.

Hoeger, *The Convent Mirror*, p. 100.

ALPHABETICAL INDEX